LAW AND BIOETHICS

CURRENT LEGAL ISSUES 2008
VOLUME 11

Law and Bioethics

Current Legal Issues 2008

VOLUME 11

Edited by

MICHAEL FREEMAN

Professor of English Law
University College London

OXFORD
UNIVERSITY PRESS

OXFORD

UNIVERSITY PRESS

Great Clarendon Street, Oxford OX2 6DP

Oxford University Press is a department of the University of Oxford.
It furthers the University's objective of excellence in research, scholarship,
and education by publishing worldwide in

Oxford New York

Auckland Cape Town Dar es Salaam Hong Kong Karachi
Kuala Lumpur Madrid Melbourne Mexico City Nairobi
New Delhi Shanghai Taipei Toronto

With offices in

Argentina Austria Brazil Chile Czech Republic France Greece
Guatemala Hungary Italy Japan Poland Portugal Singapore
South Korea Switzerland Thailand Turkey Ukraine Vietnam

Oxford is a registered trade mark of Oxford University Press
in the UK and in certain other countries

Published in the United States
by Oxford University Press Inc., New York

© Oxford University Press, 2008

The moral rights of the author have been asserted

Crown copyright material is reproduced under Class Licence
Number C01P0000148 with the permission of OPSI
and the Queen's Printer for Scotland

Database right Oxford University Press (maker)

First published 2008

British Library Cataloguing in Publication Data

Data available

Library of Congress Cataloging in Publication Data
Law and bioethics / edited by Michael Freeman.
p. cm. — (Current legal issues; v. 11)
Includes bibliographical references and index.
ISBN 978-0-19-954552-0 (hardback: alk. paper) 1. Medical laws
and legislation. 2. Medical care—Law and legislation. 3. Genetic
engineering—Law and legislation. 4. Bioethics. I. Freeman,
Michael D. A.
K3601.L37 2008
344.04'1—dc22   2008031129

Typeset by Newgen Imaging Systems (P) Ltd., Chennai, India
Printed in Great Britain
on acid-free paper by
CPI Antony Rowe, Chippenham, Wiltshire

ISBN 978-0-19-954552-0

1 3 5 7 9 10 8 6 4 2

General Editor's Preface

2007 saw the eleventh international inter-disciplinary colloquium convened in the UCL Law Faculty. On this occasion it was on 'Law and Bioethics'. This volume contains many of the papers delivered at the colloquium plus the contributions of a couple of persons prevented from presenting at the colloquium itself for personal reasons. Interest in examining law and its interface with other disciplines expands all the time. Twenty years ago the bringing together of law and bioethics would not have been contemplated. Bioethics itself was then in its infancy. It would be trite to remark that lawyers are more interested in bioethics than bioethicists are in law—but this is reflected in this collection. The volume offers important insights into a wide range of subjects upon which lawyers, bioethicists, and others have interest and concern. There are few areas of public policy which provoke more controversy, as witness the debates over the Human Fertilisation and Embryology Bill in the early months of 2008.

It remains for me to thank those who assisted me in putting together the colloquium and this volume, in particular Lisa Penfold, the Faculty's Events Organiser, and Linda Thomas without whose secretarial assistance the volume would not have reached fruition. I am also grateful to those who chaired sessions, in particular Baroness Warnock who has graced the stage of this subject for a generation.

The 2008 colloquium is on 'Law and Anthropology'. That in 2009 will probably be on 'Law and Neuroscience'. Further information may be sought from me at <uctlmdf@ucl.ac.uk>.

Michael Freeman

March 2008

Contents

Notes on Contributors

Amel Alghrani is a Research Associate at the University of Manchester. Amel studied law as an undergraduate and went on to qualify as a Barrister in 2003, having been awarded the Yarborough Anderson Benefactors and Scholarship Award. She went on to work in the General Medical Council, but left to pursue her interest in medical law. She completed a Masters in Healthcare Ethics and Law before going on to do a PhD under the supervision of Professors John Harris and Margaret Brazier.

Richard Ashcroft is Professor in the School of Law at Queen Mary, University of London. For most of the previous ten years he taught medical ethics in the medical schools of Queen Mary, Imperial College London, and Bristol University. He trained in history and philosophy of science at Cambridge University, and has published widely on ethical and social issues in the development of new medical technologies. His major area of interest is now ethical issues in public health and health policy, nationally and internationally. He is a deputy editor of the *Journal of Medical Ethics*, and serves on several other editorial boards, and as a member of the ethics committee of the Medical Research Council and the Gene Therapy Advisory Committee. The work presented here forms groundwork for a book in preparation on human rights and bioethics.

Angela Ballantyne has a BSc (genetics and molecular biology) and a PhD in bioethics. Her work has focused on global justice, health, and research ethics. She has worked internationally, in Australia, England, and America, and at the World Health Organization in Geneva. Dr Ballantyne is currently a visiting scholar at the Yale University Interdisciplinary Center for Bioethics.

Margaret P Battin is Distinguished Professor of Philosophy and Adjunct Professor of Internal Medicine in the Division of Medical Ethics and Humanities at the University of Utah. The author of prize-winning short stories and recipient of the University of Utah's Distinguished Research Award, she has authored, edited, or co-edited fifteen books, among them a study of philosophical issues in suicide (Prentice-Hall, 1982); a scholarly edition of John Donne's *Biathanatos* (Garland, 1982); *Puzzles About Art*, a volume of case-puzzles in aesthetics (St Martin's Press, 1989); a text on professional ethics (Prentice-Hall, 1989); *Ethics in the Sanctuary*, a study of ethical issues in organized religion (Yale University Press, 1990); two collections of essays on end-of-life issues, entitled *The Least Worst Death* (Oxford University Press, 1994) and *Ending Life* (Oxford University Press, 2005); an anthology on ethics and infectious disease (Blackwell, 2006); and is senior author of the multi-authored volume *Drugs and Justice: Seeking a Consistent, Coherent, Comprehensive View* (Oxford University Press, 2008). She has also been engaged in research on active euthanasia and assisted suicide in the Netherlands. She was recently named one of the 'Mothers of Bioethics'.

Belinda Bennett is Professor of Health and Medical Law at the University of Sydney and Director of the Faculty's Centre for Health Governance, Law and Ethics. Her research explores legal and ethical issues arising from new health care technologies and the interface between health law and globalization. She is the author of *Health Law's Kaleidoscope: Health Law Rights in a Global Age* (Ashgate, 2008); co-editor with George Tomossy of *Globalization and Health: Challenges for Health Law and Bioethics* (Springer, 2006); and editor of *Health, Rights and Globalisation* (Ashgate, 2006), and *Abortion* (Ashgate, 2004).

Margaret Brazier graduated in law in 1971 and was called to the Bar in 1973. She has taught at the University of Manchester since 1971 and became Professor of Law in 1990. She is joint Director of the University's Centre for Social Ethics and Policy and has participated in or directed a range of research projects, including EU-funded research into the ethics of control of communicable diseases and reproductive choice. She edits the Medical Law Review.

She has written widely on medical law and ethics, with a particular interest in problems of autonomy and consent, the use of human body parts, reproductive medicine, and public health. The fourth edition of her book *Medicine, Patients and the Law* (with Emma Cave) was published by LexisNexis and Penguin in 2007. From 1996 to 1998 she chaired a review into the laws relating to surrogacy. From 2001 to 2004 she chaired the Retained Organs Commission, and from 2004 to 2006 she chaired a Nuffield Council Working Party on critical care decisions in foetal and neonatal medicine. She was elected a fellow of the Academy of Medical Sciences in 2007 and appointed QC (*honoris causa*) in 2008.

Jo Bridgeman is a senior lecturer in the Sussex Law School, University of Sussex. Jo has researched and published in the field of health care law and the law regulating the care of children, including work on the health care of teenagers, analysis of the issues arising from the Bristol Royal Infirmary Inquiry and, in *Parental Responsibility, Young Children and Healthcare Law* (Cambridge University Press, 2007), a critical analysis of moral, social, and legal responsibilities for the health care of babies, infants, and young children. This body of work adopts a critical feminist perspective informed by, and developing, the feminist ethic of care in the analysis of the responsibilities of parents, professionals, and the state to children through the development of a conceptual framework of relational responsibility.

Roger Brownsword is Professor of Law at King's College London and Director of TELOS (researching the interfaces between law, ethics, and technology). He is a member of the Nuffield Council on Bioethics. Together with Deryck Beyleveld, he is the co-author of *Human Dignity in Bioethics and Biolaw* (Oxford University Press, 2001) and *Consent in the Law* (Hart, 2007); and his most recent book is *Rights, Regulation and the Technological Revolution* (Oxford University Press, 2008).

Cynthia R Daniels is Professor of Political Science at Rutgers University in New Brunswick, New Jersey. She is the author of *Exposing Men: The Science and Politics of Male Reproduction* (Oxford University Press, 2006) and *At Women's Expense: The Politics of Fetal Rights* (Harvard University Press, 1993). She is also the editor of *Lost Fathers: The Politics of Fatherlessness* (St Martin's Press, 1998) as well as a number of other volumes, and the author of many articles on reproductive rights, masculinity, and the politics of new reproductive technologies.

Leslie P Francis is Professor and Chair, Department of Philosophy, and Alfred C Emery Professor of Law at the University of Utah. She works on areas at the intersection of law, legal and ethical theory, bioethics, and disability. She is particularly interested in issues of distributive justice, partial compliance theory, and discrimination. She is co-editor of six volumes, including the *Blackwell Guide to Medical Ethics* (Blackwell, 2006) and *Americans With Disabilities* (Blackwell, 2000); co-author of *Land Wars: Property, Community and Land Use in an Interconnected World* (Lynne Rienner Publishers, 2003); and author of *Sexual Harassment: Ethical Issues in Academic Life* (Rowman & Littlefield, 2001).

Michael Freeman is Professor of English Law at University College London. He is the General Editor of this series. He is also the General Editor of the *International Library of Medicine, Ethics and Law* and of three volumes in the series: *Ethics and Medical Decision-Making* (Ashgate, 2001); *Children, Medicine and the Law* (Ashgate, 2005); and *The Ethics of Public Health* (Ashgate, 2008). He has written on sterilization, surrogacy, assisted suicide, saviour siblings, and medically assisted reproduction more generally.

Patrick Hanafin is Professor of Law, Director of Research and Director of the LLM Programme in Human Rights at Birkbeck Law School, and is a Visiting Professor in the School of Law at the University of Oporto, Portugal. He has held research fellowships at the European University Institute in Florence (2002–03) and at the Human Rights Program at Harvard Law School (1998–99). His books include: *Conceiving Life: Reproductive Politics and the Law in Contemporary Italy* (Ashgate, 2007); *Constituting Identity: Political Identity Formation and the Constitution in Post-Independence Ireland* (Ashgate, 2001); *Last Rights: Death, Dying and the Law in Ireland* (Cork University Press, 1997); and *Identity, Rights and Constitutional Transformation* (with Melissa Williams) (Ashgate, 1999).

Shawn HE Harmon is currently a Research Fellow at SCRIPT and InnoGen, and a PhD student at the University of Edinburgh. His research interests include the process of rule-making in the biotech field, the regulation of biotechnology internationally, regionally and domestically, and the translation of moral values into legal rules in diverse jurisdictions and cultural settings, and he has written on various aspects of these issues. In 2008, he commenced an ESRC-funded project which examines the rule-making process and the role and content of values in regulatory instruments governing stem cell research in Argentina. He is Editor-in-Chief of 'SCRIPT-ed—A Journal of Law, Technology & Society', and a barrister and solicitor of the Nova Scotia bar, Canada.

John Hearn is Vice President (International) Professor of Physiology at the University of Sydney, responsible for the University's international engagement and internationalization. He initiated and directed the primate embryology and stem cell programme at the University of Wisconsin from 1990 to 1997. A committed international citizen, he has worked extensively in China, India, Thailand, Kenya, and Brazil.

Mark Henaghan is Dean and Professor of Law at the University of Otago, New Zealand, specializing in family law. He is a Barrister and Solicitor of the High Court of New Zealand. Professor Henaghan is the Principal Investigator for the Human Genome Research Project—*Te Kaupapa Rangahau Ira Tangata*—Law, Ethics, and Policy for the Future—sponsored by the New Zealand Law Foundation. The Project has produced two reports: *Choosing Genes for Future Children* (Human Genome Project, 2006) and *Genes, Society and the Future* (Human Genome Project, 2007). Professor Henaghan's publications also include *Family Law Policy in New Zealand* (LexisNexis, 2008); and *Relationship Property on Death* (Thomson Brookers, 2004).

Jonathan Herring is a Fellow in Law at Exeter College, University of Oxford. He is author of several books including *Criminal Law: Text, Cases and Materials* (Oxford University Press, 2008); *Medical Law and Ethics* (Oxford University Press, 2008); *Family Law* (Pearson, 2007); and *Criminal Law* (Palgrave, 2006). He has also written widely on issues relating to criminal law, family law, and medical law.

Dr Myriam Hunter-Henin is a lecturer in French Law at University College London. Her work is at the intersection of human rights, family law and bioethics with a comparative and private international laws perspective. Her main publication on personal status, *Pour une redéfinition du statut personnel*, published by the Presses universitaires d'Aix-Marseille in 2004, includes chapters on the 2004 French legislation on Bioethics, in particular as regards access to assisted procreation and the concept of personhood.

Emily Jackson is Professor of Law at the London School of Economics. She is a Member of the Human Fertilisation and Embryology Authority, the BMA Medical Ethics Committee, and the Ethics Committees of the Royal College of Physicians and the Royal College of Pathologists. Her publications include *Regulating Reproduction* (Hart Publishing, 2001) and *Medical Law* (Oxford University Press, 2006).

Jay A Jacobson is Professor of Internal Medicine; Chief, Division of Medical Ethics and Humanities; and member, Division of Infectious Diseases, University of Utah School of Medicine and Intermountain Medical Center. He is a Master of the American College of Physicians and past member of its Ethics and Human Rights Committee; Fellow, Infectious Diseases Society of America; and Director, Utah Partnership to Improve End of Life Care. In 2004, he was given the American Medical Association Isaac Hayes and John Bell Award for Leadership in Medical Ethics and Professionalism.

Caroline Jones is a Lecturer at the School of Law, University of Southampton. Her research interests lie in assisted conception and the regulation of reproductive technologies; constructions of kinship and family; and in the fields of family, tort and health care law generally. She is a founder member and coordinator for the Health, Ethics and Law (HEAL) network at the University of Southampton, and the author of *Why Donor Insemination Requires Developments in Family Law* (Edwin Mellen, 2007).

Isabel Karpin is a senior lecturer in the Faculty of Law at the University of Sydney. She specializes in feminist legal theory and laws regulating the body. Her research examines laws governing reproductive and other biotechnologies, including genetics, and the challenges these pose to legal understandings of individuality, identity, disability, and family. She is involved in major research projects on: gender equity in health research; regulation of preimplantation genetic diagnosis; and Canadian and Australian legislative responses to reproductive genetics and embryo research.

Bruce M Landesman is an Associate Professor at the University of Utah. His specialties are political philosophy, ethics, and applied ethics, especially bioethics, and he has published in those areas. He is Executive Director of the American Section of the international Association for Philosophy of Law and Social Philosophy (AMINTAPHIL).

Robin Mackenzie is the Director of Medical Law and Ethics at the University of Kent. Her research interests include the regulation of new biotechnologies, death and the dying process, psychoactive substances regulation and research, body alteration, and somatechnics.

Alasdair R Maclean is a senior lecturer in law at the University of Dundee. He worked for eight years in clinical medicine before studying law. He has published widely on issues including autonomy and consent, negligence, research ethics, and the patient's right to treatment. His forthcoming book, *Autonomy, Informed Consent and the Law*, is soon to be published by Cambridge University Press. He is currently co-authoring a text on Scots Medical Law and is updating Kennedy and Grubb's *Medical Law*.

Jean V McHale is Professor of Law at the University of Leicester. Her research interests are in the area of health care law. Recent books include *Health Care Law Text and Materials* (Sweet and Maxwell, 2nd edn, 2007) (with Fox) and *Health Law and the European Union* (Cambridge University Press, 2004) (with Hervey).

Wendy Rogers is Associate Professor of Medical Ethics and Health Law in the School of Medicine at Flinders University. Her research interests include feminist bioethics, research ethics, issues to do with organ transplantation, and public health ethics. She has published widely on these and other topics in a range of medical and bioethics journals. Wendy is currently the Co-coordinator of the International Network on Feminist Approaches to Bioethics and leader of the health ethics theme of the Ethics Centre of South Australia.

Dr Katerina Sideri is lecturer in law and associate research fellow at the Centre for Socio-legal studies at the University of Oxford. She is the author of *Law's Practical Wisdom* (Ashgate, 2007). She is currently working on a book which explores the relationship among virtue bioethics, governance, and justice.

Charles B Smith MD is Emeritus Professor of Medicine at the University of Utah School of Medicine. He previously served as Chief of the Division of Infectious Diseases at the University of Utah School of Medicine, and Associate Dean at the University of Washington School of Medicine. His research has focused on respiratory, viral, and bacterial infections, and in recent years particularly on ethical issues related to infectious diseases. He is co-editor of *Ethics and Infectious Disease* (Blackwell, 2005) and co-author of *The Patient as Victim and Vector* (Oxford University Press, forthcoming, 2009).

Dr Stephen W Smith is a lecturer in law at the Birmingham Law School and the Deputy Director of the Institute of Medical Law, University of Birmingham. He specializes in medico-legal issues at the end of life and has published articles on end of life practices in the *Medical Law Review*; *American Journal of Law and Medicine*; *Medicine and Law*; and *Clinical Ethics*.

Daniel Sperling is an assistant professor of philosophy of law and bioethics at Netanya Academic College, and teaches at the Hebrew University of Jerusalem and Tel-Aviv University. He holds an LLB and BA (Philosophy) from the Hebrew University of Jerusalem and LLM and SJD from the University of Toronto. Sperling is the author of *Posthumous Interests: Legal and Ethical Perspectives* (Cambridge University Press, 2008); *Management of Post-Mortem Pregnancy: Legal and Philosophical Aspects* (Ashgate, 2006); and numerous articles in the area of law and bioethics.

List of Abbreviations

General

AATB	American Association of Tissue Banks
ACE	Association of Clinical Embryologists (UK)
AMA	American Medical Association
APA	American Psychological Association
ART	assisted reproductive technology
BMA	British Medical Association
CHD	coronary heart disease
CHRE	Council for Healthcare Regulatory Excellence (UK)
CIHR	Canadian Institutes of Health Research
CIOMS	Council for International Organizations of Medical Sciences
CNHC	Complementary and Natural Healthcare Council
CNR	cell nuclear replacement
CORE	Comment on Reproductive Ethics (UK)
CST	Council for Science and Technology (UK)
DHA	District Health Authority (UK)
DNR	do not resuscitate
DPP	Director of Public Prosecutions (UK)
DTCA	direct-to-consumer advertising
ECHR	Europe Convention on Human Rights
ECJ	European Court of Justice
ECtHR	European Court of Human Rights
EMB	evidence-based medicine
ESCs	embryonic stem cells
FAS	Foetal Alcohol Syndrome
FDA	Food and Drug Administration (US)
FINRRAGE	Feminist International Network of Resistance to Reproductive and Genetic Engineering
GMC	General Medical Council (UK)
HART Act 2004	Human Assisted Reproduction Technology Act 2004 (NZ)
hESCR	human embryonic stem cell research
HFEA 1990	Human Fertilisation and Embryology Act 1990
HFEA	Human Fertilisation and Embryology Authority
HLA	human leukocyte antigen
HREOC	Human Rights and Equal Opportunity Commission (Australia)
HSE	Health and Safety Executive (UK)
HHS	Department of Health and Human Services (US)
HTA	Human Tissue Authority (UK)
IBC	International Bioethics Committee
iPS	induced pluripotent stem cells

IVF	in vitro fertilization
JCAHO	Joint Commission on Accreditation of Healthcare Organizations (US)
LCF	Lawyer's Christian Fellowship
MHRA	Medicines and Healthcare Products Regulatory Agency
NGO	non-governmental organization
NHMRC	National Health and Medical Research Council (Australia)
NICE	National Institute for Health and Clinical Excellence
NIH	National Institutes of Health (US)
OHSS	ovarian hyperstimulation syndrome
ORWH	Office of Research on Women's Health
PAS	post-abortion syndrome
PGC	Principal of Genetic Consistency
PGD	preimplantation genetic diagnosis
PTSD	post-traumatic stress disorder
PVS	persistent vegetative state
QALY	Quality Adjusted Life Years
R&D	research and development
RCN	Royal College of Nursing
RCOG	Royal College of Obstetricians and Gynaecologists
RCP	Royal College of Physicians
RCPCH	Royal College of Paediatrics and Child Health
SARS	Severe Acute Respiratory Syndrome
SCNT	somatic cell nuclear transfer
SCR	stem cell research
SCs	stem cells
SING	Senior Infertility Nurses Group (UK)
SPUC	Society for the Protection of Unborn Children
SSCs	somatic stem cells
SynBERG	Synthetic Biology Engineering Research Centre
TRIPS	Agreement on Trade-Related Aspects of Intellectual Property Rights (WTO)
UNCRC	UN Convention on the Rights of the Child
WFDWRHL	World Federation of Doctors Who Respect Human Life
WHO	World Health Organization
WTO	World Trade Organization

Publications

AJ fam	Actualité juridique famille
AJIL	American Journal of International Law
Anglo-Am LR	Anglo-American Law Review
BMJ	British Medical Journal
CFLQ	Child and Family Law Quarterly
CLJ	Cambridge Law Journal
Harvard JLT	Harvard Journal of Law and Technology
JAMA	Journal of the American Medical Association

JCP	La semaine juridique Edition générale
LQR	Law Quarterly Review
MLR	Modern Law Review
Notre Dame JLEPP	Notre Dame Journal of Law, Ethics and Public Policy
OJLS	Oxford Journal of Legal Studies
RJPF	Revue juridique personnes et famille
RTD	Revue trimestielle de droit civil
RTD eu	Revue trimestrielle de droit européen

1

Law and Bioethics: Constructing the Inter-Discipline

Michael Freeman

Ethical thinking about medical decision-making has roots that go deep into history.

Tradition pursues this to Hippocrates whose 'oath' dates from between the fifth and third centuries BCE, but the origins are more than a millennium older.[1] Rules about the payment of fees to physicians are found as early as the Code of Hammurabi (who ruled Babylon between 1728 and 1686 BCE). Thus, we read: 'If a physician has performed a major operation on a lord with a bronze lancet and has saved the lord's life...he shall receive ten shekels of silver.'[2] If, however, he caused his death, his hand was to be chopped off.

A number of early statements of medical ethics have their foundations in pagan religion. A monument in a sanctuary of Asclepius tells doctors to be like God, and so 'saviours equally of slaves, of paupers, of rich men, of princes, and to all a brother'.[3]

Early ethical codes often took the form of oaths: the Hippocratic oath is, of course, the most famous. The physician is to abjure abuse of his position, and to keep professional confidences. He is to use his power to help the sick to the best of his ability and judgement—perhaps the earliest statement of the principle of beneficence—and to abstain from harming or wronging any man when using his medical expertise (which may be seen as the seed of the principle of non-malfeasance). There is also a prohibition on active euthanasia and one on abortion: so bioethics questions are anticipated as well.

The impact of religion on ethical thinking about medicine remains an important undercurrent. Its influence is seen in a number of papers in this

---

[1] See generally R Porter, *The Greatest Benefit to Mankind* (London, 1997), See also PJ Carrick, *Medical Ethics in the Ancient World* (Washington, DC, 2001).
[2] See JB Pritchard, *Ancient New Eastern Texts Relating to the Old Testament* (Princeton, NJ, 1969) 27.
[3] See MB Etziony, *The Physician's Creed: An Anthology of Medical Prayers, Oaths and Codes of Ethics* (Springfield, Ill, 1973).

collection.[4] Its influence on the origins of bioethics is considerable. Muslim, Jewish, and Christian scholarship of the twelfth century and earlier attests to this.[5] The Jewish polymath, Moses Maimonides (1125–1204), in his *Medical Aphorisms*, emphasized the duties of physicians: 'may I never see in the patient anything but a fellow creature in pain'.[6] Islamic scholars such as al-Razi (865–925) emphasized the importance of reason (*al-'aql*), but this did not deflect him from the view that noblemen were entitled to special consideration when it came to the prescribing of drugs.[7] However, he did not neglect the poor for whom his treatise *Man La Yahdurah al-tabib* (Who Has No Physician To Attend Him) was written.[8] Meanwhile, Christianity was modifying the Hippocratic oath to make it acceptable to Christians. No longer are physicians required to swear to Greek gods and goddesses.

Christianity's emphasis on loving one's neighbour as oneself[9] was reflected in the establishment of 'hospitals' by religious institutions such as monasteries. Crusading orders—though they had a strange concept of love for one's neighbour[10]—also built hospitals throughout the Mediterranean and German-speaking lands.[11] The Benedictine rule emphasized that the care of the sick was to be placed above and before every other duty 'as if indeed Christ were being directly served by waiting on them'.[12] Moreover, Christian teaching stressed that doctors were to cultivate the virtues of compassion and charity. A treatise,[13] thought to date from the early twelfth century, urges doctors not to heal 'for the sake of gain, nor to give more consideration to the wealthy than to the poor, or to the noble than the ignoble'. Aquinas condemned the demanding of an excessive fee, or even the refusal to give free treatment to a patient who could die without it.[14]

Questions of bioethics were also beginning to be addressed. St Augustine in the fifth century had condemned suicide.[15] Aquinas did so also.[16] A leading

[4] See also LE Sullivan (ed), *Healing and Restoring: Health and Medicine in the World's Religious Traditions* (New York, 1989). See also (1989) 20(4) *Hastings Center Report* (supplement).

[5] See JM Gustafson, *The Contributions of Theology to Medical Ethics* (Milwaukee, Wisc, 1975).

[6] Quoted in Porter (n 1 above) 101. See also J Preuss, *Biblical and Talmudic Medicine* (New York, 1978).

[7] See Porter (n 1 above) 97 noting that in this he echoed Galen.

[8] See Porter (n 1 above) 97.

[9] This is first found in *Leviticus* 19:18.

[10] Consider, eg, the Crusades, on which see S Runciman, *A History of the Crusades* (3 vols) (Cambridge, 1951–54).

[11] See NG Siraisi, *Medical and Early Renaissance Medicine: An Introduction to Knowledge and Practice* (Chicago, 1990).

[12] Quoted in Porter (n 1 above) 111.

[13] See LC Mackinney, 'Medical Ethics and Etiquette in the Early Middle Ages: The Persistence of Hippocratic Ideals' (1952) 26 *Bulletin of the History of Medicine* 1 (reproduced in M Freeman, *Ethics and Medical Decision-Making* (Aldershot, 2001) 11).

[14] ibid 37.

[15] See G Minois, *History of Suicide* (Baltimore, 1999) 27–8.

[16] *Summa Theologica*, part II–II, q 64, art 5.

sixteenth-century canonist, Navarrus, condemned euthanasia, whatever its motive.[17] On abortion there was greater equivocation than we have been led to believe. Thus, Aquinas's position, following Aristotle, was that it was only homicide to abort an animated foetus. Animation was deemed to occur at forty days in the case of male foetuses, and 90 days with female ones.[18] It was another six centuries before Pope Pius IX outlawed all abortions, regardless of the stage reached by the foetus.[19]

The birth of modern medical ethics can be traced to the Enlightenment, in particular to John Gregory (1725–73)[20] and Thomas Percival (1740–1804).[21] The publication (in 1772) of Gregory's *Lectures on the Duties and Qualifications of the Physician* is pivotal. Gregory stressed that doctors had a duty to be humane: 'It is as much the business of a physician to alleviate pain, and to smooth the avenues of death, when unavoidable, as to cure diseases.' Percival published his *Medical Jurisprudence* in 1794, and, in 1803, expanded this into *Medical Ethics*. He stressed that: 'Every case, committed to the charge of a physician or surgeon, should be treated with attention, steadiness and humanity.' The book also offered practical advice on how doctors could reinforce paternalism, even admitting that charity patients could be treated with a degree of authority which might be unacceptable where the patient was wealthy. The latter's foibles had to be humoured!

The nineteenth century saw the birth of professional nursing,[22] and, by 1901, the first book on nursing ethics had been published.[23] But, until the resurgence of feminist thinking, the nurse's primary obligation was perceived as the carrying out of the doctor's orders.[24] Reformulated in 1973, her or his primary responsibility is now to those who require nursing care.[25]

By the 1970s, modern bioethics had emerged, partly as a response to developments in medicine—in particular the heart transplant carried out by Dr Christiaan Barnard in Cape Town in 1967.[26] The ability to harvest organs

---

[17] See Philippe Ariès, *The Hour of Our Death* (London, 1981).

[18] And see, more generally, JM Riddle, *Eve's Herbs* (Cambridge, Mass., 1997).

[19] See A McLaren, 'Policing Pregnancies: Changes in Nineteenth Century Criminal and Canon Law' in GR Dunstan and MJ Seller (eds), *The Human Embryo: Aristotle and the Arabic and European-Traditions* (Exeter, 1990) 187. See also JT Noonan, 'Abortion and the Catholic Church: A Summary History' (1967) 12 *Natural Law Forum* 105.

[20] See LB McCullough, *John Gregory's Writings on Medical Ethics and History of Medicine* (Dordrecht, 1998).

[21] See T Percival, *Medical Ethics* (Manchester, 1803). And see, generally, T Hankins, *Science and the Enlightenment* (Cambridge, 1985).

[22] B Abel-Smith, *A History of the Nursing Profession* (London, 1960).

[23] I Hampton Robb, *Nursing Ethics for Hospital and Private Use* (Cleveland, Ohio, 1928) (1st edn published in 1901).

[24] See H Kuhse, *Caring: Nurses, Women and Ethics* (Oxford, 1997) ch 2.

[25] ibid 32.

[26] Roy Porter's remark that it may be no accident that South Africa got in first; the fact that the land of apartheid had fewer ethical rules hedging what doctors could do is highly pertinent: Porter (n 1 above) 621.

Michael Freeman

from cadavers to save lives necessitated a rethink about the definition of death,[27] and although this has almost universally centred on the cessation of brain stem functions,[28] the debate continues,[29] in particular in relation to those in a persistent vegetative state and anencephalic babies.[30]

The development of the contraceptive pill in the 1960s and the growth of laws permitting safe abortions (in the United Kingdom with the Abortion Act of 1967, in the United States with the watershed decision of *Roe v Wade* in 1973),[31] and their interaction with the women's movement challeged the medical profession to confront the issue of women's reproductive rights.[32]

Biomedical technology helped to procreate the reproduction revolution:[33] *in vitro* fertilization (the first 'test-tube' baby, Louise Brown, was born in 1978) produced (and continues to stimulate) innumerable ethical issues and led to the establishment of commissions of inquiry, the best known of which, the Warnock Commission in the United Kingdom, produced its report in 1984.[34] Although essentially a liberal statement endorsing a range of autonomy, its stand on surrogacy—that it was 'totally ethically unacceptable'[35]—reflected a paternalistic moralism.[36] Whilst the report can be criticized on the grounds of its incoherence, perhaps surrogacy is different: a case-by-case approach may be called for. Although surrogacy took on a very high profile,[37] other consequences of the reproduction revolution, such as embryo research[38] and the possibility of human cloning[39] and genetic enhancement,[40] now raise more profound ethical concerns.

At the other end of 'life', medicine's ability to preserve life for those who cannot, or no longer can, live in any meaningful sense (at one extreme, the anencephalic

---

[27] French neurologists coined the term *coma dépassé* in 1959. On the Harvard Medical School's definition see (1968) 205 JAMA 337. For a 'rethink' see M Lock, *Twice Dead* (Berkeley, Calif, 2002).

[28] See AM Capron and LM Kass, 'A Statutory Definition of the Standards for Determining Human Death: An Appraisal and A Proposal' (1978) 121 *University of Pennsylvania Law Review* 87.

[29] eg RD Truog, 'Is It Time To Abandon Brain Death?' (1997) 27(1) *Hastings Center Report* 29. Contrast JL Bernat, 'A Defence of the Whole-Brain Concept of Death' (1998) 28 (2) *Hastings Center Report* 14.

[30] On which see E Jackson, *Medical Law* (Oxford, 2006).

[31] 410 US 113 (1973).

[32] See eg S Sherwin, *No Longer Patient: Feminist Ethics and Health Care* (Philadelphia, Pa, 1992).

[33] See P Singer and D Wells, *The Reproduction Revolution* (Oxford, 1984).

[34] And see M Warnock, *A Question of Life* (Oxford, 1985).

[35] ibid para 8.17.

[36] As I argued in 'After Warnock—Whither the Law' (1986) 39 *Current Legal Problems* 33.

[37] The 'Baby M' case in the US attracted a lot of attention: *In The Matter of Baby M* 537 A 2d 1227. In England there was 'Baby Cotton': *Re C* [1985] FLR 846.

[38] See S Holland, K Lebacqz, and L Zoloth, *The Human Embryonic Stem Cell Debate* (Cambridge, Mass., 2001).

[39] See G McGee, *The Human Cloning Debate* (Berkeley, Calif, 1998); N Agar, *Perfect Copy* (Cambridge, 2002).

[40] See G McGee, *The Perfect Baby* (Lanham, Md, 1997), M Mehlman, *Wondergenes* (Bloomington, Ind., 2003).

baby, at the other the person in a persistent vegetative state) opened up an important debate which pitted absolutist 'sanctity of life' principles against 'quality of life' considerations.[41] In 1973, two paediatricians, Duff and Campbell, questioned whether severely ill or disabled neonates should receve life-sustaining treatment.[42] This raised the further question whether, if treatment were withheld, did we have to wait for individuals to die or could we assist/accelerate their deaths, and, if so, in what manner? Thus, the active/passive debate was born.[43] England had had the John Bodkin Adams case in the mid-1950s[44]—I recall it as being discussed within a legal framework rather than a bioethical one. The issues were addressed by prominent jurists, Glanville Williams[45] and Lord Devlin,[46] and they took up some of the bioethical issues. But it wasn't until the Karen Quinlan case (in New Jersey in 1976),[47] and the 'Baby Alexandra' case (in the United Kingdom in 1981 in the context of disabled newborns),[48] that any sustained legal and bioethical thinking took place. The issues of double effect, the ordinary/extraordinary treatment distinction, killing (and physician-assisted suicide), and allowing to die emerged as central questions within bioethics.

Ethical thinking about medical decision-making thus has deep roots. However, prior to the 1970s, there are few examples of what we would now regard as bioethical thinking. Beecher's famous essay 'Ethics and Clinical Research', published in 1966 in a medical journal—there were no journals devoted to bioethical questions as such—is the first modern discourse targeted at a fundamental ethical issue on the interface between law and medicine.[49] Beecher, it should not be forgotten, was a Professor of Research in Anaesthesia, but may have been the first to emphasize the importance of informed consent. Journals on the subject were to emerge later—the establishment in the United States of the Hastings Center leading to the first of these—the *Hastings Center Report*. This was followed in 1974 by the *Journal of Medical Ethics* in the United Kingdom, and there are now in excess of ten or more major journals in the English-speaking world. Monographs, of course, abound: it is doubtful whether anyone can have read them all.

There are few, if any, areas in which there is a closer interface between law and ethics than in the area of medicine. Law and ethics (and bioethics) employ

---

[41] See DW Brock, *Life and Death: Philosophical Essays in Biomedical Ethics* (Cambridge, 1993).

[42] RS Duff and AGM Campbell, 'Moral and Ethical Problems in the Special-Care Nursery' (1973) 279 *New England Journal of Medicine* 890.

[43] Initially stimulated by J Rachels, 'Active and Passive Euthanasia' (1975) 292 *New England Journal of Medicine* 78.

[44] Unreported. The trial judge, Lord Devlin, subsequently wrote an account with the title *Easing The Passing* (London, 1985).

[45] G Williams, *The Sanctity of Life and the Criminal Law* (London, 1958).

[46] See n 44 above.

[47] *In the Matter of Karen Quinlan* 353 A 2d 647 (1976).

[48] *Re B* [1981] 1 WLR 1421. This coincided with the prosecution of Dr Arthur for attempted murder in a similar case: *R v Arthur* (1981) 12 BMLR 1.

[49] 'Ethics and Clinical Research' (1966) 274 *New England Journal of Medicine* 1354.

many of the same conceptual categories: rules, principles, right. In addition, they use the same language, though not, or not necessarily, the same sources. In an article published in 1997,[50] Wilbren Van der Burg traced the relationship between law and bioethics through two staged models, a moralistic-paternalistic model, and what he perceives as a flawed liberal model. His own preference (he uses ideal-types, of course) is a post-liberal model in which the relationship will be more loose than it is within liberalism. When this phase is envisaged is not made clear. Certainly, the last years have, on one interpretation, seen a resurgence of liberalism, both in philosophy where Ronald Dworkin's impact grows,[51] and also in law in the United Kingdom with the passing of the Human Rights Act in 1998. On the other hand, Van der Burg is right to draw attention to the limits of law—and certainly the 1998 Act and the European Convention on Human Rights has not had the impact on medical decision-making that some anticipated. It was Carl Schneider who noted, back in 1994, that there were 'limits to the extent to which the language of the law may safely be imported into bioethical discourse and to which bioethical ideas may be effectively translated into law'.[52]

Bioethical issues are commonly expressed for public discourse in legal terms. This is in part because bioethical issues are frequently tested in legal claims: whether someone should be allowed assisted suicide,[53] whether a prisoner has the right to reproduce,[54] whether treatment can be withdrawn from a person in a persistent vegetative state, and what constitutes treatment.[55] It is also explained by the fact that the law is experienced with analysing and solving social problems. It has both method and language. In the common law world that method is the common law process. It is not suprising that 'the case approach' has been so appealing to bioethicists.[56] It has an obvious appeal both to common lawyers and the medical profession.[57] Like the common lawyer and, in most cases, the doctor, the casuist reasons from the paradigmatic case to find the 'right' result in the new, perhaps perplexing, situation. This is done by means of analogical reasoning. The case at hand is compared with the paradigm case (or cases), and similarities and differences are focused upon. So, where the question is whether a grossly disabled newborn baby should be allowed to die, the paradigmatic cases would be, on the one hand, a case such as 'Baby Alexandra' (a Down Syndrome

---

[50] 'Bioethics and Law: A Developmental Perspective' (1997) 11 *Bioethics* 91.

[51] eg S Hershowitz, *Exploring Law's Empire* (New York, 2006).

[52] C Schneider, 'Bioethics in the Language of The Law' (1994) 24(4) *Hastings Center Report* 16.

[53] *Pretty v United Kingdom* [2002] 35 EHRR 1. See also *Rodriguez v British Columbia* (1993) 107 DLR (4th) 342; *Washington v Glucksberg* 117 S Ct 2258 (1997).

[54] *Dickson v United Kingdom* [2008] 1 FLR 1315.

[55] *Airedale NHS Trust v Bland* [1993] 1 All ER 821.

[56] RB Miller, *Casuistry and Modern Ethics: A Poetics of Practical Reason* (Chicago, 1996); MG Kuczewski, *Fragmentation and Consensus: Communitarian and Casuist Bioethics* (Washington, DC, 1997).

[57] But contrast J Baron, *Against Bioethics* (Cambridge, Mass., 2006).

child with an intestinal blockage who, of course, must be treated, whatever her parents think),[58] and, on the other, a child for whom any treatment is futile and who will die anyway in a matter of months.[59] What, then, of the many cases in between these two paradigms, for example, the child who is not dying and can easily be resuscitated but who can experience little else but pain? The casuist—as also the common lawyer—will try to find arguments to categorize the case in terms of its proximity to one or other paradigm. This is a 'bottom-up', as opposed to a 'top-down' approach.[60] It is inductive and particularist, and, it would appear to be, dismissive of principles.

For some casuists principles are nothing more than what we have learnt from our intuitive responses to a series of cases. To others, they can guide actions. In John Arras' view, casuistry can be regarded as complementary to the development and use of principles, emphasizing the importance of details of cases.[61] Casuists differ from those who espouse a principle-based approach in arguing about where the principles come from. It is the contention of casuists that principles do not emerge from some 'celestial vault', as Arras puts it, but rather develop out of the methodology of a case-based approach over a period of time.[62] Common lawyers see principles in a similar way, as found embedded in rules which themselves are the product of a case-tested process. Casuists argue that principles cannot just be applied, but need fine-tuning to tackle the individual case. Thus, for example, the principle of patient autonomy may have greater or lesser weight depending upon the circumstances. It may have less pulling power when the patient is a child (where it may be thought to have a differential impact on decisions to consent to or refuse treatment),[63] or where the interests of others are threatened (as in the case of a pregnant woman who refuses a medically-indicated caesarean section).[64]

The criticisms of casuistry mirror those voiced by critics of common law methodology too. The potential for bias.[65] Casuistry, it is said, is committed to the thinking of the past, and therefore wedded to unjust social practices and prejudices: does it have the ability to challenge the inherent biases in the paradigm cases to which it must return? Similar criticisms are made of common law methodology by critical legal scholars,[66] within feminist jurisprudence,[67] and

[58] See n 48 above.
[59] As in *Re J* [1991] Fam 33.
[60] So described by J Arras, 'Getting Down To Cases: The Revival of Casuistry in Bioethics' (1991) 16 *Journal of Medicine and Philosophy* 29.
[61] ibid. [62] ibid.
[63] And see S Elliston, *The Best Interests of the Child in Healthcare* (London, 2007).
[64] See *St George's Healthcare NHS Trust v S* [1998] 3 All ER 673.
[65] See L Kopelman, 'Case Method and Casuistry: The Problem of Bias' (1994) 15 *Theoretical Medicine* 21.
[66] eg P Gabel, 'Reification in Legal Reasoning' (1980) 3 *Research in Law and Sociology* 25.
[67] eg L Finley, 'Breaking Women's Silence in Law: The Dilemma of the Gendered Nature of Legal Reasoning' (1989) 64 *Notre Dame Law Review* 886.

critical race theory.[68] But casuistry does not have to be conservative, any more than does common law reasoning. Analogical reasoning is a tool, and, like all tools, its effectiveness depends on who handles it. Casuistry is also criticized for its indeterminacy.[69] As a methodology, it depends on the mind-set of its practitioners. When there was consensus (as when there was common Christian belief), casuistry was workable. But, the argument goes, can it work in pluralistic societies? The common law works, but it has clearly defined authorities to which it can appeal (judges, a hierarchy of courts, a system of precedent, well-established methods of interpreting statutes and reading cases). Casuistry may work within the bounds of a particular religion, but its appeal to a secular, pluralistic, post-modern society may be limited by the difficulties it has in surmounting this hurdle.[70]

One does not have to adopt casuistic ethical thinking to see the value of law to bioethicists. Schneider points to law's 'most beguiling aspect' as being that it is 'not just talk'.[71] It is, as he puts it, 'a way of actively, directly trying to change the world'.[72] It is a structure of regulation backed by force. It enjoys social and moral authority. It is a symbol of legitimacy. This is one defence of the law of informed consent: doctors may not always comply with its imperative, but it nevertheless 'symbolizes society's aspirations for medicine'.[73] Of course, Schneider concedes law may fail to translate hopes into reality. It is, however, likely to produce the right result more often than leaving decisions to the discretion of decision-makers. Justice, says Schneider, 'may require that an agency of social regulation substitute rules for discretion'.[74] Rules can be over-rigid: for example, that which states that surrogacy arrangments are unenforceable contracts.[75] But we know (or think we know) that such a rule is likely to produce more just results than a rule which offers scope for discretion.

But do law's attempts at precision offer too little guidance to the medical profession? Take the *Bolam* standard[76] or the 'transatlantic' prudent patient test.[77] Do these tests tell doctors enough about what they are supposed to do? Would it be better if they weren't constrained by legal norms and relied instead

---

[68] See K Crenshaw, N Gotanda, G Pelter, and K Thomas, *Critical Race Theory* (New York, 1995) Part 4.

[69] But see KW Wildes, 'The Priesthood of Bioethics and the Return of Casuistry' (1993) 18 *Journal of Medicine and Philosophy* 33.

[70] ibid.

[71] Schneider (n 52 above) 20.

[72] ibid.   [73] ibid.

[74] ibid. But, as Ronald Dworkin has shown, it is not either rules or discretion. An understanding of 'law's empire' is not so simple.

[75] Surrogacy Arrangements Act 1985, s 1A (inserted by the Human Fertilisation and Embryology Act 1990, s 36).

[76] *Bolam v Friern Hospital Management Committee* [1957] 2 All ER 118.

[77] *Canterbury v Spence* 464 F 2d 772 (1972).

on professional ethical codes of practice? These often seem to be more patient-focused than case law.[78]

In looking at the relationship between law and bioethics it must not be forgotten that the law purports to pronounce on legalities, and not therefore necessarily on what is morally right. When courts ruled against Dianne Pretty,[79] Leslie Burke,[80] and Natallie Evans,[81] they were not saying that these were the most desirable results, merely the right legal conclusions. Sometimes, indeed, courts will 'stretch' the law to reach a conclusion that intuition or common sense tells them (and us) is right, even if it involves a distortion of conventional doctrine. The reasoning adopted in the conjoined twins case is the clearest example of this in recent years.[82] Whether the judges in this case reached the 'right answer' has been vigorously debated.[83] Much—perhaps everything—depends upon what is understood by 'right'. The debate divides positivism, natural law, and interpretivism—though perhaps less so than was the case.[84] Ronald Dworkin has called for 'integrity'.[85] A judge committed to integrity is required to decide a case by seeking a principle that both 'fits and justifies some complex part of the legal practices'.[86] The judge ought to seek both 'fit' and what sees the doctrine in its 'best light'.[87] But what if there is a conflict between convictions about 'fit' and convictions as to which interpretation shows legal practices in their 'best light'? And 'fit' and 'best light' are, it should not be forgotten, themselves interpretive questions.[88]

It is not surprising that biomedical disputes lend themselves so well to discussions about the judicial role. They are disputes about the truly moral questions, about the beginning and the end of life. They are polycentric disputes.[89] They raise issues about the limits of the law (and indeed as to the limits of medicine).[90] About the uses to which law can be put: this is seen as its starkest when litigation is pursued to challenge the allocation of medical resources.[91] It is significant that

---

[78] eg in relation to what information a doctor should give a prospective patient before treatment.
[79] *R (on the Application of Pretty) v DPP* [2002] 1 All ER 1.
[80] *R (on the Application of Burke) v GMC* [2005] 3 WLR 1132.
[81] *Evans v Amicus Healthcare Ltd* [2004] 2 FLR 766.
[82] *Re A (Conjoined Twins)* [2001] Fam 147.
[83] In particular in (2001) 9 *Medical Law Review* Special Issue.
[84] See HLA Hart, *The Concept of Law* (Oxford, 2nd edn, 1994), Postscript.
[85] *Law's Empire* (London, 1986).
[86] ibid 228.   [87] ibid 228.
[88] See S Guest, *Ronald Dworkin* (Edinburgh, 2nd edn, 1997) 40.
[89] The term is Michael Polanyi's: *Logic of Liberty* (London, 1951). See also M Freeman, 'Standards of Adjudication' (1973) 26 *Current Legal Problems* 166, and J Stone, *Social Dimensions of Law and Justice* (London, 1966) 653–4.
[90] On which see A Stark, *The Limits of Medicine* (New York, 2006).
[91] As recently in the Herceptin case: *R (on the Application of Rogers) v Swindon NHS Primary Care Trust and Another* [2006] EWCA 392.

in an earlier case[92] Laws J had conceptualized the question in rights language: the health authority had to do more than 'toll the bell of tight resources'.[93] And this was before the Human Rights Act 1998 came into operation. But it was John Ladd who pointed many years ago to bioethics' own legalistic tendencies. Writing in 1977, he thought 'it is hardly an exaggeration to say that discussions of medical ethics often amount to little more than glosses on the rights to life, liberty and the pursuit of happiness'.[94]

I am reluctant to decry the use of rights language.[95] But we must ask why it is coming to impose itself on bioethics thinking. Part of the explanation is the secularization of society. With this, religion has lost much of its authority. The debate over human-animal hybrids which erupted in March 2008[96] may be seen as the death throttle of religion's attempt to impose its answer on profound bioethical questions.[97] But many of the founders of contemporary bioethics were theologians, for example Joseph Fletcher[98] and Paul Ramsey.[99] Not suprisingly, in an era of increasing secularization this is less prevalent today. But there are still theological voices in bioethics, and these are not confined to any one religion: there is, for example, a continuing tradition of bioethical thinking within Judaism.[100] But the secularization of bioethics has left us increasingly dependent on the law as a 'working source of morality'.[101] Daniel Callahan has warned that pluralism can become a form of oppression if 'we are told to shut up in public about our private lives and beliefs and talk . . . moral esperanto'.[102] On the other hand, as Courtney Campbell emphasizes, it is important to recognize 'a wall of separation between religious

[92] *R v Cambridge DHA, ex p B* [1995] 2 All ER 129.

[93] On the case see C Ham, 'Tragic Choices In Healthcare: 'Implications of the Child B case' (1999) *British Medical Journal* 1258. More generally see A Friedman, 'Beyond Accountability for Reasonableness' (2008) 22 *Bioethics* 101; and M Stein, 'The Distribution of Life-Saving Medical Resources' (2002) 19(2) *Social Philosophy and Policy* 212.

[94] J Ladd, 'Legalism and Medical Ethics' in JW Davis, B Hoffmaster, and S Shorten (eds), *Contemporary Issues in Biomedical Ethics* (Totowa, N J, 1977) 6.

[95] As a passionate advocate of children's rights, eg in M Freeman, *The Rights and Wrongs of Children* (London, 1983).

[96] The first example of which is reported in *The Guardian*, 2 April 2008, 1. See further JS Robert and F Baylis, 'Crossing Species Boundaries' (2003) 3(3) *American Journal of Bioethics* 1.

[97] But perhaps the same thing was said when Papal authority tried to squash Galileo's scientific revelations! Who knows where it will strike next?

[98] J Fletcher, *Morals and Medicine* (Boston, 1960).

[99] P Ramsey, *The Patient As Person* (New Haven, Conn, 1970). See also now M Kuczewcki, 'Talking About Spirituality in the Clinical Setting: Can Being Professional Require Being Personal?' (2007) 7(7) *American Journal of Bioethics* 4.

[100] eg JD Bleich, *Bioethical Dilemmas—A Jewish Perspective* (Hoboken, NJ, 1998); D Sinclair, *Jewish Biomedical Ethics* (Oxford, 2003). Both authors are rabbis.

[101] PD Callahan, 'Religion and The Secularisation of Bioethics' (1990) 20(4) *Hastings Center Report* 2, 4.

[102] He is quoting from J Stout, *Ethics After Babel: The Languages of Morals and Their Discontents* (Boston, 1988) 294.

and public concerns'.[103] This is particularly so where public policy is being developed by public commissions (NICE or HFEA for example).[104] Ethics consultation must embrace moral engagement.[105] Law's concern with justice, fairness, rights, 'the rule of law' provides it with opportunites to make important contributions to such engagement.

[103] 'Religion and Moral Meaning in Bioethics' (1990) 20(4) *Hastings Center Report* 4, 6.
[104] See R Deech and A Smajdor, *From IVF to Immorality* (Oxford, 2007); LP Knowles and GE Kaebnick, *Reprogenetics: Law, Policy, and Ethical Issues* (Baltimore, 2007) (in particular T Caulfield 'Stem Cells, Clones, Consensus and the Law' ibid 105).
[105] And see J Moreno, 'Ethics Consultation as Moral Engagement' (1991) 5 *Bioethics* 44.

2

Bioethics: Bridging from Morality to Law?

Roger Brownsword*

I. Introduction

There is no older, nor more deeply contested, jurisprudential question than that of how we should understand the relationship between law and morality.[1] Should we side with the legal idealists, according to whom there is an essential conceptual connection between law and morals, such that legal reason is a sub-species of moral reason, legal obligation a sub-species of moral obligation, and so on; or should we follow the legal positivists in denying any such essential connection? With the modern emergence of bioethics, we might now ask an even more complex question, namely: how should we understand the relationship between law, morality, and bioethics?[2]

If bioethics is understood as a second order discourse (as a meta-ethic) concerning the nature of morality and the nature of moral judgments, it does little to interfere with our understanding—whatever that particular understanding might be—of the relationship between law and morality. However, if (as is the case with my untutored assumption) we understand bioethics as operating, so

---

* Professor of Law and Director of TELOS, King's College London and Honorary Professor in Law at the University of Sheffield. An earlier draft of the paper which forms this chapter was presented at the Twelfth Annual Interdisciplinary Colloquium, on 'Law and Bioethics', that was held at University College London on 2–3 July, 2007. While I am grateful for comments made by those who participated in the Colloquium, I should say that the usual disclaimers apply to the published chapter. I should also make it absolutely clear that I am in no sense speaking for, nor indeed against, the Nuffield Council on Bioethics (of which I am a member) in this chapter.

[1] Seminally, in the modern Anglo/American jurisprudential canon, see HLA Hart, 'Positivism and the Separation of Law and Morals' (1957–58) 71 *Harvard Law Review* 593, and LL Fuller, 'Positivism and Fidelity to Law—A Reply to Professor Hart' (1957–58) 71 *Harvard Law Review* 630. For my own position in the 'Sheffield school of natural law', see D Beyleveld and R Brownsword, *Law as a Moral Judgment* (London: Sweet and Maxwell, 1986; reprinted Sheffield: Sheffield Academic Press, 1994).

[2] cf J Montgomery, 'The Legitimacy of Medical Law' in SAM McLean (ed), *First Do No Harm* (Aldershot: Ashgate, 2006) 1.

to speak, 'between' law and morality, then it is not so obvious how it fits into our conceptual mapping of law and morality. On this latter understanding of the matter, what kind of intermediary is bioethics? Should we view bioethics as some sort of corrective for failures in legal and/or moral guidance? If bioethics is a 'product', is it a force for conservation and constraint or is it a force for change? If bioethics is a process, is its purpose to build consensus or to build bridges from defensible moral principles to practical legal positions? And, whatever we make of bioethics, how does it then relate to our understanding of the relationship between law and morality?

This chapter is in four parts. In the first part, I take as my foil the view of ethics presented in the Nuffield Council on Bioethics' report, 'Critical Care Decisions in Fetal and Neonatal Medicine: Ethical Issues'.³ For convenience, I will refer to this as the 'Nuffield view'. However, to avoid any misunderstanding, it is important that I emphasize that this is not some *ex cathedra* declaration by the Council; rather, this is simply the view sketched in a short section of one of the Council's many reports. According to this view, bioethics has a dual function. On the one hand, it is a critical discipline that 'investigates the underlying reasons or justifications for specific moral beliefs or moral codes.'⁴ On the other hand, bioethics should also seek out platforms and pockets of moral convergence and consensus. In the second part, I sketch how I see things from a particular rights-led legal idealist perspective. From this perspective, bioethics is much more concerned with developing practical guidance (whether in a hard or soft law form) based on particular moral beliefs and codes rather than with investigating the underlying reasons or justifications for such beliefs and codes. In the third part, I consider the nature of the plurality that a critical bioethics will construct, the extent to which that operates against consensus, and the scope for bioethics to play a practically useful role. Finally, I suggest some ways in which the critical capacity of bioethics might be further deployed. Above all, so I contend, bioethics needs to transcend the plurality by developing a critical understanding of moral community itself. Equipped with such an understanding, we can debate the possibility that developments in the biosciences might threaten the very possibility of such a community and how we think we should respond to such a threat.

One other introductory remark is in order. When I started the paper on which this chapter is based, my intention was to try to map the relationship between law, morality, and bioethics; and that line of inquiry was prompted by what I am calling the Nuffield view. However, papers have a habit of taking on a life of their own. In this case, the further that I have gone into the topic, the more I have

---

³ Nuffield Council on Bioethics, 'Critical Care Decisions in Fetal and Neonatal Medicine: Ethical Issues' (London, November 2006 hereinafter 'the Report'). Although the discussion in paras 2.2–2.7 is headed 'The role of ethical analysis in considering practical problems', I take it that what is said here about 'ethics' applies equally to 'bioethics'. In other words, I take it that for 'ethics' we can read 'bioethics'.

⁴ ibid para 2.2.

become aware of an acute tension in bioethics between the philosophical impulse towards critique and the practical need for workable consensus. In my concluding comments, I will endeavour to bring these threads together, sketching how I think that this tension in the bioethical project plays relative to the background conceptual debate between legal idealists and legal positivists.

II. Bioethics as a Critical Discipline

Bioethics, I take it, is concerned that those who engage in biopractice should make every effort to avoid doing the wrong thing and should always attempt to do the right thing. The standard directive that, above all, clinicians and researchers should do no harm to their patients and participants (*primum non nocere*) is bioethical in spirit even if its origins go back many centuries before the modern discipline of bioethics was conceived. However, if we were to seek a clear conceptual fix on 'bioethics', we would need to establish the scope of the 'bio'—bioethics being ethics with a particular, bio, focus—as well as settling the relationship between '(bio)ethics' and its fellow travellers, morality and law. It is this latter question that I want to focus on.

It is relatively unusual, I think, for those who are 'doing bioethics' to pause to reflect on what precisely it is that they are doing. However, the Nuffield Council on Bioethics' Working Party on Critical Care did just this. According to the Report that was subsequently published by the Council:

The critical discipline of ethics or moral philosophy investigates the underlying reasons or justifications for specific moral beliefs or moral codes. It does this by various means: it seeks clarity in the uses of important terms, such as 'quality of life'; and it requires consistency in the practical application of moral claims or values. Ethics also requires coherence in the defence of any moral framework, that is, a demonstration of how it conforms to other beliefs held to be true. This requirement leads to the formulation of ethical theories, which aim to give a systematic explanation of how arguments about moral issues can be resolved, through appeals to some general criterion according to which moral claims can be assessed.[5]

As I read this, it would mean that bioethics, as a critical discipline of ethics, would operate to impose some rigour on those so-called 'moral' beliefs or judgments that relate to some aspect of biopractice. For example, those who contend that it is immoral to use cytoplasmic hybrid embryos as research tools would not be allowed to get away with a mere 'yuk'.[6] Before mere negative or positive attitudes

---

[5] ibid para 2.2.
[6] See House of Commons Science and Technology Select Committee, *Government Proposals for the Regulation of Hybrid and Chimera Embryos (Fifth Report of Session 2006–07)* (HC 272-I 5 April, 2007). See, too, the Academy of Medical Sciences, 'Inter-Species Embryos' (London, July 2007) 28–30 (especially para 8.3.1, for consideration of the objection that 'the creation of human

could be treated as 'moral', they would need to survive various tests relating to their consistency and coherence as candidate moral beliefs.[7] In the process, proponents of these views would be channelled towards one of the recognized general moral theories (principally, so the Report has it, utilitarian, deontological, or virtue-based).[8]

At once, it is conceded in the Report that bioethics of this kind 'may not appear to be immediately helpful to those seeking practical solutions to the kind of dilemmas which may arise in fetal and neonatal critical care.'[9] Indeed, this seems to be so. For, if bioethical scrutiny of an ostensible moral belief results in that belief being dismissed as a mere positive or negative attitude, the holder of the belief now knows that moral reason is more demanding; but precisely what moral reason demands in the particular case has still to be determined. Alternatively, if an ostensible moral belief passes muster formally speaking, the holder of the belief is at least engaging in moral reason; but how well the belief fares in guiding the holder towards doing the right thing depends upon how it stands relative to more general criteria of right action (and how defensible those criteria are). Having taken readers through the leading moral theories, the Report warns that, where values run deep, we should not expect unanimity. In other words, even if a belief offers a passable and reasonable account of what it is to do the right thing in a particular case, there might be rival beliefs, just as passable and just as reasonable, offering different moral guidance. Spelling this out, the Report continues: 'we must acknowledge that there is a plurality of moral beliefs and assumptions and that each has the function of providing tools for examining the moral permissibility of certain acts. At the same time, we should try to seek agreement on substantive matters wherever possible, even if we disagree about the reasons behind these shared conclusions'.[10]

So, as a critical discipline, bioethics tries to sort out the moral wheat from the non-moral chaff, assisting those who wish to do the right thing to develop a deeper understanding of their moral convictions as well as an appreciation of the way in which their moral commitments hold together as a coherent set. For those who wish not only to do the right thing but also to be able to articulate a defensible justification of their particular positions on doing the right thing, this is fine. However, because there are a number of competing master criteria of rightness, this exercise in bioethical education tends to generate a well-articulated conflict of moral beliefs and positions. Faced with such conflict, how are we to move forward in practice? The answer seems to be to seek out those positions where views

embryos containing animal material is unacceptable because it subverts the animal-human species distinction and undermines human dignity and human rights').

[7] cf Ronald Dworkin's distinction between morals in an 'anthropological' and in a 'discriminatory' sense: RM Dworkin, *Taking Rights Seriously* (revised edn) (London: Duckworth, 1978) 248–53.

[8] Report (n 3 above) para 2.3.

[9] ibid.   [10] ibid para 2.5.

converge and where, as Cass Sunstein would put it, there is the possibility of 'incompletely theorized agreement'.[11]

For readers who are not yet persuaded that bioethics, so conceived, has much practical value, the Report offers the following three reasons for thinking otherwise:

- First, by carefully examining the concepts used within different ethical theories, ethical analysis can help to clarify their scope and validity. A better understanding of the strengths and weaknesses of those concepts can reduce ambiguities and confusion. It may also reveal that there is more agreement among people than they might think.

- Secondly, by demanding ethical consistency, ethical analysis can reveal ways in which people may be responding instinctively or with a 'gut' reaction to some situations, rather than examining them in terms of their general moral beliefs.

- Thirdly, by insisting that reasons or justifications for our decisions are provided, ethical analysis can lead to a shift in our views, as we come to appreciate the basis on which those with different opinions make their judgments.[12]

What are we to make of this? It seems to me that, in the light of this analysis, we might see bioethics as having a trio of critical and constructive functions as follows. First, in its critical filtering capacity, bioethics seeks to expose those views that masquerade as moral when they are no more than instinctive or gut reactions. Secondly, it aids those who aspire to do the right thing to develop an understanding of the particular justifying moral reasons for their practical views. Thirdly, having cultivated a genuinely moral community, bioethics has a role in developing a consensus where moral pluralism might otherwise lead to dissensus—although, quite how bioethics, having clarified and sharpened moral differences, is to bring biopractitioners together around a consensus is not yet clear. We might conclude, therefore, that the Nuffield view of bioethics is neither fish nor fowl, neither a full-blooded critique that goes beyond pluralism nor a clearly developed strategy for consensus-building. Is this the view that we should accept?

III. Bioethics as a Bridge

My initial reaction to the Nuffield view was not so much that it does not go as far as it might with critique but, rather, that it mislocates bioethics. Without a doubt, moral philosophy has an important role to play in clarifying the elements of a moral position (or standpoint) in the formal sense. However, my sense was

---

[11] CR Sunstein, *Legal Reasoning and Political Conflict* (Oxford: Oxford University Press, 1996) ch 2.
[12] Report (n 3 above) para 2.6.

that bioethics is much more proximately concerned with developing working guidance for those who wish to do the right thing but who are unclear what they should actually do in particular cases—such, for example, seems to be the inspiration for much of the interest in clinical ethics committees.[13] In part, the reason for this, I suspect, was that I was contrasting the Nuffield view with the way that I see bioethics operating in what I take to be an ideal-typical legal-moral community, namely a 'community of rights'.[14] Stated summarily, the essential characteristics of such a community are as follows.

First, because the community of rights is a particular kind of *moral* community, it must systematically embed a *moral* standpoint (in the formal sense). No doubt, there could be considerable debate about the precise specification of the generic characteristics of the formally-speaking 'moral'. However, in line with the Nuffield account, I take it that a community of rights, as a moral community, must hold its commitments sincerely and in good faith, that it must treat its standards as categorically binding and universalizable, and that there must be an integrity and coherence about its commitments as a whole.

Secondly, because the community is a community of *rights*, the substantive moral approach embedded is rights-led, being committed to the protection and promotion of individual rights. In this respect, the community distinguishes itself from two other rival instances of moral community, these being utilitarian and duty-driven communities.[15] Virtue ethics is also, as the Nuffield Report reminds us, a recognized approach. However, in my view, it is not directly in competition with utilitarian, rights-based, or duty-driven ethics. Rather, it focuses on agent, not act, morality and, in principle, there could be a utilitarian virtue ethics, a rights protecting virtue ethics, and a duty respecting virtue ethics.

Thirdly, a community of rights, so specified, might take quite a wide range of forms. Let me also stipulate, then, that, in a community of rights, a will (or choice) theory of rights, rather than an interest theory of rights, is adopted.[16]

---

[13] See eg D Beyleveld and R Brownsword, 'Clinical Ethics Committees in the United Kingdom: First Wave, Shock Wave, Second Wave?' in G Lebeer and M Moulin (eds), *Ethical Function in Hospital Ethics Committees* (Working Papers: Workshop 2) (Brussels: Free University of Brussels, 2001) 17; and 'Ethics Committees: Public Interest, Private Interest, and the Ethics of Partnership' in G Lebeer (ed), *Ethical Function in Hospital Ethics Committees* (Amsterdam: IOS Press, 2002) 135.

[14] See further R Brownsword, *Rights, Regulation and the Technological Revolution* (Oxford: Oxford University Press, 2008) passim.

[15] For the most part, positions argued for in bioethical debates reflect one of three principal approaches, namely: utility-maximizing, rights-led, and duty-led. See eg R Brownsword, 'Three Bioethical Approaches: A Triangle to be Squared', paper presented at international conference on the patentability of biotechnology organized by the Sasakawa Peace Foundation, Tokyo (September 2004) available at <http://www.ipgenethics.org/conference/transcript/session3. doc>; 'Making People Better and Making Better People: Bioethics and the Regulation of Stem Cell Research' (2005) 1 *Journal of Academic Legal Studies* 3; and 'Cloning, Zoning and the Harm Principle' in SAM McLean (ed), *First Do No Harm* (Aldershot: Ashgate, 2006) 527.

[16] On will and interest theories of rights, see HLA Hart, 'Bentham on Legal Rights' in AWB Simpson (ed), *Oxford Essays in Jurisprudence* (Second Series) (Oxford: Clarendon Press, 1973) 171;

It follows that, in such a community, the paradigmatic bearer of rights is one who has the developed capacity for exercising whatever rights are held, including making choices about whether to give or to refuse consent in relation to the rights that are held.

Fourthly, a community of rights is to be understood as a reflective and interpretive society, not so much a finished product as an ongoing process. By this, I mean that it is a community that constantly keeps under review the question of whether the current interpretation of its commitments is the best interpretation.

Even with these specific features, the general concept of a community of rights might be articulated in a variety of particular conceptions (including, of course, a human rights conception). Accordingly, we might find conceptions of such a community with various epistemological bases (some more foundationalist than others), with different views about the status of non-paradigmatic rights-holders, with different arrays of recognized rights, with different approaches to conflicting and competing rights, and with different views about precaution, and so on.[17]

Before I comment on how bioethics fits into such a community, it needs to be said that, within such a community, all forms of regulation (including both hard and soft law forms) are understood as being vertically integrated with the overarching rights commitments.[18] This is not just a matter of checking that positive legal enactments are compatible with the community's rights commitments, the integration, both in regulatory practice and in jurisprudential theory, is more complete. In practice, all participants in the regulatory enterprise view themselves as moral stakeholders with a responsibility to articulate the community's moral convictions in the most compelling way; and, as a matter of jurisprudential theory, if positive enactments clearly violate the community's background moral commitments they are not to be regarded as legally valid.

What role would bioethics play in such a community and how would it triangulate relative to law and morals? As I conceive of it, bioethics is a bridge that connects the very general, and rather abstract, moral convictions of the community to the day-to-day practical guidance that biopractitioners require if (as is the case in such a community) they are to be confident that they are doing the right thing. The point is that, as Charles Fried once put it, it is a long drop from general principles to particular applications.[19] Bioethics, in a community of

---

and DN MacCormick, 'Rights in Legislation' in PMS Hacker and J Raz (eds), *Law, Morality, and Society* (Oxford: Clarendon Press, 1977) 189.

[17] cf D Beyleveld and R Brownsword, 'Principle, Proceduralism and Precaution in a Community of Rights' (2006) 19 *Ratio Juris* 141.

[18] cf R Brownsword, 'The Ancillary Care Responsibilities of Researchers: Reasonable but Not Great Expectations' (2007) 35 *Journal of Law, Medicine and Ethics* 679.

[19] See C Fried, 'Rights and the Common Law' in RG Frey (ed), *Utility and Rights* (Oxford: Basil Blackwell, 1985) 215, 231: 'The picture I have...is of philosophy proposing an elaborate structure of arguments and considerations that descend from on high but stop some twenty feet above the ground. It is the peculiar task of law to complete this structure of ideals and values, to bring it down to earth...'

rights, endeavours to close this gap and articulate the general scheme of rights at a more particular level (much as the jurisprudence of the European Convention on Human Rights (ECHR) is articulated in particularly troublesome cases).[20] Let me give some short illustrative examples.

Let us assume that, in a community of rights, the range of basic rights together with their paradigmatic applications is pretty much settled. Nevertheless, bio-practitioners encounter cases where they are unclear what course they should take if they are to do the right thing (relative to their community's rights-based constitutive morality). What kinds of cases might these be?

They might be cases involving the interpretation of the scope of a recognized right (for instance, the scope of privacy and confidentiality), or the priority between conflicting recognized rights (for instance, a conflict between confidentiality and the rights of a third party to be notified that they are at risk), or between competing claims under the same right (for instance, claims to scarce health care resources), and so on.

Another cluster of practical questions might arise from the community's commitment to a will theory of rights according to which the benefit of rights may be waived by a rights-holder who gives a free and informed consent. But what precisely are the ingredients of an unforced choice? Do incentives or inducements ever militate against unforced choice? What kind of disclosure is required before a consent is informed? What kind of signal of consent (opt-out as well as opt-in) will suffice? What kind of justificatory force should be attributed to third-party authorization or consent?[21]

There are also many difficult questions arising from the community's view that rights-holders are the exemplars of those who have moral status. This invites questions about the moral status of fetuses and young children, non-human higher animals, smart robots, and, in some future world, hybrids, cyborgs, and chimeras of various kinds. Each community of rights must debate such matters. Moreover, not only must it respond to the inclusionary question (who has rights?) but it must also determine its approach to those life-forms that are to be excluded. What attitude does the community have to those who are judged not to qualify as rights-holders? Given the frailty of human reasoning, how precautionary should the community be? Is there a margin in which the benefit of doubt applies? If so, how wide is the margin to be?

Even if a community of rights starts with a substantial degree of high-level agreement, there is still a great deal of interpretive work to be done. The devil really is in the detail and, as I see it, it falls to bioethics to help to ease some of these practical dilemmas.

---

[20] cf Montgomery, (n 2 above) 9–12.
[21] See generally D Beyleveld and R Brownsword, *Consent in the Law* (Oxford: Hart, 2007); and (for inducements, information, and third parties) Roger Brownsword, 'Informed Consent: To Whom it May Concern' (2007) 15 *Jahrbuch für Recht und Ethik* 267.

IV. Bioethics and Moral Pluralism

The Nuffield view does not presuppose a community of rights nor, indeed, any kind of ideal-typical moral community. Rather, it presupposes the inevitability of moral pluralism. Indeed, there are distinct echoes of the setting (and the push for consensual solutions) presupposed (and prescribed) by the House of Commons' Science and Technology Committee in its controversial report, *Human Reproductive Technologies and the Law*:[22]

We accept that [in] a society that is both multi-faith and largely secular, there is never going to be consensus on...the role of the state in reproductive decision-making. There are no demonstrably 'right' answers to the complex ethical, moral and political equations involved.... We recognise the difficulty of achieving consensus between protagonists in opposing camps.... We believe, however, that to be effective this Committee's conclusions should seek consensus, as far as it is possible to achieve.[23]

Under such conditions, unless regulatees are either not politically engaged or they are simply prepared to trust the judgments of regulators, the capacity of the regulatory system will be put to the test—or, at any rate, in the absence of happenstance consensus or convergence of views, this will be so.

If moral pluralism is one of the regulatory facts of life, the bridging task of bioethics in the ideal-typical community of rights is *relatively* (I repeat, *relatively*) straightforward: in such a community, protagonists at least share the same deep commitments and it is for bioethics to fine-tune the detailed articulation of the rights regime. However, where the community is deeply divided with no agreement as to basic commitments, the bridge-builders will be working over seriously troubled waters.[24] If this is the real world, how does bioethics fit into it?

As I have said, I take it that we at least agree that bioethics is a discourse that enjoins biopractitioners to steer clear of doing the wrong thing and, instead, always to try to do the right thing. I also take it that, in the real world, bioethics operates on a large canvas. The dominant motif of modern bioethics is that fundamental and egregious wrongdoing should be named and constrained. Thus, bioethics has articulated two fundamental and cosmopolitan constraints: one is that biopractice should never override human rights for the sake of the larger

---

[22] HC 7-1, Science and Technology Committee, *Human Reproductive Technologies and the Law* (*Fifth Report of Session 2004–05*) (London: TSO, 24 March 2005). Ironically, the report was judged newsworthy not simply for its permissive recommendations (especially concerning sex selection) but also for the fact that the Committee, with its quest for consensus, was actually divided down the middle, 5 of the 11 members disagreeing with the report: see HC 491, Science and Technology Committee, *Inquiry into Human Reproductive Technologies and the Law* (*Eighth Special Report of Session 2004–05*) (London: TSO, 29 March 2005) Annex A.

[23] Report of 24 March 2005 (n 22 above) para 46.

[24] For an excellent discussion, see A Plomer, *The Law and Ethics of Medical Research—International Bioethics and Human Rights* (London: Cavendish, 2005).

social or scientific good; and the other is that biopractice should never support activities that compromise human dignity. These constraints are systematically embedded in the guidance issued by UNESCO and most recently so in the Universal Declaration on Bioethics and Human Rights 2005.

Even (or especially) in such grand declarations, however, we find the counter-tendencies that we can detect in the Nuffield view of bioethics as a critical discipline. If we subject the UNESCO axioms to critical analysis, we soon find that human dignity in particular is susceptible to many competing interpretations.[25] And yet it is around this very concept that UNESCO is seeking to build an international consensus. To put this another way, it is relatively easy to agree that we should regulate against biopractices that compromise human dignity; but, as soon as we take a harder look at what human dignity signifies or at which practices might compromise that value, we find that the agreement unravels. The point is that, where there is a deep-seated pluralism, whatever differences we manage to cover over are always liable to erupt. Again, as Sunstein cautions, we can be too critical for our own collective comfort.

It might be thought that there are some neutral values that can be unproblematically embedded in bioethical practice. For example, it might be thought that the principle of informed consent, or the principle that one should not harm others, is neutral in this sense and that principles of this kind are supported in the same way right across the moral plurality. If there are such values, informed consent and harm to others certainly are not two of them. As the Nuffield Report points out, there are several systematic moral theories and these generate a conflicting plurality.

In my view, the form, substance, and implications of this plurality can be summarised as follows. At root, we have a basic matrix that sets the form, rather than the substance, of ethical reasoning. This matrix, setting the mould for ethical debates, involves three essential *forms*: namely, goal-orientated (consequentialism), rights-based, and duty-based forms. Each of these forms is open to a variety of *substantive* articulations, with various goals, various rights, and various duties being advocated. Currently, the substantive articulation in bioethics highlights three views—utilitarian, human rights, and dignitarian—comprising what I have called the bioethical triangle.[26] While this triangle fully expresses the *form* of the matrix (because it is constituted by a particular goal-orientated ethic, a particular rights-based ethic, and a particular duty-based ethic), it is by no means exhaustive of all substantive ethical possibilities. In other words, the

---

[25] See the analysis in D Beyleveld and R Brownsword, *Human Dignity in Bioethics and Biolaw* (Oxford: Oxford University Press, 2001).

[26] See R Brownsword (n 15 above); R Brownsword, 'Ethical Pluralism and the Regulation of Modern Biotechnology' in Francesco Francioni (ed), *Biotechnologies and International Human Rights* (Oxford: Hart, 2007) 45; and R Brownsword, 'Human Dignity, Ethical Pluralism, and the Regulation of Modern Biotechnologies' in Therese Murphy (ed), *New Technologies Human Rights* (Oxford: Oxford University Press, 2008) forthcoming.

bioethical triangle should be viewed as a particular conjunction of ethical form and substance that reflects the way in which certain positions have come to dominate modern bioethical discourse and debate. Nevertheless, the implications of this conjunction are that we have a three-cornered and conflictual bioethics; that what one makes of 'harm' or who one counts as an 'other' depends upon where one is coming from in the triangle;[27] and that the same applies to what one makes of consent and the conditions of valid consent.[28] In other words, although the rhetoric of harm and consent, and the like, might be shared across the plurality, each constituency reads these concepts in its own distinctive way.

This is not to say that bioethics is incapable of offering any practical guidance, the plurality notwithstanding. Let me suggest four ways in which practical guidance can be developed.

First, bioethics can articulate the detailed script for a particular ethical constituency. For example, in their recent book, *Rethinking Informed Consent in Bioethics*, Neil Manson and Onora O'Neill have tried to explicate the notion of informed consent from a certain kind of (essentially Kantian) duty-driven perspective;[29] and this is very much what Deryck Beyleveld and I did in *Consent in the Law*,[30] save only that we were assuming a rights-driven perspective. In other words, bioethicists might anchor their detailed guidance to a particular ethical view. Similarly, in the Critical Care Report, we might interpret the detailed guidelines proposed for resuscitation and intensive care in relation to babies born below twenty-six weeks of gestation as concretizing an essentially utilitarian ethic. Of course, in a plurality, such notes of guidance would be embraced only by those who adopt the particular ethic; but this is not to say that the exercise would lack all practical utility.

Secondly, bioethics might identify areas of substantial convergence within the plurality. For example, although there are shades of difference between the analyses of consent stemming from a Kantian duty-led approach and a rights-based approach, there is a substantial convergence. In particular, these analyses reject the idea that consent is a fundamental value: rather, consent assumes importance relative to a background regime of rights and duties, but it is secondary to such background standards. One might then argue for a revised regulatory understanding of consent, based on such a convergence. Again, though, such a proposal would commend itself only to those parts of the plurality implicated in the convergence.

---

[27] See R Brownsword, 'Cloning, Zoning, and the Harm Principle' in SAM McLean (ed), *First, Do No Harm* (Festschrift for Ken Mason) (Aldershot: Ashgate, 2006) 527.

[28] See R Brownsword, 'The Cult of Consent: Fixation and Fallacy' (2004) 15 *King's College Law Journal* 223.

[29] NC Manson and O O'Neill, *Rethinking Informed Consent in Bioethics* (Cambridge: Cambridge University Press, 2007).

[30] D Beyleveld and R Brownsword, *Consent in the Law* (Oxford: Hart, 2007).

Thirdly, it might be possible for bioethicists to broker a compromise between competing interests or conflicting moral theories. For example, the ethics and governance framework for UK Biobank respects the interest in voluntary participation and the need for privacy and confidentiality but the interests of researchers and their sponsors are prioritized when it comes to matters of property and commercial exploitation.[31] The resulting package is necessarily a bit pragmatic but any such compromise will need to deviate from pure principle.[32]

Fourthly, bioethics might become much more procedural and facilitative in its approach. Bioethics would concede that it lacks the power to prescribe a substantive cure for the plurality. There is no magic bullet. Instead, bioethics can clarify the hotspots in bioethical debate, set out the contending considerations, and encourage protagonists to keep on talking.[33] In this vein, the Critical Care Report, having set out a number of key considerations (such as the value of life and the best interests of the fetus or child) declares that its focus 'is on not so much *what* is the "right" decision, but *how* should one proceed if people hold different views concerning substantive matters raised by critical care decisions, and *who* should be responsible for taking decisions...'[34] This kind of facilitative approach is also evident elsewhere in the Nuffield Council's work—for example, in its Report on 'The Ethics of Research Involving Animals',[35] where there is a very explicit appeal to discussion and dialogue (opening with a commitment to replacement, reduction, and refinement) that promises to generate some version of an overlapping consensus; and, in the Council's most recent report, on 'Public Health: Ethical Issues',[36] it is facilitation of ethical decision-making that underlies the proposed 'stewardship' framework.

In such conditions of plurality, then, how does bioethics relate to morality and law? Certainly, bioethics cannot simply act as a conduit bridging from shared moral principles to general laws, let alone to detailed practical guidance. Any substantive practical guidance that bioethics gives is necessarily partisan; and it might well be judged that bioethics does better to play the role of a non-partisan facilitator. Nevertheless, if what we want is a way of smoothing and stabilizing the plurality, then bioethics might have a more fundamental role to play.

---

[31] 'UK Biobank Ethics and Governance Framework,' (version 2.0, July 2006). For a helpful overview and critical comparative survey of the various governance structures adopted by biobanks in Europe, see S Gibbons, 'Are UK Genetic Databases Governed Adequately? A Comparative Legal Analysis' (2007) 27 *Legal Studies* 312.

[32] See R Brownsword, 'Biobank Governance: Property, Privacy, and Consent' in C Lenk, N Hoppe, and R Andorno (eds), *Ethics and Law of Intellectual Property: Current Problems in Politics, Science and Technology* (Aldershot: Ashgate, 2007) 11.

[33] For a nice recent example of such a bioethical contribution, see British Medical Association, 'Boosting Your Brainpower: Ethical Aspects of Cognitive Enhancements' (London, November 2007).

[34] Report (n 3 above) Executive Summary, para 14.

[35] May 2005.   [36] London, November 2007.

V. Bioethics as a Critical Discipline Revisited

The Nuffield view emphasizes the critical nature of bioethics; but the more intensely we turn the spotlight of a critical bioethics on putative moral positions, the less likely it seems that we will achieve a consensus. Arguably, though, the instincts behind the Nuffield view are correct and, if there is a mistake, it is to call off the critique for fear that it will altogether wreck any prospect of consensus or compromise. Yet, if we were to persist with a critical approach, what kind of contribution might bioethics then make? I suggest that bioethics might, in this enhanced critical capacity, make three contributions.

First, on the Nuffield view, we should not admit a position as 'moral' unless it satisfies various conditions concerning its coherence and consistency. A person who claims to have a 'moral' position on some issue will be disqualified unless these conditions are met. If one claims to stand on the moral high ground, this means that one must leave behind low ground special pleading, opportunism, ad hockery, and the like. But, this analysis can, and should, be scaled up. It is not just the supposed moral positions of individuals that should be subjected to this kind of critical analysis, it is also the positions taken up by whole communities or governments and regulators who speak on their behalf. So, for instance, in *Mice, Morality and Patents*,[37] Deryck Beyleveld and I argued that, unless the signatories were to give up their moral commitments under the ECHR these obligations necessarily carried through into their subsequent activities. Hence, when such parties signed up to the European Patent Convention 1973, they necessarily did so subject to their human rights commitments. It follows that, when the parties expressly provided in Article 53(a) for European patents to be excluded where commercial exploitation of an invention would be contrary to morality, the background human rights commitments must be focal for the interpretation of that Article.[38]

Secondly, bioethics might venture beyond immanent critique—ie beyond critique that is limited to evaluating the internal consistency of a position, or the congruence of practice with declared principle. Bioethics might stake out a position that it maintains is categorically defensible. In communities where pluralism is laced with moral relativism, it would be a bold move to take such a step. Foundationalist rationalism is short of supporters. Nevertheless, this is precisely what Deryck Beyleveld and I tried to do in *Human Dignity in Bioethics*

---

[37] D Beyleveld and R Brownsword, *Mice, Morality and Patents* (London: Common Law Institute of Intellectual Property, 1993).

[38] cf, too, J Harris, *Enhancing Evolution* (Princeton, NJ: Princeton University Press, 2007) 156–8, for a critique of the Human Fertilisation and Embryology Authority's readiness, following the public consultation on sex selection, to give priority to unfiltered public opinion rather than the moral principle of reproductive autonomy (backed by the democratic presumption).

and Biolaw.[39] In that book, our argument against the dogmatic conservativism of the dignitarian alliance is not simply a case of jumping on a certain (human rights) bandwagon; our critique rests on a particular (Gewirthian) argument in moral philosophy that maintains that there is a necessary connection between agency and a rights-led morality that demands respect for the generic conditions of agency. Granted, there is no shortage of critics of this (Gewirthian) argument, but nothing ventured nothing gained.

The third contribution that a critical bioethics can make is perhaps the most important: this is to monitor biopractices that might undermine values or conditions that underlie all versions of moral community. Our critical gaze here is on practices that challenge those ideas of responsibility and respect that are absolutely fundamental to any such community. Here, we are dealing with the lowest common denominators of ethical deliberation and the challenge is to identify which biopractices, if any, truly threaten to corrode the viability of moral community itself. If bioethics is able to wrest ideas such as human dignity and vulnerability from the partisan grip of the dignitarian alliance,[40] and if it is able to give us a clear fix on how these ideas relate to the infrastructure of moral community itself, it might yet arrest a drift towards collective self-destruction. In this light, the recent Nuffield Report, on 'The Forensic Use of Bioinformation: Ethical Issues',[41] sides with those who draw attention to the way in which the culture of security and surveillance can rapidly change as biotechnology and information technology is deployed for regulatory purposes.[42]

Taking up this particular issue,[43] the authors of an important report for the Information Commissioner have recently maintained that the development of a surveillance society is not so much a conspiracy as 'a part of just being modern'.[44] In such a society,[45] as the technologies of surveillance[46] become increasingly

---

[39] D Beyleveld and R Brownsword, *Human Dignity in Bioethics and Biolaw* (Oxford: Oxford University Press, 2001).

[40] See R Brownsword, 'Bioethics Today, Bioethics Tomorrow: Stem Cell Research and the "Dignitarian Alliance".' (2003) 17 *Notre Dame JLEPP* 15.

[41] London, September 2007.

[42] See R Brownsword 'Genetic Databases: One for All and All for One?' (2007) 18 *King's College Law Journal* 247. For a very helpful review of the range of technologies now deployed in the criminal justice system, see B Bowling, A Marks, and C Murphy, 'Crime Control Technologies: Towards an Analytical Framework and Research Agenda' in Roger Brownsword and Karen Yeung (eds), *Regulating Technologies* (Oxford: Hart, 2008) (forthcoming).

[43] Here, I am drawing on R Brownsword, 'Human Dignity: Empowerment, Constraint, and the Conservation of Moral Community' (paper given at IUA Workshop on 'Human Dignity: Sociological, Ethical and Bioethical Aspects', Royal Academy of Morocco, Rabat, 26–27 June, 2007).

[44] K Ball, D Lyon, DM Wood, C Norris, and C Raab, A Report on the Surveillance Society (September 2006) para 1.6.

[45] Ball *et al*, (n 44 above), identify the key characteristics of such a society as one in which 'we find purposeful, routine, systematic and focused attention paid to personal details, for the sake of control, entitlement, management, influence or protection' (para 3.1).

[46] For a review of the range of such technologies, see ibid at para 9.3 *et seq.*

sophisticated, less obtrusive and more embedded, citizens will not always be aware that they are being monitored and regulated. Thus:

[The] continuous software-sorting of people and their life chances in cities is organised through myriad electronic and physical 'passage points' or 'choke points', negotiated through a widening number of code words, pass words, PIN numbers, user names, access controls, electronic cards or biometric scans. Some are highly visible and negotiated willingly (a PIN credit card purchase or an airport passport control). Others are more covert (the sorting of internet or call centre traffic). On still other occasions, the passage point is clear (a CCTV camera on a street or a speed camera on a motorway), but it is impossible to know in practice if one's face or car number plate has actually been scanned.[47]

More generally, the 'combination of CCTV, biometrics, databases and tracking technologies can be seen as part of a much broader exploration . . . of the use of interconnected "smart" systems to track movements and behaviours of millions of people in both time and space'.[48]

So, imagine that, in addition to this range of smart technology, the state has access to population-wide genetic databases to which it applies a profiling technology that is so sophisticated and reliable that there is little chance that, where a criminal offence is committed, the offending agent will not be detected. Even if such a community has a fairly limited criminal code, the fact that almost all offenders will be detected might be a cause for concern in a moral community.[49] But why? If the code penalizes conduct that we judge to be immoral, what is the problem with such an effective detection strategy? For years, we have bemoaned the fact that, where crime and punishment is concerned, nothing works. So, why look for problems when we find a criminal justice strategy that actually works?

The problem, stated shortly, is that agents in a moral community expect to make a choice between compliance and non-compliance with their legal-moral criminal code. To be sure, even with the hypothesized profiling, agents have the paper option of non-compliance. But the reality is that agents who do not obey almost certainly will pay. For a moral community, the concern is whether such a state of affairs interferes with the development of agent virtue, particularly the virtue of choosing to do the right thing for the right reason. For, if agents comply only because they fear near-certain detection and punishment, there is little room for the promotion of the desired virtue.

Against this, it might be argued that such a view is 'idealistic'. Even without such profiling technology, agents rarely do the right thing for just the right reason. In practice, for many agents it is the background (albeit uncertain) threat of penal sanctions that deters the commission of crime. On this view, where agents rarely

---

[47] ibid para 9.10.2.   [48] ibid para 9.10.3.
[49] cf V Tadros, 'Power and the Value of Privacy' in E Claes, A Duff, and S Gutwirth (eds), *Privacy and the Criminal Law* (Antwerp and Oxford: Intersentia, 2006) 105 (especially Tadros' discussion of what he calls Camerania).

do the right thing for the right reason, profiling (by converting a low-risk threat of punishment into a high-risk threat of punishment) simply extends the logic of the existing arrangements—this is no real change in kind, simply a change in degree. Even in a morally disposed community, there has to be some sanction to compensate for weakness of the will.

Countering this injection of realism, those who hope for a morally progressive evolution will protest that profiling makes it much more difficult—in fact, nigh impossible—for that evolution to take place. For, when the threat of detection and punishment is relatively low, there is still space for moral reason to play a part in influencing the decision to comply or not. Indeed, in the Platonic fable of the Ring of Gyges,[50] it was precisely where there was no risk of detection and punishment that moral reason (if it were to have a significant role to play) came into its own. If, by extreme contrast, the threat of detection and punishment is overwhelming, this prudential consideration will dominate practical reason—inevitably, in most cases, the right thing will be done but not for the right reason.[51]

Underlying this idealist approach is the sense that the doing of the right thing for the right reason speaks to what it is to be human. As Terry Eagleton puts this way of thinking: 'Being human is something you have to get good at, like playing snooker or avoiding the rent collector. The virtuous are those who are successful at being human, as a butcher or jazz pianist are successful at their jobs. Some human beings are even virtuosi of virtue. Virtue in this sense is a worldly affair; but it is unworldly in the sense that success is its own reward.'[52]

But, if we argue against the surveillance society, DNA profiling, and the like, on the grounds that it compromises what it is to be essentially human, or by asserting that the moral life is its own reward, this is liable to be rejected as mystical, or metaphysical, or just plain puzzling.[53] The danger with arguing that the virtue of doing the right thing has an expressive value is that we reduce what the community prizes to little more than a modus vivendi, leaving advocates of this way of life simply to preach to the converted.

[50] Plato, *The Republic* (Harmondsworth: Penguin, 1974) 105–6 (Book II).

[51] But, what if, with smart design, the penal threat is merely background and does not intrude too much into the foreground? In such a setting, would it not be perfectly feasible for a morally disposed community to cultivate moral virtue? Support for such a view is offered by the leading regulatory theorists Ian Ayres and John Braithwaite, who conceive of socially responsible deliberation—by 'directors of nursing who deliberate in terms of the well-being of patients instead of self interest, mine managers pondering how to secure maximum safety for their employees, [and] factory managers weighing how to minimize the pollution caused by their operation'—in the shadow of the background penal law: see I Ayres and J Braithwaite, *Responsive Regulation* (Oxford: Oxford University Press, 1992) 47.

[52] T Eagleton, *After Theory* (London: Allen Lane, 2003) 125.

[53] Not that this deters the (US) President's Council on Bioethics in its report, 'Beyond Therapy' (Washington: Dana Press, 2003), the leitmotiv of which is that reliance on biotechnology to go beyond therapy (towards 'perfections' of one kind or another) may turn out to be at best an illusion but 'at worst, a Faustian bargain that could cost us *our full and flourishing humanity*' (at 338, emphasis added).

However, so long as we are presupposing (as we are) an aspirant moral community, we do not need to be more foundationalist. In such a context, agents are committed to the ideal that their regulatory framework should present each developed agent with the option of doing the right thing for the right reason—such is the dignity of moral choice. In turn, agents should learn to act in other-regarding (fellow agent-respecting) ways because they understand that this is morally required. In a sense, agents who do the right thing for the right reason self-regulate. For such an aspirant moral community, the question is whether the development of a surveillance society, like the prospect of genetic engineering or detailed brain imaging, threatens to chip away at the ideas of personal choice and responsibility that are fundamental to the vision of any kind of moral community.[54] While this is not a question that I can hope to answer here,[55] my point is that an appreciation of human dignity as a fundamental condition for the possibility of such a community at least alerts us to this being a question that we need to address.

In summary, if the principal raison d'être of critical bioethics is to steer bio-practitioners and nation states away from fundamental wrongdoing, then it needs no apologia. Moreover, if in so doing bioethics remains resolutely defensive of human dignity as an expression of the conditions that are essential, not just for a particular version of civilized life but for any kind of moral community, then we should not accuse it of being partisan. To the contrary, bioethics then speaks for all aspirant moral communities.

VI. Conclusion

What should we conclude from these short remarks on rather a large subject? Should we conclude, for example, that those who practise bioethics should simply get on with 'doing bioethics' rather than stopping to reflect on the nature and practical contribution of their activities? After all, the Nuffield view, as I have termed it, is a relatively rare example of such reflection and, if my analysis is correct, we might see it as something of a Pandora's Box. Yet, if 'doing bioethics' is a growth industry that seems to be set to continue growing,[56] it is surely right that we engage in such reflection. Moreover, if the worst thing that pops out of the box

---

[54] For a clear and cautious assessment, see Peter Lipton, 'Genetic and Generic Determinism: A New Threat to Free Will?' in D Rees and S Rose (eds), *The New Brain Sciences—Perils and Prospects* (Cambridge: Cambridge University Press, 2004) 88; and, for a robust defence of agency-based models of responsibility (applicable to both law and morals), see S J Morse, 'Moral and Legal Responsibility and the New Neuroscience' in J Illes (ed), *Neuroethics* (Oxford: Oxford University Press, 2006) 33, and SJ Morse, 'Uncontrollable Urges and Irrational People' (2002) 88 *Virginia Law Review* 1025.

[55] I take this further in R Brownsword, *Rights, Regulation and the Technological Revolution* (Oxford: Oxford University Press, 2008) ch 10.

[56] cf N Rose, *The Politics of Life Itself* (Princeton, NJ: Princeton University Press, 2007).

is a plurality of moral viewpoints, if we simply have too many cooks spoiling the moral broth, that is not too awful—at least, these are people who believe that it is important to do the right thing.[57]

What, though, of our opening question, concerning the relationship between law, morals, and bioethics? While legal positivists and legal idealists are destined to disagree about the conceptualization of law, I suggest that their practical disagreements tend to stem from their *substantive moral positions* rather than from their *conceptual* understanding of the relationship between law and morals.[58] For example, consider my own legal idealist position. As I have said, I treat the community of rights as the practical instantiation of my legal idealism. In such a community, legal reason is understood to be a sub-species of moral reason; but the key feature for present purposes is the rights-based morality that the community recognizes as its ethical benchmark. For it is the general principles of this substantive morality that the community will endeavour to concretize in bioethical practice, regardless of whether the practical standards are formally legislated. By contrast, legal positivists—or, at any rate, legal positivists who are broadly speaking Hartian in their approach—will reject my characterization of legal reason; they will accept that, on occasion, legal reason might incorporate moral reason, but they will insist that this is not a necessary (defining) condition for law. However, if they accept a rights-based morality of the kind that I take to be required, we will share the same (critical) moral vantage point and we will agree that bioethics, as a concretization of general moral principles, should strive to apply these principles. In other words, provided that we apply the same moral principles in much the same way, we should generally agree about the bioethically approved action in particular cases.

In the light of this, we can see that moral pluralism is not so much a difficulty for bioethicists, whether legal positivists or legal idealists, who are committed to a particular substantive morality; rather, the difficulty is for those who have no particular substantive moral attachments. The question for the latter is whether they can make a useful contribution to practical debates—which is precisely the puzzle prompted by the reflections associated with the Nuffield view. I have suggested that, pluralism notwithstanding, bioethicists can offer limited assistance to practical deliberation by thinking through the logic of particular principles, by identifying points of potential convergence and consensus, by brokering compromises, and by facilitating the process of practical decision-making.

Finally, I have also suggested that, even under conditions of serious moral plurality, there is an extremely important way in which bioethicists can assume a role that involves a good deal more than under-labouring or facilitating. Recognizing that many aspirant moral communities are fractured and

---

[57] cf A MacIntyre, *After Virtue* (London: Duckworth, 1981) especially ch 9.
[58] As argued in D Beyleveld and R Brownsword, 'The Practical Difference Between Natural-Law Theory and Legal Positivism' (1985) 5 *OJLS* 1.

conflictual, bioethicists should focus on the conditions that give meaning to the underlying shared (moral) aspiration of such communities, being especially alert to the risk that such conditions are compromised by the drive towards more effective technological fixes. When citizens no longer debate and legislate standards for their community; when regulators bypass practical and moral reason; when regulatees have no option (literally) but to do the thing that regulators have decreed to be the acceptable thing (ie the thing to be done), then we know that the moral life is being extinguished. If moral communities cannot regroup around the shared nature of their (moral) project, then they are liable to be divided and ruled—and ruled, moreover, not by morals or by law but by code, design, architecture, and technology.[59] For an aspirant moral community, as for any kind of bioethicist, if there is one thing worse than the noisy friction of pluralism, it surely must be the frictionless calm of the patterned and perfectly techno-ordered world.

[59] See R Brownsword, 'What the World Needs Now: Techno-Regulation, Human Rights and Human Dignity' in R Brownsword (ed) *Human Rights* (Oxford: Hart, 2004) 203; R Brownsword, 'Code, Control, and Choice: Why East is East and West is West' (2005) 25 *Legal Studies* 1; R Brownsword, 'Neither East Nor West, Is Mid-West Best?' (2006) 3 *Script*-ed 3, available at <http://www.law.ed.ac.uk/ahrb/script-ed/issue3-1.asp>; and R Brownsword, *Rights, Regulation and the Technological Revolution* (Oxford: Oxford University Press, 2008).

3

The Troubled Relationship Between Bioethics and Human Rights*

Richard Ashcroft

A plausible symbolic moment for the genesis of modern international human rights is the opening of the International Military Tribunal in Nuremberg in 1945. A plausible symbolic moment for the genesis of modern bioethics is the trial of the 'Nazi doctors' under the auspices of that Tribunal, again in Nuremberg, in 1946–47.[1] Bioethicists often take the Nuremberg Doctors' Trial and the Nuremberg Code enunciated in the judgment at that trial as being the originary moment of bioethics. Given the coincidence of historical circumstances, timing, intellectual and social approach, and even location, someone unfamiliar with modern bioethics might presume that would share a common form and approach with international human rights law and its philosophical foundations. Yet this is far from being the case. In this chapter I will examine some of the reasons for this, and consider how far some convergence might be possible between the two discourses and communities of bioethics and human rights.

To illustrate how far these two approaches to human wellbeing and misery are distinct, consider as a case study the debate which followed the publication by UNESCO of its Universal Declaration on Bioethics and Human Rights in 2005.[2]

On the face of it, the Declaration was a consolidation of previously adopted positions and statements of a wide range of international bodies, and followed a trend of the adoption of international declarations and conventions such as UNESCO's International Declaration on Human Genetic Data (2003), Universal Declaration on the Human Genome and Human Rights (1997),

---

* An early version of the paper which forms this chapter was presented at the UCL Current Legal Issues Colloquium in July 2007. A subsequent version was presented to a seminar of students from Syracuse University, and the School of Law, Queen Mary, University of London. I have had useful discussions in addition with Roger Brownsword, Conor Gearty, Patrick Hanafin, Heather Widdows, and Janet Dine. All errors of fact and interpretation are mine.

[1] GJ Annas and MA Grodin (eds), *The Nazi Doctors and the Nuremberg Code: Human Rights in Human Experimentation* (Oxford: Oxford University Press, 1992).

[2] UNESCO, Universal Declaration on Bioethics and Human Rights (Paris, 2005).

and the Council of Europe's Oviedo Convention on Human Rights and Biomedicine (1997).[3,4] In addition to the international organizations, influential non-governmental organizations such as the World Medical Association had promulgated authoritative guidance on medical ethics and human rights (such as the latter's periodically revised Declaration of Helsinki on the ethics of research on human subjects). Yet the UNESCO Declaration, in both its draft and final forms, was widely criticized, or even derided, in the bioethics literature.

It is my contention that this derision, though often put into terms of criticism of the drafting, was founded on fundamental differences of approach to the problems which one might take to be common foci of bioethics and human rights thinking. In the first part of this chapter, I will briefly present the debate over the value of the UNESCO Universal Declaration on Bioethics and Human Rights. In the second part of the chapter I will propose an account of the intellectual, sociological, and institutional differences between advocates of bioethical and human rights approaches to moral and social issues in health, medicine, and the life sciences. In the third part of the chapter, I will discuss recent arguments that bioethics can be subsumed under the human rights umbrella. In the final part of the chapter, I suggest some issues for future work on the relationship between human rights and bioethics.

I. The Controversy Over the 2005 Universal Declaration

In October 2003, UNESCO was mandated by its member states to draw up a declaration of fundamental principles in the field of bioethics.[5] A draft declaration was published in early 2005 and attracted considerable academic discussion (for a sample, see a special issue of *Developing World Bioethics* devoted to the draft, introduced in the editorial by Landman and Schüklenk.[6] This draft went through considerable amendment when considered by the national representatives to

---

[3] All of these texts and many relevant others are collected for reference in SP Marks (ed), *Health and Human Rights: Basic International Documents* (Cambridge, Mass.: Harvard School of Public Health, 2nd edn, 2006).

[4] Readers may wonder why I choose to focus on the UNESCO Declaration rather than on the Oviedo Convention and European Court of Human Rights jurisprudence. It would certainly be important to pay close attention to the evolving ECHR jurisprudence as a case study of the relationship between law, human rights, and bioethics. For present purposes, however, UNESCO's work better illustrates the nature of the debate over international human rights, their range and force, and the point that legal constructions of human rights are only one strand in the wider discourse of human rights.

[5] H ten Have, 'The Activities of UNESCO in the Area of Ethics' (2006) 16 *Kennedy Institute of Ethics Journal* 333.

[6] W Landman and U Schüklenk, 'UNESCO "Declares" Universals in Bioethics and Human Rights—Many Unexpected Universal Truths Unearthed by UN Body' (2005) 5(3) *Developing World Bioethics* iii.

UNESCO, and the finalized Declaration was adopted 'unanimously and by acclamation' by UNESCO on 19 October 2005.[7]

The Declaration has a long preamble of reflecting, recognizing, recalling, and noting clauses, linking it to the major international and regional human rights instruments, and to the research ethics guidelines of the World Medical Association and the Council for the International Organizations of Medical Sciences. As such, the Declaration is clearly intended to be taken as a further contribution to this genre of international law and human rights. The problems framing the preamble are on the one hand, expanding access to scientific, technological, and medical advances on a more equitable basis worldwide, while on the other controlling scientific and technological change and its impact on human rights and human dignity. While the focus is on human-related research, the Declaration notes the importance of the environment or biosphere, and the welfare of animals. It also notes the importance of groups such as families and communities, the fact of cultural diversity, and the economic differences between developing and developed world countries.

The Declaration in its main part is divided into General Provisions stating the aims and addressees of the Declaration (Articles 1 and 2), Principles (Articles 3 to 17), guidance on the Application of the Principles (Articles 18 to 21), guidance on Promotion of the Declaration (Articles 22 to 25), and Final Provisions relating to the relationship between principles in the Declaration and limitations on their scope (Articles 26 to 28).

The content of the principles is a mixture of statements of moral principle and statements which have the form of human rights familiar from older human rights declarations and treaties. We can find three broad classes of statements in the articles. First, there are statements of principle, for example, Article 13 reads: 'Solidarity among human beings and international cooperation towards that end are to be encouraged'. Second, there are prescriptive statements similar in form to classical human rights proclamations. For instance, Article 11 reads: 'No individual or group should be discriminated against or stigmatised on any grounds, in violation of human dignity, human rights and fundamental freedoms'. Third, there are what we could call articulating norms, bridging the gap between statements of principle and human rights norms. For instance, Article 3 sub-section 1 reads: 'Human dignity, human rights and fundamental freedoms are to be fully respected'. This sort of article underlines the difference between this Declaration and other human rights instruments. Some of these statements of principle are prior to rights statements (thus, Article 5 is a principle of respect for autonomy, which would then be cashed out in specific rights assignments). Others are interpretative statements indicating how human rights norms are to be understood and applied (Article 6 on consent in medicine and scientific research can be taken this way). Moreover there is a wide range of degrees of specificity and of prescriptiveness in the articles. Article 7 gives a very detailed

---

[7] Ten Have (n 5 above).

specification of the protection of individuals who lack capacity to consent to participation in research or to medical treatment, whereas Article 10 gives a very abstract principle of equality ('The fundamental equality of all human beings in dignity and rights is to be respected so that they are treated justly and equitably'), and Article 16 is both abstract and only minimally prescriptive ('The impact of life sciences on future generations, including on their genetic constitution, should be given due regard').

The Declaration is therefore a complex hybrid in form, and was the outcome of a political process. As such it can hardly be expected to be either intellectually coherent or a particularly fine example of the legal draftsman's art. Yet coherence is not necessarily a desideratum for a statement of principles, so long as a minimum internal consistency is achieved.[8] As Professor Henk ten Have, Director of UNESCO's Division of Science and Technology, puts it:

The Declaration on Bioethics aims to determine those principles in the field of bioethics that are universally acceptable, in conformity with human rights as ensured by international law. It does not pretend to resolve all the bioethical issues presently raised and that evolve every day. Rather, its aim is to constitute a basis or frame of reference for states wishing to endow themselves with legislation or policies in the field of bioethics. It also aims, as far as possible, to inscribe scientific decisions and practices within the framework of a certain number of general principles common to all. And it aims to foster dialogue within societies on the implications of bioethics and the sharing of knowledge in the field of science and technology.

Further:

... it anchors the principles it endorses in the rules that govern respect for human dignity, human rights, and fundamental freedoms. By drawing on the 1948 *Universal Declaration of Human Rights*, it clearly enshrines bioethics in international human rights law in order to apply human rights to the specific domain of bioethics

Beyond these practical and legal aims, ten Have goes on to say that:

The Declaration on Bioethics ... reiterates the need to place bioethics within the context of reflection open to the political and social world. Today, bioethics goes far beyond the codes of ethics of the various professional practices concerned. It implicates reflection on the evolution of society, indeed world stability, induced by scientific and technological developments. The Declaration on Bioethics paves the way for a new agenda of bioethics at the international level.[9]

---

[8] This makes for an interesting interpretative debate. If principles are, on the face of it, in contradiction, how far should we construe them as mutually consistent? Or do we take the interpretative work here as a question of balancing principles which are taken to be in tension rather than in logical contradiction? Or do we instead convict the statements in the text as in actual contradiction, and a sign of poor drafting? Bioethicists are inclined, I think, to the last approach, whereas human rights advocates, especially those with legal training, would prefer the more charitable construction approaches.

[9] Ten Have (n 5 above) 341.

Given these various aims it is unsurprising that the Declaration is as complex as it is, even were its process of preparation purely scholarly and not a political process of intergovernmental negotiation.

Ten Have's account of the purposes of the Declaration gives us an important insight into the controversies which greeted the publication of the draft Declaration and then the adoption of the finalized version itself in the course of 2005. Does the Declaration codify best practice? Or reflect international consensus only? Or interpret higher order human rights norms for this specific context? Or declare a new agenda somewhat ahead of current policy and state practice? Is it mainly addressed to states currently lacking bioethical law and regulation, or does it also speak to states in the bioethical vanguard but whose practice departs from this policy, or to the community of states taken altogether? More fundamentally, how does it situate bioethics with respect to human rights law and doctrine? Does bioethics precede human rights (for instance by giving it a philosophical foundation or a specification of which entities have human rights) or provide a language for application of human rights to concrete problems at a level of specificity greater than human rights norms can address? Or, more ambitiously, does the Declaration intend to make human rights into the master language for doing bioethics?

This complexity, or perhaps opacity, has been taken by some commentators in the way ten Have hopes, as opening a new agenda for international bioethics. Thus Mônica Serra, a Brazilian bioethicist, while noting some weaknesses (the absence of any statement on animal welfare or rights and the vagueness of its principles regarding the future of the environment), praises its breadth, its awareness of the way bioethical concerns should range from nanotechnology and cloning through to access to clean water, and the need to improve global health equity. And at a political level, she finds most hope in the way the Declaration was shaped by the representatives of the developing countries, to whom she attributes the extension of the scope of the Declaration beyond advanced biomedicine to social and environmental bioethics. On the one hand, the UNESCO process gave equal weight to all member states' representations (or, if not equal weight, at least some weight). On the other hand, by actively promoting consensus on the Declaration, it avoided division between the developed and developing countries.[10] This could be contrasted with (for instance) the revisions of the Declaration of Helsinki and the Council for International Organizations of Medical Sciences (CIOMS) guidelines on international biomedical research, which were produced and steered almost exclusively by first world bioethicists and researchers, with developing world views presented reactively.[11] Japanese bioethicists Atsushi Asai and

---

[10] M Serra, 'UNESCO has given bioethics a human face', Scidev.net, 1 December 2005, available at <http://www.scidev.net/content/opinions/eng/unesco-has-given-bioethics-a-human-face.cfm> (accessed 2 June 2008).

[11] RJ Levine, S Gorovitz, and J Gallagher (eds), *Biomedical Research Ethics: Updating International Guidelines—A Consultation* (Geneva: CIOMS, 2000); U Schüklenk and RE Ashcroft, 'Background Report: International Research Ethics' (2000) 14 *Bioethics* 158.

Sachi Oe argue that the Declaration can be seen as an 'up-to-date compendium of bioethical knowledge' and moreover that 'the world would be a better place for everyone to live, if human beings would become aware of the serious implications of every sentence in UDBHR and acquire the habit of making all possible efforts to identify ethical action in the midst of the mutually conflicting norms and principles'.[12] They acknowledge the philosophical weaknesses of the Declaration but hold that this not the important point about it, which is that it represents a call to live a more ethical life and to practise ethical reflection in the face of problems and contradictions of principle. Interestingly they take it to be as much addressed to private individuals as to scientists, professionals and states. Writing from South Africa and the United States, respectively, Loretta Kopelman and Ruth Macklin, while again noting conceptual and drafting weaknesses, praise the Declaration as both internationally authoritative and clear in its rejection of cultural relativism: by framing the bioethical issues in the human rights structure, a clear rejection of female genital mutilation is stated, for instance.[13] Macklin highlights for particular praise Article 21, which requires states to hold their nationals *and other private non-state actors* responsible for their activities overseas under the Declaration's principles. This article is of particular importance both for multinational clinical trials, a matter of heated debate over the past ten years, and for so-called 'bioethical tourism', where researchers search for the regulatory regime least restrictive of their proposed research (a particularly problematic issue with regard to assisted human reproduction, for example).[14]

However, even these positive readings of the Declaration are not unequivocal in their support for it, and the balance of academic commentary on the Declaration has been critical. Criticisms include charges that the Declaration involves a narrowly Western view of human rights[15] and a narrowly intellectual approach to human rights which misunderstands and overlooks inequalities in wealth, gender oppression, and the exclusion of the voices of the poor and vulnerable from participation in political processes nationally and internationally.[16] To that extent, one could say that the Declaration is no better and no worse than other human rights instruments since 1948, and that these criticisms are hardly specific to this most recent Declaration. On the other hand, its recency may

[12] A Asai and S Oe, 'A Valuable and Up-to-date Compendium of Bioethical Knowledge' (2005) 5 *Developing World Bioethics* 216, 218.

[13] LM Kopelman, 'The Incompatibilty of the United Nations' Goals and Conventionalist Ethical Relativism'(2005) 5 *Developing World Bioethics* 234; R Macklin, 'Yet Another Guideline? The UNESCO *Draft Declaration*' (2005) 5 *Developing World Bioethics* 244.

[14] G Pennings, 'Reproductive Tourism as Moral Pluralism in Motion' (2002) 28 *Journal of Medical Ethics* 337.

[15] J-B Nie, 'Cultural Values Embodying Universal Norms: A Critique of a Popular Assumption about Cultures and Human Rights' (2005) 5 *Developing World Bioethics* 251.

[16] MC Rawlinson and A Donchin, 'The Quest for Universality: Reflections on the *Universal Draft Declaration on Bioethics and Human Rights*'(2005) 5 *Developing World Bioethics* 258.

make these charges (if valid) more rather than less serious, since it must have been framed in full awareness of the general import of these criticisms.

Such criticisms can be considered as *Ideologiekritik* addressed to the social, economic, and cultural conditions of production of the Declaration and the way it arguably mystifies its objects and the processes which support and sustain its effects. Another more directly political criticism of the Declaration points to the way in which it was drafted and adopted. Several commentators question why UNESCO, rather than the World Health Organization, was charged with this task, given the different work of the two organizations and their greatly differing statuses and reputations internationally.[17] More seriously, they criticize the way the draft was finalized by negotiation between 'experts' from UNESCO's member states' governments, most of whom had no credentials *as bioethicists*, and which process, by its unavoidably political character, bore no relation to the standard practice of bioethical analysis and debate. These criticisms are a little odd, partly because 'bioethics' is not a profession and there are no credentials agreed upon to entitle someone to call themselves a bioethicist, but mainly because there is not and never could be an international process which was left entirely to the technical experts of all nations.[18] The nearest case to this suggested way of producing guidelines would be the revision of the Declaration of Helsinki by the World Medical Association—which in its turn has been strongly criticized (often by some of the same people criticizing UNESCO for its lack of academic rigour) for the lack of openness and the technocratic character of its decision-making.

Leaving aside the ideological and political critique of the Declaration, most criticisms it has faced are intellectual and complain about vagueness, poor drafting, contradictions between principles, inadequate attention to social and environmental issues, lack of specificity or prescriptiveness, imposition of a consensus view where an issue remains open or controversial, banality, importation of problematic concepts (for instance, human dignity), and so on.[19] Some commentators have difficulty making any sense of the relationship between bioethics as a practice (a way of thinking about moral problems) and bioethics as represented in the Declaration (a list of principles), and the relationships between those principles and human rights.[20] Most seriously, it is alleged by several commentators that the Declaration simply fails to understand the field it proposes to regulate, a claim which is urged with particular force by those who have an interest in

---

[17] H Wolinsky, 'Bioethics for the World' (2006) 7 *EMBO Reports* 354; Landman and Schüklenk (n 6 above); J Williams, 'UNESCO's Proposed Declaration on Bioethics and Human Rights—A Bland Compromise' (2005) 5 *Developing World Bioethics* 210.

[18] D Benatar, 'Bioethics and Health and Human Rights: A Critical View' (2007) 32 *Journal of Medical Ethics* 17.

[19] D Benatar, 'The Trouble with Declarations' (2005) 5 *Developing World Bioethics* 220; M Häyry and T Takala, 'Human Dignity, Bioethics and Human Rights' (2005) 5 *Developing World Bioethics* 225.

[20] Benatar (n 18 above).

public health and health equity. Michael Selgelid, for instance, argues that the Declaration privileges liberty in an unreflective way, thus down-playing substantial (rather than merely formal) equality and the role of collective action, backed by coercive sanction, in infectious disease control and in measures designed to promote health equity.[21] Given all of these criticisms, these commentators might be pleased to find that the Declaration lacks legal force or enforcement mechanisms—but indeed this is also a commonly levelled criticism. The Declaration merely 'invokes' principles and human rights, lacking any of the legal or moral punch of earlier Declarations and binding treaties and conventions.[22]

The issue that I wish to discuss is not the merit or otherwise of these criticisms, but rather the signal they give of the mutual incomprehension of those who, on the one hand, drafted or supported the Declaration as bringing together human rights and bioethics agendas and agreeing a common framework of principles and approach to further policy and legislation, and those who criticize the Declaration for its intellectual, ideological and political inadequacies. I claim that what this debate demonstrates is that rather than the Declaration bringing bioethics and human rights discourses and practitioners together, it in fact forced them to confront their differences. In the next part of this chapter I wish to sketch those differences, better to grasp what may be at stake in trying to bring about a convergence of bioethics and human rights.

II. A Comparison of the Institutional and Intellectual Features of Bioethics and Human Rights

There is a bioethical critique of human rights; and a human rights critique of bioethics. Some writers, as we shall see in the third part of this chapter, below, think that bioethics and human rights can come together either in partnership or through merger. Here I want to examine some of the reasons why so far this has not happened.

The most central criticisms made of human rights from within bioethics are theoretical. This is unsurprising, to the extent that bioethics presents itself as a branch of applied moral philosophy.[23] The first and perhaps most important bioethical criticism of human rights is that bioethicists tend not to find much merit in the concept of 'human rights' itself. There are of course bioethicists who work with one version or another of rights theory as their preferred account of normative moral theory. But for the most part, bioethicists are either eclectic in

[21] M Selgelid Universal Norms and Conflicting Values (2005) 5 Developing World Bioethics 267–273.
[22] Rawlinson and Donchin (n 16 above).
[23] More precisely, we should distinguish between bioethics considered as a field of problems, to which philosophers, lawyers, social and natural scientists, politicians, priests and the public contribute, and bioethics considered as an academic field. The latter is our concern here.

their moral theorizing (taking elements of consequentialist theories, virtue theories, principle-based ethics, and so on, considered as different tools appropriate to the solution of different problems) or work within Kantian or consequentialist traditions.[24] Bioethicists working with rights usually do not take these as moral primitives, but as legal or political rules founded on some other moral theoretic footing. Those bioethicists who do take moral rights as primitives would largely see themselves as libertarians, but this not all that common a stance in bioethics.[25] Some bioethicists do adopt libertarian positions in political philosophy, but for the most part bioethicists adopt liberal or some form of communitarian or feminist position in political theory. Feminists in bioethics represent an exception to my claim here, insofar as they are more likely to advocate a defence of women's rights, but again this is arguably a position in political philosophy rather than a claim that rights are morally fundamental. Thus, to the extent that bioethicists do work with rights-based arguments, rights are taken as derivative rather than fundamental moral concepts, therefore founded in something else, be that autonomy, or interests, or community membership. So the notion that human rights are somehow fundamental to human identity and moral status is relatively unfamiliar, and indeed provokes a sceptical response at least within bioethical theory-building.

Prior theoretical commitments aside, the notion of human rights can provoke a bioethicist's scepticism in part because of the nature of bioethical inquiry. Given that bioethics is partly speculative inquiry into the nature and boundaries of the human, concerned with determining the status of embryos, the brain dead, modification of human genomes, and so on, privileging the category of human *a priori* poses intellectual difficulties, since it seems to assume that which is to be proved. While few bioethicists would deny that we have obligations to respect and not to mistreat humans in any category of vulnerability (especially given bioethics's roots in medical ethics), most bioethicists are far more comfortable at a theoretical level with seeing this as a specification of duties rather than working back from rights claims vested in the vulnerable 'patient'. Thus, the most influential theory in modern bioethics, the Four Principles theory of Beauchamp and

---

[24] Bioethicists working outside the Anglo-American world draw on a wider range of theories, but are even less likely to be (moral) rights theorists. However, they may be dignitarians, who share some concepts with human rights theorists, without being rights theorists: (D Beyleveld and R Brownsword) *Human Dignity in Bioethics and Biolaw* (Oxford: Oxford University Press, 2001).

[25] Deryck Beyleveld and Roger Brownsword are notable exceptions here, in that while being committed moral rights theorists they are liberals rather than libertarians, who see rights theory as bringing together moral philosophy, political philosophy, and legal theory. Most bioethicists are less ambitious, and usually argue separately about the moral permissibility of some biomedical practice and the appropriate political or legal approach to that practice. My current view is that Beyleveld and Brownsword's theory is the most promising approach for a reunification of bioethics and human rights theory, but that in terms of the present account it is their exceptional status which interests me rather than the merits of their position. (See Beyleveld and Brownsword, n 24 above).

Childress, focuses on agent-relative obligations to respect the autonomy of the other, to act beneficently, to avoid harming the other, and to act justly.[26]

In addition to these sociologically contingent features of bioethics, we should note that bioethicists share with most philosophers a degree of intellectual caution about human rights even on the terms posed by human rights advocates themselves: the difficulties in enumerating human rights, the variety of kinds of claims they make, the vagueness of some of the central concepts of rights theory (notoriously, the concept of human dignity), the degree of abstraction that statements of rights possess, and the metaphysical problems of identifying which subjects have them and in virtue of what features of their humanity and personal existence.[27] Bioethicists tend not to proffer a critique based on the claim that human rights are a Westernizing discourse of false universality, or one based on the improper emphasis given to the individual and his or her demands as opposed to the community and his or her obligations thereto. They tend to be neutral on the question of the priority of civil and political over economic, social, and cultural rights.[28] The reason for these silences or neutral stances is not far to seek: it is because bioethicists are frequently tarred with the same brush! Moreover, where bioethicists have begun to argue that there should be a closer liaison between bioethics and human rights it is often because human rights offers what appears to be a universal or at any rate international *lingua franca* for the discussion of bioethical and global justice issues.[29] They see human rights discourse as a way of posing questions and setting up problems for analysis and resolution, even where they do not see human rights as a useful set of theoretical tools for that analysis or for defining solutions to moral and political problems.[30] And they point out that if you look at lawyers' constructions of human rights, for instance in European Court of Human Rights jurisprudence, the real work starts, rather than finishes, where the Court agrees that a particular right is engaged. For that is the point at which ethical argument is required in order to deploy concepts of balance, proportionality, margin of appreciation, and so on.[31]

---

[26] TL Beauchamp and JF Childress, *Principles of Biomedical Ethics* (Oxford: Oxford University Press, 5th revised edn, 2001).

[27] See for example, the detailed discussions of the concept of dignity, which bioethicists tend to approach in a spirit of conceptual analysis, while noting the political role of the concept in pushing the boundaries of respect for human life in one direction or another. Beyleveld and Brownsword (n 24 above); RE Ashcroft, 'Making Sense of Dignity' (2005) 31 *Journal of Medical Ethics* 679; H Schmidt, 'Whose Dignity? Resolving Ambiguitites in the Scope of "Human Dignity" in the Universal Declaration on Bioethics and Human Rights' (2007) 33 *Journal of Medical Ethics* 578. See also JW Nickel, *Making Sense of Human Rights* (Oxford: Blackwell, 2nd edn, 2007).

[28] A Woodiwiss, *Human Rights* (London: Routledge, 2005).

[29] LP Knowles, 'The *Lingua Franca* of Human Rights and the Rise of a Global Bioethic' (2001) 10 *Cambridge Quarterly of Healthcare Ethics* 253.

[30] D Schroeder, 'Human Rights and their Role in Global Bioethics' (2005) 14 *Cambridge Quarterly of Healthcare Ethics* 221; DC Thomasma, 'Proposing a New Agenda: Bioethics and International Human Rights' (2001) 10 *Cambridge Quarterly of Healthcare Ethics* 299.

[31] MB Dembour, *Who Believes in Human Rights? Reflections on the European Convention* (Cambridge: Cambridge University Press, 2006).

This is an important point: where bioethicists do consider human rights, it is generally in terms of seeing human rights scholars and practitioners as advocates and activists, who work with a specific range of concerns which may pose interesting questions for bioethicists, who tend to be academics and teachers rather than activists.[32] Thus, in addition to the practical utility of human rights language as a medium of communication and persuasion (taken to be distinct from the cleaner business of analysis and reasoning, it is supposed), bioethicists are beginning to look to human rights topics of concern as a way of broadening out the focus of bioethics from its traditional concerns with issues in the doctor-patient relationship and the challenges posed by new technologies. Thus bioethicists look to human rights as setting the agenda in thinking about the problems of public health, global health inequalities, access to essential medicines, the impact of environmental change on health, and especially the treatment of women and reproductive rights.[33] Even here, however, the philosophical caution of bioethicists has tended to limit their engagement with human rights theory and practice. A good example is the much debated 'right to health'. There has been limited engagement with this debate on the part of bioethicists, in part because they tend to find the very idea of a right to health implausible, while acknowledging that the problems taken up under this rubric are real and serious.[34] So inequalities in life expectancy, access to clean water, access to medicines, and so on are all important. What the bioethicist finds either misleading or otiose is the notion that we need to—and can coherently—frame all of these different problems under a single overarching 'right to health'. The concomitant concept of 'health' has itself been widely criticized as well.[35] While many human rights activists would point to the pragmatic nature of these claims and argue that what is needed is not so much analytical coherence as practical value in shaping political and economic policy, this kind of argument is anathema to philosophical bioethicists.

Bioethicists are even more cautious about accepting that human rights as an analytical and normative discourse is helpful in illuminating the problems so identified. For example, bioethicists, though frequently accused by social scientists of importing American models of autonomy and legal rights to settings which are very different in structure and culture, are relatively quick to accuse human rights advocates of similar failings.[36] Consider the notorious debate

---

[32] Recall that we are focusing on the intellectual field of bioethics. The work of political and advisory bodies in bioethics blurs this boundary between theory and practice considerably. However, one question worth considering is whether states establish bioethics committees precisely when they do not want to see an issue in human rights terms. Where a committee or commission is invited to consider bioethical and human rights issues, this tends to be within a framework of seeing them as complementary rather than synonymous.

[33] A Donchin, ' Converging Concerns: Feminist Bioethics, Development Theory, and Human Rights' (2003) 29 *Signs: Journal of Women in Culture and Society* 299.

[34] Benatar (n 18 above).

[35] *Per* the Alma Ata Declaration of the World Health Organization, health 'is a state of complete physical, mental and social wellbeing, and not merely the absence of infirmity' (1978) Art 1; and see Marks (n 3 above) 99.

[36] Nie (n 15 above).

about standard of care in clinical trials in the developing world. On the one hand, human rights activists have been in the vanguard of attempts to argue that research subjects have rights to the highest achievable standard of care in the context of such trials, so that prima facie there can be no defence of the use of placebo controls where active therapy exists and is the current standard of care in the developed world. While many bioethicists would agree, they would nonetheless argue that this is controversial and simply cutting to the human rights chase does not settle the argument. On the other hand, many human rights advocates would admit that human rights norms, especially with regard to economic, social, and cultural rights, are aspirational rather than binding, leaving many bioethicists puzzled as to what human rights advocates are willing to assert and defend.[37] While this instability and tactical argumentation is appropriate to the political world, it seems out of place in intellectual analysis and theory. The very abstraction of many human rights norms means that on the one hand, taken literally, they impose universalizing solutions which do not fit well with local and specific problems; but on the other hand the open texture of these principles allows perhaps too much flexibility in interpreting these norms in order to produce apparently acceptable solutions to such local problems in practice.[38] Thus the bioethicist may be willing to accept that her human rights colleagues pose the right problems, while rejecting their claim to be able to solve them in theory.

What, then, do the human rights community make of bioethicists? Here my account is necessarily more brief, as I write as an insider to bioethics discourse and an outsider to human rights discourse. My view is that human rights practitioners and theorists have had much less to say about bioethics than bioethicists have had to say about human rights. Nonetheless, some noted contributors to the literature on health and human rights have responded to the bioethicists' challenges.

A standard criticism levelled at bioethics by many critics, not only human rights theorists, is that bioethics, by concentrating on *ethical* questions about specific moral *problems* is blind both to the structural causes of these problems and to the structural solutions that may be available.[39] Bioethicists tend to concentrate on either the behaviour of individuals or on the effect of specific policies focused on the issue of concern. There are many reasons for this. Partly it can be accounted for in the way bioethics arises as applied moral, rather than political, philosophy. A second factor is the roots of bioethics as a field of problems in

[37] Levine, Gorovitz, and Gallagher (n 11 above).

[38] Thereby allowing considerable horsetrading and grandstanding by states parties in international for a, without necessarily committing them to very much or subjecting them to much accountability or possibility of punishment for norm violation, beyond the usual methods of Realpolitik. To that extent, I think the human rights community are more 'realist' than are bioethicists, who often have rather romantic notions of political possibility and political processes. (Nickel n 27 above).

[39] P Farmer and NG Campos, 'New Malaise: Bioethics and Human Rights in the Global Era' (2004) 32 *Journal of Law, Medicine and Ethics* 243.

medical ethics, and the doctor-patient relationship.[40] This has two consequences, first that even in public policy questions, there is a tendency to focus on individuals' claim rights and liberties, rather than considering social interests and patterns. And second, there is a tendency to consider 'horizontal' rather than 'vertical' rights claims, which is quite inconsistent with the way human rights are actually handled in law and policy.[41] The bioethicist can readily argue that if structure and social power are what the human rights theorists are concerned with, then they should find another word to use than 'rights'. But this is partly because most bioethicists are ignorant of the intellectual history of human rights as a language of the relationship between subjects and sovereigns.[42]

A related complaint is that bioethicists' constructions of ethical problems in their individualism are ideologically in hock to a prevailing discourse of 'neoliberalism', in their focus on individuals' liberties, responsibility for their own health and well-being, and so on.[43] Feminist and 'pro-poor' critics of bioethics, such as Anne Donchin and Paul Farmer, point out that this leads bioethicists to concentrate on the—as they see it—mythical figure of the autonomous subject, whose choices are not constrained and structured by the actual experience of poverty, illness or disability, gender, race, class and sexual orientation, but only by their values and preferences.[44] Bioethicists may sometimes advert to 'cultural' variation, but only as something to be respected on one level while taken as problematic in most other ways.[45] This line of criticism then focuses on the unintended social and economic consequences of bioethicists' recommendations. This is something which many bioethicists accept (and there is a flourishing community of scholarship in feminist bioethics, for example), but even while doing so they would point to the irony of rights advocates deploying a consequentialist logic which evaluates proposals by their effects rather than by their respect for rights. Be that as it may, the combination of blindness to structure and inability to deal effectively with the social nature of human existence, and the arguable charge of unacknowledged complicity in an ideological position which subverts human rights and human dignity is a serious criticism which bioethicists have only begun to acknowledge.[46]

Another kind of challenge from human rights to bioethics addresses the intellectual stance of bioethics as one of detached sceptical analysis rather than one of active advocacy of the vulnerable and miserable. Substantively, the human rights

---

[40] TA Faunce, 'Will International Human Rights Subsume Medical Ethics? Intersections in the UNESCO *Universal Bioethics Declaration*' (2004) 31 *Journal of Medical Ethics* 173.

[41] C Gearty, *Principles of Human Rights Adjudication* (Oxford: Oxford University Press, 2004).

[42] C Douzinas, *The End of Human Rights* (Oxford: Hart Publishing, 2000).

[43] G Berlinguer, 'Bioethics, Health and Inequality' (2004) 364 *Lancet* 1086.

[44] Donchin (n 33 above); Farmer and Campos (n 39 above).

[45] Kopelman (n 13 above); Nie (n 15 above); Rawlinson and Donchin (n 16 above).

[46] In part this is because bioethics is still sufficiently self-conscious and vulnerable as a newly emerging intellectual field, the reponse to criticism is often enough denial or defensiveness rather than acknowledgement and incorporation.

critique takes issue with the tendency of bioethics to dissolve accepted categories such as dignity, humanity, and rights, replacing them, if at all, by more abstract concepts of liberty, preferences, and well-being. These theoretical remainders of bioethical analysis, argue the human rights theorists, pose a number of problems. First, it is hard to see how they act as any kind of constraint or even common ground for public discourse, since they privatize the discussion of the basic goods of human life to individual subjects' preferences and interests. Second, to the extent that they do create a common ground, it is one that may take a rather economistic form, rather than a legal or human rights form, and thus is open to the charge that bioethical argument perpetuates rather than helps to deconstruct the intellectual form and social content of policies which undermine the security and welfare of the most vulnerable in society. Third, they risk undermining the most vulnerable by shifting the ground of moral entitlement from those who are the subjects of human rights to those who are able to have and express preferences and interests. While bioethicists would dispute the claim that the focus on persons in place of humans actually leads to the loss of concern for the severely disabled, the very young, the very old, and the otherwise marginal, human rights advocates argue that a door is opened to questioning whether a specific individual or class of individuals is equal in status to the ideal typical autonomous adult. Fourth, human rights theorists have a general concern that theoretical inquiry into the philosophical basis of human rights undermines the force of rights claims and instruments in practice, since abusers can claim that what advocates allege is universal and non-derogable is neither of those things, and cite philosophers in their support.

On a political level, human rights advocates point out that these theoretical problems have a practical correlate in the political quietism of bioethics. Aside from one or two issues (abortion, euthanasia, embryo research, certain issues in international research ethics), bioethicists are largely politically unengaged. This is perhaps because bioethics is a mixture of philosophical argument (where the attempt is to establish truth, or at any rate our ignorance thereof) and consensus building. There is an internal tension here: can we build a valid consensus where the truth is uncertain or controversial? Can we be committed to seeking the truth when we are willing to compromise in practice before the truth is known or even in the teeth of the facts? So, on the one hand, bioethics is quietist because it refuses political strategy and engagement in the name of philosophy. And on the other, it is quietist because it tries to translate issues of real political conflict into moral questions upon which all reasonable people ought to agree or at least grant recognition to their interlocutors. Human rights advocates, on the other hand, are willing to take on some issues in a conflictual way, seeing them as political struggles in the service of moral right. Perhaps this is merely a difference in degree or emphasis; after all, many bioethicists are willing to take personal stances on issues, and to give bioethical arguments for those stances. But there are definite differences in self-understanding and social function between bioethicists and human rights advocates. And whatever differences exist between human rights advocates, it is clear that to be a human rights advocate is to take a political stance, whereas this is not true of bioethicists, save perhaps at a rarefied and unconscious ideological level (if the criticism given above sticks). So, the human rights advocate can reasonably ask, perhaps even complain, about what bioethics, or bioethicists, actually stand for and want.[47]

Much more practically, the human rights community can point to its reality in terms of institutions, law and jurisprudence, communities of practice, and so on, and say: criticize us if you wish, but this is who and what we are, and what we do and how we do it—but what does bioethics have?

This criticism or question is, I think, rather illuminating with regard to the differences between bioethics and human rights. Thus far I have described the contrast almost entirely in intellectual and ideological terms. There are also very significant material and practical differences. At the institutional level, bioethics is largely academic and philosophical, with a few institutions nationally and internationally which are normally advisory rather than executive or juridical in nature. Human rights, on the other hand, has a vast national, international, public, and private range of institutions, from the United Nations institutions to national and international courts to civil society organizations like Amnesty. Indeed, it is hard to see how bioethics could acquire a 'fan club' for its approach to human problems and human suffering in any way analogous to Amnesty, considered as the international fan club for human rights. While some have tried to argue that bioethics has acquired some characteristics of a secular religion, it is far more plausible to see human rights *that way*; similarly, it is much more credible to claim that human rights is a sort of social movement than it would be to see bioethics in such terms. On the other hand, for the professions, for governments, and for certain kinds of institutions (hospitals, research institutes, universities, some industrial concerns), bioethics does represent a more attractive vehicle for consultation and dispute resolution than would a human rights-oriented institution, precisely because of the lower ideological temperature of bioethics relative to human rights and the lesser likelihood that it can be taken up by a possibly rather protean social movement. Note the way in which some religious bioethics groups can be efficiently marginalized as being *parti pris*, rather than 'analytical and objective', the way bioethics is supposed to be.[48]

This institutional basis is often missed by bioethical critics of human rights. They tend to focus on the textual representations of rights—the whole literature of

---

[47] For some years I have been working on the notion of bioethics as a style of utopian thought, with a particular form of desire inherent in its approach to science, technology, and medicine, and to argument about developments in these areas. For a first tessera in the mosaic; see RE Ashcroft, 'American Biofutures: Ideology and Utopia in the Fukuyama-Stock Debate' (2003) 29 *Journal of Medical Ethics* 59.

[48] JH Evans, *Playing God? Human Genetic Engineering and the Rationalization of Public Bioethical Debate, 1959–1995* (Chicago: Chicago University Press, 2002).

Declarations, Covenants, and Conventions. This is well illustrated by the debate on the UNESCO Declaration discussed above, for instance. Even on its own terms, this is arguably a misreading of this corpus of human rights documents, since they are not framed as a deductively closed system of norms, but rather as an open-textured system of rights. A right is only sometimes best expressed as an injunction or prohibition.[49] Rather, rights are something which their subjects can 'enjoy', which implies something more practical and three-dimensional than a block on some actions and an obligation to perform some others.

Another feature of human rights theory and practice often missed by bioethicists is the degree to which human rights advocates are frequently engaged in a highly reflexive and often historically minded analysis of their own praxis.[50] In particular, there are wide-ranging debates about the theoretical foundations of human rights practice in law, jurisprudence, and political and social theory. To that extent, the bioethical critique of human rights is not at odds with human rights, but could become part of this self-understanding of human rights. What is at risk for *both* discourses if this convergence is not possible, or if it is brought to a conclusion in a way which forgets the proper 'end of human rights' is well described by Costas Douzinas:

The triumph of human rights and the accompanying 'end of history' may conceal a final mutation in the long trajectory of natural law, in which the call of nature has turned from a defence against conventional wisdom and institutional lethargy into the legitimating device of some of the most sclerotic regimes and powers. As human rights start veering away from their initial revolutionary and dissident purposes, as their end becomes obscured in ever more declarations, treaties and diplomatic lunches, we may be entering the epoch of the end of human rights and of the triumph of a monolithic humanity.... When the apologists of pragmatism pronounce the end of ideology, of history or utopia, they do not mark the triumph of human rights; on the contrary, they bring human rights to an end. The end of human rights comes when they lose their utopian end.[51]

III. Recent Proposals for Bringing About Convergence Between Bioethics and Human Rights

This overview of the criticisms levelled by bioethicists of human rights and of human rights theorists and practitioners of bioethics I hope gives some explanations of the current failures of the two discourses to confront each other

---

[49] Perhaps the root of this misunderstanding may be traced to the fact that the only philosophical rights theorists most Anglo-American bioethicists have come across are Robert Nozick and Ronald Dworkin, whose headline accounts of rights posit them as trumps or side-constraints (as does the deontologist Frances Kamm). Some human rights are trumps (eg ECHR, Art 3; the non-derogable right against torture and other inhuman and degrading treatment). But most are not.

[50] Douzinas (n 42 above); Dembour (n 31 above); C Gearty, *Can Human Rights Survive?* (Cambridge: Cambridge University Press, 2006).

[51] Douzinas (n 42 above) 380.

with much more than mutual incomprehension, save on rare occasions. In another place I have discussed how, in practice, this plays out in the contrasting approaches taken by human rights and bioethics to a specific problem involving paid participation in human experimentation.[52] Some recent work suggests that this situation may be about to change, albeit gradually, again in the wake of the UNESCO Declaration. In this section I discuss the leading contributions to this argument, before concluding with some reflections of my own on the prospects for bringing about a convergence of human rights and bioethics.

For some time, international organizations have been trying to bring bioethics and human rights together, as the UNESCO Declaration and the Oviedo Convention illustrate. At a more practical level as well, we can find examples of specific projects within international organizations. For example, in 2003 the Sub-Commission on the Promotion and Protection of Human Rights of the Commission on Human Rights considered an expanded working paper on human rights and bioethics.[53] This paper concentrated specifically on issues relating to the Universal Declaration on the Human Genome and Human Rights, in particular the treatment in the Declaration of the human genome under the international law concept of the 'common heritage of humanity'; the manipulation of the human genome and human rights; discrimination and the human genome; and intellectual property and human rights. Strikingly, all the references in this paper to academic publications are to legal journal articles, and no mention is made of articles in the bioethics literature. So this approach to bringing bioethics and human rights together takes bioethics as the field of problems, rather than the intellectual or disciplinary approach to those problems, and the correct framework for analysing those problems is considered to be legal. The recommendations included in the paper are frequently normative, however, and the argument of the paper is not positivist in its approach to the law. To that extent, the paper presents the field as open for the use of bioethical analysis to interpret and shape the regulation of human genome science and technologies, especially since the author argues for the role of soft law. For reasons of space, analysis of the specific recommendations of the paper will not be pursued here. The importance of the paper lies, for my purposes, in its recognition of the field of bioethics, the placing of bioethics and human rights jointly on the agenda of international agencies, and the scope there is for bioethical argument to interpret and supplement human rights law-driven approaches to bioethical issues.

A number of bioethicists have proposed moving bioethics in a more human rights-led direction. A number of reasons have been given for this. First, it is proposed that human rights concerns give a better focus for bioethical work than some of its more traditional concerns. It is increasingly recognized that a focus

---

[52] In preparation. A version has been presented at a human rights seminar at the London School of Economics (January 2007).
[53] E/CN.4/Sub.2/2003/36.

on the health and welfare issues of the global majority is important, and that this would have implications for the problems we choose to work on, the concepts we use (paying more attention to justice-related concepts, for instance), and the level of attention that we pay to social structure and social power. Second, it is argued that bioethics should recognize the value of human rights as a global language for the discussion of social, legal, and moral issues, in contrast to the arguably ethnocentric language of bioethics. Whether or not one accepts this as a matter of intellectual principle, it can certainly be acknowledged that the language of human rights is a much more frequently deployed resource in international negotiation than any equivalent in bioethics or philosophy. Third, it is argued that the range of issues covered by human rights is so much broader than those covered in bioethics that the use of human rights would offer a much more integrated approach to the issues bioethics discusses by putting those issues back into human context. Fourth, it is possible to argue that this reframing of the issues would be more a matter of change of discourse than greater engagement with lived reality, but even so, bioethics would benefit in another way from engaging with the reflexive critique of human rights practised by human rights theorists, and this would both improve bioethics by forcing it to attend to its own social conditions of possibility and structural blind-spots, and by bringing in a wider range of philosophical sources (notably the resources of history of philosophy and continental European philosophy and social theory).[54]

These approaches to bringing human rights and bioethics together concentrate on bringing them together as complements—looking at bioethics issues using human rights tools, or encouraging bioethicists to learn from human rights agendas, and to present arguments in a human rights-friendly way for the purposes of persuasion and negotiation. Is there scope for something more like a merger?

I suggest that if there is a way that bioethics and human rights can merge, it is more likely that bioethics would become subsumed under human rights, such that human rights is the combination of law, institutions, and dominant language for addressing human well-being in the international public sphere, and bioethics comes to occupy a role as the jurisprudence to human rights law. For historical, political, cultural, and intellectual reasons make it quite unlikely that the protean and essentially contested nature of bioethics would make it a convenient international *lingua franca* or render it suitable for international or even national rendition into institutional forms and social mobilization.[55]

The most straightforward approach to this possible merger is that taken by Roberto Andorno. He argues that the UNESCO Universal Declaration and other human rights instruments provide the approach language for analysing

[54] Thomasma (n 30 above).
[55] Kopelman (n 13 above); H Widdows, 'Is Global Ethics Moral Neo-colonialism? An Investigation of the Issue in the Context of Bioethics' (2007) 21 *Bioethics* 305.

bioethical problems, and further that the norms they articulate are more than the negotiated outcomes of international political processes but actually represent international consensus not merely on legal minimum standards but actually on ethical principle.[56] We can take him to be arguing for a human rights ethic, which takes the processes of consensus formation as either discovering or constructing the fundamental principles for handling bioethical problems. Andorno's argument receives its most sophisticated philosophical form in a series of publications by Robert Baker, writing against principle-based deductive approaches in bioethics and in favour of a constructivist approach in ethics (sharing some features with Onora O'Neill's Kantian ethics and Timothy Scanlon's contractarian ethics).[57] For Baker, negotiated consensus around human rights both produces a moral consensus on the contents of and relationships between those rights, and requires recognition of all parties, entitlements to contribute to that negotiation and to have their interests considered. Moral principles are, then, the outcomes of these negotiations, rather than their origins and axioms. In this way, bioethics becomes part of the practice of human rights, rather than external or prior to it.[58] Thomas Faunce does not go so far as Baker in holding that human rights and bioethics can be unified at the level of moral theory, but argues that the stablization of bioethical principles in the form of human rights law nationally and internationally enhances the power and effectiveness of bioethics and medical ethics by requiring judges to take them into account in adjudication, and political decision-makers to take note of them in policy-making. Even if they do not become a closed and coherent moral system, they can by being taken up in human rights form become part of a coherent public morality. The merits of this proposal partly depend on how far one accepts that the legalization of human rights is such a good thing that one wants bioethics to go the same way; and how far one thinks that legal processes do or should embody moral principles. If one sees the incorporation of human rights into English law, for instance, as establishing certain moral principles as foundational principles of the legal system, and as putting the constitution

---

[56] R Andorno, 'Biomedicine and International Human Rights Law: In Search of a Global Consensus' (2002) 80 *Bulletin of the World Health Organization* 959; R Andorno, 'Global Bioethics at UNESCO: In Defence of the Universal Declaration on Bioethics and Human Rights' (2006) 33 *Journal of Medical Ethics* 150.

[57] R Baker, 'A Theory of International Bioethics: Multiculturalism, Postmodernism, and the Bankrupcy of Fundamentalism' (1998) 8 *Kennedy Institute of Ethics Journal* 201; R Baker, 'A Theory of International Bioethics: The Negotiable and the Non-negotiable' (1998) 8 *Kennedy Institute of Ethics Journal* 233; R Baker, 'Bioethics and Human Rights: A Historical Perspective' (2001) 10 *Cambridge Quarterly of Healthcare Ethics* 241.

[58] Naturally this rule of recognition of parties raises certain philosophical problems. Beyleveld and Brownsword find the best way through these problems to be the work of Alan Gewirth and his argument for the 'dialectical necessity of morality': Beyleveld and Brownsword (n 24 above): A Gewirth, *Reason and Morality* (Chicago: University of Chicago Press, 1978). I have not discussed their work in any detail in the present chapter, although it is clearly the most important attempt to bring bioethics, human rights, and legal theory together, mainly because it deserves detailed treatment in its own right. My initial thoughts are presented elsewhere: Ashcroft (n 47 above).

onto a moral (rather than simply political or historical) footing, then one would certainly find Faunce's approach attractive.[59]

IV. Conclusion

It is clear that purely in academic terms, the relationship between bioethics and human rights deserves further and deeper investigation. First, it would be very interesting to consider in detail the extent to which a philosophical bioethics constructed on human rights principles would be possible and informative. Although some initial scholarship has been produced (notably the on-going work of Deryck Beyleveld and Roger Brownsword), there are numerous leads which could be followed up, for instance in developing Amartya Sen and Martha Nussbaum's capability theory of human rights and global justice to cover a wider range of topics in bioethics and international human rights,[60] or in further development of Baker's contractarian account of human rights. Related to this inquiry would be further examination of the relationship between human rights and bioethics as foundations for national and international legal regulation of medicine, public health, and biomedical technologies.[61] Finally, it would be useful to consider what intellectual relationships would exist between bioethics and human rights if it were concluded that merger or subsumption of one under the other were impossible for some reason: what would a theory of the complementarity of the two discourses look like?

Another inquiry which would be interesting and productive would be a social scientific investigation of the relationship between bioethics and human rights in a variety of contexts (international organizations; academic conferences; published literature) the better to document the contours of the ways actors construct the relationship between the two fields as incommensurable or convergent, and the ways various kinds of professional and civil servant use the different languages of bioethics and human rights for different purposes in different contexts.

A third kind of inquiry would consider how bioethical arguments are—or could be—used in the jurisprudence of human rights and biomedicine. While courts are typically loath to make explicit ethical arguments in deciding even on matters of principle or public policy, it is clear that the new human rights

---

[59] For sceptical responses to this idea and associated notions, see T Campbell, KD Ewing, and A Tompkins (eds), *Sceptical Essays on Human Rights* (Oxford: Oxford University Press, 2001); Gearty (n 50 above). See also Faunce (n 40 above).

[60] AK Sen, 'Elements of a Theory of Human Rights' (2004) 32 *Philosophy and Public Affairs* 315; S Anand, F Peter, and AK Sen (eds), *Public Health, Ethics and Equity* (Oxford: Oxford University Press, 2004); MC Nussbaum, *Frontiers of Justice: Disability, Nationality, Species Membership* (Cambridge, Mass.: Harvard University Press, 2006).

[61] A Plomer, *The Law and Ethics of Medical Research: International Bioethics and Human Rights* (London: Cavendish Publishing, 2005); B Capps, 'Authoritative Regulation and the Stem Cell Debate', *Bioethics* online preprint. DOI: 10.1111/j.1467-8519.2007.00589.x.

jurisprudence invites them to do so, even if the European Court of Human Rights or UK jurisprudence is stylistically and culturally very different from the moral rights-based 'practice of principle' in US Supreme Court jurisprudence.[62] Initial contributions to the scholarly examination of UK human rights jurisprudence in the medical field have tended to take a very narrow, Human Rights Act and ECHR based approach to understanding medical law.[63] Informative as this is, if there is one area where a 'black letter' approach to law sells us short, intellectually, it is the area of human rights law.[64] Of course, it is equally important to consider how far the way in which human rights and bioethics issues and approaches have been taken up in the legal system distorts or at any rate frames those issues and how they are henceforward considered.[65]

Finally, a rich seam of investigation would consider how different issues can be resolved under different bioethical and human rights approaches. In another place I am considering how, in broad terms, bioethics and human rights approaches to human experimentation may come to different conclusions. Other fields ripe for this sort of analysis include access to essential medicines in international public health; infectious disease control in the contexts of the United Kingdom and the international health regulations; genetic databases and their control; and the classical issues of medical law and ethics relating to the beginning and end of life.

It is clear that neither human rights nor bioethics are going away. Whether or not they converge is interesting historically, legally, institutionally, and philosophically. What is equally interesting, I think, is what comes about when they clash. Either way, the normative concerns they share will continue to have a significant impact on national and international law—and, I hope, a positive impact on global human well-being.

---

[62] J Coleman, *The Practice of Principle: In Defence of a Pragmatist Approach to Legal Theory* (Oxford: Oxford University Press, 2001).

[63] Plomer (n 61 above); E Wicks, *Human Rights and Healthcare* (Oxford: Hart Publishing, 2007).

[64] SD Pattinson, *Medical Law and Ethics* (London: Sweet & Maxwell, 2005); D Morgan, *Issues in Medical Law and Ethics* (London: Cavendish Publishing, 2001).

[65] Wolf SM Law and Bioethics: From Values to Violence (2004) 32 *Journal of Law, Medicine and Ethics* 293–306.

4

Law and Bioethics:
A Rights-Based Relationship and
Its Troubling Implications

Daniel Sperling*

Some argue that law is the discipline which has mixed most prominently with bioethics,[1] and that 'bioethicists can be seduced by the law and by legal procedures'.[2] While there is a great consensus that law has influenced bioethics in significant and important ways, certainly much more than it influenced other 'law and...' disciplines,[3] scholars dispute as to the exact role which the law plays in bioethics, the goals it purports to achieve, and the implications of its relationship with the discipline of bioethics. This chapter aims to explore the relationship between law and bioethics and calls for a careful evaluation of the law's contributions to bioethics. Specifically, it will be argued that while the law contributed extensively to the development of bioethics it introduced a language and a way of thinking that are not necessarily appropriate to handle and resolve bioethical issues, and which, in a significant portion of cases, was irrelevant and had little impact on decision-making and behavioural patterns of patients. Moreover, law's interference with and shaping of bioethical issues resulted in serious threats to some of the major characteristics of such issues and brought about other societal concerns which the law did not consider seriously.

* SJD, LLM (University of Toronto); LLB, BA (Philosophy) (The Hebrew University of Jerusalem). Senior Lecturer, The Federmann School of Public Policy and Government and Braun School of Public Health & Community Medicine, The Hebrew University of Jerusalem, Israel <dsperling@pluto.mscc.huji.ac.il>.

[1] AR Jonsen, *The Birth of Bioethics* (New York: Oxford University Press, 1998) 342. See GJ Annas, *Standard of Care: The Law of American Bioethics* (New York: Oxford University Press, 1993) 3: ('American law, not philosophy or medicine, is primarily responsible for the agenda, development and current state of American bioethics') (hereinafter 'Annas, *Standard of Care*'). See also W Van Der Burg, 'Bioethics and Law: A Developmental Perspective' (1997) 11(2) *Bioethics* 91, 93.

[2] G Annas, 'From Selection to Rationing: Policy' Birth of Bioethics Conference, Seattle, Washington, 24–25 September 1992, 75–80, mentioned in Jonsen (n 1 above) at 343.

[3] AM Capron and V Michel, 'Law and Bioethics' (1993–4) 27 *Loyola of Los Angeles Law Review* 25, 32–3.

The chapter will conclude that it is now time to re-evaluate the direction which bioethics should take in the next years, specifically whether it should continue to integrate with law or other disciplines, or alternatively become a more autonomous and independent discipline.

I. Law's Contributions to Bioethics

There are two main areas in which the law has significantly contributed to the field of bioethics. The law facilitated the transformation and evolution of the field of medical ethics into the discipline of bioethics. More importantly, that law has introduced the rights discourse to the therapeutic relationship and bioethical issues more generally.

A. From Medical Ethics to Bioethics

As soon as the practice of medicine began to evolve, ethical questions concerning the limits of the therapeutic authorization were raised mainly by healthcare providers. The traditional area of medical ethics was developed to meet the challenges made by an omni-competent doctor and dependent patient derived from an inherent inequality of members of the two groups.[4] However, under such ethics the practice of medicine was paternalistic so that the right thing for the patient was to do what her physician thought best.[5] The traditional practice of medicine involved little communication between physician and patient.[6] In the old era, physicians used to withhold therapeutic information from their patients believing that the latter would not understand it or would be better off not knowing it. As explained by a bioethics historian David Rothman:

Well into the post-World War II period, decisions at the bedside were the almost exclusive concern of the individual physician, even when they raised fundamental ethical and social issues...
...Moreover, it was usually the individual physician who decided these matters at the bedside or in the privacy of the hospital room, without formal discussion with patients,

---

[4] DW Brock, 'Legal Rights and Moral Responsibilities in the Health Care Process' in SF Spicker, JM Healey, and HT Engelhardt (eds), *The Law-Medicine Relation: A Philosophical Exploration* (Boston: Reidel, 1981) 279.

[5] Of course, some paternalism is and must be embedded in the physician-patient relationship, the latter of which is premised on the specific technical training and competency of the physician. As Mark Siegler and Dudley Goldblatt note, such specialized knowledge and proficiency serves to assist the patient in her illness and suffering and is an inherent part of the therapeutic context. M Siegler and D Goldblatt, 'Clinical Intuition: A Procedure for Balancing the rights of Patients and the Responsibilities of Physicians' in SF Spicker, JM Healey, and HT Engelhardt (eds), *The Law-Medicine Relation: A Philosophical Exploration* (Boston: Reidel, 1981) 5, 6.

[6] cf D Oken, 'What to Tell Cancer Patients: A Study of Medical Attitudes' (1961) 175(13) *JAMA* 1120 (a study showing that only 12% of physicians told patients they had cancer while most patients wanted to know).

their families or even with colleagues, and certainly without drawing the attention of journalists, judges or professional philosophers. And they made their decisions on a case-by-case basis, responding to the particular circumstances as they saw fit, reluctant by both training and practice to formulate or adhere to guidelines or rules.[7]

It is suggested that the law was responsible for the redefinition of what was then regarded as the principle of beneficence to paternalism.[8] Such a shift in language and in goal was part of a larger effort to redress the balance of power between doctor and patient. Various reasons have contributed to the dramatic change and development of the area of medical ethics into bioethics.

As significant advances were made in medical knowledge and technology, contributors to these advances have raised concerns that medical ethics is too weak to meet the ethical challenges posed by these developments. The traditional Western medical ethics attached absolute respect for the sanctity of life. However, modern developments, such as the population explosion and the appearance of new medical technologies, forced society and physicians particularly to balance that value and confront it with other competing values, such as quality of life and respect for persons.[9] In addition, traditional medical ethics mainly focused on the qualities of a good physician and on what Jonsen calls 'bedside manners' such as the requirements that the doctor be gentle, pleasant, comforting, discreet, firm, etc. Gradually, these requirements were perceived as being trivial and mere gestures. A more grave morality was sought, that which was best articulated in a language of duties imposed on the medical profession and which was rooted in deep moral beliefs about the nature of the act of healing itself and its effects on persons subjected to it, namely the patients.[10] A new ethic for medicine and bio-logical sciences was necessary. Bioethics thus became 'the systematic study of the moral dimensions—including moral vision, decisions, conduct and policies—of the life sciences and health care, employing a variety of ethical methodologies in an interdisciplinary setting'.[11] The law helped in transforming medical ethics to bioethics by imposing duties on physicians and empowering patients and human subjects with privacy, freedom of choice, autonomy, and the like.

---

[7] DJ Rothman, *Strangers at the Bedside: A History of How Law and Bioethics Transformed Medical Decision Making* (New York: Basic Books, 1991) 1,2 (hereinafter 'Rothman, *Strangers*').

[8] DJ Rothman, 'The Origins and Consequences of Patient Autonomy: A 25-Year Retrospective' (2001) 9 *Health Care Analysis* 255, 257 (hereinafter 'Rothman, *Origins* and *Consequences*').

[9] Jonsen, (n 1 above) 5.

[10] ibid 6.

[11] WT Reich, 'Introduction' in Reich (ed), *The Encyclopedia of Bioethics* (revised edn). (New York: Simon Schuster Macmillan, 1995), mentioned in Jonsen (n 1 above) vii. The term 'bioethics' was first suggested by Van Rensselaer Potter, a biochemist and professor of oncology at the University of Wisconsin (Madison) in 'Bioethics: Bridge to the Future' (C P Swanson, (ed), 1971) mentioned in MA Rothstein, 'The Growth of Health Law and Bioethics' (2004) 14 *Health Matrix* 213. Some attribute the first use of the word 'bioethics' to the Kennedy Institute of Ethics, which was estab-lished in 1971. Others claim that Sargent Shriver was the first to introduce the term 'bioethics' to Andre Hellegers who was organizing the Kennedy Institute of Ethics at Georgetown University. Capron and Michel, (n 3 above) 26, n 6.

Along with these substantial changes there were few scandals, the most serious of which took place during the Nazi regime, which discredited the faith in health providers, exposed an inherent potential for exploiting the patient or the human subject of clinical trials, and challenged the idea that the physician's main purpose is to benefit the patient. A series of disgraceful actions revealed how a medical team may be self-interested and mainly concerned with pursuing the reputation of its members, and gaining professional credit and wealth even at the cost of the patient's well-being.[12] Examples of these scandals include the Nazi medical experiments on inmates in concentration and extermination camps aiming to ascertain how long individuals survive in freezing water and how well they function at different pressure levels existing at high altitudes. Other dreadful experiments included the practicality of various sterilization techniques, the development of new vaccines, and novel surgical techniques. In addition, Nazi physicians were involved in implementing the 'euthanasia programme' which involved 'the systematic and secret execution of the aged, insane, incurably ill, or deformed children and other persons, by gas, lethal injections and diverse other means in nursing homes, hospitals and asylums'.[13] After the Second World War, twelve US military trials were held in Nuremberg from 1946 to 1949. One of the trials (*US v Karl Brandt et al*) was concerned with the prosecution of twenty-three physicians responsible for carrying out of these medical experiments. The trial ended with fifteen defendants found guilty and sentenced to death and with the enactment of the Nuremberg Code, leading to the establishment of the Declaration of Helsinki regarding the rights of human research subjects in 1964.

A few years later, an article published in the *New England Journal of Medicine* revealed a series of studies undertaken by medical researchers in the United States. The studies were concerned with experiments subjecting normal newborns to catheterization and multiple x-rays to study their bladders, examining the period of hepatitis infectivity after children with mental defects were given the virus, and exploring the rheumatic fever of men in service who were denied treatment for streptococcal respiratory infection.[14]

During the same years, between 1932 and 1972, a large clinical study was conducted in Tuskegee, Alabama, in which almost 400 poor and illiterate African American were denied treatment for syphilis. The study was performed without the subjects' informed consent and was terminated after it was leaked to the press.[15]

---

[12] See generally G Annas and M Gordin (eds), *The Nazi Doctors and the Nuremberg Code* (Oxford: Oxford University Press, 1992).

[13] T Taylor, 'The Nuremberg War Crimes Trials' (April 1949) 450 *International Conciliation* 282, mentioned in SD Stein, 'Nuremberg Trials Held by the United States of America Under Control Council Law No. 10', available at <http://www.ess.uwe.ac.uk/genocide/cntrl10_trials.htm#Overview> (accessed 18 July 2008).

[14] HK Beecher, 'Ethics and Clinical Research' (1966) 274 *New England Journal of Medicine* 1354.

[15] Centers for Disease Control and Prevention, 'U.S. Public Health Service Syphilis Study at Tuskegee', available at <http://www.cdc.gov/tuskegee/timeline.htm> (accessed 18 July 2008).

The shift from medical ethics to bioethics can also be explained by more general developments, most prominently the emancipation process in which citizens claimed their rights and freedoms mainly by an appeal to the law.[16] With the advent of the civil rights movement in the second half of the twentieth century, public opinion has changed substantially with regard to the rights of individuals as against the state and other individuals and social or political institutions. The civil rights movement called for the increase of rights for and within health care.[17] This movement, along with the information revolution which took place at that time, brought about a profound distrust and suspicion of authority and led to a general resistance to paternalism.[18] Other events contributing to these general developments include the feminist critique of medical care institutions by womens' groups in the1960s and 1970s,[19] and the new claims of people with mental and physical disabilities and the subjects of medical research to be treated equally and with respect.

The law facilitated and encouraged the dramatic development and transformation of the area of medical ethics into the new interdisciplinary field of bioethics as advocacy for rights within health care has been advanced mainly through courts.[20] Beginning with case decisions in torts, the law developed the idea of integrity of the body, implying that no individual should be touched, let alone treated without her prior consent. Any unapproved appropriating of the body was regarded as battery and breach of duty of care.[21] Gradually, the law established and developed the requirement of consent, which not only protected patients from unwanted touching but also empowered them with new and advanced rights, in particular the right to autonomy and self-determination.[22] Next, the law expanded the requirement of consent to include the obligation to provide the

---

See generally JH Jones, *Bad Blood: The Tuskegee Syphilis Experiment* (New York: Macmillan Publishing, 1993); SM Reverby (ed), *Tuskegee's Truths: Rethinking the Tuskegee Syphilis Study* (Chapel Hill, North Carolina: University of North Carolina Press, 2000).

[16] Van Der Burg (n 1 above) 96.

[17] P Starr, *The Social Transformation of American Medicine: The Rise of a Sovereign Profession and the Making of a Vast Industry* (New York: Basic Books, 1982).

[18] Rothman, *Origins and Consequences*, (n 8 above) 256.

[19] S B Ruzek and J Becker, 'The Women's Health Movement in the United States: From Grass-Roots Activism to Professional Agendas' (1999) 54 *Journal of American Medical Women's Association* 4, 5.

[20] Even when advocacy was not pursued by lawyers, it focused on securing legal or statutory change. MA Rodwin, 'Patient Accountability and Quality of Care: Lessons from Medical Consumerism and the Patients' Rights, Women's Health and Disability Rights Movements' (1994) 20 *American Journal of Law and Medicine* 147.

[21] See eg *Schloendorf v Society of NY Hospital* 105 NE 92, 93 (NY 1914) ('Every human being of adult years and sound mind has a right to determine what shall be done with his own body; and a surgeon who performs an operation without his patient's consent commits an assault, for which he is liable in damages.'). For the duty of care in connection with the duty to provide information to patients, see eg *Bolam v Friern Hospital Management Committee* [1957] 1 WLR 582; *Canterbury v Spence*, 464 F 2d 772 (DC Cir 1972).

[22] Most notably this right was acknowledged in the area of abortion law as part of a woman's constitutional right to privacy: *Roe v Wade* 410 US 113 (1973).

patient with sufficient knowledge about treatment, risks, and alternatives so that her giving of consent should not only be free but also informed.[23] Finally, case law and advance directive legislation established the right to refuse treatment, including life-sustaining treatment, and more generally to participate actively in medical decision-making.[24]

There were few reasons for the incorporation and active involvement of law in bioethical matters.[25] On the personal level, many scholars who are concerned with issues in medical ethics and bioethics have strong legal academic backgrounds.[26] A partial list of these scholars includes Gerorge Annas, Alexander Carpron, Bernard Dickens, Michael Freeman, Lawrence Gostin, Angela Holder, Jay Katz, John Robertson, Patricia King, William Winslade, and Joseph Healey.[27] These and many other legal scholars have framed and reshaped the bioethical questions in legal language, and offered original ways to address the moral problems raised in the clinical setting as if they were legal problems deserving a 'right' justifiable answer. Along with this line, Carl Schneider argues that the language of law 'enriched bioethical discourse by generating vivid and pressing instantiations of bioethical issues, by scrutinizing them—in part—in moral terms, and by proffering means of resolving them'.[28] Along with the development of health law and the increased jurisprudence in this latter area of law, legal scholars contributed their personal knowledge and familiarity with case law and legislation and used it as a means to structure decision-making processes in bioethics.[29]

Second, the methodology used in law to develop and sustain legal rules and principles and to resolve disputes was found to be close enough to that used in medical ethics. As a practical discipline providing guidance for clinical decisions, bioethics was receptive to the methodologies of both principlism and casuistry.[30] While the first methodology calls for the application of four major moral abstract

---

[23] *Salgo v Leland Stanford Jr University Board of Trustees* 317 P 2d 170 (Cal Ct App 1957). See also J Katz, *The Silent World of Doctor and Patient* (New York: Free Press, 1984) 59–84. But cf Annas, who argues that the doctrine of informed consent was not born at case law but at Article 1 of the Nuremberg Code ('The voluntary consent of the human subject is absolutely essential'). GJ Annas, 'American Bioethics after Nuremberg: Pragmatism, Politics and Human Rights' (Boston University Lecture, 2005), 8 (hereinafter 'Annas, *University Lecture*').

[24] For the discussion of a patient's right to make health-related decisions under the autonomy model see CE Schneider, *The Practice of Autonomy: Patients, Doctors, and Medical Decisions* (New York and Oxford: Oxford University Press, 1998) 11–32 (hereinafter 'Schneider, *Autonomy*').

[25] See also RB Dworkin, *Limits: The Role of Law in Bioethical Decision Making* (Bloomington and Indianapolis: Indiana University Press, 1996) 2.

[26] CE Schneider, 'Bioethics in the Language of the Law' (1994) 24(4) *Hastings Center Report* 16 (hereinafter 'Schneider, *Language*').

[27] Jonsen, (n 1 above) 342.

[28] Schneider, *Language* (n 26 above). However, Schneider also argues that since the law has social goals and limits arising from its social purpose, the effect on and usefulness of law's language to bioethics are incomplete.

[29] For the development of health law see Rothstein (n 11 above).

[30] Other less dominant methodologies in bioethics include virtue ethics, the narrative method, and the phenomenological method. See, ED Pellegrino, 'Bioethics at Century's Turn: Can Normative Ethics Be Retrieved?' (2000) 25(6) *Journal of Medicine and Philosophy* 655, 663–5.

principles to almost every issue in bioethics,[31] the second focuses on ad hoc analysis of concrete cases.[32] Both methodologies have their counterparts in law.

Third, since the law has binding effect on people's preferences, it usually enjoys the public faith and respect confirming its social and moral authority. This is why the law was mostly suitable to redress the loss of estimation and suspicion in health providers and researchers by bringing in new objective and credible legal language to regain trust in health providers.[33] From this perspective, law's involvement and interference with the physician-patient relationship was not seen as special given that 'whenever there is a social sense of wrong, or injustice, or an abuse of power by some people or some institutions (including government), those who feel abused often turn to the law for protection.'[34]

Fourth, law's integration with bioethical issues and moral dilemmas in the medical context was facilitated by a false assumption that law reflects ethics. Charity Scott, for example, makes such an assumption when he argues that the law reflects a consensus statement by our society on what we believe to be ethically appropriate behaviour. In his view, the law reflects society's idealism.[35] However, in the light of Legal Positivism this is a partial understanding of the law. Whereas law obliges people to comply with society's normative requirements, ethics is a tool for making such requirements specific, thereby obliging persons to make their conduct conform, in a non-obligatory fashion, to such norms.[36] An example for the separation of law from morals is seen in the writings of HLA Hart. Hart argued that 'the most prominent general feature of law at all times and places is that its existence means that certain kinds of human conduct are no longer optional, but in *some* sense obligatory.'[37] The assumption that law is not distinguished from ethics is easy to make when there is a vacuum in other areas which may have integrated with bioethics, as explained by Daniel Callahan:

I suspect that there has come to be some enormous moral vacuum in this country, which for lack of better institutional candidates has been left to the law to fill. The churches are either too sectarian or too morally bland, the universities too caught up in professionalism or culture wars, the journals of opinion tiresomely focused on the religious right (the

---

[31] The major advocates of principlism are Tom Beauchamp and James Childress. See TL Beauchamp and JF Childress, *Principles of Biomedical Ethics* (New York: Oxford University Press, 4th edn, 1994).

[32] The prominent advocates of that methodology are Albert Jonsen and Stephen Toulmin. See AR Jonsen and S Toulmin, *The Abuse of Casuistry: A History of Moral Reasoning* (Berkeley: California University Press, 1998). Interestingly, the authors note that some regard such methodology as 'common-law ethics model' (ibid 330).

[33] MA Hall, 'Law, Medicine, and Trust' (2002–3) 55 *Stanford Law Review* 463, 469.

[34] C Scott, 'Why Law Pervades Medicine? An Essay on Ethics in Health Care' (2000) 14 *Notre Dame Journal of Law, Ethics and Public Policy* 245, 272.

[35] ibid.

[36] MC Sullivan and DF Reynolds, 'Where Law and Bioethics Meet...and Where They Don't' (1997–8) 75 *University of Detroit Mercy Law Review* 607.

[37] HLA Hart, *The Concept of Law* (Oxford: Oxford University Press, 2nd edn, 1994) 6.

left) or assaulting politically correct liberals (the right), and political life reduced during this campaign year to nasty negative attach on anything and everyone. That leaves the law. It is relatively free of scandal, still generally respected, national and relatively uniform in its scope, and ready to take on ethics if that is what gets served up to it for the making of decisions. It may be the best institution we have, but it is a poor substitute for moral consensus and public debate on ethics.[38]

B. The Rights Movement in Bioethics

The most significant contribution the law has made to bioethics lies in the incorporation of the idea and language of rights to bioethical issues.[39] The rights movement in bioethics began with case law and sporadic legislation, but also gained weight by commentaries especially written by legal scholars and lawyers. One of the prominent leaders of the rights movement in bioethics is George Annas. In a leading article published in 1974, which marks the beginning of this movement, George Annas and Jospeh Healey introduce for the first time the idea of protecting the patient's interests in the exercise of her rights. Such an idea would provide, towards the end of this article, a bill of rights in the medical context:

We begin with two fundamental propositions: (1) The American medical consumer possesses certain interests, many of which may properly be described as 'rights', that he does not automatically forfeit by entering into a relationship with a doctor or a health care facility; and (2) most doctors and health care facilities fail to provide for their protection or assertion, and frequently limit their exercise without recourse for the patient.[40]

A few years later, Annas publishes another essay where he writes:

... Both the health care provider *and* the patient will be better off if the status of the law regarding both the patient's *and* provider's rights is understood, and the means of change or challenge well delineated. I would go even further. An understanding of the law can be as important to the proper care of patients as an understanding of emergency medical procedures or proper drugs dosages.[41]

Although originally the rights movement in bioethics was addressed both to patients' and physicians' rights, its most powerful effect was on patients, who

---

[38] D Callahan, 'Escaping from Legalism: Is It Possible?' (1996) 26(6) *Hastings Center Report* 34.

[39] A call to ensure patients' rights in health care was also made by some medical sociologists, most notably Eliot Freidson. See LR Staffen, 'Heroic Medicine, Physician Autonomy, and Patient Rights' (1994) *Law and Social Inquiry* 753.

[40] GJ Annas and JM Healey, 'The Patient Rights Advocate: Redefining the Doctor-Patient Relationship in the Hospital Context' (1974) 27 *Vanderbilt Law Review* 243, 245. See also GJ Annas, *The Rights of Hospital Patients: The Basic ACLU Guide to a Hospital Patient's Rights* (New York: Discus, 1975).

[41] G Annas, 'Legal Rights in the Health Care Setting' in SF Spicker, JM Healey, and HT Engelhardt (eds), *The Law-Medicine Relation: A Philosophical Exploration* (Boston: Reidel, 1981) 265, 266 (hereinafter 'Annas, *Legal Rights*').

were regarded defenseless and in need of legal protection. The introduction of the new rights discourse to bioethics, which partly involved the acknowledgement of constitutional rights,[42] was purported to reflect a societal consensus over how the ethical balance ought to be weighed between doctors and patients.[43] Such a discourse was thought to be necessary in an area where people are most vulnerable and hopeless. Acknowledging, respecting, and enforcing rights in the medical context was seen as a useful way to give some power to incapable patients and guarantee that they would be treated with respect and dignity.[44]

The language of rights added to the moral discourse in bioethics statements providing vital protections of life, liberty, expression, and property and was extremely important.[45] It was successful in its conjunction with medical ethics in part because traditional medical ethics was understood to deal with the protection of individuals' interests as against their physicians, and rights were primary instruments to achieve this end. As a reaction to medical authority and paternalism, the language of rights seemed the best way to empower patients as against their doctors and to confer on them a sense of control and responsibility wherefrom they could gain some benefits that were not dependent on the physician's good will, on chance, or on money. As explained by Beauchamp and Childress, strong advocates of the rights movement in bioethics:

Being a rights-bearer in a society that enforces rights is both a source of personal protection and a source of dignity and self-respect. By contrast, to maintain that someone has an *obligation* to protect another's interest may leave the recipient in a passive position, dependent upon the other's good will in fulfilling the obligation. When persons possess enforceable rights correlative to obligations, they are enabled to be independent agents, pursuing their projects and making claims. What we often cherish is not that someone is obligated to us, but that we have a right that secures for us the opportunity to pursue and claim as ours the benefit or liberty that we value.[46]

The rights discourse in general, and the right to autonomy and self-determination specifically, focused on three levels of relationship. First and foremost is the relationship between the patient and her physician. Within this context the rights discourse empowered the patient by providing her rights which her physician has had duties to fulfil. Through that discourse the patient regained her position and standing vis-à-vis her health provider, making both parties more or less equal within that relationship. This level of relationship was influenced by the liberal thought respecting a person's rights to privacy, autonomy, and bodily integrity.

A second level of relationship concerns the relationship between the patient and the state, the latter of which represents the public interest. The rights discourse

---

[42] For the importance of constitutional rights in adjudication see Dworkin (n 25 above) 15–18.
[43] Scott (n 34 above) 263.
[44] Annas, *Legal Rights* (n 41 above) 268.
[45] TL Beauchamp and JF Childress, *Principles of Biomedical Ethics* (New York: Oxford University Press, 5th edn, 2001) 355.
[46] ibid 362.

at this level provided individuals, who needed access to medical technology or treatment, or required some assistance in order to achieve their health-related goals, a sense of security from state interventions and limitations. Rights in this category were mainly established in abortion or end-of-life legal cases and include the right to cease or refuse treatment and, more generally, the rights to privacy and bodily integrity. Such rights were usually constitutional, protecting and promoting a zone of privacy from the state's interventions. This level of relationship was influenced by the libertarian philosophy, and was most dominant in American case law.

A third level of relationship within which the rights discourse was developed concerns the rights of an individual patient as against her state in the light of a more general understanding of human rights and the right to access health care, mainly established in international treaties and conventions. Such a level of relationship was influenced by arguments concerning the equal access to health services and the enhancement of one's freedom, especially one's freedom of reproduction. Examples of rights developed in this context include Diane Blood's right to export her deceased husband's sperm for insemination in Belgium,[47] and more recently Ms and Mr Evans' rights to respect for both decisions to (correspondingly) become and not to become a parent under Article 8 of the European Convention.[48]

Although the rights discourse is now dominant in bioethics, there are many problems and difficulties which such discourse gives rise to. The following section will discuss the most important of these.

II. Critique of the Rights Movement in Bioethics

Much of the criticism against the rights movement in bioethics expressed in this section can be explained by the more general critique of the Critical Legal Studies movement of liberalism.[49] However, it is possible to identify five major areas of criticism which are highly appealing to rights in the medical context.

A. Missing Right-Holder

First, since ethical dilemmas in the medical context were formed and articulated in a language of rights, such a language was found inapplicable to certain parties affected by bioethical issues who were incapable of holding rights. These include

---

[47] *R v Human Fertilisation and Embryology Authority, ex p Blood* [1997] 2 WLR 806.

[48] *Evans v Amicus Healthcare Ltd and Ors* [2004] 2 WLR 781; *Evans v UK* (Application No 6339/05) European Court of Human Rights (7 March 2006) available at <http://www.familylawweek.co.uk/library.asp?i=1776> (accessed 18 July 2008).

[49] See eg D Kennedy, 'Form and Substance in Private Law Adjudication' (1976) 89 *Harvard Law Review* 1685.

aborted embryos, frozen eggs, brain-dead patients, etc. Hence, for example, if a frozen embryo is not a human being and does not hold rights how can one justify the special respect we owe to it while making a decision on whether to discard or donate it to others,[50] to produce from it stem cells for research, or to select its sex before it is implanted?[51] If a person does not have a proprietary right in her body or bodily parts, how can we compensate her for an unauthorized but profitable use of her cells and bodily parts?[52] Or, if a brain-dead pregnant woman cannot be said to hold rights, what prevents us from artificially sustaining her life for the sake of her foetus and society's general interest in safeguarding life?[53] These questions and many more reflect the fact that the rights discourse could not provide a satisfactory and complete mechanism through which ethical dilemmas in bioethics can be resolved.

B. Balance of Rights and Emphasis on Procedure

The concept of rights involves the viewing of the world in terms of contradictory dualities and values. The law facilitates the hiding of the conflicts inherent in such dualities and values through, for example, moving from one possible result to another without any consistent normative theory.[54] The rights discourse has proved impractical and insufficient since it requires the balance of competing rights involved. The result of such a balance is nevertheless unnecessary and in any event gives no answer or solution to the kind of problem at stake. Moreover, since more issues in bioethics have been resolved on a case-by-case basis and on an individual balance of competing rights, the law of one state on a particular issue may be opposite to that of another, while a third state may not have considered the issue at all.[55]

Furthermore, the rights discourse in bioethics refers more to the question of *who* is the right-holder and explores less about the *content* of the right at

---

[50] *Davis v Davis*, 842 SW 2d 588 (Tenn 1992).
[51] Van Der Burg (n 1 above) 105–6.
[52] *Moore v Regents of the University of California*, 793 P. 2d 479 (Cal 1990).
[53] D Sperling, 'Maternal Brain-Death' (2004) 30(4) *American Journal of Law and Medicine* 453. For a detailed account of posthumous rights and interests, see D Sperling, *Posthumous Interests: Legal and Ethical Perspectives* (Cambridge: Cambridge University Press, 2008). Other issues related to the use of dead bodies include the suggestion of having their organs automatically available for transplantation or practising resuscitation procedures on those bodies without informing families or seeking consent. See correspondingly J Harris, 'Law and Regulation of Retained Organs: The Ethical Issues' (2002) 4 *Legal Studies* 527; KV Iserson, 'Teaching without Harming the Living: Performing Minimally Invasive Procedures on the Newly-Dead' (2005) 8 *Journal of Health Care, Law and Policy* 216; D Sperling, 'Breaking Through the Silence: The Illegality of Performing Resuscitation Procedures on the Newly-Dead', (2004) 13(2) *Annals of Health Law* 393.
[54] Ed Sparer, 'Fundamental Human Rights, Legal Entitlements, and the Social Struggle: A Friendly Critique of the Critical Legal Studies Movement' (1984) 36 *Stanford Law Review* 509, 517.
[55] JL Dolgin and LL Shepherd, *Bioethics and the Law* (New York: Aspen Publishers, 2005) 7.

stake.[56] The discourse provides a mere *procedure* to resolve disputes in bioethics or better articulate them but fails to address substantive issues raised by those disputes.[57] The mechanism of rights puts emphasis on *how* conflicts are settled rather than *why*. As a result, bioethics has come to be characterized by a lack of substantive reflection represented by its difficulty in establishing a normative ethics for the biomedical sciences.[58] One of the prominent scholars who is disturbed by this lack of normative moral background to bioethical questions is Eduard Pellegrino. Pellegrino critically claims that bioethics has become a procedure for resolving 'value' conflicts whether those values are moral or not, and that bioethics is now concerned with 'what "works" or what is "useful", ie what is justifiable to the parties making the decision irrespective of whether or not the conflict resolution is true or good'.[59]

C. A Social Justice Critique

An emphasis on rights in bioethical issues encouraged an atomistic approach to ethical issues raised in the medical context. Although rights may have enhanced personal enrichment through personal and individual freedom, the idea of rights often leaves behind other individuals and groups, thereby ignoring important segments of the population who are depleted by their inability to fulfil their powers.[60] Moreover, the rights movement in bioethics made it easy for health providers to ignore the social implications, effects, and causes of the various decisions and dilemmas they are confronted with, and to take no notice of the way in which the medical institutions and legal doctrines shape and influence the social life and behaviour of individuals and patients in society. The language of rights has thus depressed any attempt to subsume individual interests under broader social interests, thereby communicating a clear message that bioethics—like law more generally—is all about rights, duties, and sanctions.

The rights discourse in bioethics discouraged a rich and broad understanding of the social factors affecting the dilemmas at issue and the possible solutions

[56] AM Capron, 'What Contributions Have Social Science and the Law Made to the Development of Policy on Bioethics?' (1999) 128(4) *Daedalus* 295, 297.

[57] cf Wendy Mariner, who argues: 'Of course, law is not a tool to enforce understanding. Just as law cannot make people kind or generous, it cannot make them understand something. The best it can do is require the presence of objectively observable factors that make understanding possible.' WK Mariner, 'Informed Consent in the Post-Modern Era' (1988) 13 *Law and Social Inquiry* 385, 402. For the general role of procedure in law, see Dworkin (n 25 above) 6.

[58] JP Bishop and F Jotterand, 'Bioethics as Biopolitics' (2006) 31 *Journal of Medicine and Philosophy* 205, 206.

[59] Pellegrino (n 30 above) 657.

[60] cf Halpern, who writes that membership of patient-rights advocacy groups is overwhelmingly white, well-educated, and middle class, as patients in these demographic groups are most interested in participating in medical decision-making. SA Halpern, 'Medical Authority and the Culture of Rights' (2004) 29(4–5) *Journal of Health Politics, Policy and Law* 835, 845.

available.[61] More generally, the rights movement led to an approach ignoring the social detriments to health and health inequalities. The emphasis on legal standing and the need merely to characterize one's legal entitlements (rights) against the other or the state and establish an alleged mechanism to balance between them made a shift in the interest of bioethics from the right to health to the right to health care. Such a shift left bioethicists considerably silent on the moral issues faced when limited health care resources are prioritized.[62] While bioethics seemed to have developed through cases establishing the freedom of choice of individuals, whether patients or the subjects of clinical trials, it remained far behind with regard to issues relating to access to medical treatment, for example access to assisted reproductive technologies, and to cases concerning the distribution of health care such as the allocation of organs for transplantation.

Moreover, emphasis on autonomy and individual rights supported the Rawlsian belief that justice is concerned with individual actions, social institutions, and outcomes which are within human control.[63] Such a belief made it difficult to justify a right to health given that the latter may be influenced by factors which are not controlled by the individual, such as her genetic inheritance, poverty, racial and national background, exposure to infectious diseases, etc. Instead, the rights movement in bioethics was able only to justify a right to health care leading to health factors controlled by the autonomy of the person in need. A precondition for that right would now be the individual's ability to participate in social life and to be able to enhance her primary goods (civil and political liberties) through such participation. Under such an understanding, any individual who, for her medical condition, could not take active measures in social life or for whom treatment is not aimed to restore the ability to be socially active, for example a terminally ill patient receiving palliative care, could not be justified in having a right to health or to that specific health treatment/ procedure.

D. General Conceptual Difficulties

Although law in general and the rights movement in particular were developed to resolve ethical issues in bioethics and were erroneously perceived as a substitute to ethics,[64] they did not succeed in establishing infrastructure to resolve

---

[61] WM Sage, 'The Lawyerization of Medicine' (2001) 26(5) *Journal of Health Politics, Policy and Law* 1179, 1186.

[62] DW Brock, 'Broadening the Bioethics Agenda' (2000) 10(1) *Kennedy Institute of Ethics Journal* 21, 22.

[63] J Rawls, *A Theory of Justice* (Cambridge, Mass.: Harvard University Press, 1971).

[64] cf Charity Scott who writes: 'Law pervades medicine because ethics pervades medicine, and in America, we use the law to resolve ethical dilemmas in health care', and 'In health care, our society has used the law to ask (and answer) questions about what are ethically appropriate behaviors among those who provide, or receive, or pay for health care services.' Scott (n 34 above) 245, 248. See also Annas, *Standard of Care* (n 1 above) 3: 'It seems natural for Americans, for example, that

ethical dilemmas in bioethics because of substantive conceptual difficulties lying in the differences between law and ethics. First, ethical dilemmas in bioethics are always between two competing alternative conducts both of which are right things to do. When law interferes with a conflict between two actions that are right, writes Roger Dworkin, the law's job is very difficult in mediating between the 'rights' and in attempting to sacrifice as little as possible of what is 'right' on both sides.[65]

Second, the law in itself demands for and is satisfied with minimum requirements and does not aspire to create or produce a praiseworthy moral conduct.[66] So, in the area of informed consent, for example, the law sets the conditions for the patient to be informed about diagnosis, treatment, and alternatives but it is not concerned with the question of whether the patient has in fact understood the information she was given. On this issue Robert Levine comments: 'A focus on rights and rules… has a tendency to yield a "minimalist ethics". In a minimalist ethics, much of the behavior we value in the caring physician is regarded as supererogatory or optimal—nice but not morally required.'[67] In addition to these different standpoints of law and morals, rights also run the risk of creating a poor understanding of the moral significance of motives, supererogatory actions, virtues, and the like characterizing the field of ethics.[68]

Third, as a result of institutional differences between law and ethics, legal conceptions and legal terms do not always fit the bioethical discourse. Developed under tort law, the law of informed consent for example, can have only limited power by retrospectively compensating victims for their injuries rather than prospectively reforming the relationship between physicians and patients so that it would include the duty to share and communicate to the latter substantive information and treatment.[69] Additionally, the legal language of rights associated with and developed through case law (especially torts) usually employs the idea of wrongs. Such language focuses on the fulfilment of those rights and the satisfaction of the subject of rights, thereby allowing physicians to separate themselves from their patients. Indeed, rights may be vested in the therapeutic relationship

---

the morality of abortion has been recast as the "right to abortion" and that the morality of medical treatment near the end of life is now called simply "the right to die".'

[65] Dworkin (n 25 above) 7, 165.

[66] 'By addressing what we have generally agreed is wrong behavior or bad actions, the law sets the legal minimums for behavior; it does not address the ethical maximums. The law provides sanctions for wrongdoing; it does not tend to provide rewards for doing good or even sanctions for failing to do good.' Scott (n 34 above) 260. The tendency to regard the physician-patient relationship as a contract may also indicate the minimalism of the law. Van Der Burg (n 1 above) 102, n 30. The contract model is also explained by the patient's exercise of rights vis-à-vis her health provider. See Brock (n 4 above) 280.

[67] R Levine, 'Medical Ethics and Personal Doctors: Conflicts between What We Teach and What We Want' (1987) 13 *American Journal of Law and Medicine* 351, 362.

[68] Beauchamp and Childress (n 45 above) 361.

[69] Schneider, *Language* (n 26 above).

but their conferral is at the expense of a genuine and caring dialogue between physicians and patients.[70]

E. Rhetorical Contribution

Rather than having practical effects on ethical issues, the main contribution of the rights movement to bioethics was its strong rhetorical and expressive function. The language of rights helped articulate and construct a balance between competing interests, making the empowerment of patients more visible, but it had limited consequences. In this important respect, the legal interference with bioethics can exemplify how the 'law in books' stands in contradiction to 'the law in action'.

The limited effect of the rights movement in bioethics is best observed in the right to refuse treatment which was regarded as correlative to the right to give consent and consequently led to the establishment of three related patient rights: the right to die with dignity and to refuse treatment; the right to receive assisted suicide; and the right to leave a valid advance directive.

Although case law developed and made it a legal obligation to obtain patients' approval for medical treatment, having explored the full consequences of such treatment, empirical studies suggest that only a few physicians view consent as integral to medical practice or give it much attention.[71] Studies show that physicians prefer some treatments over others and are sceptical regarding whether informed consent can bring any gain to their patients. Moreover, it is reported that most patients prefer to leave treatment choices to their physicians, and that less than a third want veto power over those decisions.[72] Recent studies reveal that almost half of respondent patients prefer to rely on physicians for medical knowledge rather than seeking out information themselves.[73] Leading to these data is the fact that many patients are incapable of comprehending and manipulating complex information about risks associated with proposed treatment and alternatives to it.[74] Hence, physicians frequently do not genuinely embrace the goals of informed consent and these are not implemented within the physician-patient relationship.[75] The lack of patients' participation in medical decisions is also observed in studies of intensive care units, where physicians insist that decisions require understanding of technical information and that patients' families

[70] ibid. [71] Halpern (n 60 above) 840–1.

[72] CW Lidz, A Meisel, M Osterweis, JL Holden, JH Marx, and MR Nunetz, 'Barriers to Informed Consent' (1983) 99 *Annals of Internal Medicine* 539.

[73] W Levinson, A Kao, A Kuby, and RA Thisted, 'Not All Patients Want to Participate in Decision Making' (2005) 20(6) *Journal of General Internal Medicine* 531.

[74] DI Shalowitz and MS Wolf, 'Shared Decision-Making and the Lower Literate Patient' (2004) 32 *Journal of Law, Medicine and Ethics* 759.

[75] A Meisel and M Kuczewski, 'Legal and Ethical Myths about Informed Consent' (1996) 156 *Archives of Internal Medicine* 2521.

are too emotional to give or make medical choices.[76] Finally, in the context of biomedical research, studies also show that researchers rarely supply broad information about the process and goals of the type of research being conducted, and as a result human subjects make false assumptions about the studies in which they participate.[77]

Beginning with Karen Ann Quinlan's case, which addressed the right of an unconscious patient to withdraw life-sustaining treatment as expressed by her father,[78] courts have acknowledged a patient's or surrogate's right to accept or refuse medical treatment, including a constitutional right to die with dignity.[79] Courts have also recognized the right of mentally competent patients to refuse treatment even at the cost of death. Examples of the latter cases include the right of a Jehovah's Witness to refuse a blood transfusion,[80] and the right of a patient with a disability to refuse nutrition and hydration.[81]

Indeed, the Quinlan case symbolizes the beginning of a new era where the courts expand the patient's rights to decline life-sustaining treatment, compel physicians to respect patients' Do-Not-Resuscitate demands, and eventually require physicians' assisted help to terminate individuals' lives. But, as illuminated by Tina Stevens, this is a false genealogy since this era marks the beginning of a fatal turn from the ambit of patients, health providers, and communities to the sphere of the courtroom and the language and limitations of rights.[82] The court's refusal to acknowledge Nancy Cruzan's right not to be fed by her doctors and its requirement for clear and convincing evidence to demonstrate the wishes of an incompetent adult patient,[83] as well as the reluctance of the US Supreme Court to recognize a general constitutionally protected right to commit suicide with the help of her physician[84] suggests that the movement is misdescribed.

The right to refuse treatment was not as fully acknowledged as its rhetorical presentation might have suggested. Such a right was not respected by courts when the interests of a minor were at stake or for the protection of a foetus. For example, the court ordered that a mother of an infant who was a Jehovah's Witness should receive a blood transfusion,[85] and that doctors are free to force

---

[76] Halpern (n 60 above) 841.

[77] JA Fisher, 'Procedural Misconceptions and Informed Consent: Insights from Empirical Research on the Clinical Trials Industry' (2006) 16(3) *Kennedy Institute of Ethics Journal* 251.

[78] *Re Karen Ann Quinlan* 355 A 2d 647 (NJ 1976).

[79] *Cruzan and Ors v Director, Miscuri Department of Health* 497 US 261, 110 S Ct 2841 (1990).

[80] *Norwood Hospital v Munoz* 564 NE 2d 1017 (Mass. 1991).

[81] *Bouvia v Superior Court* 225 Cal Rptr 297 (Ct App 2d Dist 1986).

[82] MLT Stevens, *Bioethics in America: Origins and Cultural Politics* (Baltimore and London: The Johns Hopkins University Press, 2003) 151.

[83] *Cruzan and Ors v Director, Missouri Department of Health* 497 US 261, 110 S Ct 2841 (1990).

[84] *Washington v Glucksberg* 521 US 702 (1997); *Vacco v Quill* 521 US 793 (1997).

[85] *Application of the President and Directors of Georgetown College Inc* 331 F 2d 1000 (DC Cir 1964).

pregnant woman to have a cesarean section to save the life of her foetus.[86]
Moreover, empirical studies suggest that 34 per cent of 879 surveyed physicians practicing in adult intensive care units in the United States continue to
provide life-sustaining treatment against the wishes of patients or their surrogates.[87] In the area of Jehovah's Witnesses' right to refuse blood transfusions,
careful analysis shows that some cases acknowledging such a right were held
after the patient was successfully transfused, after she successfully recovered
without needing the transfusion, or when the decision was rendered moot by
the patient's 'willingness to be coerced'.[88] The rhetorical function of the rights
discourse is explained by Lisa Staffen:

> Despite the presence of the law in defining the nature of some of the patient's rights, the
> evidence from the books under review here clearly suggests that the rights of patients
> depend on the actions of physicians. Physicians may fulfill their obligation to seek con-
> sent for some medical interventions, but this obligation does not extend to full disclosure
> of the range of treatment options or full access to the decisions about which course of
> treatment is appropriate. In addition, physicians have a great deal of discretion in decid-
> ing when treatment is futile and whether a decision is the kind that requires patient and
> family participation.[89]

Moreover, since the rights discourse in bioethics hardly involved the establishment of positive rights, no right to *receive* medical treatment, let alone to
be given assistance that will hasten one own's death was acknowledged. This
is especially puzzling since the law did recognize other rights protecting the
very same interest justifying those positive rights, namely the privacy interest of patients. Although empirical studies suggest that around 16 per cent of
surveyed oncologists participated in euthanasia or physician-assisted suicide,[90]
courts (including the US Supreme Court) ruled that there is no constitutional
right to receive a physician's assistance in committing suicide.[91] Courts declined

---

[86] *Jefferson v Griffin Spalding County Hospital Authority* 274 SE 2d 457 (Ga 1981). For a detailed
analysis of legal interventions involving the bodies of pregnant women, see D Sperling, *Management
of Post-Mortem Pregnancy: Legal and Philosophical Aspects* (Aldershot: Ashgate, 2006) 15–34.

[87] DA Asch, J Hansen-Flaschen and PN Lanken, 'Decisions to Limit Life-Sustaining Treatment
by Critical Care Physicians in the US' (1995) 151(2) *American Journal of Respiratory and Critical
Care Medicine* 288.

[88] Siegler and Goldblatt (n 5 above) 24.

[89] Staffen (n 39 above) 756. cf Robert Zussman, who writes that law's impact is largely cere-
monial in that it influences how physicians document their decisions on DNR orders but not the
process through which such decisions are made. R Zussman, *Intensive Care: Medical Ethics and
the Medical Profession* (Chicago: Chicago University Press, 1992), mentioned in Halpern (n 60
above) 841.

[90] EJ Emmanuel, ER Daniels, DL Fairclough, and BR Clarridge, 'The Practice of Euthanasia
and Physician-Assisted Suicide in the Uninted States' (1998) 280(6) *JAMA* 507.

[91] *Vacco v Quill* 521 US 793 (1997); *Washington v Glucksberg* 521 US 702 (1997); *R (on the
Application of Pretty) v Director of Public Prosecutions* [2002] 1 AC 800. Oregon is the only state in
the US which has passed a law (in 1994) permitting physician-assisted suicide under certain circumstances: Or Rev Stat §§ 127.800–127.897 (2005). The Act allows physicians to prescribe lethal
medication for competent terminally ill patients who make a written request, but removes the

to promulgate a new liberty interest in having assistance to end one's own life and saw no violation of the equal protection of the law by preventing competent terminally ill patients from receiving assistance as opposed to incompetent patients. Moreover, courts concluded that every state might rationally forbid anyone from assisting another to commit suicide.[92] To secure the inexistence of such a right, US Federal law prohibits the use of funds to subsidize physician-assisted suicide,[93] and states also include a ban of physician-assisted suicide in their national legislation.[94]

The mere rhetorical function of the rights movement in bioethics is also evidenced in the area of the right to leave a valid advance directive for the determination of health treatment to be provided or withdrawn in the state of incompetency. Such a right was acknowledged by national and federal legislation in the United States,[95] Canada,[96] United Kingdom,[97] and many other Western countries.[98] However, studies show that the law has had little effect on the issuing and use of advance directives; that it is implemented by medical institutions and personnel in a passive manner; and that the involvement of physicians in its implementation is lacking.[99] Beside the fundamental flaws in and unexpected problems of advance directives, usually associated with the handing of authority regarding incompetent patients to persons other than the person who issues the directive,[100] completion rates among most patient groups run at only 4 to 25 per cent and intensive education and promotion barely improve those rates.[101] Other studies suggest that the concept of advance directives may

physician from civil or criminal liability in compliance with such a request. A recent majority decision of the US Supreme Court held that an interpretive rule regarding the Controlled Substances Act, making the use of a controlled substance to assist suicide not a legitimate medical practice and an unlawful act, could not prohibit physicians from prescribing drugs for use in suicide under Oregon law permitting the procedure, *Gonzales and Ors v Oregon and Ors* 546 US 243 (2006).

[92] See Capron (n 56 above) 314–15.

[93] Federal Assisted Suicide Funding Restriction Act, 42 USC (1997).

[94] Scott (n 34 above) 279, n 90.

[95] Patient Self Determination Act, 42 USC (1992). The Act requires that hospitals and other health providers inform their patients of their right to make end-of-life decisions and issue an advance directive.

[96] For an exhaustive description of legislation in Canada, see <http://www.utoronto.ca/jcb/outreach/documents/JCB_Living_Will.pdf> (accessed 18 July 2008).

[97] Mental Capacity Act 2005, ss 24–26.

[98] Recently, Israel has enacted the Dying Patient Act 2005 which legalizes the withdrawal of medical treatment from a patient suffering from an incurable medical condition and whose life expectancy is no more than 6 months. Sections 31–36 regulate the issuing and validation of an advance directive relating to such a physical state.

[99] JL Yates and H Glick, 'The Failed Patient Self Determination Act and Policy Alternatives for the Right to Die' (1997) 9(4) *Journal of Aging and Social Policy* 29.

[100] R Dresser, 'Relitigating Life and Death' (1990) 51 *Ohio Law Journal* 426–37; Allen E Buchanan and Dan W Brock, *Deciding for Others: The Ethics of Surrogate Decision Making* (Cambridge: Cambridge University Press, 1989) 185.

[101] Henry S Perkins, 'Controlling Death: The False Promise of Advance Directives' (2007) 147(1) *Annals of Internal Medicine* 51.

appeal only to certain subsets of the population (mostly the white middle-class population), limiting the effectiveness of such legal mechanism.[102]

The legal policy about end-of-life decisions and ethical dilemmas, mostly manifested through the areas of refusal of treatment, the right to be given end-of-life assistance, and the issuing of advance directives demonstrates how the rights discourse in bioethics was adopted without much empirical reason to believe it could be effective and of real use.[103] The main rhetorical function of the rights discourse in bioethics can be explained more generally by the limits of the law's ability to shape and influence individuals' behaviour deriving from society's complexity and the diversity in patients' expectations regarding disclosure of their diagnosis or prognosis, the general importance they give to truth-telling, and the way in which they deal with the nature of their illness and treatment options.[104] As Carl Schneider commented:

People are enticed by many pressures beyond those the law creates. They have their own agendas and, more important, their own normative systems. The law writes rules, but the governed—when they know the rules—often have the incentives, and energy to avoid them...

...While the language of law may have penetrated into the bosom of society, it must still, in quotidian life, compete with the many other languages that people speak more comfortably, more fluently, and with much more conviction. These are the languages of religion and morality, of love and friendship, of pragmatism and social accommodation, of custom and compromise. The danger of bioethicists, then is believing too deeply that law can pierce the Babel, can speak with precision, can be heard.[105]

III. Implications of the Rights Movement in Bioethics

In addition to the difficulties associated with the incorporation and application of legal rights to bioethics, there are several other implications which the consideration of rights in the medical context has brought about. Some of these implications took different directions than those originally intended by the rights movement. Four major implications will be now identified.

A. Change of the Therapeutic Relationship

The rights movement in bioethics brought dramatic changes to the therapeutic relationship. First, strange parties were suddenly involved in and became part of the therapeutic relationship and stood in between the patient and their physician.

---

[102] Capron (n 56 above) 312.   [103] ibid 306–25.

[104] ibid 312–13, 318. The court's assumption in the *Quinlan* case that hospital ethics committees were common institutions for resolving ethical problems is an example of a legal proposition made in bioethics which is not grounded on empirical data (ibid 321).

[105] Schneider, *Language* (n 26 above).

As a result, physicians turned into strangers and became a group apart from their patients. Emphasis on patient rights invited lawyers, clinical bioethicists, and hospital ethics committees to protect and strengthen the patient's role in medical decision-making.[106] While the rights discourse was aimed at recovering the physician-patient relationship, which suffered from excessive paternalism and possible exploitation and abuse of patients, such discourse created an atmosphere under which medicine becomes adversarial practice and physicians lack trustworthiness. As observed by Richard Sherlock: 'The language of rights and the language of trust move in opposite directions from one another. The scrupulous insistence on observance of one's rights is an admission that one does not trust those at hand to care properly for one's welfare.'[107] The physician's response to the increase in legal intrusions and control of medical practice also resulted in viewing such an interference as an attack upon physicians' competence, leading to defensiveness and suspicion among physicians.

Second, emphasis on rights in bioethical issues, and especially an admiration of autonomy, allowed physicians to detach themselves from the consequences of their actions and involve themselves less in the exercise of discretion. As a result, physicians became more remote from their patients and preferred to focus on formal communication with them. William Sage summarizes this point nicely when he comments: 'Why grapple with moral dilemmas when one can concentrate on achieving a technical result and let the patient decide if it is good or bad?'[108]

B. A Shift to Patient-controlled Medicine

It would not be an exaggeration to argue that the rights movement in bioethics resulted in a patient-controlled medicine whereby patients are not only empowered to choose between various courses of treatment but they may compel health providers to provide them with treatment or medical procedures which are not necessarily for their benefit. In this new position, the patient has become a 'consumer' of health, while 'health' is regarded as a 'product' which the physician must supply to her. Under such a view the patient is motivated by her self-interests and these allow her to choose who should provide medical services and what kind of services or products to purchase.[109] The physician, on the

---

[106] Rothman, *Strangers* (n 7 above) 108–9.

[107] R Sherlock, 'Reasonable Men and Sick Human Beings' (1986) 80 *American Journal of Medicine* 2, 3. See also Rothman, *Strangers* (n 7 above) 109: 'Physicians who were strangers could not be trusted to exercise discretion over weighty matters of life and death; hence, a growing contingent insisted that physicians would be compelled to tell patients the truth, no matter how grim the diagnosis.'

[108] Sage (n 61 above) 1185. Next, he writes: 'bioethics pushed medicine toward a lawyer-like approach to fact-finding through formal deliberative bodies and frank judicial oversight, overcoming the medical profession's traditional preference for empiricism and deference to experience'.

[109] Rodwin (n 20 above) 153. For a critique of patients' consumerism and the market metaphor, see G Annas, *Some Choice: Law, Medicine and the Market* (Oxford: Oxford University Press, 1998). See also Schneider, *Autonomy* (n 24 above) 207–10.

other hand, is regarded as the patient's passive agent and her responsibilities and expertise are relevant insofar they coincide with the patient's desires.

A good example of the shift to patient-controlled medicine facilitated by the rights movement would be the recent development of direct to consumer advertising (DTCA). This is an area where a cynical use of rights language is made by drug companies to enhance their profits at the cost of health providers' professional autonomy, making the vast majority of physicians accommodate patients' requests for an advertised drug.[110] Alan Holmer cites a survey showing that more than 53 million Americans asked their physicians about advertised drugs, arguing that patients have the right to receive such advertised information and ask their doctors about new treatment.[111] According to a telephone poll conducted among 199 primary care doctors in the United States, whose patients asked them about drugs advertised in the media, in 36 per cent of the cases doctors gave in to the patient's pressure, even when the drug was not their first choice.[112] As Sydney Halpern notes, 'directed marketing provides a reminder that multiple constituencies can adopt the rhetoric of rights for a variety of purposes—not all of them consistent with consumers' interests'.[113] The patient sometimes demands a certain medication which is not necessarily in her best interest. The result of such a phenomenon is a decrease in public confidence and trust in their health providers,[114] which may also lead to violent attacks on physicians.[115]

Another area where medicine's cognitive authority is being challenged and controlled by patients, and more generally by the public, concerns the creation of medical knowledge through clinical trials. Two recent examples include the effect of AIDS activists on research into new treatments for HIV/AIDS, by, for example, hastening the speed with which new drugs are available for testing and broadening the eligibility for those drugs, and the involvement of groups of patients with genetic disorders and their families in the promotion and design of genetic research.[116] These examples reflect the fact that patient rights, which were first understood as a way to stand up to physicians' intervention with patient freedoms (negative rights) transformed to and are perceived as patients'

---

[110] *Thompson and Ors v Western States Medical Center and Ors* 535 US 358, 383 (2002) (referring to a poll where 84% of patients reported that doctors accommodated such requests).

[111] A Holmer, 'Direct-To-Consumer Marketing of Prescription Drug Advertising Builds Bridges between Patients and Physicians' (1999) 281(4) *JAMA* 380. See also MF Hollon, 'Direct-to-Consumer Marketing of Prescription Drugs' (1999) 281(4) *JAMA* 382.

[112] D Spurgeon, 'Doctors Feel Pressurised by Direct to Consumer Advertising' (1999) 319 *BMJ* 1321.

[113] Halpern (n 60 above) 846. See also J Donohue, 'A History of Drug Advertising: The Evolving Roles of Consumers and Consumer Protection' (2006) 84(4) *The Milbank Quarterly* 659.

[114] M Schlesinger, 'A Loss of Faith: The Sources of Reduced Political Legitimacy for the American Medical Profession' (2002) 80(2) *The Milbank Quarterly* 185.

[115] See generally JL Morrison, JD Lantos, and W Levinson, 'Aggression and Violence Directed Toward Physicians' (1998) 13(8) *Journal of General Internal Medicine* 556.

[116] Halpern (n 60 above) 838–9.

entitlements as against their providers (positive rights), imposing duties on the latter, the fulfilment of which is not always in the best interests of the patient.

C. Expansion of the Idea of Rights Outside the Therapeutic Relationship

The rights movement in bioethics has brought about that the idea of rights not only applies to the therapeutic relationship but also to the concept of managed care,[117] thereby positing the physician and the patient in one place as against managed care organizations and other entities paying for health care services. Rights to and within that concept make managed care 'the battlefield on which physicians applied the accumulated legal experience of prior decades'.[118] Hence, for instance, the rights discourse and legalization of medicine more generally has made it possible for physicians to employ lawyers to form corporations, negotiate contracts, secure their intellectual property rights, and focus more on providing technical services to clients and less on playing a social role. It also transformed physicians to serve as patient advocates, thereby protecting their 'clients' from the possible conflicts of interest of their colleagues and from unnecessary costs.[119] Under such an approach health care is now seen as an industry rather than a profession and so issues arising within the therapeutic relationship are now subjected to antitrust law and policy considerations.[120]

Some expansion of the idea of rights outside the traditional therapeutic relationship is noticed in issues concerning public health, and more specifically with the rise of preventive medicine. This area, which is primarily concerned with prevention of diseases and the promotion and preservation of health in the individual, may also serve as an indicator of the emphasis on the rights discourse.[121] Recognition by the courts of a liberty right, the right to privacy in medical decision-making or the more general freedom to act in accordance with one's religious beliefs, is used as a claim against the state interest in regulation of mandatory

---

[117] Managed care programmes are: 'Health insurance plans intended to reduce unnecessary health care costs through a variety of mechanisms, including: economic incentives for physicians and patients to select less costly forms of care; programs for reviewing the medical necessity of specific services; increased beneficiary cost sharing; controls on inpatient admissions and lengths of stay; the establishment of cost-sharing incentives for outpatient surgery; selective contracting with health care providers; and the intensive management of high-cost health care cases. The programs may be provided in a variety of settings, such as health maintenance organizations and preferred provider organizations.' Medical Subject Headings, US National Library of Medicine's controlled vocabulary, available at <http://www.ncbi.nlm.nih.gov/sites/entrez> (accessed 25 November 2007).

[118] Sage (n 61 above) 1189. Interestingly, the US federal legislation reform in managed care was referred to as a 'patient's bill of rights'. Scott (n 34 above) 235, n 23.

[119] Sage (n 61 above) 1190–1.

[120] AJ Rosoff, 'Antitrust Law and the Health Care Industry: New Warriors into an Old Battle' (1979) 23 *St Louis University Law Journal* 446.

[121] Van Der Burg (n 1 above) 106.

vaccination.[122] Recently, more cases of personal objections to vaccination have also been witnessed, especially those of parents who exercise their autonomy by choosing to leave their children unvaccinated on the basis of personal concerns about the risks of vaccination. Privacy concerns are also frequently raised against reporting infected individuals for the treatment and prevention of transmitted diseases and an argument for a breach of autonomy is raised against forced checks of arrested prostitutes or other groups in danger of epidemiological diseases.[123] These and many other cases raise the serious costs and the cumulative effect of respecting patients' rights in the area of public health.

D. Rights Understood Internationally as Means to Achieve Global Health

The inclusion of the concept of rights in bioethics paved the way for breaking free from the focus on the physician-patient relationship and medical technology and aspiring to global force for health and human rights.[124] The concept of rights made it easy for Western medicine and ethical norms to engage and influence developing countries and Eastern cultures in the name of the protection of international human rights. The enormous effect of law on bioethics, especially through the rights movement, demonstrating how law shapes ethical discourse and medical practice, initiated the development of an international agenda for human rights in health. Such an ambition has been mostly directed by George Annas in recent years.[125] Annas argues that American bioethics should be reborn as a global force by accepting its Nuremberg Code and actively engage in a human rights agenda. This would be made possible by the harmonization of three disciplines: bioethics, health law, and human rights.[126] The development of such a view seeks to recognize and employ two interrelated forces which shape the world, thereby providing new frameworks for ethical analysis and action: these are globalization and public health. By globalization, Annas refers merely to a new focus on international human rights law and its aspirations as manifested in the Universal Declaration of Human Rights and subsequent treaties.[127] What is meant by public health, on the other hand, is the emphasis on populations

---

[122] KM Malone and AR Hinman, 'Vaccination Mandates: The Public Health Imperative and Individual Rights' in RE Hoffman, W Lopez, GW Matthews, MA Rothstein, and KL Foster (eds), *Law in Public Health* (Oxford and New York: Oxford University Press, 2nd edn, 2007) 338–60.

[123] See eg *Reynolds v McNichols* 488 F 2d 1378 (10th Cir 1973).

[124] Annas, University Lecture (n 23 above) 4.

[125] See GJ Annas, *American Bioethics: Crossing Human Rights and Health Law Boundaries* (Oxford: Oxford University Press, 2004).

[126] For a critique, see A Jonsen (Book Review) (2005) 5(3) *American Journal of Bioethics* 71–2.

[127] UNESCO's Declaration on Bioethics and Human Rights is regarded as an attempt to develop an international bioethics framework based on the Universal Declaration of Human Rights. See <http://portal.unesco.org/shs/en/ev.php-URL_ID=1883&URL_DO=DO_TOPIC& URL_SECTION =201.html> (accessed 18 July 2008).

and prevention, global health inequalities, and widespread diseases.[128] From this perspective the rights revolution in bioethics is only just beginning.

IV. The Future of Law and Bioethics

The previous sections discussed one of the greatest contributions of law to bioethics, namely the integration of rights in ethical dilemmas and issues arising within the medical context. Such a contribution nevertheless creates many difficulties and has various implications, some of which go in different directions from those originally expected. It is possible to anticipate three paths which bioethics may take as a result.

The first is the search for support and justification of some substantive theory and the conceptualization of basic principles to realize ethical dilemmas in the medical context. Such theory may be developed from the area of ethics and the disciplines of philosophy and religion more generally. By providing a universal, applicable, and acceptable normative content, bioethics will regain faith as a branch of ethics involving moral norms to evaluate human conduct. The normative theory will complement the procedural mechanism suggested by the rights discourse and will become more dominant than law's influence and interference with bioethics.[129] Under such an alternative, law and ethics would become more independent and distinct. The more there is a plurality of ethical approaches and normative understanding of ethics, the more we can supplement the rights model in bioethics and minimize the law's strong effect on problems in medical ethics. If we follow this approach we will not have to regress to the pre-rights model of bioethics. Instead we will progress to a post-rights model under which morality becomes a more important component of resolving problems and moral dilemmas in bioethics.[130]

A second approach would be the search for a better understanding of ethical issues in bioethics by an appeal to the social sciences and other related disciplines. A social science critique of bioethics argues that traditional bioethics idealizes rational thought and ignores social and cultural factors which shape one's thought and choices. As this chapter shows, this is made possible with the guise of the rhetorical language of rights. The social science critique asks bioethicists to support their claims in more empirical research, to be reflexive, and to challenge theories which are based on evidence.[131] A better understanding of social implications for and construction of health and disease and a closer look at the role social science plays in framing and resolving decisions in bioethics may address serious

---

[128] Annas, *University Lecture* (n 23 above) 3.
[129] Pellignero (n 30 above).
[130] Van Der Burg (n 1 above) 111–14.
[131] AM Hedgecoe, 'Critical Bioethics: Beyond the Social Science Critique of Applied Ethics' (2004) 18(2) *Bioethics* 120.

problems in justice and equality that are left unresolved by a pretext of rights and by the law's interference with bioethics more generally.[132] Along with this argument, Albert Jonsen invites bioethicists in the new millennium to consider institutional structures, organizational patterns, financial and economic calculations, etc in addressing their questions.[133] However, such an approach may lead to the result that bioethics will become an amorphous expansion of discipline consisting of a mix of preferences, opinions, value choices, and more. Under such terms, it will be hard to isolate a concrete and acceptable normative content which will make bioethics a unique and autonomous field, and from this perspective this second proposed approach seems less appealing than the first.

A third possible direction may be to withdraw the use of legal rights discourse and more generally the legal regulation of issues in bioethics, and to resolve disputes in bioethics by an appeal to constitutional rights only in exceptional cases. Generally, constitutional rights are regarded as a mechanism to contest the abuse of power by government or the majority.[134] An alternative and perhaps more appropriate discourse in bioethics may be that which emphasizes health providers' responsibility and the considerations of a multitude of factors such as risk and benefits; the physician-patient and other relationships occurring within the medical context; concerns, needs, and abilities of patients and third parties who may be affected by the proposed medical decision, etc.[135] The best way to create such discourse would be to have ethics committees resolving and determining specific cases in bioethics.

Leaving the decision-making processes to ethics committees rather than lawyers or judges could not only lead to a more neutral and inclusive discussions of these matters but also reduce chances to err and minimize the risk to parties involved. Following this suggestion, Roger Dworkin argues that ethics committees are a very attractive decision-making group, combining expertise and popularity. It is argued that these institutions are able to work quickly, informally, and inexpensively and their advantage lies in the fact that they lack the power to submit people to stigmatizing or inappropriately severe sanctions.[136]

Although the institutionalization of ethics committees was encouraged by case law and legislation and was mandatory for every institution conducting experimentation with human subjects,[137] its major purpose was to free doctors from

---

[132] Capron (n 56 above) 305.

[133] AR Jonsen, 'Why Has Bioethics Become So Boring?' (2000) 25(6) *Journal of Medicine and Philosophy* 689, 693.

[134] 'The institution of rights is therefore crucial, because it represents the majority's promise to the minorities that their dignity and equality will be respected. When the divisions among the groups are most violent then this gesture, if law is to work, must be most sincere... If the government does not take rights seriously, then it does not take law seriously either.' R Dworkin, *Taking Rights Seriously* (Cambridge, Mass.: Harvard University Press, 1978) 205.

[135] See eg J Ladd, 'Legalism and Medical Ethics' (1979) 4(1) *Journal of Medical Philosophy* 70.

[136] Dworkin (n 25 above) 168.

[137] Despite the fact that some Catholic hospitals already maintained ethics committees, the first call for the establishment of such committees was made by a pediatrician in a law review

taking responsibility in difficult cases.[138] For example, in *Re Quinlan*, the court referred with agreement to the argument that 'it would be more appropriate to provide a regular forum for more input and dialogue in individual situations and to allow the responsibility of these judgments to be shared'.[139] Such a recommendation was followed only scarcely, and in some instances it also created tensions and a sense of uneasiness.[140] While in 1983 only 1 per cent of American hospitals had ethics committees, and existing committees reviewed an average of one case per year,[141] in 1998 over 90 per cent of a random sample of 1,000 hospitals in the United States had ethics committees.[142] Gradually, hospital ethics committees developed guidelines and principles and their tasks were progressively defined.[143] As Albert Jonsen remarks: 'In hundreds of hospital ethics committees, discourse about ethics went on; thousands of persons became familiar with the issues and arguments. When asked to consider a question, many committees had already developed the competence to respond in an informed and orderly manner.'[144]

However, the functioning of ethics committees was criticized by scholars and little was known about them. Bernad Lo, for example, argued that hospital ethics committees are biased and have no procedure to deal with questions and problems raised.[145] John Fletcher and Dianne Hoffman commented that ethics committees and committee members often lack the requisite education and skills for effective participation in committee meetings and called for the establishment of quality standards to govern the operation of committees.[146] As a result, in 2000,

---

article. K Teele, 'The Physician's Dilemma: A Doctor's View: What the Law Should Be' (1975) 27 *Baylor Law Review*.

[138] 'Physicians, by virtue of their responsibility for medical judgments are, partly by choice and partly by default, charged with the responsibility of making ethical judgments which we are sometimes ill-equipped to make . . . [The concept of ethics committees] diffuses the responsibility of making these judgments. Many physicians, in many circumstances, would welcome this sharing of responsibility' Teele (n 137 above) 8–9.

[139] *Re Quinlan* 355 A 2d 647, 668 (NJ 1976). See also *Re Colyer* 660 P 2d 738 (1983).

[140] eg Tina Stevens mentions that legal counsel for the AMA, BJ Anderson, commented that such ethics committees are unnecessary because 'a treating physician is certainly able to determine whether a patient is in a terminal condition. If he is unsure of anything, the doctor can ask for consultation with another doctor.' Stevens (n 82 above) 142. See also *Superintendent of Belchertown State School v Saikewicz* 373 Mass. 728, 370 NE 2d 417 (1977).

[141] Jonsen (n 1 above) 363.

[142] G McGee, JP Spanogle, AL Caplan, D Penny, and DA Asch, 'Successes and Failures of Hospital Ethics Committees: A National Survey of Ethics Committees Chairs' (2002) 11 *Cambridge Quarterly of Healthcare Ethics* 87. The increase in the number of ethics committees was a response to a 1991 mandate by the Joint Commission on Accreditation of Healthcare Organizations and state legislation raising the status of such committees.

[143] cf Annas, who argues that the law contributed immensely to the development of ethics committees mainly through the threat of legal liability and community disapproval, which could have led to new laws. Annas, *Standard of Care* (n 1 above) 6.

[144] Jonsen (n 1 above) 364.

[145] B Lo, 'Behind Closed doors: Promises and Pitfalls of Ethics Committees' (1987) 317(1) *New England Journal of Medicine* 46.

[146] JC Fletcher and DE Hoffman, 'Ethics Committees: Time to Experiment with Standards' (1994) 120(4) *Annals of Internal Medicine* 335–8.

the Society for Health and Human Values—Society for Bioethics Consultation Task Force on Standards for Bioethics Consultation issued a position paper detailing the core competences for members involved in ethics consultation.[147] Despite these guidelines other problems relating to the legitimacy and accountability of those committees remain unresolved.[148]

V. Conclusion

One of the major characteristics of the relationship between law and bioethics, and probably the most important contribution of law to bioethics, concerns the introduction of the idea and language of rights. As David Rothman argues, the patient rights movement in bioethics was 'highly democratizing, removing, as it were, the hallow around the expert and giving encouragement to the laymen'.[149] The rights movement in bioethics seemed promising indeed. However, as this chapter shows, the idea of rights is objectionable and creates many difficulties all of which reflect the limits of the law in terms of shaping and influencing decision-making in bioethical issues. Such a movement was proved too narrow to encompass and realize many of the issues raised by new technologies and changing therapeutic relationships in the modern era. The specific role the rights movement has played in bioethics is therefore disputable and hinges upon, *inter alia*, our understanding of the origins and future of bioethics. Did bioethics grow out of the need to control scientific change and medical progress, purporting to deliver exotic technologies into social acceptance?[150] Or did it evolve out of the necessity to control and protect the basic freedoms of patients and human subjects? Should bioethics continue to integrate with law or other disciplines, or should it become a more autonomous and independent discipline? While scholars may continue debate on these substantial questions it is clear that the time to re-evaluate the direction which bioethics should take in the next years has come.

[147] MP Aulisio, RM Arnold, and SJ Youngner, 'Health Care Ethics Consultation: Nature, Goals and Competences' (2000) 133(1) *Annals of Internal Medicine* 59.
[148] Dworkin (n 25 above) 170.
[149] Rothman, *Origins and Consequences* (n 8 above) 263.
[150] Stevens (n 82 above) 149.

5

Health, Global Justice, and Virtue Bioethics

Katerina Sideri

I. Introduction

The current discussion on bioethics includes issues such as health, quality of life, identity, dignity, belonging in communities, and ensuring the equitable progress of science and technology. Euthanasia, abortion, the environment, gene therapy, patents on diagnostic tests, surrogate mothers, health care, all present us with important ethical and policy dilemmas. To answer relevant questions, it has been proposed to use Kantian ethics of moral agency, Mill's utilitarianism, and Aquinas' account of the good.[1] Schools of thought as diverse as deontology, consequentialism, intuitionism, hypothetical choice, hypothetical contractor arguments, rational choice, game theory, natural law, or middle level principle analysis, have provided the theoretical tools to approach relevant questions.[2]

Currently, various documents on bioethics promote the principles of respect for human dignity, autonomy, justice, beneficence, proportionality, solidarity, social subsidiarity, and deliberation, as important parameters in defining what counts as 'life', 'reproduction', and 'death', and how they should be regulated.[3] From the vantage point of procedural justice and discourse ethics, Habermas and Rawls point to the importance of objective legal processes and consensus.[4] The

---

[1] HT Engelhardt, *The Foundations of Bioethics* (New York and Oxford: Oxford University Press, 2nd edn, 1996) 33.

[2] ibid 40–65.

[3] For instance, see the Belmont Report, The National Commission for the Protection of Human Subjects of Biomedical and Behavioral Research, 18 April 1979 (USA); TL Beauchamp and JF Childress, *Principles of Biomedical Ethics* (Oxford and New York: Oxford University Press, 5th edn, 2001); J Rendtorff, 'Basic Ethical Principles in European Bioethics and Biolaw: Autonomy, Dignity, Integrity and Vulnerability/Towards a Foundation of Bioethics and Biolaw' (2002) 5(3) *Medicine, Health Care and Philosophy* 235.

[4] Engelhardt (n 1 above) 50, 59–63. For a critique see also K Sideri, *Law's Practical Wisdom: The Theory and Practice of Law Making in New Governance Structures in the European Union* (Aldershot: Ashgate, 2007) ch 6.

topical question in modern fragmented societies seems to be: how do we all agree on basic principles, so that co-existence becomes possible?

Jonsen and Toulmin suggested that casuistry and practical reason could provide the grounds for consensus in a morally fragmented world.[5] In the same spirit, Clouser brings up the importance of examining particular cases instead of formulating abstract rules.[6] Following the neo-Aristotelian tradition, virtue bioethics brings to the foreground the importance of considering the context of particular circumstances, as it reveals a variety of options available for action.[7] According to Beresford, one must focus on both the details of the case and the central substantive goods at stake.[8]

The following sections will reflect on the philosophical tradition of virtue ethics to link the relevant discussion to bioethics, the idea of human flourishing, and the principles of practical reason, justice, and equity. The thesis advanced is that a dynamic understanding of *health*, promoting empowerment and capacity building, should present us with a primary bioethical endeavour. This position brings to the foreground important questions as to the ways bioethics should be governed at the international level, whilst capturing the pluralist content of secular bioethics by means of stressing the importance of participation and deliberation when facing relevant regulatory dilemmas. In this framework, health does not simply present us with the external conditions necessary to promote happiness and well-being. The proposition in what follows is that health *is bio-*ethics, as it embodies our pursuit of happiness and balance, a process requiring an understanding of ethics as a personal journey to discover who we are, involving the need to pay attention to the particular, and any relations of power and interdependence implied therein. As such, health and virtue bioethics present us with interesting connections amongst ethics, governance, and law-making.

II. Ethics and Praxis

Aristotle's philosophy of practical reasoning will be the starting point of the present analysis. According to this, there is no need for a universal theory to determine ethical conduct. Practical reasoning, *phronesis,* encapsulates a long process of accumulating experience; the latter guides deliberation on the choice

---

[5] AR Jonsen and S Toulmin, *The Abuse of Casuistry: A History of Moral Reasoning* (Berkeley: University of California Press, 1988).

[6] B Gert, CM Culver, and KD Clouser, *Bioethics: A Return to Fundamentals* (New York: Oxford University Press, 1997); see also T Chambers, *The Fiction of Bioethics* (New York: Routledge, 1999). The latter author suggests the use of literary theory to come to grips with illness and healing.

[7] See eg R Hursthouse, 'Virtue Theory and Abortion' (1991) 20(3) *Philosophy and Public Affairs* 223; P Foot, *Virtues and Vices and Other Essays in Moral Philosophy* (Berkeley and Los Angeles: University of California Press, 1978).

[8] E Beresford, 'Can Phronesis Save the Life of Medical Ethics?' (1996) 17(3) *Theoretical Medicine* 209.

of appropriate conduct in the context of the particular circumstances of the situation at issue. Achieving the telos of good life implies that life is a personal journey, a quest to discover how our lives can be lived more satisfactorily. In this sense, the telos of life consists of learning to lead a happy life, constantly begging the question: 'who should I be?', as opposed to the Kantian categorical imperative guiding conduct according to what should be done, independently of the particular circumstances.

The study of ethics unlike other branches of philosophy, has a practical aim, for we are not investigating the nature of virtue for the sake of knowing what it is, but in order that we may become good...We have to consequently carry our inquiry into the region of conduct and to ask how we are to act rightly, since our actions determine the qualities of our dispositions.[9]

And if this is true of the general theory of ethics, still less is exact precision possible in dealing with particular cases of conduct...[10] These though good in the absolute sense, are not always good for a particular person.[11]

Aristotle's philosophical tradition is followed in Gadamer's hermeneutics,[12] stressing the importance of praxis and accumulated experience in providing horizons of meaning. It is also followed by American pragmatists, such as Peirce's and James's work challenging Kant's and Descartes' models of thinking. Rorty and Bernstein also emphasize the importance of examining the particular as opposed to the universal, accepting the importance of the interpretative endeavour, and the practical character of the ethical enterprise.

Rorty refers to Nietzsche's *Gay Science*, where the reader is presented with the argument that in pre-Socratic Greece polytheism provided the necessary space for the free expression of individuality, as the worship of one god did not preclude the parallel worship of other deities.[13] Rorty also reads the work of

---

[9] Aristotle, *The Nicomachean Ethics* (trans, H Rackham) (Cambridge, Mass.: Harvard University Press, Loeb Classical Library, 1982) 77; *Αριστοτέλης – Ηθικά Νικομάχεια* (3 τόμοι, Αθήνα: Κάκτος, 1992).

[10] ibid Harvard University Press edition, 75.

[11] ibid 257.

[12] Gadamer's practical philosophy revolves around the notions of praxis and dialogue, and explicitly addresses the question of understanding between cultures and religions. Gadamer uses the Aristotelian concept of phronesis to describe the interaction between different systems of meaning as a process pregnant with the possibility of fusion, exchange, and dialogue. Dialogue brings in contact different historically constructed systems of meaning. It implies a process triggering the simultaneous reproduction of tradition and its exposure and transformation in view of external challenges. Our selves are socially constructed, yet, we constantly renegotiate the properties of the process of construction by acting or speaking; this being the interpretative component of our everyday existence, see HG Gadamer, *Philosophical Hermeneutics* (trans, DE Linge (Berkeley: University of California Press, 1976); HG Gadamer, *Dialogue and Dialectic: Eight Hermeneutical Studies on Plato* (trans, PC Smith) (New Haven: Yale University Press, 1980); HG Gadamer, *Truth and Method* 2nd revised edn (1st English edn, 1975), (trans, J Weinsheimer and DG Marshall) (New York: Crossroad, 1989).

[13] R Rorty, *Philosophy as Cultural Politics: Philosophical Papers, Volume 4* (Cambridge, Mass.: Cambridge University Press, 2007) 29.

Berthelot, who was the first to consider James, Dewey, Nietzsche, Bergson, Mill, and Poincaré as belonging to the same intellectual movement, pragmatism, in this instance particularly revealing itself as romantic utilitarianism. Rotry further compares Nietzsche's with James' version of polytheism to find considerable similarities, as they both agree that there is no will to truth distinct from the will to happiness, and together with Mill, all three philosophers consider the notions of true and right to be anchored in the effort to achieve happiness.[14] Ethical existence becomes an individual endeavour, and we have the responsibility to allow others to worship their own Gods. Toleration then becomes the operating principle of the responsibility towards the other. This approach repudiates the distinction between the real and the apparent world as Nietzsche showed in the *Twilight of the Idols*.[15]

This approach begs a series of difficult questions relating to law, justice, and governance. In a society where loyalties spring from multiple localities, we are left puzzled as to the substantive content of law. Thinkers inspired by the Kantian moral philosophy would say that loyalties belong to the realm of sentiment, and should be surpassed by reason. Sentiment's character reveals its contingency as it is rooted in society; rationality begs us to release the bonds of the ephemeral, to rise above the particular circumstances and short-lived moralities, to recognize and criticize injustice stemming from transient interests. This is a process requiring us to look inwards in search of the one truth. However, Nietzsche bitterly militates against established systems of thinking and altruism, where guilt is 'cruelty turned backwards', toward oneself, as sentiment and rationality necessarily interweave. Spinoza, whose thinking directly anticipates Nietzsche, speaks of the need to criticize the ascetic ideal of the clergy, positioning joyous self-affirmation over the oppression of imposed duty.

The proposition here is that Aristotle's virtue ethics contains a pre-modern conception of ethics, justice, and politics where the difference between interdependence and autonomy, form and substance, subject and object, universal and particular coexist and complement each other in the course of our quest for a complete life, lived according to instinct and wisdom. The basic tenets of his theory are the following: first, man wishes one thing: to live happily. Second, man's choice is mostly driven by habit. Therefore, a theory of ethics is necessary as man has to learn to master appetites by means of learning habitually to seek satisfaction in the right way. This is because appetites can be both good and evil, depending on whether they are expressed in a manner that is too much or too little. To illustrate this with respect to fear, courage is the right condition positioned between recklessness (too much courage) and cowardice (too little courage). Liberality is the right condition positioned between prodigality and miserliness. High-mindedness is the right condition between vanity and humility. Gentleness is positioned between timidity and boldness.

---

[14] ibid 28.   [15] ibid.

Virtue, then, is a trained faculty implying the exercise of moderation, in other words the observance of the mean relative to the person concerned, as determined by reason and the particular circumstances of the situation at hand. In a nutshell, appetites, if we consider their positive side, are good, if their negative side, evil. The only rule is the doctrine of the golden mean relative *to us*, whose exercise implies results that are not the same for all individuals, pointing to moderation, μηδέν ἄγαν (nothing in excess).

Durkheim's thought is relevant here, as it can help us explain the religious underpinnings of the golden mean. This is because, in *The Elementary Forms of Religious Life*, Durkheim suggested that the mystical foundations of our most basic categories of thought are religious. In his genealogy of human thought, categories of perception, such as categories of time and space and classifications of nature, emerged from that first distinction between the sacred and the profane.[16]

This is happening as religious organization reflects the passage from the mere effort to survive to the formulation of the first forms of socialization and the first varieties of collective representation. In this instance, the unity of the group is glorified, by means of religious symbols and rituals to be regularly performed, simultaneously reminding and demanding from the members of the group their commitment to be active members of the collectivity. Hence, religion crystallizes effervescent sentiments of belonging. It follows that institutions, concepts, categories, all reflect the ways in which a particular society (in particular sociopolitical circumstances) imagines itself as collectivity through archetypal religious divisions.

Such an archetypal division is presented by the sacred/profane taxonomy. Human intervention was required to keep the two realms separate or to help to change the nature of profane forces to sacred, and prevent the opposite from happening. In this instance, Gods need man to survive as much as man needs them; and human intervention in nature is important to restore balance, due to the fluid character of the elements of the sacred and profane, reflecting nature's ambivalence, or rather a conception of nature as being ambivalent, which is mediated by socially constructed categories of thought, reflecting the ambivalence and irregularity of society's organization, concealed in short-term stability, while simultaneously implying the potentiality of rupture. Nature and truth revealed its plural character, its contingency. Categories of thought were made, unmade, and remade relentlessly, instincts were to be tamed, souls to be cleansed to approach the divine, but the role of humans in the process was complementary. Gods were a part of nature, in plants, animals, and stones. Society was imaging

---

[16] E Durkheim, *The Elementary Forms of Religious Life* (trans, KE Fields) (New York: The Free Press, 1954). As some categories of thought became autonomous, science acquired its objective vocabulary. Although Durkheim thought that societies perceive the world differently, and that our cognition is a cultural creation, he also maintained that as science progresses, its system of concepts increasingly converges (but always fails to coincide) with the world as it is.

itself as being a part of nature, Gods being dependent on humans for their existence and vice versa.

The doctrine of the golden mean endorses this position: man is positioned in
the middle, between the sacred and profane, as his intervention (not by means of
religious rites this time, but through her individual genius) is required to transform the profane into sacred and keep the sacred unspoiled. Human genius is
required to restore balance within oneself, so that men can live in harmony with,
and do the most out of, both their natural and social constraints. Subsequently,
in this formulation we accept that ethics is the particular instantiation of the
universal. In other words, this approach, which locates ethics in the contingent,
implies the universal as in the pursuit of happiness, the doctrine of the golden
mean, the need for individual contemplation leading to freedom from mere
natural caprice and untrained habit.

These latter points link to MacInytre's work and in particular his notion of
interdependency.[17] The ethical enterprise involves contemplation upon the
characteristics of good life. However, this is realized in the context of particular communities and implies a conceptualization of individuals as being interdependent. According to McIntyre, in heroic society there is no 'outsider' except
for the stranger.[18] His views remind us of the social character of our existence
that gives rise to interdependency, the impossibility of separating the private
from the public realm, and the canopies of meaning that make our everyday
lives make sense.

Why is our current understanding of ethics so hostile to the notions of interdependency? The reason for this is that man's relation to his animal nature has
been transformed. The Enlightenment offered scientific rationality as the way
out of prejudice stemming from the unreflective reproduction of tradition. It
promoted a critique of the established systems of thought, revealing prejudice,
inequalities, religious fanaticism. In the same spirit, Kantian ethics postulate
that human freedom would emerge as a result of subjecting established morality to reason by autonomous human agents. This position seeks to strip human
beings of their social attributes, to separate the individual from the injustice
of the parochial and mundane character of their social existence, to subject it
to critique. Still, Durkheim taught us that when old Gods die, new ones take
their place. Autonomy and individualism currently present us with new types
of religions, demanding a new telos of human life. However, they are categories of thought, characteristic of our present socio-historical circumstances.
Universalism is rooted in the religious belief that the contingent character of any
morality stemming from man's ephemeral forms of social organization should be
replaced by the quest for transcendental rules untouched by the profanity of the

---

[17] A MacIntyre, *After Virtue; A Study in Moral Theory* (Notre Dame, Ind.: University of Notre
Dame Press, 1981).
[18] ibid.

social. If nature, which gave birth to the doctrine of original sin, directs impulse, then man (and man made law) should rise above it.

With respect to the modern bioethical debates over the right to life of a foetus, deformed newborns, or comatose patients, answers as to who lives and who dies can vary considerably from society to society, or even from family to family in multicultural societies. However, the present investigation does not seek to entertain a view of ethics that collapses into extreme particularlism. Still, even if we agree on a form of contingent universalism, on set of ethical values that seem to hold currency in our current social organization, the process of their actualization in concrete circumstances (when making ethical decisions) implies individual contemplation and judgment of what the best course of action is. The following sections will reflect on the latter point, while trying to articulate the link between bioethics, human flourishing, justice, and governance.

III. Bioethics, Justice, and Human Flourishing

In the light of the analysis in the previous section, the main propositions for a virtue ethics approach to bioethics and justice are the following:

(1) Ethics is about the individual ways in which man could be at peace with himself, the way to contemplate the personal path to happiness in accordance with natural endowance and individual genius. This is a conceptualization of ethics which discards a notion of autonomy as stemming from the universal 'ought'.

(2) Justice relates to ethics, since, whether as a state of mind or as in rules and principles, it involves the exercise of *'ethical intention towards the others'.*[19] This last point is also echoed in Ricoeur's work,[20] where he suggests that the relationship between ethical intention and justice can be formulated as 'aiming at the good life with and for others, in just institutions',[21] as the self is constituted via its relationship with the 'other'. Therefore, justice always involves relationships, regulating belonging and co-existence in collective forms of life.[22]

(3) If ethical intention involves opening ourselves up to the needs of others, as we find ourselves in relations of interdependence, then it logically follows

[19] Aristotle (n 9 above).

[20] P Ricoeur, *Oneself as Another* (trans, K Blamey) (Chicago: University Of Chicago Press, 1992).

[21] ibid 172.

[22] Spinoza's *Ethics*, Part IV, is also relevant here: 'my own self-realization is enhanced by the self-realization of others with whom/which I am internally related…whereas human freedom arises from intellectual intuition about our interdependence/ interrelatedness', see B Spinoza, *Ethics* (trans, RHM Elwes) (London: Penguin Books, 1996). Also see MacIntyre's views (n 17 above), attributing the loss of belonging to the advent of individualism (as manifested in the language of rights and the utilitarian discourse) as marking the contemporary crisis of justice.

that ethics and justice should be sensitive to the particular circumstances, the specific context where the needs of others are anchored. To reformulate this, the needs of others cannot be defined in abstract terms, but are anchored in culture.

(4) According to the rule of the golden mean, justice (δικαιοπραγία) not only involves relationships and the examination of particular circumstances, but also implies the position between two extremes: suffering and doing injustice to the 'other'. To this effect, justice requires striking the right balance between giving unfair advantage and inflicting too much disadvantage. Transactions of economic nature and penal cases both involve relationships, where the state of the mean between too much justice and injustice, between unfair advantage and disadvantage, must be preserved.

(5) The principle of equity is crucial when applying the rule of the golden mean. Legislation is drafted in general terms, and in certain cases the law may not fit the circumstances. In this instance, equity implies that an outcome should be proportional to another contribution, and requires the judge or law-maker to reach a decision as if they were in the same position as the defendant or interested party. This is a process that implies the exercise of tolerance, επιείκια.[23] In other words, the notion of equity offers useful guidance as to how to flesh out the properties of the golden mean. The following section will consider the latter point in more detail.

IV. Equity and Bioethics: Towards a Dynamic Notion of Health

The principle of equity figures prominently in the debates in the United Nations. For instance, with respect to environmental law, equity links to sustainability in the use of natural resources and begs the question of unequal distribution of access to resources such as food.[24] Moreover, the concept of equity is mentioned in recent important international agreements, such as the United Nations Convention on the Law of the Sea, the Convention on Biological Diversity, and the Universal Declaration on Bioethics and Human Rights, and there have been adjudicative attempts to interpret it,[25] following the Aristotelian conceptualization of equity as having both distributive and corrective functions.

[23] Aristotle (n 9 above). For the definitions of equity in law, economics, psychology, and other disciplines see A Smagadi, 'Analysis of the Objectives of the Convention on Biological Diversity: Their Interrelation and Implementation Guidance for Access and Benefit Sharing' (2006) 31(2) *Columbia Journal of Environmental Law* 244.

[24] Smagadi (n 23 above) referring to the report of the Brundtland Commission on sustainable development. (UN General Assembly document A/42/427).

[25] CR Rossi, *Equity and International Law: A Legal-Realist Approach to International Decision Making* (New York: Transnational Publishers Inc, 1993). Rossi analyses the meaning of equity

The Universal Declaration on Bioethics and Human Rights relates equity to human rights and capacity building. For instance, Article 10 of the Declaration states that 'the fundamental equality of all human beings in dignity and rights is to be respected so that they are treated justly and equitably'. The Declaration also recognizes that 'decisions regarding ethical issues in medicine, life sciences and associated technologies may have an impact on individuals, families, groups or communities and humankind as a whole'.[26] In the same spirit, it acknowledges that 'health does not depend solely on scientific and technological research developments, but also on psycho-social and cultural factors'. Finally, the notion of equity points to the sharing of benefits and conservation for future generations,[27] self-determination, empowerment, and participation in decision-making.[28]

The proposition in what follows is that if one chooses to apply the principle of equity in the context of bioethics, while accepting the importance of bridging the universal with the local and the theoretical with the practical, then it is important to translate into the theoretical language of ethics and justice the stark reality of socio-economic equalities, poverty, and suffering, with the aim to promote empowerment and capacity building.

We are now in a position to summarize the arguments presented so far:

- If bioethics concerns the ethical relationship with our bodies and the environment, and the ways in which this is affected by modern biomedical technologies[29]

- If the telos of bioethics concerns well-being and flourishing

- If bioethics requires attention to cases, hence presenting us with the interpretive and practical component of the ethical enterprise

- If this exercise implies situating ethical intention and justice in the context of existing relationships, aiming at the good life with and for others, in just institutions

- If justice requires the application of the rule of the golden mean and the doctrine of equity in the course of regulating relationships

as a source of international law discussing the decisions of international courts such as the ICJ. Moreover, Smagadi (n 23 above) discusses the importance of the principle of equity in the law of the sea, as it has been applied to balance the interests of both developing and developed countries with respect to the use of ocean resources.

[26] Universal Declaration on Bioethics and Human Rights, adopted by UNESCO's General Conference on 19 October 2005.

[27] ibid.

[28] On these points also see TM Franck, *Fairness in International Law and Institutions* (New York: Oxford University Press, 1995).

[29] See also the wide definition of bioethics in the Universal Declaration on Bioethics and Human Rights, which includes all issues relating to our understanding of life, for instance issues relating to animal, vegetable, and human life, such as health, quality of life, identity, dignity, belonging in communities, and ensuring that progress in science and technology contributes to justice, to equity, and to the interest of humanity, see Declaration, 2–3.

- If the doctrine of equity implies the need to pay attention to socio-economic inequalities and to the promotion of empowerment

Then, it follows that bioethics should be concerned with regulating the relationship with our bodies and the environment, promoting a balanced approach to life so that we become good and lead a happy life, by means of being trained in habits that empower and do not enslave the spirit. Justice, on the other hand, should be concerned with bridging the universal with the local (as when it takes into account the stark reality of socio-economic inequalities), while promoting the notions of interdependence, deliberation, and empowerment. In the light of this proposition, the following sections will advance the thesis that the promotion of a dynamic notion of *health* should be a primary aspiration for bioethics and justice, as it can fruitfully tie together all the above-mentioned qualities of virtue bioethics.

The following sections will examine in detail the latter proposition.

A. Health and Bioethics

The following paragraphs merely present elements of a genealogy of health, justice, and ethics to be undertaken in detail elsewhere.

Health has always been perceived as a good of incommensurable value. In classical antiquity health was a good above beauty and wealth, as it was directly related to man's well-being. Concerns about healthy living interweaved with the supernatural. In antiquity, sickness was the realm of activity for traditional healers (using spells, herbs, and magic), powerful deities, and physicians, all seeking to alleviate the pain of disease and fear of death. Physicians were involved in the prognostics of the body, just as seers were concerned with the prognostics of external events.[30] True, Hippocratic principles were opposed to religious ritual. Yet, the popular cult of Asclepius throughout antiquity in the Mediterranean indicates that medicine and health were never fully divorced from religion. Asklepia were health sanctuaries, and the cult of Asclepius was simultaneously a religion and a system of healing.

With the advent of Christianity, the activity of traditional healers was conducted alongside the cult of relics and Saints, but the relationship with medicine was difficult, as they were both seeking to attain health and well-being in a holistic sense implying the pursuit of balance between soul and body.[31] The uneasy nature of this relationship can be attributed to the passage from

---

[30] R Bartz, 'Remembering the Hippocratics: Knowledge, Practice, and Ethos of Ancient Greek Physician-Healers' in MG Kuczewski and R Polansky (eds), *Bioethics. Ancient Themes in Contemporary Issues* (Cambridge, Mass.: MIT Press, 2000) 4.

[31] See for instance Plato's *Charmides* (trans, TG Tuckey) (New York: Cambridge University Press, 1951). This connection was dear to Greek philosophers, for attitudes in Byzantium, see AC Eftychiadis, 'Byzantine Psychosomatic Medicine (10th–15th century)' (1999) 1(2) *Med Secoli* 415.

a polytheistic model of plural possibilities as to the attainment of health to the monotheistic understanding of singularity, where God and nature are separated, as nature is potentially demonic. This rupture is best illustrated in attitudes towards the administration of drugs, pharmaka, (φάρμακα), in early Christian times. Although Galen and others insisted on the unity of the three aspects of medicine (pharmacology, dietetics, and surgery) not all physicians agreed with him: it is not possible to say how many physicians denied administering drugs during the late Hellenistic and early Roman Empire eras. However, the denial reflects the view that drugs, pharmaka (φάρμακα), are matter and can be used both as poisons (δηλητήρια) and therapeutic substances (ἰώμενα), in other words, both for good and evil, as matter can always be manipulated by demons to deceive people. The problem can be located in the ambivalence of the meaning of the pharmakeia word group, which pointed at the same time to sorcery in both the Septuagint and the New Testament.[32] Yet, the ambivalence of the word pharmaka simultaneously implies the ambivalence of the sacred and profane character of nature in pagan times, this being unacceptable to the Christian mind, as good and evil had to be situated above the contingency of the social.

Contrary to the latter understanding, Hippocratic medicine sought to assist nature and to fill in what nature has failed to provide. In fact, man's purpose was to assist nature, in an attempt to achieve a harmonious and symbiotic relationship with it, while with Christianity, man is called to break the bonds with any deceiving natural forces.[33] This is why, in classical antiquity the task of religion and philosophy was to understand the order of nature and live in accordance with it, while with Christianity the telos of human existence is salvation and not happiness. Still, resort to traditional healers never disappeared in Byzantium and Western Europe during the Middle Ages.[34]

Nowadays, religion and science still seem to intertwine in interesting ways. Nelkin and Lindee observe that scientists describe the genome as the Holy Grail and the Holy Book and arguments relevant to cloning are made against the backdrop of ultimate meaning.[35] In the face of the extraordinary capacities of modern medicine, touching on the supernatural to the popular mind, the medical profession is expected to prolong life and cure disease, in the same way that Christian saints did, Christianity being the healing religion par excellence, and miracles

[32] DW Amundsen, *Medicine, Society and Faith in the Ancient and Medieval Worlds* (Baltimore and London: John Hopkins University Press, 1996) 158.

[33] R Polansky, 'Is Medicine Art, Science, or Practical Wisdom? Ancient and Contemporary Reflections' in MG Kuczewski and R Polansky (eds), *Bioethics. Ancient Themes in Contemporary Issues* (Cambridge, Mass.: MIT Press, 2000).

[34] Amundsen (n 32 above) and B Baldwin, 'Beyond the House Call: Doctors in Early Byzantine History and Politics' in J Scarborough (ed), *Symposium on Byzantine Medicine. Dumbarton Oaks Papers* (Washington, DC: Dumbarton Oaks, 1985).

[35] D Nelkin and LS Lindee, *The DNA Mystique: The Gene as Cultural Icon* (New York: Freeman, 1995).

being important in inspiring faith.[36] In the era of science, the same metaphors continue to agitate people's imaginations when entertaining the primordial fear of death.

In this sense, it can be said that man rediscovers its animality and nature its divinity,[37] as man seeks a life of quality, while contemplating multiple possibilities and being prepared to engage in experimentation. Health belongs not only to the realm of science or to religion, but also to the realm of ethics; it entails choice, it encloses potentialities, it demands reflection. For instance, we are currently witnessing the emergence of the *curious patient*, who is empowered, well-informed, and demands a new ethical relationship with her body and the environment, as health appears to be the prerequisite to a life of quality.[38] Health embodies the quest for happiness and balance, as humans are better positioned to contest authoritative knowledge, by becoming increasingly aware of their uniqueness. Hence, biotechnology and the wide availability of information on relevant developments make possible a wide definition of health as being not only concerned with well-being, but also as implying multiple diverse choices to attain happiness.[39,40] This results in opening to public debate relevant policy questions. For instance, deaf parents may choose to give birth to a deaf child by selecting a deaf sperm donor.[41]

---

[36] Amundsen (n 32 above).

[37] HG Gadamer, *The Enigma of Health: the Art of Healing in a Scientific Age* (trans, J Gaiger and N Walker) (Cambridge: Polity Press, 1996). However, note that Gadamer uses this quotation in a different context.

[38] P Rabinow, 'The Third Culture' (1994) 7(2) *History of the Human Sciences* 53.

[39] C Novas and N Rose, 'Genetic Risk and the Birth of the Somatic Individual' (2000) 29(4) *Economy and Society* 484.

[40] The flip side of this approach is that clinical medicine and life sciences, such as biotechnology, may give birth to techniques for the monitoring and control of life and death, whose ultimate aim is to control a population: 'If genocide is indeed the dream of modern powers, this is not because of a return of an ancient right to kill; it is because power is situated and exercised at the level of life, the species, the race, and the large scale phenomena of population', see M Foucault, *The History of Sexuality Volume 1: An Introduction* (trans, R Hurley) (New York: Pantheon, 1978) 136. For instance, such power may be exercised by means of techniques such as risk management, N Rose, 'The Politics of Life Itself' (2001) 18(6) *Theory, Culture and Society* 1. Post-modernists such as Baudrillard warn against the risk of transforming mankind into mere mechanistic simulacra, see J Baudrillard, *The Vital Illusion* (New York: Columbia University Press, 2000). Derrida, on the other hand, is concerned about the future of eugenic practices, yet he questions the extent to which humans will be able to absolutely master and control the human genome, see J Derrida, 'The Aforementioned So-called Human Genome' in E Rottenberg (ed), *Negotiations* (Stanford: Stanford University Press, 2002). Habermas argues that modern technologies may negatively affect the way we perceive ourselves as free agents, see J Habermas, *The Future of Human Nature* (Oxford: Polity Press, 2003). Finally, Fukuyama calls for the careful regulation of modern technologies, see F Fukuyama, *Our Posthuman Future. Consequences of the Biotechnology Revolution* (London: Profile, 2002).

[41] Story reported by Liza Mundy in the *Washington Post Magazine* (31 March 2002) and refers to Sharon Duchesneau and her partner Candace McCullough. On these issues, see also M Greco, 'The Politics of Indeterminacy and the Right to Health' (2004) 21(6) *Theory, Culture and Society* 1.

The following sections will elaborate in more detail on the possibility of conceptualizing health in terms of empowerment.

B. Health and Empowerment

Foucault's work on the genealogy of the right to health cites the Beveridge Plan of 1942, which set the foundations for the welfare state in the United Kingdom and in many other European countries. This is important as it marked the transformation of health into an object of state concern, not for the benefit of the state, but for the benefit of individuals.[42] In this sense, it marked the genesis of a new politics of the body, as 'we live in a regime that sees the care of the body, corporal health, the relation between illness and health, etc as appropriate areas of State intervention'.[43]

However, Osborne[44] makes the argument that health policies advancing direct intervention cannot grasp the indeterminate character of health. To substantiate this argument Osborn relies on the work of Canguilhem,[45] advancing the importance of dynamic normativity, as opposed to the notion of normality, to discuss the epistemological properties of health. Taking the example of the discovery of the DNA structure, and assuming that the normal corresponds to the procedures of positivist science and medicine, it is naive to suggest that there is direct correlation between the information carried by DNA and disease. In this framework, the normal is synonymous with the mechanical, suggesting a lack of capacity of any dynamic adaptability, variation, and creativity.

Contrary to this approach, the notion of dynamic normativity implies that health can be described as a set of possibilities available to an organism; the normal then being always subject to transformation, as it embraces potentialities, one of which will be actualized in response to the particular circumstances of a given situation. The dynamic element of normativity lies in the understanding that organisms do not merely respond to a set of normal, objective, capacities; instead there is constant communication between these and the environment, a process involving reflection and uncertainty. Reflection implies the choice to live according to one's norms; yet normative intention may not follow the normality inscribed in the mechanical understanding of life.[46]

---

[42] M Foucault, 'The Crisis of Medicine or the Crisis of Antimedicine?' (trans, EC Knowlton, WJ King, and C O'Farrell) (2004) 1(1) *Foucault Studies* 5.

[43] ibid 7.

[44] Greco (n 41 above) citing T Osborne, 'Of Health and Statecraft' in A Petersen and R Bunton (eds), *Foucault, Health and Medicine* (London: Routledge, 1997).

[45] See eg M Foucault, Introduction to Georges Canguilhem, *The Normal and the Pathological* (New York: Zone Books, 1991); See also special issue (1998) 27(2) *Economy and Society* dedicated to Georges Canguilhem.

[46] Current discussions on eugenics and cloning sometimes reflect a mechanistic understanding of life and health.

Katerina Sideri

Bergon's influence on the articulation of Canguilhem's thought is important.[47] Bergson militates against any conceptualization of the conditions of genesis of observed phenomena as being both independent of human experience and based on pre-existing essences, hence presenting us with the dystopia of a world of pre-defined possibilities. The same applies in a world where every new material object under observation simply needs the invention of a new category in order to reveal its qualities. Entering the realm of experience is the only way to grasp the real, which is found both in bodies and in things. It is only then that we can come to grips with the *possible* that is never *real*, even though it may be *actual*, as soon it is crystallized in action. However, the *virtual*, understood as the myriad diverse and multiple possibilities that have not become *actual*, is nonetheless very much real, as real as the possibilities finally actualized in the course of action.[48]

It then follows that every observed action exhibits something that is really free and creative, something spontaneous and innovative, yet limited by the particular circumstances of its actualization.[49] Bergson also suggests that every

---

[47] Bergson asserted that there should be a different way to inquire into the conditions of the real, apart from the solutions offered by mechanism and finalism. He strongly attacked both models for failing to account for unforeseeable creation and creative force. He argued that since mechanism is providing a model of the world that works on the basis of mathematical laws that explain repetition, and finalism furnishes explanations that follow the realization of an organized plan, they both confuse order with freedom, and as such the notion of creative change is trapped in the already given. This is happening since both theories offer the point of view of someone who simply observes action, the final product of a process whose attributes they fail to grasp. Bergson then assumed that the fallacy involved in the conceptualization of creation as something that one can think of, and not something that is lived and experienced. He then offered a model of a world that has been made open, by means of human intervention, as soon as it gave up its objectivity. Nonetheless, material objects retain a dual character by existing both in minds and in themselves. In *Matter and Memory*, Bergson asserts that his philosophy intends to overcome difficulties raised by both idealistic and materialistic conceptions of matter, see H Bergson, *Matter and Memory* (trans, NM Paul and WS Palmer) (New York: Zone Books, 1990) 12.

[48] This distinction between the *virtual/actual* and the *possible/real* is to remind us that the real is only an instant of a passage from the multiplicity to the unity, a moment of order that would have been impossible to predict because of the dazzling creative force encapsulated in the virtual. This is why Bergson attacks the logic found in the possible/real couple as being governed by resemblance and limitation since it prescribes that the possible existed before its realization and it is only through the process of limitation that it becomes real, thus the real is understood as simply reflecting the possible. On the contrary, the passage from the virtual to the actual is always something unpredictable, as it follows no laws. Therefore, Bergson attacks Darwin and his notion of species adaptation as he considers it 'being passive, a mere repetition of what the conditions give to the mould, (and as such) it will build nothing more that what one asks it to build', Bergson (n 47 above) 62.

[49] It is beyond the scope of the present chapter to discuss the viability of the doctrine of vitalism. As Greco notes: 'It is an error, but an error endowed with a positive, perhaps even necessary, function.' To this effect, Greco cites Michel Foucault's introduction to *The Normal and the Pathological*: 'if the "scientificization" process is done by bringing to light physical and chemical mechanisms . . . it has on the other hand, been able to develop only insofar as the problem of the specificity of life and of the threshold it marks among all natural beings was continually thrown back as a challenge. This does not mean that "vitalism" . . . is true . . . It simply means that it has had and undoubtedly still has an essential role as an "indicator" in the history of biology', Foucault (n 44 above). Greco further notes that: 'Canguilhem endorses vitalism conditionally, in that the historicity of vitalism allows for a resignification of its value for the science of biology,' see M Greco, 'On the Vitality of

creation is based on something, and as such there is no creation *ex nihilio*, as creation always finds its premises on what is already present in life. Following the same line of thought, he understands the problematique between order and disorder as being a pseudo-problematique, since it is generated by the failure to regard both concepts as manifesting different states of order.[50] It is simply that the intellect fails again to grasp the real nature of things, and judges as disorder what does not fit into the existing categories of thought. In short, reality is a perpetual becoming, a continual change of form, 'it makes itself or it unmakes itself, but it is never something made'.[51] 'Life is a movement... to movement then everything will be restored and into movement everything will be resolved.'[52]

Foucault's position with respect to medicine effectively links the above abstract philosophical discussion to our present enquiry: 'In a certain sense, "social medicine" does not exist because all medicine is already social. Medicine has always been a social practice. What does not exist is non-social medicine, clinical individualizing medicine, medicine of the singular relation. All this is a myth that defended and justified a certain form of social practice of medicine: private professional practice.'[53]

Health is something lived, experienced, something reproduced and contested, subject to objectified constraints, and grounded on different interpretations resulting in the making of choices. Thus, uncertainty is inserted in a world under constant change. Conceiving health as such is at odds with both the conceptualization of it as something that can be pursued by clear criteria and as being positioned in a realm beyond the one of everyday struggles. Accepting that the norms regulating our perception of health reflect socially constructed knowledge, implies that both patients and biomedical experts possess considerable freedom as to how they are to respond to the authority of expert scientific knowledge. Life conceals possibilities that remain hidden from the gaze of scientific classification.

This position accords with the classical Greek conceptualization of medicine as an art, which was at the same time related to natural science and to practical wisdom.[54] The Hippocratic physician was considered a healing craftsman, the outcome of any intervention being limited by the quality of materials (the patient, the disease) to be worked upon. In this sense, the doctor assisted nature, and therefore abstained from doing too little or too much; the physician could

---

Vitalism' (2005): 2(1) *Theory, Culture and Society* 15, 17. A full discussion on vitalism falls outside the scope of this chapter.

[50] H Bergson, *Creative Evolution* (trans, A Mitchell) (New York: MacMillan and Co, 1928) 242.
[51] ibid 262.
[52] ibid 263–4. The influence of Heraclitus' philosophy on this passage is obvious, see also Heraclitus, *Fragments: The Collected Wisdom of Heraclitus* (trans, B Haxton) (New York: Viking Penguin, 2001).
[53] Foucault (n 42 above) 8.   [54] Polansky (n 33 above) 31.

only do what the patient would do for himself.[55] Plato and Aristotle agreed that working with the forces of nature implies that physicians are the medium though which nature can be transformed to reveal both its goodness and profanity; the healing craftsman has the power in his soul to achieve both outcomes, and as such the best doctor can be the best poisoner.[56]

In the same spirit, Gadamer points out that 'medicine is not an art that implies the invention or planning of something new...It is from the beginning a particular way of doing and making which produces nothing of its own...The art inserts itself entirely in the process of nature in so far as it seeks to restore this process when it is disturbed, and to do it in such a way that the art can allow itself to disappear once the natural equilibrium of health is restored.'[57] This is why the physician's job was also to engage in the art of *prognostics*, reading the signs of the body; if signs foretold that the body was able to overcome disease, he would abstain from any intervention.

Moreover, medical practice also relates to practical wisdom, as it involves much deliberation; it has to take into account ways of life and character, as a variety of treatments is available. 'Matters of conduct and expediency have nothing fixed or invariable about them, any more than have matters of health...Agents have to consider what is suited to the circumstances of each occasion just as is the case with the art of medicine or of navigation.'[58] In other words, medical knowledge is not only knowledge of universal principles; diagnosis and treatment call for phronesis, the application of principles to specific cases.[59]

We are now in a position to flesh out the properties of a dynamic notion of health: the first aspect of the definition involves coming to grips with it as the pursuit of happiness and balance by individuals who strive to live full-fledged moral lives. This understanding brings to the foreground the importance of deliberation and empowerment of individuals to control their health. The second aspect of the definition points to the exercise of power relations underpinning our conception of health. Both aspects of the proposed definition will be considered in turn in the following two sections.

Health and the Pursuit of Well-being

Nowadays, with the advent of modern technologies, we are witnessing the resort to various diverse avenues to attain heath. Health does not simply present us with the external conditions necessary to promote happiness.[60] Health *is* bio-ethics, as it embodies our pursuit of happiness and balance. This implies contemplation

---

[55] ibid 46.

[56] ibid 37, citing Plato's *Republic* and *Lesser Hippias*, and Aristotle's *Metaphysics* and *Nicomachean Ethics*.

[57] Gadamer (n 37 above).   [58] Aristotle (n 9 above) 77.

[59] K Montgomery, 'Phronesis and Misdescription of Medicine: Against the Medical School Commencement Speech' in MG Kuczewski and R Polansky (eds), *Bioethics. Ancient Themes in Contemporary Issues* (Cambridge, Mass.: MIT Press, 2000) 61.

[60] Aristotle (n 9 above).

in the context of the particular circumstances of the issue at hand, as to what constitutes the best course of action, and how to conduct one's life. As Rose and Novas argue:

Like earlier practices of confession and diary writing, the practices of posting, reading and replying to messages in these web forums and chat rooms are techniques of the self, entailing the disclosure of one's experiences and thoughts according to particular rules, norms, values and forms of authority...In HD [Huntington disease], key issues concern the decision as to whether to have children, the decision to get married, and disclosure to other family members that they face the prospect of developing a debilitating neurological disorder. These informal practices of mutual disclosure around such issues among those who identify themselves with a virtual community are significant because they constitute a novel form of authority—an authority based not on training, status or possession of esoteric skills, but on experience. And, like those older forms of authority, experiential authority, the experiential authority of others, can be folded into the self. As we shall see, relations with older forms of authority, such as medical and genetic expertise, mutate. These small, yet important mutations are starting to shape the ways in which novel life strategies are formulated and developed. Within such life strategies, the governance of risky genes is intimately tied to identity projects, the crafting of healthy bodies, and the management of our relations with others, in relation to a wide range of authorities that are folded into the self.[61]

Citizens increasingly tend to understand themselves in biological terms.[62] Rose refers to the complex decision-making process for women and men on the issues of amniocentesis and AIDS.[63] These people are moral pioneers, as they have to critically evaluate and manage a variety of diverse information in order to come up with decisions as to what the best course of action is. Expert advice, expectations from their immediate environment, even established social stereotypes are subjected to critique.[64]

Bioethics, Human Rights, Governance: Health and Power

The manner in which power relations pertain to health can be best illustrated by examining the link between human rights and bioethics. Human rights and

---

[61] C Novas and N Rose, 'Genetic Risk and the Birth of the Somatic Individual' (2000) 29(4) *Economy and Society* 485, 503.

[62] P Rabinow, 'The Third Culture' (1994) 7(2) *History of the Human Sciences* 53.

[63] N Rose and C Novas, 'Biological Citizenship' in A Ong and S Collier (eds), *Global Anthropology: Technology, Governance, Ethics* (New York: Blackwell, 2003), citing S Epstein, *Impure Science: AIDS, Activism, and the Politics of Knowledge* (Berkeley: University of California Press, 1996), E Martin, *Flexible Bodies: Tracking Immunity in American Culture from the Days of Polio to the Age of AIDS* (Boston: Beacon Press, 1994), and R Rapp, *Testing Women, Testing the Fetus: the Social Impact of Amniocentesis in America* (New York: Routledge, 1999).

[64] However, some might say that these techniques of the biomedical self are a kind of narcissistic self-absorption, see Engelhardt (n 1 above) 414. Also, some argue that this process may also imply normalization as 'The enactment of such responsible behaviours has become routine and expected, built in to public health measures, producing new types of problematic persons, those who refuse to identify themselves with this responsible community of biological citizens', see M Callon and V Rabeharisoa 'Gino's Lesson on Humanity: Genetics, Mutual Entanglements and the Sociologist's Role' (2004) 33(1) *Economy and Society* 1.

bioethics interweave in interesting ways, as in the 2005 UNESCO Universal Declaration on Bioethics and Human Rights, the European Convention on Human Rights and Biomedicine, the UN Covenant of Social and Economic rights, and the Comment on Article 14 by the UN Committee on socio-economic rights.[65]

It is beyond the scope of this chapter to discuss in detail the various forms of criticism addressed against human rights, including the problems relating to their theoretical justification, and the debate surrounding socio-economic rights.[66] However, one line of criticism relevant to the present analysis concerns the abstract nature of rights, failing to come to grips with the everyday realities of people. Yamin's position is relevant here: 'International human rights instruments both reflect and create an unfinished world made by men and women who are themselves unfinished'.[67] This is particularly obvious in the developing world, as the concepts of dignity, autonomy, and informed consent[68] often do not take into account the reality of extreme conditions of poverty in some developing countries. The example of informed consent and HIV drug clinical trials is illuminating. Farmer asks the simple question: how can we expect a poor and sick person in the developing world to exercise their autonomous will when in dire need of medication?[69] A good example where prinicipalism and our current understanding of autonomy fail, as poverty provides a different canopy of meaning than the one in the West.

The 'capabilities approach' developed by Martha Nussbaum[70] and Amartya Sen, seeks to correct some of the inadequacies described earlier, by means of

[65] Proving a breach of the Hippocratic Oath's ethical obligation to 'do no harm' led to the conviction of the Nazi doctors at the Nuremberg Trials after the Second World War for non-consensual experimentation on human beings, sterilization, and non-voluntary euthanasia. Documents such as the Declaration of Geneva (updating the Hippocratic Oath), the Nuremberg Declaration on Human Experimentation, and the International Code of Medical Ethics were created afterwards, bringing to the foreground the importance of informed consent, patient autonomy, and human dignity. Human rights currently seem to intrude into many aspects of international law, due to the symbolic power attached to the language of rights.

[66] M Freeman, 'The Philosophical Foundations of Human Rights' (1994) 16(3) *Human Rights Quarterly* 491, where the author provides a detailed account of the various arguments supporting the necessary universality, contingent universality, and relativism of human rights.

[67] AE Yamin, 'Defining Questions: Situating Issues of Power in the Formulation of a Right to Health under International Law' (1996) 18(2) *Human Rights Quarterly* 398, 401.

[68] The problem is recognized by the UN. The thirteenth session of the International Bioethics Committee (IBC) of the UN held in November 2006 in Paris, was devoted entirely to examining preliminary reports prepared by working groups on two principles of the Universal Declaration on Bioethics and Human Rights, one on consent (Articles 6 and 7) and the other on social responsibility and health (Article 14). The fourteenth session of the IBC held in May 2007 Nairobi, Kenya continued the discussion, see <http://portal.unesco.org/shs/en/ev.php-URL_ID=10736& URL_DO=DO_TOPIC&URL_SECTION=201.html>.

[69] P Farmer, *Pathologies of Power: Health, Human Rights, and the New War on the Poor* (Berkeley and LA: California University Press, 2003).

[70] Nussbaum in particular has produced an open-ended list with capabilities such as: (1) Life. (Being able to live to the end of a human life of normal length; not dying prematurely, or before one's life is so reduced as to be not worth living). (2) Bodily Health. (3) Bodily Integrity. Being

bridging the abstract nature of rights with the context of everyday realities. Although their work is not on bioethics, it is important to briefly refer to it, as useful analogies can be made. Deriving inspiration from Aristotle's thinking, both thinkers bring to the foreground questions relevant to welfare and quality of life to supplement the language of rights. Their approach is liberal, distinguishing their theoretical framework from communitarian critics of rights. 'Capabilities' designate material well-being, and require that we consider what people are actually able to be and to do, when asking the question 'what policies do we need to promote human flourishing'.[71]

The capabilities approach reminds us that it is not enough to ensure that individuals have access to a certain number of resources, as resources are not valuable in themselves, but derive their value from allowing us to function in certain ways. Sen's criticism against the Rawlsian position in *The Theory of Justice* and *Political Liberalism* illustrates this latter point. John Rawls' list of primary goods presents to all individuals the necessary resources to live a meaningful life in accordance with their privately held ethical convictions as to what counts as good life. Resources include liberties, opportunities, and powers, wealth and income, the social basis of self-respect, freedom of movement, and the free choice of occupation.[72] Rawls argues that the choice of principles of justice should be

---

able to move freely from place to place; to be secure against violent assault, including sexual assault and domestic violence; having opportunities for sexual satisfaction and for choice in matters of reproduction. (4) Senses, Imagination, and Thought. (5) Emotions. Being able to have attachments to things and people outside ourselves; to love those who love and care for us, to grieve at their absence; in general, to love, to grieve, to experience longing, gratitude, and justified anger. Not having one's emotional development blighted by fear and anxiety. Supporting this capability means supporting forms of human association that can be shown to be crucial in their development. (6) Practical Reason. Being able to form a conception of the good and to engage in critical reflection about the planning of one's life. This entails protection for the liberty of conscience and religious observance. (7) Affiliation. (a) Friendship. Being able to live for and to others, to recognize and show concern for other human beings, to engage in various forms of social interaction; to be able to imagine the situation of another and to have compassion for that situation; to have the capability for both justice and friendship. Protecting this capability means, once again, protecting institutions that constitute such forms of affiliation, and also protecting the freedoms of assembly and political speech. (b) Respect. Having the social bases of self-respect and non-humiliation; being able to be treated as a dignified being whose worth is equal to that of others. This entails provisions of non-discrimination on the basis of race, sex, ethnicity, caste, religion, and national origin. (8) Other Species. Being able to live with, concern for, and in relation to animals, plants, and the world of nature. (9) Play. Being able to laugh, to play, and to enjoy recreational activities. (10) Control Over One's environment. (a) Political. Being able to participate effectively in political choices that govern one's life; having the right of political participation, protections of free speech and association. (b) Material. Being able to hold property (both land and movable goods); having the right to employment; having freedom from unwarranted search and seizure, see MC Nussbaum, 'Capabilities and Human Rights' (1997) 66 *Fordham Law Review* 273, 287.

[71] To illustrate this, a middle class girl in Europe and a girl in the developing world may both have the right to free education, in other words, equal access to a resource. However, the latter girl may not exercise her right, as a result of living in a society where women are not considered worthy of an education, or because of being a member of a poor family, requiring her to work.

[72] A Sen, *Resources, Values, and Development* (Cambridge, Mass.: Harvard University Press, 1984).

underlined by information relevant to who is better off and less well off according to his list of primary resources. However, the Rawlsian notion of resources fails to take into account the context of their social construction and the asymmetries of power involved. Sen's argument in particular is that individuals vary greatly in their need for resources. For example, differences may be of a physical nature, as nutrition needs differ according to age, occupation, and sex. Moreover, differences may imply social inequalities, an obvious candidate to illustrate this being women's literacy.[73] Hence, social inequalities may result in the inadequate use of resources, such as free public education, the right to vote, or the right to employment.

To convey some of these thoughts in the context of bioethics and human rights, the capabilities approach brings to the foreground the importance of locating the abstract language of rights within the practical context of suffering and socio-economic inequalities. Moreover the theoretical framework of virtue bioethics developed in this chapter can provide the tools to formulate a novel approach to questions relating to governance, human rights, and bioethics. In the same manner as the capabilities approach, it stresses the importance of contextual analysis taking into account conditions of inequality. It goes beyond by means of stressing the importance of translating into the language of rights a dynamic notion of health, promoting the importance of interdependence, deliberation, and empowerment.

We are now in a position to pull together the threads of the diverse strands of analysis conducted in the previous sections, to formulate them as concrete propositions indicating ways in which human rights can fruitfully engage in dialogue with bioethics. The main propositions can be summarized in the following points:

Virtue bioethics is concerned with the question: 'who should I be?', and not with the question, 'what should be done?' independently of the particular circumstances:

(a) A consideration of particular circumstances requires taking into account socio-economic inequalities, poverty, and suffering, and translating these

---

[73] Hence, both thinkers militate against crude forms of utilitarianism measuring good life in terms of a single metric; instead indeterminacy is injected in their analysis by means of allowing a plurality of goods as contributing to human flourishing, hence limiting the possibility of engaging in an analysis simply based on trade-offs. Moreover, people's individual pleasure and pain is deemed an unreliable indicator to measure their quality of life. This is because satisfaction is socially constructed; Socialization in particular communities, education, religious background, poverty, all function as canopies of meaning as to what counts as pleasure. Sen says that in 1944, the year after the Great Bengal Famine, the All-India Institute of Hygiene and Public Health did a survey on the health status of the population. The response of widowers to the survey was striking: only 2.5% of widows, as against 48.5% of widowers, reported that they were either ill or in indifferent health. This can be attributed to the social position of widows, who tacitly accept that their social status implies malnourishment, suffering, and disease, see A Sen, 'Equality of What?' in *Choice, Welfare and Measurement* (Cambridge, Mass.: Harvard University Press, 1982); Nussbaum (n 70 above).

into legal language, by means of integrating them throughout the body of documents such as the Universal Declaration on Human Rights and Bioethics, as justice always involves relationships and the observance of the mean relative to us, the mean between doing and suffering injustice.

(b) The doctrine of equity is important in delineating the boundaries of the particular when applying abstract principles. Equity points to self-determination, empowerment, capacity building, and participation in decision-making.

Proposition: From the vantage point of virtue ethics, the principal endeavour of bioethics can be best captured by formulating a dynamic notion of health, as involving the pursuit of happiness and balance by individuals who strive to live full-fledged moral lives.

(1) The proposed concept of health integrates the doctrine of equity by means of making connections between health, poverty, and education, being in compliance with Article 14 of the Universal Declaration on Bioethics and Human Rights, which defines health as a 'social and human good'. However, the notion of health proposed here should be integrated throughout the body of the document of the Declaration.

(2) Furthermore, it points towards an understanding of health as a high priority goal.[74] This position reminds us both that justice is concerned with relationships, and that there is a need for flexibility in the process of deliberation, sensitive to the context of particular circumstances, requiring dialogue between the local and international levels. Then, serious research should be conducted as to the exercise of power in the course of deliberations. This approach is in accordance with the current trend in the literature on governance stressing the importance of advancing flexible regulatory instruments in the process of implementing rights.[75] In this framework, UN committees would cooperate with national bioethics committees in search of acceptable solutions sensitive to the particular context of the case at issue. Moreover, it brings attention to the fact that large-scale centralized projects often are not as successful as projects where local organizations are involved.[76]

(3) It reminds us that although health may be currently accepted as a universal value, it acquires different meanings depending on the particular circumstances in which it is actualized. The regulatory dilemmas that the developing world faces are different from those encountered in the developed world. For instance, access to essential medicines and effective participation in deliberation of minority groups present us with distinctive problems that the

[74] This position is also adopted by Amartya Sen in respect of human rights generally.
[75] Sideri (n 4 above).
[76] Farmer (n 69 above). This approach is endorsed by the Aga Khan Foundation, working directly with communities, see <http://www.akdn.org/agency/akf.html>.

developing world currently faces, while cloning and patents on genes are hotly debated in the West. This is because different canopies of meaning, such as poverty and religion, attach different meanings to health. Yet, if we accept that health should be a central preoccupation of bioethics, it is important to reveal differences between Western and other conceptions of health and discuss how the effort to govern bioethics on the global level should embrace this difference.

(4) However, this analysis is not meant to advance an extreme view of particularlism. True, human flourishing and the attainment of health are currently accepted as universal values. However, there is an ongoing struggle to negotiate the practical meaning of the particular way in which human flourishing is to be achieved, hence the importance of promoting the importance of deliberation and cross-cultural dialogue.

V. Conclusions

In the light of the above, the proposition here was that, from the vantage point of virtue bioethics, the pursuit of *health* should present us with a primary bioethical endeavour. In this instance, the pursuit of health embodies the pursuit of happiness and balance, a position implying contemplation in the context of particular circumstances, as to what constitutes the best course of action, and how to conduct one's life. This approach promotes empowered ethical relationship with our bodies, as individuals are better positioned to contest authoritative knowledge, by becoming increasingly aware of their uniqueness. This makes possible a wide definition of health as implying multiple diverse choices to attain happiness.

Such an open-ended notion of health implies an understanding of bioethics as an individual journey to discover how life is worth living, revealing the practical character of the bioethical enterprise; the importance of the particular circumstances; the necessity of recognizing socio-economic inequalities and local needs; the need to stress the importance of deliberation, while promoting the empowerment of individuals to pursue, preserve, and ultimately define the relationship with their bodies.

In a nutshell, the aim of the present analysis is to propose a theoretical framework positioning the notion of health as a central concern in the effort to govern bioethics. Nevertheless, the present theoretical endeavour should be tested and refined by means of examining the practical ramifications of this proposition in the context of regulatory dilemmas relevant to Europe and to the governance of bioethics on the global level.

6

Law, Human Rights, and the Bioethical Discourse

Michael Freeman

Bioethics has developed more or less at the same time as the propagation of international human rights law.[1] But until recently the two discourses have not had much to say to each other. It is striking how little attention books on human rights give to bioethical issues or insights: much the same can be said about texts on bioethics.[2] This chapter—based on a paper which forms part of a larger project—takes as a case study global pharmaceutical patents to examine possible engagements between law, in particular human rights law, and bioethics. This is not a chapter on the 'AIDS holocaust', as Schüklenk and Ashcroft have called it,[3] but a central focus inevitably and justifiably is the business of AIDS in the developing world.

I. A Historical Perspective

Patents have been seen as 'a necessary evil... at odds with free trade'.[4] The system can only be properly understood in its historical and socio-political context.[5] The origin of patents differs in different legal systems, but a common feature is the idea of monopoly.[6] In Elizabethan England, the origins of patent protection can

---

[1] On the origins, see A Jonsen, *The Birth of Bioethics* (New York, 1998).

[2] A good attempt is GP Smith II *Human Rights and Biomedicine* (The Hague, 2000). But see TA Faunce, 'Will International Human Rights Subsume Medical Ethics?' Intersections in the UNESCO Universal Bioethics Declaration (2005) 31 *Journal of Medical Ethics* 173.

[3] 'Affordable Access To Essential Medication in Developing Countries: Conflicts Between Ethical and Economic' (2002) 27 *Journal of Medicine and Philosophy* 179. Over 95% of people living with HIV/AIDS are in developing countries.

[4] S Sell and C May, 'Moments In Law' (2001) 8 *Review of International Political Economy* 467.

[5] For the briefest of histories, see J Johnston and AA Wasanna, 'Patents, Biomedical Research, and Treatments: Examining Concerns, Canvassing Solutions' (2007) 37(1) *Hastings Center Report* 1, 54–5.

[6] R Brennan and P Baines, 'Is There a Morally Right Price for Anti-Retroviral Drugs in the Developing World?' (2006) 15 *Business Ethics: A European Review* 29.

be traced to the grant of 'letters patent' to merchants over commodities such as salt or coal, giving them the exclusive right to trade in those goods in exchange for cash payments. Such patents were not tied to invention, but were designed as revenue-raising devices for the Crown: sometimes to reward 'royal favourites at the public's expense'.[7] This type of patent was outlawed by the Statute of Monopolies in 1624. A similar system survived in France until the Revolution.[8]

Modern developments in patent protection were motivated by states' desires to attract inventors to their territories. The earliest example of this is a Venetian decree of 1474 which gave patent protection to 'each person who will make in this city any new and ingenious contrivance...so that it can be used and exercised'.[9] The emphasis is on the policy interests of the state, not on any natural rights of the inventor to property in what he invents.

Developments have not been linear, nor necessarily consistent. Patent laws have been repealed or substantially modified to reduce patent protection in the public interest, and later reinstated, at least partially.[10] In England the system came close to being abandoned in the 1870s. This was not because of a public health crisis, but was the result of pressure from economists and industrialists whose view it was that the system was too protectionist. In 1919, the British chemical industry, under pressure from German competition, persuaded the government to abolish 'product' patents on chemicals. The government went even further, and allowed compulsory licensing on demand for all patents relating to medicine. These changes were not reversed until after the Second World War.[11]

It has been argued that England 'escaped' its status as an economically backward nation in the Middle Ages because it practised industrial piracy.[12] The economic history of the United States is similarly tainted ('American businessmen attempted to bypass British controls on technology, by illicitly importing state-of-the-art intellectual property').[13] Switzerland too—today a giant of the pharmaceutical industry—achieved prominence initially as a 'patent piracy' haven where German patents were safely imitated. The founder of Geigy AG denounced patents as a 'paradise for parasites'—Grubb believes he meant 'patent lawyers'.[14]

Historically, a patent grant was a 'reward':[15] the state bestowed it on the investor in return for making the invention available to the public. Not necessarily of

[7] See P Grubb, *Patents for Chemicals, Pharmaceuticals and Biotechnology: Fundamentals of Global Law, Practice and Strategy* (Oxford, 2004) 8.

[8] ibid 12.

[9] ibid 10–11. The UK Patents Office traces origins to the grant to a Flemish man by Henry VI in 1449 of a 20-year monopoly over the making of stained glass.

[10] See Grubb (n 7 above) 17–35.

[11] ibid 19.

[12] C VanGrasstek, 'Trade-Related Intellectual Property Rights: United Nations Trade Policy, Developing Countries and the Uruguay Round' in UNCTAD, *Uruguay Round: Further Papers on Selected Issues* (New York, 1990) 88.

[13] ibid.   [14] Grubb (n 7 above) 25.

[15] M Heywood, 'Drug Access, Patents and Global Health: "Chaffed and Waxed Sufficient"' (2002) 23 *Third World Quarterly* 217.

course the global public. When it suits an industrial nation to impose upon a drugs manufacturer, no qualms are expressed. Thus, in the moral panic post 9/11, the governments of the United States and Canada forced Bayer, makers of ciprofloxacin, to sell the drug at substantially reduced prices after threatening to issue compulsory licenses to generic manufacturers.[16] But, as Sterckx notes, 'differences in national priorities, which are closely connected to different levels of economic development, justify [ie are used to justify] a different approach to intellectual property protection'.[17] It is offensive that many patented drugs are substantially higher priced in the developing world than they are in some developed countries. This is partly the result of price caps on pharmaceuticals in many industrialized countries. Over-pricing pharmaceuticals—putting them beyond the reach of most who need them in the developing world—actually prevents the companies themselves getting the optimal use out of their patents. In fact, it is in their best business interests to reduce prices. And so we get arguments for, and some policies to implement, price reductions and private-public partnerships.[18] But these tend to be ad hoc, and do not address fundamental ethical questions. They fail to address, most obviously, the justification for granting patents for life-saving pharmaceutical products. This is part of a bigger question as to what can be subject to ownership. The *Moore* case famously addressed this.[19] This is not a route I intend to go down here, though I have addressed it elsewhere.[20]

But the question must be raised in relation to life-saving pharmaceutical drugs. Granted that research and development has to be funded, but does it follow that the burden of paying for it—it potentially benefits all humanity—should fall on those who purchase or pay for the drugs they need to stay alive? The provision of charity and price discounts merely scratch the surface. Do we not need to go deeper and rethink and reform, in effect to start again? Article 25 of the Universal Declaration of Human Rights recognizes that all individuals have the right to medical care.[21] Section 14 of the UNESCO

---

[16] B Loff and M Heywood, 'Patents on Drugs: Manufacturing Scarcity or Advancing Health? (2002) 30 *Journal of Law, Medicine and Ethics* 621.

[17] S Sterckx, *Biotechnology, Patents and Morality* (Aldershot, 2000). See also S Sterckx, 'Patents and Access to Drugs in Developing Countries' (2004) 4 *Developing World Bioethics* 58.

[18] eg Brennan and Baines (n 6 above) 41.

[19] 793 P2d 479 (1990).

[20] M Freeman, 'Biotechnology, Patients and Profits: How Is The Law to Respond?' in I Robinson (ed); *Life and Death Under High Technology Medicine* (Manchester, 1994) 118; and M Freeman, 'Taking the Body Seriously?' in K Stern and P Walsh (eds); *Property Rights in the Human Body* (London, 1997) 13. See also CA Erin, 'Who Owns Mo?: Using Historical Entitlement Theory to Decide The Ownership of Human Derived Cell Lines' in AO Dyson and J Harris (eds), *Ethics and Biotechnology* (London, 1994) 157; SR Munzer, 'An Uneasy Case against Property Rights in Body Parts' (1994) 11(2) *Social Philosophy and Policy* 259; and D Dickenson, *Property in the Body*: *Feminist Perspective* (Cambridge, 2007).

[21] See JL Kunz, 'The United Nations Declaration of Human Rights' (1949) 43 *AJIL* 316. And see GJ Annas, 'Human Rights and Health—The Universal Declaration of Human Rights at 50' in S Gruskin, MA Grodin, GJ Annas, SP Marks (eds) ; *Perspectives on Health and Human Rights* (New York, 2005) 63.

Universal Declaration of Bioethics 2005 proclaims that all individuals have a fundamental human right to the 'enjoyment of the highest attainable standard of health'. The mismatch between these norms and practice is huge, and so long as current practices prevail will be unbridgeable.

II. Why Protect Patents: The Utilitarian Case

What is the case for protecting patents in pharmaceutical products? Most often put are arguments grounded in utilitarian ethics. The pharmaceutical companies themselves argue that without patent protection of innovative drugs, research and development (R&D) would stall. It was estimated (in 2001) that about US $24 billion a year was spent on clinical research by the world's fifteen largest pharmaceutical companies—it is certainly more now, perhaps as much as US $60 billion.[22] Thus it is argued that unless invention is fully compensated there will be sub-optimal incentives to pursue research. Of course, the availability of patents does lead to more inventions of drugs. But it also leads to price increases: the price of patented drugs can be kept artificially high. Those who put this argument assume that it applies also to drug development—for example to drugs for tropical diseases—in developing countries. But this is not happening: few drugs for diseases which are endemic to the developing world are being developed. Of the 1,223 molecules that were sold worldwide between 1975 and 1996, less than 1 per cent targeted tropical diseases.[23] That the developing world is not developing responses is not because of patent protection norms, but because of a weak economic infrastructure. Meanwhile pharmaceutical companies in the developed world would, as one critic put it, 'rather give a rich white guy an erection than help an African with AIDS'.[24] 'More money is invested in research against baldness than in research of all tropical diseases combined.'[25]

There is evidence to suggest that expenditure on R&D is grossly inflated. The fifteen largest pharmaceutical companies spend almost three times more per year on marketing, advertising, and administration than on R&D. A significant part of R&D funding is devoted to extending existing patent protection: acquiring patents and annual maintenance fees required to retain it.[26] Nor should the

---

[22] See D Resnick, 'Developing Drugs for the Developing World: An Economic, Legal, Moral and Political Dilemma' (2001) 1 *Developing World Bioethics* 11.

[23] B Pécoul, P Chirac, P Trouiller, and J Pinel, 'Access to Essential Drugs in Poor Countries—A Lost Battle?' (1999) 281 *JAMA* 365, Table 2.

[24] DG McNeil, Jr, 'As Devastating Epidemics Increase, Nations Take On Drugs Companies' *New York Times*, 9 July 2000. According to Sterckx (2004) (n 17 above) 69, the pharmaceutical industry makes its biggest profits on hair tonics, anti-impotency, drugs for cholesterol, ulcers, depression, allergies, and high blood pressure.

[25] Sterckx (2004) (n 17 above) 69.

[26] H M Haugen, 'Intellectual Property—Rights or Privileges?' (2006) 8(4) *Journal of World Intellectual Property* 445.

taxpayer's contribution to R&D be overlooked: a high level of public funding stimulates private profit. This varies from country to country—and no figure can be put on it—but we may be sure the sums involved are huge, and unaccounted for.[27] It is clear that, as elsewhere, private firms are spending public funds, and that transfers of public property to the private sector go relatively unchallenged.[28]

Defenders of pharmaceutical companies have to confront the 'super-normal' profits they garner. Profits may be as much as three times those of other industries.[29] But the only defence we get is the 'development and testing of new drugs is an expensive and risky business'.[30] Is it really that risky when pharmaceuticals have been rated first or second on the list of the most profitable industries for more than thirty of the past forty years?[31] It is very difficult to see how an industry that is so successful can justify further net gains by citing 'risk'. In what sense do they experience 'losses' as a result of lack of patent protection in the developing world? It is often unquestioned that they do. Thus, Resnik, hardly one of their defenders, writes (in 2005) that 'it is hard to say exactly how much money pharmaceutical companies lose as a result of the failure to recognise patents globally'.[32] The argument based on loss is disingenuous.

III. Patents and Natural Rights

Another defence of patent protection cites natural rights: society has an obligation to protect these rights to ideas and inventions. The source of this argument is, of course, Locke's 'labour theory of property'. According to Locke the appropriation of a thing occurs when man applies his labour to it, 'mixing' the thing with his labour. As Locke puts it, the: 'Condition of Human Life, which requires Labour and Materials to work on, necessarily introduces private Possessions.'[33] This is not the place to tease out Locke's thesis in detail—a pity because it is all too apparent that contemporary defenders of patents who cite Locke have at best a superficial understanding of him. Thus, Locke saw the invention of money as an event which changed his simple labour theory. It increased the inequality of possessions made possible by the 'different degrees of Industry'[34] which

---

[27] And see S Sell, *Private Power Public Law: Globalisation of IP Rights* (New York, 2003).

[28] But see AM Pollock, *NHS plc: The Privatisation of Our Health Care* (London, 2004).

[29] See Brennan and Baines (n 6 above) 35. See also C O'Manique, *Neoliberalism and AIDS Crisis in Sub-Saharan Africa: Globalization's Pandemic* (New York, 2004), 85.

[30] *Per* Brennan and Baines (n 6 above) 35.

[31] See O'Manique, (n 29 above) 85. See also SS Hunter, *Who Cares? Ethics and AIDS in Africa* (New York, 2003).

[32] D Resnik; 'Access to Affordable Medication in the Developing World: Social Responsibility vs Profit' in A van Niekerk and L Kopelman (eds); *Ethics and Aids in Africa: The Challenge To Our Thinking* (Walnut Creek, Calif. 2005) 111, 121.

[33] Locke, *Two Treatises of Government* II, 35.

[34] ibid 38.

men display. In Locke's view it made it possible for a man to 'possess more than he can use the product of'.[35] Labour may be an uncontentious good, but the role of money is altogether 'more ambiguous'.[36] As Dunn points out, the 'entire social and economic order of seventeenth-century England rested upon a human institution about whose moral status Locke felt deeply ambivalent'.[37] Taking away the produce of a man's labour was not justifiable, but Locke had fewer qualms about taking away the profits of speculation. Locke also defended welfare rights.[38] For example, he insisted that if a man insisted on market price for a man dying of hunger and caused his death by so doing, he was guilty of murder.[39] He even argued that charity gave every man a title 'to so much out of another's Plenty, as will keep him from extreme want' for 'God requires him to afford to the wants of his Brother'.[40]

Little attention has been paid to the implications of this for pharmaceutical companies. But Sterckx[41] doubts whether the conditions which Locke stipulates to justify a property right are met by pharmaceutical companies. These are that there must be enough left for others, and man is not permitted to appropriate more than he can use. She also disposes of Nozick's defence of Locke's first condition. Nozick's defence, which is specifically targeted at patents, is interesting, if unconvincing. Asking himself the question whether appropriation worsens the situation of others, he responds that this is not necessarily so. Nozick claims: 'If I appropriate a grain of sand from Coney Island, no one else may now do as they wish with *that* grain of sand. But there are plenty of other grains of sand left for them to do the same with or if not grains of sand, then other things.'[42] This argument—whatever its merits elsewhere—is manifestly inapplicable to patents on pharmaceutical products, most obviously because it is that grain of sand that is needed. As for Locke's second proviso—the non-waste condition—the patent system can lead to waste because it does not require patent holders to exploit their invention.

IV. Patents as Distributive Justice

The third defence of the patent system is based on distributive justice. The argument is straightforward: fairness dictates a reward for those who provide a service to society. Otherwise, the rest of us, non-inventors, would become free-riders. But inventors can be rewarded in other ways than granting them exclusive rights of ownership on their inventions. Hettinger believes the mistake is to conflate the

---

[35] ibid 50.
[36] See J Dunn, *Locke* (Oxford, 1984) 40. See also KM McClure, *Judging Rights* (Ithaca, NY, 1996) Ch. 4.
[37] ibid.   [38] As Aquinas had done in the 13th century.
[39] 'Venditio' in J Dunn, 'Justice and the Interpretation of Locke's Political Theory' (1968) XVII *Political Studies* 84.
[40] Locke (n 33 above) 42.
[41] Sterckx (n 17 above) 63.
[42] R Nozick, *Anarchy, State and Utopia* (New York, 1974) 175.

created object which makes a person deserving of a reward with what that reward should be. Property rights in the created object are not the only possible reward. Alternatives include 'fees, awards, acknowledgement, gratitude, praise, security, power, status, and public financial support'.[43] It should not be overlooked, though it frequently is, that the R&D which produces the pharmaceutical innovations is largely publicly-funded. Much of it takes place at universities and other publicly-funded institutions which sell it to companies for what are in effect derisory fees.[44] Sterckx notes that in the United States—I would expect the figure to be higher in the United Kingdom and elsewhere in Europe—55 per cent of the research projects leading to the discovery and development of the five best-selling drugs in 1995 were carried out by researchers whose work was financed with taxpayers' money.[45] For example, two key HIV/AIDS drugs were developed respectively at Yale University and the University of Minnesota, and are now licensed exclusively to Bristol-Myers Squibb and Glaxo Smith Kline.[46]

If the justification is fairness, the question still arises as to whether excessive rewards can be justified. 'Patent evergreening'—the extension of protection terms of patents—is common, and it frustrates the development of generic drugs which are, of course, much cheaper. And if the justification is fairness, then justice, may dictate that the developing world ignores product patents as a way of bridging the gap between the developed world and itself.[47]

V. Alternative Models

Many of the pro-patent arguments rest on the assumption that the private corporate model is the only one which can support the R&D required to meet global health needs. Thus, Kettler[48] purports to evaluate costs and benefits of three models of R&D—the commercial, the public-private, and the wholly public—but dismisses the public model in a paragraph. The other two, she says, have the 'greatest prospect of progressing R&D in neglected diseases'.[49] The public model is discussed by reference to an initiative by *Médicins sans frontières*, and contains the dismissive comment that MSF must demonstrate how it will be able to raise the funds necessary to duplicate the industry know-how and resources and that

[43] EC Hettinger, 'Justifying Intellectual Property' (1989) 18 *Philosophy and Public Affairs* 31, 41. See also L Becker, *Property Rights* (London, 1977).

[44] A point also made by Schüklenk and Ashcroft in Niekerk and Kopelman (n 32 above) 136.

[45] Sterckx (2004) (n 17 above) 65.

[46] And for a 'paltry' fee. See J Backley and S Ótuama, 'International Pricing and Distribution of Therapeutic Pharmaceuticals: An Ethical Minefield' (2005) 14 *Business Ethics: a European Review* 132.

[47] See also DW Brock, 'Some Questions about the Moral Responsibilities of Drug Companies in Developing Countries' (2001) 1 *Developing World Bioethics* 33.

[48] H E Kettler, 'Using Intellectual Property Regimes to Meet Global Health R&D Needs' (2002)5(5) *Journal of World Intellectual Property* 655.

[49] ibid, 657.

this is a more efficient use of scarce funds than 'negotiating agreeable terms with companies directly'.[50] Not surprisingly, there is no reference to Cuba. A recent report on this[51] notes that 'modest infrastructure investments combined with a well-developed public health strategy have generated health status measures comparable with those of industrialized countries, particularly in the control of infectious diseases, reduction in infant mortality, establishment of a research and biotechnology industry, and progress in control of chronic diseases'. A number of common diseases have been entirely eliminated. The Cuban biotechnology industry, in something like twenty years, has advanced to the point that some of its products are being licensed by foreigners, including in some cases US Corporations who have, of course, to surmount the hurdle of getting US government approval to waive the embargo on Cuba. These include the world's only type B meningitis vaccine, licensed to Smith Kline Beecham, and revolutionary cancer drugs licensed to CancerVax, a Californian biotechnology company.[52] Other Cuban-developed drugs may follow, including recombined vaccines against AIDS and hepatitis C.[53]

So where should developing countries be looking? Should they aspire to adopt the model propagated by industrialized countries though the World Trade Organization (WTO) and TRIPS? Or will they learn more by examining the Cuban experience and the evidence emerging from Cuba? Cooper *et al* believe that the Cuban public health programme is well within the reach of most middle-income countries.[54] The Cuban model can be operationalized without replicating its political context.[55] Cuban Medical Brigades are in a number of countries, including Ghana, Namibia, and South Africa. But the Cuban model has yet to spread, though it cannot be long before it takes root in countries like Venezuela and Bolivia. Of South Africa it has been said that 'a cold-hearted economic calculus on the part of the elite may conclude that it is more efficient to let people die than to raise taxes to try to save them'.[56]

The developing world may also look to Indian policies. The Patents Act in India in 1970 removed patent protection on pharmaceutical products. As a result of this, the number of domestically-registered pharmaceutical producers increased nearly

[50]   ibid.

[51]   RS Cooper, JF Kennelly and P Orduñez-Garcia, 'Health in Cuba' (2006) 35(4) *International Journal of Epidemiology* 817.

[52]   See J Randall, 'Embargos and Economics: the Birth of Biotechnology in Cuba' (2003) 13 *Journal of The National Cancer Institute* 962.

[53]   On the taboo against discussing this, see JM Spiegel, 'Commentary: Daring To Learn from a Good Example and Break the "Cuba Taboo"' (2006) 35 *International Journal of Epidemiology* 825.

[54]   Cooper, Kelly, and Orduñez-Garcia (n 51 above) 817–22.

[55]   Cuba does honour foreign patents, and it has a patent office. It did, however, achieve some notoriety when it countered the impact of HIV/AIDS by segregating those infected from the general population. See R Bayer and C Healton, 'Controlling AIDS in Cuba: the Logic of Quarantine' (1989) 320 *New England Journal of Medicine* 1022.

[56]   N Nattrass, 'Rolling out Antiretroviral Treatment in South Africa: Economic and Ethical Challenges' in Niekerk and Kopelman (n 32 above) 39, 43.

five-fold. Production multiplied by 48: a more competitive environment was created in which the prices of medicines remained 'within the reach of the common man'.[57] This supports the hypothesis that international patents block off areas of scientific development without compensating benefit to the public: according to Deardoff, 'inventive activity diminishes the more the patent spreads'.[58] But, as Schüklenk and Ashcroft put it, 'intellectual property rights are designed to promote innovation in the public interest … where they contravene the public interest, the justification for their enforcement … is removed'.[59]

VI. Towards Globalized Public Health Law—and Human Rights

This, it may be argued, is where we need to insert a human rights perspective. Current theories of public health law only rarely address the interdependency between law at the national and international levels.[60] But one cannot 'isolate a state from its global interactions and focus on the relationship between law and public health within impermeable [national] borders'.[61] There is a need for a 'globalized theory of public health law',[62] which would include multinational organizations within its parameters. As Fidler points out, 'states are no longer the only entities that possess power to act for the betterment or detriment of the public health'.[63] Just as science does not always concentrate on the most serious and widespread problems, so 'ethics committees also fail to address the needs of the poor. The majority of inter-national biomedical research has inequality as its foundation.'[64] So Farmer and Campos advocate 'a human rights approach that concerns itself especially with the poor'.[65] They point to the gap between the rhetoric of instruments like the Universal Declaration of Human Rights and practice, to 'double standards for rich and poor'.[66] In the global world order, 'global health equality must be a goal of any serious ethical charter'.[67] Governments of developed countries in particular must transcend their responsibility for protecting

---

[57] See V Shiva, 'TRIPS, Human Rights and the Public Domain' (2006) *Journal of World Intellectual Property* 665.

[58] S Deardoff, 'Welfare Effects of Global Patent Protection' (1992) 59 *Economica* 33, 47.

[59] U Schüklek and R Ashcroft, 'Affordable Access To Essential Medication in Developing Countries: Conflicts Between Ethical and Economic Imperatives' in Niekerk and Kopelman (n 32 above) 127, 137.

[60] See D Fidler, 'A Globalized Theory of Public Health Law' (2002) 30 *Journal of Law, Medicine and Ethics* 150. And see B Bennett, *Health, Rights and Globalisation* (Aldershot, 2006).

[61] D Fidler (n 60 above).

[62] In addition to Fidler (n 60 above), see J Frenk and O Gómez-Dantés, 'Globalisation and the Challenges in Health systems' (2002) 325 *BMJ* 95.

[63] Fidler (n 60 above).

[64] P Farmer and N G Campos, 'New Malaise: Bioethics and Human Rights in the Global Era' (2004) 32 *Journal of Law, Medicine and Ethics* 243.

[65] ibid. See also P Farmer, *Infections and Inequalities: the Modern Plagues* (Berkeley, 1999).

[66] Farmer and Campos (n 64 above).   [67] ibid.

the health of their own population and move instead towards a 'population-based approach that is transactional in orientation'.[68]

There is thus a need, Farmer and Campos argue, to 'resocialize the way we see ethical dilemmas in medicine'.[69] Only if we do this can we avoid ignoring large parts of the world's population. A lesson we have surely learned from human rights thinking generally is that human rights are of value only when they protect the rights of those who are most likely to have their rights violated.

Access to essential medicines is an issue of human rights. Universal access to affordable essential medicines must be recognized as a core element of the international right to health; what for the developed world is hegemony is death to the developing world. To argue, as is done, that diminution of patent protection leads to less R&D and is therefore contrary to the interests of all humanity is a form of moral blackmail. As pointed out earlier in this chapter, industrialized countries used piracy to develop their industries. Can they now deny this opportunity to the poor nations of the world? As Michael Hardt and Antonio Negri point out,[70] 'juridical concepts...always refer to something other than themselves...They point toward the material condition that defines their purchase on social reality'. Moreover, 'every juridical system is in some way a crystallization of a specific set of values, because ethics is part of the materiality of every juridical foundation'.[71] The juridical concept of a patent is nothing more than the sum of ethical, moral, and political justifications and rationalizations that animate it, together with the historical and political mechanisms that develop, evolve, and put it into practice.

The ethical debate over the enforcement of patents in developing countries faced with public health crises is a debate over the very meaning of the notion of patent.[72] Multinational pharmaceutical corporations and governments of industrialized countries have misconstrued this meaning. Intellectual property law should be considered within the body of international human rights law, and therefore be implemented consistently with human rights such as the right to health.[73] 'Any intellectual property regime that makes it more difficult for a state party to comply with its core obligations in relation to health, food, education or any other *right* set out in the covenant, is inconsistent with the legally binding obligations of the State party.'[74]

[68] JH Flory and P Kitcher, 'Global Health and the Scientific Research Agenda' (2004) 32 *Philosophy and Public Affairs* 36.

[69] Farmer and Campos (n 64 above).

[70] M Hardt and A Negri, *Empire* (Cambridge, Mass., 2000), 22.

[71] ibid 10.

[72] Itself requiring interpretation: see R Dworkin, *Law's Empire* (London, 1986).

[73] See P Cullet, 'Patents and Medicine: The Relationship Between TRIPS and the Human Right To Health' in Gruskin *et al* (n 21 above) 115.

[74] Committee on Economic, Social and Cultural Rights, General Comment No 14: The Right To The Highest Attainable Standard of Health, UN doc E/C 12/2000/4, 4 July 2000.

7

Magic, Myths, and Fairy Tales: Consent and the Relationship Between Law and Ethics

Alasdair R Maclean

I. Introduction

In a sense the relationship between law and ethics is obvious: both purport to provide guidance in our dealings with other members of our social community. As Miola opined: 'for as long as courts and ethics have existed, their interconnection has been nothing if not inevitable'.[1] However, while ethics details both the unacceptable and the desirable, law tends to focus on the minimally acceptable or what may be reasonably expected of each of us. Thus, while the law may, and arguably should, be informed by ethics, the two necessarily diverge. Furthermore, the law must provide a single standard of behaviour that provides consistent and coherent guidance. Different ethical standards, however, may coexist. Because of this, even where the law comports to one system of ethics it is always open to criticism from other ethical perspectives. In a liberal democracy, this means that the law exists in a constant state of flux under tension from the scrutiny of competing ethical views.

This is a healthy state of affairs because it means that the arrogance of infallibility never gains a foothold,[2] and the dominant norms are constantly under pressure with the possibility of revision always hovering in the background. The law, particularly the judge-made reactive common law, is always open to the influence of ethical discourses challenging the dominant view. In the context of healthcare provision, the power of the medical profession traditionally allowed the dominant approach to remain relatively safe from external challenge. More recently, with the development of the discipline of bioethics and other societal changes, the traditional norms have come under increasing

---

[1] J Miola, 'The relationship between medical law and ethics' (2006) 1 *Clinical Ethics* 22.
[2] JS Mill, 'On Liberty', in J Gray (ed), *On Liberty and Other Essays* (Oxford, 1991) 5.

scrutiny and challenge and this continuing ethical critique is at its strongest in the field of healthcare law.[3] In this chapter I will examine the possible impact that this relatively new discourse has had on the legal regulation of consent to medical treatment, focusing particularly on the legal duty to disclose information.

Before turning to consider the relationship between the law and ethics of consent, it should be noted that medical ethical discourse is not an homogenous set of influences.[4] Legal development may be affected by the professional ethical guidance issued by bodies such as the General Medical Council (GMC), the Royal Colleges, and the British Medical Association (BMA). Equally, it may be influenced by academic commentary. These different sources complicate the influence that ethics has on the developing law and may lead to inconsistencies and a lack of coherence.

The risk of inconsistency or incoherence is exacerbated because the influence may not always be direct. Ethical discourse may be presented to the courts by medical experts or by lawyers relying on expositions by legal commentators. This latter influence is likely to increase as ever more lawyers are exposed to ethics through the now obligatory chapter in new textbooks on medical law. This means that even before the ethical arguments have reached the judges they have been subject to at least one level of filtering and interpretation. The problem with this is that the courts are exposed to ethical arguments that may differ significantly from the original source. This filtering adds bias and the risk of misinterpretation even before the ethical argument is exposed to the institution of law, which may further shape the argument. Finally, this Chinese whispers effect is further exacerbated by the inconsistent appeal of the courts to ethical discourse and by its indirect impact on judicial decision-making through its influence on the politics of society.

Before looking at how the law has developed since the inception of bioethics I will briefly discuss the concepts of consent and autonomy in order to explicate the scope for influence.

II. The Concepts of Consent and Autonomy

Consent derives from the Latin *con sentire* meaning 'to feel together'. In the legal context it is used in two ways. It may be used in the sense of an agreement, which acts to alter the respective parties' obligations, and this is how the term is used in contract law. In the context of healthcare treatment, consent is used to mean permission. If I give you consent to do something I grant you permission to do

---

[3] W Van Der Burg, 'Bioethics and Law: A Developmental Perspective' (1997) 11 *Bioethics* 91, 93.

[4] J Miola, 'The relationship between medical law and ethics' (2006) 1 *Clinical Ethics* 22, 23. J Miola, 'Medical Law and Medical Ethics—Complementary or Corrosive' (2004) 6 *Medical Law International* 251, 253.

something that would otherwise be unlawful. In other words consent transforms the forbidden to the permitted, both morally and legally.[5]

For consent to work in this way the person granting consent must have the moral or legal right to grant permission: while I can give you consent to use a bicycle, unless I own the bicycle my consent is legally and morally ineffective and your use of the bike will remain illegitimate. Thus, the right—or power—to give (or withhold) consent is derivative of a primary underlying right.[6] This primary right may be broadly conceived of as the right to bodily integrity and the right to control that right is usually justified by an appeal to the value of individual autonomy. So far this is all relatively straightforward, however, matters become more complicated because neither autonomy nor consent are value neutral and the meanings of both concepts are affected by one's political suasion.[7]

Consent may be seen as a state of mind,[8] as an act of communication,[9] or as some combination of the two.[10] At the libertarian extreme, consent is simply a state of mind or propositional attitude and the rules of consent focus entirely on the autonomous individual who is conceived of as isolated from dependent relationships. At the communitarian extreme, consent is seen solely as an act of communication with the rules of consent being more concerned with the process of interaction between the parties than with the, necessarily relational, autonomy of the person giving consent. Between these two extremes the rules of consent may be more nuanced, acknowledging that consent must temper protection of the individual's autonomy with an approach that does justice to the other party involved in the communicative process that culminates in the person giving or withholding consent.

The variable nature of consent provides one axis for influence. Other axes arise because of the varied nature of autonomy. Although there are many different conceptions of autonomy,[11] it is possible to tease out three broad approaches.[12] First, autonomy may be equated with self-determination. Second, there are conceptions that include a requirement for rationality. Third, some views of autonomy include both rationality and a moral element. A related axis reflects varying degrees of dependency. At the libertarian extreme, autonomy isolates the individual as the independent frontiersman. At the communitarian extreme, individuals are so co-dependant that the idea of personal autonomy is rendered meaningless.

---

[5] L Alexander, 'The Moral Magic of Consent (II)' (1996) 2 *Legal Theory* 165.

[6] R Brownsword, 'The Cult of Consent: Fixation and Fallacy' (2004) 15 *King's College Law Journal* 223, 225.

[7] A Maclean, 'Consent and Sensibility' (2005) 4 *International Journal of Ethics* 31.

[8] HM Hurd, 'The Moral Magic of Consent' (1996) 2 *Legal Theory* 121.

[9] A Wertheimer, 'Consent and Sexual Relations' (1996) 2 *Legal Theory* 89, 94.

[10] E Sherwin, 'Infelicitous Sex' (1996) 2 *Legal Theory* 209, 217.

[11] G Dworkin, *The Theory and Practice of Autonomy* (Cambridge, 1988) 5–6.

[12] Maclean (n 7 above) 39.

Finally, where autonomy requires rationality this adds another axis of variation that could influence the way in which consent is regulated.[13] At one extreme of this axis is the Humean view of rationality, which is purely instrumental. In this view, it is only the means of achieving my desires or goals—rather than the content of those aims—that are subject to rationality. At the other extreme, compatible with communitarian and virtue ethics, is the recognitional view of rationality, which imposes an objective list of goals and values. The constructivist approach to rationality sits between these two extremes.

In Frankfurt's liberal model of reflective rationality, which is closer to Humean rationality than to the recognitional model, the individual must reflect on their first order desires to ensure that they do not conflict with higher order goals and values.[14] A second type of constructivist rationality, which moves further from the Humean approach, is Kant's view, in which rationality is constrained by the Categorical Imperative that any self-legislated law must be universalizable.[15] O'Neill's accessible-ends model is a compromise that sits between Kant's approach and the recognitional model. For O'Neill, the assessor does not need to agree with the person's decisions, however, he or she must be able to understand those choices.[16] In this model, the person's goals and values do not need to be *acceptable* to the assessor. However, they must be *accessible*.

In this brief examination of the concepts of consent and autonomy I have highlighted how these concepts are open to interpretation and how different ethical approaches favour different views. This has practical importance because the rules of consent are dependent on the normative models of autonomy and consent and any change to the models, if accepted by the courts, will affect the legal regulation of consent. As Lee argued: 'Determining the content of consent is a creative exercise. Judges interpret it according to some vision of why consent is important and of the values which the law should espouse.'[17] In the subsequent sections of this chapter, I will examine the law's approach to consent and the duty to disclose and consider how the rules have changed over the last quarter of a century. I will explore the way in which the law's development has followed the dominant ethical approach and, although I make no particular claim about a direct causal relationship between the two discourses, I will suggest that the ethical discourse has, at least, had an indirect effect. Finally, I will look at the recent ethical challenges raised against the concept of 'informed consent'.

---

[13] The following approach is based on: B Gaut, 'The Structure of Practical Reason' in G Cullity and B Gaut (eds), *Ethics and Practical Reason* (Oxford, 1997) 161–2.

[14] H Frankfurt, 'Freedom of the Will and the Concept of a Person' in R Kane (ed), *Free Will* (Malden, Mass., 2002) 127.

[15] G Cullity and B Gaut, 'Introduction' in Cullity and Gaut 1, 3–5.

[16] O O'Neill, *Towards Justice and Virtue* (Cambridge, 1996) 58.

[17] S Lee, 'Towards a Jurisprudence of Consent' in J Eekelaar and J Bell, (eds) *Oxford Essays in Jurisprudence: 3rd Series* (Oxford, 1987) 199, 201.

III. Consent and the Legal Duty to Disclose

It is trite to note that the law does not develop in a vacuum and that the ethical concerns are not the only influence affecting the construction of the regulatory rules. Other more pragmatic matters either constrain the law's ability or
temper its willingness to develop an ethically coherent jurisprudence. To begin
with, there is no statute specifically governing the law of consent to healthcare
interventions. The legal rules have developed as part of the common law and just
as there is no specific statute so there is no distinct tort that regulates those interactions.[18] This means that the judges have had to apply existing torts however
imperfectly they suit the context.[19]

Since it specifically governs intentional interference with the body of another
person, the tort of battery is perhaps the most relevant private action. However,
while battery has been used to regulate healthcare interventions there are a
number of factors that restrict its use. The primary reasons are the judiciary's
reluctance[20] to find healthcare professionals liable for battery because of its association with criminal behaviour and the need to control liability, which is easier
through the law of negligence than the law of battery.[21] The consequence of this
was that information about risks and alternative options became separated from
the knowledge required for a 'real' consent necessary to avoid liability for battery.[22] Instead, this additional information formed the basis for a duty to disclose
regulated through the law of negligence.

Because the split was made for pragmatic rather than ethically principled reasons, it has resulted in a conceptually incoherent situation, which complicates any
analysis of the influence that ethics may have on the law of consent. Furthermore,
most of the legal claims are for the physical damage resulting from a materialized
risk, rather than for the failure of consent per se. Thus, my focus will be on the
duty to disclose in negligence.

A. *Sidaway*

The House of Lords case of *Sidaway* is a useful starting point. The case, which
reached the House of Lords in 1984, concerned an operation performed some

---

[18] Similarly, there is no specific criminal offence. This chapter, however, is concerned with the
civil law.
[19] E Jackson, ' "Informed Consent" to Medical Treatment and the Impotence of Tort' in SAM
McLean (ed), *First Do No Harm* (Aldershot, 2006) 273.
[20] *Sidaway v Board of Governors of the Bethlem Royal Hospital* [1985] AC 871, 885 *per* Lord
Scarman; *Davis v Barking, Havering and Brentwood HA* [1993] 4 MedLR 85, 90.
[21] M Brazier, 'Patient autonomy and consent to treatment: the role of the law?' (1987) 7 *Legal
Studies* 169, 180; G Robertson, 'Informed consent to medical treatment' (1981) 97 *LQR* 102,
123–4.
[22] *Chatterton v Gerson* [1981] 1 All ER 257, 265.

ten years previously in 1974. The plaintiff was left partially paralysed following an operation on her neck. While it was accepted that the operation had been performed competently, she claimed that the surgeon had negligently failed to warn her of the risk. While their Lordships were unanimous in deciding that he was not negligent, the case is important to this discussion because of the different approaches adopted by their Lordships.

Prior to the *Sidaway* case, the duty to disclose the risks of a procedure was determined by the *Bolam* test. In *Bolam v Friern HMC*, McNair J directed the jury, *inter alia*, that the question of whether a failure to disclose the risks of electroconvulsive therapy was negligent depended on whether the doctor: 'acted in accordance with a practice accepted as proper by a responsible body of medical men skilled in that particular art...Putting it the other way round, a man is not negligent, if he is acting in accordance with such practice *merely* because there is a body of opinion who would take the contrary view'.[23]

This test formed the basis for the judgments of all of their Lordships except for Lord Scarman. Lord Diplock applied the *Bolam* test *simpliciter*, while Lord Bridge, with whom Lord Keith agreed, applied the test with the caveat that there were some risks so obviously relevant that it would always be negligent to fail to disclose them.[24] Lord Templeman did not actually refer to the *Bolam* test. Nonetheless, echoes of the test permeate the whole of his speech. Like Lord Bridge, he also held that there were some risks that should always be disclosed.

Lord Diplock's speech was the most paternalistic, evidencing deference to the medical profession that was the norm prior to the developing influence of the ethical challenge to the traditional hegemony. His approach was underscored by his belief that the beneficent medical profession would advise what was best for the patient and, unless the patient specifically requested the information, they should be allowed to control what the patients were told in order to ensure that they were not deterred from consenting to the recommended treatment. This was because patients—unlike the judge (a 'highly educated man of experience')—would generally lack the kind of education and training that would make it appropriate for them to want to decide for themselves.[25]

In a less paternalistic speech, Lord Bridge acknowledged 'the logical force' of the doctrine of informed consent.[26] However, he nonetheless rejected it because it was 'impractical'. For Lord Bridge, whether a particular risk should be disclosed in order to enable the patient to make a 'rational' decision was 'primarily...a matter of clinical judgment' governed by the *Bolam* test.[27] This ultimately deferential approach to the ethical conscience of the professional was qualified by an inclination of the head towards the patient's right to self-determination.

---

[23]   *Bolam v Friern Hospital Management Committee* [1957] 1 WLR 582, 587.
[24]   The one exception to this may be where disclosure would fall within the therapeutic privilege exception.
[25]   *Sidaway v Board of Governors of the Bethlem Royal Hospital* [1985] AC 871, 895.
[26]   ibid 899.   [27]   ibid 900.

As noted earlier, Lord Bridge added the caveat that 'a substantial risk of grave adverse consequences' (such as a 10 per cent risk of stroke) must be disclosed.[28] Lord Templeman arrived at a similar standard to Lord Bridge.

Lord Scarman was the only one of their Lordships willing to accept the doctrine of informed consent and incorporate the prudent patient test within English law. It is notable that he acknowledged his reliance on two articles, one written by Gerald Robertson and the other by Ian Kennedy (see below).[29] Like Kennedy, his approach was predicated on: 'The right of "self-determination"—the description applied by some to what is no more and no less than the right of the patient to determine for himself whether he will or will not accept the doctor's advice.'[30] Unlike the other Law Lords, Lord Scarman took an essentially liberal/libertarian view of autonomy conceived of as self-determination.

B. The Law Following *Sidaway*

After the *Sidaway* case the Court of Appeal followed Lord Diplock's approach in the two well-known cases of *Blyth v Bloomsbury HA* and *Gold v Haringey HA*.[31] In doing so, the Court of Appeal largely ignored the response of the academic community. Although the reaction was mixed, most commentators saw *Sidaway* as at least modifying the *Bolam* test,[32] if not rejecting it outright.[33] The support for a law that protects patient autonomy was clear. Kennedy, for example, declared that: 'The message of *Sidaway* is clear. Those who advise doctors already know it. Medical paternalism has had its day.'[34] While Williams, who was less convinced of the impact of the *Sidaway* case, argued that, although the *Bolam* test had been modified, the House of Lords' rejection of the prudent patient test left the law in an 'unsatisfactory state' because it failed to provide sufficient support for individual autonomy.[35] Given the general academic support for patient autonomy it is unsurprising that both the *Blyth* and *Gold* cases were subject to sometimes scathing criticism.[36]

---

[28] ibid.   [29] ibid 886.   [30] ibid 882.

[31] *Blyth v Bloomsbury HA* [1993] 4 Med LR 151 (decided 1987); *Gold v Haringey HA* [1988] 1 QB 481.

[32] K Williams, 'Pre-operative Consent and Medical Negligence' (1985) 15 *Anglo-Am LR* 169, 179–180; D Giesen and J Hayes, 'The Patient's Right to Know—A Comparative View' (1992) 21 *Anglo-Am LR* 101, 103; H Teff, 'Consent to Medical Procedures: Paternalism, Self-determination or Therapeutic Alliance' (1985) 101 *LQR* 432, 450.

[33] I Kennedy, 'The Patient on the Clapham Omnibus' in *Treat Me Right: Essays in Medical Law and Ethics* (Oxford, 1988) 175; A Grubb, 'Contraceptive Advice and Doctors—A Law Unto Themselves' (1988) 47 *CLJ* 12, 13. See also, S Lee, 'Operating Under Informed Consent' (1985) 101 *LQR* 316.

[34] Kennedy (n 33 above) 210.   [35] Williams (n 32 above) 179–80.

[36] See eg J Montgomery, 'Power/Knowledge/Consent: Medical Decisionmaking' (1988) 51 *MLR* 245, 248; Grubb (n 33 above); S Lee, 'A Reversible Decision on Consent to Sterilisation' (1987) 103 *LQR* 513; I Kennedy, 'Consent to Treatment: The Capable Person' in C Dyer (ed), *Doctors, Patients and the Law* (Oxford, 1992) 44, 68–69; Giesen and Hayes (n 32 above) 104.

In the 1990s the judiciary showed an increased, although by no means consistent, willingness to challenge the opinions of expert witnesses and this was as true of cases involving failing to disclose as of other cases of negligence. This less deferential approach arguably reflected an increasing dissatisfaction with the accepted paternalism of the past. In *McAllister v Lewisham and North Southwark HA*, for example, Rougier J preferred Lord Bridge's judgment in the *Sidaway* case and found the defendants liable for the surgeon's failure to disclose the serious and significant risks of the operation to repair the vascular lesion in the plaintiff's head.[37] In rejecting the opinion of the defendant's expert witness, Rougier J noted that, 'within certain limitations, a patient is entitled to be given sufficient information on the risks of an operation to allow him or her to exercise a balanced judgment: after all it is their life which is going to be affected'.[38] Rougier J accepted the opinions of the plaintiff's experts, who maintained that responsible practice required 'sufficient information to enable her to make a properly informed choice'.[39]

In *Smith v Tunbridge Wells HA* Moorland J was prepared, on the authority of Lord Bridge's and Lord Templeman's speeches in the *Sidaway* case, to reject the common practice of withholding information regarding the risks of impotence and bladder dysfunction from an operation to repair a rectal prolapse as unreasonable.[40] Although the plaintiff's counsel raised the issue of the doctrine of informed consent by reference to the Australian case of *Rogers v Whittaker*,[41] Moorland J was bound by *Sidaway*. However, he noted that since the *Sidaway* decision in 1985 there had been an ever-increasing 'emphasis on informed consent'.[42] Similarly, in *Newell & Newell v Goldenberg* Mantell J was also prepared to hold that even if it were the common practice of some doctors, it was unreasonable not to disclose the risk of failure associated with a vasectomy.[43]

In *Pearce v United Bristol Healthcare NHS Trust*, which was heard in 1998, the Master of the Rolls, Lord Woolf, had the opportunity to revisit the requisite standard of information disclosure.[44] The case before the Court of Appeal involved a pregnant woman who was post-term, distressed, and primarily concerned for the health of her unborn child. The consultant obstetrician advised her to continue with conservative treatment without explaining that this carried a 0.1 to 0.2 per cent risk of stillbirth. The issue was whether this failure was negligent. Lord Woolf followed Lord Templeman's and, in particular, Lord Bridge's judgments in the *Sidaway* case, interpreting those speeches to hold that the *Bolam* test was subject to the caveat that: 'if there is a significant risk which

---

[37] *McAllister v Lewisham and North Southwark HA* [1994] 5 Med LR 343, 351.
[38] ibid 352.   [39] ibid.
[40] *Smith v Tunbridge Wells HA* [1994] 5 Med LR 334, 339.
[41] *Rogers v Whittaker* [1993] 4 Med LR 79.
[42] *Smith v Tunbridge Wells HA* [1994] 5 Med LR 334, 339.
[43] *Newell and Newell v Goldenberg* [1995] 6 Med LR 371, 374.
[44] *Pearce v United Bristol Healthcare NHS Trust* [1999] PIQR 53.

would affect the judgment of a reasonable patient, then in the normal course it is the responsibility of a doctor to inform the patient of that significant risk, if the information is needed so that the patient can determine for him or herself as to what course he or she should adopt'.[45] In deciding the case in favour of the defendants, however, Lord Woolf agreed with the expert medical witness's opinion that the 0.1 to 0.2 per cent risk was not significant and so there was no obligation to disclose it.

Like *Sidaway* before it, the *Pearce* case has been trumpeted as heralding the birth of informed consent in the United Kingdom. Brazier and Miola, for example, argued that read in conjunction with *Smith v Tunbridge Wells HA* 'Pearce signals that announcements of the stillbirth of "informed consent" in England were premature'.[46] Brazier and Miola underplayed the fact that in the *Pearce* case the question of significance was still determined by reference to the expert medical witness's opinion rather than to what the reasonable person would have thought. However, the decisions in subsequent cases perhaps support their prophecy, although there may be an element of self-fulfilment given that Lord Woolf, speaking extra judicially, appeared to find Brazier and Miola's arguments persuasive and he suggested that if any area of medical practice was to be subject to logical analysis it would be 'informed consent'.[47]

The House of Lords in *Chester v Afshar* supported Lord Woolf's approach.[48] Lord Steyn, for example, stated that: 'Surgery performed without the informed consent of the patient is unlawful. The court is the final arbiter of what constitutes informed consent. Usually, informed consent will presuppose a general warning by the surgeon of a significant risk of the surgery.'[49] Lord Steyn went on to state that the patient had an 'important' right to an 'appropriate warning' that should be given 'effective protection whenever possible'.[50] This right was predicated on a respect for the autonomy and dignity of the patient. To support his argument, Lord Steyn made direct reference to the ethical writings of Ronald Dworkin, accepting Dworkin's liberal view of autonomy as integrity.[51]

Lord Hope also based his speech on the patient's right to autonomy, which grounded the doctor's duty to warn.[52] Making explicit reference to Professor Jones's article 'Informed Consent and Other Fairy Stories',[53] Lord Hope noted the symbolic importance of the law and suggested that: 'The "happy ending" of his title would be found if the iterative process between case law and professional

---

[45] ibid 59.
[46] M. Brazier and J Miola, 'Bye-Bye Bolam: A Medical Revolution?' (2000) 8 *Medical Law Review* 85, 113.
[47] Lord Woolf, 'Are the Courts Excessively Deferential to the Medical Profession' (2000) 9 *Medical Law Review* 1, 10.
[48] *Chester v Afshar* [2005] 1 AC 134; see the judgments of Lords Steyn, Hope, and Walker.
[49] ibid 143, para 14.   [50] ibid 144, para 17.
[51] ibid 144, para 18.   [52] ibid 162, para 86.
[53] M Jones, 'Informed Consent and Other Fairy Stories' (1999) 7 *Medical Law Review* 103.

guidance were to lead to the creation of a more substantive "right" to truly informed consent for patients.'[54]

It is clear from this statement that Lord Hope recognized the relationship between law and ethics, at least at the formal level of professional ethics. The wider relationship was perhaps implicit in Lord Walker's statement that: 'during the 20 years which have elapsed since Sidaway's case the importance of personal autonomy has been more and more widely recognised'.[55] Like Lords Steyn and Hope, Lord Walker connected this to the doctor's duty to warn.

Support for the view that the law in England is moving steadily towards the doctrine of informed consent may be found in *Wyatt v Curtis*. In discussing the standard of disclosure, Sedley LJ referred to Lord Woolf's approach in the *Pearce* case. He stated: 'Lord Woolf's formulation refines Lord Bridge's test by recognising that what is substantial and what is grave are questions on which the doctor's and the patient's perception may differ, and in relation to which the doctor must therefore have regard to what may be the patient's perception.'[56]

By specifically associating the question of significance with the patient, this goes beyond the way Lord Woolf actually applied his test, especially as Lord Woolf believed his approach to be consonant with Lord Bridge's judgment in the *Sidaway* case.[57] Furthermore, the discussion of *Pearce* was obiter to the decision.[58] Thus, it remains to be seen whether the courts will apply Sedley J's more autonomy-sensitive version or if Lord Woolf's approach will be followed. Nevertheless, the case does suggest that the courts are inexorably moving towards the doctrine.

IV. Information Disclosure and Autonomy

These cases show that over the last quarter of a century the duty to disclose has moved on from the paternalist, physician-centred duty regulated by *Bolam simpliciter*. Under this test, the standard was more sensitive to clinical judgment than to patient autonomy. Beginning with the *Sidaway* case and the judgments of Lords Bridge, Templeman, and Scarman, the law has gradually reduced the role for clinical judgment and constrained the healthcare professional's autonomy while shifting the focus towards the patient and his or her right to autonomy.[59] In most of these cases the change was not explicitly associated with bioethical discourse, with Lord Steyn's specific reliance on Dworkin's conception of

---

[54] *Chester v Afshar* [2005] 1 AC 134, 154, para 58.
[55] ibid 163, para 92.
[56] *Wyatt v Curtis* [2003] EWCA Civ 1779, para 16.
[57] *Pearce v United Bristol Healthcare NHS Trust* [1999] PIQ 53, 57–9.
[58] *Wyatt v Curtis* [2003] EWCA Civ 1779, para 19.
[59] It is arguable that law still leaves too much discretion to the medical profession: Jackson (n 19 above) 285.

autonomy in the *Chester* case a rare exception. However, even where there have been no explicit references to ethical articles on autonomy or consent, the judges are likely to have been indirectly influenced.

This influence may have filtered through the medical profession, either formally in professional guidance, or informally through the opinions of the expert witnesses. In the *McAllister* case, for example, the plaintiff's witness was noted by Rougier J to be, 'very much of the informed consent school saying that a patient should be advised of the benefits as well as the risks: it was not his role to decide: he merely gave options and the decision was that of the patient'.[60] This view of informed consent reflects a particularly defensive reaction to the demands of patient autonomy. In this approach, the more libertarian view of autonomy as obligatory independence, self-reliance, and responsibility for oneself shapes the duty to disclose which focuses entirely on autonomy as the negative right to self-determination. Thus, the doctor discloses; the patient decides.

In the *Sidaway* case, Lord Scarman's judgment was informed by the US case of *Canterbury v Spence*,[61] in which Robinson J held that the concept of informed consent required that the standard of disclosure should be determined by reference to the reasonable person in the patient's position.[62] In his judgment Robinson J referred to a number of academic articles but relied most heavily on a paper by Waltz and Scheuneman.[63]

The Waltz and Scheuneman article takes a doctrinal approach to the question, examining the issue on the basis of precedent and legal principle. There is no explicit reference to ethical discourse and no obvious direct influence of ethical discourse. However, the paper does refer to a medical text that accepted the patient's right to be informed of 'pertinent' information, which indicates an indirect influence of professional ethics if nothing else.[64] Walz and Scheuneman's article was published in 1970, when bioethics was still in its infancy,[65] so it is perhaps not surprising that there is no direct reliance on ethical commentary.

The legal origins of informed consent lie in the 1957 case of *Salgo v Leland Jr University*.[66] Before that case consent was governed by a paternalistic beneficence.[67] However, it has been claimed that the term was first used in 1947

---

[60] *McAllister v Lewisham and North Southwark HA* [1994] 5 Med LR 343, 352.

[61] *Canterbury v Spence* 464 F 2d 772 (1972).

[62] ibid 788.

[63] JR Walz and TW Scheuneman, 'Informed Consent to Therapy' 64 (1970) *North Western University Law Review* 628.

[64] ibid 644.

[65] Jonsen suggested that: 'until the 1960s, the persons called bioethicists…were unknown': AR Jonsen, *The New Medicine and the Old Ethics* (Cambridge, Mass., 1990) 128.

[66] *Salgo v Leland Jr University* 317 P 2d 170 (1957). R Faden and TL Beauchamp, *A History of Informed Consent* (New York, 1986) 58–9. MS Pernick, 'The Patient's Role in Medical Decisionmaking: A Social History of Informed Consent in Medical Therapy' in The President's Commission for the Study of Ethical Problems in Medicine and Biomedical and Behavioral Research, *Making Health Care Decisions*, Vol 3, (Washington, DC, 1982) 3.

[67] Faden and Beauchamp (n 66 above) 59.

in a letter from the US Atomic Energy Commission to a researcher advising on the requirements for research using human subjects.[68] This letter was preceded by the Nuremberg Code 1947, drafted by the prosecution's expert witness Dr Andrew Ivy for the purpose of the Nuremberg Trials of the Nazi researchers. The Code placed great emphasis on the voluntary consent of the research subject given as a result of an 'understanding and enlightened decision'. Nevertheless, despite these other sources, it was the impact of the US legal decisions and the discourse surrounding them that 'spearhead[ed] the interest in informed consent found in medicine'.[69]

While the idea of informed consent had mixed origins, its early development was primarily fuelled by the law and legal discourse. However, the nature of the ethical dialogue was about to change with the increased interest of academics in medical ethics and the development of the 'genuinely new' discipline of bioethics in the 1960s and 1970s.[70] This discourse provided a gaze external to the practice of medicine and unrestricted by the institutional constraints of the law. Founded on a rights-based approach, bioethics sought to replace a model of consent based on beneficence with one predicated on autonomy.[71]

During the 1970s the idea of informed consent was being taught to US medical students and was increasingly referred to in the medical literature.[72] Then, in the 1980s it was the focus of the landmark Report by the President's Commission for the Study of Ethical Problems in Medicine and Biomedical and Behavioral Research, which recognized its legal origins but claimed it was primarily a moral requirement, based on self-determination but involving shared decision-making.[73] Although not ignoring the importance of beneficence, the Commission emphasized the primacy of autonomy.[74]

The pressure to shift from a beneficence model to an autonomy model was picked up in the1980s by the British academics spearheading the development of the new legal discipline of medical law.[75] For example, in 'The Patient on the Clapham Omnibus', which was initially written before the House of Lords decision in the *Sidaway* case, Kennedy argued that the High Court and Court of Appeal were wrong for applying the reasonable doctor standard to the duty to disclose.[76]

---

[68] JD Moreno and SE Lederer, 'Revising the History of Cold War Research Ethics' (1996) 6 *Kennedy Institute of Ethics Journal* 223, 227.

[69] Faden and Beauchamp (n 66 above) 88.

[70] ibid 88.   [71] ibid 94–5.

[72] ibid 95.

[73] President's Commission for the Study of Ethical Problems in Medicine and Biomedical and Behavioral Research, *Making Health Care Decisions*, Vol 1, (Washington, DC, 1982).

[74] President's Commission for the Study of Ethical Problems in Medicine and Biomedical and Behavioral Research, *Deciding to Forego Life Sustaining Treatment* (Washington, DC, 1983) 44.

[75] I Kennedy, 'Emerging Problems of Medicine, Technology, and the Law' in *Treat Me Right: Essays in Medical Law and Ethics* (Oxford, 1991) 1, 3; SAM McLean, *A Patient's Right to Know: Information disclosure, the doctor and the law* (Aldershot, 1989).

[76] I Kennedy, 'The Patient on the Clapham Omnibus' (1984) 47 *MLR* 454.

Perhaps reflecting the approach of the bioethicists, Kennedy's argument was based on the claim that consent to medical treatment was an ethical doctrine, rather than a legal one, predicated on the 'Kantian imperative of respect for others'. This respect, essentially for autonomy, is given substance by the patient's right to give or withhold consent.[77] Following the House of Lords' decision in *Sidaway*, Kennedy added a postscript to his essay, predicting that Lord Scarman's acceptance of the prudent patient standard 'undoubtedly represents the law as it will be', maintaining his support for the patient's right to self-determination and claiming that 'The message of *Sidaway* is clear ... medical paternalism has had its day'.[78]

Kennedy made a further point, which is relevant to the focus of this chapter because it is fundamental to the relationship between the nature of autonomy and the physician's duty to disclose. In criticizing the use of the reasonable doctor standard, Kennedy distinguished information from advice. He argued:

The advice given by the doctor, in the context of informed consent, is not the same sort of advice as that given by the solicitor. Rather than *advice*, what is really involved is *information*. Thus Dunn LJ's conclusion [in the Court of Appeal hearing of *Sidaway*], that the standards of the medical profession are to be applied, begs the question by assuming that information giving is the same as advice giving.[79]

If the doctor's duty is seen as one of disclosing information rather than giving advice, or warning the patient then 'the proposition that it is for the profession to set standards becomes hard to sustain'.[80] While Kennedy may have seen this as the most logical way of attacking the application of the *Bolam* test, the consequence is that it is the patient's self-determination that is emphasized, rather than a more nuanced conception of autonomy. It encourages the polarization of the parties' roles and is reflected in the more arm's-length interaction that may be summed up as 'the doctor discloses, the patient decides'.

Part of the problem with the discourse that has surrounded consent and the duty to disclose over the last twenty-five years is the relatively thin view of autonomy that fails to reflect the debates in the ethical and, more recently, the bioethical literature. Kennedy, for example, equates autonomy with self-determination and this conception appears to be reflected in the approach taken by the courts.

Compared to a more relational approach to autonomy, self-determination emphasizes the patient's right, and consequently his or her responsibility to be an independent decision-maker. This allows the doctor's duty to be satisfied simply by the provision of information, and further support for the patient is largely limited only to providing the information in lay terms. Additionally, there is often

---

[77] ibid 456.
[78] I Kennedy, 'The Patient on the Clapham Omnibus' in *Treat Me Right: Essays in Medical Law and Ethics* (Oxford, 1991) 175, 210.
[79] I Kennedy, 'The Patient on the Clapham Omnibus' (1984) 47 *MLR* 454, 461.
[80] ibid 462.

a tendency to shift seamlessly from 'knowledge' to 'information'.[81] This ignores the point that knowledge implies understanding and the ability to use information, which may not be achieved simply through disclosure. However, autonomy as self-determination promotes a vision of the individual as an independent agent and may be seen as mandating a responsibility for decision-making that restricts the expert's role to information provider rather than a more supportive adviser.[82]

This effect on the doctor's duty, of focusing on autonomy as self-determination, may be exacerbated by the way that consent has been developed in the context of clinical research. Given that it is society and future patients that stand to benefit from research, especially where it is non-therapeutic, it is understandable that a more absolute approach to the duty to disclose has been taken. There is, for example, no place for the therapeutic privilege and most, if not all, commentators support a more comprehensive disclosure. This is fine provided the distinction between research and treatment is maintained. However, in both cases, the term 'informed consent' is applied and clinicians are generally involved in or exposed to clinical research. It is, therefore, easy to see how arguments that should be restricted to the research context cross over into the treatment context.[83]

This cross fertilization between consent to research and consent to treatment also occurs when commentators fail to recognize the context-sensitive nature of consent. For example, at the head of his chapter on 'Consent to Medical Procedures' Skegg reproduced the Declaration of Helsinki's statement that 'the doctor should obtain the patient's freely given consent after the patient has been given a full explanation'.[84] This emphasis on the duty to inform is continued in more recent articles. Despite noting that 'more information ... does not necessarily improve the quality of patient decision-making',[85] Jones went on to criticize the law's paternalism and argue that information is required to allow the patient to exercise his or her autonomy, which is the ethical principle underlying 'informed consent'. This meant being able to make decisions 'freely and independently',[86] which prioritizes the liberal view of the autonomous person as the independent responsible agent who is self-reliant in his or her self-determination.

The impact on the physician's duty to the patient may be exacerbated further by a consumerist approach to consent, which emphasizes the value of choice and extensive information at the expense of the mutually interactive process of good

[81] See eg S Lee, 'Towards a Jurisprudence of Consent' in J Eekelaar and J Bell (eds), *Oxford Essays in Jurisprudence, 3rd Series* (Oxford, 1987) 199, 212–13.
[82] CE Schneider, *The Practice of Autonomy: Patients, Doctors, and Medical Decisions* (New York, 1998) 10–33.
[83] That the rules of consent should be context dependent is recognized by Manson and O'Neill: NC Manson and O O'Neill, *Rethinking Informed Consent in Bioethics* (Cambridge, 2007) 78.
[84] PDG Skegg, *Law, Ethics and Medicine* (Oxford, 1984) 75.
[85] M Jones, 'Informed Consent and Other Fairy Stories' (1999) 7 *Medical Law Review* 103, 126.
[86] ibid 123.

advice.[87] The final Report of the Bristol Royal Infirmary Inquiry, for example, noted how: 'The public became more consumer-minded. They came to demand more and better care and to show a greater readiness to complain if care fell short of what they expected.'[88] The Inquiry's response to the problems encountered at the Bristol Royal Infirmary, included an emphasis on the need to engage the patient as a partner and it is unsurprising that the Report argued that: 'One of the principal ways of empowering the patient is to ensure that they have the necessary information to allow them to understand and participate in their care to the extent desired.'[89] As suggested by that statement, the whole chapter emphasized the importance of information and the informed patient.

This bias towards a liberal or libertarian conception of autonomy as independent self-determination is apparent in the majority's speeches in *Chester v Afshar*. This is understandable given that, as I noted earlier, Lord Hope relied on Jones's article and Lord Steyn referred to Dworkin's liberal conception of autonomy. As I have argued elsewhere, this approach is consistent with corrective justice and the necessary and sufficient link between consent and responsibility for outcome.[90] Thus, Lord Steyn argued that 'a patient's right to an appropriate warning ought normatively to be regarded as an important right which must be given effective protection wherever possible'.[91]

However, this emphasis on the duty to disclose information and the liberal conception of autonomy carries the risk that the doctor's duty is largely satisfied by providing the patient with the information and the patient is then abandoned to his or her own devices. Rather than being an important interest that deserves the support of others, autonomy becomes an obligation that delineates the respective roles of the doctor and the patient.[92]

The conception of autonomy as obligation rather than right is apparent in some of the more recent cases. In *Attwell v McPartlin*,[93] for example, the judge argued:

It is for the patient, not the doctor, to decide whether the risks of any particular treatment or procedure are acceptable. It would, in my opinion, be a novel and serious departure for established practice throughout a wide range of professional relationships…to hold that a doctor is under a legal duty, not just to advise and warn fairly and appropriately but to persuade.[94]

If this attitude is combined with Kennedy's view of what 'advice' means in this context, it is apparent that the healthcare professional's duty is satisfied simply

[87] P Alderson and C Goodey, 'Theories of consent' (1998) 317 *BMJ* 1313.
[88] I Kennedy (Chairperson), 'The Report of the Public Inquiry into Children's Heart Surgery at the Bristol Royal Infirmary' 1984–1995: *Learning From Bristol* (Cm5207, 2001) Ch 22, para 6.
[89] ibid Ch 23, para 17.
[90] A Maclean, 'Risk, Consent and Responsibility for Outcome' (2005) 14 *Nottingham Law Journal* 57–65.
[91] *Chester v Afshar* [2005] 1 AC 134, para 17.
[92] A Maclean, 'Autonomy, Consent and Persuasion' (2006) 13 *European Journal of Health Law* 321, 336.
[93] *Attwell v McPartlin* [2004] EWHC 829.   [94] ibid para 60.

by disclosure, albeit supported by the minimal duty to facilitate understanding
by using lay language and choosing an opportunity to disclose when the patient
is not incapacitated by the effects of drugs or illness. The consequence of this libertarian approach to self-determination is that it allows patients to be abandoned
to the vagaries of their decision-making when the conditions may be less than
ideal and the patients may be operating with misunderstandings.

This approach has arguably reached its nadir in *Al Hamwi v Johnston*.[95] The
case concerned a 34-year-old Muslim woman with a strong family history of
Down's syndrome. Early in her pregnancy, she sought genetic testing to establish whether her unborn child was affected. She was referred to a specialist who
told her that she could have an amniocentesis. Although she was accurately
advised of the risks the claimant misunderstood the risk of the procedure and she
subsequently refused amniocentesis. It was unclear how the misunderstanding
arose and the court held that, in providing the claimant with accurate information the specialist had satisfied her duty of care.

Although Simon J suggested that, 'clinicians should take reasonable and
appropriate steps to satisfy themselves that the patient has understood the information which has been provided',[96] this duty 'required only a superficial enquiry
as to whether the patient understood the information'.[97] This conclusion as to the
nature of the duty follows from Simon' J's acceptance of the defendant doctor's
argument that: 'I would never ask a patient to explain or justify the decision they
have made. I would not do so because I would be concerned that by doing so the
patient may interpret this as criticism of their choice'.[98] This is justified by the
ethos of non-directive counselling, which—in this context—reflects an acceptance of moral pluralism.[99] The idea is that the expert should not try to impose his
or her moral view on the patient and that the only way this can be ensured is by
adopting a 'neutral' position, restricting any 'advice' to the unbiased provision of
factual information.

Putting to one side the question of whether this is even possible, this
Humean approach implies that rationality consists simply in making a choice.
However, this ignores the possibility that the decision may be irrational on
the patient's own terms. A misunderstanding of the risks and benefits may
well cause the patient to make a choice that does not fit with his or her own
goals and values, as was the case in *Al Hamwi*. Furthermore, it mandates one
extreme approach to the meaning of rationality and it is one that is arguably
less supportive of individual autonomy than more moderate versions, such as

---

[95] *Al Hamwi v Johnston, The North West London Hospitals NHS Trust* [2005] EWHC 206,
[2005] Lloyd's LR Med 309.
[96] ibid para 69.   [97] Maclean (n 92 above) 327.
[98] *Al Hamwi v Johnston, The North West London Hospitals NHS Trust* [2005] Lloyd's LR Med
309, para 73.
[99] The court noted that such an approach was recommended in a standard textbook on
Obstetrics: *Al Hamwi v Johnston* (n 98 above) para 44.

Frankfurt's idea of reflective rationality or O'Neill's accessible ends model of rationality.[100]

V. Consent and Paternalism

The focus of most commentators has been on the deference to clinical judgment and the lack of respect for patient autonomy. The response has been to bolster the patient's right to self-determination by requiring a gradually increasing duty of disclosure. This shift has come both from the approach of the courts and from the response of the medical profession and has resulted in a duty on doctors to impart information and an obligation on patients to accept the information and to act as decision-maker. However, these developments have occurred with surprisingly little impact on the healthcare professional's discretion to act paternalistically. The tension between patient autonomy and the doctor's paternalism was apparent in their Lordships' judgments in the *Sidaway* case, but perhaps the clearest example is found in Lord Caplan's speech in the Scottish case of *Moyes v Lothian*.[101] He stated:

> As I see it the law in both Scotland and England has come down firmly against the view that the doctor's duty to the patient involves at all costs obtaining the informed consent of the patient to specific medical treatments. When the patient entrusts himself to the doctor he expects, and is entitled, to be kept fully informed about decisions which have to be taken.[102]

For Lord Caplan, 'the paramount expectation is that the doctor will do what is best to care for the patient's health'.[103] This is generally consistent with the patient's entitlement to be informed of the risks, especially where that risk is severe. However, Lord Caplan continued: 'I can read nothing in the majority view in *Sidaway* which suggests that the extent and quality of warning to be given by a doctor to his patient should not in the last resort be governed by medical criteria.' Essentially, the patient is entitled to be 'fully informed' but, if the doctor believes that the information will alarm or—even more paternalistically—deter the patient from giving their consent to an operation deemed necessary for his health, then the risk need not be disclosed. And it is the doctor, with his clinical experience, who is best placed to determine this.[104]

Although the duty to disclose has continued to be developed, the healthcare professional retains the discretion to undermine the patient's autonomy in the

---

[100] H Frankfurt, 'Freedom of the Will and the Concept of a Person' in R Kane (ed), *Free Will* (Malden, Mass., 2002) 127. See also G Dworkin, *The Theory and Practice of Autonomy* (Cambridge, 1988) 20; O O'Neill, *Towards Justice and Virtue* (Cambridge, 1996) 58.
[101] *Moyes v Lothian HB* [1990] 1 Med LR 463.
[102] *Moyes v Lothian HB* [1990] 1 Med LR 463, 469.
[103] ibid.   [104] ibid.

manner of the disclosure or through withholding information under the authority of the therapeutic privilege, which—despite being overtly paternalistic—has received little criticism from British commentators.[105] Consider, for example, the recent case of *Atwell v McPartlin*.[106] Despite stating that 'It is for the patient, not the doctor, to decide whether the risks of any particular treatment or procedure are acceptable', the judge also allowed that: 'Some doctors may wish to make an effort to persuade a reluctant patient to act in what the doctor sees as the patient's best interests; some doctors may even feel the need to adopt an overbearing or bullying attitude in order to secure compliance.'[107]

This laissez faire attitude to the process of communication was also apparent in *Thompson v Bradford*.[108] In this case the Court of Appeal overturned the High Court's decision that the doctor had negligently advised the claimant's parents. Wilkie J found that the actual advice—that the child should proceed to be immunized against polio—was not negligent. However, he also held that the doctor had been 'unnecessarily dismissive' of the parents' concerns and was, therefore, negligent 'for the way in which he gave advice'.[109] This more sensitive recognition of the importance of the process of communication was rejected by the Court of Appeal, which ignored the doctor's manner. The doctor's approach to the parents' concerns was irrelevant and he was not liable for negligence because his advice was consistent with that set out in the Green Book.[110]

This indifference to the process of communication between the healthcare professional and the patient compounds the law's approach to autonomy, reinforcing the idea that the healthcare professional's duty is largely satisfied by the disclosure of a certain amount of information.[111] However, the process of disclosure is entirely a matter for clinical autonomy. This means that, while the law may be applauded for increasing the protection for individual autonomy it may also be criticized for adopting a conception of autonomy that prioritizes independent self-determination over a more textured relational approach. This is reflected in two recent case commentaries published in the Medical Law Review. In a comment on *Chester v Afshar*, Devaney declares in the title 'Autonomy Rules OK'.[112] In a subsequent commentary on the *Al Hamwi* case, Miola wittily retorts with the title 'Autonomy Rued OK'.[113]

---

[105] I Kennedy, 'The Patient on the Clapham Omnibus' in *Treat Me Right: Essays in Medical Law and Ethics* (Oxford, 1988) 175, 187. M Brazier, 'Patient autonomy and consent to treatment: the role of the law?' (1987) 7 *Legal Studies* 169, 188.

[106] *Attwell v McPartlin* [2004] EWHC 829.

[107] ibid para 60.

[108] *Thompson v Bradford* [2005] EWCA Civ 1439, [2006] Lloyd's LR Med 95.

[109] *Thompson v Bradford* [2004] EWHC 2424, para 27.

[110] *Thompson v Bradford* [2006] Lloyd's LR Med 95, para 11. For information on the 'Green Book' see: <http://www.dh.gov.uk/PolicyAndGuidance/HealthAndSocialCareTopics/GreenBook/fs/en>.

[111] J Miola, 'Autonomy Rued OK?' (2006) 14 *Medical Law Review* 108, 111–12.

[112] S Devaney, 'Autonomy Rules OK' (2005) 13 *Medical Law Review* 102.

[113] Miola, 'Autonomy Rued OK?' (2006) 14 *Medical Law Review* 108–114.

VI. The Future

Recently there seems to have been a shift in the attitude to autonomy and informed consent.[114] There has been a growing criticism of the way in which informed consent has developed and affected clinical practice. For example, in a recent public meeting organized by the GMC, John Harris, a well-known bioethicist, was reported as proclaiming that: 'Informed consent is a lost cause, a hopeless ideal.'[115] Dr Phil Hammond, a fellow panel member at the meeting 'agreed that the pressure to gain patients' consent may be getting out of hand'. He is reported as saying: 'As doctors we're becoming like financial advisers, setting out all the possible options for treatment but forcing all the choice and uncertainty involved in making a decision about it on the patients themselves.'[116]

Legal commentators have also criticized the law's development, pointing to undesirable consequences such as the disclosure of excessive information that serves to confuse rather than facilitate decision-making.[117] It has also been argued that the law's focus on information and choice, far from promoting autonomy, has acted to exclude morality and allow healthcare professionals simply to transfer responsibility to the patient who is mandated to make the decision.[118] While some of the problems arise from a reliance on a liberal (or even libertarian) model of autonomy and consent, other problems arise from the defensive response of healthcare professionals[119] and risk management strategies. These problems are exacerbated by the constraints of the common law. Forcing the regulation of consent into the poorly fitting strait-jacket of the law of tort, which was not designed for such a purpose, makes it unlikely that sufficiently sensitive rules could be developed by the courts.[120]

As far as the United Kingdom is concerned, Onora O'Neill's attack on the concept of informed consent may turn out to be the most influential criticism. Her attack is two-pronged. Her first approach is based on a view of Kant's auton-omy of the will that she terms 'principled autonomy'. O'Neill sets out her object-ive by suggesting that:

Some commonly cited reasons for thinking that informed consent is of great import-ance are quite unconvincing: informed consent has been supported by poor arguments

---

[114] GM Stirrat and R Gill, 'Autonomy in medical ethics after O'Neill' (2005) 31 *Journal of Medical Ethics* 127.

[115] J Davies, 'Doctors should be allowed to offer patients a simplified form of consent, expert says' (2005) 331 *BMJ* 925.

[116] ibid.

[117] R Heywood, 'Excessive Risk Disclosure: The Effects of the Law on Medical Practice' (2005) 7 *Medical Law International* 93, 95.

[118] J Montgomery, 'Law and the demoralisation of medicine' (2006) 26 *Legal Studies* 185, 186–189. *Al Hamwi v Johnston* (n 98 above) provides visible support for Montgomery's argument.

[119] M Jones, 'Informed Consent and Other Fairy Stories' (1999) 7 *Medical Law Review* 103, 129–30.

[120] This is true for the basic duty of disclosure, respecting autonomy as self-determination, let alone the more complex approach that would be required to respect relational autonomy.

and lumbered with exaggerated claims. My intention is not to deny its importance, or to argue for any return to medical paternalism, but to take it sufficiently seriously to identify some of its limitations as well as its strengths.[121]

O'Neill's strongest attack is aimed at the idea that informed consent is ethically important because it 'secures some form of individual autonomy'. She goes on to argue that:

Informed consent procedures protect choices that are timid, conventional, and lacking in individual autonomy (variously conceived) just as much as they protect choices that are self assertive, self knowing, critically reflective and bursting with individual autonomy. Contemporary accounts of autonomy have lost touch with their Kantian origins, in which the links between autonomy and respect for persons are well argued; most reduce autonomy to some form of individual independence, and show little about its ethical importance.[122]

O'Neill concludes from this attack on the association between autonomy and consent that, because informed consent protects the patient's choices, whether autonomous or not, the ethical importance of consent lies in the more basic duty not to coerce or deceive.[123]

O'Neill's second challenge is to conceptualize consent as a non-transitive 'propositional attitude', which means that it cannot be assumed that consent to an intervention is necessarily consent to the consequences entailed by the procedure.[124] The problem of consent as a propositional attitude is that it is impossible to achieve a true, or metaphysical, consent. Because of this, and her argument that the purpose of informed consent is not to protect autonomy but to prevent coercion and deception, O'Neill argues that rather than seeking informed consent we should be aiming for 'genuine consent', which is achieved by providing limited 'accurate and relevant information' while allowing the patient to control the flow of further information.[125]

Although this approach still focuses on informing the patient rather than fostering understanding, it does highlight the importance of the process of communication that precedes a valid consent. Emphasizing the limits of consent as a propositional attitude shifts the balance back towards consent as communication and away from the libertarian monster of mandatory independent self-determination. This is a key focus of her book, co-authored with Neil Manson.[126]

If healthcare professionals take on board this appeal for genuine, rather than informed consent, then it will inevitably affect the standard of care expected by the courts, which remains parasitic on the expectations of professional ethics. This might cause a move away from the current direction of the law and pull it back towards the approach taken by Lords Bridge and Templeman. However, because a genuine consent requires the patient to control the flow of information,

[121] O O'Neill, 'Some limits of informed consent' (2003) 29 *Journal of Medical Ethics* 4.
[122] ibid 5.   [123] ibid.   [124] ibid 6.   [125] ibid.
[126] NC Manson and O O'Neill, *Rethinking Informed Consent in Bioethics* (Cambridge, 2007).

and the professional to facilitate that flow, it would modify their Lordships' arguments by restricting the role for clinical judgment, which would only be relevant insofar as it is applied to enable the patients to control how much information they want.

O'Neill's more balanced approach to consent would be a step backwards that would eliminate any tendency simply to disclose reams of information and leave the patient to get on with making the decision. The demands of communication will at least increase the interdependence of the professional and patient. However, in claiming that informed consent is about choice and avoiding coercion and deception rather than autonomy, there is a risk that O'Neill's 'genuine consent' throws the baby out with the bathwater. The problem is that O'Neill's response to the fact that there are many different conceptions of autonomy, most of which marginalize Kant's approach to autonomy of the will, is to claim that consent is not really about morally meaningful autonomy. Because of this she redirects the focus to the ethical importance of trust and trustworthiness, emphasizing the need to avoid deception and coercion. These general duties derive from Kant's Categorical Imperative and are a necessary feature of effective communication.

This approach, which shifts the focus from the patient's right to the doctor's duty, may be fine for those patients who are willing to cede the decision to the healthcare professional, or for those patients who are capable of good decision-making without assistance. However, her approach may prejudice the less able patients who want to make their own decisions but require significant input and support to enable them to make good decisions. Eliminating autonomy from the equation still allows, and perhaps encourages, the focus of the professional's duty to be on disclosure rather than understanding, but it is comprehension rather than information per se that is needed to enable good decisions to be made. While trust is necessary it is not sufficient for effective communication since it is irrelevant to whether the information is understood.

Supporting understanding would require a duty on the healthcare professional not just to avoid coercion and deception but to engage with the patient's decision and, where necessary attempt to persuade the patient to change his or her mind.[127] This duty to engage with the patient as an agent derives not from the need for trust but from a respect for the autonomy necessary for responsible moral agency. Crucially, however, this is not autonomy as independence. Rather it is a relational autonomy that recognizes not only the importance of moral agency but also the mutual interdependence of agents.

Other than the problem of undervaluing autonomy, Manson and O'Neill's approach could suffer from precisely the same problems that have distorted informed consent. Their model is entirely theoretical and no attention has been given to the practical effects of implementing the model within the current system. A combination of the restrictions of tort law, risk management, and

---

[127] See the argument in Maclean (n 92 above).

defensive practices will inevitably affect how the model works in practice and the final result is likely to be quite different from the theoretical model presented in their book.

The strong point of Manson and O'Neill's argument is their approach to information with its focus on agency and communication. However, this hugely important insight is in danger of being swamped by the three main weaknesses, which are the severing of the connection between autonomy and consent; the failure to engage with relational autonomy; and the lack of consideration given to the likely consequence of implementation. By both undervaluing the role of autonomy and inverting the focus from the patient's rights to the healthcare professional's duties, Manson and O'Neill's model of genuine consent reflects an unsupportive approach that remains focused primarily on the negative duties of avoiding deception and coercion and non-interference with the patient's control of the information made available.

While Manson and O'Neill suggest that medical performance could be judged 'by the quality of the communication achieved',[128] the model of genuine consent that they construct still allows an approach essentially focused on the outcome of disclosure rather than on the communicative process that is necessary to support autonomous decision-making, particularly for less able patients. Because it is harder to regulate the process than it is to assess the outcome of the process, there is a danger that the law will retain its emphasis on the information that constitutes an adequate disclosure at the same time as it acknowledges the danger of over informing the patient (cf Lord Templeman's speech in the *Sidaway* case). This may simply act to rein in the duty to disclose, making it more difficult for a claimant to succeed without providing any greater antecedent control of the information.

Manson and O'Neill do criticize the current approach in healthcare practice, which they term the 'conduit/container model', for '[ignoring] the importance of reciprocal communication and the opportunities that it provides to check and challenge, to correct and defend truth-claims'.[129] However, this is mentioned almost in passing and in their proposals for how informed consent should be approached the emphasis is firmly on 'intelligible', 'relevant' information that is *'adequately accurate for the purposes at hand* and not *dishonest'*.[130] This risks falling into exactly the trap they seek to avoid, which is a focus on the content of disclosure to the relative exclusion of the process or manner of disclosure. This risk may be increased by the institutional constraints that operate in the common law and tend to push the court's attention to the outcome rather than the process of any disclosure.

The consequence of subjecting their 'agency model' especially to the common law torts of battery and negligence and the erosive eddies of defensive risk

---

[128] Manson and O'Neill (n 126 above) 199.
[129] ibid 89–90.   [130] ibid 85–7 (original emphasis).

management is that it may still fail to require healthcare professionals to engage with their patients and support their decision-making through a process of mutual persuasion.[131] This may be exacerbated by the resource implications of requiring a deeper engagement with the patient and, given the emphasis of the authors themselves, that engagement may be largely subjugated to a layered, but less extensive duty to disclose. It is unfortunate, therefore, that the authors did not engage with the interaction between the law, the ethical norms, and professional practice.

An additional problem of ignoring the law's influence on professional ethics, which is evidenced by the way in which professional ethical guidance frequently refers the professional back to the legal standard,[132] is that the liability in negligence necessarily connects outcome responsibility with the presence or absence of an adequate disclosure. When risk management is included in the mix, the focus is understandably on the risks that need to be disclosed to avoid liability. There is, therefore, a constant pressure pushing the emphasis back to the outcome rather than the process of disclosure. For O' Neill's approach to have the effect she desires, the connection between disclosure and outcome responsibility must be severed.[133] Although O'Neill's model is more sensitive to the patient's need than the mutation that the more extreme versions of informed consent have become, it may—as I have argued—end up being limited in the support it provides. However, it may also be a necessary step towards developing a duty that allows the patient the benefit of assistance to support the more negative and still overly independent control of a genuine consent.

While O'Neill is right to emphasize the need to refocus on communication rather than information per se, her account is further limited by her claim that 'informed consent' is not ethically justified by autonomy. O'Neill's attack on the connection between autonomy and consent largely focuses on the undesirable consequences of the libertarian view of autonomy as independence and the inability of Kant's principled autonomy to be translated into rules governing informed consent. She ignores the relational conception of autonomy,[134] which is unfortunate because that approach would necessarily emphasize the importance of communication as an interactive process between two agents.

Those commentators who see autonomy as essentially relational point out that none of us are independent of others: the very possibility of autonomy requires the

---

[131] DH Smith and LS Pettegrew, 'Mutual Persuasion as a Model for Doctor-Patient Communication' (1986) 7 *Theoretical Medicine* 127; Maclean (n 92 above).

[132] See eg the Department of Health's guidance on consent and the GMC's insistence that doctors should be aware of major legal judgments such as that in the *Sidaway* case.

[133] This would only really be possible through legislation.

[134] Her other attack on autonomy is that there is no requirement for decisions to be rational, which undermines any connection between consent and those conceptions of autonomy that rely on rationality (Manson and O'Neill (n 126 above) 21). This is a flawed argument because, if autonomy is important because it is necessary for responsible moral agency, the agent must be free to be wrong. Thus, the relevance of rationality is to capacity and not to the actual decision.

assistance of our parents, our teachers, and the community that supports us.[135] Thus, it makes little sense to require patients to be independent decision-makers. Incorporating such a conception of autonomy into a model of consent that is situated in the context of the professional-patient relationship, and seen as central to that relationship, would require the regulatory gaze to be focused as much on the healthcare professional's positive obligations as on their negative duties. As I have suggested above, this would entail that healthcare professionals engage with their patients' decisions and assist patients in making the best decision for them, whether or not the decision is to give or withhold consent to a particular treatment, or to make a decision to cede such decisional authority to a trusted professional. Such an approach would go beyond O'Neill's proposals, but would provide a greater respect for patients' autonomy.

VII. Conclusion

The interaction between the law and the bioethical discourse that has developed around consent and the right to respect for autonomy has, predominantly through indirectly mediated effects, resulted in the balance of legal regulation shifting from the paternalistic tradition to one that tries to balance respect for autonomy and welfare. However, the bluntness of legal regulation and the institutional constraints of the common law have resulted in a distorted approach that at once sees the development of a libertarian approach to autonomy as independent responsibility for decision-making coupled with the persistence of an overtly paternalistic approach to the discretion allowed to healthcare professionals to manipulate their patients' decisions.

The effect of bioethical discourse has been shaped by the dominant liberal approach to autonomy. This sees the principle of respect for autonomy as: 'the principle of protecting and promoting patients' ability to make and act upon free, informed decisions resulting from capable and uninfluenced deliberation'.[136] On close inspection this definition reveals the problem: other than through the provision of clear information in lay terms how is it possible to avoid influencing the patient's decision and yet promote their ability to decide. Even the provision of information is difficult to do without introducing a bias. It is easy to see how this tension, when coupled with a fear of litigation and a defensive approach to consent as a legal requirement, is most easily resolved by moving towards non-directive counselling and mandatory autonomy, where the doctor discloses and the patient decides.

---

[135] See eg the collected essays in C Mackenzie and N Stoljar (eds), *Relational Autonomy: Feminist Perspectives on Autonomy, Agency and the Social Self* (New York, 2000).

[136] R Kukla, 'Conscientious Autonomy: Displacing Decisions in Health Care' (2005) 35(2) *Hastings Center Report* 34, 35.

Recently, there has been a shift in the bioethical discourse with increasing criticism of the prevailing approach to autonomy, and some commentators have even begun to challenge the connection between informed consent and autonomy.[137] If these attacks gain a foothold then we may see the law in the future pulling back from the nadir of *Al Hamwi* and perhaps finding some middle ground between the paternalism of Lord Diplock's approach in *Sidaway* and the gargoyle of informed consent. However, although this would encourage a greater attention to the process of disclosure, and so would be better than the currently developing approach to patient self-determination, it still provides insufficient support to enable rational decision-making. This would require an obligation on the healthcare professional to engage with the patient's decision and to use persuasion to maximize the patient's ability to decide.[138] In finding a suitable position along the value axes I noted earlier, there needs to be a balance between consent as a mental state and consent as communication. In redressing the imbalance that has arisen, Manson and O'Neill's approach to informed consent is an important step backwards from the attempt to achieve a metaphysically ideal consent. However, the step forward towards consent as communication, while a step in the right direction, is a step too short.

---

[137] O'Neill (n 121 above). See also JS Taylor, 'Autonomy and Informed Consent: A Much Misunderstood Relationship' (2004) 38 *The Journal of Value Inquiry* 383.

[138] It would also require an obligation on patients to allow the engagement, to be willing to give reasons for their decisions, and to accept the healthcare professional's advice in the spirit in which it was given.

8

Stem Cell Promises—Rhetoric and Reality

*John Hearn**

I. Summary

Stem cell science is proving to be prolific in new discovery and provocative in challenging ethical, religious, and regulatory boundaries. The recent achievement of induced stem cells may result in a diminished focus on embryonic stem cells. The understanding of bio-regulation and control of stem cell differentiation is still at an early stage. Some early attempts at clinical therapies are promising, while others are dubious and dangerous. The prospects for a revolution in regenerative medicine and health care are improving. The ethical and religious ripples are multiple, reflecting conflicting philosophies as well as pluralistic societies. Regulatory and legal frameworks around the world, including the management of intellectual property, are also in new territory. The communication of this science to stakeholders and to the public may be a valuable model to extend to other areas of science. The science and the ethical debate will continue to evolve rapidly, posing fundamental questions for science and medicine, government and industry, laws and ethics, society and the individual.

II. Introduction

The pace of scientific discovery in stem cell biology continues to regenerate and accelerate. Between the paper which forms the basis of this chapter being presented in July 2007 and revised in December 2007, the field has again been reshaped through the reports from Thompson[1] and Yamanaka[2] in November

* Deputy Vice Chancellor (International) and Professor of Physiology, the University of Sydney. Correspondance to <j.hearn@usyd.edu.au>. In a complex, multidisciplinary research programme, an individual can achieve nothing without the dedication and expertise of every member of team. I thank all the scientists, laboratory, and animal technicians who worked with me, and the administrators and grant agencies that supported us, through my part in the stem cell story.

[1] J Yu, MA Vodyanic, K Smuga-Otto, J Antosiewicz-Bourget, JL Frane, S Tian, J Nie, GA Johnsdottir, V Ruotti, R Stewart, II Slukvin, and JA Thomson, Induced Pluripotent Stem Cell Lines Derived from Human Somatic Cells' (2007) 318 *Science* 1917.

[2] K Takahashi, K Tanabe, M Ohnuki, M Narita, T Ichisaka, K Tomoda, and S Yamanaka, 'Induction Of Pluripotent Stem Cells from Adult Human Fibroblasts by Defined Factors' (2007) 131 *Cell* 861.

2007 to demonstrate that four genes, carried on a viral vector, can transform an adult or a neonatal cell into the equivalent of a pluripotent stem cell. This finding injects a highly significant new dimension into the field as it may enable the derivation of stem cell lines for individual patients without the ethical and social negatives associated with the derivation of embryonic stem cells. The finding also sends ripples through the ethical, religious, and regulatory dimensions of stem cell biology, where once again the rapid advance of scientific discovery flows ahead of and around the ethical debate.

The isolation of human embryonic stem cells and the cloning of 'Dolly' the sheep, published in 1997[3] and 1998[4] by Wilmut and Thomson respectively, based on primate and other animal studies from the previous twenty years, created explosions of interest that have continued with daily reports in the world's press. Over the ten years since, new advances and sources for stem cells have been defined, while the ethical and religious debates, especially on the status of the human embryo, have led to various interpretations and policy developments around the world.

Currently, scientific advances include improvements in the efficiency of the cloning process, a greater knowledge of the capacity of cells for flexibility in their development, and of the manipulation of cells for trans-differentiation. The ethical frontiers have moved beyond consideration of the use of frozen human embryos that are due for discard, to the deliberate formation of embryos for research and the cloning of embryos for genetic manipulation and for the derivation of stem cells lines. A Bill is currently going through the British Parliament that will allow the formation of 'cybrids', where human somatic cell nuclei can be placed in an animal oocyte or egg in order to study differentiation and development.

Over the same ten-year period, there have been numerous claims and promises for stem cell therapies to treat human disorders. There is an emerging industry in stem cell tourism, where costly and often dubious applications and cures are marketed on the internet by clinics in many countries. The drive for fame and fortune is sometimes outstripping the careful and rigorous use of scientific method and clinical testing, along with peer reviewed publication, as the traditional and fundamental tools that ensure the integrity of scientific and clinical research. Some stem cell promises have become the snake oil of our times.

In this chapter, I review some selected scientific advances as milestones in the development of the field; and comment on the ethical, religious, and regulatory debate that has surrounded the often startling discoveries in cell and developmental biology. This chapter reflects the status of the field at the start of 2008 in the knowledge that there will certainly be further, significant discoveries over the

[3] I Wilmut, AE Schnieke, J McWhir, AJ Kind, and KHS Campbell, 'Viable Offspring Derived from Fetal and Adult Mammalian Cells' (1997) 385 *Nature* 810.

[4] JA Thomson, J Itskovitz-Eldor, SS Shapiro, MA Waknitz, JJ Swiergiel, VS Marshall, and JM Jones, 'Embryonic Stem Cell Lines Derived from Human Blastocysts' (1998) 82 *Science* 1145.

next year and beyond that will reshape the debate further. In this brief review I have drawn on a highly selected list of key references, but these include several recent books where a much more comprehensive set of references may be found. In addition, I have included a sum of claims from numerous case reports and publications in non-refereed web journals, where it is not possible to assess the reality of a claim that has not been tested by full publication of methods and results following rigorous peer review. The reason for including some of these non-conventional sources here is to identify trends and likely developments in the field that affect the priority and choice of research, as well as the likely impact on the ethical, religious, and regulatory developments. In adopting this approach, I am responding to the request of the Editor to provide a brief status report of the scientific front lines, with a follow through in posing bioethical and legal issues that will arise in this fast changing field.

III. Selected Scientific Milestones

The birth of 'Dolly' in 1996[5] forced a new interpretation of the fundamental capacity and limits of cell differentiation in higher mammals. Previously, it was assumed that cells are conferred with a lineage (endoderm, ectoderm, mesoderm) early in embryonic development and after gastrulation there is very limited capacity for cells to transfer into a different lineage. The exceptions are adult stem cells or precursor cells, such as those in bone marrow that give rise to blood cells, and those which constantly regenerate and repair the body throughout life, where some limited diversification is possible. The production of 'Dolly' from a somatic cell, taken from the mammary gland of a sheep, transferred to an enucleated oocyte and fused with an electric pulse, was an incremental discovery proving that adult nuclei from higher mammals could revert to totipotency under specific conditions. 'Dolly' was one success from over 275 attempts, showing that the procedure is extremely inefficient. This is not surprising as the cytoplasam of oocyte must reprogramme the adult nucleus back into the equivalent of a totipotent nucleus from an undifferentiated embryo. In the ten years since, the procedure has been repeated in a wider range of animals and efficiency has been improved a little, but it is still not possible to predict success or to guarantee repetition. A whole new field is opening up in studying the proteins, growth, and other factors that can return an adult to an embryonic cell.

The isolation of human embryonic stem cells by Thomson in 1998,[6] based on his and others' previous work over twenty years in rodents and primates,[7] was

    5 See n 3 above.   6 Thomson *et al* (n 4 above).
    7 JA Thomson, J Kalishman, TG Golos, M Durning, CP Harris, RA Becker, and JP Hearn, Isolation of a Primate Embryonic Stem Cell Line' (1995) 92 *Proceedings of the National Academy of Sciences* 7844; JA Thomson, J Kalishman, TG Golos, M Durning, CP Harris, and JP Hearn, 'Pluripotent Cell Lines Derived from Common Marmoset (Callithrix jacchus) Blastocysts' (1996)

met with an explosion of interest and an immediate realization that embryonic stem cells hold the potential for a revolution in regenerative medicine and might also have applications in agriculture and conservation. The coalescence of the fields of embryonic cloning, embryonic stem cells, and genetic manipulation to investigate the development and potentially to apply new therapeutic cures, led to intense debate in international agencies and national governments about the feasibility, the funding, and the ethical and regulatory frameworks within which these advances could be interpreted and taken further. Since the initial reports, there have been numerous significant findings, of which the following present a brief summary.

The capacity and restrictions of 'cell lineage choice' in mammalian cells have become a major focus. Although Dolly was one success from 275 attempts, her birth showed that adult cells can retain and regain complete potency under certain conditions. Immediately, the search for factors in the cytoplasm of the oocyte, that could achieve regeneration of an adult cell, intensified at molecular and physiological levels. In parallel, the factors that affect the guidance and 'lineage choice' of embryonic stem cells present a rich field of inquiry with a vast amount of scope remaining.

Alongside these developments, there was a renewed emphasis on the study of adult stem cells, both in the revisiting of known stem and precursor cells, such as the haemopoietic and other precursor cells of bone marrow, and also in the trans-differentiation of cells from skin, muscle, nerve, and other tissues to follow other developmental pathways. Currently adult stem cells have been isolated and characterized from bone marrow, cord blood, and peripheral blood (where they are in extremely low concentrations) and from over twelve different organ types. Careful reprogramming of these cells and their transplantation to other organs and tissue sites indicate that there is significant capacity for cells of one type to adopt the shape and function of cells in the new site. Examples include the transformation of bone marrow stem cells to cardiac muscle cells, and of muscle cells to nerve cells. Whether these transformations will remain permanent or de-differentiate has yet to be clarified. Recent case reports indicate encouraging therapeutic results in animal models with neurodegenerative conditions (the equivalent of Alzheimers and Parkinsons) and in human patients with primary and secondary diabetes. There is a recent case report of short-term improvement of cerebral palsy in an infant following the transplantation of cord blood stem cells. Many of these claims have yet to be submitted for rigorous review and constitute 'one off' demonstrations, but the implication is that new therapies are possible and will be substantiated in due course.

---

55 *Biology of Reproduction* 254; JP Hearn, 'Embryo Implantation and Embryonic Stem Cell Development in Primates' (2001) 13 *Reproduction, Fertility and Development* 517; and AB Parson, *The Proteus Effect 2004, National Academy of Sciences* (Joseph Henry Press, 2004).

The startling results reported independently by Thomson and Yamanaka in November 2007[8] showing that small sets of four genes, carried on a viral vector, could reprogramme a neonatal foreskin cell or an adult cheek cell respectively to regain the capacity of the equivalent of an embryonic stem cell, brings a whole new depth to the science and to the debate. If it is confirmed that such cells can trans-differentiate into a broad range of cell lines and tissues; that the use of a viral vector can be neutralized or replaced; and that the resulting cell lines can be controlled to function long term in their newly assumed roles, the vision of a revolution in regenerative medicine comes closer. This new field of induced pluri-potent stem cells (iPS) may hold the welcome attribute that stem cell therapies will not require the cloning and manipulation of human embryos. There are, of course, many scientists and others who will argue that full throttle must be maintained in all areas of stem cell biology, including the deliberate formation and cloning of human embryos and cybrids for research. I will return to this point later.

Alongside the rapid advancement of knowledge in cloning, embryonic, and adult stem cell differentiation have been other, less welcome developments. These include the offering of dubious and unproven stem cell therapies from clinics in many countries, as may be seen by calling up 'stem cell therapies' on Google. These are often from laboratories and clinics that have a rudimentary or non-existent refereed publication record, but are offering cures for a range of disorders and ailments. Staying with Google, a search for 'human egg donors' will list women who are marketing their follicles and oocytes for assisted reproduction or for embryo and stem cell research. Often these offerings include a previous track record of donations, number of eggs produced and the price requested. There is now an emerging stem cell tourism where those suffering from intractable diseases can choose to take high risk and high cost treatments, possibly with undefined or uncharacterized cells and products, in the hope of recovery. When the rhetoric moves a long way from the reality, we risk losing the trust of the public in the integrity of biomedical science and scientists.

IV. Selected Ethical and Regulatory Developments

The greater part of the ethical debate in stem cell biology has focused on (1) the status of the human embryo being used for experimental research including cloning and genetic manipulation; (2) the issues surrounding and shared with assisted human reproduction; (3) the use and disposal of 'excess' embryos from *in vitro* fertilization procedures; and (4) the appropriate testing of cell therapies in patients with terminal disorders. There are also further ethical dimensions in considerations of egg and embryo donation; the use of rigorous scientific method;

---

[8] See Yu *et al* (n 1 above) and Takahashi *et al* (n 2 above).

and the requirements for properly constituted clinical trials before any wide-spread application of stem cell therapies is permitted.

It is not possible for me to present here a detailed account of each of these issues or of the differing interpretation worldwide of ethical, regulatory, and legal frameworks. Consequently, I select a few issues which I consider to be generic to the future development of the field.

The status of the early human embryo, particularly before twelve days after fertilization, which is often the estimated time of implantation and also the time when the formation of one or two primitive streaks indicates if the embryo is a single or twins, is not universally accepted. The teaching of the Roman Catholic Church is that life and personhood are established at syngamy, when the sperm nucleus fuses with the egg. This is a clear and absolute statement, which permits no arguments along gradualist lines. Interference or termination of the viable embryo from the point of syngamy is equivalent to murder. Consequently, most if not all of the manipulations of gametes and embryos around fertilization and beyond are unacceptable and proscribed. This includes most of the broader therapies of assisted human reproduction and *in vitro* fertilization, as well as the formation and destruction of embryos for research including embryonic stem cell research. The Church encourages and has funded alternatives to embryo research, especially research in adult stem cells and now the development of induced pluripotent stem cells. Apart from the immediate issues surrounding the manipulation of gametes and embryos, the Church has clearly stated the dangers of an inherent disrespect and abuse of human life that are attached to embryonic research and embryo destruction, which can cheapen and callous fundamental ethical values for individuals and for societies.

A useful summary of religious perspectives in embryonic stem call research is presented recently by Jafari *et al* in a volume edited by Monroe *et al*.[9] They analyse the views of Christian, Buddist, Hindu, Islam, Muslim, and Jewish teaching on the moral status of the embryo and foetus at day six, week eight, and at birth respectively. They conclude that perceptions of the moral status of personhood and the way those perceptions change through development hinge on social, cultural, and religious tenets. The answers are as varied as the religions and their denominations. To oversimplify their conclusions here, Roman Catholic, Eastern Orthodox, and fundamentalist Christians accord full moral status at conception. Others take a more gradualist approach from a limited moral status at conception (Protestants); and no moral status at day six is accorded by Islam, Judaism, and those interpreting karmic considerations in Buddisim and Hinduisim. These teachings can make possible embryonic stem cell research in certain circumstances and suggest that not to pursue research

---

[9] M Jafari, F Elahi, S Ozyurt, and T Wrigley, 'Religious Perspectives on Embryonic Stem Cell Research' in KR Monroe, RB Miller, and J Tobis (eds), *Fundamentals of the Stem Cell Debate: The Scientific, Religious, Ethical and Political Issues* (University of California Press, 2008) 79.

that offers great benefits would be immoral. In pluralistic and democratic societies, most shades of opinion will be presented, while the structure, makeup, and sometimes the history of a country (for example Ireland, Germany) will influence and determine the ethical and regulatory frameworks. In both of these countries, for rather different reasons, embryo and related stem cell research are not permitted.

With the above in mind, the balance between the development of embryonic and adult stem cells, along with their sources from umbilical cord, transdifferentiated cells, and now induced pluripotent stem cells, is a matter that will ensure the continuation of a vigorous debate as the front lines of scientific knowledge progress further and the choices for regulation become broader. The question is now becoming more focused on the relative costs and benefits of studying human embryos, embryo clones, derived stem cells and their products, versus the less controversial study of adult and induced stem cells. It is too early to conclude, from scientific data, whether either line of inquiry should be curtailed, so the matter becomes one for ethical balance in the review process when research proposals are given both a scientific and an ethical review.

Ethical and regulatory frameworks around the world have been subject to change as the science has progressed over the past ten years. The widespread appreciation by the public of the potential benefits of stem cell research, presented as rhetorical or realistic as the case may be, has led to a rapid and avid communication of the science and related claims for therapeutic application. The approaches range from highly moral to highly utilitarian. Let us take just three examples here of the changing climate of the debate.

In the United States there is no federal funding permitted for embryo research or for other than embryonic stem cell lines that existed before 9 August 2001. Yet individual states allow or disallow embryo and stem cell research and there is also a divergence between research permitted with public funds and research permitted with private funds, so a highly diverse and relatively unregulated environment prevails.

In the United Kingdom, a more liberal and permissive set of guidelines are in place regulated by the Human Fertilisation and Embryology Authority (HFEA), which licenses the use of human embryos only for medical research or the treatment of infertility. In legislation before Parliament in March 2008, new provisions will allow for the use of cybrid embryos, where a human nucleus may be placed and developed in an enucleated animal egg, in order to study the development of resulting cells carrying genetic abnormalities or to screen the efficacy of multiple drug types. This permissive step would overcome the shortage of human follicles and eggs for such study. Many will consider that this is a bridge too far along the already slippery line of bridges that have permitted the deliberate formation of embryos for research, the cloning of embryos, genetic manipulation of embryos, and now the hybrid embryo. In the same Bill, some legislators are appealing against the restriction in the current legislation that the HFEA is not permitted to license stem cell products for therapeutic use and to approve new treatments.

Implicit in this latter discussion in the United Kingdom is the speed of testing and ethical application of stem cell therapies for a wide range of diseases. Currently, rigorous clinical trials can be approved because these constitute research. The pressure to remove all barriers to the application of stem cells is in order to avoid having to return to Parliament for further primary legislation should any promising therapeutic line become apparent. Also implicit in this debate is the playing down of some potentially significant safety issues, such as the patency of stem cells to behave as required, when knowledge of the control and regulation of cells after transplantation cannot guarantee that they will not degenerate rapidly or re-form into cancerous cells and tissues. Implicit also is the intensifying competition to establish and develop precedence in intellectual property for future industrial and national advantage.

In Australia, a widespread review carried out by a House of Representatives committee between 1999 and 2001 resulted in legislation in 2002 that permitted the derivation of human embryonic stem cells from excess embryos, stored frozen after IVF procedures, that were to be discarded after five years. Both the investigators and research projects would need to be licensed after scientific peer review and separate ethical consideration. There was no permit for the formation of embryos for research or for the cloning or genetic manipulation of embryos. The legislation would be reviewed again in three years. In due course, the subsequent developments in science and of international legislation were revisited by the Lockhart Review in 2005,[10] with proposed recommendations and legislation passing the Australian Parliament in 2006. Among the adopted recommendations were relaxations in the availability of non-frozen IVF embryos, with the added ability to clone or to introduce genes to human embryos for the purpose of derivation of stem cells. There was no permission to form embryos deliberately for research and as yet no approval of hybrid embryos. Thus there was a relaxation of restrictions towards the British model, but with a unified national system— now adopted by most Australian states and territories—that is different from the diversity in the United States. In the interval between 2002 and 2005, there were reportedly fewer than half a dozen grant applications to derive embryonic stem cells from frozen embryos, with little to report in that short time.

An interesting facet of the Lockhart Review Committee was their argument and recommedation that the start of embryonic development should be redefined and postponed from syngamy until the completion of the first embryonic cell cleavage. The purpose of this innovation was to suggest that conception and fertilization does not occur until it is evident from the result of successful cell cleavage. The argument was attacked as sophistry by those who hold to the

---

[10] Australian Government, 'Legislation Review: Prohibition of Human Cloning Act 2002 and the Research Involving Human Embryos Act 2002' (Reports, Biotext, Canberra, 2005).

traditional view that fertilization, conception, and the investment of personhood are complete at syngamy. The argument is reminiscent of that of the Warnock Committee on *in vitro* fertilization in the 1980s in Britain, where the term 'pre-embryo' was promoted to cover developments until the expression of the primitive streak at about day fourteen after fertilization. The term 'pre-embryo' still survives in some current literature. In my opinion, there is little to be gained and much to be lost by coining new terms that are designed or could be interpreted to fudge the straightforward definitions of embryology. If one takes an absolute position on the biological and philosophical events around syngamy, then other definitions are indeed sophistry and meaningless. If one is striving to blur the terminology in order to introduce a concept of gradualisim or partial personhood, then the concept is equally meaningless as it derives from a utilitarian intent. If one is arguing the moral cost versus the potential human benefit, then surely it is still better to keep the argument clear and honest.[11]

V. Discussion and Conclusions

Anyone who tries to predict the future or even the next steps in stem cell science is liable to be surprised. The short history of human stem cell biology over the last ten years proves that fundamental change and demonstrations are likely to be the norm. Among the proximate challenges are the still nascent exploration of induced pluripotent stem cells and the ability to control their trans-differentiation and expression. The current requirement for a viral vector to facilitate gene transfer may be overcome, making it possible to tailor immune-compatible and transplantable cells for individual patients. The merging of these apparently positive findings in this new field, with those of the past ten years, can only accelerate the rate of progress and of new discovery.

The scientific challenges continue to be extremely exciting, both in understanding the plasticity of cell lineage expression and trans-differentiation and also in discovering the factors that guide cell lineage choice. It is likely that such discovery will provide defined therapeutic agents that are more effective in stimulating cell regeneration in the body than whole cell therapies that will always be expensive and hard to control. On the same theme, the control of cell differentiation and expression, through external targeting or by the use of lethal genes, may be techniques that can be developed in order to control cells that de-differentiate or are at risk of becoming cancerous.

Some centres and states are already staking ambitious claims. An example is the recent statement by the Governor of Wisconsin that the state intends to hold 10 per cent of the US$500 billion predicted stem cell industry. Underlying such

---

[11] M Ford and M Herbert, *Stem Cells—Science, Medicine, Law and Ethics* (Sydney: St Paul's, 2007).

claims will be a fierce increase in competition for intellectual property, which itself can encounter surprises from new discovery. The 'art of the possible' in framing generic patents, to defend against future scientific advances, will add further sophisticated and nuanced layers to intellectual property law. The already rich and complicated ethical dimensions related to stem cell biology will extend further along the frontiers of the field.

One remarkable and positive feature of the stem cell field and its development over the past ten years has been the rapid transmission of new information to stakeholders and the public; and the evolution of the ethical and regulatory debate resulting from new research. As an example of the communication of science to the public, this gives us a lot to learn. It is quite usual now to have complex scientific discussion on cell differentiation and transformation at social occasions and to find that the company is well versed in the fundamentals and well able to pose challenging and highly informed scientific and ethical questions. The way that knowledge of stem cell science and its ethical consequences has permeated all levels of societies is encouraging and could be extended to other debates, such as those in genetic manipulation, transplantation immunology, and assisted reproductive technologies.

The public debate on stem cells has been engaged at all levels of society, perhaps more than most other debates other than nuclear science. At an international level, UNESCO and many other organizations established early positions and policies, including the consensus position that human reproductive cloning should be banned. Legislative bans have not in fact been adopted by most countries. Some hold that the cloning of a human embryo *in vitro* for research is not human reproductive cloning, and invent euphemisms to sidestep the ethical dilemma. Others state that the human embryo is fully human from the point of syngamy. Such conflicting opinions, based on opposing philosophical premises and beliefs, cannot be resolved. At a national level there have been variations around the world. Within the United States, the current President adopted a policy and implemented a rare congressional veto, against the majority positions of politicians, academies, industry and the public. Governors of certain US states have taken contrary positions and some of these are being challenged in the courts.

At an institutional and laboratory level, the issues and their relevance in funding, intellectual property, and research strategy are daily topics.

And at a personal level, research groups and individual scientists have been confronted with the related dilemmas depending on their views of the status of the human embryo and the utilitarian benefits promised by new discovery. When I initiated and directed the primate embryology and embryonic stem cell programme at the University of Wisconsin from 1990 to 1997, after ten years of research in the 1980s to reach that point, a range of ethical issues were raised for me and for our teams as the research progressed. Initially, we dealt with the animal ethics around the recovery of early embryos from rhesus and marmoset monkeys by obviating the need for repeated surgery and by developing new techniques for the non-surgical recovery of embryos. This achievement increased production of embryos on which the subsequent programme on primate and human stem cells depended. When I was fortunate to recruit James Thomson and the methods for primate embryo culture and differentiation were fully established, we made difficult priority decisions, investing most of the embryos in the then risky stem cell programme and cutting back on other promising programmes in embryology and implantation. Once the isolation and characterization of primate embryonic stem cells was achieved,[12] the decision to move on to isolate and characterize human embryonic stem cells presented.

In facing the decision to initiate a programme of human embryonic stem cell research, I consulted with my team. The consensus was that we had gone as far as we could with the research on non-human primates. Many colleagues did not want to proceed in working with human embryos, but James Thomson was keen to follow the logical next steps. I phoned my Director at NIH, Dr Judyth Vaitukatis, who had given me strong support through the five years when our search for primate stem cells had sometimes seemed slow and quixotic, or when a few colleagues had argued that the programme was a waste and the resources should be spent on their own projects. She confirmed, with legal opinion, that as a director of an NIH supported Centre, neither I nor the Centre could engage with any research on human embryos and that 'not one pipette tip' bought with federal funds, could be used. We took the decision to establish a separate laboratory in different premises, headed by James Thomson and funded entirely from non-federal sources. Two years later, based on the non-human primate protocols, he had isolated and grown human embryonic stem cells.[13]

Now more than twenty years after I started the search for primate embryonic stem cells, I have been privileged to see the birth of a new phase in developmental biology and to participate in the scientific, ethical, religious, and regulatory dimensions as a scientist, scientific adviser to governments, and as an individual in society. The rhetoric around stem cell promises, especially in the past ten years, has sometimes been deafening. The reality, based on stringent scientific method and open public debate, is steadily gaining form and substance.

---

[12] See Thomson *et al* (1995) (n 7 above); and Thomson *et al* (1996) (n 7 above).
[13] See Thomson *et al* (n 4 above).

9

Motivating Values and Regulatory Models for Emerging Technologies: Stem Cell Research Regulation in Argentina and the United Kingdom

Shawn HE Harmon[*]

I. Introduction

It has been said that progress is an 'optional goal' rather than an 'unconditional commitment'.[1] However, progress (ie 'innovation')[2] has become the backbone of modern, knowledge-based societies. Indeed, the mounting pressure exerted on our social and environmental setting by our prevailing mode of existence (characterized by escalating population, mobility, and consumerism) has elevated innovation to an imperative role.[3] Healthcare innovation in particular is one of the cornerstones of the new (necessary) innovation-based social/political-economy.

[*] Research Fellow, INNOGEN, ESRC Centre for Social and Economic Research on Innovation in Genomics, PhD Candidate in Law, University of Edinburgh, and Member of the Nova Scotia Bar. BA, Saint Mary's University (1993); LLB, University of New Brunswick (1996); LLM, University of Edinburgh (2004). The author would like to thank Dr Graeme Laurie, Chair of Medical Jurisprudence, University of Edinburgh, and Co-Director of SCRIPT, the AHRC Research Centre for Studies in Intellectual Property and Technology Law, and Prof Fabiana Arzuaga, University of Buenos Aires. This work forms part of the ESCR-funded project RES-000-22-2678, and the author would like to acknowledge with gratitude the support of the Economic and Social Research Council.
[1] H Jonas, 'Philosophical Reflections on Experimenting with Human Subjects' (1969) 98 *Daedalus* 219, 245.
[2] Innovation is an interactive process between stakeholders with varied expertise for the purpose of achieving a desired and novel technological or developmental outcome, usually in response to a particular problem: Learning Innovation and Technology Consortium, 'Fostering Innovation for Social Change' (2004) at <http://learninginnovation.org/LITCWhite_Paper_Innovation. pdf> (accessed 29 August 2006).
[3] Technological innovation has been integral to human development since the Second World War, the first post-war period in which technological development did not experience a slowdown: J Smart, 'Measuring Innovation in an Accelerating World' (2005) at <http://www.accelerating. org/articles/huebnerinnovation.html> (accessed 30 October 2006).

And genomic innovation is viewed as the philosopher's stone of healthcare innovation; it is the base science and a primary beneficiary of our ambitions for achieving health and longevity. Not only is it a primary feature of our new innovation society, it is reshaping that society: introducing new lexicons, redefining our understanding of desirable and undesirable bodily states, re-forging our relationships with our bodies, other people, and the environment, etc.[4]

One of the most important and controversial fields of inquiry within genomics is stem cell research (SCR). Stem cells (SCs) divide asymmetrically, giving rise to an identical 'daughter' cell and to a 'differentiated' cell. Different SCs exhibit different levels of differentiability (ie plasticity) and are characterized as 'totipotent',[5] 'pluripotent',[6] and 'multipotent'.[7] Given the early developmental stage at which they become available, pluripotent SCs are called 'embryonic stem cells' (ESCs), whereas multipotent SCs, only available in the later stages of development, are called 'somatic stem cells' (SSCs). SCs are seen as important research tools because they can be cultured and used as models to study (1) the pharmacological utility and toxicity of drugs; (2) the course of pathogenic viruses and/or diseases in human tissue;[8] (3) the function of specific genes and proteins; or (4) the development of human tissue and organs more generally,[9] and, additionally, they are seen as a fundamental pillar of the anticipated 'regenerative medicine'.[10]

---

[4] C Hauskeller, 'Science in Touch: Functions of Biomedical Terminology' (2005) 20 *Bioethics and Philosophy* 815, suggests that bio-science is so closely related to the cultural milieu that they are inseparable.

[5] Totipotent SCs can give rise to an entirely new organism, including the cells needed for human development. The only known totipotent SCs are the 8 cells of the zygote at approximately 36 hours post-fertilization. A single zygote can give rise to identical twins and the necessary extra-embryonic material such as the placenta and umbilical cord.

[6] Pluripotent SCs can differentiate into any and all of the 200+ cell types which comprise the human body, but cannot give rise to the extra-embryonic cells necessary to support the development of a foetus *in utero*. They are harvested during the brief period when the inner cell mass of the blastocyst (ie the mass which could otherwise form the embryo and evolve into the foetus) reaches approximately 25 cells.

[7] Multipotent SCs, harvested from the primordial germline cells of early aborted foetuses or from mature tissue (eg from any post-foetal stage of life of the organism, including the late foetus, umbilical cord blood, children, and adults), can give rise to the cell types regenerative of the tissue in which they normally reside. Some studies suggest that they may have greater plasticity than originally thought: L Epatko, 'Adult Stem Cells: Conflicting Research' (2004) at <http://www.pbs.org/newshour/science/stem-cells/conflicting-research.html> (accessed 3 October 2006).

[8] K Devolder, 'Human Embryonic Stem Cell Research: Why the Discarded-Created-Distinction Cannot be Based on the Potentiality Argument' (2005) 19 *Bioethics* 169; S Kadereit and P Hines, 'An Overview of Stem Cell Research' (2005) 39 *New England Law Review;* 607; and E Singer, 'The Real Stem Cell Hope' (2006) at <http://www.technologyreview.com/printer_friendly_article.aspx?id=16558> (accessed 29 September 2006).

[9] A Chapman *et al*, 'Report: Stem Cell Research and Applications: Monitoring Frontiers of Biomedical Research' (1999) at <http://www.aaas.org/spp/sfrl/projects/stem/report.pdf> (accessed 2 October 2006).

[10] 'Regenerative medicine' refers to the interdisciplinary and collaborative field of healthcare focusing on the repair, replacement or regeneration of cells, tissues, and organs so as to restore function the loss of which is caused by defects, disease, trauma, and ageing: H Greenwood *et al*,

Both the increasing rates at which SC advances are being realized,[11] and the massive economic and psychological cost of chronic, degenerative, and acute diseases,[12] are making stakeholders (for example governments, researchers, commercial enterprises, healthcarers, patients groups) ever more keen to expand SC knowledge and to translate that knowledge into novel processes and treatments deliverable across the healthcare spectrum. As such, although our comprehension of SC processes is in its infancy and significant hurdles remain to our effective and efficient clinical use of them,[13] SC therapies have leapt from the lab to the clinic in defiance of the normal hypothesis-to-trial process.[14] One researcher has stated: 'Usually you do the basic science and slowly evolve to human trials. In cardiac stem cell therapy, it's happening at the same time.'[15] In short, SC treatments are being developed and administered despite significant gaps in our understanding

---

'Regenerative Medicine: New Opportunities for Developing Countries' (2006) 8 *International Journal of Biotechnology* 60, 62–3.

[11] 1981: Evans and Kaufman (Cambridge) generate mouse embryonic stem cells; 1984: Andrews *et al* (Sheffield) generate pluripotent embryonic carcinoma cells; 1993: Mountford and Smith (Edinburgh) develop a process for isolating, selecting, and propagating animal transgenic SC; 1994: Bongso *et al* (Singapore) generate human embryonic stem-like cells; 1995: Thomson *et al* (Wisconsin-Madison) generate non-human primate ESC *in vitro*; 1997: Wilmut *et al* (Edinburgh) clone an adult sheep; 1998: Thomson *et al* (Wisconsin-Madison) isolate human embryonic pluripotent SC; 1998: Gearhart (Johns Hopkins) generates ESC lines from aborted foetuses; 2001: ACT clones human embryos; 2002: National University of Singapore, Monash University, and Hebrew University propagate human ESC without use of mouse feeder cells; 2003: Minger *et al* (London) generate first UK ESC line; 2004: Hwang *et al* (Seoul) isolate ESC from cloned human cells; 2005: Hwang *et al* (Seoul) tailor hESC lines to match patients; 2005: Murdoch *et al* (Newcastle) clone human embryo. See N Perrin, 'Report: The Global Commercialisation of UK Stem Cell Research' (2005) (accessed at <http://www.fco.gov.uk/files/kfile/UKTI%20stem%20cell%20presentation2,0.pdf> (accessed 2 October 2006) 2–50.

[12] In the US alone, and for just diabetes, the cost of treatment has been estimated at US$100 billion, and this is considered a conservative estimate: see <http:// www.diabetes.org/ada/c20f.asp> (accessed 20 October 2006).

[13] Fundamental hurdles remain to our understanding of how SCs work both inside and outside the body: UK Stem Cell Initiative, 'Report & Recommendations' (2005) at <http://www.advisorybodies.doh.gov.uk/uksci/uksci-reportnov05.pdf> (accessed 3 September 2006) 25–7; Select Committee, 'Stem Cell Research Report' (UK: House of Lords, 2002), at <http://www.parliament.the-stationary-office.co.uk/pa/ld200102/ldselect/ldstem/83/8301.htm> (accessed 26 September 2006) para 2.13; J Shaw, 'Stem Cell Science: When Medicine Meets Moral Philosophy' (2004) at <http://www.harvardmagazine.com/on-line/070483.html> (accessed 29 September 2006) 37; E Singer, 'Turning Stem Cells into Tissues' (2006) at <http://www.technologyreview.com/printer_friendly_article.aspx?id=16374> (accessed 29 September 2006).

[14] Existing treatments include bone marrow transplants for leukaemia patients, corneal regeneration for eye injury patients, skin grafting for burn patients, epithelium transplants for patients requiring bladder reconstruction, foetal dopamine neuron injections for Parkinson's patients, and pancreatic islet cell transplants for diabetics: see S Kadereit and P Hines (n 8 above) 615. However, existing treatments are somewhat simplistic and their efficacy is variable at best: see Chapman *et al* (n 9 above); Select Committee (n 13 above); and M Valente, 'Argentina: MDs Use Stem Cell Technique to Treat Diabetes' (2005) at <http://www.cordblood.com/cord_blood_news/stem_cell_news/a_argentina.asp> (accessed 30 October 2006). For more on what is happening in SCR, see the Stem Cell Research Foundation's monthly updates, at <http://www.stemcellresearchfoundation.org/whatsnew/>.

[15] Epatko (n 7 above), quoting Dr Amit Patel, University of Pittsburgh Medical Centre.

of basic functionality. Given this blurring of the boundaries between SCR and SC-based clinical practice, authorities need to revisit how healthcare is advanced, planned, and delivered.[16] One aspect of this is the (re)consideration of legal regulation of healthcare-related research. Although research regulation is not the primary means of protecting patients, the uneven transition of SCs from subject of basic research to basis of clinical treatment suggests the need for clear and comprehensive (front end) SC-based research regulation.

This chapter considers and compares the SCR regulation of two different jurisdictions: Argentina, a southern developing country and technology importer with aspirations to become an SCR power, and the United Kingdom, a northern developed country and recognized SCR leader. These countries represent a valid case study in that both are participating in the common global enterprise that is biotech innovation. Indeed, because SCR, as a part of this global innovation enterprise, is so new, it represents a real opportunity for developing countries to build capacity alongside developed countries and blur the developing/developed divide.[17] They represent an interesting case study in that, despite these parallel undertakings, they are culturally, religiously, historically, and politically different, and geographically separated.

Section II explores some of the more hotly contested and persistent ethical concerns raised by human SCR. More particularly, 'human embryonic stem cell research' (hESCR) is chosen because (1) current evidence *suggests* that ESCs are superior to SSCs;[18] (2) SSCR is akin to other human tissue/subject research, and falls largely within existing associated regulation (for example its concern

---

[16] This has begun in Scotland where the need for (1) synergies between research and clinical communities; (2) enhanced genomic capacity-building amongst healthcarers; and (3) the creation of networks to facilitate technology transfer from conception to clinician has been noted: Scottish Executive, *Review of Genetics in Relation to Healthcare in Scotland* (Edinburgh: SE, 2006) at <http:// www.scotland.gov.uk/Resource/Doc/146336/0038294.pdf>.

[17] A phenomenon which is already occurring in some sectors, particularly the digital communications sector: see M Kende and O Ocholi, 'Leap-Frogging the Divide: Next Generation Networks in Developing Countries' (2006) at <http://web.si.umich.edu/tprc/papers/2006/580/ Microsoft%20Word%20-%20Leap-frogging%20the%20divide.pdf> (accessed 15 February 2007); and R Davison *et al*, 'Technology Leapfrogging in Developing Countries—An Inevitable Luxury?' (2000) at <http://www.undp.org/lstarch/sdnpaf/pdf00000.pdf> (accessed 15 February 2007).

[18] SSCs (1) can only create tissue related to their specific tissue type; (2) are completely absent or not readily accessible from some organs; (3) cannot create organs; and (4) may not be able to proliferate *ex vivo*: Devolder, (n 8 above) 169. Conversely, ESCs combine (1) versatility (ie they can differentiate into any cell type while in culture, thereby allowing the production of massive amounts of whatever cell type is desired); (2) longevity (ie they can replicate in culture indefinitely without apparently ageing, dying, or mutating); and (3) commonality (ie the genomes of derivative organisms have been shown to be genetically and functionally normal): Chapman *et al* (n 9 above) 2. For more on why researchers prefer ESC, see R Lovell-Badge, 'The Future of Stem Cell Research' (2001) 414 *Nature* 88; and A Newhart, 'The Intersection of Law and Medicine: The Case for Providing Federal Funding for Embryonic Stem Cell Research' (2004) 49 *Villanova Law Review 329*. For a contrary view, see B Capps, 'Bioethics and Misrepresentation in the Stem Cell Debate' (2005) at <http://www.ccels.cardiff.ac.uk/literature/publications/2005/capspaper.pdf> (accessed 15 March 2006).

with recruitment and individual participant protection does not raise particularly novel ethical issues); and (3) hESCR raises unique concerns relating to embryo well-being (utilization currently requires embryo destruction), and societal well-being (notionally threatened by certain practices associated with ESCR), both of which are the subject of titanic clashes between competing positions. The purpose of this exercise is to identify and articulate the 'moral values'[19] exposed by these latter concerns. Section III explores the Argentine and UK hESCR regulatory regimes. In addition to exposing the content and characterizing the model of the regulation adopted in each jurisdiction, this part considers how (and whether) the values have manifested within the regulation, and how (and whether) the regulation enhances or realizes these values 'on the ground' (ie do they translate these moral values into binding action-guiding legal rules).

By comparing the legal outputs of these socially and developmentally diverse jurisdictions, one might (1) draw some conclusions about the translation of moral values into legal rules in different settings, and (2) make some preliminary observations about the trajectory of regulation in this field.

II. The Ethical Environment: Contested Positions and Multi-Faceted Values

Technical shortfalls aside, perhaps the most significant hurdles to the widespread application of SC-based solutions to (ill)health are the serious bioethical controversies which surround the science.[20] Bioethics is generally concerned with evaluating what states of being, what levels of risks, and what predictable consequences, are good and bad in relation to biotechnological advances and applications. It endeavours to delineate morally informed behavioural norms so as

---

[19] Values are the deeply held and often unarticulated ideals, customs, and habits which we as a society and as individuals hold, and which move societies/communities to respond, either positively or negatively, to possibilities. Though rarely altered through negotiation, they are frequently transformed over time. For more on values, see A Bruce and J Tait, 'Interests, Values and Biotechnological Risk' (2003) at <http://www.innogen.ac.uk/assets_innogen/dynamic/1118847372616/working-paper-7.pdf>, and S Harmon, 'Regulation of Human Genomics and Genetic Biotechnology: Risks, Values and Analytical Criteria' (2005) at <http://www.innogen.ac.uk/assets_innogen/dynamic/1132844739842/Innogen-Working-Paper-40.pdf>.

[20] See the debates examined in J Kitzinger and C Williams, 'Forecasting Science Futures: Legitimizing Hope and Calming Fears in the Embryo Stem Cell Debate' (2005) 61 *Social Science and Medicine* 731; C Ganchoff, 'Regenerative Movements: Embryonic Stem Cells and the Politics of Potentiality' (2004) 26 *Sociology of Health and Illness* 757; B Nerlich and D Clarke, 'Anatomy of a Media Event: How Arguments Clashed in the 2001 Human Cloning Debate' (2003) 22 *New Genetics and Society* 43; and S Parry, 'The Politics of Cloning: Mapping the Rhetorical Convergence of Embryos and Stem Cells in Parliamentary Debates' (2003) 22 *New Genetics and Society* 145. In the US, ethical concerns have lead to serious funding restraints: Economist, 'Hype Over Experience' (2005) at <http://www.economist.com/business/displayStory.cfm?story_id=4427625> (accessed 12 October 2006).

to protect human freedom.[21] In the hESCR context, the bioethical discourse has coalesced into four divergent positions, which are functionally (as opposed to philosophically) characterized as 'prohibitive', 'restrictive', 'permissive', and 'facilitative'.

This part briefly outlines those positions with a view to defining the core values underlying them, and in doing so, focuses on their approach to two fundamental elements: the well-being of the embryo, which is currently destroyed in the hESC extraction process, and the well-being of society, for the moral story would be incomplete without some attention to broader social questions about the sort of society we wish to construct.[22] Considerations of embryo well-being turn on interrelated and contested questions about the commencement of human life, the moral status of the embryo, and the meaning of personhood. Considerations of societal well-being turn on interpretations of the scope of our duty to take action to alleviate the social damage caused by injury and disease (ie the limitations we must respect so as to avoid destruction of existing social relationships, structures, and rights caused by the outputs of those actions).

A. The Prohibitive Position

Proponents of this position generally consider human life and personhood to occur simultaneously at the moment of conception. For example: 'the living human embryo is—from the moment of the union of the gametes—a human subject with a well defined identity, which from that point begins it own coordinated, continuous and gradual development, such that at no later stage can it be considered as a simple mass of cells. From this it follows that . . . it has the right to its own life.'[23] Regardless of the temporal acquisition of personhood, they argue that the embryo's unique potential to develop into a complex organism substantially different from its origins, and from any other known entity, endows it with a right to 'special protection', and it is immoral to take any action which prevents the embryo from fulfilling that potential; that would be tantamount to permitting the formation of an underclass of entities otherwise destined for humanity but instead used as a means to an end.[24] In short, everyone has an absolute

[21] C MacDonald, 'Stem Cells: A Pluripotent Challenge' (2001) 13 *Bioscan* 7; and B Bryan, 'Biotechnology, Bioethics and Liberalism: Problematizing Risk, Consent and Law' (2003) 11 *Harvard Law Journal* 119, 127.

[22] J Makdisi, 'Human Cloning and Stem Cell Research: Who Should Decide Where to Draw the Line?' (2005) 39 *New England Review* 635.

[23] Pontifical Academy for Life, 'Declaration on the Production and the Scientific and Therapeutic Use of Human Embryonic Stem Cells' (2000) at <http://www.vatican.va/roman_curia/pontifical_academies/acdlife/documents/rc_pa_acdlife_doc_20000824_cellule-staminali_en.html> (accessed 18 October 2006). See also R Doerflinger, 'Destructive Stem-Cell Research on Human Embryos' (1999) 28 *Origins* 769.

[24] For a potentiality argument grounded on 'egalitarian speciesism', see J Deckers, 'Why Current UK Legislation on Embryo Research is Immoral: How the Argument from Lack of Qualities and the Argument from Potentiality Have Been Applied and Why They Should be Rejected' (2005) 19

duty to treat others—including embryos, which have 'a teleological orientation towards becoming more developed humans'[25]—in such a way as to avoid instrumentalisation (ie using others as a means to an end).[26]

Concerns over instrumentalization and discrimination also drive their assessment of the societal impact of hESCR. They attach greater weight to the risks than to the benefits of hESCR, and question the moral fabric of a society (and the position of the individual within a society) that routinely destroys early human life for inquisitive purposes. One component of this argument is their claim that hESCR is too closely tied to SCNT; advances in therapeutic SCNT (intended to increase the number of SCs available and eventually to overcome immunological responses in patients) eliminate important obstacles to the acceptability of reproductive SCNT (for example lack of safety)[27] with the result that hESCR constitutes a slippery slope to the eventual (and inevitable) application of SCNT as a means of reproduction. This could lead to alterations in (pockets of) the species. One of the few things that truly bind all humans together is our membership in a single biological species with identical needs and similar capabilities to experience and feel. The consequences of losing this could be more destructive than anything mankind has experienced to date. As such, they consider hESCR too dangerous for society to tolerate.[28]

Bioethics 251. For a critique of the potentiality argument, see K Devolder (n 8 above), who argues that its reliance on both internal and external factors is fatal. A Chapman *et al* (n 9 above) 12, question the value of 'potentiality' as a 'complex idea drawing on even more complex...notions of "nature" and "the natural"'. Select Committee, (n 13 above) para 4.10, notes that potentiality to qualify as a member of some class in the future, provided certain qualifications are met, does not confer the rights of membership until those conditions are actually met (ie a child is a potential voter but cannot vote until attaining age 18).

[25] Deckers (n 24 above) 271.

[26] One expects that the development of harvesting techniques that do not destroy the embryo will not significantly alter the stance of those who adopt this position. Presumably, their interpretation of dignity (which demands a strict view of instrumentality) will still bar the use of non-consenting embryos from 'donating' some of their SCs.

[27] Currently, SCNT is inefficient and, for reproductive purposes, both ineffective and unsafe: see the survey of scientific opinions in G Annas and S Elias, 'Politics, Morals and Embryos' (2004) 431 *Nature* 19–20, nn 13 and 90. As such, there is an international consensus to the effect that it is unethical: see UNESCO's Universal Declaration on the Human Genome and Human Rights (1997), Art 11; the Council of Europe's Additional Protocol on Cloning Protocol (1998), Art 1; and others. See also R Chester, 'Cloning Embryos from Adult Human Beings: The Relative Merits of Reproductive, Research and Therapeutic Uses' (2005) 39 *New England Law Review* 583, and others. It has been postulated, however, that once our understanding increases such that reproductive SCNT is safe, the prevailing consensus may disintegrate: R Brownsword, 'Stem Cells and Cloning: Where the Regulatory Consensus Fails' (2005) 39 *New England Law Review* 535.

[28] For more on the destructive potential of reproductive cloning, see Brownsword (n 27 above); Chester (n 27 above); D Davis, 'Genetic Dilemmas and the Child's Right to an Open Future' (1997) 28 *Rutgers Law Journal* 551; L Andrews, 'Is There a Right to Clone? Constitutional Challenges to Bans on Human Cloning' (1998) 11 *Harvard JL&T* 643; L Wu, 'Family Planning Through Human Cloning: Is There a Fundamental Right?' (1998) 98 *Columbia Law Review* 1461; and C Sunstein, 'Is There a Constitutional Right to Clone?' (2002) 53 *Hastings Law Journal* 987; R Santorum, 'The New Culture of Life: Promoting Responsible and Appropriate Medical Research'

These arguments expose the operation of two overarching core values. The first, 'human dignity', generally encapsulates the idea that individuals must be afforded honour and respect, and that the human species has a unique value which must be maintained through enhanced protection.[29] A violation of dignity occurs whenever an act directed toward another is viewed, on an *objective* basis, as humiliating, insulting, shameful, contemptuous or damaging to the whole of humanity. In this respect, dignity is deployed as a *constraining mechanism*, with its limits determined by some authority and imposed on everyone. The second value, 'sanctity of life', generally connotes an aversion to harm and an elevation of human life above all other forms of life.[30] In a similarly dogmatic vein, sanctity is interpreted such that human life is deemed intrinsically valuable/ sacred and deserving of priority over all other considerations, including comfort, health, actualization, and the advancement of knowledge.

The consequence of these interpretations for hESCR is circumscribed possibilities. Proponents of this position would prohibit procuring or using hESCs, or indeed conducting embryonic research for any purpose other than assisting reproduction.

B. The Restrictive Position

Proponents of this position adopt stances on the commencement of human life and personhood comparable to those adopted by prohibitive proponents. Their interpretations of dignity and sanctity, which values figure prominently in their ethical judgment, are also comparable, but they concede the (potential) social utility of such research. Thus, they marshal these values in support of a slightly less strict (and less internally consistent) approach to using hESCs. They would prohibit *procuring* hESCs, but would allow research to continue on those cell lines already in existence, viewing the unethical damage to have already been done.[31]

C. The Permissive Position

Proponents of this position generally believe that, while the embryo may be genetically human, it has none of the necessary characteristics of

(2003) 17 *Notre Dame JLEPP* 151; B Taylor, 'Whose Baby Is It? The Impact of Reproductive Technologies on Kinship' (2005) 8 *Human Fertility* 189.

[29] M Cutter, 'Genetic Databases and What the Rat Won't Do: What is Dignity at Law?' in G Arnason *et al* (eds), *Blood and Data: Ethical, Legal and Social Aspects of Human Genetic Databases* (Reykjavik: UIP, 2004) 217, 219.

[30] P Suber, 'Against the Sanctity of Life' (1996) at <http://www.earlham.edu/~peters/writing/sanctity.htm> (accessed 5 August 2005).

[31] The US federal funding policy of supporting research on SC lines created before 2001, but not permitting the creation of new lines represents such a bifurcated approach, which, coincidentally, leaves private sector conduct unregulated, and has been described as ethically inconsistent: see BBC, 'Bush "Out of Touch" on Stem Cells' (2006) at <http://news.bbc.co.uk/2/hi/science/nature/5197926.stm> (accessed 18 October 2006). For US opinion polls on SCR, see <http://www.pollingreport.com/science.htm>.

personhood—uniqueness, sentience, and the cognitive capabilities of consciousness, reasoning, and self-awareness (ie the means by which life is given value and meaning).[32] Drawing support from religion,[33] biology,[34] and law,[35] they argue that, although embryos are deserving of some 'moral awe',[36] they are not sacrosanct, and can therefore be utilized for worthy/virtuous ends before they are in a position to 'experience' loss.

Like proponents of the prohibitive and restrictive positions, permissive proponents rely on human dignity and the sanctity of life, thereby exposing the dualistic nature of these values. For example, dignity is viewed as an *empowering* value. Espousing a *subjective* interpretation, proponents perceive a violation of dignity whenever an act is perpetrated against another which *that other* considers humiliating, insulting, contemptuous, or damaging (ie its breach depends on the individual's sensibilities).[37] Similarly, sanctity refers not to the un-utilizable sacredness of life, but to the uniqueness of the lived human experience (beyond mere biological existence), thereby taking into account other life interests (for example health, comfort, social interaction).[38] These interpretations implicate another core value: 'autonomy', which encompasses physical and psychological liberty and the right to be free from coercion within the reasonable limitations

---

[32] For an interesting discussion on the status of the embryo, see H McLachlan, 'Persons and Their Bodies: How We Should Think About Human Embryos' (2002) 10 *Health Care Analysis* 155.

[33] In Judaic and Protestant traditions, personhood is believed to develop gradually as opposed to the instance of conception: see S Siegel, 'Fetal Experimentation' in M Kellner (ed), *Contemporary Jewish Ethics* (New York: Hebrew Publishing Co, 1978) 289; L Cahill, 'The Embryo and the Fetus: New Moral Contexts' (1993) 54 *Theological Studies* 124; and T Peters, *For the Love of Children* (Louisville: John Knox Press, 1996). In Islamic tradition, personhood is achieved after 'ensoulment', which takes place no earlier than 40 days post-fertilization: C Dabu, 'Stem-Cell Science Stirs Debate in Muslim World Too' (2005) at <http://www.csmonitor.com/2005/0622/p15s02-wogi.html> (accessed 29 September 2006).

[34] Biologically, human uniqueness and the ability to feel occurs gradually—only after the embryo can no longer split into identical twins and after it has developed a functional nervous system. However, the timeframe is very much contested: see H Greely, 'Moving Human Embryonic Stem Cells from Legislature to Lab: Remaining Legal and Ethical Questions' (2006) 3 *PLoS Medicine* e143, M Mulkay, *The Embryo Research Debate: Science and the Politics of Reproduction* (Cambridge: Cambridge University Press, 1997); and P Spallone, *Beyond Conception: The New Politics of Reproduction* (London: MacMillan Education, 1989).

[35] Legally, it has been held that an embryo is not a human life and has no right to life. In the UK, see *Evans v Amicus Healthcare Ltd* [2003] 4 All ER 903 (HC), which cites *Re F (in utero)* [1988] 2 All ER 193 (CA) and *Paton v BPAST* [1978] 2 All ER 987 (QB).

[36] A term used by A McCall-Smith and M Revel (Rapporteurs), 'Report to the IBC: The Use of Embryonic Stem Cells in Therapeutic Research' (Paris: UNESCO, 2001) at <http://portal.unesco.org/shs/en/file_download.php/64b74abda57372bdc22570b42c1718f1stemcells_en.pdf> (accessed 5 October 2006) 8.

[37] For more on this, see D Beyleveld and R Brownsword, *Human Dignity in Bioethics and Biolaw* (Oxford: OUP, 2001), A Capron, 'Indignities, Respect for Persons, and the Vagueness of Human Dignity' (2003) at <http://bmjjournals.com/cgi/eletters/327/7429/1419#44060> (accessed 2 August 2005); and D Statman, 'Human Dignity and Technology' in Arnason *et al* (n 29 above) 223.

[38] K Boyd, 'Medical Ethics: Principles, Persons, and Perspectives: From Controversy to Conversation' (2005) 31 *Journal of Medical Ethics* 481.

imposed by cherished relationships (for example familial or community).[39] The individual, exercising moral agency, must determine whether their (or the embryo's) dignity is violated.

Given the above, and evincing a sensitivity to the (perceived) need for hESCs, proponents of this position would permit the use of embryos left over from *in vitro* fertilization (IVF). Using supernumerary IVF embryos, they argue, affords respect to individuals by recognizing their autonomous choice to donate and their right to make moral judgments (about research), and affords respect to embryos by investing them with a moral status greater than if they were simply discarded/destroyed:

> ... the ethical consistency of provisions that forego their donation for ... research, while at the same time conferring 'special respect' to the human embryo is questionable.... using embryos for important scientific research would be the most coherent way to grant 'serious moral consideration' to human embryos already created for reproductive purposes [and otherwise destined for destruction].[40]

They stipulate, however, that embryos must never be *created* for the sole purpose of destruction/research; to do so would be legally to create an underclass of beings with a purely instrumental role in society.[41]

This position has several practical benefits. First, it does not call into question existing socially useful practices such as abortion (which rightly ranks the life and well-being of the living woman over that of the foetus) and IVF (which necessitates producing extra embryos which, if not used, are subject to dangerous cryo-freezing and eventual destruction). Second, it offers the potential of utility and some commercial recovery regarding tissue/products (for example embryos) that would otherwise be destroyed/wasted.[42] Third, the specific limitations it envisions are supported by existing legal instruments.[43]

---

[39] Harmon (n 19 above); T Beauchamp and J Childress, *Principles of Biomedical Ethics* (Oxford: Oxford University Press, 4th edn, 1994); R Scott, *Rights, Duties and the Body* (Oxford: Hart Publishing, 2002); S Aksoy and A Elmali, 'The Core Concepts of the "Four Principles" of Bioethics as Found in Islamic Tradition' (2002) 21 *Medicine and Law* 211. R Gillon, 'Ethics Needs Principles—Four Can Encompass the Rest—and Respect for Autonomy Should be "First Among Equals"' (2003) 29 *Journal of Medical Ethics* 307, argues that autonomy must be respected if morality is to exist.

[40] R Isasi and B Knoppers, 'Beyond the Permissibility of Embryonic and Stem Cell Research: Substantive Requirements and Procedural Safeguards' (2006) 21 *Human Reproduction* 2474, 2477.

[41] W Cheshire Jr, 'Small Things Considered: The Ethical Significance of Human Embryonic Stem Cell Research' (2005) 39 *New England Law Review* 573.

[42] MacDonald (n 21 above). In the US, in 1996, over 3,000 frozen embryos were statutorily destroyed, and another 100,000 were 'abandoned' (to meet a similar fate): Chapman *et al* (n 9 above) 14. In the UK, as of March 2004, there were some 117,619 embryos in storage: HFEA, 'Disclosure Log: March 2006' at <http://www.hfea.gov.uk/cps/rde/xchg/SID-3F57 D79B-7567D570/hfea/hs.xsl/695.html> (accessed 18 October 2006).

[43] The Biomedicine Convention (1997), Art 18 states that the creation of human embryos for research purposes is prohibited.

D. The Facilitative Position

Proponents of this position attach minimal moral status to the embryo, classifying it as a collection of cells little different from any other bodily tissue. Then, adopting the view that the acquisition of personhood is a gradual process rather than an event, they elevate its status over time. Common articulations of this position are:

[The] creation and use of a human embryo outside the context of human reproduction does not necessarily undermine...respect for the human body and human dignity, provided that the purposes involved in such creation and use are purposes which we would recognise as beneficial ones [such as] medical ones...[It is] consistent with an attitude of respect for human life to allow the use of human embryos at an early stage of development, well before the stage at which anything resembling a self can be said to come into existence. Such use promises to provide the possibility of the relief of a great deal of human suffering, a goal which in no sense calls into question respect for the human body.[44]

And:

...The respect one has for an entity does not exclude it...from being used as a resource for a goal which is believed to be important. (Research on cadavers, with the informed consent of the party in question and on the condition of respectful treatment, is entirely legitimate in most countries.) Early embryonic...cells are respected by ensuring that they are used with care in research that incorporates substantive values such as alleviation of human suffering.[45]

If it is morally acceptable to create embryos to help the infertile (or to conduct pre-implantation genetic diagnoses), they argue, it can be no less moral to create them to help the ill or injured (or for research that will benefit the ill/injured).

With respect to societal well-being, proponents of this position generally emphasize the obligation to do everything possible to alleviate the suffering of existing and future human beings; intergenerational justice demands that we enhance the life chances of emerging and future generations.[46] Although conceding that actions intended to alleviate suffering are fuelled by a complex array of factors (for example career advancement, commercial rewards, scriptural

---

[44] McCall-Smith and Revel (n 36 above) 11. See also Resolution in Support of Stem Cell Research and Education, Rabbinical Assembly Convention, (April 2003), at <http://www.rabbinicalassembly.org/docs/2003resolutions2.pdf> (accessed 3 October 2006).

[45] Devolder (n 8 above) 182–3. In Japan, respect is shown to research embryos by treating them carefully and offering prayers for them at the time of their use: M Sleeboom-Faulkner, 'Regulating "Respect" for the Embryo in Japan: Steering Scientific Explorations in hESCR' presented at EGENIS Conference, 'Governing Genomics: Interdisciplinary Perspectives on the Regulation of Biosciences', 25–27 January 2007.

[46] It is a curious juxtaposition that sees proponents of this position invoking the well-being of future individuals to justify use of embryos to which they attach no significant moral value.

directives), they suggest that actors are (additionally) motivated by moral values such as solidarity.

Proponents of this position deploy the human dignity, sanctity of life, and autonomy values in much the same way as the permissive proponents. However, they arguably attach greater importance to autonomy, giving full credit to the individual's right to make choices and take actions based on personal beliefs; indeed, they insist that the state must *enable* individuals to do so.[47] As such, donors must be empowered to gestate and offer embryos for research and the betterment of humanity. Similarly, researchers must be given latitude in exercising their moral right to pursue scientific knowledge.[48] In short, positive action must be enabled and indeed promoted even where such action incurs costs and/or creates risks.

This position also implicates another value alluded to above, namely 'solidarity', which generally recognizes that individuals are naturally and irrevocably embedded in social contexts and thus have a duty to undertake personal and collective actions to promote the welfare of individuals and society. It implicates compassion, fraternity, interest in human welfare, and a desire to construct a just and decent society where everyone's life chances are supported; enhancing the health and quality of life of living and future humans is obviously imperative.[49]

Although autonomy and solidarity often conflict, this position ties them together through its claim that the moral life requires *positive action* in response to identified, response-demanding human needs, and that individuals must therefore be empowered to undertake that positive action. Conducting controversial research in the absence of knowledge about its ultimate social impact must be permitted because such research *may* prove beneficial to society.[50] The fact that new ideas and technologies create controversy and resistance (because they challenge existing thinking, boundaries, and visions of the world) is of little consequence.

The natural consequence of this position is that the broadest approach to the acquisition and use of ESCs is supported. With respect to the former, this includes

[47] Beauchamp and Childress (n 39 above) 125.

[48] A right that is well established at international law: see provisions in the Universal Declaration of Human Rights (1948), the International Covenant of Social and Cultural Rights (1966), the Universal Declaration of the Human Genome and Human Rights (1997), and the Preliminary Draft Declaration on Universal Norms on Bioethics (2005).

[49] S Harmon, 'Solidarity: A (New) Ethic for Global Health Policy' forthcoming in *Health Care Analysis*. See also R Houtepen and R ter Meulen, 'The Expectation(s) of Solidarity: Matters of Justice, Responsibility and Identity in the Reconstruction of the Health Care System' (2000) 8 *Health Care Analysis* 355; R ter Meulen *et al*, 'Final Report: Solidarity and Care in the European Union' (2000) at <http://europa.eu.int/comm/research/biosociety/pdf/bmh4_ct8_3971_partb. pdf> (accessed 24 August 2005); and S Benatar, A Daar, and P Singer, 'Global Health Ethics: The Rationale for Mutual Caring' (2003) 79 *International Affairs* 107.

[50] Shaw (n 13 above) 39, quotes Prof R Losick making a similar argument in the context of the academic world (ie universities have a responsibility to support controversial basic research on the understanding that it may or may not be beneficial to the world).

both the use of embryos supernumerary from IVF, and the *creation* of embryos for research purposes through IVF or through 'somatic cell nuclear transfer' (SCNT).[51] With respect to the latter, only frivolous uses (for example for the creation of cosmetics) which diminish the moral respect shown to the embryo are unacceptable. Ultimately, it is reasoned that if hESCR has the potential to achieve virtuous social ends, then, despite its costs and risks, there is a moral duty to pursue it, and the limitations imposed on its pursuit must be minimal and narrow.[52] This, it is argued, is the most ethically and practically defensible position for a diverse, pluralistic society (which should not be held hostage to the restrictive beliefs of a minority).[53]

E. Summation: A Moral Foundation for Every Appetite?

The above suggests several conclusions. First, the competing ethical positions each have a moral foundation grounded in (universal) human values the purposes of which are to promote the well-being of and respect for persons and to elucidate the equality of all human life within the species (but values which have not been consistently defined and applied). Second, that moral foundation has disinclined proponents of the various positions from conceding to the others' positions, and has made arriving at a consensus on the propriety of hESCR elusive.[54] Third, the moral position to which one subscribes will determine the acceptability and scope of SCR, and translating that ethical judgment (with its particular interpretations of underlying values) into normative rules becomes a matter of democratic negotiation. In short, the moral landscape—which includes multiple positions regarding the embryo and society supported by several core values (dignity, sanctity, autonomy, and solidarity)—exposes enormous barriers to (legal) harmonization.

---

[51] SCNT is a process whereby the nucleus of an adult cell is inserted into an enucleated egg, which is then induced to divide, thereby producing a blastocyst that is a genetic match to the adult cell/nucleus donor. For SCR purposes, the resulting cloned blastocyst is not permitted to develop into a full embryo; rather the pluripotent ESCs of the blastocyst are harvested and can then be used to treat the donor/patient without fear of immunological responses. This process is called therapeutic cloning, and is contrasted with reproductive cloning only insofar as its purpose rather than its technique is different. If the purpose of SCNT is human reproduction, the blastocyst would be implanted in a woman's uterus and permitted to grow into a baby.

[52] O Corrigan *et al*, 'Ethical, Legal and Social Issues in Stem Cell Research and Therapy' (2005) at <http://www.eeescn.org.uk/pdfs/elsi_paper.pdf> (accessed 3 October 2006).

[53] J Childress, 'An Ethical Defence of Federal Funding for Human Embryonic Stem Cell Research' (2001) 2 *Yale Journal of Health Policy Law and Ethics* 157; and K Devolder, 'What's in a Name? Embryos, Entities and ANTities in the Stem Cell Debate' (2006) 32 *Journal of Medical Ethics* 43–48.

[54] McCall-Smith and Revel (n 36 above) state that personhood arguments have failed to achieve agreement, as exemplified at the international level by the prolonged attempt to realize an international declaration on cloning and the politics surrounding its eventual failure in 2005: see UN, 'Press Release: Legal Committee Recommends UN Declaration on Human Cloning to General Assembly' UN Doc GA/L/3271, 2005, at <http://www.un.org/news/press/docs/2005/ga13271.doc.htm> (accessed 10 October 2006).

III. The Legal Environment: Regulatory Options and Variable Translational Power

Various mechanisms can be used to translate moral values and ethical judgments into action-guiding rules (for example policy guidelines, professional codes, legislation). Because there is public disquiet over hESCR, an endeavour where science, health, commerce, and human identity converge, perhaps uncomfortably, 'regulation', which represents public articulation of behavioural norms supported by government-enforced sanctions,[55] is warranted. Given the divisive moral context described above, one would expect this regulation to address the embryo, the individual and the collective, and, if it is to have anything more than a nominal or incidental effect on the science, to identify the forms of research considered acceptable, influence the direction of that research to facilitate outputs, and articulate the limits of research outputs so that they are timely and socially useful. As such, regulation might appropriately adopt a framework which explicitly addresses (1) procedural matters (creation of a monitoring authority, and erection of sanctions), and (2) substantive matters (SC sourcing and SCR purposes, participant safeguards, and commercialization). Such a framework has the potential to deliver clear and flexible guidance that translates the above values into conduct. Using it, this part explores the Argentinian and UK regimes with a view to assessing (1) the moral approach exposed by them; (2) the values discernable within them; and (3) the translation of those values into legal rules enforceable through them.

A. The Developing World: Argentina

A Developing World Social Context

Although enduring periods of brutal military rule, most recently from 1976 to 1983, Argentina is a geographically large democratic federal republic comprising some 37 million inhabitants, approximately 75 per cent of whom are catholic, who (now) enjoy a variety of constitutional rights and protections.[56] Throughout

---

[55] Regulation here refers to focused control exercised by public agencies over an activity valued by the community: A Ogus, *Regulation: Legal Form and Economic Theory* (Oxford: Clarendon, 1994) 1.

[56] For more on Argentina's historic, social, and legal context, see C Lewis, *Argentina: A Short History* (Oxford: Oneworld, 2002); and E Kozameh *et al*, 'Guide to the Argentine Executive, Legislative and Judicial System' (2001) at <http://www.llrx.com/features/argentina.htm> (accessed 14 February 2007). For insights into its recent and current human rights record, see Amnesty International, '2006 Elections to the Human Rights Council: Background Information on Candidate Counties' (2006), at <http://web.amnesty.org/library/index/ENGIOR410062006?open&of=ENG-ARG> (accessed 14 February 2007); US State Department, 'Background Note: Argentina' (2006) at <http://www.infoplease.com/country/profiles/argentina.html> (accessed 14 February 2007); US State Department, 'Argentina: International Religious

the 1990s, Argentina's fledgling democratic institutions struggled with the realities of globalization and relinquished many of their economic oversight and social welfare management roles.[57] In 2001–02, Argentina's escalating economic failures and consequent recessions culminated in a multi-faceted crisis, some aspects of which include:[58]

- a failure of the government's monetary policy and default on foreign debts;
- a precipitous drop in GDP (over 20 per cent) and hyper-inflation (70 per cent);
- increased unemployment (22 per cent) and reduced earnings;
- increased poverty rates (58 per cent of population) and indigence (28 per cent of population);
- increased inequality (poor income distribution);
- a freeze on private assets resulting in civil unrest across social classes; and
- undersupply and discontinuation of health services and loss of health insurance.

The significance of this crisis for public institutions, the economy, and the national psyche cannot be overestimated, and certain consequences (for example reduced investment in education and public health, lingering distrust of state and multinational organizations, and slow commercial growth) continue to have repercussions.

Despite this turbulent background and an inefficient and underperforming innovation system,[59] Argentina views sci-tech innovation as a fundamental pillar

Freedom Report 2006' (2006) at <http://www.state.gov/g/drl/rls/irf/2006/71446.htm> (accessed 14 February 2007).

[57] L Romero, *A History of Argentina in the Twentieth Century* (Pennsylvania: PSUP, 2002) 319.

[58] See Inter-American Development Bank, 'Country Paper: Argentina' (2000) at <http://www.iadb.org/regions/re1/ar/argentinaeng.pdf> (accessed 14 February 2007); World Bank, 'The Argentine Health Sector in the Context of the Crisis', Background Paper No 6 (November 2002) at <http://wbln0018.worldbank.org/lac/lacinfoclient.nsf/d29684951174975c85256735007fef12/3d29a0ed02294a8b85256db10058dbdd/$file/argentinapabp6.pdf> (accessed 15 February 2007); World Bank, 'Argentina—Crisis and Poverty 2003', Report No 26127-AR (July 2003) at <http://wbln0018.worldbank.org/lac/lacinfoclient.nsf/d29684951174975c85256735007fef12/3d29a0ed02294a8b85256db10058dbdd/$file/argentinapamainreport.pdf> (accessed 15 February 2007); S Cesilini *et al*, 'Social Accountability Around Emergency Operations' (2004) 42 *en breve* 1; C Valdovinos, 'Growth, Inequality and Social Equity in Argentina' (2005) 82 *en breve* 1; CEDLAS, 'Monitoring Socio-Economic Conditions in Argentina, Chile' (2005) at <http://www.wds.worldbank.org/external/default/wdscontentserver/wdsp/ib/2005/07/15/000011823_20050715164315/rendered.pdf/329490v10argen1rsion0lcshd01public1.pdf> (accessed 15 February 2007).

[59] See World Bank, 'Country Innovation Brief: Argentina' (2004) at <http://wbln0018.worldbank.org/lac/lacinfoclient.nsf/8d6661f6799ea8a48525673900537f95/c403060941d238c285256dc10062b05d/$file/argentina%20innovation%20brief.pdf> (accessed 15 February 2007); and K Thorn, 'Science, Technology and Innovation in Argentina: A Profile of Issues and Practices' (2005) at <http://siteresources.worldbank.org/intargentina/resources/sciencetechnologyandinnovationinargentina.pdf> (accessed 30 October 2006); where it is noted that: (1) a significant portion of Argentine R&D is conducted by its 37 public universities; (2) though private entities are involved in R&D, only about 33% of all R&D funding comes from private sources; (3) though Argentine researchers published

of sustainable development.[60] As such, although Argentina has emphasized agro-biotech (where it enjoys a comparative advantage over other nations),[61] it is also investigating regenerative medicine possibilities,[62] and is one of a handful of developing countries taking steps to build a competitive domestic SCR market. Indeed, although its overall R&D spending is low by international standards, it is a leading spender on SCR.[63]

Given these objectives and the scientific activity already under way (for example the operation of IVF programmes since 1984 and the advancement to clinical trials of SSC treatments),[64] one might expect Argentina to have a reasonably well-developed regulatory regime. However, Argentina has not enacted a law explicitly governing SCR or the related fields of IVF or embryonic research.[65] Rather, it has permitted market forces to determine research direction in this and other fields.[66] This began to change with the adoption of the Promotion

some 5,600 articles in international scientific journals in 2003, this is a relatively low publication per full-time researcher by international standards, though an improvement over 1990s levels; and (4) there remains weak translation of government and public university funded R&D into commercializable outputs, and domestic and international patenting remains relatively low.

[60] See the Declaration of Buenos Aires, (March 2005) at <http://www.unesco.org/science/psd/thm_innov/forums/l_america.shtml> (accessed 15 February 2007).

[61] World Bank (2004) (n 59 above); World Bank, 'Argentina: Agriculture and Rural Development: Selected Issues' Report No 32763-AR (July 2006) at <http://www-wds.world-bank.org/external/default/wdscontentserver/wdsp/ib/2006/10/18/000090341_2006101808 4304/rendered.pdf/32763.pdf> (accessed 15 February 2007). Argentina now ranks in the top 4 (with Canada, China, and the US) in number of GM acres planted: National Association of State Departments of Agriculture, 'Biotechnology—A Key to Agriculture's Future' (2002) at <http://www.nasda.org/policies/three.htm> (accessed 14 February 2007).

[62] Greenwood *et al* (n 10 above) elucidate 4 categories of conduct: (1) academic; (2) corporate; (3) publication; and (4) consumer goods/products—noting that Argentina is active in each.

[63] In 2004, R&D spending represented 0.44% of GDP, and of that, 14% related to health research: Thorn (n 59 above) 6. Argentina is now listed as a world leader in SCR (see Biocrawler, 'Stem Cell' (2006) at <http://www.biocrawler.com/encyclopedia/stem_cell> (accessed 12 October 2006)), in stark contrast to the dismal state of science funding during Argentina's 2001–02 crisis: C Marzuola, 'Argentina's Crisis Heralds Time of Torment for Scientists' (2002) 415 *Nature* 104.

[64] See R Nicholson, 'In Vitro Fertilisation and Embryo Transfer at the CEGYR, Buenos Aires, Argentina' (1987) 4 *Journal of IVF and Embryo Transfer* 129. There are now Biology of Reproduction Summer Fellowships: see <http://www.ivf.net/content/index.php?page=out&id=2452> (accessed 15 February 2007). See also Valente (n 14 above); *Medical News Today*, 'Stem Cells Implanted in Brain of Patient Who Suffered a Cerebral Infarction: Argentina', (June 2005), at <http://www.medicalnewstoday.com/medicalnews.php?newsid=25613> (accessed 3 October 2006); and *Medical News Today*, 'Stem Cell Breakthrough Helps 85% of Type II Diabetes Patients' (February 2006) at <http://www.medicalnewstoday.com/medicalnews.php?newsid=37226> (accessed 3 October 2006).

[65] Isasi and Knoppers (n 40 above) 2475, and E Rivera-Lopez, 'Ethics and Genetics in Latin America' (2002) 2 *Developing World Bioethics* 11. Indeed, SCR and SCNT laws are absent in most countries: S Pattinson, *Influencing Traits Before Birth* (London: Ashgate, 2002); A Bonnicksen, *Crafting A Cloning Policy: From Dolly to Stem Cells* (Washington: Georgetown University Press, 2002); and T Caulfield, 'The Regulation of Embryonic Stem Cell Research: A Few Observations on the International Scene' (2003) Special Edition *Health Law Journal*. 87.

[66] D Chudnovsky, 'Science and Technology Policy and the National Innovation System in Argentina' (1999) at <http://www.cepal.org/publicaciones/xml/3/20113/chudnovsky.pdf> (accessed 30 October 2006).

and Development of Technological Innovation Law 1990,[67] and the Science, Technology and Innovation Law 2001,[68] but the sci-tech framework remains complex, fragmented, and uncoordinated.

SCR Regulation

Aside from the Prohibition on Human Cloning Research Decree[69] ('the 1997 Decree'), which addresses human cloning rather than SCR per se, Argentina has very little in the way of explicit public policy on SCR.[70] However, the close association of cloning with SCR makes consideration of the 1997 Decree and its (potential) influence on SCR useful.

Procedural provisions

Although it has been claimed that licensing (which generally necessitates quality control, reporting procedures, and ethics approval) is the most effective means of influencing the conduct of research,[71] Argentina has neither imposed licensing in the SCR setting nor erected any monitoring or enforcement authority. Lines of responsibility are unclear and certain functions (for example formulating a comprehensive health research strategy) are underperformed by bodies that might be expected to perform them (for example the Secretariat of Science, Technology and Productive Innovation).[72] This *laissez faire* approach towards innovation (and SCR) governance makes it difficult to infer the operation of any particular value. One *might* claim that autonomy is exposed: recall that autonomy manifests respect for others by allowing them to make decisions for themselves. Researchers (and companies) are permitted to pursue their work largely unfettered, and one hopes that they will work towards social ends. Conversely, one can argue that the prevalent researcher liberty does not 'promote' autonomy (ie it does not create space/opportunity to do a particular thing or range of things), and it is stretching the inference to claim that inactivity can masquerade as respect for autonomy. More probably, this regulatory fallowness is not the result of any motivating value, but rather a symptom of underdeveloped technical, legal, and financial capacity (a common shortcoming in developing countries).

---

[67] Law No 23.877.   [68] Law No 25.467.

[69] Prohíibense los Experimentos de Clonación Relacionados con Seres Humanos, Decreto No 200/1997.

[70] F Arzuaga, e-correspondence dated 30 October 2006, indicates that there have been no official government position papers or reports on SCR to date, though the Science and Technology Promotion Agency created an Advisory Commission on Stem Cells in October 2006, which Commission has not yet produced its opinion.

[71] Isasi and B Knoppers, (n 40 above) 2478.

[72] See Thorn (n 59 above) and Chudnovsky (n 66 above), who notes that responsibility has been improved with the creation of the National Agency for the Promotion of Science and Technology.

Substantive provisions

Sources and purposes After noting in the Recitals the state's duty to defend human dignity and the need to control all activities associated with cloning, the 1997 Decree states that 'all cloning experiments related to humans are prohibited'.[73] It is silent on all other matters relating to SCR, including, importantly, the definition of an embryo.[74] The practical consequence of this brevity would seem to be that (1) SCR (including hESCR); (2) the use of supernumerary IVF embryos for obtaining hESCs; (3) the importation and use of SC lines derived from supernumerary embryos; and (4) the importation and use of SC lines derived from therapeutic SCNT, are all permitted.

This regulatory reality exposes an apparent contradiction between Argentina's legal position towards hESCR and the broader, publicly shared values applicable to hESCR, assuming that the latter are as expressed through (a) Argentina's ratification of the American Convention on Human Rights (1969),[75] which states that every person has the right to have his life protected by law from the moment of conception,[76] and (b) its constitutional entrenchment of catholic dogma,[77] which views the creation of embryos for research purposes as the creation of 'sacrificial victims predestined to be immolated on the altar of scientific progress'.[78] Thus, although Argentina's legal and constitutional character and conservative (church-influenced) social history suggest that it should espouse the prohibitive position, its regulatory environment is not reflective of this position. This contradiction may stem from:

- an unresolved social ambiguity toward SCR;
- the conflicting pressures of an increasingly pluralist society in transition; or
- the fallout from Argentina's crisis and consequent incentives (and pressures) to undertake economy-building research, particularly in the biotech field where Argentina has already experienced success.

---

[73] Article 1 states: 'El Presidente de la Nacion Argentina en Ecuerdo General de Ministros Decreta: Prohíbense los experimentos de clonación relacionados con seres humanos'.

[74] The importance of such a definition and its absence in Argentina is noted in R Isasi *et al*, 'Legal and Ethical Approaches to Stem Cell and Cloning Research: A Comparative Analysis of Policies in Latin America, Asia and Africa' (2004) 32 *Journal of Law, Medicine and Ethics* 626.

[75] American Convention on Human Rights (1969) OAS Treaty Series, No 36.

[76] See Art 4.

[77] See the Argentinean Constitution 1853, s 2, <http:// at www.oefre.unibe.ch/law/icl/ar00000_.html>, which obliges the federal government to 'support the Roman Catholic Apostolic religion'.

[78] Pontifical Academy for Life, 'The Dignity of Human Procreation and Reproductive Technologies: Anthropological and Ethical Aspects' (2004) at <http://www.vatican.va/roman_curia/pontifical_academies/acdlife/documents/rc_pont-acd_life_doc_20040316_x-gen-assembly-final_en.html> (accessed 31 October 2006). It has been noted that Latin American legislators receive mandates from the Vatican and frequently act under Vatican morality rather than their own: F Zegers-Hochschild, 'Attitudes Towards Reproduction in Latin America: Teachings from the Use of Modern Reproductive Technologies' (1999) 5 *Human Reproduction Update* 21. This deference to the church goes so far as criminalizing abortion in all circumstances and refraining from legislating on IVF: see E Rivera-Lopez (n 65 above).

But these are questions for the social scientist to answer with empirical evidence. For present purposes, suffice it to say that, despite intense conservative catholic moral influence, the official position is that *only* the performance of SCNT (for any purpose) is forbidden. Researchers are otherwise unfettered by regulatory limitations or oversight. Presumably, local project-specific ethical review is conducted, but the bulk of SCR takes place in the penumbra and remains invisible to public authorities.

Participant safeguards SCR is well under way in Argentina, and SSC-based treatments have already moved to human trials. For example, SSC-based cerebral infarction treatment has been administered to over a hundred patients,[79] a similar treatment is being applied to restore pancreatic insulin production in diabetes patients, and multi-centre international SSC treatment collaborations are being pursued with respect to congestive heart failure.[80] However, Argentina has articulated no binding participant safeguards in the SCR, IVF, or human subject research fields.[81] The Argentinian Ministry of Health has commenced work on human subject research guidelines, but no results have yet been published.[82]

Commercialization There is no binding regulation on the commercialization of SCR.

Comments on the Argentinian Regulation

The regulatory framework proposed at the outset of section III is not exemplified in Argentina. The legal regime, to the extent that it exists, is neither comprehensive nor concise. It adopts a minimalist 'thou shalt not' approach, but circumscribes this negative directive's applicability, thereby resulting in an overarching disposition that may be characterized as 'permissive'. The lack of detail makes it difficult to identify motivating values (and therefore the effectiveness of their translation into legal rules). It also permits some discrepancy between the social values enshrined in primary legal instruments on the one hand, and the scope of the conduct permitted on the other. However, given the regulatory work that is commencing in this field, and the fact that the restrictive elements of the existing regime have already been questioned,[83] Argentina's position should not be

---

[79] See H Pilcher, 'Bone Marrow Stem Cells Help Mend Broken Hearts' (2004) at <http://www.bioedonline.org/news/news.cfm?art=936> (accessed 30 October 2006); and *Medical News Today*, 'Stem Cells Implanted in Brain of Patient Who Suffered a Cerebral Infarction' (2005) at <http://www.medicalnewstoday.com/medicalnews.php?newsid=25613> (accessed 3 October 2006). Generally, the patient's own SSCs are extracted from bone marrow and isolated, then implanted in the brain near the infarct via a micro-catheter. The whole procedure is performed in a single day.

[80] See H Greenwood *et al* (n 10 above) 68.

[81] L Baranao, President, National Agency for the Promotion of Science and Technology, representations made at an informal meeting in Edinburgh on 26 October 2006.

[82] Arzuaga (n 70 above).

[83] In April 2004, the Committee of Ethics in Science and Technology urged the government to lift its blanket ban on cloning so as to allow therapeutic cloning, and to rescind its support for the UN Resolution which would ban all forms of cloning: R Sametband, 'Argentina Urged to Support

viewed as settled. Any new regime will be the result of stakeholders battling for their positions within a conservative ethical framework faced with stiffening demands for effective healthcare and global competitiveness (ie ingrained ethical conservatism versus science policy market deference and increasing consumerism).

B. The Developed World: The United Kingdom

A Developed World Social Context

The United Kingdom is a much smaller though more populated country than Argentina, with a more socially and religiously pluralistic (though increasingly secular) society.[84] Its more enduring and consistently practised conceptions of democracy have resulted in extensive public consultation and consideration of the ethical, legal, social, and economic consequences of biotechnology, an ongoing undertaking that has been facilitated by the United Kingdom's relative prosperity and economic stability.

After almost a decade of national debate,[85] a key feature of which was the Warnock Report (1985), the United Kingdom passed the *Human Fertilisation and Embryology Act 1990* (HFEA 1990).[86] The existence of HFEA 1990 (which regulates relatively normalized practices: IVF and embryo research) has contributed greatly to the relatively smooth uptake of new sciences. Indeed, its use as a framing tool for the SCR debates which erupted in the late 1990s arguably served to circumscribe the exploration of issues, consequences, and alternatives:

> ... [The] rhetorical construction of SCR in the parliamentary debates slips seamlessly into existing ideas, values and practices, particularly those relating to health, illness and scientific progress. Invocations of the [HFEA 1990] have served to frame SC developments on safe ground by focusing upon embryo research. Broader implications of SCR and cloning-related developments, such as the financial cost of healthcare access to any therapies developed and implications upon sociocultural notions of life, death and nature, were largely muted.[87]

In any event, consultations culminated in the adoption of the *Human Fertilisation and Embryology (Research Purposes) Regulations 2001* ('the 2001

"Therapeutic" Cloning' (2004) at <http://www.scidev.net/News/index.cfm?fuseaction=readNews&itemid=1380&language=1> (accessed 31 October 2006). Ultimately, in March 2005, the UN General Assembly adopted (by a vote of 83-34-37) a non-binding Declaration on Human Cloning, A/59/280, which calls on states to ban all forms of cloning and genetic engineering as contrary to human dignity and the protection of life: see UN Press Release at <http://www.un.org/News/Press/docs/2005/ga10333.doc.htm> (accessed 31 October 2006).

[84] See National Statistics, at <http://www.statistics.gov.uk/CCI/nugget.asp?ID=6> (22 February 2007); 10 Downing Street, at <http://www.number-10.gov.uk/output/Page843.asp> (accessed 22 February 2007); and BBC, at <http://news.bbc.co.uk/>.

[85] Corrigan *et al* (n 52 above) 6.

[86] (UK) 1990, c 37.   [87] Parry (n 20 above) 165.

Regulations'),[88] by which SCR was explicitly brought within the existing legal regime.[89] Parallel to this exercise, and conscious of the demands of the new innovation society, the United Kingdom attempted to position itself as a global SCR leader.[90] As such, it has invested significant and increasing sums in SCR (for example over £47.2 million between 2002 and 2005),[91] created the UK Stem Cell Bank, which will serve as custodian for clinical-grade adult, foetal, and embryonic SC lines,[92] and formulated a ten-year action plan for SCR.[93]

SCR Regulation

As noted above, the governance of SCR in the United Kingdom is conducted through HFEA 1990 and the 2001 Regulations, both of which are considered below.

Procedural Provisions

The Human Fertilisation and Embryology Authority ('the HFEA') administers HFEA 1990. This is a statutory body separate from the Crown[94] which must (1) keep under review information about embryos, embryo development, IVF and related treatment; (2) inform/advise the Secretary of State on such information; (3) inform/advise licensees about the purposes of HFEA 1990-governed activities; (4) inform/advise patients and the public about HFEA 1990 and licensed services; and (5) provide both an annual statement of accounts and an annual report of activities.[95]

The HFEA is authorized to grant, vary, suspend, and revoke licences, including licences to undertake research, and a licence must be obtained before any research commences.[96] Although its authority relates primarily to creating, storing, and using embryos, a broad interpretation of its power to license embryo

---

[88] SI 2001/188.

[89] See R Twine, 'From Warnock to the Stem Cell Bank—Evaluating the UK's Regulatory Measures for Stem Cell Research' (2005) 2 *Journal of International Biotechnology Law* 1, for a review of that consultation process.

[90] For consideration of public consultation efforts, see M Jones and B Salter, 'The Governance of Human Genetics: Policy Discourse and Constructions of Public Trust' (2003) 22 *New Genetics and Society* 21. For consideration of ethical, legal, and social implications go to the Human Genetics Commission, at <http://www.hgc.gov.uk/Client/index.asp?ContentId=1>; the Public Health Genetics Unit at <http://www.phgu.org.uk/>; the Wellcome Trust, at <http://www.wellcome.ac.uk/>; and see Nuffield Council, *Human Tissue: Ethical and Legal Issues* (London: NCB, 1995); Nuffield Council, *Stem Cell Therapy: The Ethical Issues* (London: NCB, 2000); Medical Research Council, *Stem Cells—MRC Research for Lifelong Health* (London: MRC, 2006); and Medical Research Council, *The UK—The Place to be for Stem Cell Research* (London: MRC, 2006).

[91] For example, the MRC invested £26m, the BBRC invested £10m, the ESRC invested £1.8m, the DTI awarded £4.9m in SCR-related technology and collaborative R&D grants, and the Wellcome Trust spent £4.5m on 15 SCR projects: Perrin (n 11 above) Ch 2.

[92] Though domestically focused, the UKSCB has forged international links and is the first of its kind in the world: see <http://www.ukstemcellbank.org.uk>.

[93] UKSCI (n 13 above).   [94] See HFEA 1990, Sch 1.

[95] See ibid ss 5–8.   [96] See ibid ss 3, 4, 9–12.

research supports its authority to oversee and license hESCR, the derivation of hESC lines, and the use of hESCR.[97] With respect to granting a licence, the HFEA 1990 stipulates that:[98]

- the application must be accompanied by the appropriate fee;
- the designated facilities must be suitable (and can be inspected pre-issuance); and
- the applicant must be the project supervisor (or some other satisfactory person).

Further, the research must be undertaken within a licensed project, comply with licence conditions, and be undertaken at the licensed premises.[99]

In addition to licensing, the HFEA must also maintain a Code of Practice which offers guidance on the ethical conduct of licensed activities.[100] The Code of Practice stipulates that all projects must undergo ethical review prior to licensing, and academic peer review as part of licensing.[101] Additionally, hESCR must comply with the Stem Cell Bank's (UKSCB's) Code of Practice and researchers must deposit a sample of any SC line with the UKSCB.[102]

Although over thirty bodies govern research approval in the United Kingdom, the HFEA is one of only five that has enforcement powers.[103] HFEA

---

[97] This has already been suggested by K Liddell and S Wallace, 'Emerging Regulatory Issues for Human Stem Cell Medicine' (2005) 1 *Geonomics, Society and Policy* 54. A broad interpretation of the HFEA's power has already been rendered in *R (on the Application of Quintavalle) v HFEA* [2003] 3 All ER 257 (CA), affd [2005] 2 All ER 555 (HL).

[98] See HFEA 1990 ss 9, 10, 16, 17. For more on procedures relating to the grant, supervision, variance and revocation of licences, and appeals from HFEA decisions re the same, see HFEA 1990, ss 16–22 and <http://www.hfea.gov.uk/cps/rde/xchg/SID-3F57D79B-8081B446/hfea/hs.xsl/373.html> (accessed 25 October 2006).

[99] For more on licence conditions, see HFEA 1990, ss 13–15 and ss 3 and 4; Sch 2.

[100] See ibid s 25. For the most recent research directions, see the HFEA Code of Practice (6th edn, 2003) part 10, at <http://www.hfea.gov.uk/cps/rde/xbcr/SID-3F57D79B-8FE105BF/hfea/Code_of_Practice_Sixth_Edition_-_final.pdf>.

[101] See the HFEA Code of Practice (2003) paras 10.7–10.10.

[102] Liddell and Wallace (n 97 above). Once ESC lines are generated, in addition to UKSCB oversight, regulatory responsibility over their use vests in the Human Tissue Act 2004 (in force April 2006), which requires donor consent to the storage and use of any human material, including ESCs, and which creates the Human Tissue Authority, which licenses activities and will issue a Code of Practice. Other regulatory instruments relevant to ESCR include the MRC Code of Practice for the Use of Human Stem Cell Lines (2004); the MHPRA, Code of Practice for the Production of Human-Derived Therapeutic Products (2003); the DoH Code of Practice for Tissue Banks (2001); the MRC Good Research Practice (2000); the DoH Guidance on the Microbiological Safety of Human Organs, Tissues and Cells Used in Transplantation (2000); and the UKCCCR Guidelines for the Use of Cell Lines in Cancer Research (1999).

[103] J Kaye, 'Practising Consent' presented at the ESRC Genomics Forum, 'Social and Legal Aspects of Collecting, Storing and Owning Human Tissue', London, 28 June 2006. The other bodies with enforcement capabilities are the National Health Service operating under various instruments, the General Medical Council operating under the Medical Act 1983 (and other instruments), the Information Commissioner operating under the Data Protection Act 1998, and the Human Tissue Authority operating under the Human Tissue Act 2004. The Medical Products Agency is less concerned with research and more concerned with the consumer safety of medical products ready for market.

representatives can enter and inspect licensed facilities and take possession of anything, including recorded information, which they have reasonable grounds to believe may be required for carrying out the HFEA's responsibilities.[104] Where evidence of an offence is provided under oath (by an HFEA representative), the judiciary can issue a warrant permitting HFEA representatives and constables to enter and search premises and seize and preserve material.[105] With respect to offences, the HFEA 1990 identifies both summary[106] and indictable[107] offences, and it imposes civil liability with respect to certain defined wrongful acts.[108]

Regarding the values engaged, it might be said that the administrative provisions suggest a tendency towards justice, an encompassing value which, when given a functionally-weighted definition, emphasizes the democracy, transparency, and independence of governing institutions.[109] The HFEA, with its enumerated powers and its authority to monitor compliance and punish non-compliance, is defensibly characterized as transparent in operation and independent of function. Similarly, the licensing criteria, which emphasize lines of responsibility, promote transparency. Finally, the detailed procedural provisions relating to appeals suggest a tendency towards the rule of law.

Substantive provisions

Sources and purpose In the United Kingdom, ESCs can be obtained from a number of sources. HFEA 1990 authorizes: (1) the storage and use of embryos for research, which de facto permits the use of supernumerary embryos from IVF treatment for hESCR;[110] (2) the creation of embryos *in vitro* specifically for research;[111] and (3) the use of SCNT to create embryos for research, though not in explicit language.[112] However, embryos are only to be used where they are

---

[104] See HFEA 1990, s 39.

[105] See HFEA 1990, s 40. A power which was recently exercised against two London clinics operated by Mohamed Taranissi: see *Guardian*, 'Watchdog Investigates Fertility Clinics' (15 January 2007) at <http://www.guardian.co.uk/medicines/story/0,,1991056,00.html> (accessed 15 February 2007); and Short Sharp Science, 'IVF Clinics Raided by UK Regulator' (15 January 2007) at <http://www.newscientist.com/blog/shortsharpscience/2007/01/ivf-clinics-raided-by-uk-regulator.html> (accessed 15 February 2007).

[106] See HFEA 1990, s 41(2), (3), and (4). These are punishable by a fine, imprisonment for up to 6 months, or both.

[107] See HFEA 1990, s 41(1). These are punishable by a fine, imprisonment for up to 10 years, or both.

[108] See ibid s 44.   [109] S Harmon (n 19 above).

[110] See HFEA 1990, s 3(1)(b), Sch 2. In 2002, the HFEA granted the first two licences permitting the use of supernumerary embryos from IVF for hESCR: see <http://www.hfea.gov.uk/research/> In 2003, the first hESC lines were derived from spare embryos donated from a couple undergoing pre-implantation genetic diagnosis, an early pre-natal diagnosis intended to identify serious disorders and which results in surplus embryos: Twine, (n 89 above).

[111] See HFEA 1990, s 3(1)(a), Sch 2. By the end of 2005, the HFEA had issued 9 licences relating to the derivation of ESCs: see <http://www.hfea.gov.uk/research> (accessed 23 March 2006).

[112] People, Science & Policy Ltd. 'Report on the Consultation on the Review of the HFEA 1990' (2006) at <http://www.peoplesciencepolicy.com/downloads/DH_consultation.pdf> (accessed 4 October 2006); and L Knowles, 'A Regulatory Patchwork—Human ES Cell Research

absolutely necessary, conditions on their use may be stipulated, and licences are limited to a maximum duration of three years.[113] Researchers must identify the purpose of their proposed research and the HFEA may only issue licences for research the purposes of which are to:[114]

- promote advances in the treatment of infertility;
- increase knowledge about the causes of miscarriages;
- develop more effective techniques of contraception;
- increase knowledge about congenital, genetic, and chromosomal disease;
- develop methods for detecting congenital, genetic, or chromosomal abnormalities;
- increase knowledge about the embryo development or 'serious' disease;[115]
- enable knowledge to be applied in developing treatments for serious disease.

Prevailing public sentiment and the Human Reproductive Cloning Act 2001,[116] which prohibits the implantation of a cloned embryo in a woman, makes the advancement of reproductive cloning an unlicensable purpose.

Although the UK regime has been criticized for vagueness as it relates to hESCR,[117] provisions relating to sources and purposes do expose underlying values. The obvious objectives of promoting women's and children's health and relieving human suffering implicate solidarity, a value intimately linked with motivating positive action toward the well-being of others. The empowering interpretation of dignity and the contextual interpretation of sanctity are also apparent in the enumerated research purposes, the obvious consequences of which are to relieve patients from painful, debilitating, and humiliating symptoms. However, the primary value underlying the regime is probably autonomy. The freedom given to individuals to shape their research (within the enumerated limits) enhances the personal pursuit of human knowledge. Similarly, references to developing (1) knowledge about contraception, miscarriage and congenital disease, and (2) methods to treat disease, point to an overarching goal of enhan-

---

Oversight' (2004) 22 *Nature Biotechnology* 157. Others include Belgium, China, Finland, India, Israel, the Netherlands, the Republic of Korea, and Singapore: UNESCO, 'National Legislation Concerning Human Reproductive and Therapeutic Cloning' (2004) at <http://unesdoc.unesco.org/images/0013/001342/134277e.pdf> (accessed 3 October 2006). By the end of 2005 the HFEA had issued 2 licences relating to SCNT, and 2 relating to parthenogenesis: see <http://www.hfea.gov.uk/research> (23 March 2006); and R Twine (n 89 above) 10.

[113] See HFEA 1990, s 3(6), (7), and (9), Sch 2.

[114] See HFEA 1990, s 3(2) and (3), Sch 2, and the 2001 Regulations, s 2(1).

[115] The determination of whether applications are directed at qualifying (ie 'serious') diseases is left to the HFEA on a case-by-case basis: Twine (n 89 above) 10.

[116] (UK) 2001, c 23.

[117] See R Brownsword, 'Stem Cells; Superman and the Report of the Select Committee' (2002) 65 *MLR.* 568–87; and D Morgan and M Ford, 'Cell Phoney: Human Cloning After Quintavalle' (2004) 30 *Journal of Medical Ethics* 524.

cing/enabling personal choice.[118] Ultimately, the regime is utilitarian insofar as the values it embodies are deployed so as to facilitate research by offering multiple sources of SCs and multiple purposes for hESCR.

Participant safeguards Given that the procurement of hESCs is usually linked with (in)fertility treatment, hESCR is reliant on individuals; particularly vulnerable individuals who are under severe emotional, social, marital, and financial strains as they grapple with and make decisions regarding infertility.[119] Thus, special attention must be paid to participant safeguards, the primary component of which is informed consent. Contextually interpreted, this comprises a process involving information exchange, absence of duress, and adequate measures for privacy protection.

Under the HFEA's regime, before consent is given, individuals who store tissue which is ultimately used for research or who donate tissue specifically for research must be given the opportunity to receive oral counselling regarding the medical, scientific, legal, and psychological implications of their actions, during which they must receive written material and be encouraged to seek further information.[120] In addition, donors must be given (1) assurances that neither donation nor research will compromise treatment; (2) confirmation that they are not obliged to donate (for research); and (3) details about research funding and benefits to researchers or related staff.[121] If tissue is to be used in secondary research or genetic research, further information is provided.[122]

Having received this information, donors who give their consent for storage/research must do so in writing.[123] The written consent must address, *inter alia*, the maximum period of storage and limitations on use (including limitations on export).[124] Donors are entitled to vary or withdraw their consent at any time before the embryo is actually used in research.[125] No money or other benefit shall be given or received in respect of the supply of embryos unless authorized by an HFEA Direction (which is considered a licence condition).[126] Even then, payments must not be offered at such a level as to constitute an inducement which

---

[118] *Evans v Amicus Healthcare Ltd* [2004] 3 All ER 1025 (CA), an IVF treatment case in which the court relied on consent rather than a more contextual and socially sensitive basis which gave heed to the moral considerations, is useful for highlighting the autonomy emphasis of the regime.

[119] Chapman *et al* (n 9 above).

[120] See HFEA 1990, s 3, Sch 3 HFEA and, HFEA Code of Practice (2003) para 5.2.

[121] See HFEA Code of Practice (2003) paras 5.8, 10.11.

[122] See HFEA Code of Practice (2003) paras 5.9, 5.10.

[123] See HFEA 1990, ss 1, 2, Sch 3.

[124] See HFEA 1990, ss 24(2), 2, Sch3. and HFEA Code of Practice (2003) part 8.

[125] See HFEA 1990, s 4, Sch 3.

[126] ibid s 12(e). For more on Directions, see HFEA 1990, ss 23,24(4). Note that, pursuant to the HFEA Code of Practice (2003) Part 4 and Appendix G, donors of gametes can be paid £15, plus travel expenses, modest absence from home/business subsistence payments, financial loss allowance to a maximum of £50 per day, childminding expenses to a maximum of £50 per day, and miscellaneous and accommodation expenses in exceptional circumstances.

might prompt participants to take risks they wouldn't otherwise take or to volunteer more frequently than is advisable or against their better judgment.[127]

With respect to privacy, the HFEA is obliged to maintain a register of information relating to treatment services and the storage and use of embryos (and gametes) from identifiable individuals.[128] Information on the register must be kept confidential, particularly with respect to the identity of those who donate, although certain classes of people can apply for access to certain of the information.[129]

All of these provisions disclose an underlying reference to the autonomy value. They enhance the personal rule of the participant, offering measures to shelter the participant from the controlling influences of others and from limitations that prevent meaningful choice. They also offer some peace of mind that, having chosen to participate, one's personal choices and information will remain confidential. Although the HFEA regime might be accused of not taking enough notice of the various categories of participants (ie their differing moral status and needs),[130] its detailed management of participant interaction with the research environment clearly discloses concerns for individual safety and scientific integrity.

Commercialization The HFEA 1990 says very little about commercialization. It stipulates that participants cannot receive money or benefit for the supply of embryos unless authorized by HFEA directions.[131] With respect to researchers, there are no limits, only duties to disclose commercial interests. Similarly, there are no conflict of interest guidelines which prohibit fertility clinics benefiting financially from embryos, nor anything specific about standards (or enforcing the same) for cross-border collaborations. In 2003, the UK Patent Office issued a notice stating that neither processes for obtaining SCs from human embryos nor human totipotent cells are patentable, but patents can issue for pluripotent SCs.[132] In

---

[127] See HFEA Code of Practice (2003) para 10.11. Unfortunately, there is nothing (1) requiring the separation of IVF treatment personnel from hESCR personnel; (2) about the timing of inquiries into donation preferences; (3) requiring a minimum 'cooling off' period between inquiry and donation or the need for reconfirmation (ie once it is clear the couple have completed their family), all of which have been identified as special concerns in this context. See Select Committee (n 13 above); and L Knowles, 'Comparative Primordial Stem Cell Regulation: Canadian Policy Options' (2001) at <http://cbac-cccb.ic.gc.ca/epic/internet/incbac-cccb.nsf/en/ah00165e.html> (accessed 23 October 2006) 632.

[128] See HFEA 1990 s 31(2).   [129] ibid ss 31–35.

[130] Greely (n 34 above) identifies 6 different categories of participants/donors in SCR, each having their own particular ethical needs and requiring variations on the consent process. For more on individual consent and privacy, see also B Lo *et al.* 'A New Era in the Ethics of Human Embryonic Stem Cell Research' (2005) 23 *Stem Cells* 1454; and D Magnus and M Cho, 'Issues in Oocyte Donation for Stem Cell Research' (2005) 308 *Science* 1747.

[131] See HFEA 1990, s 12(e).

[132] UKPO, 'Inventions Involving Human Stem Cells' (2003) at <http://www.patent.gov.uk/patent/p-decisionmaking/p-law/p-law-notice/p-law-notice-stemcells.htm> (accessed 25 October 2006).

short, the regime is very sketchy on this matter, which may be reflective of the liberal, market ideology which drives Western science and regulation.

Comments on the UK Regulation

The HFEA 1990 pre-dated SCR and, as such, did not explicitly address hESCR or SCNT. However, intended to be strong, risk-conscious, and pragmatic, it encompasses much of the framework offered above and was (therefore) flexible enough to capture the new science when it emerged. Indeed, it has become one of the most debated and emulated examples of legislation affecting this field.[133] Though perhaps not comprehensive, it is nevertheless consistent insofar as, through its adoption of the facilitative position, it appears to reflect the values expressed in the society in which it operates. Although it appears to embody notions of dignity, sanctity, and solidarity, justice and autonomy are clearly the primary or default motivating values. That is not to say that UK legislators should be complacent; areas of potential improvement include amendments to: (1) clarify and streamline the statutory regulation of SCR (including clinical trials); (2) statutorily define 'embryo'; (3) centralize/unify the list of accepted SC sources and SCR purposes; (4) extend maximum storage periods for embryos donated for research; and (5) further enhance the HFEA's power to promote compliance (for example by issueing breach of regulations notices).[134]

C. Summation: Morally Grounded Command and Control?

In section II I suggested that the diversity of the moral landscape represented a serious barrier to legal harmonization in the SCR arena. The two jurisdictions examined in section III exemplify this lack of harmonization. Although both jurisdictions endeavour to respect embryos (and humans) and allay public fears about research abuses, their approach is wildly different.

Argentina's regulatory approach can be characterized as a 'black box model' whereby the minimal regulation that exists does nothing more than prohibit a specified activity viewed to be particularly reprehensible. Aside from this legislatively-enclosed conduct, the science takes place beyond the scope of the regulation. The absence of an oversight mechanism means the science is largely invisible to regulators and the regulation has little chance of shaping research trajectories; choice of SCR direction remains a bottom-up process

---

[133] Perrin (n 11 above) 5; UKSCI (n 13 above) Knowles (n 127 above). It has formed the basis for similar legislation in Canada, New Zealand, and France: L Knowles, 'Stem Cell Policy: Where Do We Draw the Lines?' (2005) 39 *New England Law Review*, 623, 627.

[134] Various reforms are discussed in HFEA, 'Response by the HFEA to the Department of Health's Consultation on the Review of the HFEA' (2005) at <http://www.hfea.gov.uk/cps/rde/xbcr/SID-3F57D79B-D50E227B/hfea/2005-11-23_review_of_the_Act_response_FINAL.pdf> (accessed 7 November 2006).

with authorities relying on individual researchers to police themselves and to act both virtuously and with utility. Further, as new technologies (processes, practices, capabilities) emerge, there is no institutional means by which to measure the social unease which they incite or manage the research in response thereto.

Whereas Argentinian SCR occurs outwith the narrow regulatory framework, British SCR occurs wholly within the regulatory framework. The UK approach can be characterized as a 'matrix model'; a complex regulatory structure which envelopes and shapes the science. The regulation is therefore, by necessity, more complex (ie permissibility demands greater specificity). It clarifies the scope of SCR (ie dissuades 'bad science'); minimizes risk (ie articulates and punishes unfair practices); encourages utility (ie identifies how research is expected to benefit society); and promotes markets (ie creates spheres of un/acceptability and lines of responsibility). Further, this model allows legislators to alter the scope of scientific endeavour with much less controversy and effort by simply contracting or expanding the matrix. Finally, because SCR is monitored by statutorily empowered regulators, the regime relies less on the goodwill of researchers; it demands compliance with a publicly-set policy aimed at achieving an identified utility.

One can speculate that the divergence in models is explained by the combined effect of economic disparities (economic crisis versus relative affluence), uneven capabilities (shortfall in skilled regulators versus pipeline of sophisticated regulators), and cultural variances (social conservatism and homogeneity versus social diversity and secularism). I would suggest that their reliance on different ethical positions and conflicting interpretations of moral values—primarily dignity, sanctity, and autonomy—is also fundamentally relevant. Argentina's 'black box model' relies rhetorically on sanctity and dignity as constraint (which figure prominently in the recitals) and, to a lesser extent, on autonomy, although in practice it does little to ensure promotion of any of them. Conversely, the United Kingdom's 'matrix model' relies heavily on autonomy (by enhancing personal choices and consent-based vetoes), but gives an explicit nod to solidarity (by requiring researchers to meet publicly set objectives deemed useful to the population).

IV. Conclusion

Future claims that innovation is optional, and future calls for its deceleration, will almost certainly fall on deaf ears. However, it must be recognized that the pressure to move forward, particularly in SCR, takes us further from an environment where we know (or can identify) the unknowns, to one where the unknowns are unknown. In such an environment, it is understandable that we might 'act as children trembling in the blind darkness, fearing everything and holding in terror all those things we imagine might come true'.[135] But this need not be the reality. Regulation which recognizes both the beneficial possibilities of SCR and the need to avoid the potential human catastrophe of the unknowables would go a long way in salving the terror.[136] This chapter has examined the regulatory responses of two jurisdictions, Argentina and the United Kingdom, with a view to (1) drawing some conclusions about the translation of moral values into legal rules in different settings, and (2) making some preliminary observations about the trajectory of regulation in this field.

Regarding the first line of inquiry, the analysis justifies characterizing the UK approach as a matrix model with ambitious and effective directive capabilities. It adopts the facilitative position and has the means to translate the natural consequences of its overarching value (for example: autonomy) into practice. The analysis justifies characterizing Argentina's approach as a simplistic black box model which, while deploying the rhetoric of the restrictive position, allows, by default, the permissive position to obtain. It does not translate its motivating values into action-guiding rules as effectively as the former; imprecision and lack of oversight means that researchers, emphasizing different values supportive of their moral position, can conduct prohibited research with little fear of discovery.[137] Regulation as fallow as Argentina's could be seen as irresponsible in the SCR setting where outputs are translated (very quickly) into medical applications some of which will undoubtedly encounter technical hiccups and concomitant social backlashes. Neither the existence of minimal public funding nor only a fledgling industry is an excuse for under-regulation. To its credit, Argentina has recognized this and is taking steps to remedy its regulatory lacunae.

Regarding the second line of inquiry, regulatory trajectory, it has been claimed that newly drafted policies tend towards convergence and greater permissiveness, and that, as scientific understanding increases, SC science becomes more effective, and the reputation of SCR becomes more established, international norms may emerge.[138] This chapter demonstrates that the morality of SCR (particularly

---

[135] Imagery courtesy of Lucretius, 'On The Nature Of Things, Book I' (50 BCE) at <http://etext.library.adelaide.edu.au/mirror/classics.mit.edu/Carus/nature_things.1.i.html> (accessed 18 October 2006).

[136] On this point, it is worth pointing out that regulating SCR represents only part of the governance task. Appropriately dovetailing SCR regulation with the regulation of SCR outputs (ie SC-based medicinal products and devices) so as to form a streamlined regulatory framework of the SC pipeline (eg: from conception, to research, to market, to clinic) is of critical importance if the benefits of SCR are to be realized and the pitfalls avoided.

[137] However, again, one might argue that Argentina's drive toward recovery from its crisis and its success in other genomic fields (eg GM crops) is a relevant factor in its disconnect between apparent values and actual conduct. Economics is a strong motivating factor. For example, Argentine farmers support GM crops in large part because it keeps them in business: see Commentary, 'Argentine Farmers Embrace Biotech' (2001), at <http://www.biotech-info.net/embrace.html> (accessed 14 February 2007).

[138] Isasi *et al* (n 74 above) 627; L Knowles (n 133 above) 627; and B Salter and C Salter, 'Bioethics and the Global Moral Economy: The Cultural Politics of Human Embryonic Stem Cell Science' (2006) at <http://www.ioh.uea.ac.uk/biopolitics/publications/working_papers/wp3.pdf>

hESCR) remains contested, and so long as this situation endures, the chance of formal legal harmonization of *substantive practices* remains remote.[139] Given the legitimate moral disagreement in this field, such harmonization, in addition to being unattainable,[140] may be unwarranted. A more practical pursuit may be to promote greater symmetry of *regulatory models*. In the absence of consensus around the acceptable scope of SCR, harmonization might be achieved (and is desirable) around *matters addressed* by regulation. As a start, we might agree that all domestic regulation (and indeed international instruments) must include provisions addressing: lines of authority for research conduct; public oversight/monitoring of research; enforcement of standards and prohibitions; participant consent and privacy; and rights in and responsibilities over SC lines. Given the international nature of SCR, it would also be advisable to include uniform direction on: the limits of legal extra-jurisdictional conduct of nationals (ie liability shields); the conduct of international collaborations, including knowledge diasporas; and research standards for ESCR-derived products or tools subsequently imported.

Ultimately, what is needed is concise regulation with clear limitations and strict sanctions for conduct identified as illegal/unethical, whatever conduct that may be. Such modest hopes for harmonization may actually be achievable in the short and medium term, and their realization is critical, not only so we avoid the most detrimental outcomes of SCR, but so we ensure that we better the lives of *everyone* through SCR.[141]

(accessed 5 October 2006) 14–15. L Turner, 'Bioethics Inc.' (2004) at <http://genetics-and-society. org/resources/items/200408_naturebt_turner.html> (accessed 10 October 2006), argues that this shift toward permissiveness is due to bioethicist 'capture' by corporate interests, and says that the ties being forged between ethicists and industry have 'deeply problematic consequences', namely, improving the reputation of private entities without necessarily improving their practices, and spawning conflicts of interest (eg bioethical conclusions may well become less analytical/critical of corporate paymaster activities). Annas and Elias (n 27 above), argue that bioethics, at least in the US, tends to be pragmatic and market-oriented.

[139] This polarization persists even within Europe: Twine (n 89 above).

[140] eg note the abortive UN attempts to draft a cloning convention: see P Goodenough, 'Effectiveness of UN Cloning Declaration in Dispute' (2005) at <http://www.cnsnews.com/ viewculture.asp?page=%5cculture%5carchive%5c200502%5ccul20050224a.html> (accessed 15 February 2007). For more on the work of the UN Ad Hoc Committee on an International Convention Against the Reproductive Cloning of Human Beings, see <http://www.un.org/law/cloning/>.

[141] Some have suggested that SCR has limited potential for *global* utility. However, evidence suggests that diabetes, cancer, cardiovascular diseases, and accident/injury (target conditions) are all rising in the developing world. For example, non-communicable diseases now account for more deaths annually than infectious diseases, with developing countries accounting for 80% of all disabled people, 80% of cardiovascular deaths, 90% of injury/trauma deaths, and 66% of diabetes sufferers: H Greenwood *et al* (n 62 above). Accepting the relevance of the research, there remains the question of whether regenerative medicine solutions will ever be cost-efficient enough to be widely accessible in the developing world.

10

Cultures of Life: Embryo Protection and the Pluralist State

Patrick Hanafin

The neutral state, confronted with competing claims of knowledge and faith, abstains from prejudging political decisions in favor of one side or the other.[1]

...the politics of biotechnology serves as a theater for observing democratic politics in motion.[2]

...the not-yet-born intermittently press their...demands with an unmistakable but invisible power, a power that exceeds our conventional formulations of agency.[3]

I. Introduction

In 2004, the Italian legislature approved a law on assisted reproduction which narrowed the scope of women's reproductive freedom by according symbolic legal recognition to the embryo.[4] The law prohibits testing of embryos for research purposes, donor insemination, freezing of embryos, and outlaws pre-implantation diagnosis for preventing genetically transmitted diseases. It also denies access to assisted reproductive technologies to single women and ordains that no more than three cells may be fertilized *in vitro* and that these be transferred to the womb simultaneously. Once couples agree on the treatment they will not be allowed to withdraw their consent. Moreover, those doctors who attempt to carry out procedures prohibited by the legislation face prison terms or fines, in addition to suspension from the medical register. The text of the law has at its heart an ideal of the family which is at odds with current societal realities.

---

[1] J Habermas, *The Future of Human Nature* (Cambridge, 2003) 105.
[2] S Jasanoff, *Designs on Nature: Science and Democracy in Europe and the United States* (Princeton, NJ, 2005) 6.
[3] W Brown, *Politics Out of History* (Princeton, NJ, 2001) 149.
[4] Law No 40 of 19 February 2004, 'Norme in materia di procreazione medicalmente assistita', *Gazzetta Ufficiale* No 45 of 24 February 2004.

The phenomenon of embryo protection in Italy has come about as the result of a particular conflation of circumstances, namely, a successful campaign on the part of the Church and lay Catholic interest groups which placed the issue of the sanctity of embryonic life on the legislative agenda; the lack of any ideological commitment on the part of the main political parties in this area, the continued reliance of politicians on Church support, and the gradual weakening of the influence of feminism as a mass political movement. This law can be seen as an intriguing case study in the way in which patriarchal institutional power can overcome accepted norms of autonomy in a pluralist society. In this recent episode, the Church has re-emerged as a political force or at the very least the mouthpiece of a resurgent conservatism, aided and abetted by a political class who would prefer to follow the Church's line on bioethics rather than formulate models of bioethical governance which regulated the area in a non-partisan manner. This strategy was, in part, provoked by the defeat of traditionalist groups in the struggle for legalized abortion in the 1970s and 1980s. This characterization of the state of reproductive medicine in Italy had as its aim not the effective governance of the field but the reinstating of Roman Catholic family values in law.

II. Conceiving Life in Law

Since the birth of the first test tube baby in Italy in 1983, politicians of all ideological hues have been making calls for the regulation of reproductive medicine. The first attempt to regulate the sector came in 1985 when the then Minister for Health, Costante Degan, introduced a circular, which prohibited all forms of donor insemination within the Italian national health service. This prohibition was not extended to clinics in the private sector, which were growing rapidly without any regulation. Many of those clinics were exploiting the desire of couples to have a child by any means. The circular also prohibited the freezing and preservation of embryos for use in the industrial or research sectors. As Ramjoue and Kloti have observed, the Circular resulted 'in unequal access to ART. Wealthy patients [could] afford faster access to a wider range of ART than those who depend[ed] on the [Italian National Health Service] for treatment and financial coverage. In the absence of a comprehensive regulation on ART, many techniques [were] available to a few, and few [were] available to many.'[5]

This state of affairs gave the religious right the grounds on which to attack the paucity of regulation of the assisted reproductive sector. In the 1990s neo-conservative politicians began to refer to the unregulated assisted reproduction sector as the 'far

[5] C Ramjoue, and U Kloti, 'ART policy in Italy: Explaining the lack of comprehensive regulation' in I Bleiklie, M Goggin, and C Rothmayr (eds), *Comparative Biomedical Policy: Governing Assisted Reproductive Technologies* (London, 2004) 59.

west'.[6] This characterization of the state of reproductive medicine in Italy had as its aim not the effective governance of the field but the reinstating of Roman Catholic family values in law. By creating this scene of chaos, which required immediate taming by the law, the political right was engaging in a politics of immunity, which attempts to erect symbolic boundaries between what is considered natural and that which is seen as excessive.[7] Conservative political elites have had a powerful ally in the Roman Catholic Church in their attempt to introduce restrictive policy in this area. Despite the fact that Article 7 of the Italian Constitution states explicitly that Church and State are separate entities, the Vatican has wasted no time in lobbying assiduously for a law which protects life itself in the abstract.

This campaign has succeeded in transforming the way in which reproductive medical services are governed by restricting reproductive freedom. This '*vita*politics' is not a politics of empowerment but a politics of entrapment in an imagined natural order. In this paradigm, as Barbara Duden notes: 'flesh is extinguished and replaced by a disincarnate notion'.[8] This '*vita*politics' does not refer to life in the material sense but to what Duden has called 'synthetic life'.[9] For Duden, 'synthetic life' has become the idol of the present, not only for the Church but also for ethicists, politicians, journalists, and advertising executives, among others. In this new ideogram 'life', Duden detects a wider concern with endangered life. She observes that 'this idolatry of life' is a consequence of 'a surreptitious shift in social and medical management concerns about the importance of "survival"'.[10]

Duden sees two cult objects as currently exemplifying this concern with survival, the planet Earth and the foetus. Each in their own way reflects a concern about mortality, survival and extinction. In this sense she notes that: 'The four-letter word [life] is meaningless and loaded; it can barely be analysed, yet it is a declaration of war'.[11]). For the religious right, the embryo is also invested with such great symbolic value. It is seen as the promise of the survival of the hetero-patriarchal family narrative. The notion of embryo citizenship includes the *what* of the embryo, thus further undermining the unique *who* of the female citizen. It creates a model of citizenship based on the future interests of an unborn entity and diminishes the current interests of the individual woman. Woman is, in Drucilla Cornell's words, reduced to the position of 'a what ... not a who, a self.'[12]

---

[6] The Northern League deputy and conservative Catholic, Irene Pivetti, coined this phrase in 1994 in order to put on the political and legislative agenda a restrictive response to what she perceived as a legislative lacuna. See E Cirant, *Non si gioca con la vita: Una posizione laica sulla procreazione assistita* (Rome, 2005) 180.

[7] See further F Neresini and F Bimbi, 'The Lack and the Need of regulation for assisted fertilisation: The Italian Case' in A Rudinow Saetnan, N Oudshoorn, and M Kitejczyk (eds), *Bodies of Technology: Women's Involvement with Reproductive Medicine* (Columbus, Oh, 2000).

[8] B Duden, *Disembodying Women: Perspectives on Pregnancy and the Unborn* (Cambridge, Mass., 1993) 100.

[9] ibid 99–106.   [10] ibid 110.   [11] ibid 104.

[12] D Cornell, 'Dismembered selves and wandering wombs' in W Brown and J Halley (eds), *Left Legalism/Left Critique* (Durham, NC, 2002) 350.

III. Church, State, and Bioethics

The Roman Catholic Church in Italy has consistently constructed woman as being synonymous with the private sphere. In 1987, the papal instruction *Donum Vitae*, penned by the then Cardinal Ratzinger, now Pope Benedict XVI, which outlined the Catholic Church's position in relation to artificial reproductive technologies, noted that the legitimate desire for a child should not be seen as a right to have a child at all costs. That would be to treat such a child as merely a means to an end. In the 1995 papal encyclical *Evangelium vitae*, which called for the protection of life, IVF was seen as contrary to Church teaching because it constituted a danger to human life in the form of the embryo.

If the embryo was seen as an entity deserving of unconditional respect in Church teachings, women were seen in an altogether different light. In 2004, Cardinal Ratzinger was the key drafter of the condescending Papal Letter to Women.[13] This document reveals current Vatican thinking on the role of women in society. The papal letter referred to the conflict between women's biological role and her role in the public sphere. It noted how an effective balance could be struck, but worried mostly about the way in which women's role as mother and carer was being diluted by wider changes in society. In the letter the following observation is made:

...the obscuring of the difference or duality of the sexes produces enormous consequences at different levels. [Feminism] which favoured equal opportunities for women, freeing her of every biological determinism, has in fact inspired ideologies which promote, for example, the questioning of the family in its natural two parent form, made up of a mother and a father, equalising homosexuality and heterosexuality, a new model of polymorphic sexuality.

Here the Vatican calls up the spectre of what it calls 'polymorphic sexuality' in its declaration of war on feminism in the name of Life itself. This spectral phenomenon is seen as disruptive of the two parent heterosexual family model. The Church here characterizes the feminist movement as being responsible for the decline of the heteropatriarchal family. In its rhetoric the Church accords more importance to woman's biologically determined role as reproducer and carer rather than as autonomous citizen. Woman are recognized as being different but not equal.

Many of those in secular political quarters have not seen the position of the Church as irrational. In fact, in 1996, the Italian National Commission on Bioethics published a report entitled 'The Identity and Status of the Human Embryo' which called for the embryo to be treated as a person from the moment

---

[13] Congregazione per la dottrina della fede, *Lettera ai vescovi della Chiesa cattolica sulla collaborazione dell'uomo e della donna nella chiesa e nel mondo* (31 July 2004).

of conception.[14] The report was to become influential in subsequent attempts at legislating in the area of assisted reproduction. It was much discussed in the media and the then president of the Bioethics Commission, Francesco D'Agostino, became a frequent guest on talk shows and news programmes, propounding the message that the embryo was 'one of us'.[15]

In January 1998, the then centre-left coalition government proposed a law on medically assisted reproduction. In its original form the draft legislation allowed both donor insemination and embryo research for therapeutic purposes. It also provided that the number of embryos produced in each treatment cycle should be limited to that amount strictly necessary for a single implantation, and in any case not more than four. During its passage through both houses of the Italian Parliament, the Bill was subject to several amendments, which would transform its structure and tone radically. The amendments were added by a cadre of Roman Catholic conservative parliamentarians whose aim was to ensure that the rights of the embryo be firmly implanted in the Bill. The Bill was amended to include a stipulation that in the carrying out of assisted reproductive services, regard should be had to the rights of all parties involved, including in particular those of the embryo.

The draft legislation was further amended by the introduction of a ban on the freezing of embryos, the limiting to three as the maximum number of embryos to be produced and implanted in any one treatment cycle and even more alarmingly an amendment was added which would allow the adoption of embryos as if they were children. The Chamber of Deputies approved the amended Bill by a majority of 266 to 153 on 26 March 1999. In the Senate certain parts of the text, which had been amended in the lower house, were further amended, including the removal of the reference to the embryo as being possessed of rights. This law was finally abandoned due to the fall of the coalition government.[16] This debacle showed the possibility of translating the extreme views of the Vatican and neo-conservatives into legislative reality and set the scene for the current law.

IV. The Embryo in Legal Space

In 2001, a relatively stable centre-right government under Silvio Berlusconi came to power. This proved a propitious development for advocates of embryo protection. By 2002 the new government had secured the approval of a draft Bill to govern the assisted reproduction sector in the Chamber of Deputies. The revised Bill granted the embryo symbolic legal recognition, and prohibited both embryo

---

[14] See Comitato Nazionale di Bioetica, *Identita e statuto dell'embrione umana* (Rome, 1996). The Commission was set up in 1990 by the then Prime Minister, Giulio Andreotti, and in its early years was an all male and predominantly conservative body.
[15] See further C Valentini, *La fecondazione proibita* (Milan, 2004) 110–22.
[16] See further Cirant (n 6 above) 182–4.

freezing and donor insemination. After its initial approval, the Bill remained in limbo awaiting further discussion in the Senate. The government did not appear to be in a hurry to speed the Bill through to final approval. However, the Vatican decided to expedite matters and once more exerted its influence on an apathetic government. In February 2003, on the occasion of the anniversary of the signing of the Lateran Pacts of 1929, representatives of the government attended a meeting with Vatican officials.[17] On this occasion, the Pope's displeasure at government policy in relation to its support for the war in Iraq, the implementation of discriminatory legislation on immigration, the so-called Bossi-Fini law (named after its instigators, the leaders of the separatist Northern League and of the former neo-fascist National Alliance respectively), and the government's opposition to the introduction of a system of clemency for prisoners, was communicated to the government. The Vatican pointed out that the swift approval of a law on assisted reproduction in line with its thinking would go some way to winning back its political backing.[18]

After this meeting, the government's lethargic position on assisted reproduction legislation, coincidentally or not, underwent a sea-change. By December 2003, the government had obtained approval of the draft legislation on assisted reproduction in the Senate, without any significant amendments. The Bill became law on 10 February 2004 after final approval by the Chamber of Deputies. Significantly, the centre-left opposition did not act to oppose the legislation. In fact, there seemed to be no major difference between the opposition and the government on the issue when it came to the final vote. They seemed to have a common interest in pushing the law forward based on shared patriarchal values.[19]

The 2004 law gives implicit legal recognition to what is termed the *concepito*, literally 'that which is conceived'.[20] Article 1(1) of the law states: 'subject to the conditions and according to the means set out in this Act, which guarantee the rights of all subjects involved, including the *concepito*, access to assisted human reproduction services is permitted in order to facilitate the resolution of reproductive problems caused by human sterility or infertility'.

---

[17] The Lateran Pacts were concluded between the Vatican and the fascist regime on 11 February 1929. The pacts gave official recognition to the special position of the Church in Italian politics. The Pacts recognized Roman Catholicism as the state religion as well as giving many concessions to the Vatican, including tax exemptions for employees of the Holy See, exemption from jury service for the clergy, and providing for the teaching of Christian doctrine in primary schools. The Pacts were given continued recognition in the post-fascist republic by virtue of the Constitution of 1948, art 7 which provides as follows: 'The State and the Catholic Church are, each within its own ambit, independent and sovereign. Their relations are regulated by the Lateran Pacts. Such amendments to these Pacts as are accepted by both parties do not require any procedure of Constitutional Revision'.

[18] See further C Flamigni and M Mori, *La legge sulla procreazione medicalmente assistita: Paradigmi a confronto* (Milan, 2005) 39–42.

[19] There were of course exceptions, including the Radical Party, and some dissident voices in the larger parties. See further, Cirant (n 6 above) 190–204.

[20] The term *concepito* is also used in the 1978 Abortion Act (Law no 194 of 22 March 1978, 'Norme per la tutela sociale della maternita e sull'interruzione volontaria della gravidanza').

This broad term *concepito* encompasses all stages of pre-natal development, including both the embryo and the foetus. In article 1(1), the legislation speaks of assuring the rights of all subjects involved in the process, including the *concepito*. In this way, the law implies, without explicitly stating, that the embryo has rights of some kind, which are deserving of protection.

However, this is the only article in which the term *concepito* is employed. In the rest of the Act the object of legal protection is named as the *embrione*, the embryo. The fact that the more vague term *concepito* is used only in the opening article could be seen as the signalling of a particular ideological view in relation to the manner in which life is conceived. In this case using the term *concepito* could imply that all unborn life once conceived is deserving of protection. As Fenton points out: 'Nowhere in Italian law is it stated that the embryo has legal status; nonetheless, the effect of the new law and subsequent case-law may well be to give the foetus legal status by the back door. The law establishes the rights of the unborn from the moment when the woman accepts the fertilization of her eggs.'[21]

By claiming that the embryo was already a member of the community of human persons, the government conferred on the embryo the status of a subject worthy of rights. This model sits uncomfortably with a properly pluralist model of bioethical regulation. As Jurgen Habermas has observed in this regard:

As a member of a species, as a specimen of a community of procreation, the genetically individuated child *in utero* is by no means a fully fledged person from 'the very beginning.' It takes entrance in the public sphere of a linguistic community for a natural creature to develop into both an individual and a person endowed with reason.

In the symbolical network constituted by the relations of mutual recognition of communicatively acting persons, the neonate is identified as 'one of us.' He gradually learns to identify himself—simultaneously as a person in general, as a part or a member of his social community [or communities], and as an individual who is unmistakably unique and morally nonexchangeable.[22]

The law also conflicts with the provision in article 31(2) of the Constitution of the Italian Republic, which states that no protection independent of the mother shall be accorded to the unborn.[23] Moreover, the Constitutional Court has held that the welfare of the embryo or foetus does not override a woman's right to health.[24]

---

[21] R Fenton, 'Catholic Doctrine Versus Women's Rights: The New Italian Law On Assisted Reproduction' (2006) 14 *Medical Law Review* 73, 104.

[22] Habermas (n 1 above) 35.

[23] Art 31 states in full: The Republic furthers family formation and the fulfilment of related tasks by means of economic and other provisions with special regard to large families. The Republic protects maternity, childhood, and youth; it supports and encourages institutions needed for this purpose.

[24] See the decision of the Constitutional Court of 18 February 1975, *Corte Costituzionale*, sentenza n 27 of 18 February 1975.

Under the 2004 law, access to *in vitro* fertilization is limited to those categorized as infertile or sterile couples. Couples who are not so defined but who are carriers of a hereditary genetic condition cannot have access to assisted reproductive services. Ironically, it is such couples who have no other choice but to seek such services given the risk of transmitting the condition to their offspring if they conceive 'naturally'. This has caused great difficulty for couples who are carriers of hereditary genetic illnesses, who are now no longer able to obtain pre-implantation genetic diagnosis in order to determine whether their embryos are affected by such illnesses. This interferes both with the couple's right to receive information in relation to making health care decisions, and their ability to consent fully to such procedures based on a complete knowledge of all the consequences involved in going ahead with the pregnancy.

Article 4 prohibits donor insemination.[25] Here the law allows only assisted reproduction using the egg and sperm of the couple involved (*homologous* reproduction) and prohibits the use of genetic material from third parties (*heterologous* reproduction). This reflects a particular ideological narrative, which sees *homologous* reproduction, ie reproduction using genetic material from the couple, as natural, and *heterologous* reproduction, that which uses donated genetic materials, as offending against nature. This is a socially imposed affinity based on an officially recognized social tie, ie marriage or a stable relationship.[26] In article 5, the law limits access to assisted reproductive services to adult heterosexual couples who are either married or in a stable relationship, are of a potentially fertile age, and are both living. The law makes it clear that the value of the heterosexual couple is accorded recognition over and above other familial formations. In addition the arbitrary inclusion of the term 'potentially fertile age' which is not further defined would appear to bar access to the procedure to older women in particular.[27]

Article 6(3) allows consent to the procedure to be withdrawn only up to the point at which the egg is fertilized. This leads to a bizarre result whereby the woman involved could potentially be forced to go through with the procedure once the egg is fertilized.[28] This forced consent measure, as well as going against all principles of autonomy, also breaches article 32(2) of the Italian Constitution which states that no person shall be subjected to medical treatment without legal

---

[25] Art 4(3) notes: 'È vietato il ricorso a tecniche di procreazione medicalmente assistita di tipo eterologo'.

[26] See further B Latour, *Les microbes: Guerre et paix* (Paris, 1984).

[27] Art 5 states in full: 'Fermo restando quanto stabilito dall'articolo 4, comma 1, possono accedere alle tecniche di procreazione medicalmente assistita coppie di maggiorenni di sesso diverso, coniugate o conviventi, in età potenzialmente fertile, entrambi viventi'.

[28] Art 6(3) states: 'La volontà di entrambi i soggetti di accedere alle tecniche di procreazione medicalmente assistita è espressa per iscritto congiuntamente al medico responsabile della struttura, secondo modalità definite con decreto dei Ministri della giustizia e della salute, adottato ai sensi dell'articolo 17, comma 3, della legge 23 agosto 1988, n.400, entro tre mesi dalla data di entrata in vigore della presente legge. Tra la manifestazione della volontà e l'applicazione della tecnica deve intercorrere un termine non inferiore a sette giorni. La volontà può essere revocata da ciascuno dei soggetti indicati dal presente comma fino al momento della fecondazione dell'ovulo'.

sanction and that the law can in no manner violate the limits imposed by the need to respect human dignity. Article 13 of the law prohibits experimentation on human embryos. Specifically, the law prohibits the production of embryos for research, all embryo selection for eugenic purposes, cloning, and inter-species fertilization. This aspect of the legislation has curtailed research into genetic illnesses. It also operates in conjunction with article 12 to prevent pre-implantation genetic diagnosis, as, under a rigid interpretation of the law, such a procedure could be seen as being for 'eugenic' purposes. The law falls into the model of what Roger Brownsword has called 'regulated prohibition'.[29] This prohibition is brought about by the particular socio-cultural influences which the government chose to acknowledge, in this case the views of the Roman Catholic Church.

V. Embryo Protection and Constitutional Rights

The draconian implications for couples who seek access to assisted reproductive services of the rigid implementation of the law can be seen clearly in the first case to test the provisions of the Act, which was heard in Catania in May 2004.[30] In this case a couple, who were both healthy carriers of the genetic condition *beta thalassaemia*, requested approval of pre-implantation embryo selection to ensure that the child born as a result would not suffer from this condition. The judge ruled that this was not permissible under the Act, and noted that the fertilized eggs be implanted whether or not there is the risk that they may carry this disease. This ruling was based on article 14 of the Act which prohibits the creation of a number of embryos greater than that strictly required for one contemporaneous transfer. The number created should be no greater than three.[31]

The couple argued that the 2004 Act was incompatible with the rights guaranteed in article 2 (the guarantee of inviolable human rights) and article 32(2) (the right not to be forced to submit to unwanted medical treatment) of the Constitution.[32] The judge dismissed these claims, noting that the obligation to

[29] R Brownsword, 'Regulating Human Genetics: New Dilemmas for a New Millennium' (2004) 12 *Medical Law Review* 14, 17.

[30] Tribunale di Catania, 1 sezione civile, (3 May 2004) at <http://www.diritto.it/sentenze/ magistratord/trib_ct_40_19_03_04.html>: See further P Abbate, 'Vittima di una legge crudele' *Il Manifesto*, 27 May 2004, 13, and R Fenton, 'Catholic Doctrine Versus Women's Rights: The New Italian Law On Assisted Reproduction' (2006) 14 *Medical Law Review* 73, 100–4.

[31] Art 14 also outlaws cryopreservation, the destruction of embryos, and embryo reduction. This, of course, leaves those embryos frozen and placed in storage prior to the coming into force of the Act in a state of limbo. On the one hand, they cannot remain as such, on the other, they cannot be destroyed. The Italian National Bioethics Committee has come up with a typically Jesuitical solution to this dilemma, namely that such frozen embryos be put up for 'adoption'. See further, Stefano Rodotà, 'Se l'embrione e più importante di una donna' *La Repubblica*, 21 November 2005, 1 and 18.

[32] Art 2 states: 'The Republic recognizes and guarantees inviolable human rights, be it as an individual or in social groups expressing their personality, and it ensures the performance of the unalterable duty to political, economic, and social solidarity.'

transfer three embryos into the womb simultaneously (notwithstanding the fact that one or more might be carriers of the genetic condition suffered by the parents), did not constitute unconsented to medical treatment contrary to article 32(2) of the Constitution.[33] Moreover the judge also dismissed the claim that the couple's inviolable human rights were being interfered with, noting that there was no fundamental right to have a child of one's desires. The judge argued that the child in this case is a potential child rather than an actually existing one. For the judge, the couple are interested not in the health of any child born as a result of the procedure, but in their wish to have the child of their desires, ie a healthy child, something which in his reading the Constitution does not guarantee.[34]

The judge here wilfully refuses to see that, by rigidly enforcing the three embryo transfer rule, there was the possibility that a child suffering from *beta thalassaemia* could be born as a result. The future child's physical condition is disregarded in the service of the protection of 'Life' itself in the abstract.[35] If the couple were to continue with the implantation and subsequently discover that the future child would suffer from such a condition, the only option left open to them would be a therapeutic abortion.[36] The process would then have to start over again with no guarantee that a similar outcome would not eventuate. As Fenton has rightly pointed out, in her discussion of this case:

The theme running throughout the judgement can be identified as the need to give effect to a strict and literal interpretation of the new law, driven by a misconception that use of [Pre-Implantation Genetic Diagnosis] is disguised eugenics, because a child can never be better off by not being born. The religious influence, the misplaced criticism of the parents' desire to have a 'designer baby', the disrespect for the rights of the mother and her subjugation to the rights of the foetus, illustrate that this judgement is the mirror image of the reasoning of the majority in Parliament who approved this law.[37]

Art 32 (2) states: 'Nobody may be forcefully submitted to medical treatment except as regulated by law. That law may in no case violate the limits imposed by respect for the human being.'

[33] On this point the judge noted:

L'argomento è illogico sotto un duplice profilo. Per un verso, infatti, non può in alcun modo dirsi che l'obbligo di trasferimento degli embrioni nell'utero costituisca un 'trattamento sanitario obbligatorio', per il semplice fatto che l'aspirante madre è posta, dalle disposizioni normative di cui all'art. 6 della legge 40/2004, nelle condizioni di scegliere liberamente e consapevolmente se sottoporsi o no alle tecniche di procreazione medicalmente assistita...

Per altro verso, quand'anche quello di cui si discute potesse essere ritenuto...un trattamento sanitario obbligatorio, poiché sarebbe previsto e disciplinato dalla legge, non violerebbe il 2 comma dell'art. 32 della Costituzione' Tribunale di Catania, 1 sezione civile, 3 May 2004, at <http://www.diritto.it/sentenze/magistratord/trib_ct_40_19_03_04.html>, 17.

[34] Here the judge stated: Ed è certo che la Costituzione non prevede un diritto assoluto dei genitori di avere un figlio come lo desiderano. *Tribunale di Catania, 1 sezione civile,* (3 May 2004) at <http://www.diritto.it/sentenze/magistratord/trib_ct_40_19_03_04.html>, 16.

[35] See Valentini (n 15 above) 139–58.

[36] See further M Fusco, 'Il "caso" Catania e la legge sulla procreazione assistita: Il referendum e davvero l'unica strada' *Diritto & Diritti* at <http://www.diritto.it/articoli/dir_famiglia/fusco1. html>.

[37] Fenton (n 30 above) 103–4.

A further challenge to the law was heard in Sardinia in July 2005. In this case, article 13 of the Act was the subject of the challenge.[38] In this case the *Tribunale Civile* of Cagliari referred the question of the constitutionality of article 13 to the Constitutional Court (*Corte Costituzionale*) for review. Here, a couple, XY and ZJ, who had been refused access to pre-implantation genetic diagnosis by their attending consultant in accordance with article 13 of the 2004 Act, claimed that this refusal was contrary to articles 2, 3, and 32(1) of the Italian Constitution.[39] XY had, on a previous occasion, undergone IVF treatment and had discovered in the eleventh week of her pregnancy that the foetus was affected by *beta thalassaemia*. As a result she decided to undergo a pregnancy termination. On this occasion the couple wanted to make sure that the embryo was not affected by the condition before implantation. They refused to go ahead with the implantation before receiving a pre-implantation genetic diagnosis. However, the doctor involved refused this service as it was contrary to article 13 of the 2004 Act.

The judge in this case (unlike the judge in the Catania case) noted that the question of the constitutional legitimacy of the law was not manifestly without foundation. In referring to decisions of the Constitutional Court in relation to abortion, the judge noted that the Constitutional Court had always declared in favour of the right to health of the woman when it came into conflict with the protection accorded to the foetus. In addition, the judge spoke of the right of a woman in such a case to receive the fullest information on the state of health of the embryo. In this case the general right to receive information in relation to medical procedures would apply to information obtained via pre-implantation genetic diagnosis in relation to the state of health of the embryo. The judge noted that this was the case in relation to determining the health of a foetus *in utero*. If couples in the position of the applicants were to be refused access to pre-implantation genetic diagnosis then this would place them in a different position to couples who had a right to obtain access to tests to determine the state of the foetus *in utero*. This raised the question of whether this ban was in accord with the equality provisions in article 3 of the Constitution, as well as the human rights provisions of article 2, and the specific provisions in relation to the right to

[38] A copy of the decision can be found at <http://www.lucacoscioni.it/?q=node/5796>. For further discussion see E Palmerini, 'Corte costituzionale e procreazione assistita (Trib. Cagliari, ord. 16.7.2005)' 6 *La Nouva Giurisprudenza Civile Commentata* 613.

[39] Art 3 provides as follows:

All citizens have equal social status and are equal before the law, without regard to their sex, race language, religion, political opinions, and personal or social conditions.

It is the duty of the republic to remove all economic and social obstacles that, by limiting the freedom and equality of citizens, prevent full individual development and the participation of all workers in the political, economic, and social organization of the country.

Art 32 (1) states: 'The republic protects individual health as a basic right and in the public interest; it provides free medical care to the poor.'

health in article 32(1). The judge referred the matter to the Constitutional Court for a consideration of the constitutionality of this aspect of the law.

The matter was eventually heard by the Constitutional Court on 24 October 2006.[40] The Court refused to allow lawyers for various interest groups (both pro-life groups and patients' rights groups) to present submissions. After very little deliberation the Court declared inadmissible, in the same evening, the question of the constitutional legitimacy of article 13. The rationale for the decision was to come on 9 November 2006, and was an even greater affront to justice and to the idea of constitutional adjudication. The rationale was without rationale. In an alarming decision, the Court, without actually stating why they were doing so, noted that the reference of the lower court in Cagliari was not admissible. The decision merely stated that the Cagliari court's assumption was contradictory in that the constitutionality of the impugned article could be deduced from other articles in the legislation and in the light of the interpretation of the entire law against the background of its stated intent. This circular and problematic non-decision merely states, in effect, that 'we cannot review the admissibility of this request because we think the law is constitutional, because of its stated aims'. In other words, the law is intended to protect the embryo and, as such, any procedure which would harm the embryo is not legitimate. However, the Constitutional Court refused to actually measure the constitutional validity of article 13 against the principles of equality and the right to health in the Constitution. It merely stated that the law itself was justified by its legitimating principles.

As far as the Constitutional Court was concerned, the law was constitution-proof. This is indeed a highly controversial and unacceptable outcome, a decision without a justification, not a critical analysis of the law but a rubber-stamping of an unconstitutional law by a Constitutional Court. Clearly unwilling to judge the constitutionality of the issue, the Court (in a decision which was not unanimous) stated that the law is legitimate because of its ideological premise.[41] Nonetheless, the Court in deciding not to decide and by bypassing any form of what one could reasonably call constitutional adjudication is doing exactly this. It is stating that

---

[40] Corte costituzionale, Ordinanza 369/2006, at <http://www.cortecostituzionale.it/ita/attivitacorte/pronunceemassime/pronunce/>. For further analysis, see L Trucco, 'La Procreazione Medicalmente Assistita Al Vaglio Della Corte Costituzionale' (2006) *Consulta Online*, at <http://www.giurcost.org/studi/trucco.html>; S Morsiani, 'A buon intenditor poche parole' (2006) *Forum di Quaderni Costituzionali*, at <http://www.forumcostituzionale.it/site/index2.php?option=com_content&task=view&id>; and A Morelli, 'Quando la Corte decide di non decidere. Mancato riorso all'illegitimità conseguenziale e selezione discrezionale dei casi (nota a margine dell'ord. N. 369 del 2006)' (2006) *Forum di Quaderni Costituzionali*, at <http://www.forumcostituzionale.it/site/index2.php?option=com_content&task=view&id>.

[41] The Court noted: 'pertanto, è evidente la contradizione in cui il Tribunale incorre nel sollevare una questione volta alla dichiarazione di illegittimità costituzionale di una specifica disposizione nella parte relativa ad una norma...che, secondo l'impostazione della stessa ordinanza di rimessione, sarebbe pero, desumibile anche da altri articoli della stessa legge...nonche dall'interpretazione dell'intero testo legislativo alla luce dei suoi criteri ispiratori'. *Corte costituzionale*, Ordinanza 369/2006, at <http://www.cortecostituzionale.t/ita/attivitacorte/pronunceemassime/pronunce/schedaDec> 4.

constitutional principles such as equality or a right to health do not matter in this case because the embryo's rights are paramount.

The decision could have been scripted by the Attorney-General, who appeared at the hearing on 24 October 2006 to defend the law. On that occasion he noted outrageously and in flagrant disregard of constitutional principles: 'considering that the right to have a "healthy child" does not exist and has no legal basis, and as such, one cannot accord any relevance to the element regarding the psycho-physical balance of the woman'.[42] This highly unconscionable piece of legal rhetoric disregarded the very being of women. The rhetoric follows the clinical, fleshless style of the lower court judge in the earlier case in Catania in May 2004, who spoke of no such thing as a right to have a healthy child and, in so doing, displayed a total disregard for both the rights and desires of parents and the suffering of any child born as a result. According to such a view, parents should be happy to give birth to chronically ill children with reduced quality of life even when it is possible (albeit legally prohibited) to attempt to give birth to a healthy one. This betrays a mentality amongst legal elites that we must accept what nature intended and this must be imposed by the state if need be.

In this case we are faced with the exception in which normal constitutional principles do not apply. The reasoning of the judge in the Catania decision, the Attorney-General, and the Constitutional Court all betray the same logic. We can suspend or forget the Constitution in this case. The physical and mental well-being of the woman is of no importance in a state whose guiding principles include the protection of 'Life' in the abstract. The valuing of *true* abstract life over the *mere life* of women, who must sacrifice their health and their desires, is evident here. This is so because some men think it is right that one should not have a healthy child and dismiss with such callousness the psychological and physical well-being of women. This is a very strange outcome to say the least. The Court, in engaging in such an exercise, acted neither in the interests of the health of any future child born as a result of such an intervention, nor in the interests of the health of the woman. Nor indeed, did it act in the interests of justice, in its lamentable failure to carry out its duty to scrutinize the constitutionality of this law.[43]

VI. The Possibility of Bioethical Pluralism

After the passing of the law in February 2004, the Radical Party acted as the main promoter of the call for its repeal. The means by which the opposition sought to

---

[42] '...tenuto conto che non essiste e non ha fondamento giuridico la pretesa di avere 'un figlio sano' e che, pertanto, non può assumere alcuna rilevanza l'elemento attinente all'equilibrio psico-fisico della donna' Cited in E Martini, 'Consulta "inteconda"' *Il Manifesto* (October 2006) at <http://www.ilmanifesto.it/Quotidiano-archivio/25-Ottobre-2006/art46.html>.

[43] See further C Lalli, 'Legge 40, articolo 13: le motivazioni della Corte Costituzionale sulla questione di legittimità', at <http://www.bioetiche.blogspot.com/2006_11_01_bioetiche_archive.html>.

modify the law was through the mechanism of the repeal referendum (*referendum abrogativo*); a mechanism used over twenty years previously by the right to life alliance in its attempt to repeal the 1978 abortion law. This mechanism requires that the petitioners for a referendum obtain at least 500,000 signatures of citizens with the right to vote. This form of referendum allows the petitioners to outline their proposals for either partial or total repeal of the legislation in question. Once the requisite number of signatures is obtained the referendum proposals are then scrutinized for admissibility by the Constitutional Court.[44]

Subsequently, a referendum committee was formed made up of an alliance of the Radical Party, representatives of parties of the centre-left, the Green Party, and other interested parties, including scientists, doctors, and patients' groups. In their original set of referendum proposals the referendum committee called for the total abrogation of the legislation. In addition, and in the event that the Constitutional Court would reject this proposal, four proposals, which would partially repeal the legislation, were also proffered. The first of these would partially repeal articles 12, 13, and 14 of the Act, and thereby remove the ban on embryo freezing and embryo experimentation. The second proposal would lead to the partial amendment of articles 1, 4, 5, 6, 13, and 14, thereby repealing the limitation on three embryos to be transferred simultaneously, and removing the limitation on access to such procedures to sterile or infertile couples alone. This would allow couples who were carriers of genetic disease access to such services. The third proposal would remove the legal recognition of the embryo. This would have led to the total repeal of article 1 and partial repeal of articles 4, 5, 6, 13, and 14. The final proposal would remove the ban on donor insemination. This would lead to the repeal of articles 4, 9, and 12.

Once the required signatures were obtained, the referendum proposals were submitted to the Constitutional Court to test admissibility. The Court decided to allow four out of the five proposed referendum proposals. The proposal that was rejected was that which called for the total repeal of the Act. With the four referendum proposals admitted the referendum campaign began. The main opposition to the referendum came from the Church itself. The Church set up an anti-referendum committee called 'Science and Life' to campaign on its behalf. The anti-referendum campaign, instead of calling for a no vote, called for voters to abstain so that the required quorum of 50 per cent plus 1 of voters would not be reached and the ballot would be declared invalid. This tactic was seen as a far more effective way of allowing the law under question to remain untouched but was also a subversion of the so-called deliberative democratic process. Having used the legislative process to secure their aims, the Church and the conservative right now tried to sabotage the democratic system again because it did not serve their ends.

---

[44] See Law No 352 of 1970, 'Norme sui referendum previsti dalla Costituzione e sulla iniziativa legislativa del popolo'.

The anti-referendum campaign proved to be successful. The quorum was not reached with only 25.9 per cent of voters turning out.[45] The battle for values in this case was won by default. The reason for the large abstention cannot be attributed simply to the Church's call for a boycott of the polls. The issue of assisted reproduction was not one which excited the enthusiasm of many voters. They saw it as an issue which affected a minority of the population. Moreover, the recent history of referendums in Italy has been marked by a high rate of abstention. Of the eighteen referendums held between 1997 and 2003, none have achieved a quorum.[46] This might be attributed to fatigue on the part of the electorate in relation to the use of the referendum, for example in 2000 alone there were seven referendums.[47] Notwithstanding the debate over the appropriateness of the referendum as a means of bringing about democratic change, the wider issue of the introduction of a law which erases autonomous reproductive decision-making has demonstrated the success of the Vatican's strategy of engaging explicitly in political action.

With the victory of the centre-left alliance led by Romano Prodi in the general election of April 2006, a new era, as far as bioethical governance, does not appear to have commenced in Italy. The situation seems to have continued in the same way as previously, with bioethical matters not being addressed in a mature and objective manner. The ranks of the government alliance are made up of many members with Roman Catholic ethical values, as ideological division in the Italian party system has always been transcended by a common Catholic faith. The Prime Minister, Romano Prodi, was previously the leader of the Popular Party, a party with strong Catholic allegiances, and has expressed his opposition to stem cell research and has spoken of his support for the sanctity of life of the embryo. Indeed, one of Prodi's first acts in relation to bioethics was to reprimand his Minister for Research who had removed the Italian veto from the vote in the European Union on the approval of stem cell research in 2006.[48] The Minister for the Interior, Giuliano Amato, has supported the notion of embryo rights and has written of the need to accord certain limited rights to the embryo. His point

---

[45] See G Luzi, 'Procreazione, quorum fallito' *La Repubblica*, 14 June 2005, 2.

[46] See A Barbera and A Morrone, *La Repubblica dei referendum* (Bologna, 2003) 209–51.

[47] Silvia Ballestra, in a provocative intervention, speaks of the unwillingness of the Italian electorate to engage with the vital issues raised by the referendum campaign. Instead, drained of curiosity or civic responsibility, in a polity which had become a mediocracy, they simply couldn't be bothered to inform themselves of what exactly was at stake in this referendum. She observes: 'Capire, dibattere, valutare le implicazioni tecniche, troppo faticoso. Toccava impratichirsi con termini quali citoplasma, blastociti, morula, ootidi, zigoti e gameti, avere una vaga idea di come funzionassero le cose, maneggiare daccapo le sigle FIVET, PMA, IPS, DIPI, TRA, e quindi occorreva un glossario da tenere sottomano. Bisognava, insomma, *studiare*. Pazzesca pretesa per un paese dove l'informazione si fa un vanto della più sfrenata superficialità, dove persino di fronte alla lista della spesa, al conto della tintoria, qualunque caporedattore ti può dire: troppo difficile! La gente non capirebbe!' S Ballestra, *Contro le donne nei secoli dei secoli* (Milan, 2006) 30–1.

[48] See further on this F Alberti, 'Ricerca sugli embrioni, Prodi richiama Mussi' *Corriere Della Sera*, June 2006, 10.

of departure is that the embryo should be protected by law and any law on assisted reproduction should be based on such a view.[49]

It is indeed ironic that Amato was appointed chair of an ad hoc committee set up by Prodi to look at the area of bioethical governance.[50] This ad hoc committee was set up to try to find common ground within the coalition government on issues of bioethical concern, given the diverse views ranging from those of theo-dems like Amato and Prodi to the more liberal views of other coalition partners such as *Rifondazione Communista* and *Rosa nel Pugno*. The ad hoc committee is a means by which to try to hammer out a common government view on bioethical issues. This, in itself, is hardly a sign that radical change on the issue of assisted reproduction is imminent. If the government is spilt internally on such issues, then the likelihood of a liberal model being introduced is slim.

Further evidence of the new government's lack of willingness to take this area seriously was its stalling on the appointment of the new members of the National Committee on Bioethics. The outgoing committee ended its term in June 2006 and was not replaced until December 2006. However the new government has not transformed the National Committee on Bioethics into a more radical body willing to take new approaches to the governance of issues of bioethical controversy. Within the governing coalition the names of several candidates to act as President of the Committee were circulated. The government was reluctant to appoint a candidate who might appear 'too secular' as opposed to being too Catholic.[51] Candidates of high-standing within the field of bioethics, such as Stefano Rodotà, Grazia Zuffa, and Tamar Pitch, were seen as 'too secular' for the new theo-democratic left-wing alliance. This shows an inability to deal with the question of bioethical regulation in an objective and open manner. The government views bioethics policy as the ultimate hot potato and has neither the courage nor the political will to act in a manner independent of the Church on these issues. One cannot expect reform to come from the organs of state as far as assisted reproduction is concerned. The appointment of an elderly male retired Constitutional Court justice, Francesco Paolo Casavola, as the new President of the National Bioethics Committee does not signal a radical transformation. The government has paid lip-service to the needs of women by appointing fourteen women to the thirty-five strong committee. Can this be anything more than tokenism from a government which supported the law on assisted reproduction and has made no move to repeal it?[52]

---

[49] G Amato, 'I dogmatici dell'embrione lo trattano come "muffa"' *Corriere Della Sera*, 11 April 2005, at <http://www.corriere .it/Primo_Piano/Documento/2005/04_Aprile/10/index.html>.

[50] See further, S Bianchi, 'La bioetica, nervo scoperto dell'Unione' *Il Sole 24 Ore*, 13 June 2006, at <http://www.ilsole24ore.com/fc?cmd=anteprima&artId=790169&chId=30&artType= Artico>.

[51] See further Editorial, 'Comitato di bioetica, *le diable probablement*' *Il Manifesto*, 30 November 2006, at <http://www.lucacoscioni.it/node/7675>.

[52] See further on the composition of the new National Bioethics Committee, 'Italia. Nominato nuovo Comitato nazionale di bioetica, Francesco Paolo Casavola il presidente' (2006) 128 *Cellule*

VII. Religiosity, Embryo Protection, and the Pluralist State: Comparative Perspectives

The existence of a culturally Catholic context alone is not enough to lead to a restrictive policy on assisted reproductive technologies. If we look at the stance of, for example, Belgium and Spain with regard to policy on assisted reproductive technology this becomes clear. In Belgium, another country with a large Catholic population, the government did not address the issue of assisted reproductive technologies in legislation until 2003. Until then the situation was marked by governmental non-decision.[53] Belgium had a relatively similar liberal model to that of Italy throughout the 1990s. In the words of one study 'everything [was] allowed, since nothing [was] strictly forbidden'.[54] Belgium has been and continues to be one of the leading centres for the development of reproductive technology in Europe. In fact it has been observed that Belgium has the highest density of assisted reproductive centres in the world.[55] Until legislation was finally introduced, the sector was governed by ministerial decrees which provided for a licensing and reporting framework.

Historically, the Belgian political system has been made up of Catholic, Socialist, and Liberal cleavages. However, due to the predominance of coalition governments in the post-war period, the need to seek compromise on policy issues has been foremost. As Schiffino and Varone have observed: 'the political system allows compromise to resolve the conflict among such a plural and segmented society as the Belgian one. It is by negotiating, and *not* by imposing the opinion of the majority, that the groups—and mainly the political parties—overcome their oppositions.'[56] This has led the Social-Christian (Catholic) parties to avoid putting bioethical issues on the political agenda. If these parties were to adopt an extreme conservative position on such matters then they would lose their ability to work with more liberal coalition partners and if they adopted a more liberal compromise position on bioethics they would lose their core Catholic vote. As a result, the most pragmatic political position to take on bioethical policy was to avoid it. This effectively led to a situation where issues such as IVF were not tackled in an explicit manner by coalition partnerships which included the Social-Christian parties as majority partners.

In 1999, for the first time since 1945, the Social Christians failed to enter a coalition government. The new coalition made up of Socialists, Liberals, and Greens adopted a different attitude to bioethical policy. This led to the

---

Staminali: Notiziario Quattordicinale sulla clonazione terapeutica, 8 December, at <http://www.staminali.aduc.it/php/stampa.php?id=5766>.

[53] N Schiffino and F Varone, 'Belgium: a bioethical paradise?' in I Bleiklie, M Goggin, and C Rothmayr (eds), *Comparative Biomedical Policy: Governing Assisted Reproductive Technologies* (London, 2004) 21.

[54] ibid 21.   [55] ibid 22.   [56] ibid 31.

introduction in 2003 of legislation in relation to assisted reproductive technologies. Unlike the Italian case, the pressure placed on central government by the Church is not as strong and neither is the degree of religiosity. The existence of a strong Social-Christian party for most of the post-war period impeded the political discussion of controversial bioethical issues but in the assisted reproductive technology sector did not impede development of a more liberal model of provision. The value pluralism which prevented the Social Christians from engaging in a more conservative governance style in relation to bioethical policies is also present within the medical profession, which did not push for restrictive legislation in this field. Indeed, given Belgium's leading position in this sector worldwide, those in reproductive medicine were quite happy to have as little central regulation as possible. Unlike Italy, then, the grassroots Catholic culture did not impose itself on policy-making in relation to reproductive technology in Belgium.

In Spain, another traditionally Catholic state, the approach varies widely from the one taken in Italy. Spain was one of the first European states to introduce legislation in this area. The legislation itself is not restrictive in nature. Like Italy, there is a clear split between conservative Catholic thought on assisted reproductive technology and the more liberal stance taken by many in the medical profession. Unlike Italy, the more liberal views of medical actors prevailed when legislation was introduced. The Spanish Law 35/1988 on Assisted Reproduction Techniques (*Ley sobre Tecnicas de Reproduccion Asistid*) is aimed at the objective regulation of assisted reproductive technologies and does not include any provision which would give special legal protection to the embryo. In terms of access, women are not required to be married or indeed in a stable relationship in order to be eligible for treatment.[57] As Dubouchet and Kloti observe, the legislation's objectives:

…are primarily of a medical nature…and there is…no reference to embryos and the protection due to them…One of the law's goals is to ensure progress and the expansion of scientific research, which must in no way be hindered unless this is justified by reasonable and objective criteria and in order to prevent conflict with human rights or the dignity of the human being…It can therefore be summed up as 'offering a framework without constraints'.[58]

Such a liberal framework was facilitated by a number of factors. First, the medical community acted in a clear and cohesive manner in putting forward proposals for legislation. The medical sector was of the opinion that regulation of this field was necessary in the interests of scientific progress. Medical actors succeeded in putting their ideas across to the parliamentary committee set up to look into the matter in 1984. Indeed the President of the Committee, Marcelo

---

[57] See J Dubouchet and U Kloti, 'ART in Spain: Technocratic inheritance and modernist aspirations' in I Bleiklie, M Goggin, and C Rothmayr (eds), *Comparative Biomedical Policy: Governing Assisted Reproductive Technologies* (London, 2004) 102–19.

[58] ibid 105.

Palacios was himself an expert in the area of bioethics and a medical doctor, and supported a liberal framework for this area. Secondly, Spain was in a period of transition after the Franco dictatorship and the ruling Socialist Party in this period was favourable to both liberal models of governance as a reaction to the repressive Catholic conservatism of the Franco period and to progressive scientific development. The model for the regulation of the assisted reproductive technology sector proffered by the medical community was in harmony with these objectives. Thirdly, Catholic opposition to the legislation was weak. The Church in Spain failed to initiate a coherent campaign against the new law and failed to gain support amongst members of the special parliamentary committee on the topic in the same way that the medical community did. In this regard, the position was the reverse of that in Italy. When legislation was being formulated in Italy the Church drove the design and implementation of legislation on its terms.

VIII. Conclusion

The case of Italy is both unique and also evokes many questions of enormous current import for other societies in relation to how one can or should govern bioethical issues. The Italian experience in relation to the governance of human reproduction forces us to ask how law can accommodate different views on bioethical policy in 'multiethical'[59] societies. Can there be such a thing as impartial governance of such issues in a state which, despite transformations, remains symbolically and materially masculine and culturally Catholic?[60] Successive Italian governments have tended to avoid addressing issues of bioethical controversy in an objective and honest manner due to a fear of a conservative backlash and a subsequent loss of political support. As Stefano Rodotà has so astutely pointed out in this regard:

...today we live in an era characterized by a proliferation of values and of disputes about how to give recognition to pluralism...Can one make [such values] live together, avoiding the transformation of such disputes into a more serious conflict?...In this regard, vehement demands are made for certainties at any cost, and of course, short-cuts [are made]. This leads to the imposition of an incontestable Truth, by way of the law...in this way the law takes on an authoritarian hue, and appears as an imposition and not as a reflection of a shared feeling.[61]

---

[59] This term is borrowed from Enzo Bianchi, who used it to describe Italian society in an interview on the radio programme 'Fahrenheit', Rai Radio 3, Monday 10 July 2006, at <http://www.radio.rai.it/radio3/fahrenheit/mostra_evento.cfm?Q_EV_ID=182142>.

[60] For an illuminating analysis of this theme in relation to the question of violence against women in contemporary Italy, see S Plesset, *Sheltering Women: Negotiating Gender and Violence in Northern Italy* (Stanford, Cal., 2006).

[61] S. Rodotà, *La vita e le regole: Tra diritto e non diritto* (Milan, 2006) 16.

This sums up very well the manner in which bioethical issues have been dealt with, or rather not dealt with in Italy over the past twenty years. Instead of attempting to gain community consensus on an issue and working towards a solution which expresses the values of all sectors of society, governments have tended to see such matters in very simplistic terms: either they are morally supportable or morally suspect. In all this the pluralist state's moral guide has been the Vatican.

There is an unwillingness on the part of political elites to engage in open deliberative consensus politics on issues of bioethical controversy, particularly where Roman Catholic ethical values are at stake. This experience differs markedly from developments in this field in other culturally Catholic European states such as Spain and Belgium, where a more open and consensual model of bio-ethical policy-making has evolved. This would lead one to conclude that despite high degrees of secularization in Italian society, the levels of religiosity remain high and particularly influential when it comes to particular areas of bioethical policy. One could argue that a resurgent and more overtly politically active Church establishment is coordinating a mass backlash politics against what it sees as an unwelcome secularization of Italian politics. In doing so they have tapped into and harnessed an already existing religiosity amongst a significant percentage of the citizenry.

11

Precautionary Reasoning in Determining Moral Worth

Stephen W Smith[1]

I. Introduction

Deciding which individuals matter morally is one of the most important foundational issues in any field of ethics. In bioethics this can be a particularly difficult issue considering the wide range of entities[2] which may need to be considered in a specific problem. Generally, though, approaches to deciding on moral worth may be seen as falling into two broad categories. The first asserts that moral worth is connected with species membership. In this approach, provided an entity happens to be a member of a particular species, for example human beings, they are granted all of the rights associated with that species.[3] This approach may be associated with religious viewpoints where human beings 'are created in God's image' and are 'given dominion' over all other things.[4] Other secular views may also be based upon the fundamental premise that moral worth is based upon species membership. These viewpoints held sway for a long period during human history and have, as one benefit, that they are easily applied (even if we may disagree with the applications of the method by previous generations).

[1] Deputy Director, Institute of Medical Law, University of Birmingham. I would like to thank Roger Brownsword, Gavin Byrne, Steven Cammiss, Rob Cryer, Mary Ford, and the participants of the *Law and Bioethics* colloquium at University College London for helpful comments on earlier drafts of this chapter. The usual disclaimers apply.

[2] For reasons of clarity and ease of expression, in this chapter I will be referring to 'that thing which we are deciding if it is morally relevant or not' as an 'entity'. This is, by deliberate choice, a vague content-less term to use. However, a more specific term, such as 'human' or 'individual' would not include all of the relevant things to which we might wish to ascribe moral worth and the definition of 'person' is one of the important concerns for this chapter. Other terms which would probably have also been reasonable choices are 'being' or 'creature', although those might also suffer from problems. In any case, the term entity is merely a placeholder for the thing which might or might not be morally relevant prior to the determination of moral worth.

[3] G Meilaender, *Bioethics: A Primer for Christians* (Grand Rapids, Mich., 2nd edn, 2005) 6; H Kuhse and P Singer, *Should the Baby Live?: The Problem of Handicapped Infants* (Oxford, 1985) 121.

[4] Meilaender, (n 3 above) 30–2; Kuhse and Singer (n 3 above) 124.

The other way to determine moral worth is not based upon membership in a particular group but by the entity having certain characteristics or abilities.[5] This is because the simple fact that one has the basic genetic structure of a particular species does not appear to be a relevant ethical criterion when determining which moral rights to grant to a specific party.[6] So, the mere fact that one has the basic genetic structure of a human being does not mean, in and of itself, that one should be given full moral worth because the simple fact that one has a specific number of chromosomes in a particular pattern does not seem to have any overwhelming relevance. Therefore, what is important is the possessing of particular criteria. The relevant criteria may consist of any number of things, but are most likely to be cognitive or other mental characteristics of the entity.[7] The reasons mental and cognitive characteristics are given such prominence is that those granted full moral worth are seen to be those entities which are most likely to be able to value their own existence.[8] In other words, we cannot act against the interests of things which do not have interests at all. I can do what I want to a rock, for example, because it has no interests to protect and is not harmed in any way by my actions even if I break it into tiny pieces. If an entity can value its own existence, however, we can harm it by adversely affecting those interests. Thus, breaking into small pieces an entity which does value its own existence is a harm to that entity. We may also grant lesser moral status to other entities which do not rise to the level of person based upon other factors (for example the ability to feel pain) but we are unlikely to grant to those entities the full moral value that we grant ourselves because, while acting against their interests may harm those entities to some extent, it is unlikely to harm them to the full extent that it does us.[9]

By far, one of the most dominant of these types of theories of moral worth is personhood.[10] According to this theory, only entities called persons are entitled to full moral worth. A person is not necessarily synonymous with a human being

---

[5] Kuhse and Singer (n 3 above) 119.

[6] J Harris, *The Value of Life* (London, 1985) 12–19.

[7] Kuhse and Singer (n 3 above)121–3.

[8] ibid 130–1.   [9] Harris (n 6 above) 18–19.

[10] John Harris has, in the past, disputed the place of personhood theory as the 'dominant view' of bioethics. J Harris 'Four Legs Good, Personhood Better' (1998) IV(1) *Res Publica* 54. However, it appears that Harris' claim was that personhood theory cannot claim pre-eminence in any field of bioethics because of the vast diversity of ethical theories, but does not make claims about its place within theories which ascribe moral worth based upon certain characteristics of the individual. Even if Harris meant the claim to extend to the viewpoint that personhood theory is not the dominant theory of this type, one needs only to look at the vast array of personhood theorists such as John Harris, Peter Singer, Helga Kuhse, Michael Tooley, Jonathan Glover, and others to realize that personhood theory is an incredibly important theory of moral worth. It therefore may not be *the* dominant theory of moral worth based upon the characteristics of the entity, but it is certainly *a* dominant theory in the literature. Singer has, for example, stated that 'Among philosophers and bioethicists, the view that I was to defend [his view on moral worth] is by no means extraordinary; if it has not quite reached the level of orthodoxy, it, or at least something akin to it, is widely held, and by some of the most respected scholars in the fields of both bioethics and applied ethics.' P Singer, *Applied Ethics* (Cambridge, 2nd edn, 1993) 343–4.

but is instead an entity which has the capacity for certain criteria.[11] Among them are: self-awareness, self-control, a sense of the future, a sense of the past, the capacity to relate to others, concern for others, communication, curiosity, rationality, the use of language, or autonomy.[12] It is worth emphasizing that it is not the discernable presence of the specific criteria that is necessary for personhood but the capacity to exercise such criteria.[13] Thus, a competent human adult[14] may still be a person even if that adult never seems to utilize a particular characteristic necessary for personhood or if the adult is currently unable to exercise that particular characteristic such as when he or she is sleeping. There may also be differences between different types of personhood theories about the relevant criteria, whether one must possess all of the criteria or only a percentage of them (for example can someone suffering from permanent amnesia be a person?) and other issues but, by and large, the basics of personhood theory are relatively stable.

Personhood theory thus provides a reasonably flexible approach to determining moral worth. Additionally, it eliminates concerns about speciesism, the concern that we are preferring our species over other ones merely because it is our species. That does not mean, however, that there are no problems with personhood theory. One of the primary problems with personhood theory is the position it takes on certain human entities such as those in persistent vegetative states (PVS) or newborns. Under the most common versions of personhood theory, these human entities are not persons because they lack the relevant criteria.[15] Thus, these entities are not entitled to the full moral status that persons (again such as competent adult human beings) have.[16] That means we *qua* moral actors may be allowed to act towards these entities in ways in which we are not allowed to act towards persons.

The problem with this approach is not that such a viewpoint is logically inconsistent (which it is not) but because it seems to conflict with the intuition of the ordinary member of the moral community about moral status in these

[11] Kuhse and Singer (n 3 above) 130–1.

[12] ibid. It should be noted that Kuhse and Singer are actually referencing a Protestant philosopher by the name of Joseph Fletcher, who states that the list of criteria are 'indicators of humanhood'. Kuhse and Singer, however, see these as possible criteria for personhood although they place prime importance on self-awareness and sense of the past and future. See also J Harris, 'Euthanasia and the value of life' in J Keown (ed), *Euthanasia Examined*, (Cambridge, 1995) 9.

[13] J Harris, 'Final thoughts on final acts' in J Keown (ed), *Euthanasia Examined* (Cambridge, 1995), 58–9.

[14] By competent human adult, I simply mean those human beings which the law would consider able to make contracts and the like. In medical terms, these would be those who are capable of making health care decisions without resorting to the courts for a determination about the best interests of the patient. This, of course, does not mean that those who are not competent human adults are not persons, just that the standard example used of a person is a competent human adult.

[15] J Harris, 'The philosophical case against the philosophical case against euthanasia' in J Keown (ed), *Euthanasia Examined* (Cambridge, 1995) 36–45; J Glover, *Causing Death and Saving Lives* (London, 1977) and Kuhse and Singer (n 3 above).

[16] Harris (n 15 above) Glover (n 15 above); and Kuhse and Singer (n 3 above).

cases.[17] The ordinary member of the moral community is likely to see the case of newborns to be particularly troubling. The general viewpoint would be that newborns are not deserving of a lower moral status than adult humans but are actually worthy of greater protection due to their limitations. While this feeling may be less pronounced in the case of adults in a persistent vegetative state, the recent case of Terry Schiavo in Florida shows it is far from absent.[18] This does not mean, obviously, that we necessarily provide them with all of the rights that we might provide competent human adults in areas such as decision-making. In fact, providing greater protection means we take decision-making power away from entities such as newborns because they are incapable of making decisions. Note, however, that the protection of these entities is not because of a belief that they are less morally worthy, but based upon perceived incapacities that the entity possesses to act in their own best interests.

What we have, then, is a fundamental disagreement between at least some of those in the field of bioethics and those purporting to be acting for those in the 'real world' who must deal with the application of bioethics. This is presented perhaps most starkly in the treatment that Peter Singer, one of the most prominent proponents of personhood theory, seems to get in various parts of the world. His talks or lectures have been subject to a number of attempts to have them cancelled, including the very successful campaign in Germany described in *Practical Ethics*.[19] These attempts continue to this day.[20] Whatever you might think of Singer's particular take on personhood, it should be noted that most of the concerns expressed about Singer's viewpoint are about points which would not differ from most personhood theories. In other words, they are probably inherent in the theories themselves, not within Singer's expression of that theory. It is thus a global problem for bioethics.

The issue can be summarized as follows. Personhood theory is one of the dominant theories about moral worth in bioethics. Additionally, it provides a number of benefits over the more traditional species-based theory. It avoids concerns about speciesism. It provides a measurable basis for determining moral worth and that basis appears to be more closely aligned with relevant criteria about moral worth. Unfortunately, it also reaches results which appear to many to be counter-intuitive, clearly wrong, or morally abhorrent. Of course, merely because

---

[17] One possible way we can gauge the opinions of the average member of the moral community on a particular issue is to see how the question is treated under the law. This will not, of course, always provide a compelling answer but is likely to provide a general response. In the case of neonaticide, while the withdrawal of treatment from a severely disabled newborn is acceptable in many legal jurisdictions, the deliberate killing of a severely disabled newborn is not. See eg *R v Arthur* (1981) 12 BMLR 1; *Portsmouth NHS Trust v Wyatt* [2005] 1 FLR 21, [2004] Fam Law 866.

[18] See eg the comment in *The Nation* posted by Laura Hershey, available at <http://www.thenation.com/doc/20050502/hershey> (accessed 11 September 2007).

[19] Singer (n 10 above) 337–59.

[20] See eg the website of the disability rights group Not Dead Yet <http://www.notdeadyet.org>, which has a whole section on Singer (accessed 11 September 2007).

a particular theory reaches results which might not be considered acceptable to a particular part of the population at large does not make it invalid per se. In this particular case, that might be even more true as a number of the protests appear to be based upon either an inaccurate understanding of what certain bioethicists (including Singer) have said, what those bioethicists have said has been taken out of context or, most importantly, the arguments presented against particular theories do not appear to be based on anything that those bioethicists have actually said.[21] Even so, it is worth exploring in greater depth the disparity between the dominant viewpoint in bioethics and the dominant viewpoint of ordinary members of the moral community. Consequently, this chapter will examine whether this disparity results from a fundamental premise in personhood theory or whether it is possible to keep the essential elements of personhood theory while moving that position towards a more acceptable one from the perspective of ordinary members of the moral community.

One of the essential elements of personhood theory is the determination of a specific entity as a person. Thus, if we created a more inclusive definition of personhood, many of these problems would disappear. In fact, there has been a large amount of research on just this concern. For example, one argument that has been used to expand the number of possible persons is the idea of potentiality, often used with arguments relating to embryo research or abortion. Under this sort of argument, while it is conceded that the entity in question (ie the embryo or foetus) does not possess the characteristics necessary for personhood at the moment, it will become a person given appropriate circumstances.[22] Thus, we should treat it as if it is a person now because it has the potential to be one.[23]

There are a number of possible problems with this type of approach. First, the foundational premise of the argument that something with the potential to belong to category X should be treated as if it currently belongs to category X is far from obvious.[24] John Harris has noted that every living human being has the potential to be a corpse because given the appropriate circumstances—death—a human being will become a corpse.[25] That does not mean that we should currently treat all living human beings as if they were corpses.[26] Consequently, there would appear to be little reason to treat entities with the potential to be persons as if they were currently persons. Even if this particular counter-argument can be resolved, it would be necessary to decide how far this concept of potentiality goes. What about foetuses which will develop into anencephalic babies and will therefore be incapable of the higher brain functions required of persons? Do we consider them to have the potential for personhood even if they will never

---

[21] See eg Singer (n 10 above) 346–7, 350, where he describes various attempts by various groups to protest against his views where the objections are, at least in part, based upon misconceptions of those views.

[22] Harris (n 6 above) 11.   [23] ibid.

[24] ibid.   [25] ibid.   [26] ibid.

become persons?[27] What about sperm or unfertilized eggs?[28] Given the appropriate circumstances, they too will become persons. If the question is potential for personhood, why do we not consider them to be persons as well? If one wishes to expand the possible criteria for personhood, these and other problems will need to be addressed.

However, the necessary criteria for personhood is only part of the task when determining personhood. It is also necessary that those criteria be applied in an appropriate manner. Otherwise, there might be a situation where we have the best possible criteria (however we wish to decide that) but still reach untenable conclusions because those criteria are not applied correctly. One important aspect of any method of determining personhood is the applicable burden of proof. Is it up to the entity to prove that it is a person or must those wishing to offer a specific entity less moral protection prove that it is not a person? While not explicitly stated in many cases, a majority of personhood theories, including those by Singer, Harris, and others, appears to place the burden of proof on the entity and not on those doing the evaluation.[29]

This may seem to be a minor concern because, after all, the real issue is to get the determination correct. Thus, in a perfect world, it would not really matter where the burden of proof lies; what matters is that the evidence is assessed appropriately and personhood assigned according to that assessment.[30] Unfortunately, we do not live in a perfect world. In particular, we have issues with both our knowledge about the world and our perception of it. One need only consider the number of times throughout history when the standard beliefs about nature, the world, and our place in the universe have been shown to be incorrect even though the general consensus was that those beliefs were unassailable.[31] Additionally, one

---

[27] If we wish to argue that even those foetuses which have almost no chance of developing into a person have the potential to be persons, then what might be at work is an attempt to dress up a theory of moral worth based upon species membership as one based upon characteristics. In other words, if all human beings, regardless of their current or potential characteristics are to be considered persons, then it appears that the fact that an entity is a human being is what is doing the real work. This kind of argument, then, would be subject to all of the concerns previously raised about species-based theories of moral worth. For an example of argument which appears to be something of this type, see J Finnis, 'The fragile case for euthanasia, a reply to John Harris' in J Keown (ed), *Euthanasia Examined* (Cambridge, 1995) 48.

[28] Harris (n 6 above) 11–12.

[29] See eg J Harris and S Holm, 'Abortion' in H Lofollette (ed) *The Oxford Handbook of Practical Ethics* (Oxford, 2003) 116, where they state that 'we want *detectable evidence of personhood*...we need to know whether and why we should assume that the sorts of creatures that we know to be normally capable of developing self-consciousness—namely, human creatures—are persons at some time prior to the manifestation of the "symptoms" of personhood,' (emphasis in original).

[30] This presumes that there is a correct answer to the question of personhood in relation to a particular entity. Whether that necessarily requires that I or a reader who accepts that premise must make any greater commitment about things such as mind-independent truths is a question beyond the scope of this chapter.

[31] As one example, we could consider the work done on animal behaviour and, in particular, on animal behaviour which appears to be based upon some sort of cognitive ability. This includes work done with primates on language capabilities. See eg Singer (n 10 above) 110–17. Additionally,

need only consider the times, such as on encountering mirages, when our percep-tions have been faulty to understand how those can sometimes fail. So, even if we generally get things right there will be occasions where either our perceptions or the knowledge that results from those perceptions is likely to be flawed or at least incomplete.[32]

What becomes important, then, is how we deal with these knowledge deficien-cies that arise. One of the ways in which we can deal with this is to examine how we assign the risk of error. In legal settings, of course, one of the ways in which we assign the risk of error is through the previously mentioned burden of proof. If the costs of being incorrect are seen as being quite high, then we set the burden of proof fairly stringently. This is what we do in criminal cases, where the cost of an incorrect judgment is that an innocent person loses their liberty. On the other hand, if we do not consider the risks of being incorrect as being that high, we might assign a lower burden of proof to a particular case. Furthermore, the legal system also takes note of who must do the proving in a particular case.

If we examine moral status in the same way, we might examine claims differently from the way outlined above where the burden of proof is placed on the entity. First, since claims about personhood ground many of our moral judgments, it would be a decision where the costs of failure would be reason-ably high. If we decide that an entity which is a person is not a person, then we have acted incorrectly towards that entity. We have not treated it in ways that it deserves and this is a very serious ethical problem. So, we might begin to examine moral worth by putting the burden of proof quite high. Additionally, we might consider where we have placed the burden of proof. If it is us who is interested in deciding whether a particular entity is morally worthwhile, why should the entity itself have to prove its worth? Why could we not place the burden of proof on us to show an entity is not worthy of the status of person? In other words, why not assert that it is better for us to assume the risk of being incorrect than it would be to assign that risk to the entity in question? That way, an incorrect decision

---

it includes work with both bottlenose dolphins and elephants on whether they are able to recog-nize themselves in mirrors. See D Reiss and L Marino, 'Mirror self-recongnition in the bottle-nose dolphin—A case of cognitive convergence' (2001) 98 *Proceedings of the National Academy of Sciences* 5937; J Plotnik, F de Waal, and D Reiss, 'Self-recognition in an Asian elephant' (2006) 103 *Proceedings of the National Academy of Sciences* 17053. Finally, there have also been the recent studies dealing with New Caledonian crows. What is of particular interest with the crows is their ability to use tools, including the ability to use one tool to manipulate another. See A Taylor *et al*, 'Spontaneous Metatool Use by New Caledonian Crows' (2007) 17 *Current Biology* 1504; See also L Bluff *et al*, 'Tool-related Cognition in New Caledonian Crows' (2007) 2 *Comparative Congition and Behaviour Reviews* 1 (although the article by Bluff *et al* is more reluctant to make claims about the cognitive abilities of the crows).

[32] There is, of course, a whole field of philosophy, epistemology, which deals with just these sorts of concerns. However, most of the debates within epistemology are beyond the scope of this chapter. Instead, the essential point for our purposes is that our knowledge about the world, and in particular, our knowledge about other entities is not perfect and we need to adjust our ethical decision-making accordingly. Those interested in the debates about theories of knowledge gener-ally should consult J Dancy, *An Introduction to Contemporary Epistemology* (Malden, Mass., 1985).

will cause problems for us as opposed to causing them for the entity. This would increase the chances of mistakenly deciding a non-person is a person, but would decrease the chance of deciding a person is not a person. If this kind of system has some sort of appeal, at least initially, we should consider it in more depth. What would such a system look like? How would it operate? The purpose of this chapter is to begin to analyse that point by presenting one possible method by which we could switch the burden of proof while still maintaining the essential elements of personhood theory. We can then analyse whether it would provide a reasonable way of determining personhood.

II. Precautionary Principles and the Gewirthian Approach

To do that, though, we need an ethical system capable of dealing with these sorts of proof problems. To make things a bit easier, it would also be useful to use a system already in existence instead of creating one from scratch. Unfortunately, there is none that I am aware of that deals specifically with personhood. What does exist, however, is one described by Beyleveld and Brownsword in *Human Dignity in Bioethics and Biolaw* which is based upon Gewirthian agency theory.[33] This approach will be used in this chapter because of the following factors: (1) it is already in existence; (2) Gewirthian agency theory is similar to personhood theory on the factors important to this analysis; and (3) it is relatively easy to use. Before applying it to personhood theory, though, it will be useful to examine the theory to provide a basic framework.

As noted above, Beyleveld and Brownsword's approach is based upon the philosophy of Alan Gewirth. Gewirth was an American philosopher attempting to create an ethical theory which did not suffer from the flaws of Kantian ethics. He therefore based his theory, not upon persons, but upon agents. An agent is someone who is capable of doing voluntary actions and does them for a reason. Thus, an agent is someone who can create and implement a life plan. Gewirth then works from the initial statement an agent would make (I do action X for purpose E) to arrive at what is referred to as the Principle of Generic Consistency (PGC)—ie the idea that an agent must provide the 'generic rights' (a basic set of moral rights) to all other agents at the risk of denying his or her own agency.[34] We thus have something with some relatively compelling parallels to personhood theory. First, it is based upon criteria which are separate from species membership. Second, they are criteria which are primarily cognitive or mental

---

[33] D Beyleveld and R Brownsword, *Human Dignity in Bioethics and Biolaw* (Oxford, 2001). A previous version of this argument is presented by D Beyleveld and S Pattinson, 'Precautionary Reason as a Link to Moral Action' in M Boylan (ed) *Medical Ethics* (Upper Saddle River, NJ, 2000) 39–53.

[34] ibid 72. For a good summary of the fairly complex philosophical argument about the PGC, see Beyleveld and Brownsword, (n 33 above) 72–82.

in nature. Third, the categorization of something as an agent grounds a set of moral rights and the lack of agency means that the entity lacks those rights. Thus, the determination of whether an entity is or is not an agent is a fundamentally important one.

Up until this point in the argument, Beyleveld and Brownsword follow Gewirth's approach. However, they begin to deviate and do so in an important way for our consideration. Gewirth originally suggested that there could be something called a partial agent.[35] These were not full agents because they did not meet the criteria but were granted some of the generic rights because they had some of the criteria necessary for agency.[36] Beyleveld and Brownsword disagree with the idea that one can be a 'partial' agent.[37] According to them, one either is or is not an agent. It is not something you can be in part. Instead of there being something called a 'partial' agent, however, Beyleveld and Brownsword do think there can be other categories of agent like 'potential' or 'ostensible' agents.[38] The difference between a partial agent and a potential one is a question of knowledge. According to Beyleveld and Brownsword, we should accept the fact that the only agent we can be sure of is our self. We can only guess about the other possible agents in the world because it is theoretically possible, even if not probable, that there are no other agents in the world. All other things which act like agents may only be entities which look and act like agents but are not. Alternatively, things may not look or act like agents but turn out to be agents. Considering our imperfect knowledge of the world, what we are left with is a guess, educated though it may be, about the possible agency of other entities. A potential agent, then, is an entity which we think might be an agent; an ostensible agent is an entity which we are fairly convinced is an agent but we are not completely sure.[39]

What it is important to realize, though, is that the consequences of a mistaken determination are not the same. If I assume a particular entity is an agent, granting to the entity all of the generic rights of agency, and it turns out the entity is not actually an agent, then nothing really bad happens. I have granted agency rights to something which does not necessarily deserve them, but that, in and of itself, is not morally problematic. On the other hand, if I deny a particular entity to be

---

[35] ibid 117.   [36] ibid.

[37] ibid 118. While it is not necessary to make a firm judgement on whether Beyleveld and Brownsword's view is more persuasive than Gewirth's about partial agents, it is at least more facially compelling. It seems as if one is either able to make the relevant judgement about life plans and purposive action or one is not able to make those judgements at least in regard to a distinct action in a distinct period of time. This does not mean that a specific entity is unable to fluctuate between having the relevant abilities to be an agent at certain points in time or in regard to certain actions but not to others. However, nothing in Gewirth's theory seems to be based upon the idea that one must be an agent at all times and in relation to all actions.

[38] ibid 119–21.

[39] ibid. The difference, then, between a potential agent and an ostensible agent is our confidence in the entity's status as an agent. We are more confident that ostensible agents are agents than we are with regard to potential agents. For the ease of understanding, both groups will be referred to as potential agents for the purposes of this chapter.

an agent and deny it the generic rights of agency as a result, and it turns out that the entity was an agent, then I have created real problems for myself. Since I have denied the generic rights of agency to something that deserves them, through the PGC I have denied my own agency because it requires that I grant all the generic rights to other agents at the expense of denying my own agency. So, according to Beyleveld and Brownsword, it is always better to err on the side of caution and grant an entity the status of agent if that is possible.[40]

That, of course, greatly expands the possible number of agents. With that expansion also comes the greater chance of a conflict between the generic rights of different agents. In fact, since taking the principle to its logical conclusion means everything needs to be treated as an agent, there appears to be little we could actually do that would not violate some entities' generic rights (eating, for example, might become a very big problem). Beyleveld and Brownsword's approach, however, is more sophisticated than is indicated by the statement above. They argue that we should grant the rights of agency to anything which might possibly be an agent provided it does not conflict with the generic rights of something that is more probably an agent. In other words, we have a probability exercise to conduct. Since granting the generic rights of agency increases the number of agents (and thus the potential conflicts), we must at some point choose between potential agents. When we do so, we should decide on the basis of which potential agent is more likely to be an agent. If we have two possible agents with conflicting rights and one of them is more likely to be an agent, then we should respect the rights of the entity which is more likely to be an agent because that gives us the greatest chance of preserving our own generic rights.[41]

In summary, the argument works as follows. Gewirthian theory requires that we grant all agents the generic rights of agency at the risk of losing our own agency. But, we have imperfect knowledge and there will be a risk that we violate the PGC by denying agency to something which later turns out to be an agent. Thus, the best way to deal with this problem is to treat as many things as possible as agents even if we are uncertain about their status as agents. When conflicts arise, as they invariably will, we respect the generic rights of those things which are more likely to be agents at the expense of those things which are less likely to be agents even though the preferred response is to treat both of them as if they were agents. In other words, only in cases where it is not possible to grant moral rights to all potential agents do we engage in a balancing process and provide rights only to the entity which is more likely to be an agent.

A. Application to Personhood Theory

All of this might seem wildly off the point. Whatever the merits of the argument, the theory of Beyleveld and Brownsword is not one based on personhood.

---

[40] ibid.   [41] ibid 122–5. See also Beyleveld and Pattinson (n 33 above).

Instead, it is based on agency and while there are some similarities, there are also some considerable differences. Foremost among them is the PGC, which does not have a comparison within most forms of personhood theory. Additionally, the PGC is often one of the most controversial elements of Gewirth's agency theory and thus it will also be a controversial part of Beyleveld and Brownsword's approach. More importantly, the PGC plays an important role in the precautionary argument outlined above. It provides a reason to exercise caution in the way suggested and also provides the 'punishment' of a failed judgment. What is necessary, then, is to see whether this sort of approach is one that can be used in personhood theory as well.

In order to do that, it is worth clearing up exactly what part the PGC plays in the argument. This is likely to be the sticking point and thus a clear understanding of its role is vital. It should be noted that the PGC does not play a foundational role in the argument in the way that the PGC plays a part in the Gewirthian argument generally. Instead, the main foundational claim in the precautionary argument is the lack of certainty in the knowledge we possess. The purpose of the PGC in the precautionary argument is merely to provide us the subsidiary role of giving us a compelling reason to order our preferences in a particular way. It does this by performing two specific functions. First, it provides the consequences for mistakes. If we deny moral rights to something which turns out to be worthy of them, we deny our own status as agents. On the other hand, if we grant moral rights to something which turns out not to be worthy of them, then nothing particularly bad happens as a result. Because of this, the second function of the PGC is that it provides us with a reason to exercise caution by erring on the side of determining something to be a person instead of determining them not to be a person. In other words, it gives us a reason to prefer an error on the side of granting personhood to an error on the side of not granting personhood in situations where personhood is unclear. All that is necessary, then, to turn the precautionary argument into one consistent with personhood is to find principles within personhood which replicate those tasks. If that is possible, then the PGC becomes a non-essential element of the argument.

The first function seems to be one that can be readily taken up by another principle. All it really indicates is that treating morally relevant entities as if they were not morally relevant is bad while treating morally irrelevant entities as morally relevant is neutral provided that one does not infringe on the moral rights of morally relevant beings in the process. This, however, does not appear to be an idea fundamentally linked to the PGC but would appear to be a constant across ethical theories. It is always considered to be bad in ethical theories to treat morally relevant beings as if they were not morally relevant.[42] That is why so much time is spent arguing on whether particular things (for example foetuses,

---

[42] MA Warren, *Moral Status* (Oxford, 1997) 3.

animals, the environment) are morally relevant entities.[43] If they are, they are granted moral rights based upon their status as a morally relevant being and to deny the entity those rights is seen as being problematic if it is not subject to some justification. We do not, therefore, need the 'punishment' of denying our own agency in order to see that treating morally relevant beings as if they were not morally relevant is ethically bad. Nor does it appear to be ethically problematic if one grants moral rights to those entities which do not deserve them, at least as a general rule. If I decide a particular entity is worthy of a moral status it does not deserve then I may have done something unnecessary but I do not appear to have done anything bad.[44] There are, of course, two provisos to this. First, my grant-ing of moral rights to entities which do not deserve them should not be arbitrary. Thus, there might be concerns if I treat my own dog as being morally relevant but do not treat any other dog in a similar manner. If I did this, others could jus-tifiably argue that I was not acting in a consistent ethical manner. The problem lies, though, in the arbitrary treatment of entities, not in treating non-morally relevant entities as if they were morally relevant. Secondly, treating non-morally relevant entities as morally relevant may create ethical problems if one infringes on the moral rights of morally relevant entities in the process. Thus, I may not be acting in an ethical manner if I prefer the moral rights of non-morally relevant beings to those of morally relevant beings. Provided these two provisos are met, there appears to be nothing ethically unjustifiable in treating as morally relevant those entities which are not.[45]

This can be distinguished from a case of granting non-morally relevant entities moral responsibilities, which may turn out to be bad. In particular, it might be bad to assign moral responsibilities to non-morally relevant entities which are incapable of acting in a way that fulfils those moral responsibilities (for example if we decided that animals were morally responsible for killing other animals). That is different, however, from the granting of moral rights which may be applied on behalf of an entity. Thus, while we might be acting in a morally incorrect manner to assign moral responsibilities to non-morally rele-vant entities, there appears to be nothing ethically wrong with granting moral rights to non-morally relevant entities.

If it is correct that it is ethically wrong to treat morally relevant entities as if they were not morally relevant, but not ethically wrong (even if unnecessary) to treat non-morally relevant entities as if they were morally relevant, then it would appear to be a logically consistent conclusion that we ought to err on the side of deciding that questionable cases are persons instead of deciding that they are not. This means there is sufficient reason to accept the second necessary function for

---

[43] For a very brief summary of some of these questions, see ibid 3–9.

[44] ibid 241.

[45] eg the multi-criterial view about moral obligations put forth by Mary Anne Warren seems to suggest that there is benefit to treating entities which might not be entitled to moral status, or at least full moral status, as if they had some moral relevance. See ibid 241–2.

the precautionary argument to work without resorting to the PGC. This is not to indicate that it is the only possible logically consistent conclusion, as it presumes that one wants to minimize risk in such circumstances, but it is one possible logical conclusion that results.

Nor does there appear to be any reason for either conclusion to be inconsistent with personhood theory generally. The first conclusion, that it is ethically wrong to treat morally relevant entities as if they were not morally relevant while it is not ethically wrong to treat non-morally relevant entities as if they were, would seem to be a sound conclusion from personhood theory. Otherwise, we would not, as mentioned above, spend so much time arguing about whether particular entities were persons. Since that is consistent with personhood theory, the second conclusion, which logically follows (although not as a necessary conclusion) would also seem to be consistent with personhood theory. Thus, we appear to be able to utilize the precautionary argument of Beyleveld and Brownsword (or at least something very similar) in personhood theory. Consequently, we have a way in which one can shift the burden of proof from the entity under question to those wishing to deny that entity the status of person without losing any of the essential elements of personhood.

We can see how this applies in situations by considering the treatment of severely disabled newborns and severely disabled foetuses. Under this theory, while we do not think that severely disabled newborns are persons (in fact, no newborns are necessarily persons), we cannot be completely sure about that conclusion. A newborn is thus a potential person. Since it is better for us to act as if potential persons were persons, we should grant them the same moral rights as persons so far as this is possible. That would include the right not to be killed and thus infanticide (or neonaticide) would not be morally justified provided there is no intractable conflict with other entities which are more likely to be persons. There are, perhaps, several other potential persons involved in any decision about the severely disabled newborn. For example, any parental figures involved are more likely to be persons than the newborn and are also likely to have interests that may be affected by any decision we make about the rights of the newborn. However, it is important to note that while other potential persons' interests are involved, important rights are probably not impacted in a way where we could not protect the rights of both parties. For example, a mother might argue that caring for a severely disabled newborn impacts her right to liberty because she cannot do everything she could do previously and that this right is of primary importance to her personhood.[46] However, that right could be protected in a way that does not mean we infringe upon the right to life of the newborn—we could take the child into state care or allow it to be cared for by the father, for instance.

---

[46] Other entities, such as the father, might have similar viewpoints about the newborn in question. The mother is the entity used in this particular example because it will make comparisons with the abortion case referred to below easier.

Thus, since we can avoid infringing on the rights of any potential persons, we ought to use that option instead of an alternative which infringes the rights of potential persons.

The case of a severely disabled foetus is more complex. In this case, we are also likely to think that while a foetus is not a person, we cannot be sure. They are likewise potential persons and we should grant them the same moral rights as far as is possible. In the case of abortion, however, the question of other entities becomes more problematic. The other entity in question, of course, is the mother and she is also a potential person but much more likely to be a person than the foetus.[47] We would have a conflict, then, if the mother wanted an abortion because her rights would conflict with the rights of the foetus. Unlike the case of severely disabled newborns, however, there is not a way to recognize the rights of both parties and avoid a conflict of rights. One party must prevail in such a case in a way that is different from the case of a severely disabled newborn. Since it is more likely that the mother is a person than the foetus is a person and it would be impossible to protect both of their rights, the mother's moral rights would be respected instead of those of the foetus. If another potential person interferes, however, then we could grant the moral rights to the foetus without any adverse effect on the mother's rights.[48] We therefore appear to have a way to justify the prevention of infanticide/neonaticide for severely disabled newborns but still allow the termination of severely disabled foetuses. Not only does this correspond to the standard legal position in the United Kingdom, it also appears to fit more closely with the standard intuition of many ordinary members of the moral community. Thus, we have a system which seems to do what we want—provide a coherent justification of moral worth which corresponds more closely to the intuitions of the average member of the moral community.

B. Possible Problems

Even if the use of the precautionary argument within a general personhood framework is workable and results in decisions which are more similar to those of an ordinary member of the moral community, it does not mean that there are no resulting problems. In fact, there are several that result from the use of the precautionary argument in this way. While it is not possible within the confines of this chapter completely to consider possible resolutions to these concerns, some are worthy of mention.

---

[47] In fact, the mother is what Beyleveld and Brownsword would term an ostensible agent. In our terminology, then, the mother would be an ostensible person.

[48] See eg *Vo v France* (2005) 10 EHRR 12, 79 BMLR 71, [2004] 2 FCR 577, where a pregnant woman went into a French hospital for a routine pre-natal check-up and due to a mix-up between two patients, her foetus was aborted. The mother in question did not want a termination of pregnancy.

The first concern that arises is that the precautionary argument to some extent goes against our current scientific knowledge about the world. At the very least, it puts it in doubt. What it is important to realize, though, is that the precautionary argument is merely stating the fact that scientific knowledge progresses and that things we used to believe to be true are no longer seen as being true. In other words, it merely emphasizes the point that we have not learned everything possible.[49]

The second concern is probably best personified by the *Bland* case. As Anthony Bland had no higher brain function (indeed everything but his brain stem had become 'a mass of watery fluid')[50] it would seem to stretch the limits of credibility to suggest that there is any possibility that he could fulfil the criteria necessary for personhood. The only way to argue against that would be to suggest that it is possible that the brain is not actually the location of rational thought and the other criteria necessary for personhood. While that is conceivable, the chance of that assertion being correct is negligible. Therefore, even under the precautionary approach to personhood, there may be some individuals which are still considered to be non-persons.

A third concern that arises is the treatment of animals. Here there are two particular problems worth mentioning. The first is that some animals appear to be more likely persons than infants.[51] If we are utilizing the precautionary argument and there is a conflict between such an animal (such as a great ape) and a child, whose rights should win? One possibility is to consider how best to accomplish the probability assessment. For example, one could argue that since the only individual we can be sure is a person is oneself, and since we were once infants but were never apes, that the infant, despite current evidence, is more likely to be a person than the ape. That, however, is an argument that requires further research and firm conclusions cannot be drawn at this stage. A related argument which also requires further research is whether this precautionary argument means we must all become vegetarians as animals should be more likely treated as persons and thus killing them for food is a violation of their moral rights.

Finally, to some, this might bring us back to the potentiality argument used to justify abortion restrictions. As stated previously in the introduction, this argument suggests that since a foetus is a potential person we ought to treat it as such, which would make abortion morally wrong. Harris, however, has shown this argument to be false by pointing out that we are all potential corpses but that does not mean we should be treated as such. There is a fundamental difference between the potentiality argument (as it is normally run) and the precautionary argument I am outlining here. The potentiality argument trades on the idea of potential as 'given appropriate circumstances, X will happen.' That

---

[49] Again, see the animal studies cited in n 31 above.
[50] *Airedale NHS Trust v Bland* [1993] All ER 821, 859 (*per* Lord Keith).
[51] See eg the animal studies cited in n 31 above, particular the primate studies mentioned in *Practical Ethics*.

is why the counter-argument by Harris is so effective because given appropriate circumstances, we will all become corpses. The precautionary argument, on the other hand, works differently. It does not trade on the idea of what will come to pass given appropriate conditions. Instead, it is a probability exercise based upon the possibility that our current knowledge is incorrect. It is thus not a question about future events, but of a current misunderstanding. A foetus is a possible person in the sense that there is a chance greater than 0 per cent but less than 100 per cent that, despite our current knowledge, the foetus actually fulfils the criteria for personhood. There is conversely, not a chance greater than 0 per cent that I am currently a corpse. Possible personhood might ground a claim of moral rights; potentiality does not.

III. Conclusion

In conclusion, what I have outlined here is a possible personhood theory which shifts the burden of proof away from the entity under consideration. I have done this by arguing that we ought to exercise caution when making determinations about personhood and hold that things are persons when we are unsure, as opposed to determining that they are not. This way is likely to provide an ethical system with fewer bad results and one that is ultimately more consistent with the viewpoint of the average member of the moral community. This provides the added benefit of increasing the potential pool of persons to include entities such as foetuses, newborns, and those in PVS states while not taking away any rights from existing persons.

12

Marketing Masculinity: Bioethics and Sperm Banking Practices in the United States

Cynthia R Daniels

On California Cryobank's webpage prospective customers will find a wealth of information about potential sperm donors. One can click on a link to the 'Donor of the Month' club to see a spread of donor pictures as babies. Laid out in high school yearbook fashion, subtitles on each picture capture the sperm donor's top selling trait: 'Best smile', 'Most talkative', 'Most athletic', 'Most likely to win the Nobel Prize', 'Most intellectual', and 'Mr. Congeniality'. The website declares: 'It's fun! It's easy! It's a new list every month! This month we present a CCB Yearbook voted on by our donor department. Each donor features a baby picture, Up Close and Personal information, and interesting fun facts.' According to his 'Up Close and Personal', Donor 2467 'lights up a room like a warm fire on a cold winter night with an electric smile, dimples, blond hair and blue eyes'. With a degree in advertising, 'this future Madison Ave. Ad Man is an intriguing combination of sweetness and devilish charm that no doubt have him destined for great things'.[1]

The free market in sperm in the United States has produced marketing practices such as these which raise important bioethical considerations. Are we to sell sperm like any other market product? And what are the implications of donor selection practices which, this chapter argues, increasingly select donors based on a narrow range of hierarchical physical and social traits? This chapter addresses these questions through analysis of the recruitment and marketing practices of the sperm banking industry in the United States. These practices raise ethical questions about the increasing commodification of sperm donors and, I argue, the increasing stratification of sperm donors, whose value is determined not just by their health and vitality, but by the extent to which they mirror idealized traits of masculinity. Sperm banking practices combined with

---

[1] California Cryobank: www.cryobank.com.

consumer demand for men with certain characteristics, elevate in status those men who are taller, fitter, and better-educated than the average male—or as one donor 'ad' put it 'the perfect combination of both brains and brawn'.[2] These social processes raise serious bioethical questions as they are reminiscent of an American eugenic past, where 'selective breeding' was promoted in the interest of 'improving American stock'. The advantages of accessibility to a relatively large pool of sperm donors must be weighed against the price of human commodification which donor recruitment, payment, and marketing practices seem to have produced.

I. Sperm Banking Overview

In the United States, sperm banking is big business. All but one sperm bank in those surveyed here are 'for profit', the exception being one bank which serves primarily lesbian populations and operates as a 'known donor' bank (Rainbow Flag Reproductive Health Services in Oakland, California). This chapter surveys the top twelve sperm banks in the United States—those which both collect and distribute sperm nationally and internationally, to assess the marketing practices of the industry and the collective profile of sperm donors in the United States from 2001 to 2006.

Sperm banks recruit young men for donation primarily from college-enrolled students. Most banks also limit donation to those men between the ages of 19 and 39. Sperm banks rigorously screen for family history of disease and test donors for a variety of contagions and genetic disorders, retesting active donors every three months. With the exception of Rainbow Flag, all sperm banks exclude men who have had sexual contact with other men, even though Federal law requires the quarantining of cryopreserved semen for at least six months while donors can be repeatedly tested for all sexually transmitted diseases, including HIV. Once past this screening process, donors are paid by 'acceptable donation', often approximately US$75 to $100 per donation. A single donation may produce four to six vials of sperm, which may then be sold to reproductive consumers for US$125.00 per vial or more, depending on special social traits of donors, such as one programme which markets 'Doctorate Donors' for a higher price.[3]

Sperm banks rely heavily on repeat donations, as the screening of new donors can be a cumbersome and expensive process. As such, the national market in sperm relies upon the donations of a core of 'repeat' donors, whose seminal

---

[2] California Cryobank: www.cryobank.com: Donor #11031.
[3] Fairfax Cryobank markets 'Doctorate Donors' who are either attending graduate school or who have completed graduate training.

product may be distributed both nationally and internationally to other centres for insemination. Sperm banks vary in their practices regarding how many of one donor's samples can be sold. One bank, for instance, limits donor participation to three years.[4] But others set no limits on donor contributions. Often, the most 'popular' donor on a given list will be listed as 'sold out'. There are no Federal regulations or guidelines regarding the number of vials which can be sold from a single donor in his lifetime.[5]

Donor catalogues categorize donors by physical characteristics, like race, height, weight, and hair and eye colour. In addition, donor lists provide information regarding a wide range of social traits like ethnicity, religion, educational achievement, musical and artistic talents, personality, and hobbies—traits of questionable genetic origin.

II. Sperm Bank Donors

Surveys were conducted of all sperm donors available at twelve of the largest and longest-standing sperm banks in the United States in 2001 and 2006. A number of national trends are illustrated by this data, as analysed below.

Broken down by bank, Table 12.1 illustrates the number of donors available at each site, as well as total donor availability for these twelve banks and comparisons between 2001 and 2006 totals. Also broken down by bank is the racial distribution of all sperm donors.

The figures in Table 12.1 indicate a number of important points. The total pool of sperm donors has grown in size over these five years, from 901 in 2001 to a total of 1,156 in 2006, a 28 per cent increase. Aggressive recruitment practices combined with the enticement of payments to young men (who, through some banks, may earn up to US$1,000 per month for donations), have led to a steadily growing supply of sperm for sale.[6] No doubt the high cost of college tuition in the United States has also combined with an increasing US cost of living to make sperm donation an attractive form of income-earning for young men.

---

[4] Biogenetics in New Jersey, for instance limits anonymous donors to three years of participation, expecting contributions of one to two donations per month. In their 'known donor' programme, where the identity of the donor is released to conceived children, donors are limited to two pregnancies per state in the US. See <http://www.sperm1.com/biogenetics/donor.html>.

[5] The American Society for Reproductive Medicine recommends a limit of 25 live births per population of 850,000, but since many sperm banks provide services nationally, this limit is not relevant to births per donor. In addition, this limit is not grounded in law and there is no tracking mechanism to ensure such limits. Rainbow Flag is the only sperm bank to limit donors to six different women as recipients of the same donor.

[6] See California Cryobank website, where donors are informed that they may earn up to US$1,000 per month, at $75.00 per donation per month: www.cryobank.com.

Table 12.1. Total donors and distribution by race/ethnicity

Bank name	All donors		White		Black		Hispanic		Asian		Other	
	2001	2006	2001	2006	2001	2006	2001	2006	2001	2006	2001	2006
Biogenetics Corporation—NJ	35	33	29	30	3	3			2		1	
California Cryobank—CA	168	296	117	236	7	5	2	2	27	27	17	27
Cryobiology, Inc—OH	96	69	78	52	3	3	1	2	5	11	8	1
Cryogam Colorado, Inc—CO	45	49	38	41	1	1		2	3	2	2	3
Cryogenic Laboratories, Inc—MN	90	120	65	100	8	2		1	17	15		2
Fairfax Cryobank—VA	119	128	95	100	9	9	4	4	8	13	3	2
Fertility Center of California—SanD—CA	45	52	30	36	2	2	5	5	8	8		1
Idant Laboratories—NY	33	42	24	34	1	1	1	2	6	4	1	1
New England Cryogenic Center—MA	120	128	114	119	2	1	1	3	2	4	2	1
Pacific Reproductive Services—CA	37	78	28	51	2	3	5	8	4	9	2	7
Xytex—GA	59	116	44	96	7	11	4	3	3	6		
Zygen Laboratory—CA	54	45	40	36					3		7	9
TOTAL	901	1156	702	931	45	41	23	32	88	99	43	54

Source: Calculations based on data collected by author from each sperm bank's website.

III. Race and Ethnicity

In terms of ethnicity and race, the donor population in 2006 contained a higher proportion of white donors than those surveyed in 2001. Table 12.2 shows race/ethnicity percentages for all surveyed sperm banks for both years.

A number of trends in donor availability are apparent in this data. The percentage of white donors has increased from 77.9 to 80.4 per cent of all donors, while African American donors have decreased from 5 to 3.5 per cent. The percentage of those donors categorized as Asian has decreased, while those categorized as Hispanic or 'other' (including those of 'mixed race') has remained about the same.

These percentages are not reflective of general population rates by race and ethnicity in the United States. Whites are disproportionately represented, making up approximately 75 per cent of the total US population but just over 80 per cent of all sperm donors. Asians are also overrepresented, constituting 4 per cent of the US population but 8.6 per cent of the donor list. By contrast, African Americans and Latinos are both underrepresented. For instance, African Americans make up approximately 12 per cent of the population, yet represent only 3.5 per cent of all donors. Hispanics make up 14.4 per cent of the US population, yet represent only 2.8 per cent of all donors.[7]

Given higher levels of poverty, malnutrition, exposure to toxins from work and the environment, and lack of access to adequate medical and reproductive heath care, it is likely that lower income populations, disproportionately

Table 12.2. Race and Ethnicity

Year	2001		2006	
White	702	77.9%	930	80.4%
Black	45	3.5%	41	3.5%
Hispanic	23	2.6%	32	2.8%
Asian	88	9.8%	99	8.6%
Other	43	4.7%	54	4.7%
Total	901	100.0%	1156	100.0%

Source: US Census Bureau, *Census 2000 Summary File 1 (SF 1) 100-Percent Data* and 'Population of the U.S. by Race/Hispanic/Latino Origin, Census 2000 and July 1, 2005' National Population Estimate, US Census.

---

[7] On Hispanic population numbers also see Table 1.1, 'Population by Sex, Age, Hispanic Origin, and Race: 2006', US Census Bureau, Current Population Survey, Annual Social and Economic Supplement, 2006, Ethnicity and Ancestry Statistics Branch, Population Division.

including minority populations, might have greater levels of male infertility than higher income, disproportionately White and Asian populations. Sperm donor availability by race might in fact be in inverse relation to need based on health.[8]

Given the significant expense of these services, lack of economic resources must play a large role in skewing donor availability by race and ethnicity. With significantly fewer economic resources, lack of access to health care and health insurance, and with health insurance companies rarely covering the costs of such 'voluntary' reproductive procedures, Black and Hispanic populations have less access to the resources necessary to take advantage of sperm banking services. Sperm banks may thus be less inclined to provide donor semen from African-American and Hispanic donors.

In summary, donors both in 2001 and 2006 have been skewed in favour of White donors, with Black and Hispanic donors significantly underrepresented. In addition, since 2001, the 2006 donor catalogues indicate a decreasing representation of Asian donors as well as approximately the same percentage of donors of 'other' or 'mixed' race.

IV. Body Mass Index/Height/Weight

How do sperm donors compare to the average man in weight and height? Table 12.3 analyses data for proportional height and weight, assessed through calculations of all donors by 'Body Mass Index'.

According to the US Centers for Disease Control (CDC) analysis using BMI as a measure, 58 per cent of all US males between the ages of 20 and 34 are overweight. Nearly one-quarter of men in this age range are obese (24 per cent). Men in this age group have a rate of 'healthy weight' at 39 per cent. With sperm donors

Table 12.3. Body Mass Index (BMI)

	Donors—2001		Donors—2006		All US Males (age 18–24)
Underweight	4	0.3%	12	1.0%	5%
Healthy weight	840	64.5%	716	61.9%	39%
Overweight	380	29.2%	369	31.9%	58%
Obese	79	6.1%	59	5.1%	24%
	1303	100.0%	1156	100.0%	

Source: Chart Data from <http://www.cdc.gov/nchs/data/hus/tables/2003/03hus068.pdf>.

---

[8] Lack of statistics on male infertility rates in general, as well as by race, make it difficult to determine what the true level of need for these services might be.

Table 12.4. Height

Height	Donors—2001	Donors—2006	All US males
%>6ft.	38%	44%	10%

Source: Table built from the CDC Growth Charts, '2 to 20 years: Boys—Stature for-age and Weight-for-age percentiles', Developed by the National Center for Health Statistics in collaboration with the National Center for Chronic Disease Prevention and Health Promotion (2000) < http://www.cdc.gov/growthcharts>.

at 64.5 per cent at 'healthy' weight, 29 per cent at 'overweight' and only 6 per cent obese, donors clearly are selected from men well above average on body mass index scales. This is in marked contrast to overall weight trends in the United States, where rates of obesity have doubled in the past twenty-five years.[9]

Sperm donors are also dramatically taller than the average young American male. In the general population, only 10 per cent of all men are six feet tall or taller. In 2001, sperm donors were more than three times as likely as the national average to be this tall (38 per cent). By 2006, this rate had increased to 44 per cent of all sperm donors, over four times as likely to be six foot tall or taller. This represents a fairly significant increase in the supply (and perhaps the demand for) donors of greater height. And, of course, there is no reason to believe that those men who need sperm donor services are significantly taller than the national average and thus simply trying to 'match' their own taller-than-average height.

V. Education

How do sperm donors compare to national averages in terms of educational achievement? The data shows sperm donors to be well above average in their proportions having college degrees.

Table 12.5. Education

Education Level	Donors—2001 %	Donors—2006 %	All US males %
High School	1.5	2	32
Some college	36	31	26
BA, BSc or higher	61	65	26

Source: US Department of Education, National Center for Education Statistics, Digest of Education Statistics 2001, based on US Department of Commerce, Bureau of the Census, March Current Population Surveys, various years. (Originally published on p 107 of the complete report from which this data is excerpted.)

[9] CL Ogden *et al*, 'Obesity Among Adults in the US' NCHS Data Brief No 1: National Center for Health Statistics, 2007.

First, if we look at the trends from 2001 to 2006, we see the percentage of donors with completed college degrees has risen slightly from 61 per cent to 65 per cent. The level of those with only 'some college' has dropped by similar proportions, from 36 to 31 per cent. And those with only a high school education have stayed about the same and remain a very small percentage of the total donor pool at 2 per cent of all donors.

As in other measures, these are significantly above average compared to all males in the United States. If we look at national averages for all men we see that 32 per cent of all males have achieved only a high school degree; and 26 per cent of all males have either 'some college' or have completed a college degree. These numbers show a disjuncture between national averages and the total donor pool, with a decided preference of sperm banks for young men who are either pursuing or have completed a college degree.

If we cross-reference education and race, we see even greater distances between sperm donors and national averages for gender and race. For instance, only 18 per cent of all African American men achieved a college degree. For Hispanic men these numbers are even lower, with 8 per cent of all Hispanic men achieving a college degree. And on average 32 per cent of White men achieved college degrees. With a higher average than sperm donors were Asian and Pacific Islander men in the United States, an average of 54 per cent achieving a college degree.

This disparity in educational achievement is in large part a reflection of the recruiting practices of sperm banks, which often place ads in college newspapers to recruit new donors. Some practices even restrict donors to those who are currently attending or have a degree from a four-year university.[10] This practice is also reflected in perceptions of sperm banks that consumers are more likely to purchase the sperm of men who are college educated, presuming that the transmission of intelligence might be tied to the genetic material in sperm. This 'bias' of consumers then exaggerates racial differentiations in donor lists, perpetuating the notion that the highest quality sperm is produced by men of those races (and classes) who have the opportunity to attend four-year colleges or universities. The preference, therefore, for donors with certain educational achievement thus skews donor lists in favour of men of particular races and economic classes.

In sum, donor profiles tend to reflect traits often associated with idealized norms of masculinity. Preferences are clearly for those men who are above average in educational attainment, with healthier body mass indexes, exceedingly above average in height, and disproportionately selected from White populations.

VI. Donor Compensation

Since 2001, sperm banks have become more explicit about sperm 'donation' as a form of income-earning. For instance, on California Cryobank's website, while

---

[10] California Cryobank imposes such restrictions, for instance.

potential donors are informed that 'compensation should not be the only reason for becoming a sperm donor', the bank makes the following bid for donor sperm: 'Earn up to $1,000/month; Be your own boss—Donate at your convenience up to 3 times a week.' In addition, the site tells us: 'We periodically offer incentives such as movie tickets or gift certificates for extra time and effort expended by participating donors.' Only at the bottom of the list of donor 'compensation' does the site appeal to donor altruism, in its plea to 'Help people fulfill their dreams of starting a family.'[11]

While some care is taken by most websites to avoid wage-based language by referring to 'compensation' or 'reimbursement', clearly, the bottom line is, literally, the bottom line: income-earning. Indeed, in recognition of this form of 'work,' the US federal tax system now requires all sperm donors to file IRS tax forms as 'independent contractors' for those earning more than US$600 a year from sperm donation.[12] Nothing could say more than the 'logo' appearing on the California Cryobank's website for new donor recruitment: a colorful image of a dollar sign, being swarmed by thousands of sperm trying to 'penetrate' the $ symbol.[13]

Many sperm bank websites also focus their recruitment on the potential earnings of sperm donors. At Idant lab, donors are compensated US$60 per acceptable specimen. In addition, donors can receive a 'bonus' of US$100 for every friend they refer who is accepted into sperm donation service.[14] Similarly, Fairfax Cryobank offers donors a very substantial bonus of '$400–1,000' for referring a friend or 'coworker' to their donation centre (after acceptance of the new recruit into their donor programme).[15] As is common on all of the sperm donor websites, Fairfax combines financial appeals with appeals to reproductive altruism in its recruitment of new donors. As Fairfax states on their donor recruitment website: 'As a donor, you will receive excellent compensation, as well as the knowledge that you are truly making a difference in someone's life.'[16] Fairfax also varies its payments to donors, as stated on their recruitment site: 'Donors are compensated for their time and effort. The average donor is compensated $100 per acceptable ejaculate, although many are compensated more. Each donor's commitment to the program thru healthy life style and abstinence has a direct impact on his individual compensation.'[17]

New England Cryobank combines its pitch for income and altruism in this way: 'While donors receive financial compensation, the ultimate reward for becoming a sperm donor is the knowledge that you are helping couples experience

---

[11] <http://www.cryobankdonors.com/newdonors/index.cfm?ID=4>, bold in the original.
[12] ibid, see section 'About Taxes'.
[13] ibid, for image, see top right-hand corner of page.
[14] <http://idant.com/fertilityServices/anonymousDonorProgram.html>;   see   section   on compensation.
[15] <http://www.123donate.com/>.
[16] ibid. This website is run by Fairfax Cryobank to recruit both egg and sperm donors.
[17] <http://www.123donate.com/donorfaqs-sperm.htm>.

the joy of conceiving and having a child.' Like most other banks, NE Cryobank 'expects donors to commit to at least 12 months of donation' and at least one donation per week. At US$85 per acceptable donation, this adds up to a significant source of income for young college-aged students—potentially an income of over $4,400 per year for a single donation per week.[18]

Unlike payment for donation of other body products, such as blood and even ova, payment for sperm donation in the United States has engendered no public debate. In fact, blood that is received from paid donors must be marked as such before it is distributed to those in need. And recipients must be informed that the blood they are receiving has come from a 'paid donor'.[19] No such concerns have been raised regarding sperm donation. The Food and Drug Administration, which regulates sperm banks, has no regulatory standard for the payment of sperm donors. The professional association which certifies sperm banks, the American Association of Tissue Banks (AATB), has only the most general guidelines for donor compensation, requiring that compensation 'promotes voluntary, non-remunerated tissue donation as an autonomous informed choice free of coercion and pressure,' and asks banks 'to affirm the altruism of donation'.[20] Yet clearly this principle is not upheld by banks offering potential earnings of thousands of dollars for cash-strapped college students.

VII. Marketing Practices

An increasingly competitive free market in sperm has led sperm banks to promote their sperm donors by providing a wide range of traits questionably associated with genetic transmission through sperm. Sperm banks, for instance, often sell sperm by advertising the availability of donor handwriting samples, lists of their hobbies and interests, grade point averages, religion, occupation, Keirsey personality testing, and 'staff impression' reports. The lack of regulation of this industry in the United States has led to the exaggeration of the importance of sperm in transmitting social traits to offspring. With appropriate caveats that sperm banks make no promises about the transmission of such traits to offspring, sperm banks are left to use to their advantage (or exploit) suspect beliefs about the social traits carried in sperm.

Even those physical traits which may be transmitted genetically are 'packaged' in marketing materials that have the feel of special ordering a piece of expensive merchandise. For instance, California Cryobank provides potential consumers with 'Facial Features Reports' on all potential sperm donors. Such

---

[18] <http://www.necryogenic.com/become_a_donor/index.php>.
[19] Compliance Policy Guide Guidance for FDA Staff and Industry, CHAPTER–2 SUB CHAPTER–230: Sec. 230.150 Blood Donor Classification Statement, Paid or Volunteer Donor, 2005.
[20] American Association of Tissue Banks, 'Statement of Ethical Principles, 1994'.

reports specify configurations for eye shape (round, almond or round-almond), eye size, eye setting, length of eye lashes, eyebrow shape and direction (curved, straight or angled), facial shape (round, oval or square), skin color and tone (fair, medium or dark), forehead setting and size, freckles or dimples, nose shape or profile (straight, round or wide), nose width, length and 'nostril flare', ear size and shape of lobes (attached or detached), mouth size, with separate distinctions for upper and lower lip shape (thin, medium or large), chin shape and prominence, hair texture and color, cheekbone setting and teeth size and appearance (small, medium or large; gapped, straight or crooked).

While such practices may allow consumers to choose donors who mirror their own family traits, they are reminiscent of eugenic practices which historically subcategorized human value according to dominant class and racial hierarchies. Given that there is no evidence that reproductive consumers are also well above average on donor scales, this mirroring practice cannot fully explain the drive of sperm banks to promote donors in this way. Rather, it appears to be driven by broader social processes which attribute higher value to those donors bearing specific traits—traits that mirror not just individual consumers but gender, racial, and class hierarchies. And the flip side is also here implied: those young men not sharing these traits are less valuable as human beings, less worthy of having their genetic material passed on to future generations.

VIII. Conclusion

A revisit to the California Cryobank website in February 2008 finds an image which perfectly exemplifies the problematic nature of sperm banking practices in the United States. The February 'Donor of the Month Club' features an image of a large heart-shaped box of chocolates, presumably in recognition of Valentine's Day (celebrated in the United States on 14 February). But set inside some of the small compartments in the box are not all chocolates, but baby photos of sperm donors, ready to be 'consumed' by infertile couples.

Such an image might be seen simply as a clever marketing strategy in a very competitive health industry. But it belies a deeper problem produced by leaving to the free market the responsibility of serving the reproductive health needs of men and women. Left unregulated, these marketing practices create a reproductive marketplace where donors are lured by cash into donating and, perhaps, fathering hundreds of children as a result. No doubt young college-aged men may not clearly see the consequences of their participation in such processes until long after college when they father their own children who may wonder if they have a hundred 'half-siblings' across the country.

The lack of regulation of the industry has meant that sperm businesses may provide unlimited lures for such young men; lack of regulation means also that sperm banks may use unlimited numbers of vials from 'popular' donors; lack of regulation has also meant no limit on marketing practices which turn donors, literally, into pieces of reproductive 'candy'.

Reaching a new balance in the provision of this important reproductive health service requires the imposition of limits on an 'industry gone wild'. Ideally, this would mean maintaining some level of autonomy for sperm banks so they may continue to recruit adequate numbers of donors, but setting limits on the level of compensation provided to those men who chose to donate. No doubt, any restrictions on donor payment will shrink the donor pool. But it will ensure that young men are not selling their reproductive consciences for the price of their rent.

Regulations might also limit the marketing practices of sperm banks. The attribution of social traits to the genetic material in sperm verges on 'false advertising' practices, where sperm is cast as the magic elixir that carries the cure for all social ills. It also feeds a social climate increasingly focused on subcategorizing human beings by presumably intractable ethnic, racial, and human difference. Marketing practices should return to the principles established by the AATB in 1994: respect the altruism of the donation. Principles of altruism have been so fundamentally undermined that it is hard to see how they might now apply to the US sperm banking industry. But alternatives do exist in non-profit provision of such services, where payments to donor are quite limited, but where supply nevertheless remains steady. In the end, it may be that the price of preventing the exploitation of human beings requires restrictions on human reproduction. Yet the alternative—perpetuation of hierarchical norms of gender, race, and class—seems an unacceptable price to pay for access.

13

Bioethics and Law in Action—Mining the Gaps: The Human Genome Research Project

*Mark Henaghan**

I. Introduction

There is a gap between stating ethical principles and choosing which one to apply in a particular situation. Even when the choice of ethical principle is made, there is a gap between the expression of the principle and its interpretation when it is applied. At the point of application there is also a gap between the interpretation of the facts and the application of the principle. The focus of this chapter is on these gaps in the context of making law for new developments which are now available because of advances in genetic science. It is in the gaps where the action happens. Mining the gaps exposes where power really lies in terms of deciding outcomes for issues where there are a variety of different views in society.

Ethics has a long history,[1] stretching back to Aristotle.[2] Ethics began the moment there was a choice between two different value positions. The phenomenon of bioethics as a field of inquiry is more recent.[3]

* Professor and Dean of the Faculty of Law, University of Otago, Dunedin, New Zealand. E-mail <mark.henaghan@stonebow.otago.ac.nz>. The author thanks Kellee Clark, LLB (Hons)/ B Com graduate of the Faculty of Law, University of Otago for her exceptional research assistance for this chapter.
[1] The origins of ethics can be seen in the moral reflection underlying early moral codes such as the Code of Hammurabi and the Ten Commandments. An explosion of ethical thought in Ancient Greece gave birth to Western philosophical ethics, developing from the writings of, for example, Socrates (c470–399 BC), Plato, and Aristotle (384–322 BC). For a greater exposition of the history of ethics, see Henry Sidgwick, *Outlines of the History of Ethics for English Readers* (London, 1931; reissued 1996).
[2] Aristotle, *Nicomachean ethics* (trans, JAK Thomson) (New York, 1976); Aristotle, *Eudemian Ethics* (trans, M Woods) (New York, 1992).
[3] J-C Galloux, A T Mortensen, S de Cheveigné, A Allansdottir, A Chatjouli, and G Sakellaris, 'The Institutions of Bioethics' in M W Bauer and G Gaskell (eds), *Biotechnology: The Making of a Global Controversy.* (Cambridge, 2002) 129, cites oncologist Van R Potter as coining the term in 1971. They trace the history of bioethics from the 'discovery of genetic recombination techniques'

The prime purpose of ethics and bioethics is to give us values upon which we can make choices of how we should act. Ethics and bioethics provide a menu as to what is right and what is wrong—a very powerful role in any society. Ethics and bioethics are simply the names of fields of inquiry. They are built up on the work and thought processes of individual thinkers over time. That is their strength. As Einstein said: 'A hundred times every day I remind myself that my inner and outer lives are based on the labors of other people...'[4]

In an open society, ethics and bioethics are not static. They have not reached the point where the final word has been written and that hallowed grail of 'objectivity' has been reached. Yet if ethics and bioethics are to play a role separate from politics their appeal must be to something more than status or the power of the speaker. Thrasymachus posed the following dilemma to Plato in the *Republic*:[5] reason alone does not provide ethical truth and even if it did it would only be an academic exercise. In the real world, what orders society is politics, and the underlying value of politics is that might makes right. Academia has its own political world of power and hierarchy and might is right in the sense of 'dominant discourses' being given the most air time.[6] In an ideal society, Plato[7] assumed that there would be some method that 'generates unity of opinion about the good'.[8] But once we have found that method we have destroyed the very thing many of us treasure most—'that we are wholly free, not only to choose for ourselves what we ought to do, but to decide for ourselves, individually and as a species, what we ought to be'.[9] As Flynn puts it, there is a 'necessary consequence of truth-tests—the fact that they elevate a non-partisan criterion of right and wrong above humane ideals necessitates the downgrading of humane ideals... It would strip humane ideals of their capacity to generate humane reasons for the goodness of acts.'[10]

in the 1970s. They explain that bioethics developed within the scientific community—that it first evolved from the 'diverse and sometimes paradoxical anxieties within a scientific community trying to come to terms with the enormity of the power it was acquiring'. Public debate over bioethical issues followed on from this.

[4] A Einstein, 'What I Believe' (1930) 84 *Forum and Century* 193; reprinted as 'The World as I See It' in C Seelig (ed), *Ideas and Opinions* (New York, 1954).

[5] Plato, *Republic*, I 338–339, (trans, AD Lindsay) (London, 1992).

[6] This has been most visible in the US with the debate in legal circles between the Law and Economics movement and the Critical Legal Studies school. See eg G Minda, 'The Law and Economics and Critical Legal Studies Movements in American Law' in N Mercuro (ed), *Law And Economics* (Boston/Dordrecht/London, 1989) 87; AC Hutchinson and PJ Monahan, 'Law, Politics, and the Critical Legal Scholars: The Unfolding Drama of American Legal Thought' (1984) 36(1/2) Stanford Law Review 1/2, 199; D Kennedy, 'Law-and-Economics from the Perspective of Critical Legal Studies' in P Newman (ed), *New Palgrave Dictionary of Economics and the Law* (New York, 1998) 465.

[7] *Republic*, VI 506, (trans, AD Lindsay) (London, 1992).

[8] JR Flynn, *How to Defend Humane Ideals* (London, 2000) 27.

[9] AA Leff, 'Unspeakable Ethics, Unnatural Law' (1979) *Duke Law Journal* 1229.

[10] Flynn (n 8 above) 68.

Matters such as whether and when preimplantation genetic diagnosis (PGD) can be rightly used, whether young children should be tested for genetic diseases which they may be susceptible to later in their lives, and how findings of genetic research should be released if they indicate potential negative characteristics for a particular ethnic group, all create choices of values. The sequencing of the human genome has made these choices possible.[11] A major research project in New Zealand, 'The Human Genome Project (Te Kaupapa Rangahau Ira Tāngata)',[12] has focused its research and thinking on how, and on what basis, these choices should be made. The Project research team approaches the choices from different theoretical and methodological lenses. There are two bioethicists, two lawyers, one scientist, and an expert in Māori[13] culture and practices.[14] We have made recommendations on PGD, genetic testing of children, and community genetic testing of an ethnic group. We have used a variety of bioethical, legal, and scientific principles to justify our conclusions. A spirit of open inquiry and empathy for different viewpoints combined with dispassionate (as is humanly possible) analysis were our lenses for the research. There is no foolproof way of showing why one choice of principle is more right than choice of another.

II. Principles and Gaps

A range of principles emerge from bioethics. As Campbell has said: 'Each captures different dimensions of our moral universe, but one is not better than the other in settling finally how we make correct mind judgements.'[15] The principles

---

[11] The sequencing of the human genome was achieved by the Human Genome Project, an international undertaking coordinated by the US Department of Energy and US National Institutes of Health. The project began in 1990 and was completed (early) in 2003. See the Human Genome Project's website at <http://www.ornl.gov/sci/techresources/Human_Genome/home.shtml>.

[12] The Project is funded by the New Zealand Law Foundation, a charitable body. The website for the project is <http://www.otago.ac.nz/law/genome>.

[13] Māori are the indigenous people of New Zealand. Their ancestors were a Polynesian people originating from south east Asia, and they are typically thought to have settled in New Zealand between 950 and 1130 AD, with the first mass arrival of Polynesian settlers, the 'Great Fleet' of waka (canoes), estimated to have occurred in 1350.

[14] The principal investigator is Professor Mark Henaghan. Senior investigators are Professor Donald Evans (Director of the Bioethics Centre, University of Otago); Professor Stephen Robertson (Paediatrics and Child Health, Department of Women's and Children's Health, University of Otago); Dr Ian Morrison and Dr Tony Merriman (Biochemistry Department, University of Otago); Bevan Tipene-Matua (Director of Māori Research and Development, Christchurch Polytechnic Institute of Technology); Professor Nicola Peart (Law Faculty, University of Otago); Professor Grant Gillett (Bioethics Centre, University of Otago); and Dr Nicki Kerruish (Paediatrics and Child Health, Department of Women's and Children's Health and the Bioethics Centre, University of Otago). International collaborators include the Institute of Law and Ethics in Medicine at the University of Glasgow, Scotland (Director: Professor Sheila McLean), and Stanford Centre for Biomedical Ethics at Stanford University, US (Associate Director: Professor Mildred Cho).

[15] AV Campbell, 'The virtues (and vices) of the four principles' (2003) 29 *Journal of Medical Ethics* 292.

do not contain within themselves any criterion of how they should be prioritized if they conflict. They leave a gap as to when they should be applied. For example, if we give priority to autonomy then we cannot interfere with actions even though they are causing great harm and would generally be accepted as unjust, so there comes a point where there must be some constraint on autonomy.

Flynn describes ethics in terms of 'six great goods with multiple trade-offs between them'.[16] We are like jugglers who want to keep six balls in the air, sometimes one flying to the top, sometimes another, knowing that it is fatal to become pre-occupied with one ball to the neglect of the others. Flynn describes the 'six great humanist goods' at a minimum as: the greatest happiness principle; justice with more emphasis on desert[17] than merit; the creation of beauty; the pursuit of truth; the perfection of the human species; a regard for human diversity and the integrity of various groups.[18] Flynn is prepared to trade off the happiness ball if it diminishes the pursuit of truth, 'even if it were proved that a happier humanity would be of low intelligence'.[19] The tolerance ball would be traded off less easily: 'I would tolerate considerable internal misery within another society before I would interfere if interference meant shattering that society's cultural integrity... If alleviating mild privation among a people means the equivalent of exterminating them and replacing them with happy Europeans, the price is too great.'[20] In the same breath Flynn accepts there are 'levels of intragroup misery, say the more horrible forms of female circumcision, at which tolerance may have to give way'.[21]

Campbell's conclusion to the dilemma of ordering principles and juggling moral balls is to say that: 'We need a diversity of approach in these complex human scenarios and no theory should be seen as dominant.'[22] Flynn says that ultimately we look within ourselves and find 'certain moral ideals acceptable and other moral ideals loathsome',[23] and that we should be honest and explicit about our choices rather than hiding behind some such device as recommending respect for all of the diverse moral principles that divide humanity. That merely leads to a truncated form of humanism totally dominated by the tolerance ball.[24]

Until the 1970s the primary spokespersons on social and ethical issues in genetics were scientists.[25] Diane B Paul and Hamish G Spencer in an article

---

[16] Flynn (n 8 above) 169.

[17] The term 'just deserts', meaning 'that which is deserved' has been used in English since at least the 13th century. An early example is the phrase in the anonymous play, *Warning Faire Women* (1599): 'Upon a pillory—that all the world may see, A just desert for such impiety.' See G Martin, 'The Phrase Finder' at <http://www.phrases.org.uk/meanings/just-deserts.html> (accessed 5 December 2007).

[18] Flynn (n 8 above) 169.   [19] ibid.

[20] ibid 170.   [21] ibid.

[22] Campbell (n 15 above) 296.   [23] Flynn (n 8 above) 170.

[24] ibid.

[25] DB Paul, 'From Reproductive Responsibility to Reproductive Autonomy' in LS Parker and RA Ankeny (eds), *Mutating Concepts, Evolving Disciplines: Genetics, Medicine, and Society* (Dordrecht, The Netherlands, 2002) 87–8.

in *Nature*, 'The Hidden Science of Eugenics',[26] show that these scientists did not share our social values. For example, geneticists in the 1920s and 1930s generally favoured eugenic policies. Herbert Spencer Jennings said in his book, *The Biological Basis of Human Nature*, that 'to stop the propagation of the feebleminded by thoroughly effective measures is a procedure for the welfare of future generations that should be supported by all enlightened persons. Even though it may get rid of but a small proportion of the defective genes, every case saved is a gain, is worthwhile in itself.'[27] Linus Pauling, a revered American scientist, advocated compulsory testing for defective recessive genes such as sickle-cell anemia before marriage to prevent carriers from marrying other carriers.[28]

Autonomy[29] is currently the dominant value in bioethical[30] and legal literature[31] on genetics. Arguments from the viewpoint of social responsibility are put in different forms in today's contest of social values. How the gap between these two opposing value positions is closed will be considered in the context of making legal policy about PGD, genetic testing of children and genetic testing of whole communities.

III. Choosing Genes for Future Children

The title of the Human Genome Research Project's first report—'Choosing Genes for Future Children: Regulating Preimplantation Genetic Diagnosis'[32]— was carefully selected. We wanted the report to be accurate about what is being done when PGD is used. PGD allows the choice of an embryo that will not have genes for a particular genetic disorder. The fact that embryos are specifically created for selection in the use of PGD entails their possible rejection. Interference with the 'natural order' is an objection which comes both from a Christian perspective—in terms of rejecting human life as a gift, which the embryo is considered to be[33]—and a secular view that the intrusion creates risks such as a

---

[26] DB Paul and HG Spencer, 'The Hidden Science of Eugenics' (1995) 374 *Nature* 302.

[27] HS Jennings, *The Biological Basis of Human Nature* (London, 1930) 238–42.

[28] L Pauling, 'Reflections on the New Biology: Foreword' (1968) 15(2) *UCLA Law Review* 267.

[29] JS Mill, *On Liberty* (London, 1859) 22.

[30] See Paul (n 25 above) 95–98; AR Jonsen, *The Birth of Bioethics* (New York, 1998); PR Wolpe, 'The Triumph of Autonomy in American Bioethics: A Sociological View' in R DeVries and J Subedi (eds), *Bioethics and Society: Constructing the Ethical Enterprise* (Englewood Cliffs, NJ, 1998).

[31] S McLean, *Modern Dilemmas Choosing Children* (Edinburgh, 2006); M Freeman, 'Saviour Siblings' in S McLean (ed), *First Do No Harm* (London, 2006) 389.

[32] 'Choosing Genes for Future Children: Regulating Preimplantation Genetic Diagnosis/ Human Genome Research Project' (Dunedin, NZ.: Human Genome Research Project, 2006) (hereinafter '*Choosing Genes for Future Children*').

[33] See *Choosing Genes for Future Children*, (n 32 above) 174–6; and eg RA Mohler, 'The Brave New World of Cloning: A Christian Worldview Perspective', at <http://www.mercola.com/2001/ mar/10/cloning.htm> (accessed 3 December 2007); 'Instruction on Respect for Human Life in

reduction in biodiversity.[34] Contrasted with these perspectives is the liberal view that no moral status should be accorded to the embryo.[35] Citizens of goodwill sit at various points on the spectrum of views. Given these philosophic differences and the political realities, a 'gradualist' approach fills the gap.[36] The gradualist approach sees the embryo as more than a collection of cells but as less than a full person. It puts a brake on liberal autonomy. The embryo is entitled to 'respect'. What this means in practical terms is that any interventions into the embryo will be controlled by regulation designed to ensure that there is a socially acceptable and responsible reason for the intervention.[37]

Selecting embryos on the basis of their genetic status is a matter of particular concern for those speaking for the disability rights community.[38] There is concern that the availability of PGD to screen out genetic conditions will result in disrespecting people with disabilities. The place of people with disabilities does deserve special protection. It is not possible to quantify the effect that choosing an embryo without Huntington's disease has on a person who does have Huntington's disease, or the choice of an embryo that does not have Downs Syndrome has on a person who has Downs Syndrome. However, the New Zealand Organisation for

Its Origin and on the Dignity of Procreation Replies to Certain Questions of the Day', Statement from the Congregation For The Doctrine Of The Faith, 22 February 1987, at <http://www.vatican.va/roman_curia/congregations/cfaith/documents/rc_con_cfaith_doc_19870222_respect-for-human-life_en.html> (accessed 3 December 2007).

[34] See *Choosing Genes for Future Children* (n 32 above) 179–81; and eg G McGee, *The Perfect Baby: Parenthood in the New World of Cloning and Genetics* (Lanham, Md: 2002); National Biological Information Infrastructure, 'Introduction to Genetic Diversity', at <http://www.nbii.gov/portal/community/Communities/Ecological_Topics/Genetic_Diversity/Introduction_to_Genetic_Diversity/> (accessed 3 December 2007).

[35] See *Choosing Genes for Future Children* (n 32 above) from 186; and eg R Wertheimer, 'Understanding the Abortion Argument' (1971) 1(1) *Philosophy and Public Affairs* 67, 74; MF Goodman (ed) *What is a Person?* (Clifton, NJ, 1988); PA King, 'The Judicial Status of the Fetus: A Proposal for Legal Protection of the Unborn' (1979) *Michigan Law Review* 77.

[36] See *Choosing Genes for Future Children* (n 32 above) 186, 195–6, 198; and eg J Robertson, 'Procreative Liberty in the Era of Genomics' (2003) 29(4) *American Journal of Law and Medicine* 439–87; J Robertson, 'Ethics and Policy in Embryonic Stem Cell Research', (1999) 9(2) *Kennedy Institute of Ethics Journal* 109, 136.

[37] New Zealand's (see *Choosing Genes for Future Children* (n 32 above) 229–72) Human Assisted Reproduction Technology (HART) Act 2004 establishes an Ethics Committee and Advisory Committee. The Ethics Committee approves applications for PGD. The Advisory Committee has policy-making authority, under which the Committee may declare certain procedures to be 'established procedures' not requiring Ethics Committee approval. This has been done for PGD in certain circumstances. The United Kingdom's more liberal approach is governed by the Human Fertilisation and Embryology Act 1990 and the Act's Code of Practice (see *Choosing Genes for Future Children* (above) 272–94). There is currently no federal or state regulation of PGD in the US (see *Choosing Genes for Future Children* (above) 294–301). For a general summary of the various positions taken by other counties, see *Choosing Genes for Future Children* (above) 302, 336.

[38] See *Choosing Genes for Future Children* (n 32 above) 169–72; E Parens and A Asch, 'The Disability Rights Critique of Prenatal Genetic Testing' in E Parens and A Asch (eds), *Prenatal Testing and Disability Rights* (Washington, DC, 2000), 13; M Saxton, 'Why Members of the Disability Community Oppose Prenatal Diagnosis and Selective Abortion' in Parens and Asch (eds) (above) 148.

Rare Disorders is open to the use of emerging genetic technologies for parents to choose to avoid the birth of children with disabilities, which shows that there is also a gap between disability rights groups on this issue.

Each country's response to PGD and whether there should be limits to it very much reflects the political make-up of that country, rather than any generally accepted universal principle. The United Kingdom was one of the first jurisdictions in the world to introduce legislation.[39] The Human Fertilisation and Embryology Act has been described as one of the most liberal schemes in Europe.[40] This has no doubt enabled the United Kingdom to enjoy the benefits of PGD and maintain a leading position in scientific developments. The United States goes further with *no* regulation of PGD. It is an 'open market'. It is 'essentially unmonitored, unstudied, and unregulated'.[41] The consequence is that only the wealthy have access to PGD in the United States.

In the United Kingdom there is an unwritten rule that the Human Fertilisation and Embryology Authority will consult with the public before developing a significant new policy. The New Zealand Human Assisted Reproductive Technology (HART) Act 2004 works from the premise that public consultation is an essential element of making legal policy where individual and social interests are at stake.[42] The public consultation is carried out by an Advisory Committee.[43] The Committee is guided by principles,[44] with the

[39] Human Fertilisation and Embryology Act 1990 (UK).

[40] R Morgan, 'Ethics, Economics and the Exotic: The Early Career of the HFEA' (2004) 12 *Health Care Analysis* 7, 20.

[41] The President's Council on Bioethics, 'Reproduction and Responsibility: The Regulation of New Biotechnologies' (Washington, DC, 2004) 103, at <http://www.bioethics.gov/reports/reproductionand responsibility/index.html> (accessed 4 December 2007).

[42] HART Act 2004, ss 36(1), 39–41.

[43] The Advisory Committee is established under of the HART Act 2004, s 32. It consists of 8–12 members (s 33), who are appointed by the Minister of Health (s 34(1)). Half must be laypersons (meaning not associated with health practice or research), and the members must include *at least*: one member with expertise in assisted reproductive procedures, in assisted reproductive research, in ethics, and in law; one member with the ability to articulate issues from a consumer perspective; a Māori member with expertise in Māori customary values and practice and the ability to articulate issues from a Māori perspective; and the Children's Commissioner or a representative or employee of the person holding that office (s 34). The Committee is expected, *inter alia*, to issue and review guidelines and give advice to the Ethics Committee on matters relating to any kind of assisted reproductive procedure or human reproductive research; to advise the Minister on issues arising from assisted reproductive procedure or human reproductive research (including the need for legislative or regulatory action or whether a certain procedure should be an 'established procedure'); and to monitor the application and health outcomes of assisted reproductive procedures and established procedures, and monitor developments in human reproductive research (s 35). See 'Genes, Society and the Future: Volume I/Human Genome Research Project'. (Dunedin, NZ: Human Genome Research Project, 2007 (hereinafter '*Genes, Society and the Future: Vol I*') 147–95.

[44] These principles are set out in the HART Act 2004, s 4 as being: the importance of the health and well-being of the children born as the result of an assisted reproductive procedure when making decisions about such procedures; that human health, safety, and dignity of present and future generations should be preserved and strengthened; that the health and well-being of women must be protected; the need for an informed choice and informed consent before assisted reproductive

health of women given particular emphasis (women being more 'directly and significantly affected' by assisted reproductive procedures).[45] The current regulatory provisions for PGD in New Zealand allow its use when there is a familial single gene condition which causes 'serious impairment'.[46] A plain reading of the wording means that late onset and low penetrance conditions—where not all individuals with the mutation will manifest symptoms of the condition—are included.[47] This guideline was drawn up before the Advisory Committee and the public consultation was put in place. There was no planned intent to put PGD on such a wide basis—it is more a case of the wording being wider than intended. By way of contrast, human leukocyte antigen (HLA) tissue typing is restricted to situations where embryo biopsy for a genetic condition is clinically indicated, and HLA tissue typing is an add-on to the primary procedure. The Guidelines restrict tissue typing to cases where the sick child is suffering from a genetically heritable disorder.[48] The 'Choosing Genes for Future Children' report recommends that, for the sake of consistency, HLA tissue typing should be available where the child is suffering from a condition which is severe or life-threatening.[49]

The underlying premise which is filling the gap between autonomy and social responsibility in the case of PGD is that there is little evidence that the use of PGD for serious genetic conditions, and the use of HLA tissue typing for life-threatening conditions, are causing medical[50] or social harm. The benefits to the families who use the procedures are given preference. This is best summed up by one of the Māori participants we surveyed about the use of PGD: 'If you knew that your child was going to have a terminal disease that would kill them by the age of two or three and be in absolute pain and agony for that two or three years. If I had had that choice, I wouldn't want to see anybody go through that pain, child or not...'[51]

procedures or research are conducted on an individual; that donor offspring should be informed of their genetic origins and be able to access information on these; and that the needs, values, and beliefs of Māori, and the different ethical, spiritual, and cultural perspectives in society, should be considered and treated with respect.

[45] HART Act 2004, s 4(c).

[46] Section 1 of the Guidelines on Preimplantation Genetic Diagnosis (hereinafter 'Guidelines on Preimplantation Genetic Diagnosis'), prepared by the National Ethics Committee on Assisted Human Reproduction (March 2005), and since designated as interim ACART Guidelines under the HART Act 2004, s 83.

[47] *Choosing Genes for Future Children* (n 32 above) 234–7, 296.

[48] Section 2 of the Guidelines on Preimplantation Genetic Diagnosis (n 46 above) See *Choosing Genes for Future Children* (n 32 above) 261–2.

[49] *Choosing Genes for Future Children* (n 32 above) 261–2.

[50] JC Harper, K Boelaert, J Geraedts, G Harton, WG Kearns, C Moutou, N Muntjewerff, S Repping, S Sengupta, P N Scriven, J Traeger-Synodinos, K Vesela, L Wilton, and KD Sermon, 'ESHRE PGD Consortium Data Collection V: Cycles from January to December 2002 with Pregnancy Follow-Up to October 2003' (2006) 21 *Human Reproduction* 3. See also *Choosing Genes for Future Children* (n 32 above) 51–4.

[51] Hana Oregan, quoted in *Choosing Genes for Future Children* (n 32 above) 88.

But who decides whether the impairment is serious enough for PGD to be used? In the current New Zealand Guidelines, that decision is the responsibility of PGD providers in collaboration with a clinical geneticist.[52] The gap at the point of application is closed by giving power to the medical profession. In the United Kingdom, 'the seriousness of a condition should be a matter for discussion between the people seeking treatment and the clinical team'.[53] A detailed empirical study of how the UK approval works concludes that: 'Overall, these health professionals and scientists showed great empathy with the experiences of prospective parents and were likely to defer to their views.'[54] However, the study did find that if the health professionals and scientists truly doubted the seriousness of a given condition, 'they would act as a check on their views, and would be likely to deny the provision of PGD'.[55] Seriousness was interpreted generally in terms of parents' interests, which meant that conditions such as Cystic Fibrosis and Downs Syndrome were seen to be sufficiently serious to meet the criteria for PGD.[56] In the end, the study recommends that where there is a 'reasonable' disagreement of whether a condition is serious enough, the benefit of the doubt should be given to the parents' views.[57]

IV. Genetic Testing of Minor Children[58]

The genetic testing of minors who cannot give their own consent raises the gap between parental responsibility and the future autonomy of the child.[59] It raises new issues for those involved in ethical medical decision-making contexts. Genetic testing may have far greater practical implications for other family members than decisions made in other medical contexts. Additionally, genetic information has the power to be more predictive of future health than other

---

[52] Guideline 6 of the Guidelines on Preimplantation Genetic Diagnosis (n 46 above).

[53] Human Fertilisation and Embryology Authority and Human Genetics Commission, 'Outcome of the Public Consultation on Preimplantation Genetic Diagnosis' (18 June 2001) recommendation 11. The recommendation continues, 'information provided to those seeking treatment... should include genetic and clinical information about the specific condition; its likely impact on those affected and their families; information about treatment and social support available; and the testimony of families and individuals about the full range of experiences of living with the condition'.

[54] R Scott, C Williams, K Ehrich, and B Farsides, 'The Appropriate Extent of Pre-Implantation Genetic Diagnosis: Health Professionals' and Scientists' Views on the Requirement for a "Significant Risk of a Serious Genetic Condition"' (2007) 15 *Medical Law Review* 320, 355.

[55] ibid.

[56] ibid 354.   [57] ibid 356.

[58] 'Genes, Society and the Future: Volume II/Human Genome Research Project', (Dunedin, NZ: Human Genome Research Project, 2007) (hereinafter '*Genes, Society and the Future: Vol II*'). The report deals in detail with minors who can give consent as well as minors who cannot. For the purposes of this chapter, the focus is on minors who cannot give consent.

[59] For the most thoroughly developed and articulated theory on the future autonomy of children, see M Freeman, *The Rights and Wrongs of Children* (London, 1983).

medical tests or interventions. Yet the predictive aspects are not easily understood and may be over- or underrated by parents.

Testing for medical conditions where there is treatment available creates no problem: it will enhance the child's future autonomy to have the testing. However, with respect to minors who cannot consent, predictive genetic testing for early onset conditions for which there is *no* beneficial medical intervention does raise difficult ethical considerations. Benefits of such testing may include: relieving the anxiety of uncertainty for both the child and the parents in high risk family situations; allowing the child time to adjust to having the condition; and giving parents the ability to prepare the child's environment before the onset of the condition.[60] Yet, the gaps in interpreting predictive genetic test results leave considerable residual uncertainty. For example, the risk that a child will develop a genetic condition they have been tested as being susceptible to depends on a number of factors, such as the particular gene(s) affected and environmental features. Equally, testing often cannot predict the severity of the disorder that the person will develop, or *when* they will develop it.[61] The inability to treat the condition means that any knowledge is largely unproductive. In these circumstances, the benefits may be outweighed by possible harms, such as the possibility that parents will treat the child differently (in terms of negative attitudes consequent on perceiving the child to be 'ill', or by subjecting the child to severe health regimes or treatments with negligible established benefits).[62] Such reactions can have severe consequences for a child's future autonomy. Unless there is evidence that the testing of the child for an early onset untreatable condition will harm the child's well-being, the final decision for such testing should be with the parents.[63]

The most difficult situation of testing of minors who are not able to give consent is for *late* onset conditions for which there is no medical intervention. Some people argue that, given parents know their child best and bear primary responsibility for their care, they should have the right to consent to testing.[64] Also, parenting involves exercising considerable discretion and parents need to be able to do this in an informed manner.[65] Conversely, social and psychological harms to the child may arise from: early awareness that one will inherit the untreatable

---

[60] *Genes, Society and the Future: Vol II* (n 58 above) 211, 216–17. See also 'GIG Response to the Clinical Genetics Society Report: The Genetic Testing of Children' (1995), at <http://www.gig.org.uk/docs/gig_testingchildren.pdf> (accessed 5 December 2007).

[61] *Genes, Society and the Future: Vol II* (n 58 above) 217.

[62] ibid 212, and 212–17. See also S Robertson and J Savulescu, 'Is There a Case in Favour of Genetic Testing of Young Children' (2001) 15(1) *Bioethics* 26, 34.

[63] Robertson and Savulescu (n 62 above) 26.

[64] *Genes, Society and the Future: Vol II* (n 58 above) 212. See also EW Clayton, 'Genetic testing in Children' (1997) 22 *The Journal of Medicine and Philosophy* 233; and Robertson and Savulescu (n 62 above) 26.

[65] *Genes, Society and the Future: Vol II* (n 58 above) 212–13. See also R Duncan 'Holding Your Breath, Predictive Genetic Testing in Young People', PhD Thesis, Department of

condition; lack of control over the decision to be tested; the possibility of detrimental differential parental treatment; or the inability to control the extent to which one's parents disclose one's genetic information.[66] The child may develop low self-esteem or depression, the parents may suffer feelings of guilt (to the detriment of the child), and the child may be discriminated against socially, such as in employment and insurance access.[67] Testing in childhood violates the child's future autonomy as it precludes the individual from choosing later in life that they prefer to live with the possibility as opposed to finding out for certain.[68] Therefore, 'Genes, Society and the Future concludes' that testing in these situations should be postponed until the minor can consent.[69] The power of deciding should be left to the child.

V. Warrior Genes[70]

A headline, '"Warrior Gene" Blamed for Māori Violence',[71] was breaking news around the world in August 2006. An Australian scientist, Dr Rod Lea, who was working in New Zealand, said that Māori men have a 'striking over-representation' of the monoamine oxidase gene that is 'strongly associated' with risk-taking and aggressive behaviour—'it definitely predisposes people to be more likely to be criminals'.[72] A member of our Human Genome Research Project team, Dr Tony Merriman, a genetic scientist, was of the view that Dr Rod Lea's claims did not stack up scientifically. Dr Merriman, and his colleague, Dr Vicky Cameron, found the longitudinal studies which showed that the crucial fact was whether or not the person had been severely mistreated as a child, and that 'high' monoamine oxidase-A (MAO-A) alleles were protection against antisocial behaviour even where there had been severe maltreatment.[73] Many Māori were

[66] *Genes, Society and the Future: Vol II* (n 58 above) 217.

[67] ibid 212; and Robertson and Savulescu (n 62 above) 26.

[68] *Genes, Society and the Future: Vol II* (n 58 above) 215. cf Robertson and Savulescu (n 62 above) 38–42, who argue that childhood testing does not reduce the options for the individual in later life; it just creates different options. They also contend that autonomy may be enhanced by a greater self-knowledge.

[69] *Genes, Society and the Future: Vol II* (n 58 above) 217.

[70] *Genes, Society and the Future: Vol I* (n 43 above).

[71] *The Age*, 8 August 2006, at <http://www.theage.com.au/news/National/Warrior-gene-blamed-for-Maori-violence/2006/08/08/1154802879716.html> (accessed 6 December 2007).

[72] ibid. cf R Lea and G Chambers, 'Monoamine Oxidase, Addiction, and the "Warrior Gene" Hypothesis' (2007) 120(1250) *The New Zealand Medical Journal*, 5–10, at <http://www.nzma. org.nz/journal/120-1250/2454/>, where Rod Lea retreats from the inferences drawn by the media.

[73] T Merriman and V Cameron, 'Risk-taking: behind the warrior gene story' (2007) 120(1250) *The New Zealand Medical Journal*, 62–7, citing A Caspi, J McClay, TE Moffitt,

rightfully upset by the findings that appeared to say they had a gene which made them more likely to be criminals. With Māori having the highest proportion of their people in prison in New Zealand,[74] the 'warrior gene' headline furthers a stereotype that some sections of New Zealand Society believe anyway. The gap between the headline and the realities of the longitudinal studies potentially disempowers Māori people in New Zealand.

In our report, 'Genes, Society and the Future: Volume I',[75] we find that there are a number of areas of criticism of genetic studies involving indigenous people. These comprise the exclusion of indigenous people from the planning and design of such research; disregard of different cultural values about conditions; insufficient reporting to communities of research results, and the potential for community stigmatization as a result of badly managed publication of research results; arguments over who owns DNA; community perceptions of exploitation; and fears about the unauthorized research use of stored DNA and cell lines.[76] We conclude that, in order to restore the balance of power between the community and the researchers, test results should be reported back to the community and the data should either be mutually owned by the community and researchers, or owned by the community with the researcher having access to it as a steward.[77] Some researchers will say that this gives too much power to the community. But if the researcher builds a good relationship with the community then, from that trust, the researcher is much more likely to carry out better research.[78]

J Mill, J Martin, IW Craig, A Taylor, and R Poulton, 'Role of Genotype in the Cycle of Violence in Maltreated Children' (2002) 297(5582) *Science* 851–4, at <http://www.sciencemag.org/cgi/content/full/297/5582/851> (accessed 6 December 2007); J Kim-Cohen, A Caspi, A Taylor, B Williams, R Newcombe, IW Craig, and TE Moffitt, 'MAOA, Maltreatment, and Gene-Environment Interaction Predicting Children's Mental Health: New Evidence and a Meta-Analysis' (2006) 11 *Molecular Psychiatry* 903, at <http://www.nature.com/mp/journal/v11/n10/abs/4001851a.html> (accessed 6 December 2007); C Spatz-Widom and LN Brzustowicz, 'MAOA and the "Cycle of Violence": Childhood Abuse and Neglect, MAOA Genotype, and Risk for Violent and Antisocial Behavior' (2006) 60(7) *Biological Psychiatry* 684, at <http://www.journals.elsevierhealth.com/periodicals/bps/article/PIIS0006322306004732/abstract> (accessed 6 December 2007).

[74] See New Zealand Department of Corrections, 'Annual Report 2004/05: Strategic Context: Environment, Issues and Implications', at <http://www.corrections.govt.nz/public/news/statutory-reports/annualreport/annual-report-2004-2005/part-1/environment-issues-and-implications.html>. People who identify as Māori constitute 14.5% of the general population of New Zealand but 50% of the prison population.

[75] *Genes, Society and the Future: Vol I* (n 43 above).

[76] *Genes, Society and the Future: Vol I* (n 43 above) 359, citing L Arbour and D Cook, 'DNA on Loan; Issues to Consider When Carrying Out Genetic Research with Aboriginal Families and Communities' (2006) 9 *Community Genetics* 153.

[77] See *Genes, Society and the Future: Vol I* (n 43 above) 17.

[78] See eg P Guilford, J Hopkins, J Harraway, M McLeod, N McLeod, P Harawira, H Taite, R Scoular, A Miller, and AE Reeve, 'E-cadherin Germline Mutations in Familial Gastric Cancer' (1998) 392(6674) *Nature* 6674, 402.

VI. Conclusion

Bioethics cannot solve the disagreements we have among ourselves over contentious matters. It can provide a menu of principles to look at the issues, but, in the end, it comes back to the dilemma Thrasymachus posed to Plato—that, on its own, reason does not supply ethical truth.[79] Might is ultimately right, in the sense that a particular principle is dominant, and it is by exploring the gaps between principles at the point of application—both in terms of choice and of principle—that we see how that might is applied—whether it be the might of the specialist in deciding whether to allow PGD, the parents in genetically testing their young child, or the scientist releasing research results without working closely with the community. It is only by constantly 'mining the gaps' that we can see where and how power operates, and whether new restraints on power may need to be instigated.

[79] See *Republic* (n 5 above).

14

Synthetic Biology and (Re)productive Liberties: Biosecurity, Biosecrecy, and Regulating New Technologies with Futures in Mind

Robin Mackenzie[1]

Biology as it's classically presented is God's domain, and biotechnology is dangerous turf so we need to keep it safe, lock it up in the lab so only scientists at institutions that have biosafety committees can access it...

A lot of our technology gets developed and presented in a social framework that is explicitly exclusionary and this promotes passive consumerism. What if instead we made biotechnology available, so that more people could learn about what was possible and could be involved in figuring out what to do? What if we made biotechnology not scary?

At the moment, we're trying to distribute the technology, we're trying to teach as many people as possible, we're trying to internationalize the technology for political reasons, to be direct about it, because we think that this is the path to a future that is secure.

Drew Endy, synthetic biologist.[2]

There is no such thing as too much security.

Stephen Collier, Andrew Lakoff and
Paul Rabinow on biosecurity.[3]

[1] The author wishes to acknowledge Thomas Saalfeld for ongoing thoughtful, stimulating, and perceptive conversations. His helpful remarks on terrorism, systems theory, and metaphor transformed the approach taken in this chapter. All its shortcomings are, naturally, my own.
[2] Bulletin of the Atomic Sciences, 'Drew Endy: the Bulletin Interview' (2007) 63 *Bulletin of the Atomic Scientists* 28.
[3] S Collier, A Lakoff, and P Rabinow, 'Biosecurity: Towards an Anthropology of the Contemporary' (2004) 20 *Anthropology Today* 2.

I. Introduction

The aim of this chapter is to map relatively unexplored territories within the discursive environment surrounding the ethics and regulation of (re)productive liberties associated with synthetic biology. In that regulatory oversight is involved in the use of technologies to create new living entities, as well as in the industrial production of commodities, regulation may be seen as curtailing or containing our freedom to reproduce and produce. In that synthetic biology involves the creation of new types of living entities, potentially on an industrial scale, the liberty to (re)produce in this way raises ethical and regulatory issues which may not easily be subsumed under past practices and presumptions over the governance of new biotechnologies. In this sense, our liberty to (re)-produce regulatory governance is also called into question. How we are to decide upon forms of regulation, mechanisms to translate opinions into decisions, and how to integrate the ethical, economic, and socio-cultural contexts of governance once the knowledge and means required to create synthesized life becomes widespread is by no means self-evident. Nor is agreement on the appropriate relationship between these capacities and concerns over biosafety and biosecurity easy to arrive at. In this light, the degree to which we may be required to (re)produce regulation is also at stake, as is the salience of the engineering model of (re)production for this enterprise. This chapter sets out to explore these issues, in order to argue that options for regulation should be evaluated in the light of the possible futures to which they are most likely to lead. How we might best synthesize regulation, in order to produce the future we would most wish for in a time of synthesized life, is a question to which we must all turn our minds, if one we might not wish for at all is not to eventuate.

II. Equipments, Ethics, and Engineering Life

Also known as synthetic genomics, synthetic biology is the use of technology to create life which is novel in the sense of an engineering of new biological systems that do not exist in nature, or a redesigning of existing living beings in order that a specific problem might be solved by them.[4] Such function-oriented entities might include microbes engineered to express medicines, to provide biofuels which could replace oil, or to clean up the environment. These utopian technofixes are mirrored by their dystopian images: microbes which could spread new or established diseases, via either bioterror or bioerror—deliberate or accidental releases. As will be described below, collectivities of synthetic biologists seek to make this technology accessible to all, so that ingredients for

---

[4] J Pleiss, 'The Promise of Synthetic Biology' (2006) 73 *Applied Microbiology Technology* 735.

making these synthesized entities may be able to be ordered freely online from the Massachussetts Institute of Technology Registry of Spare Parts at <http:// www.parts.mit.edu> to be assembled in modular form and produced in industrial quantities.[5] Thus (re)production refers to the fact that the entities are being reproduced, in the sense that they represent a new way of solving a problem, or the new improved version of whatever they are being set up to replace, and also to the fact that their creation may take place on a production line basis.

How we are to choose an ethical framework appropriate for these developments, and which regulatory consequences flow from this are questions central to this chapter. In order to explore them, I shall draw upon Paul Rabinow's reading of 'equipment'.[6] As delineated below, this signifies the ways in which truth claims, affects, and ethical orientations constitute contingent sets of practices. Much post-Foucauldian theory has addressed the part played by truth claims, affect, and ethical orientations in regulatory practices.[7] In this light, my cartography will involve the superimposition of work on considerations of scientific citizenship and the regulation of new technologies[8] over theorizations of biosecurity and biosecrecy. I will conclude by arguing that new technologies must be regulated as ongoing iterative acts of choice between possible futures.

Synthetic biology takes an engineering approach not only to life, but to shaping its own disciplinary future. A collaborative research centre, SynBERC (Synthetic Biology Engineering Research Centre, at <http:www.synberc.org>), has been established with this in mind.[9] Paul Rabinow and Gaymon Bennett explain that SynBERC, 'represents an innovative assemblage of multiple scientific subdisciplines, diverse forms of funding, complex institutional collaborations, an orientation to the near-future looking, intensive work with governmental and non-governmental agencies, focused legal innovation, imaginative use of media. More unusual still, SynBERC has built in ethics as an integral and co-equal if distinctive component.'[10]

In the engineering economy of nature, natural components may be isolated, identified and assembled anew.[11] Rabinow and his colleagues are engaged in

[5] 'Drew Endy: the Bulletin Interview' (n 2 above).

[6] P Rabinow, *Anthropos Today: Reflections on Modern Equipment* (Princeton: Princeton University Press, 2003) (hereinafter, *'Anthropos Today'*).

[7] M Horst, 'Public Expectations of Gene Therapy: Scientific Futures and Their Performative Effects on Scientific Citizenship' (2007) 32 *Science, Technology and Human Values* 150; N Brown, C Douglas, L Eriksson, E Rodrigues, S Yearly, and A Webster, 'Researching Expectations in Medicine, Science and Technology: Theory and Method', Position Paper for the York Workshop of the Expectations Network (June 2005); C Novas, 'The Political Economy of Hope: Patients' Organisations, Science and Biovalue' (2006) 1 *BioSocieties* 289.

[8] P McNaghten, M Kearnes, and B Wynne, 'Nanotechnology, Governance and Public Deliberation: What Role for the Social Sciences?' (2005) 27 *Science Communication* 268.

[9] J Keasling, 'Synthetic Biology' Paper given at Synthetic Biology 3.0, Zurich, June 2007.

[10] P Rabinow and G Bennett, 'From Bio-ethics to Human Practice' (2007) 11 *ARC Working Papers* 1, 7.

[11] P Rabinow, 'The Biological Modern' (2006) 6 *ARC Concept Notes* 1, (hereinafter *'The Biological Modern'*).

what appears to be a homologous process to construct an anthropology of the contemporary ethics of technology. Arguing that ethics takes specific forms as shaped by the science of technologies, Rabinow characterizes the conceptual tools involved in the production of ethical, legal, and cultural interventions and their standardization as 'equipment'.[12] He and Bennett expand on the role of equipment as follows: 'what is distinctive about equipment is that its task is to connect a set of truth claims, affects and ethical orientations into a set of practices. These practices, which have taken different forms historically, are productive responses to changing conditions brought about by specific problems, events and general reconfigurations'.[13]

Discussing the ethical component of equipment within the anthropology of the contemporary, Rabinow and Bennett explain that equipment signifies the recalibration of bioethics as it operates as an authoritative producer of truths and procedures within official bodies, such as the President's Council on Bioethics, in order to provide the means of decision-making over reconceptualizations provoked by new technologies. A recent example of this recalibration would be the ways in which the controversy within the United Kingdom over whether cybrids (inter-species cytoplasmic hybrids) formed from denucleated cow eggs and human genetic material should be permissible both informed and formed the ongoing social negotiations over the moral significance of life, as well as the socio-legal construction of distinctions between persons and things, or human and non-human animals.[14] Claiming that bioethics has suffered from a reluctance to incorporate the insights of science into such recalibrations, Rabinow and Bennett suggest that a collaboration of ethics, anthropology, and science holds promise for a human flourishing (eudaemonia) which is built upon phronesis, or practical wisdom. They stress that:

...eudaemonia should not be confused with technical optimization as we hold that our capacities are not already known and that we do not understand flourishing to be uncontrolled growth or the undirected maximization of existing capacities. Here we are merely insisting that the question of what constitutes a good life today, and the contribution of the bio-sciences to that form of life must be vigilantly posed and re-posed. Which norms are actually in play and how they function must be observed, chronicled and evaluated in an ongoing fashion. It is plausible that engaged observation stands a chance of contributing positively to emergent scientific formations. It is worth seeing if such observation can be effectively realized by conducting ethical inquiry in direct and ongoing collaboration with scientists, policy makers and other stake holders. We are persuaded that within such collaborative structures biology, ethics and anthropology can orient practice to the flourishing as both telos and mode of operation.[15]

---

[12] Rabinow, *Anthropos Today* (n 6 above).
[13] Rabinow and Bennett (n 10 above) 7.
[14] R Mackenzie, 'Queering Spinozan Somatechnics: Stem Cells and Strategic Sacralisations' in N Sullivan (ed), *Queering Somatechnics* (London: Ashgate, 2008) forthcoming.
[15] Rabinow and Bennett (n 10 above) 5.

How synthetic biology might contribute to eudaemonia and phronesis, and the degree to which our regulating with the future in mind should involve iterative processes wherein we exercise practical wisdom in drawing upon scientific and other knowledges to maximize human flourishing, are questions which will be explored more fully below.

Before doing so, I wish to turn to the equipment producing and produced by synthetic biology. A salient factor here is the framing of risk, uncertainty, biosafety, and biosecurity. Filippa Lentzos has suggested a research agenda for biosecurity incorporating three types of denaturalization: the process whereby biorisk is problematized, the movement from risk/insurance to uncertainty/security configurations and the 'path-dependent' consequences of frame choice.[16] Applying this to synthetic biology reveals ongoing negotiations over the form which problematization of associated biorisks should take, differing national and international orietations towards biosafety or biosecurity measures mediated by cultural factors and a growing awareness of difficulties associated with choices determining path-dependence. These will now be assessed in greater depth.

III. Synthetic Biology, Biorisk, Biosafety, and Biosecurity

(Bio)risks associated with synthetic biology include not only the accidental or intentional construction and release of synthetic life forms which pose a threat to other life forms or the environment but also inappropriate regulation, economic competition, dispossession of poor farmers in the third world, and the implications of adoption of an engineering perspective on life and living. Indeed, the new ability to create artificial life renders it is unlikely that all existing and potential (bio)risks are capable of being conceptualized, recognized, or assessed at present.[17] Nonetheless, all of those listed above constitute concerns expressed by groups involved in the problematization of biorisk and synthetic biology. For example, the ETC Group, an NGO seeking to support rural agriculturalists, has mounted a campaign to increase public debate on synthetic biology, arguing that the promised benefits of such new technologies are likely to prove ineffectual and to further disadvantage already vulnerable peoples and eco-systems.[18] In the

---

[16] F Lentzos, 'Rationality, Risk and Response: a Research Agenda for Biosecurity' (2006) 1 *BioSocieties* 453.

[17] J Vallverdu and C Gustafsson, 'Synthetic Life: Ethics for a New Biology', Paper given at Synthetic Biology 3.0, Zurich, June 2007.

[18] ETC Group, 'Broad International Coalition Issues Urgent Call For Strong Oversight of Nanotechnology',at<http://www.etcgroup.org/en/materials/publications.html?pub_id=651> (accessed 25 September 2007); ETC Group, 'Patenting Pandora's Bug: Goodbye Dolly...Hello Synthia! J. Craig Venter's Institute Seeks Monopoly Patent on World's First-Ever Human-Made Life Form', at <http://www.etcgroup.org/en/materials/publications.html?pub_id=631> (accessed 25 September 2007); ETC Group, 'Synthia's Last Hurdle?',at <http://www.etcgroup.org/en/materials/publications.html?pub_id=648> (accessed 25 September 2007); ETC Group, 'Extreme Genetic Engineering: An Introduction

wake of a successful campaign against Monsanto, the ETC Group oppose the view that self-regulation would suffice to contain the risks they perceive synthetic biology as posing.

Past controversies over new technologies such as genetically modified organisms impact upon strategies deployed by actors seeking to problematize biorisk aspects of synthetic biology. Certainly the synthetic biology community's ongoing engagement with perceived stakeholders may be seen in this light. Scientists working on synthetic biology have for some years consciously adopted strategies based upon collaboration and disclosure to ensure public acceptance of the technologies involved.[19] The Synthetic Society Working Group describe themselves as 'a group of individuals working together to directly address societal issues embedded in and surrounding the new emerging field of synthetic biology' on the website they maintain, where their goals include making 'unbiased progress on the issues' and 'collecting and organizing resources to facilitate widespread understanding and consideration of the issues'.[20] Continuing efforts have been made to demystify synthetic biology, to make its standardized constituents available to all via an open source licensing scheme and to promote its use among young scientists by publicizing a highly successful annual international student competition iGEM (Genetically Engineered Machines).[21] A comic strip on the joys of synthetic biology, the first comic to be published in the prestigious science journal *Nature*,[22] was co-created by Drew Endy, one of the foremost scientists in the field, who has engaged in a campaign of impression management not only in order to render synthetic biology accessible to all but also to sideline knee-jerk opposition to it from the public at large.[23] Indeed, a salient concern has been to forestall what the supporters of synthetic biology conceptualize as overly stringent governmental regulation which would stifle further research. To this end, collaborative gatherings of supporters of synthetic biology have repeatedly sought to propose self-regulatory measures which would be found acceptable as a substitute.[24]

to Synthetic Biology' (2007) at <http://www.etcgroup.org/en/materials/publications.html?id=602> (accessed 25 September 2007).

[19] H Breithaupt, 'The Engineer's Approach to Biology' (2006) 7 *EMBO Reports* 21; G Church, 'A Synthetic Biohazard Non-proliferation Proposal', at <http://arep.med.harvard.edu/SBP/Church_Biohazard04c.htm> (accessed 26 September 2007).

[20] R Rettberg, 'iGEM: the International Genetically Engineered Machine Competition'; J Keasling, 'Synthetic Biology', Paper given at Synthetic Biology 3.0, Zurich, June 2007. See also <http://openwetware.org> (accessed 26 September 2007).

[21] M Campbell, 'Meeting Report: Synthetic Biology Jamboree for Undergraduates' (2005) 4 *Cell Biology Education* 19.

[22] D Endy and I Deese, 'Adventures in Synthetic Biology' (2005) 438 *Nature* 449.

[23] 'Drew Endy: the Bulletin Interview' (n 2 above); D Endy, 'Foundations for Engineering Biology' (2005) 438 *Nature* 449.

[24] S Maurer, K Lucas, and S Terrell, *From Understanding to Action: Community Based Options for Improving Safety and Security in Synthetic Biology* (Berkeley, Calif: University of California Press, 2006); Synthetic Biology 3.0 Conference, Zurich, June 2007. Proceedings at <http://www.syntheticbiology3.ethz.ch/proceedings.htm> (accessed 25 September 2007).

At stake is the undoubted possibility that synthetic biology could be used to produce self-replicating, evolving entities which could give rise to biohazard.[25] Measures to protect against accidental release (biosafety) or intentional biowarfare or bioterrorism (biosecurity) are accepted as necessary by most stakeholders. The choice between these exemplifies the second point made by Lentzos, the move from a biosafety to a biosecurity frame as appropriate for containing biorisk. Much discussion over the ethics and potential of synthetic biology thus has as its focus these risks, and ways in which they might be contained.[26] Synthetic biology is not alone amongst the life sciences in having both civilian and military potential uses. A burgeoning literature on what is known as the 'dual use dilemma' seeks to rationalize controls over access to salient bioscience facilities, equipment, constituents, and information.[27] Concerns over the consequent surveillance of populations, and the shift from prevention to preparedness abound.[28]

Potential risks, such as those posed by dual use biological technologies, provoke new responses in several ways. In that they are unable to be contained by individual sovereign state measures, prevention of their menace to nation state populations is problematic. Insofar as their threat is unable to be located, except in the malice or carelessness of anonymous 'others', or the unforeseen outcome of acts performed in good faith (like refrigeration using CFCs), assessing the likelihood of their occurrence is impossible. Thus, many nation state and international bodies charged with dealing with catastrophes have altered their focus from the prevention of predictable perils, such as war and pestilence, to preparing for catastrophic events by ensuring that protective measures to preserve infrastructures and public services are in place.[29] Stephen Collier and Andrew Lakoff assess the theoretical significance of this move in collective security measures towards vital systems security as follows: 'it might be more analytically productive not to ask how much or how little security is appropriate, or whether security must be at the expense of other values such as liberty or welfare. Rather, it is more appropriate to ask which forms of collective security are in question, what kinds of expertise are being mobilized to provide security, and how the politics of security are changing.'[30]

Policies of preparedness and an orientation towards preserving vital systems security are likely to focus on generic catastrophic threats, increased surveillance,

[25] Breithaupt (n 19 above).

[26] G Mukunda, S Mohr, and K Oye, 'Biosecurity Implications of DNA Synthesis and Synthetic Biology', Paper given at Synthetic Biology 3.0, Zurich, June 2007.

[27] R Atlas and M Dando, 'The Dual-Use Dilemma for the Life Sciences: Perspectives, Conundrums and Global Solutions' (2006) 4 *Biosecurity and Bioterrorism: Biodefence Strategy, Practice and Science* 276.

[28] L Fearnley, 'From Chaos to Controlled Disorder: Syndromic Surveillance, Bioweapons and the Pathological Future' (2005) 5 *ARC Working Papers* 1. L Fearnley, 'Pathogens and the Strategy of Preparedness' (2005) 3 *ARC Working Papers* 1.

[29] A Lakoff, 'From Population to Vital System' (2007) 7 *ARC Working Papers* 1.

[30] S Collier and A Lakoff, 'Vital Systems Security' (2006) 2 *ARC Working Papers* 1.

the administrative logistics of response, and the modelling of singular catastrophic events in such a way as to exclude non-technical factors from the framing of potential risk factors.[31] One example of this would be the assumption that
those subjected to Hurricane Katrina would own vehicles which would allow
them to leave the afflicted area, despite the poverty of many of the residents
affected. Ethical difficulties associated with this elision are obvious, as are the
homologies with engineering perspectives which frame problems in terms of
efficient manipulation of industrial quantities of modular, equivalent parts in
abstract contexts where social, emotional, and environmental factors tend to be
excluded as irrelevant. How this impacts on the regulation of synthetic biology
will now be explored.

Using Collier and Lakoff's frame to map how the politics of security impacts
on synthetic biology reveals an ongoing concern over the degree of regulatory
security which it is feared would be imposed on the field should a catastrophic
event occur, and the need to take a proactive approach to prevent this. This has
been described by Rabinow as follows:

> Roger Brent has named such a situation as the 'crossing the valley of death' moment
> before anything like a set of regulations, surveillance mechanisms, standard practices,
> community control mechanisms and policing can be developed. The years to come are
> therefore likely to be full of danger. The task then becomes establishing a risk terrain so as
> to begin the process of turning amorphous and fear producing dangers into risks that are
> at least somewhat calculable and predictable.[32]

The assumption among members of the synthetic biology community is that
there is a significant risk that stultifying restrictions are likely to be imposed on
the field of synthetic biology unless a proactive approach to establishing collaboration between stakeholders leading to an acceptance of self-regulation is followed, and that self-regulation depends upon agreement on measures which
would contain risk. Proffered suggestions in a recent White Paper written for the
synthetic biology community have included that best practice screening procedures be adopted by all commercial gene synthesis houses, that industry screening programmes be improved, that members affirm an ethical duty to investigate
and report dangerous behaviour, that a confidential hotline for biosafety and
biosecurity issues be set up, that a community wide clearing house for identifying
and tracking potential biosafety/biosecurity issues be set up and that biosafety/
biosecurity R&D priorities be endorsed.[33] Such measures correspond with many
current practices as dictated by national and international regulations and guidelines.[34] A subsequent report on options for the governance of synthetic genomics

---

[31] Lakoff (n 29 above).   [32] Rabinow, (n 11 above) 15.

[33] S Maurer, K Lucas, and S Terrell (n 24 above).

[34] M Graf and R Wagner, 'Synthetic Biology and Biosafety: Insight into Control Mechanisms
on Worldwide Distribution of Synthetic DNA from an Industrial Perspective', Paper given at
Synthetic Biology 3.0, Zurich, June 2007.

identified security challenges linked to technical issues of safety, access to information on the internet by bad faith users, and emergent or unknown dangers.[35] The report recommended moving from a safety to a security framework, and responding to uncertainty with preparedness. Yet, as Rabinow, Bennett, and Stavrianakis point out, control of access via screening and licensing and promoting best practice among scientists constitute technological safeguards which fit within a frame of safety rather than security. They contend that a frame of security and preparedness render necessary 'vigilant observation, regular forward thinking and ongoing adaptation'.[36] Asserting that 'the next challenge is to design and develop continuous forms of collaboration as a mode of science governance' they conclude:

What is needed today is mutual reflection on the significance of work being done in synthetic genomics, the environment in which this is being done, and what problems might be on the horizon. The aim of such collaborative reflection would be to identify challenges and opportunities in real time, and to redirect scientific, political, ethical and economic practice in ways that would, hopefully, mitigate future problems and actualize possible benefits.[37]

The iterative process the synthetic biology community are attempting to instantiate, as well as that envisaged by Rabinow and Bennett where equipment is continually created and modified through engaged observation, are both typical features of a systems theory or engineering approach. Indeed, it has been suggested that this desire to design and test via simulation before instantiation is one of the defining characteristics of synthetic biology.[38] As such, it represents an attempt to avoid the path-dependence viewed by Lentzos as problematic. How this should relate to the ethics of collective security systems and the optimum forms of regulating reproductive liberties in relation to synthetic biology is the issue to which I shall now turn.

The shift from prevention to preparedness within nation state and international bodies charged with collective security matches an increasing recognition that, given the increasing extra-territoriality of threats to populations, forms of global governance involving multilateral cooperation and disclosure, stakeholder participation in decision-making, and internalization of professional ethics by scientists represents the sustainable way forward.[39] Yet while scientists

---

[35] M Garfinkle, D Endy, G Epstein, and R Friedman, 'Synthetic Genomics: Options for Governance', Report of the Project Synthetic Genomics: Risks and Benefits for Science and Society (Berkeley, 2006).

[36] P Rabinow, G Bennett, and A Stavrianakis, 'Response to "Synthetic Genomics: Options for Governance"' (2006) 10 *ARC Concept Notes* 1, 15.

[37] ibid 16.

[38] R Brent, 'A Partnership Between Biology and Engineering' (2004) 22 *Nature Biotechnology* 1211.

[39] N Sims, 'The Future of Biological Disarmament: New Hope After the Sixth Review Conference of the Biological Weapons Convention' (2007) 14 *Nonproliferation Review* 351; J Whitman, 'Governance Challenges of Technological Systems Convergence' (2006) 26 *Bulletin*

in the synthetic biology community favour these measures on the grounds that openness, dissemination, internationalization, and popularization represent the best path to a secure future, not all agree.[40]

Biosecrecy is espoused by those who fear that sharing the technical information and constituents of synthetic biology (re)-production would increase the likelihood of threats to global and national biosecurity. Michael Selgelid has expressed concerns that biological research which is openly published may encourage bioterrorists by providing the instructions to create bioweaponry. Arguing that some studies should not be published, he considers that the recommendations of the United States National Research Council in 2003 that pre-publication review and self-censorship by scientists should provide security would prove insufficient, contending that normative values within a scientific field are not necessarily appropriate to govern it.[41] Selgelid supports the American Medical Association's Council on Ethical and Judicial Affairs Guidelines to Prevent the Malevolent Use of Biomedical Research, which hold that physicians/researchers should avoid projects where the likely social harms outweigh the likely social benefits.[42] Admitting that governments cannot always be trusted to balance the competing interests, he nonetheless supports a degree of government censorship, as their possession of classified information may allow them to assess the potential of dual use research most accurately.

In similar vein, Laurie Zoloth, a bioethicist who has focused on dual use and synthetic biology, argues for what she has called a Jedi theory of governance, where only a chosen few from the synthetic biology community are permitted access to information with potential for bioweaponry.[43] A central issue which has been perceived as being at stake here is how far the ethical issues of synthetic biology may be reduced to those pertaining to risk and biosecurity. Nicola Biller-Andorno finds that there has been an impasse reached here between two camps, the 'cool' scientists, who favour open disclosure and the 'concerned', who argue that matters of risk and safety are not the sole ethical concerns.[44] Biller-Adorno sees the central difficulty as establishing criteria for which arguments are legitimate in pluralistic societies.

---

of Science, Technology and Society 398–409; World Health Organization, *Scientific Working Group on Life Science Research and Global Health Security: Report of the First Meeting* (Geneva: WHO, 2006).

[40] 'Drew Endy: the Bulletin Interview' (n 2 above).

[41] M Selgelid, 'A Tale of Two Studies: Ethics, Bioterrorism and the Censorship of Science' (2007) 37 *Hastings Center Report* 35.

[42] M Selgelid, 'Commentary: the Ethics of Dangerous Discovery' (2006) 15 *Cambridge Quarterly of Healthcare Ethics* 444.

[43] L Zoloth, 'Hide and Seek: the Ethics of Curiosity and Security in Synthetic Biology', Paper given at Synthetic Biology 3.0, Zurich, June 2007.

[44] N Biller-Andorno, 'Debating the Ethics of Synthetic Biology: Transcending the Current Impasse', Paper given at Synthetic Biology 3.0, Zurich, June 2007.

Yet, I would suggest, any severing of issues of risk and security from other ethical concerns is artificial. In my view, the set of practices advocated by the 'cool'—disclosure, dissemination, and self-governance—constitute equipment, assemblages transversed by axes of opposing views on economic competition, propertization, and citizen participation in policy decisions. National and international bodies are seeking to coordinate research strategies with a view to maximizing the economic potential afforded by synthetic biology.[45] This will inevitably involve a form of economic modelling of the value of biosecurity and biosafety measures, where moves towards harmonization are tempered by economic competition and cultural differences. Thus the balance between under- and over-regulation necessary in order to attract venture capital, the ideological baggage associated with the open source/intellectual property rights debate, and distinctions between providing information and engaging in impression management are evidently ethical issues which underpin disagreements over risk and biosecurity.[46] Similarly, the moral economy of various jurisdictions, past debates over new genetic technologies, and perception and location of risk will affect the degree to which necessary action is framed in terms of biosafety (Europe) or biosecurity (United States).[47] Indeed, Schmidt sees synthetic biology as resembling a large scale Rohschach test for detecting attitudes to non-technical issues of technology development in the United States, Europe, and the rest of the world.[48]

Thus how far, by which means, and upon what basis we might regulate new technologies is problematic. In part, this stems from structural difficulties inherent in the regulatory process in democratic nation states in a globalizing world. Limitations of national sovereignty in world trade networks, together with tensions over envisioning regulation as a means of preventing market failure which simultaneously promotes social solidarity and trust, continue to provoke soul searching within regulatory jurisprudence.[49] Issues of inclusion, knowledge dissemination, reflective deliberation and civic participation are well known, as are those surrounding risk, professional self-regulation, accountability, and transparency.[50] Both the European and the English imperatives associated with

---

[45] S Gaisser, H Bernauer, A Linkes, K Muller, T Reith, and B Buhrien, 'Towards a European Strategy for Synthetic Biology: the TESSY Project' Paper given at Synthetic Biology 3.0, Zurich, June 2007; J Stelling, 'EMERGENCE: a Foundation for Synthetic Biology in Europe', Paper given at Synthetic Biology 3.0, Zurich, June 2007.

[46] J Henkel, 'On the Economics of Synthetic Biology: Is Openness Feasible?', Paper given at Synthetic Biology 3.0, Zurich, June 2007; S Maurer, 'The BP Deal: a Policy Analysis', Paper given at Synthetic Biology 3.0, Zurich, June 2007; A Rai and J Boyle, 'Synthetic Biology: Caught Between Property Rights, the Public Domain and the Commons' (2007) 5 *PLoS Biology* 389; J Tait, 'Riding a Roller Coaster: Policy, Public and Science Interactions in Synthetic Biology', Paper given at Synthetic Biology 3.0, Zurich, June 2007.

[47] Lentzos, (n 16 above); M Schmidt, 'Framing the Safety and Security Aspects of Synthetic Biology', Paper given at Synthetic Biology 3.0, Zurich, June 2007.

[48] ibid.

[49] T Prosser, 'Regulation and Social Solidarity' (2006) 33 *Journal of Law and Society* 364.

[50] J Black, 'The Emergence of Risk Based Regulation and the New Public Risk Management in the United Kingdom' (2005) Public Law 512; J Black, 'Tensions in the Regulatory State' (2007) *Public Law* 58.

the better regulation initiative have been extensively canvassed, and the promise of what is termed 'smart' regulation noted.[51] Marrying the regulation of new technologies, especially biotechnologies, with these concerns is far from simple, as the new technologies give rise to separate ethical and legal problematics which centre upon a plethora of views on the place of dignity, human rights, and conceptions of nature and morality within regulatory discourse.[52] Finally, there are the idiosyncratic characteristics of the new technologies themselves. Each is embedded in a complex assemblage of constructed narratives and framings which both influence and are influenced by public perceptions of the possible futures they offer.[53]

It is easy in the abstract to see regulation as tasked with connecting a clutch of truth claims, affects, and ethical orientations into a set of practices which are productive responses to contingency, ie as related to equipment as the term is used by Rabinow and Bennett. Another relevant piece of equipment in this sense is the utility of the engineering model, which embodies a set of truth claims, affects, and ethical orientations into a set of practices which excludes as irrelevant non-technical factors, operates on a closed system methodology, and may be condemned as reductionist for its insensitivity to context. Nonetheless, its emphasis upon self-correction through iteration, openness to new input, and task-oriented efficiency are arguably valuable characteristics which might serve to improve regulatory effectiveness. Indeed, as will be seen in the following section, issues of self-correction, responsiveness, and efficacy are some of the current preoccupations in regulatory jurisprudence. I shall turn to these after a further consideration of the relationship between (re)-productive liberties and regulation.

IV. (Re)-productive Liberties, Regulation, and Synthetic Biology

As sketched out above, the term '(re)-productive liberties' in the title of this chapter signifies the difficulties associated with the placing of an appropriate frame on the regulation of synthetic biology. 'Reproductive liberties' usually denotes the exercise of autonomy to decide when, how, and whether we might decide to use gametes which are our own, or which we have acquired, to create a new entity. In other words, when we reproduce life. We may do so using

---

[51] R Baldwin, 'Is Better Regulation Smarter Regulation?' (2005) *Public Law* 485.

[52] D Beyleveld and R Brownsword, 'Principle, Proceduralism and Precaution in a Country of Rights' (2006) 19 *Ratio Juris* 141; R Brownsword, 'Regulating Human Genetics: Dilemmas for a New Millenium' (2004) 12 *Medical Law Review* 14; R Brownsword, 'Reproductive Opportunities and Regulatory Challenges' (2004) 67 *MLR* 304; R Brownsword, 'What the World Needs Now: Techno-Regulation, Humanity, Human Rights and Human Dignity' in R Brownsword (ed), *Global Governance and the Quest for Justice* (Oxford: Hart, 2004).

[53] C Tourney, 'Narratives for Nanotech: Anticipating Public Reactions to Nanotechnology' (2004) 8 *Techne* 88.

human gametes, if we wish to become a parent, or animal gametes should we be involved in animal production, or breeding. As seen above, synthetic biology allows life to be reproduced in a fundamentally different sense. It is often characterized in terms of applying an engineering perspective to designing life, as distinct from genetic engineering.[54] Rather than relying upon gametes to produce a life whose form is constrained by boundaries associated with existing life forms, synthetic biologists assemble synthesized building blocks of genetic materials into life forms which have not existed before in order that they might fulfil a pre-existing function. The job which needs to be done determines the design and form of the engineered entity. Synthetic biologists may also use such building blocks to redesign existing life forms. Moreover, in that they are able to do so on an assembly line basis, mass production of new forms of 'life itself' may take place in the very near future. The infrastructure for the supply of standardized modular synthesized building blocks, together with assembly services for new parts, devices, and systems, already exists, in the MIT (Massachussetts Institute of Technology) Registry of Standard Biological Parts. Although currently the contents of the repository are in the form of synthesized DNA (sDNA), it is envisaged that as synthetic biology becomes more common and costs reduce, economies of scale will enable components to be stored as information and synthesized on request.[55] (Re)-production, then, in this sense, implies the manufactured generation of novel life forms which synthetic biology renders possible for the first time. How far, in what way, and on what basis might such new (re)-productive liberties be limited by regulation?

Regulation over activities involving the use of technologies to reproduce life tend to focus on a mixture of ethical and procedural safeguards. In the United Kingdom, for instance, the Human Fertilisation and Embryology Act 1990 regulates the provision of fertility treatment to humans, while the European Convention for the Protection of Animals Kept for Farming Purposes has been ratified and Directive (EC)98/58 implemented into national legislation as governing the use of reproductive technology within animal husbandry breeding. As new possibilities to use genetic technologies to alter the characteristics of human and non-human animal populations have emerged, regulations have been fine tuned to prohibit certain techniques, such as reproductive cloning of human embryos, while permitting others, such as pre-genetic diagnosis of embryos for specific disorders. Legal oversight in both cases focuses upon the protection of the humans or animals reproducing through technological means, and sets limits on the technologies and procedures which may be used in this light. Regulating synthetic biology differs here in that any protective measures are likely to focus on the need to preserve not the reproduced life forms

---

[54] Synthetic Society, Distinguishing and Defining Synthetic Biology', at <http://openwetware.org/wiki/Synthetic_Society/Distinguishing_and_defining_Synthetic_Biology> (accessed 26 September 2007).

[55] Rai and Boyle (n 46 above).

themselves, but rather the public and the environment at large. In this sense, although synthetic biology is conceptually distinct from the genetic modification of organisms, the potential for the two to be conflated exists. As outlined above, this is a concern for supporters of synthetic biology, who wish to ensure that its reception by the public is more favourable than that accorded to genetically modified organisms.

My suggestion in this chapter is that the creation of novel or redesigned life forms raises specific ethical issues which are part of ongoing social negotiations over the moral significance of life and the socio-legal construction of the distinction between persons and things.[56] The degree to which the process involved in setting regulation in place is a site for such negotiations may perhaps best be seen in relation to the consultations on inter-species cytoplasmic hybrids, or cybrids in the United Kingdom during 2007.[57] In addition, the (re)-production of synthetic life forms raises issues over how far this might be framed in terms of biopower, and the relationship between biopower and biosecurity.[58] I will draw upon the work of anthropologists, social scientists, and science studies scholars in order to suggest that, in order for the regulation of new technologies to be carried out in an iterative fashion, it must be done with the need to choose between possible futures in mind. This resonates with current calls within the philosophy of technology and regulatory theory for a social ethics of technology,[59] together with an emphasis on 'smart' rather than 'better' regulation.[60] It is also homologous with Nowotny's quest to delineate the characteristics of institutions capable of developing their own reflexivity,[61] as well as with Rabinow and Bennett's vision of an iterative input from biosciences into questions of what constitutes the good life, eudaemonia, and phronesis. Regulation of new technologies would thus proceed upon a basis of participatory choices among possible futures. Such an iterative process would involve creating, adjusting, and maintaining an ongoing variety of possible futures as scenarios as a basis for negotiated meanings which lead on to regulatory structures which continually alter as a result.

---

[56] I expand on this aspect of the chapter in a companion piece, 'Hopes and Fears: the Impact of Synthetic Biology on the Regulation of Socio-Legal Constructions of Persons, Things, Dreams and Nightmares in the Affective Economy'; see also R Mackenzie, 'Queering Spinozan Somatechnics: Stem Cells and Strategic Sacralizations'; A Pottage, 'Introduction: the Fabrication of Persons and Things' in A Pottage (ed), *Law, Anthropology and the Constitution of the Social* (Cambridge, 2004), 1.

[57] Academy of Medical Sciences, *Inter-species Embryos* (London, 2007); House of Commons, Science and Technology Committee, *Fifth Report* (London, 2007); Human Fertilisation and Embryology Authority, *Hybrids and Chimera* (London, 2007), at <http://www.hfea.gov.uk/en/1517.html> (accessed 26 September 2007).

[58] B Braun, 'Biopolitics and the Molecularization of Life' (2007) 14 *Cultural Geographies* 6; L. Holloway and C Morris, 'Exploring Biopower in the Regulation of Farm Animal Bodies: Genetic Policy Interventions in UK Livestock' (2007) 3 *Genomics, Society and Policy* 82.

[59] R Devon, 'Towards a Social Ethics of Technology: a Research Prospect' (2004) 8 *Techne* 99.

[60] Baldwin, 'Is Better Regulation Smarter Regulation?'.

[61] H Nowotny, 'How Many Policy Rooms Are There?' (2007) 32 *Science, Technology and Human Values* 479.

V. Regulating in Times of Uncertainty: the Unexamined Technology is Not Worth Having[62]

Regulating innovative technologies is paradoxical in that the difficulties associated with assessing their impact must be overcome in order to regulate with the future in mind. This demands drawing on a base of informed expectations to construct alternative futures and a choice of the regulatory framework which would most happily manifest the chosen outcomes. Yet doing so under conditions of uncertainty is problematic. In that risks come with known or knowable probabilities, they may be calculated, despite the inevitability of certain margins of error. Nonetheless, the decisions under uncertainty associated with novel technologies must be taken where probabilities are unknown, as indeed are the range of unforeseeable and unwelcome outcomes. Hansson suggests in this light that criteria whereby we might decide when to worry about unforeseen outcomes and when to ignore them might include asymmetry of information (or the degree of uncertainty), the degree of unfamiliarity, spatial and temporal limits on the potential effects, and the degree of interference with complex systems in balance.[63] Nonetheless, when we don't know what we don't know, as is inevitable with new technologies, estimating the degree of uncertainty, their potential effects, and possible disruptions of complex systemic balances is problematic. One regulatory response to this is to draw upon the precautionary principle, ie to err on the side of caution, although support for its opposite, the proactionary principle, is also to be found among transhumanists.[64]

How far citizen or stakeholder involvement in governing science might anchor regulation as a negotiation process of world making is an ongoing preoccupation for policy-makers. Jasanoff has argued that technologies of hubris, where information from experts was communicated to inexpert citizenries, should be replaced by technologies of humility, where acknowledgement of ongoing uncertainties over prediction and control takes place.[65] She sees as essential, here, formal mechanisms of participation, provided in an intellectual environment where the resolution of common problems benefits from citizens' knowledge and skills. Regulation may then take place in a shared fashion wherein stakeholders focus on the questions: what is the purpose, who will be hurt, who will benefit, and how do we know? In similar vein, the regulation of new technologies has been framed as the co-production or co-evolution of

---

[62] Devon (n 59 above) 112.

[63] S Hansson, 'The Epistemology of Technical Risk' (2005) 9 *Techne* 68.

[64] J Schummer, 'Societal and Ethical Implications of Nanotechnology: Meanings, Interest Groups and Social Dynamics' (2004) 8 *Techne* 56.

[65] S Jasanoff, 'Technologies of Humility: Citizen Participation in Governing Science' (2003) 41 *Minerva* 223.

science and society,[66] and as a move from the public understanding of science to public engagement with science.[67]

Integrating extra-academic types of knowledge, interests, and values into the production of scientific knowledge, known as transdisciplinarity, or the construction of socially robust knowledge, is an associated effort to find a new mode of governing science.[68] However, empirical research suggests that the participation of various groups may be provoked by disparate motives, and the likelihood of epistemic integration of different perspectives small without a mediated negotiation or 'epistemediation'.[69] Nonetheless, this kind of public engagement with science may be framed as embodying a 'new deal' between science and society involving more shared responsibility for outcomes.[70] It may also be valuable in that it contributes to a more realistic assessment of the benefits which can be expected from new technologies.[71]

Yet where policy is thought to gain legitimacy from public input, such decisions demand a degree of informed engagement by citizens which is often considered to be problematic. Participation may be read differently by policy-makers and citizens in terms of differing ideas over how far the citizenry should be involved in the decision-making process.[72] While policy-makers seek to fix citizens with a degree of accountability for unwelcome outcomes based upon civic participation in policy decisions, citizens cannot assume that they will be accorded decision-making power unless mechanisms to ensure this have been put in place.[73] One of the difficulties is the varying conceptions of democracy as embodied in models of scientific citizenship. Mark Elam and Margareta Bertilsson argue that advanced consumer, deliberative, and radical/pluralist models are partly complementary and partly competing frameworks within

[66] S Franklin, 'Interview: Visions of Frontier Knowledge: an Interview With Helga Nowotny' (2007) 2 *BioSocieties* 375.

[67] M Elam and M Bertilsson, 'Consuming, Engaging and Confronting Science: the Emerging Dimensions of Scientific Citizenship' (2007) 6 *European Journal of Social Theory* 233.

[68] S Maasen and O Lieven, 'Transdisciplinarity: a New Mode of Governing Science?' (2006) 33 *Science and Public Policy* 399.

[69] A Wiek, 'Challenges of Transdisciplinary Research As Interactive Knowledge Generation—Experiences From Transdisciplinary Case Study Research' (2007) 16 *GAIA: Ecological Perspectives For Science and Society* 52; W Zierhofer and P Burger, 'Transdisciplinary Research—a Distinct Mode of Knowledge Production? Problem Orientation, Knowledge Integration and Participation in Transdisciplinary Research Projects?' (2007) 16 *GAIA: Ecological Perspectives For Science and Society* 29.

[70] O Lieven and S Maasen, 'Transdisciplinary Research: Heralding a New Dawn Between Science and Society' (2007) 16 *GAIA Ecological Perspectives for Science and Society* 35.

[71] D Barney, 'The Morning After: Citizen Engagement in Technological Society' (2006) 9 *Techne* 23; H Nowotny, 'High and Low Cost Realities for Science and Society' (2005) 308 1117; H Nowotny, 'Wish Fulfilment and its Discontents' (2003) 4 *EMBO Reports* 917.

[72] S Davenport and S Leitch, 'Agoras, Ancient and Modern, and a Framework for Science-Society Debate' (2005) 32 *Science and Public Policy* 137.

[73] G Abels, 'Citizen Involvement in Public Policy Making: Does It Improve Democratic Legitimacy and Accountability?' (2007) 13 *Interdisciplinary Information Sciences* 103.

which the rights and responsibilities of scientific citizens may be negotiated.[74] As such frameworks give rise to different expectations from science, each constructs the objectives of scientific governance and citizenship differently.[75]

Citizens who feel that the effort to inform them about novel technologies has not been made may be more likely to reject them, whereas opportunities to engage in informed reflective deliberation and the perception of direct potential benefits are likely to lead to increased acceptance,[76] as well as a more realistic appreciation of what the technologies offer.[77] Nonetheless, redressing democratic disengagement may prove more complex. Culver argues that there is 'a more general unfocussed and inexplicit unease' which encourages opposition to new biotechnologies.[78] Condemning the OECD's model of citizen engagement for equating providing information with democratic partnership in decision-making, he argues for a sharing of authority. As he explains, 'a merely consultative process cannot be satisfactory as long as governments retain agenda-setting and decision-making authority, and fail to engage in a kind of partnership which offers both capacity to contribute and power to ensure that contributions are meaningfully reflected in eventual policy'.[79]

It is thus all too plausible to argue that many of the strategies adopted by policy-makers to encourage a degree of public input, such as programmes seeking to inform public opinion, or consultative exercises, in fact are fundamentally unethical where they substitute for the kind of power sharing envisaged by Culver. Claiming that the bond between democratic citizens and their governments rests not upon consent to be governed but rather consists of 'meaningful participation, as equals, in decisions that matter',[80] Barney argues that few nation states provide the pre-conditions for exercising democratic citizenship. In his view, these are constitutional arrangements which distribute meaningful political power equally among citizens, equal sharing of material resources of effective citizenship, such as leisure, a culture which habituates citizens to the practice of democratic citizenship, and an arena wherein this might be exercised. From this perspective, given the speed at which technological developments take place, citizen engagement in regulation located in deliberative democratic engagement appears decreasingly likely.

Devon joins such concerns with a condemnation of engineering ethics as typically narrowly focused upon individual responsibilities while ignoring as externalities the wider contexts within which these operate in his call for research

---

[74] Elam and Bertilsson (n 67 above).

[75] Horst (n 7 above).

[76] D Castle, 'The Balance between Expertise and Authority in Citizen Engagement About New Biotechnology' (2006) 9 *Techne* 1.

[77] N Brown, 'Shifting Tenses: From Regimes of Truth to Regimes of Hope', SATSU Working Paper No 30 (York, 2006).

[78] K Culver, 'Adoption and Governance of Biotechnology in Democracies' (2006) 9 *Techne* 32.

[79] ibid 39.   [80] Barney (n 71 above) 23.

into 'the ethics of how people collectively make decisions about technology'.[81] Similarly, Juillard contends that the integration of ethical reflection into industrial processes rests upon the question of the means by which ethical responsibilities might be socially assigned to the involved parties.[82] Both the use and misuse of technologies would form part of the research agenda of an ethics of technology in this model, which seeks to redress many of the shortcomings of the engineering approach such as decontextualization explored above. How far, then, a marrying of the participatory regulation of new technologies and an ethics of engineering and technology which set out to incorporate context might prove fruitful is a question which would bear further investigation.

VI. Conclusion

I have argued that new technologies place an obligation upon us to regulate with possible futures in mind. Reading path-dependence as opportunity cost, if the adverse consequences of unfortunate choices are to be minimized, we must engage in the continuous iterative evaluations of regulatory structures variously characterized in terms of being 'smart' regulation[83] or the denaturalization of biorisk.[84] Finding the mechanisms to do so and putting them in place is essential, but unlikely to be straightforward, given the difficulties associated with regulatory inflexibility,[85] integrating deliberative participation of scientific citizens in decision-making over policy, and the conflicting obligations of policy-makers. Such an outcome would demand commitment from all concerned to instantiate iterative regulatory structures and sustainable mechanisms to ensure accompanying participatory decisions. One example of this might be the model put in place by the community of synthetic biologists, but how this might be translated to wider regulatory contexts is not a simple matter. Nor does regulatory (re)production take place at the speed of scientific discovery.

How, then, are we to regulate synthetic biology? The possible futures it affords are directly related to the regulatory structures we choose to govern it. Self-regulation, open disclosure of technologies, and open access to parts, according to synthetic biologists, presages a future where security rests upon trust, sharing, and ongoing discoveries.[86] Yet the ETC Group views this prospect as dangerous techno-hype with the potential to disadvantage further the agriculturalists in poorer countries.[87]

---

[81] Devon (n 59 above) 100.
[82] Y Juillard, 'Ethics Quality Management' (2004) 8 *Techne* 117.
[83] Baldwin (n 51 above).   [84] Lentzos (n 16 above).
[85] Baldwin (n 51 above).
[86] 'Drew Endy: the Bulletin Interview' (n 2 above).
[87] ETC Group, 'Broad International Coalition Issues Urgent Call For Strong Oversight of Nanotechnology', at <http://www.etcgroup.org/en/materials/publications.html?pub_id=651>

Biosecrecy and vital systems preparedness seem to usher in an acceptance of catastrophe and an exclusion of contextual factors which would foster further sacrifices of the domestic unfortunate, as with Hurricane Katrina, as well as the global dispossessed, who would fall outside national protective measures. Any guarantees of safety such measures might promise would thus be partial, morally compromising, and ethically reductionist. Nonetheless, this focus and the degree of oversight of such regulatory structures characterize much of the equipment of new technologies and biosecurity in the United States today. As both this approach and the focus upon mechanisms to ensure coordination of information flows and decision-making, iterative correction, and ongoing change recommended in this chapter characterize the engineering approach to (re)production, which has been criticized as framing issues in such a way as to exclude context, finding ways to integrate context and (re)production becomes crucial.

In this sense, regulators, citizens, and policy-makers are in a situation homologous with that of synthetic biologists. Both groups are faced with making (re)productive choices. Life, or regulations, may be synthesized in such a way as to bring about new improved versions of old entities. From an engineering perspective, this may seem relatively simple. Once a system is created from known parts in order to perform a specific function, its ability to do so may be measured, monitored, and improved by iterative correction through feedback. This model of intervention and creation in the material world operates best in the context of closed systems. Extra elements may not enter the equation and contextual factors may be deemed as irrelevant. (Re)production is straightforward. The extent to which this model may prove helpful when (re)producing regulation is debatable. Regulatory systems are not closed systems. To regulate demands taking action in an imperfect world, on the basis of imperfect information. The consequences of action are uncertain and pose unknown and unknowable risks. The way forward depends upon normative choices which will result in manifestions of possible futures. To the degree to which these are to be evaluated in terms of security, choices over safety are both ethical and epistemological. Who, or which knowledges, are to be included, valued, and protected, and the mechanisms which will ensure this are, ultimately, leaps of faith towards the futures we wish to realize.

(accessed 25 September 2007); ETC Group, 'Patenting Pandora's Bug: Goodbye Dolly...Hello Synthia! J. Craig Venter's Institute Seeks Monopoly Patent on World's First-Ever Human-Made Life Form', at <http://www.etcgroup.org/en/materials/publications.html?pub_id=631> (accessed 25 September 2007); ETC Group, 'Synthia's Last Hurdle?', at <http://www.etcgroup.org/en/materials/publications.html?pub_id=648> (accessed 25 September 2007); ETC Group, 'Extreme Genetic Engineering: An Introduction to Synthetic Biology' (2007), at <http://www.etcgroup.org/en/materials/publications.html?id=602> (accessed 25 September 2007).

15

Exploring the Routes from Consultation to (In)forming Public Policy

Caroline Jones[1]

> What gives lawmakers, in Parliament . . . the right to promote or proscribe a particular course of action in the face of controversy?[2]

> There are obvious limitations to the use of public opinion and feeling; not least is the question as to how public opinion can effectively form part of the normative process . . . if public consultation is an existing component in policy making in the area of assisted conception, its actual role and impact is not apparent.[3]

I. Introduction

The focus of this chapter is the analysis of the routes by which Parliamentary bodies move from consultation to formulating public policy in the controversial field of assisted conception and related technological developments. These quotes illustrate rather different concerns about policy-making processes, not least because Montgomery's question points to issues of legitimacy for law per se, whereas Callus's comments are made in reference to the Human Fertilisation and Embryology Authority's (HFEA) track-record as a policy-maker, rather than that of Parliament. Nevertheless, both commentators address issues that have proved crucial to this chapter. That is, how do Parliamentary bodies recommend particular policy stances in controversial areas and are these legitimate? Further, given

[1] School of Law, University of Southampton. I am grateful to Jonathan Montgomery and the participants at the Law and Bioethics Colloquium for comments on an earlier draft of the paper which forms the basis of this chapter. I am also indebted to the Health Ethics and Law (HEAL) network at the University of Southampton for funding this research, and to Hiroko Onishi for her research assistance.

[2] JR Montgomery, 'The Legitimacy of Medical Law' in SAM McLean (ed), *First Do No Harm, Law Ethics and Healthcare* (Ashgate, 2006) 1.

[3] T Callus, 'Patient perception of the Human Fertilisation and Embryology Authority' (2007) 15 *Medical Law Review* 62, 69.

the emphasis on public confidence in the regulatory framework in this field, how and in what ways are the public's opinions—as expressed in responses to the relevant consultations—taken up and used in the construction of policy?

These vexed issues have spawned significant academic commentaries, to which there is insufficient space to give due consideration to here. Nevertheless, it is possible to highlight some key issues that have influenced this analysis. In the context of the regulation of human genetics, Brownsword has argued that the 'stand-off between...the ruling synthesis of utilitarian and human rights thinking and...the dignitarian alliance is a key feature of the current debates'.[4] The 'dignitarian alliance' refers to a grouping united by the view that human dignity ought not to be compromised; a stance reached by one of a number of possible routes, and therefore not merely based on religious beliefs.[5] In Brownsword's account this stand-off creates particular problems for regulators trying to justify the policies they adopt as legitimate to all interested stakeholders; particularly as a permissive regulatory framework will not assuage the concerns of the dignitarian alliance.[6] Hence, he portrays the dignitarians as holding the 'ethical last stand' against potential developments like hybrid embryo research. Drawing on Michelman's work, he notes that there are limits to citing procedural justice as a legitimating factor, and works through this argument with reference to the recent modification of the regulatory framework to permit human embryonic stem cell research under the auspices of the HFEA licensing procedures. Brownsword articulates three grounds upon which—even in the absence of any procedural impropriety—a challenge might be made: namely, incrementalism; lack of opportunity to enter all the relevant deliberations and challenge assumptions held by committee members; and the difficult balance of expertise and detachment where expert advisers are necessary.[7] Hence, the challenge posed for regulators by the dignitarians is that where no consensus exists, their dissent accentuates the difficulty of providing justification for policy-making via the usual appeals to legitimacy.[8]

Consequently, one of the key questions informing this research is the legitimacy of the routes through the consultation processes; in particular the extent to which public responses inform, or are at least seen to inform, the resulting policy recommendations. For example, are 'representative' or 'majority' opinions either portrayed as influential, or proved to be in practice when policies are announced? Further, is the status of particular respondents accorded greater significance, or to put it rather bluntly—whose opinion counts, and which, if any, count more

---

[4] R Brownsword, 'Regulating Human Genetics: New Dilemmas for a New Millennium' (2004) *Medical Law Review* 14, 22. Other relevant commentaries include J Steele, 'Participation and Deliberation in Environmental Law: Exploring a Problem-solving Approach' (2001) *OJLS* 415; and K Syrett, 'Deconstructing Deliberation in the Appraisal of Medical Technologies: NICEly Does it?' (2006) 69 *MLR* 869.

[5] Brownsword (n 4 above) 20.

[6] ibid 22.   [7] ibid 26–7.   [8] ibid 38.

than others? These questions are addressed through the analysis of a bounded example of public consultation, the Department of Health *Review of the Human Fertilisation and Embryology Act* (HFEA 1990), which resulted in the publication of the Human Tissue and Embryos (Draft) Bill in May 2007; eventually placed before the House of Lords by Lord Darzai in November 2007 as the Human Fertilisation and Embryology Bill (HFE Bill).

The reasons for choosing this particular regulatory framework are twofold. First, it is a controversial area where achieving consensus on the appropriate framework is highly unlikely. As a consequence, it is a particularly useful example to consider the routes from consultation to policy-making, as polarized views are often held and expressed by a diverse range of stakeholders. The need for legitimacy in such an area is particularly stark. Second, in this instance, both the government and the House of Commons Science and Technology Committee highlighted the importance of the role of the public in policy development; but, as outlined further below, the latter cautioned against using the weight of opinion to determine policy recommendations. This cautionary note is a familiar one, be it JS Mill's concern over the 'tyranny of the majority',[9] or HLA Hart's view that 'it seems fatally easy to believe that democratic principles entail acceptance of what may be termed moral populism: the view that the majority have a moral right to dictate how all should live'.[10] Consequently, one question raised here is what role does this leave for the public to inform policy-making? Given this focus, two specific areas of the consultation have been chosen for analysis and comparison; the retention or removal of a statutory reference to the welfare of the child in the HFEA 1990 and the (im)permissibility of hybrid embryos for research purposes. These aspects were chosen as they have both proved to be controversial, in the latter case not least because of the policy u-turn performed by the government in May 2007, which is examined closely below.[11]

The intention of this chapter was to look beyond the published reports and provide a close reading of the responses to this consultation in order to try and assess the extent to which this input informed policy-making, rather than necessarily developing themes and concepts under the broad umbrella of democratic theory, though there is clearly the scope to do so at another juncture. A number of commentators whose work has proved influential in writing this chapter were cited above but, given the subject matter, one final example is particularly pertinent. Dodds and Ankeny[12] undertook a similar review of the processes informing

---

[9] JS Mill, *On Liberty* (1859).

[10] HLA Hart, *Law, Liberty and Morality* (Oxford University Press, 1963) 79; cited by the Joint Committee on the Human Tissue and Embryos (Draft) Bill, *Human Tissue and Embryos (Draft) Bill Volume 1: Report (Session 2006–07)*, HL Paper 169-I, HC Paper 630-I, para 21.

[11] I am grateful to Professor Donna Dickinson for her questions on this issue at the UCL Colloquium.

[12] S Dodds and RA Ankeny, 'Regulation of HESC Research in Australia: Promises and Pitfalls for Deliberative Democratic Approaches' (2006) *Bioethical Inquiry* 95. I am grateful to Professor Wendy Rogers for alerting me to this article.

the enactment of federal legislation on human embryo research in Australia. They noted the various calls for the need for public consultation, debate, and education, suggesting that 'at least symbolically' this discourse of public participation indicated a desire for policy development to be 'responsive' following a 'process of deliberation'. However, they concluded that there was 'little evidence that those involved in the legislative process genuinely sought broader public involvement and engagement with the issues raised by the science or the legislation'.[13] Their focus in the article, therefore, was on whether concepts from democratic theory *could* inform policy-making processes in contentious fields like human embryo research. Further, their attention was focused in the main on official documentation, reports, and relevant debates in Senate. In contrast, the analysis below not only considers the relevant documentation, but looks to the responses that informed these reports in order to examine the ways in which this data was presented, and to question whether or not there was an accurate (re-)presentation of the views expressed by the public therein.

II. The History of the Consultation Process

The timeline for the consultation process began on 24 October 2003 when, citing the 'limp response' of the Department of Health to an earlier Report from the House of Commons Science and Technology Committee ('the Committee')[14] as a driving factor, the Committee announced its intention to undertake an inquiry into human reproductive technologies and the law. On 22 January 2004 an online consultation was launched by the Committee 'to listen to and gauge the public's views, both to help us frame the inquiry's terms of reference and to allow new voices to contribute to the debate'.[15] The on-line consultation ran between 22 January and 15 March 2004. On 30 March 2004, the Committee announced the terms of reference for its inquiry, which consisted of twelve oral evidence sessions held between 14 June 2004 and 19 January 2005. The Committee's findings were published on 24 March 2005.[16]

The day before the Committee's e-consultation was launched, the Department of Health announced its intention to review the legislation governing this field.[17] However, its consultation, entitled *Review of the Human Fertilisation and Embryology Act: A Public Consultation*,[18] was not launched until approximately

---

[13] ibid 96; see also 99–101.

[14] Department of Health, *Government Response to the Report from the House of Commons Science and Technology Committee: Developments in Human Genetics and Embryology* (Cm 5693, 2002), cited in House of Commons Science and Technology Committee, *Human Reproductive Technologies and the Law (Fifth Report of Session 2004–05)*, March 2005, HC 7–1, para 2.

[15] House of Commons Science and Technology Committee (n 14 above) para 3.

[16] ibid.   [17] ibid para 2.

[18] Department of Health, 2005, available via the Department's website, at <http://www.dh.gov.uk>.

five months after the Committee's findings were made public (on 16 August, and ran until 25 November 2005); and around the same time the government published its response to the Committee's Report.[19] March 2006 saw the publication of a summary of results, analysed and prepared by People Science and Policy Ltd for the Department of Health,[20] prior to a White Paper in December of the same year.[21] The Human Tissue and Embryos (Draft) Bill[22] was presented to Parliament in May 2007 and scrutinized by the Joint Committee on the Human Tissue and Embryos (Draft Bill), which reported in July 2007.[23] Lord Darzai introduced the HFE Bill to the House of Lords on 8 November 2007 and, at the time of writing, the Bill had reached the Report stage in the House of Lords, with the third reading scheduled for 4 February 2008. One other development worth mentioning at this stage is that in April 2007 the Committee published its report on the regulation of the creation and use of hybrid and chimera embryos,[24] an issue that proved particularly problematic during the consultation.

III. Observations on the Committee's Findings

In the introduction to its report, *Human Reproductive Technologies and the Law*, the Committee expressed concern about whether or not the regulatory framework adopted in HFEA 1990 remained fit for purpose.[25] In a chapter devoted to the status and uses of human embryos, the Committee's ethical standpoint was outlined thus:

We accept that (sic) a society that is both multi-faith and largely secular, there is *never going to be consensus* on the level of protection accorded to the embryo or the role of the state in reproductive decision-making. There are no demonstrably 'right' answers to the complex ethical, moral and political equations involved. We respect the views of all sides on these issues. *We recognise the difficulty of achieving consensus between protagonists in opposing camps in this debate, for example the pro-life groups and those advocating an entirely libertarian approach to either assisted reproduction or research use of the embryo. We believe, however, that to be effective this Committee's conclusions should seek consensus, as far as it is*

[19] HM Government, *Human Reproductive Technologies and the Law: Government Response to the Report from the House of Commons Science and Technology Committee* (Cm 6641, 2005).

[20] People Science and Policy Ltd, 'Report on the Consultation on the review of the Human Fertilisation and Embryology Act 1990', (March 2006).

[21] Department of Health, *Review of the Human Fertilisation and Embryology Act: proposals for revised legislation (including establishment of the Regulatory Authority for Tissue and Embryos* (Cm 6989, 2006).

[22] Department of Health, *Human Tissue and Embryos (Draft) Bill* (Cm 7087, 2007).

[23] Joint Committee on the Human Tissue and Embryos (Draft) Bill, *Human Tissue and Embryos (Draft) Bill Volume I: Report*, HL Paper 169-I, HC Paper 630-I, July 2007.

[24] House of Commons Science and Technology Committee, Government proposals for the regulation of hybrid and chimera embryos (Fifth Report of Session 2006–07), April 2007, HC 272-I.

[25] n 14 above, House of Commons Science and Technology Committee, paras 2 and 7.

possible to achieve. Given the rate of scientific change and the ethical dilemmas involved, we conclude, therefore, that we should adopt an approach consistent with the gradualist approach, of which the Warnock Committee is one important example. This does not mean that we will shy from criticism of regulation to date, where we believe it warranted. *But it does mean that we accept that assisted reproduction and research involving the embryos of the human species both remain legitimate interests of the state. Reproductive and research freedoms must be balanced against the interests of society but alleged harms to society, too, should be based on evidence.*[26]

Three significant points are made here. The first two, namely the perceived desirability of achieving consensus on these issues and the difficulty in so doing, are considered together; whereas the third issue, raising the precautionary principle and need for evidence-based regulation, will be dealt with further below.

The Committee's statement begins by noting the *impossibility* of achieving consensus on issues relating to human embryos, and then moves towards an acknowledgement as to the *difficulty* of attaining consensus between parties with opposing views on these issues, suggesting that some middle ground might be found (in the Committee's case via the gradualist approach adopted in the Warnock Report). It is interesting to note, therefore, that precisely the same difficulties beset the Committee (noted by Laing and Oderberg; Montgomery),[27] albeit that this is not immediately apparent in reading the Report. The only clue to any internal disagreement lies in the formal minutes provided after the conclusions and recommendations,[28] and further information is contained in a separate document—the *Eighth Special Report* of the Committee.[29]

The aforementioned formal minutes relate to the Committee's meeting on March 14 2005 to read and agree the draft Report, where five members and the Chair were present.[30] A number of possible amendments to various aspects of the report were tabled, mostly by Paul Farrelly, though Dr Evan Harris made four (recorded) proposals. All of Mr Farrelly's proposals failed whereas all of Dr Harris's succeeded. On first examination this might appear to be a simple division among the Committee members present at that particular meeting. However, the sequence of events summarized in the *Eighth Special Report* tells a rather more complex tale.[31] Nine members were present at a meeting on 28 February where Paul Farrelly successfully tabled an amendment radically changing the written summary of the Committee's ethical standpoint, typified as 'a shift from an extreme libertarian position to one that was more

---

[26] ibid para 46 (emphasis added).

[27] JA Laing and DS Oderberg, 'Artificial Reproduction, the "Welfare Principle", and the Common Good' (2005) 13 *Medical Law Review* 328; JR Montgomery, (n 2 above).

[28] n 14 above, House of Commons Science and Technology Committee, 190–208.

[29] House of Commons Science and Technology Committee, *Human Reproductive Technologies and the Law (Eighth Special Report of Session 2004–05)*, March 2005, HC 491.

[30] Those present were Dr Ian Gibson (Chair), Paul Farrelly, Dr Evan Harris, Dr Brian Iddon, Mr Robert Key, and Dr Desmond Turner, ibid 3.

[31] ibid 3–6.

precautionary and saw more of a continuing role for the state and regulation'.[32] The original text read as follows:

We have listened with interest to a wide range of views. However, it was necessary to adopt a position on them, based in principle. While we recognise the significance of each ethical position articulated, *we are persuaded that the State's role in regulating assisted reproduction should primarily be guided by the human rights or libertarian approach.* The justification for the extent of the regulatory intervention which currently exists was appropriate to a time when the outcome of reproductive decisions in assisted reproduction was unknown and the state arguably had a legitimate interest in policing this area of medical practice. *However, the evidence now suggests that the scale of the intrusion into the private choices of individuals seeking to have a family can no longer be justified.* We do, however, accept that the research use of the embryo of the human species remain [sic] a legitimate interest of the state. The difference between these two approaches is justified by the fact that the first is a private matter between individuals seeking to attain an accepted social goal, whereas the latter satisfies a social or public aim. *We conclude that the most appropriate principle that should be used to provide a framework for our conclusions and recommendations is that as far as possible the state should withdraw from people's reproductive decision-making. Parents rather than the State must be assumed to be the right decision-makers for their families.* While this reproductive freedom must be balanced against the impacts against other individuals and society, any such claims must be clearly demonstrable.[33]

Therefore, it is clear that the initial stance was very much a libertarian one, with a reduced role for the state in regulating assisted conception and related technologies. Yet, during subsequent meetings when amendments were tabled that were concordant with the *revised* ethical standpoint, or which highlighted potential alternative constructions to those aligned with the *original* stance, these were either negatived or disagreed to.[34] Furthermore, due to the guillotine, inadequate time was allocated for discussion, leading to one Committee member leaving the meeting[35] and to Paul Farrelly voting against the entire Report at the conclusion of the meeting.

In the light of this background, it is perhaps unsurprising to read of the disquiet expressed by half the Committee's members[36] during the 16 March meeting, the purpose of which was to agree the Report and (intended) accompanying press release. 'Strong reservations about the process by which the Report had been considered and agreed' were expressed; including criticism of the fact that in the light of the amendment agreed on 28 February no other redrafting of the Report was undertaken which 'invalidated' the Report; the 'guillotine' severely restricted the time available to consider changes; where consensus was difficult to achieve an extreme libertarian approach should not be adopted merely because of

---

[32] ibid 4.   [33] ibid 6, Annex A (emphasis added).
[34] eg Farrelly's proposal to amend para 32 to read, 'according to a libertarian interpretation of [Article 8]...' rather than 'in line with [Article 8]' (n 14 above) 190–1.
[35] Tony McWalter MP (n 29 above) 4.
[36] Paul Farrelly, Kate Hoey, Tony McWalter, Geraldine Smith, and Bob Spink.

the unlikelihood of reaching a unanimous approach; the lack of balance regarding the utilization of 'libertarian interpretations'; and perhaps most significantly in this context, '*insufficient regard was given in the Report to public opinion and the evidence submitted to the inquiry*'.[37] These are damning indictments indeed, and consequently the findings outlined in the Report are particularly problematic for two reasons.

First, it is clear that despite the complete redrafting of the ethical standpoint no further amendments were made to the remainder of the Report, notwithstanding the fact that the ethical approach would undoubtedly prove influential on some, if not many, conclusions and recommendations. One example of how this failure to re-draft might operate is the relevance, or otherwise, of the welfare of the potential child in determining access to treatment services. The Committee concluded that the reference in section 13(5) of HFEA 1990 to the perceived need of a child for a father 'is too open to interpretation and unjustifiably offensive to many. It is wrong for legislation to imply that unjustified discrimination against "unconventional families" is acceptable.'[38] Further:

The welfare of the child provision discriminates against the infertile and some sections of society, is impossible to implement and is of questionable practical value in protecting the interests of children born as a result of assisted reproduction... The welfare of the child provision has enabled the HFEA and clinics to make judgements that are more properly made by patients in consultation with their doctor. It should be abolished in its current form. The minimum threshold should apply but should specify that this threshold should be the risk of unpreventable and significant harm. Doctors should minimise the risks to any child conceived from treatment within the constraints of available knowledge but this should be encouraged through the promotion of good medical practice not legislation.[39]

The influence of this statement is clearly evident in the framing of the Department of Health's consultation questions (discussed below). However, Paul Farrelly proposed a number of possible amendments to this paragraph during the ill-fated 14 March Committee meeting. These included replacing 'discriminate' with 'may be considered to discriminate'; 'impossible' with 'is difficult'; 'dubious' with 'questionable practical'; and crucially 'it should be abolished' with 'The government should, therefore, consider the case for its abolition rather than retention in any new Act. It should also carefully consider the case that... [the minimum threshold should apply].'[40] None of these amendments was passed. However, in reading the original version and the associated commentary in the formal minutes, it is apparent that another amendment was made and agreed to, yet further details are not provided. Nevertheless, the text changes from 'It should be abolished. Doctors should minimise the risks...', to the version cited above in the final report. The lack of transparency as to how these changes evolved is problematic,

---

[37] n 29 above, 5–6, (emphasis added).
[38] n 14 above, House of Commons Science and Technology Committee, para 101.
[39] ibid para 107.   [40] ibid 199–200.

particularly in the light of the acknowledged lack of consensus within the Committee. Furthermore, the sentiments expressed in the final version strongly accord with the *initial* framing of the ethical stance of the Committee *rather* than the *revised* standpoint.

Second, no press release was made regarding the 'balance of views' held by the Committee. Rather, this dissent was made 'public' in the *Eighth Special Report*. On the one hand this provides scope to deal with this matter in greater depth and with the status of a House of Commons paper; yet, on the other hand, in terms of ensuring transparency and for the public to be informed accordingly, it is problematic to bury this information in a separate document. It also contrasts with the approach adopted by the Warnock Committee where 'three formal expressions of dissent' were highlighted in Dame Mary Warnock's introduction to the Report,[41] and full versions thereof were included in the Report and highlighted as such in the Table of Contents.[42] This matter is particularly significant when one sees in the government's consultation process the reliance placed on many of the Committee's findings, apparently unquestioningly. It also sits uneasily with the Committee's emphasis on the desire for achieving consensus when it could not do so, although it should be made clear that the lack of consensus per se is not the troubling aspect here. Rather, given the status and importance of the exercise, the procedures adopted were problematic (for example the use of the guillotine), and did not necessarily facilitate the possibility of the Committee efficaciously achieving its reported goals.

The third issue arising out of the Committee's ethical standpoint was the emphasis on purported harms to society being proved rather than assumed.[43] This was reiterated in the consecutive paragraph:

This [precautionary principle] means different things to different pressure groups, and to different sides of the argument. In respect of medical advances it has never meant 'proceed only where there is evidence of no harm'. If it did many of the advances would never be made. In medical research practice it means proceeding through carefully regulated and tightly overseen research stages, requiring—among other things—vigilance and peer review. In clinical practice it means proceed cautiously and in a manner amendable to ethical oversight and clinical audit while there is no evidence of sufficiently serious harm or potential harm to outweigh benefit or potential benefit, while being vigilant in looking for unintended and otherwise adverse outcomes. **We do not see why the area of human reproductive technologies should do anything other than proceed under a precautionary principle currently prevalent in scientific, research and clinical practise (sic).**

---

[41] Department of Health and Social Security, *Report of the Committee of Inquiry into Human Fertilisation and Embryology* (Cmnd 9314, 1984 iv).

[42] It is interesting to note that in its report on abortion, the current Committee specifically highlighted the lack of agreement over an initial draft of *that* report at the outset; see further House of Commons Science and Technology Committee, Scientific Developments Relating to the Abortion Act 1967 (Twelfth Report of Session 2006–07), November 2007, HC 1045–1, 3.

[43] n 14 above, para 46, cited above.

This means—as specified in paragraph 46 above—that alleged harms to society or to patients need to be demonstrated before forward progress is unduly impeded.[44]

Whilst the construction of the precautionary principle outlined early in this quotation is correct, the concluding statement (highlighted in italics) provided a blunt oversimplification of the principle which is misleading. This was highlighted in the government's response to the report, which noted that:

The Government disagrees, however, with the Committee's interpretation of the precautionary principle. *The potential harms that should be taken into account may not necessarily be susceptible to demonstration and evidence in advance.* For example, in our view the application of a precautionary principle requires that consideration of harms to society or to patients must include the consideration of *potential harms* to future offspring.[45]

Indeed, they defended the consideration of the welfare of the potential child as a 'central tenet of the HFE Act, and one of the key guiding principles which informs the operation of the HFEA and the contents of its Code of Practice'. The government went on to note that the current approach 'recognises that whereas patients are entitled to sensitive consideration of their wishes, *the welfare of children cannot always be adequately protected by concern for the interests of the adults involved*'.[46] The assumption here is that the welfare of the child assessment is useful, nay essential, and that an extreme libertarian standpoint with a reduced role for government is not appropriate in this field. The government indicated that it would seek wider views on securing the welfare of children conceived through assisted conception, suggesting a continued retention of this provision.[47]

Therefore, as one might expect in this field, it was clear at an early stage in the consultation process that it was going to be difficult to find agreement amongst democratically elected members of Parliament, let alone the public at large. Interestingly, therefore, no mention of this disparity in viewpoint—ie *within* the Science and Technology Committee, and *between* the Committee and the government—was made in the Department of Health consultation document that followed. As a consequence the public, whether so-called 'experts' or laypersons, may have assumed that the recommendations of the Science and Technology Committee referred to in the consultation document were unanimous. It is not possible to ascertain whether or not this would have influenced

---

[44] ibid para 47 (original emphasis).
[45] n 19 above, para 6 (emphasis added).
[46] ibid para 37 (emphasis added).
[47] This provision is not universally accepted by commentators; see in particular E Jackson, 'Conception and the Irrelevance of the Welfare Principle' (2002) 65 *MLR* 176; J Wallbank, 'The Role of Rights and Utility in Instituting a Child's Right to Know Her Genetic History' (2004) 13 *Social and Legal Studies* 245; E Jackson, 'Rethinking the Preconception Welfare Principle' in K Horsey and H Biggs (eds), *Human Fertilisation and Embryology: Reproducing Regulation* (Routledge Cavendish, 2006) 47; A Alghrani and J Harris, 'Reproductive liberty: should the foundation of families be regulated?' (2006) 18 *CFLQ* 191; but in contrast see JA Laing and DS Oderberg (n 27 above).

particular respondents' answers. However, it sits rather uneasily with the notion of the importance of transparency in regulation and the need to educate the public, and may call into question the actual importance of public contributions to policy-making despite this being highlighted by both the Committee and the government.

IV. What Role Does This Leave for the Public?

Two main features emerge from the relevant literature; the need for public confidence in the regulatory framework adopted, and the practical issue of how public responses should be used in forming policy, which are now addressed in turn.

In 1985, Dame Mary Warnock highlighted the fine balancing act in achieving public confidence in this contentious area succinctly, thus 'the law must not outrage the feelings of too many people, but it cannot reflect the feelings of them all'.[48] As Thérèse Callus has noted, more than two decades later policy-makers remain concerned about the need for public confidence in the regulatory regime.[49] Whereas the Committee highlighted the role of Parliament in providing the public with 'greater confidence' that ethically sensitive issues were being addressed adequately,[50] the government in turn placed emphasis on re-affirming the 'broadly acceptable' status of the proposed framework.[51] Callus correctly states that there has been scant attention as to whether or not the regulatory framework provided by the HFEA 1990 is 'in fact' accepted by the public;[52] an issue recently acknowledged by the government.[53] The government also made clear that public responses to its consultation would be used to 'inform any proposals for changes' in the legislation.[54] This begs the question of *how* public responses ought to be used in order to *inform* public policy-making?

A. Quantification of the Consultation Findings?

In addressing the role of the public, the Committee highlighted the fact that it had not quantified the views submitted to its on-line consultation. Indeed, following a critical assessment of the HFEA's record on public consultations, it concluded that: 'Surveys and opinion polls provide useful input to policy development, but

---

[48] M Warnock, *A Question of Life: The Warnock Report on Human Fertilisation and Embryology* (Basil Blackwell, 1985) Introduction xvi, cited in Callus (n 3 above) 62.

[49] Callus (n 3 above). See eg Caroline Flint's comments in the Foreword to the White Paper and Draft Bill, respectively: Department of Health, *Review of the Human Fertilisation and Embryology Act: Proposals for Revised Legislation (including establishment of the Regulatory Authority for Tissue and Embryos)*, (Cm 6989, 2006) v; Department of Health, *Human Tissue and Embryos (Draft) Bill 2007* (Cm 7087, 2007) v.

[50] n 14 above, para 356.   [51] n 18 above, para 1.4.
[52] Callus (n 3 above) 62.   [53] n 18 above, para 1.8.
[54] ibid.

are essentially anecdotal and represent the views of a self-selecting group of indi-viduals; often activists. Additionally we would caution about using the weight of response to determine the outcome of any policy review.'[55]

This note of caution is a familiar one (see 'Introduction' above). Further, this advice was followed by People, Science and Policy Ltd in the production of its report on the responses to the 2005 consultation for the Department of Health; in which it was noted that 'since responses to the consultation were self-selecting and could not therefore be said to be representative, it has not been the intention of this analysis to quantify frequencies of argument or to generalise about par-ticular actor groups'.[56] As a qualitative researcher one can readily identify with the concern expressed by the Committee as to the use of figures and statistics to determine policy, particularly in such a controversial field where some activism is to be anticipated, and where some groups will be more organized than others. However, in the White Paper the government drew on a quasi-quantitative analysis of the responses, using vague terms such as 'generally favoured' to cite support for some proposed changes and/or the retention of current aspects of the regulatory framework; yet there is no further indication of what 'generally favoured' might mean in this context.

B. Status of Respondents

An interest in whose opinion counts (or at least appears to do so) was piqued by the statement in White Paper, on the issue of the welfare of prospective children, that 'retention of a duty to consider the welfare of the child was *well supported* by responses to the government's consultation, including some from *representa-tives of the medical profession*'.[57] This support for retention was consistent with the government's proposals. Yet, in the paragraphs that followed, reference was also drawn to:

Responses... from *individual members of the public generally favoured retention* of a refer-ence to a child's need for a father, as part of the consideration of the welfare of the child. *Many thought* that the legislation should be revised to refer to a need for *both a mother and a father*.[58] The government has carefully considered this matter, and in particular has taken into account considerations of the proper role of the State, and of clinicians, in seeking to determine family forms via controls on access to medically-assisted con-ception, particularly in light of more recent enactments such as the law relating to civil partnerships...**On balance, the Government has decided to propose that the reference to the need for a father...should be removed from the Act.**[59]

Consequently, it would seem that where responses to the Department of Health's consultation *supported* the retention of an arguably controversial aspect

---

[55] n 14 above, paras 357–361 (emphasis added).
[56] n 20 above, para 1.2.
[57] n 21 above, para 2.24 (emphasis added).
[58] Emphasis added.
[59] ibid paras 2.25–2.26 (original emphasis).

of HFEA 1990 in the face of sustained academic and stakeholder criticism, this evidence was used accordingly. Specific attention was drawn to some 'represent-atives' of the medical profession, yet it is not clear who they were and whether or not they were, *in fact*, responding as *representatives* of the profession (for example the BMA) or simply as individual *members* putting forward their own views. The emphasis on 'representatives' rather than 'members' is significant, as even if the Department did not necessarily intend to indicate a *representative* response, the manner in which the data is presented here is certainly suggestive of this. Further, this statement privileges the responses from the medical pro-fession as having particular status or significance regarding (in)forming policy, notwithstanding the fact that without further context this quasi-quantitative portrayal of the data is grossly vague.

This privilege is compounded by the Department of Health's recommenda-tion to remove the reference to the need of a child for a father, which flies in the face of the views of 'many' 'individual members of the public'. At this juncture it is important to make clear that my views lie in support of this recommen-dation. However, the purpose of this chapter is to draw out the ways in which the consultation processes fed into public policy-making, and not to deliberate the content of those policies per se. Therefore, it is interesting to note in contra-distinction the *lack* of attention drawn to representatives of the medical profes-sion or indeed any other groups which supported the retention of the reference to a father and/or the proposed extension to include reference to a mother also. Rather, the data is presented in a way that indicates that *only* individual members of the public supported this policy stance. In doing so, the Department disem-powered the responses of those individuals, whose status is portrayed as being less significant than that of 'representatives' of the medical profession. This raises questions as to who those people were, and whether or not the medical profession was represented in their midst. Furthermore, it highlights issues around how the data from public consultations should be analysed and presented as this could prove crucial when (in)forming policy.

C. Method

Dissatisfaction with this approach led to the analysis of the 505 publicly available responses to the consultation published on the Department of Health website (of a reported total of 535 responses).[60] The was led by a curious interest in the ways in which expressions of support or opposition had been taken up and uti-lized by the government in defence of some proposed changes or the retention of existing measures, yet downplayed at other junctures. For the reasons outlined in the introduction, this analysis was limited to the questions pertaining to child

[60] Available at <http://www.dh.gov.uk/en/Consultations/Responsestoconsultations/DH_4132358> (accessed December 2007).

welfare considerations and hybrid embryos. In order to extract the relevant information, the full transcripts of all the responses made available by the Department were printed off and the relevant sections were read and analysed. Whilst this data is presented in numerical formats below, the purpose of this exercise was not merely to number crunch, but rather to draw out some of the richness of this data including who was responding, what drivers were apparent/stated for their standpoints, and to question whether particular viewpoints proved influential. It should be noted that the use of the term 'responses' here is deliberate and follows the lead set by People, Science and Policy Ltd in their report,[61] ie a single 'response' might be from an individual, from a couple or family, or from groups of individuals, professionals (acting in that capacity), or organizations. Therefore, to refer to 'respondents' would suggest that each submission related only to a single person, which would be misleading.

V. Responses to the Consultation: 'I trust that you will take people's views into consideration and that this is not an exercise in spin'[62]

This section is concerned only with the five questions on the statutory welfare of the child provisions, and will conclude with a brief discussion of hybrid and chimera embryos. Noting a range of criticisms of the application of the welfare principle to assisted conception,[63] the Department of Health sought views on the legal requirements for this field including whether or not the welfare of the child should remain a statutory obligation; whether it ought to be a matter of 'good medical practice' rather than within the regulatory framework of the HFEA; if so, if it should be limited to medical welfare concerns; or, if it remained a legal obligation, it should be limited to risks of serious harm only; and finally, whether the reference to a need for a father in section 13(5) of HFEA 1990 should be retained or replaced with reference to both a mother and a father.[64]

In the report produced by People, Science and Policy Ltd, the electronically submitted responses were analysed using Atlas-ti, a qualitative analysis using a grounded theory approach in order to present an 'overall landscape' of responses (whereas non-electronic responses were read and analysed).[65] Having read the publicly available responses it would seem to be a fair claim by People, Science and Policy Ltd, and it fulfilled the guidance issued by the Committee as to the undesirable possibilities of permitting the mere weight of opinion to determine

---

[61] n 20 above, para 1.2.
[62] Nora Brown, response to the Department of Health consultation; see n 60 above.
[63] n 18 above, paras 3.4, 3.10–3.18.
[64] ibid paras 3.19, 3.23, 3.24, 3.26, and 3.32 respectively.
[65] n 20 above, para 1.3.

or unfairly influence policy formation. However, in the White Paper it was stated that:

This [Report] was designed to draw out the landscape of arguments being presented and to place contrasting views side by side. The responses covered a wide diversity of opinions and arguments. However, it was clear that responses *generally favoured* measures such as a ban on sex selection for offspring for non-medical reasons, retention of a 'welfare of the child' consideration in some form in decisions to provide fertility treatments, and controls on the potential use of so-called 'artificial gametes' in the future. Respondents were *generally less convinced* of the need to make changes to the scope of permissible embryo research.[66]

Hence, despite the Committee's guidance against pure quantitative analysis, there is a vague quasi-quantitative description of the data here. Further, as outlined above, under the discussion of the welfare of potential and existing children, the Department of Health reiterated this quasi-quantitative approach, stating that retention of this provision was *'well supported'*, including by *'some [responses] from representatives of the medical profession'*.[67] What does 'generally favoured' or 'well supported' actually mean in this context?

A. Well Supported?

Analysis of the 505 available responses indicated that 241 responses (47.7 per cent) were in favour of retention of a statutory obligation; 40 (7.9 per cent) were actively in favour of its removal; and 9 (1.8 per cent) suggested alternatives (as there is no information on the 30 non-publicly available responses they have been excluded here). Therefore, at first glance it appeared that 'well supported' might refer to a popular viewpoint, but not an unequivocal one. However, on closer inspection the popularity of this standpoint can be contextualized further; 215 responses left this question blank. Consequently, if one recalculated using only responses that *actually addressed this question*, then the support for retention is far more convincing, standing at 83 per cent. Viewed this way it is far from a minority viewpoint. Further, the numbers of those responses which actively sought removal translated to 14 per cent, whereas only 3 per cent suggested alternatives. Whilst a counter-analysis might look to the lack of interest indicated by the other 215 *blank* responses, it is clear that the most strongly supported standpoint on this issue fell in favour of continued retention of welfare considerations. It is possible to see, therefore, how the Department of Health concluded that the proposed retention was 'well supported'. However, this exercise has also highlighted the difficulties that a statistical/percentage analysis would have created for the Department (or People, Science and Policy Ltd on their behalf). After all, circa 48 per cent support sounds rather less convincing than 83 per cent, yet a case

---

[66] n 21 above, para 1.11 (emphasis added).
[67] ibid para 2.24 (emphasis added).

could legitimately be made for the latter figure to be utilized in support of the retention of this provision in an official report. Clearly, the way in which data is presented is crucial to its potential influence, so if a statistical approach were to be adopted, such choices would need to be explicit and transparent.

B. Representatives of the Medical Profession?

Analysis of the responses indicated that this issue mattered enough for 290 responses to comment on it, but it revealed little about the so-called 'representatives' of the medical profession highlighted by the Department of Health. It is clear that the Department had a fuller data set including, for example, contact information which might relate to a person's or organization's status within the medical or indeed other fields. Therefore the information that follows has been deliberately couched to reflect the lack of clarity as to the classification of some responses.

With this caveat in mind, 44 potential 'representatives' of the medical profession were noted, including responses from individuals and organizations. There were a further 28 individual 'doctors', but it was unclear whether or not they were medical professionals. An obvious example that highlighted the difficulties in determining an individual's status was the response submitted on behalf of the Health, Ethics and Law network at the University of Southampton (HEAL UoS), by Jonathan Montgomery and myself. In the publicly available information we are referred to by our titles, Professor and Dr respectively, yet neither of us is medically qualified. This would not be readily apparent to an uninformed third party. Therefore, in reading other responses where the title 'Dr' was used, a healthy cynicism was adopted as to whether or not those persons were 'representatives' of the medical profession. Unless comments about, for example, their experience in this field were expressly stated in the response they were discounted. Were one being less cautious it would be possible to count a total of 72 potential 'representatives' (including individuals *and* organizations) of the medical profession. That figure does not, of course, include any person(s) that did not use the title 'doctor', nor does it include the other 30 responses that could not be accessed.

To provide further context on the 44 responses categorized here as 'representatives' of the medical profession, this figure included an NHS GP but none of the reported Reverend Doctors as it was unclear whether or not they were medically qualified; it included a doctor representing a fertility clinic but not a counsellor at another fertility clinic. Also included were organizations such as the British Fertility Society, British Medical Association (BMA), Royal College of Physicians (RCP), Royal College of Paediatrics and Child Health (RCPCH), Royal College of Nursing (RCN), Senior Infertility Nurses Group (SING), and (perhaps controversially) the HFEA, but not the British Infertility Counselling Association, British Association of Counselling and Psychotherapy, and British Psychological Society. It is conceded that the case could be made for the latter groups to be included in the broad umbrella term 'medical profession'. However, for the purposes of this chapter, a narrower definition has been adopted. The responses from the BMA, the HFEA, the RCP, the RCPCH, and the RCN all *supported* the continued retention of the statutory welfare provision, whereas the Royal College of Obstetricians and Gynaecologists (RCOG) and SING did not. Interestingly, there was a division of opinion among responses from fertility clinics; some supported retention as a statutory obligation (for example the Department of Reproductive Medicine (no affiliation given), King's College Hospital—but see discussion below), whereas others called for its removal citing good medical/clinical practice as providing sufficient protection for potential children (for example Guy's and St Thomas' Assisted Conception Unit, the London Fertility Centre, the Centre for Reproductive Medicine, University of Bristol). Whilst it is contended that the Department of Health's reference to 'some' representatives of the medical profession ascribed privileged status to those responses when (in)forming policy, but was so vague as to be almost meaningless, it is clear that the Department could legitimately claim that some *members* of the medical profession were indeed in favour of the continued retention of a statutory welfare provision.

However, whilst undertaking this analysis further problems with the data were uncovered. In the list of responses provided by the Department of Health, some responses were categorized by the individual's name whereas others were categorized by organization. Some responses made clear that the submission was representative of a group or organization, for example, through the provision of a mission statement or description of the group (see BMA, HEAL UoS), but others did not. For instance, Michele Harris of King's College Hospital, cited above and listed as the latter on the Department website, may well be an individual's response but it is categorized as an organizational one. The Department of Health presumably had access to further information that determined how people/organizations were listed. Yet, for an external researcher it provided some difficulty in ascertaining the accuracy of the listings, particularly for the purpose of examining whether or not the status of responses appeared to be influential on policy proposals drafted as a result of the consultation.

Further examples can be provided. These include Dr David Morroll who was listed as an individual, but whose response suggested a submission on behalf of the Association of Clinical Embryologists (ACE); similarly Damien Sarsfield was listed under that name, but in his response (by way of a letter) he stated that he was the Public Relations Officer of the Labour Life Group and, with two exceptions, referred to the collective 'we' throughout his letter. Alternatively, Robin Carter was listed under 'COTS—Robin Carter', as was Vivien Grimes (for a separate response), yet it is unclear from the responses whether either of them were acting as representatives of that organization. Arguably if one (as the Department of Health had purportedly sought to) counted these as different responses and was unconcerned by the statistical prevalence of particular viewpoints and the *status* of respondents, then these discrepancies are irrelevant. However, as the Department of Health specifically drew attention to the medical standing of 'some' responses, this data attained greater significance and the need for accuracy became rather more salient.

C. Other Questions on the Welfare Issue

In the White Paper, the Department of Health glossed over the responses to the next three questions, stating 'Clinicians expect to consider a range of factors relating to patients' circumstances as a matter of "good medical practice", and guidance from the regulator will continue to encourage consistent good practice among professionals'.[68] No further comment is made on the range or strength of support for continued guidance. However, as noted above, on the 'need' for a father the Department of Health was rather more expansive, referring to '*individual members of the public [who] generally favoured*' retention, and '*many*' who wished to see revisions to include reference to '*both a mother and a father*'. Yet, the government proposed the removal of any reference to either mother or father in the legislation. Whilst public *confidence* in the proposed system is said to be important, clearly public *opinion* is far removed from being the overriding factor when it does not accord with government policies. This finding is unsurprising, but it does highlight the problematic use of public opinion in the vague manner found in the White Paper. Whereas in the preceding example attention was drawn to the medical profession, in this instance it was 'individual *members* of the public' that were highlighted; hence there is a clear shift from notable 'representatives' to mere 'members' whose responses are downplayed. Once again, the questions raised included what was meant by 'generally favoured' and 'many thought', and who were those members of the public?

D. Generally Favoured?

There was some difficulty in analysing the responses to this question in numerical terms as a number of responses ignored the distinction between the two options or did not directly address the question as put by the Department of Health. The non-electronic forms provided by the Department further complicated matters as following the question it included the following text:

I think that the consideration of 'the need of the child for a father' **should/should not** be removed from the Act (Delete as applicable)

I think that the consideration of 'the need for a father' **should/should not** be replaced with 'the need for a father and mother' (Delete as applicable)[69]

---

[68] n 21 above, para 2.24.
[69] Original emphasis, see eg the form submitted by Mrs Catherine Blatchley.

This was followed by space to provide written feedback giving reasons for the response submitted. People, Science and Policy Ltd noted 408 electronically received submissions and 127 non-electronic responses.[70] Leaving aside potential criticisms regarding setting out the questions and space for answers differently depending on the method of submission, it meant that a number of responses indicated that they would not sanction the removal of the reference to the need for a father, but that they also expressed a preference for its replacement with the need for both a father and a mother. Therefore, whilst the questions were initially asked as alternative options, this is not necessarily how they were responded to (it should be added that this was the case for both electronic and non-electronic submissions, therefore the forms were not entirely to blame).

Consequently, in a pragmatic move, where responses indicated support for the retention of the need for a father *and/or* replacement with reference to a father and a mother they have been counted together. Accordingly, to retain or replace found favour with 228 responses (45 per cent), whereas 70 (14 per cent) were in favour of its removal; 16 (3 per cent) wished to see retention of a reference to fathers only, and 40 (8 per cent) made alternative suggestions (for example the need for secure family life; need for parents/family; stable loving environment or, at the other extreme, the removal of any reference to welfare entirely). 151 responses (30 per cent) left this question blank. Therefore, it is clear that this matter concerned *more* of those responding than the issue regarding the inclusion of welfare as a statutory obligation. One interpretation of this difference in response rates might be that many of those who answered question 17 but not 13 *presumed* that the latter would be a prerequisite of the former. After all, if there was no statutory welfare consideration then its precise parameters would be irrelevant. In keeping with the analysis of question 13, of those that responded to question 17, 64 per cent were in favour of retention/replacement; 20 per cent were in favour of removal; 5 per cent sought retention of a reference only to fathers; whereas 11 per cent made alternative suggestions.

A couple of issues remain: who were these 'individual members of the public'? Was the medical profession—or indeed any other interest group—represented within these figures and if so, in what way?

E. Individual Members of the Public?

Upon examination of the responses from medical professionals including the BMA, the HFEA, the RCOG, the RCPCH, the RCP, the RCN, and the SING, it is clear that *none of these organizations* supported the retention of a specific reference to the need for a father, albeit not necessarily for the same reasons. For example, the BMA expressed concern over 'blanket restrictions applied to certain categories of people'; whereas the HFEA noted (among other comments) the

---

[70] n 20 above, para 1.3.

conflict with the law relating to adoption and civil partnerships, and the RCOG and SING highlighted this as a matter for general clinical assessment rather than legislation.

However, these groups were *not* the only ones pertaining to members of the medical profession. Responses from both Doctors Who Respect Human Life, reported to be the British Section of the World Federation of Doctors Who Respect Human Life (WFDWRHL),[71] and Doctors for Life Northern Ireland[72] expressed support for the presence of fathers *and* mothers. The latter's response was rather more equivocal than that of the former, and although they did *not explicitly* state that the statutory requirements should stipulate a need for a mother *and* a father, it is contended that this interpretation would certainly be justified.

In contrast, the British Section of WFDWRHL made clear that:

Children conceived by assisted reproduction, who survive to birth, need the protection of the law. The requirement that no treatment be given unless account is taken of the welfare of any child born, *including the child's need for a father* (Questions 13, 17) *should be retained… The 'welfare of the child' provision must include a reference to the need of the child for both a father and a mother* (Question 17).[73]

According to its website, WFDWRHL is 'an affiliation of doctors throughout the world who support the traditional medical ethic of service to life'; one of their primary aims is 'to call for legal protection for all members of the human race, from conception/fertilisation until natural death, in accordance with the U.N. Declaration of Human Rights 1948 and the Declaration of the Rights of the Child 1959'.[74] There is certainly scope for WFDWRHL to be portrayed as a 'representative' of the medical profession in the manner alluded to by the Department of Health in the White Paper. However, this group clearly does not have the official standing or status of the BMA and the Royal Colleges, and of the medical viewpoints expressed in the responses its views were in the minority. More significantly, it would be inconvenient for the Department of Health to highlight this response as it would undermine the impression given by them that this was a view favoured only by 'individual members of the public'.

Consequently, this analysis indicates that the Department of Health's presentation of this data was factually correct insofar as it was clear that there were indeed a number of individuals who advocated the retention of the reference to a father (including, in most cases, an extension to refer to a mother also). However, in addition to Doctors for Life Northern Ireland and WFDWRHL, there were other organizations—*and not merely*

---

[71] See <http://www.doctorsfed.org.uk> (accessed December 2007).

[72] At the time of writing I could not ascertain whether or not this group was affiliated with Doctors for Life International <http://www.doctorsforlifeinternational.com> (accessed December 2007).

[73] Emphasis added.

[74] Taken from <http://www.doctorsfed.org.uk/content/view/169/49> (accessed December 2007).

individuals—that also supported these proposals. This list included Affinity, the Catholic Bishops' Joint Bioethics Committee (listed as Bishop of Plymouth), the Christian Medical Fellowship, Comment on Reproductive Ethics (CORE), Evangelical Alliance, Family Education Trust, the Lawyer's Christian Fellowship (LCF), LIFE, the National Council of Women of Great Britain (by majority), the Scottish Council on Human Bioethics, the Society for the Protection of Unborn Children (SPUC), and the Centre for Ethics in Medicine at the University of Bristol (this is a non-exhaustive list). It is clear that those responding from a religious standpoint were well-represented, but this list also includes secular, pro-life, humanist groups.[75] This observation leads neatly into the issue of how 'other' viewpoints were addressed in this consultation (and, of course, raises the question of how, in future, 'other' viewpoints *should* be used to (in)form public policy, although there is no scope to consider this matter further here).

F. Religious and 'Other' Viewpoints

In the White Paper, the Department of Health noted at the outset that 'churches and faith communities' had responded to the consultation.[76] Yet, in the discussion of responses on the welfare of the child and regarding hybrid embryos, there is no mention of religious input whatsoever; *nor*, in fact, is there any indication of the views expressed by these churches and faith communities at any point in the document. How then, if at all, were such responses used to 'inform' policy?

This is a difficult question to address. In their response to the consultation, the LCF launched a scathing attack on the Committee's 2005 report, arguing that despite a fifteen-month consultation 'the evidence it received was almost totally ignored in its report' (which is a stronger version of the argument of the dissenting Committee members, outlined above). The LCF went on to state that 'with such important issues at stake for the family and the whole of society it is essential that the Department takes notice of the responses it received in this consultation'. The LCF's vociferous criticism was by no means a view held only by those who responded from a religious perspective. LIFE, a secular organization advocating respect for the rights and dignity of persons from conception until natural death,[77] highlighted the significance of the Department of Health consultation as 'an important opportunity for legislators, scientists and opinion-formers to reconnect with public opinion, which has so often been neglected in the past as scientists forge ahead with controversial and little-understood new techniques'. Despite the LCF and LIFE's misgivings and call for action, it seems clear that the

---

[75] This is an example of Brownsword's 'dignitarian alliance' (n 4 above) 20.
[76] n 21 above, para 1.10.
[77] See <http://www.lifecharity.org.uk/about/values> (accessed December 2007).

Department of Health took particular note of responses from one faction—the medical profession—but not others. This utilization and further prioritization of *some* responses over others to justify policy stances is problematic if the purported aim of ensuring continued public confidence in the (actual and proposed) regulatory framework is to be met.

Two further points can be made at this juncture. First, one explanation for the absence of an account of the religious or humanist responses might be the government's firm avowal that certain topics were not open to re-negotiation, including the issue of embryo research, portrayed as being one of the 'fundamental aspects of the law that are widely accepted in our society or which have been recently debated and conclusively resolved in Parliament'.[78] Given that a number of responses from individuals and organizations were overtly from religious or humanist standpoints, and consequently they were writing against the use of *any* technology that would result in the destruction of human embryos, this left a conundrum for policy-makers as to how these responses ought to be used to (in)form their processes. The approach seemingly adopted here is to marginalize those responses *in toto* due to their problematic status, as it is difficult to reconcile outright objection with a permissive[79] regulatory framework. Therefore it seems that permitting the public the opportunity to respond to the proposals sufficed,[80] whereas Brownsword has made clear that merely enabling stakeholders to participate in proceedings does not ensure the agreed legitimacy of the findings.[81] Second, in reading the responses to question 13, the phrase that 'children are uniquely vulnerable and uniquely valuable' was repeated by a number of responses from individuals, and was also ascribed to the LCF, indicating that its members were motivated to respond individually also. It is for precisely this reason that reliance *solely* on the weight of opinion in constructing public policy would be a dangerous move indeed.[82]

---

[78] n 21 above, para 1.9.

[79] 'Permissive' is taken here to mean permitting these technologies to be used in spite of objections from some quarters. It is patently clear that not all stakeholders or commentators would necessarily view the current or proposed regulatory framework as permissive in the sense of being laissez-faire.

[80] Though there were criticisms of the consultation process, for example, in his response Stephen Lenane inquired: 'how are you ensuring that enough people are consulted on this matter? What about those who do not have internet access, or who do not know what technical terms like gamete means, or who did not happen to listen to or read the news on the day that the so-called consultation was announced?'

[81] n 4 above, 22–4; see Steele (n 4 above) 429 on the problems of making a person merely a 'speaker'.

[82] Dodds and Ankeny (n 12 above) 101, noted a similar finding in their study of similar consultation processes in Australia. See also examples of multiple responses apparently from members of the same family (in the absence of access to their address the similarity or indeed identical submissions lends weight to this inference), eg Elizabeth, Roy, and Susan Quispe; also John, Matthew, Rachel, and Sally Ann Keane—although only the Keanes' is explicitly influenced by religion.

G. Addendum: Policy Developments in 2007

Notwithstanding the Joint Committee on the Human Tissue and Embryos (Draft) Bill recommendation that the proposed removal of the reference to the 'need for a father' be 'put to a free vote in both Houses',[83] it surfaced as clause 14(2)(b) of the Human Fertilisation and Embryology Bill introduced to the House of Lords on 8 November 2007. However, during the first sitting of the second reading Baroness Deech moved swiftly to re-establish the reference to a need for a father, and indeed moved for an extension to include reference to a mother also.[84]

VI. Hybrids

As outlined in the Introduction above, the purpose of comparing the approach taken by the government in relation to the welfare of the child with that regarding the permissibility of hybrid research is to examine the ways in which consultation responses appear to (in)form policy-making. In the White Paper, the government's stance was prohibitive, albeit that it simultaneously recommended that provision be made for future changes to be addressed under delegated legislation (akin to the removal of donor anonymity), rather than undertaking revision of the entire statute.[85] This recommendation was made in recognition of the 'considerable public unease' over hybrid research, but with the awareness of possible advantages for research into serious illnesses.[86] However, a policy reversal occurred in May 2007 with the publication of the Human Tissue and Embryos (Draft) Bill, which proposed that some inter-species entities be permitted for research purposes.[87] The reasons given for the policy u-turn are of particular interest here.

A. Timing

The timing of developments around the hybrid issue was rather complex. The Department of Health's proposals were published in the White Paper in December 2006. However, a month *earlier* the HFEA had received two applications from groups of researchers at Newcastle University (led by Dr Lyle Armstrong)[88] and King's College London (led by Dr Stephen Minger) for licences to permit the

---

[83] n 10 above, para 243.
[84] *Hansard*, HL, 19 November 2007: col 673.
[85] n 21 above, para 2.85.
[86] ibid para 2.83.
[87] DH, *Human Tissue and Embryos (Draft) Bill*, (Cm 7087, 2007) ix–x: paras 1.10–1.14.
[88] The application by Newcastle University nominated Dr Majlinda Lako as the person responsible, but in the media coverage it has been stated that the team is led by Dr Armstrong;

use of these technologies for specific projects. On 11 January 2007, the HFEA released a statement to the effect that these applications fell within the regulatory framework and therefore under its remit.[89] However, prior to deciding whether or not to grant the requisite licences, the HFEA undertook an extensive public consultation between April and July 2007, as summarized in the resulting report.[90] Almost simultaneously, and reportedly as a consequence of these developments, the House of Commons Science and Technology Committee decided to undertake an urgent inquiry into this issue,[91] officially launched on January 10 2007. The Committee's Report was published on April 5 2007, followed shortly by the Draft Bill in May 2007.

B. Evidence

The Committee's Report was crucial in sealing the government's volte-face; as the introduction to the Draft Bill clearly illustrates:

Having regard to the *scientific evidence* produced during the Committee's inquiry, and that the recommendations are the *consensus view of a Parliamentary Committee*, we intend to accept the principle that legislation should provide for [certain] inter-species entities... This list includes the cytoplasmic hybrids that the Committee particularly wants to see allowed, and for which the HFEA has received two licence applications,...[92]

Therefore, the *consensus* achieved by the elevenfold Committee was highlighted by the Department of Health as being particularly significant. This lies is in stark contrast to the Department of Health's *failure* to highlight the discord of the previous Committee which, incidentally, *also* supported the use of hybrid embryos for research. Two further issues are of particular interest—the emphasis on scientific evidence and references to public opinion/confidence found within the Committee's Report.

The Department of Health privileged the *scientific* evidence provided to the Committee in 2007. It is unsurprising that a greater amount of scientific data would be given to an inquiry focused solely on hybrid embryos, as opposed to its broader focus in 2005, and justifiable given the Committee's remit, including explicit consideration of the potential impact of regulatory reform on science

see eg, the BBC coverage at <http://news.bbc.co.uk/1/hi/health/7193820.stm> (accessed January 2008); D Batty, 'Hybrid embryos get go-ahead' *Guardian*, 17 May 2007.

[89] <http://www.hfea.gov.uk/en/1478.html> (accessed December 2007).

[90] HFEA, 'Hybrids and Chimeras: A report on the findings of the consultation' (October 2007) Ch 4, at <http://www.hfea.gov.uk/docs/Hybrids_Report.pdf> (accessed December 2007). See also the homepage for the HFEA consultation, at <http://www.hfea.gov.uk/en/1517.html>.

[91] n 24 above, paras 1–3.

[92] n 22 above, paras 1.12–1.13 (emphasis added). Details of the applications by Newcastle University and King's College London and the Licence Committee Minutes can be found at <http://www.hfea.gov.uk/en/1640.html> (accessed January 2008).

in the United Kingdom.[93] This focus is evident throughout the process of the inquiry, which began with a 'private seminar' to educate the Committee on the scientific issues around this subject[94] and continued with visits to a laboratory. Given the complexity of the subject matter, these procedures were laudable. While no suggestion of any impropriety is evident, nor intended in this discussion, it is interesting to note that Dr Stephen Minger was one of only three persons involved in educating the Committee at the outset, and it was his laboratory that was visited to examine the facilities for stem cell research. In addition another member of the King's College London group, Professor Chris Shaw, together with Dr Lyle Armstrong of Newcastle University, participated in one of the three oral evidence sessions,[95] and both doctors gave written submissions. Given that these researchers/groups had live applications to the HFEA on the very issue being examined by the Committee, the outcome of which was likely to be influenced by its recommendations, a critical audience might view the *extent* of their involvement in the inquiry as problematic.[96]

This is particularly salient when one considers that, of six panels of oral evidence held over three sessions, only one panel was given over to persons known to oppose or to be likely to oppose these developments, in part or in full.[97] Yet, a cursory glance over the written submissions to the inquiry illustrates greater discontent than the oral evidence sessions alone would indicate. Without the opportunity to appear before the Committee, dissenters could not expand on their arguments in the way that the scientists were able to promulgate their research.[98] Furthermore, whilst scientific debate was acknowledged, it was swiftly marginalized: 'We recognise the scientific debate among experts about the potential usefulness of the research under discussion in this Report but we conclude that the scientific community as a whole is supportive of the work being licensable, even where there may be doubts about its likely success.'[99]

Another facet of concern for the Committee was the potential loss of competitive edge in this field of research; although it recommended that the government view this as a contributory factor and not a determining one.[100] However, such assurances that a potential brain drain should not be the overriding factor are unlikely to appease those who expressed concern over the lack of consideration

---

[93] n 24 above, para 5.   [94] ibid para 7.
[95] ibid para 8.
[96] See also Brownsword (n 4 above) 27, on the difficult balance between detachment and expertise.
[97] See the third panel with Dr David King, Dr Calum MacKellar, and Reverend Dr Lee Rayfield. However, the grilling of Caroline Flint, MP, Minister of State for Public Health, in the final session should also be noted.
[98] Although it should be recognized that it is for the Committee members to ask the questions and not the reverse, as illustrated by the exchanges between Dr MacKellar, Dr Turner, and the Chair; House of Commons Science and Technology Committee, *Government proposals for the regulation of hybrid and chimera embryos (Fifth Report of Session 2006–07) Volume II Oral and Written Evidence*, HC 272-II, ev 23.
[99] n 24 above, para 58.   [100] ibid para 107.

of the moral and ethical objections to this research—issues which did appear in the Committee's report, but were accorded limited time in the oral evidence sessions.[101]

Another major consideration was the matter of public opinion and confidence. The first issue here concerns the quantification of responses to the Department of Health consultation. In 2005, the Committee could hardly have been clearer in its *opposition* to drawing on the weight of response to determine policy outcomes. However, in 2007, the current Science and Technology Committee (retaining four original members)[102] in commenting on the ethical and moral points of view on the government's proposed ban of hybrid embryo research, drew attention the Department's consultation as the 'most extensive study of public opinion' on this topic. The Committee then provided a *scathing account* of the perceived failure of the government to provide a full breakdown of the results: 'We regret that the Department of Health did not seek to specify more clearly in its consultation what views it was seeking, nor to evaluate fully the responses of the public consultation exercise. We recommend that in future a more systematic statistical or scientific approach is developed to quantify and qualify the results of the public consultation.'[103]

This volte-face by the Committee raises questions as to how changes in the constitution of relevant bodies and/or advice to government departments ought to be taken into account in developing public policy and defending its legitimacy. The analysis undertaken by People, Science and Policy Ltd for the Department of Health followed the criteria outlined by the previous Committee, and the Department's question was posed in the context of the government's (then) intention not to revisit the issue of embryo research; therefore, this attack seems misplaced.

The second issue concerns the way the Committee analysed the breakdown of results provided by the Department of Health, whereby of 336 responses to this question, 277 were opposed, and of the remaining 59 responses 'most...were in support'.[104] The Committee placed emphasis on the fact that those 59 responses included some that '*represented* the collective views of multiple membership

---

[101] Dodds and Ankeny (n 12 above) 100, noted the separation of economic and financial aspects of human embryo research from the scientific, social, and ethical issues in the Australian consultation process. However, the former issues were *not* put to public debate, in what they describe as a 'tightly circumscribed' 'mandate for public debate'. Nor did this form part of the UK debates, emerging only in the Committee's 2007 Report.

[102] The Committee in 2004–05 comprised the following members: Dr Ian Gibson (Chair), Paul Farrelly, Dr Evan Harris, Kate Hoey, Dr Brian Iddon, Robert Key, Tony McWalter, Dr Andrew Murrison, Geraldine Smith, Bob Spink, Dr Desmond Turner. In 2006–07 the membership had changed accordingly: Phil Willis (Chair), Adam Afriyie, Robert Flello, Linda Gilroy, Dr Evan Harris, Dr Brian Iddon, Chris Mole, Brooks Newmark, Dr Bob Spink, Graham Stringer, Dr Desmond Turner.

[103] n 24 above, para 41.

[104] ibid. The Department of Health's analysis can be found under Memorandum 68 (n 98 above) evi 167 *et seq*.

organizations',[105] although it did not provide further information as to which groups it was referring to. Yet, in Memorandum 68 it is clear that the questions posed (by the Committee) to the Department of Health were directed to assessing the 'proportion of responses... from the scientific community', and 'how many of the respondents opposed to the creation of human-animal chimera or hybrid embryos for research were also against use of human embryos for research purposes'.

In a fairly even-handed response, the Department of Health noted that a *range of views* were taken by those responding to this question, but did list ten bodies which could fall within the definition of 'scientific community' for the purposes of the Committee's inquiry (including, for example, The Royal Society, the Medical Research Council, the Wellcome Trust, and the University of Newcastle). They also noted that 227 responses either were explicitly or implicitly opposed to *all* forms of embryo research. It is clear that the purpose of asking the latter question was to delineate between persons concerned with the development of hybrid embryos per se rather than with embryo research in general. Those in the latter group might justifiably feel riled as a consequence of this compartmentalization, as the Report (at least as I read it) suggested that it was only a small number of persons who were opposed to hybrid embryos per se—particularly as there was no mention of 'multiple membership organizations' in opposition. This very conveniently overlooks the submission of the RCP, for example, which indicated that 'at present we would be very unhappy for this sort of research to be allowed in humans', although they also indicated that research on animals might be beneficial, and in future delegated legislation might address this matter. Therefore, the presentation of the data in the Report is problematically selective.

The final issue concerns the discussion of public engagement—confidence, opinion, and understanding.[106] On the one hand the Committee drew attention to the need for full consideration of the views of the public, which it characterized as 'essential' to public confidence in the regulatory framework.[107] However, almost in the same breath, the Committee went on to argue that the views of the public on this area remain unclear, in part relying on its analysis of the responses outlined above; ie pointing out the difficulty in determining the reasons for the opposition to hybrids per se. In general the comments made by the Committee were critical of the self-selecting sample for the Department of Health consultation.[108] This does raise significant questions about the role of the public in informing policy; is it 'merely' to 'inform' policy or is there a more onerous role—that of being representative of society in general? If so, should government departments be seeking representative samples for every consultation they undertake, notwithstanding the attendant costs, delays, and other implications this

---

[105] ibid (emphasis added).　　[106] n 24 above, Ch 6, paras 108–115.
[107] ibid para 109.
[108] See also similar comments by the Joint Committee on the Human Tissue and Embryos (Draft) Bill (n 10 above) paras 14–15, and 21.

would incur? Indeed, Steele makes this very point; that 'the purpose of establishing participation rights, processes or requirements... is less often addressed, and yet the purposes in question will have a large impact on the types of participation which are thought to be appropriate'.[109] Interestingly, in all the negative commentary on the self-selecting (public) sample, there was no consideration whatsoever of whether or not the responses by industry and other stakeholders (for example scientific bodies) were representative, either of their respective industries or in general. Self-selection matters, it seems, only in relation to individual members and lay groups within society.

C. Addendum

The Joint Committee on the Human Tissue and Embryos (Draft) Bill was critical of the government's stance on this issue, arguing that it 'rests on no sound point of principle', and accordingly recommended that the HFEA should determine which inter-species entities should be permitted for research under licence.[110] On 15 January 2008, a proposal by Lord Alton[111] to prohibit the creation of hybrid embryos was defeated by a majority of 172 (a vote of contents: 96, non-contents: 268),[112] and shortly thereafter, on 17 January 2008 the HFEA announced its decision to grant licences to Newcastle University and King's College London (as a result of meetings on 28 November 2007 and 9 January 2008).

VII. Conclusion

The intention for this chapter was to undertake exploratory research into the findings of the Department of Health consultation as reported in the subsequent reports. Hence, attention was paid not only to the official interpretation of the data, but to alternative constructions and problems created by the quasi-quantitative representation of the material at some junctures. On the one hand this process has led to greater empathy for the Department of Health and other official bodies in sifting through the myriad responses, but on the other hand a creeping cynicism has also taken hold. It is clear that there are significant issues about the way that data is presented by governmental and Parliamentary bodies, and even in the absence of the use of statistical data it remains feasible to skew the presentation of data in ways that are strictly speaking factually correct but simultaneously misleading about the dataset as a whole.

---

[109] Steele (n 4 above) 416. Contrast, eg, the Committee's consultation on hybrid embryos with that of the HFEA in 2007, where the latter involved 12 deliberative groups, a day event, a public debate with a variety of stakeholders and an opinion poll. Further details and downloads are available at <http://www.hfea.gov.uk/en/1517.html> (accessed January 2008).

[110] n 10 above, para 161.

[111] Hansard HL, 15 January 2008: col 1202.

[112] Hansard HL, 15 January 2008: col 1224.

Perhaps more questions have been raised here than have been answered. These include issues around addressing marginal or oppositional viewpoints, be they from a 'dignitarian' or any other alliance, a problem highlighted eloquently by Brownsword. Is it legitimate not to portray data in statistical formats, yet then to go on to develop quasi-quantitative analyses without providing further context? Also, is it acceptable to highlight the responses from some factions whose views happen to support the recommended policy outcome but disempower responses from 'others'? One issue, which was not expressly addressed above but which featured heavily in critiques of the Department of Health consultation process, was how responses ought to be compared. That is, where there are responses from single individuals or families and others from multiple-membership organizations, ought they to be directly compared in the consultation data analysis? Certainly the view of those responding from industry was that they should not,[113] on the basis that self-selecting samples were not representative of the UK population and also due to the unfair weighting accorded to individuals.

This correlates with questions regarding the appropriate role of the public in the consultation process. Much was made of the lack of a representative sample for the DH consultation,[114] yet there was no suggestion at the outset that this—nor indeed other consultations in this field in recent years (for example donor anonymity removal, or the child welfare revisions in the HFEA's Code of Practice)—was intended to fulfil such a role. Perhaps in the light of the attention this matter has received from the Committee in recent years, it seems that the HFEA, at least in *its* recent consultation on hybrid embryos,[115] has sought to ameliorate this situation and avoid similar critiques of its findings. Not only does the HFEA make explicit the purpose of the various facets of the consultation process but also what inferences might reasonably be drawn from different datasets. Hence, the written consultation and public dialogue work was intended to provide 'insight into those with a specific interest in the issues', but it makes clear that these findings are *not* representative of public opinion.[116] In contrast, the opinion poll of a random sample of a representative group of 2,000 residents of Great Britain and 60 from Northern Ireland was intended to provide 'an indication of the views of the UK population'.[117] Perhaps these explicit statements go some way to addressing Callus's comments at the outset of the chapter, although it remains to be seen whether or not the HFEA approach will become or remain the gold standard for public policy-making in contentious areas in the future.

---

[113] eg the BioIndustry Association, cited (n 24 above) para 111.

[114] ibid. See also House of Commons Science and Technology Committee, *Scientific Advice, Risk and Evidence Based Policy Making (Seventh Report of Session 2005–06)*, October 2006, HC 900-I, paras 133–136, especially 136.

[115] HFEA, 'Hybrids and Chimeras: A report on the findings of the consultation' (October 2007) available from the HFEA website (n 109 above).

[116] ibid. paras 4.1–4.4.   [117] ibid.

16

The Donation of Eggs for Research and the Rise of Neopaternalism

Emily Jackson

I. Introduction

The trigger for this chapter was the reaction to the revelation, towards the end of 2005, that Professor Woo-Suk Hwang's apparently remarkable achievements in the field of human embryonic stem cell research were not what they had seemed.[1] Some of his results had been deliberately faked, and there was also evidence that he had been involved in recruiting PhD students and junior lab technicians to act as egg donors.[2] It was these twin elements of research fraud and the possible exploitation of egg donors which were the focus of the opprobrium which was heaped on Professor Hwang and some of his collaborators. What I found intriguing, however, was the relative lack of concern about the *embryos* that had been wasted in his laboratory. It is, I would argue, noteworthy that the interests of female egg donors seemed to be of more concern than the possibility that embryos were created and destroyed for no good purpose.

In this chapter, I want to reflect further upon this new focus on egg donation for research purposes, which has, I will argue, reignited some old debates about reproductive technologies' potential to exploit women, and breathed new life into the so-called 'unholy alliance' between feminists and pro-life activists. Drawing analogies with a similar shift in pro-life campaigners' strategic focus in relation to abortion, I highlight, and criticize, the development of a new sort of paternalism towards women's decision-making.

---

[1] WS Hwang *et al*, 'Evidence of a Pluripotent Human Embryonic Stem Cell Line Derived from a Cloned Blastocyst' (2004) 303 *Science*; Hwang *et al*, 'Patient-Specific Embryonic Stem Cells Derived from Human SCNT Blastocysts' (2005) 308 *Science* 1777.

[2] This almost certainly amounted to a breach of the Helsinki Declaration, Act 23 which specifies that when a research subject is in 'a dependent relationship' with the researcher, consent should be obtained by an independent physician, who is not involved in the research project.

II. Eggs for Research: a Novel Issue

It is only within the last few years that the question of egg donation for human embryonic stem cell research (hESCR) has arisen. In 1984, the Warnock report did not concern itself with the sources of eggs for research because it was assumed that surplus IVF embryos would be the principal source of embryos for research, and that it would only very occasionally be necessary to create embryos specifically for research. The demand for eggs, as opposed to embryos, was assumed to be extremely low, and could almost certainly be met, in any event, by using the eggs which are not successfully fertilized during an IVF cycle (known as 'failed to fertilize' eggs).

Consent to the use of 'spare' IVF embryos or 'spare' eggs is importantly different to consent to becoming an egg donor solely for the purposes of embryo research. Because it was assumed that only the former was likely in relation to embryo research, the rules take for granted that the gamete providers' only interest in consenting to the use of their eggs or embryos in research is that they should have some control over the destination and use of their genetic material. Donation itself poses absolutely no risk to them, and the leftover eggs or embryos would otherwise be destroyed or allowed to perish. The 'subjects' of this sort of research are not egg donors, but rather embryos, which were, according to Warnock, said to require some protection against being used frivolously or profligately.

We can tell that it simply had not occurred to the Warnock Committee, or to Parliament when it debated the Human Fertilisation and Embryology Act in 1990, that women might go through ovarian stimulation purely in order to provide eggs for research because the Human Fertilisation and Embryology Authority's (HFEA) regulatory remit over the use of gametes in research is limited. Researchers only need a licence from the HFEA if their research project involves creating embryos *in vitro*, or keeping or using embryos for the purposes of a project of research.[3] A research project which just used freshly donated eggs, where there was no chance that any of the eggs would subsequently become embryos, would not need a licence from the HFEA, and would not be subject to any special regulatory control. Again in 1984 and 1990, it is clear that it was embryos and not egg donors which were the principal objects of concern.

So what has changed? The short answer is stem cell research. In 1990, it was assumed that research using embryos would generally be directed towards improving assisted conception techniques, not curing disease, although sensibly the drafters of the Human Fertilisation and Embryology Act 1990 (HFEA 1990) left open the possibility that new purposes for embryo research might

[3] HFEA 1990, Sch 2(3).

subsequently emerge. The birth of Dolly the sheep in 1996,[4] and the extraction of the first human stem cell line in 1998,[5] radically altered the field of embryo research by creating the possibility that stem cell lines might, in the future, be extracted from embryos created using cell nuclear replacement (CNR), and, once the process of differentiation has been properly understood, lead eventually to stem cell therapies for a wide range of degenerative diseases.

Whether or not the 'holy grail' of creating patient-specific stem cell lines capable of generating genetically-matched replacement tissue ever becomes a reality, it seems clear that within a few years there will be a stem cell bank containing clinical-grade stem cell lines which might be able to produce new tissue for patients suffering from certain degenerative conditions such as Parkinson's disease. Before we get to that point, however, scientists need to perfect the currently extremely inefficient process of extracting stem cell lines, and for this basic research, they need eggs.

In the United Kingdom, three possible sources of eggs have recently been the subject of considerable controversy: altruistic egg donors, egg sharers (women who receive reduced price IVF in return for egg donation), and animals. In the past year, there have been two major HFEA public consultations on these potential sources of eggs for research.[6] The creation of hybrid embryos was the subject of a special Science and Technology Select Committee Report, and forms one of the central and most contentious aspects of the Human Fertilisation and Embryology Bill. While all these potential sources of eggs raise important issues, in this chapter I will focus on the question of whether women should be permitted to donate their eggs altruistically for research. The reason for my interest in this question is that it seems to have prompted the increasing use of 'pro-women' rhetoric by pro-life campaigners, and has also resulted in the emergence of an at first sight counter-intuitive alliance between feminists and pro-life activists.

III. Should Women be Allowed to Donate Their Eggs to Research?

My own starting point is that competent adult women should be allowed to do whatever they like with their bodies, provided what they choose to do is not going to hurt other people, and provided that they have voluntarily given consent, after having been provided with all the information they need to make this

---

[4] I Wilmut, AE Schnieke, J McWhir, AJ Kind, and KHS Campbell, 'Viable offspring derived from foetal and adult mammalian cells' (1997) 385 *Nature* 810.

[5] JA Thomson, J Itskovitz-Eldor, SS Shapiro, MA Waknitz, JJ Sweirgiel, VS Marshall, and JM Jones, 'Embryonic stem cell lines derived from human blastocysts' (1998) 282 *Science* 1145.

[6] 'Donating Eggs for Research: Safeguarding' Donors (2006) available at <http://www.hfea.gov.uk/en/1417.html> (accessed 19 September 2007); HFEA, 'Hybrids and Chimeras' (2007) available at <http://www.hfea.gov.uk/en/1517.html> (accessed 19 September 2007).

decision. In relation to egg donation for research, then, it would be important to ensure that consent is both voluntary and informed. The potential benefits of stem cell research should not be oversold: for example, a woman who offers to donate eggs because she has a close relative suffering from Parkinson's disease should not be misled into believing that a cure is likely within the next year or so. The discomfort and risks involved in the process of egg donation should also be explained clearly and frankly. But provided women have given fully informed and voluntary consent, what justification could there be for preventing them from donating eggs to research?

I shall first deal with the scientific objection: namely that it is premature to ask women to donate their eggs to research because the inefficiency of the process of stem cell extraction will inevitably mean that many eggs are 'wasted' while scientists practise the difficult task of extracting viable stem cell lines. A further practical objection might be that it is simply not sensible to invest time and money in setting up a programme for egg donation for research given that, without payment, the number of women who might be expected to volunteer is likely to be very low indeed. Payment for donation is not permitted in the United Kingdom, so scientists wanting to recruit egg donors must rely on women's altruism. Since egg donation is time-consuming, uncomfortable, and carries the risk, albeit a small one, of ovarian hyperstimulation syndrome (OHSS), very few women are likely to volunteer to donate their eggs altruistically, so investment in an egg donation programme is likely to have a fairly poor return.

But the question of whether it is sensible to ask women to donate their eggs to stem cell research is importantly different from the question of whether they should be *allowed* to make this decision at all. Scientists who currently argue that it is premature to recruit egg donors are not necessarily against egg donation in the future, once the processes are better understood, and there is a better chance that a woman's eggs might lead to the creation of a valuable stem cell line. Similarly, someone who argues that women are not likely to want to donate eggs altruistically, meaning that investment in a donation programme may not be a productive use of resources, is not saying that there would be something intrinsically *wrong* with a woman donating her eggs for research purposes.

Practical arguments against egg donation for research can, I would argue, be distinguished from the neopaternalist arguments against egg donation, which I discuss below. A scientist who says that it is too early to use women's eggs is not saying that a woman cannot take this decision for herself, rather he is saying that he does not think it is currently sensible to ask her to do so, perhaps because he believes that another source of eggs, such as animal eggs, could be used instead. Someone who argues that most women would not want to go through egg donation is also not contending that a woman who decides to donate her eggs is incapable of making this choice.

It may be true that few women would want to donate their eggs to basic research at this stage, but if they do want to do so, after receiving full and frank disclosure that the likelihood that their donation will result in a valuable stem cell line is, at this stage, relatively small, it is hard to see why the woman should not be permitted to make this choice for herself. In any event, whether it is true now or at some point in the near future, we can predict that there will be scientists who will want to recruit female egg donors for hESCR research, even if the numbers are always likely to be fairly small. It is therefore important to tackle the question of whether women should be permitted to donate eggs for research, since there are clearly many people who believe that, whatever the scientific merits of egg donation, the answer should always be 'no'. Those who object, *in principle*, to egg donation for research fall into two different camps. First, there are those who adopt feminist analysis, reminiscent of FINRRAGE's (Feminist International Network of Resistance to Reproductive and Genetic Engineering) opposition to reproductive technologies in the 1980s and 1990s. Second, pro-life campaigners, whose principal concern has traditionally been embryos rather than women, have realized that their arguments may reach a wider audience if they adopt women-friendly (as opposed to embryo-friendly) language.

IV. Feminist Objections to Egg Donation

In the 1980s, and into the 1990s, it was not unusual to come across feminist arguments against the use of assisted conception techniques. FINRRAGE, for example, argued that reproductive technologies reinforced the cultural assumption that a woman's primary purpose is to become a mother.[7] It was argued that these technologies (or rather scientists, doctors, and partners) put women under considerable pressure to undergo uncomfortable, invasive, and risky treatment, even when they themselves are fertile.[8] Some feminists therefore claimed that men—both women's partners and the medical/scientific establishment—were using these techniques to exploit women. The fact that treatment was risky, experimental, and had some unpleasant side-effects tended to be downplayed, it was argued, thus compromising women's ability to give truly informed consent.

These sorts of arguments are much less common now. Fertility treatment has become almost routine, and its ability to help create unconventional families—in particular single mother families and lesbian families—mean the majority of feminists do not now believe the use of assisted conception techniques is *always* against women's interests.

Yet in relation to egg donation for research purposes, these sorts of feminist arguments against the use of reproductive technologies have resurfaced.

---

[7] For an excellent summary of FINRRAGE's opposition to reproductive technologies, see N Lublin, *Pandora's Box: Feminism Confronts Reproductive Technology* (Lanham, Md: Rowman and Littlefield, 1998) 61–74.

[8] See, eg G Corea, *The Mother Machine* (London: The Women's Press, 1985); R Arditti, RD Klein, and S Minden (eds), *Test-tube Women* (London: Pandora Press, 1984).

FINRRAGE's hostility towards scientists' use of women's bodies appears to have found a new target. Egg donation for research does not have any subversive potential in helping women conceive without men, rather at present it serves only the interests of science and scientists. In the longer term, there may be therapeutic applications from stem cell research, but at present this is basic research, where the goal is simply the advancement of knowledge.

Feminists have criticized proponents of stem cell research for emphasizing the scientific and therapeutic potential of stem cell lines extracted from CNR embryos without mentioning that this research would be impossible without a plentiful supply of women's eggs. Ingrid Schneider, for example, has argued that 'clone research involves an immanent, but unspoken tendency towards a social obligation of the female body'.[9] She argues that women will be expected to provide the material resources for the treatment of the old and sick.[10] Renate Klein—one of the founding members of FINRRAGE—talks about 'the biotech industry's voracious appetite for eggs',[11] and argues that 'women's lives and bodies should not be invaded for the so-called "public good" ... Women should not be sacrificed to the vested interests of the biotechnology industry.' In particular, Klein is worried about the capacity of women to give properly informed consent. She suggests that 'with a focus not on women's health but on promised cures, women distressed by the suffering of a loved one will be under pressure to do the right thing and altruistically donate eggs'.[12] Beeson and Lippman are similarly concerned about women coming under pressure to consent to egg donation.[13] They argue that 'the apparently purposeful use of misleading language to describe this research has the potential to be coercive'.[14] Their proposed solution, however, is not to insist that women are given clear and comprehensive information, instead they propose 'a moratorium on egg harvesting for cloning purposes'.

An analogy might be drawn between women's agreement to donate eggs to a research project and participation in clinical trials. Where the participants in a clinical trial are also patients, it is widely recognized that they may be easily misled into believing that they will benefit from the research as a result of what is described as the 'therapeutic misconception'. Consent forms which set out what the study intends to achieve for *future* patients may exacerbate this problem, leading to confusion between the goals of the research and what patients hope to gain for themselves. The solution normally adopted to this problem is not, however, to

---

[9] 'Women as raw material suppliers for science and industry' in Reprokult (Women's Forum for Reproductive Medicine) *Reproductive Medicine and Genetic Engineering: Women between Self-determination and Societal Standardization* (2002) 76.

[10] ibid.

[11] 'Rhetoric of choice clouds dangers of harvesting women's eggs for cloning', at <http://www.onlineopinion.com.au/view.asp?article=5229> (accessed 14 June 2007).

[12] ibid.

[13] 'Egg harvesting for stem cell research: medical risks and ethical problems' (2007) *Reproductive Biomedicine Online* at <http://www.keinpatent.de/doc/RBM.pdf> (accessed 23 August 2007).

[14] ibid.

prevent patients from participating in research at all, but rather to ensure that information sheets and consent forms are as clear and frank as possible.

For altruistic egg donors, the therapeutic misconception does not arise in quite the same way, because they could be under no illusion that the process of egg donation will improve their own health. Rather it is possible that egg donors could be under the misapprehension that their donation is likely to benefit a sick relative. But just as in relation to patients taking part in clinical trials, the solution should be to inform women clearly and unambiguously that clinical applications of this sort of research are not likely to be available in time to treat someone who has already been diagnosed with a disease like Parkinson's. It is surely perfectly plausible that someone who has watched a close friend or relative suffer as a result of a degenerative disease might want to participate in a research trial in the certain knowledge that their participation will not lead to a cure for their loved one, but that it might improve scientists' knowledge of processes which have to be understood before therapies are developed, many years down the line.

It is also, of course, true that there are risks associated with ovarian stimulation, but proper monitoring should be able to minimize the chance of a woman suffering from OHSS. A parallel might again be drawn with participation in clinical trials, where subjects expose themselves to often unknowable risks. In relation to egg donation, the risks are at least well known, and the donor can be properly informed in advance. To say that women are not capable of weighing these risks up in advance, and of understanding clear information about the fact that this would be basic research, with no immediate therapeutic application, is, in my view, unacceptably paternalistic.

V. Pro-life Campaigners' (Strategic) Focus on Women

In the United Kingdom, pro-life activists who are against all research on embryos, have virtually no chance of getting Parliament to reopen the question of whether research on embryos should be permitted at all. Opinion polls consistently show that there is fairly widespread public support for embryo research, which may be due, at least in part, to the fact that research has been tightly regulated for the last seventeen years.

In recent years, the government has embarked on the lengthy process of reforming HFEA 1990. At the time of writing, it is anticipated that the Human Fertilisation and Embryology Bill will be introduced to Parliament in early 2008. This Bill will substantially amend some parts of the 1990 Act—for example, by offering new definitions of embryo and gametes—but importantly it simply takes for granted the legitimacy of carrying out research on embryos. When the Bill is debated in Parliament, opponents of embryo research will undoubtedly be among its most vocal critics, but there is, I would predict, virtually no chance that any new legislation will prohibit all research on embryos.

When the draft Bill was scrutinized by a Joint Committee of both Houses of Parliament, the Committee laid out a series of questions for those giving evidence. These questions were concerned with controversial issues like the creation of inter-species embryos; organizational questions about the proposed merger of the HFEA and the Human Tissue Authority; and definitional issues, such as how 'embryo', 'gamete', 'motherhood', and 'fatherhood' should be defined. The Committee did not ask people for their views as to whether embryo research should be permitted at all because banning all embryo research is simply no longer open for discussion as a realistic policy option.

In short then, with the exception of a few committed pro-life activists, there is little public or Parliamentary appetite for rehearsing the arguments for and against research on human embryos. The Bill, it could be argued, reflects the official consensus that embryo research is acceptable and that Britain should continue to facilitate, within a strict regulatory framework, scientific progress which depends upon the instrumental use of human embryos. If anything, as we can see from the worldwide reaction to the Korean stem cell scandal, the interests of the embryos themselves are *less* visible as an object of concern than they were seventeen years ago.

It might therefore be concluded that there is very little political mileage in a campaign against hESCR which is grounded in the moral status of a five-day-old embryo. Very few people in the United Kingdom are against all embryo research, but it might be predicted that more are concerned about risks to women's health. By focusing on the risks to women, rather than risks to embryos, it is therefore possible to appeal to a constituency which is considerably larger than the section of society which believes that a five-day-old embryo is a person.

This turn towards a focus on women's interests and women's health has facilitated a coalition with feminists best exemplified in the 'manifesto' and 'mission' of a campaign with the catchy name 'handsoffourovaries.com'. Its mission is explicitly to bring together 'pro-life' and 'pro-choice' activists in order 'to find and give expression to a voice of common concern: making the health and welfare of women central to the planning of any biotechnological research that seeks to use their bodies or tissues'.[15] In placing women's interests at the centre of pro-life opposition to human embryonic stem cell research, we can see an interesting parallel with pro-life opposition to abortion, which has also, as I explain in the next section, sought to focus on harms to *women*, rather than harms to foetal or embryonic life.

VI. From Foetus-centred to Women-centred Arguments Against Abortion

Just as in relation to embryo research, in the United Kingdom there must be virtually no chance that pro-life campaigners will succeed in having abortion

---

[15] <http://handsoffourovaries.com/mission.htm> (accessed 14 August 2007).

recriminalized. In the United States too, despite the fairly constant chipping away at the principle in *Roe v Wade*[16] through funding restrictions, waiting periods, directive counselling, and restrictions on certain abortion procedures, it is unlikely that abortion will be completely banned. Very few people in fact believe that the foetus has exactly the same moral status as a human person. The widespread acceptance that abortion is legitimate where the pregnancy is the result of rape, for example, offers evidence that the vast majority of people do not think that an eight-week-old foetus has the same moral status as an eight-year-old child. Pro-life activists have not abandoned their fundamental belief in the foetus's full moral status, but it is clear that the section of the community which shares this belief is too small to have much impact upon law reform. Many more people are, however, concerned about women's health and well-being.

Until fairly recently a common strategy of anti-abortion campaigners was to pit the life of the foetus against the 'desires' or 'wishes' of pregnant women. In the debates which preceded the passage of the Abortion Act 1967, Jill Knight MP claimed that women who sought abortions treated babies... 'like bad teeth to be jerked out just because they cause suffering... simply because it may be inconvenient for a year or so to its mother'.[17]

Since the 1990s, there has been an interesting change of focus, which has been particularly evident in the United States. Rather than arguing that the foetus's interest in continued life should take precedence over the pregnant woman's interest in deciding what happens to her body, the new strategy involves the claim that abortion is bad for women too. With this, Emily Bazelon argues, pro-life campaigners hope to:

...accomplish what the anti-abortion movement has failed to do for more than three decades: persuade the 'mushy middle' of the American electorate—the perhaps 40 to 50 per cent who are uncomfortable with abortion but unwilling to ban it—to see that, for women's sake, abortion should not be legal.[18]

David Reardon, a prominent anti-abortion campaigner in the US, has argued that the 'solution' to bad publicity is:

...to *always*—ALWAYS—place our arguments for the unborn in the middle of a pro-woman sandwich. Our compassion for the women must be voiced both first and last in all our arguments, and in a manner which shows that our concern for women is a primary and integral part of our opposition to abortion. (emphasis in original)[19]

---

[16] 410 US 113 (1973).
[17] Knight, HC Deb, Vol 732, col 1100, 1966 (22 July).
[18] E Bazelon, 'Is there a post-abortion syndrome' *The New York Times,* 21 January 2007.
[19] D Reardon, *Making Abortion Rare: A Healing Strategy for a Divided Nation'* (Acorn Books, 1996) 26.

Rather than denigrating women who choose abortion, Reardon's strategy is to increase public sympathy for women, and 'align it with our own outrage at how women are being victimized'.[20]

So instead of urging us to accept that abortion is equivalent to murder, and that women who seek to terminate unwanted pregnancies are feckless and irresponsible, pro-life activists have sought to persuade us that abortion is bad for women's health. It is argued that women suffer psychological harm as a result of abortion: they regret their abortions, and are wracked by guilt and bereavement for years afterwards. Campaigners have claimed that post-abortion syndrome (PAS) is a species of post-traumatic stress disorder (PTSD). Links between abortion and infertility are often made, and it has even been claimed that abortion causes breast cancer. Websites with the testimonies of abortion 'survivors', who recount their regret, and the ill-effects they have suffered, have proliferated.[21]

The claim that abortion is bad for women's health is not, however, backed up by the evidence.

In 1989, the American Psychological Association (APA) convened a panel of psychologists to review the data on the psychological consequences of abortion. They concluded that the most scientifically rigorous studies could find no evidence of 'post-abortion syndrome', and that PAS is not recognized by scientists or doctors. Their conclusion was that abortion has 'no lasting or significant health risks'. Many studies have taken place since, and they have all tended to confirm the APA's conclusions. In one eight-year study of 5,295 women, it was evident that the most important predictor of emotional well-being in women who have terminated unwanted pregnancies was their well-being before the abortion took place.[22] Russo and Dabul conclude that 'the experience of having an abortion plays a negligible, if any, independent role in women's well-being over time, regardless of race or religion'.[23]

In another study, Schmiege and Russo found 'no evidence of an association between abortion and depression'.[24] They compared women who carried an initially unwanted pregnancy to term with those that had chosen termination, and 'found no evidence that terminating compared with delivering an unwanted first pregnancy changes risk for subsequent depression'. Gilchrist *et al* carried out a similar study in which the health of 13,261 British women who had either continued or aborted unintended pregnancies was tracked for eleven years. They

---

[20] ibid 27.
[21] See, eg <http://www.afterabortion.org/> (accessed 14 August 2007) and <http://www.operationoutcry.org/> (accessed 14 August 2007).
[22] NF Russo and KL Zierk, 'Abortion, childbearing, and women's well-being,' (1992) 23(4) *Professional Psychology: Research and Practice* 269.
[23] NF Russo and AJ Dabul, 'The relationship of abortion to well-being: Do race and religion make a difference?' (1997) 28(1) *Professional Psychology: Research and Practice* 1.
[24] S Schmiege and NF Russo 'Depression and unwanted first pregnancy: longitudinal cohort study' (2005) 331 *BMJ* 1136.

found that rates of reported psychiatric disorders were no higher after termination of pregnancy than after childbirth. Women who had a previous history of psychiatric illness were most at risk of suffering from a mental disorder after the end of their pregnancy, regardless of whether they had given birth or had a termination.[25]

Of course since abortion and depression are both fairly common life experiences—one in three women will have an abortion at some point during their lives and one in four women will suffer from some sort of mental health problem—some overlap between these two groups of women is inevitable. But the fact that there are some women who have mental health problems after abortion does not establish a causal link. All the evidence instead suggests that pre-existing mental health is a much more important predictor of mental health after pregnancy, regardless of whether the woman has an abortion or carries the pregnancy to term.[26]

But despite the scientific and medical establishment's rejection of the claim that abortion poses a risk to women's health, it is an allegation which has had considerable purchase. In the United Kingdom, it is possible that pro-life campaigners will take the opportunity presented by the passage of the Human Fertilisation and Embryology Bill to bring forward amendments which will impose mandatory counselling requirements, whereby women would have to be told about the potential negative effects for them of terminating their pregnancies. In the United States, evidence of the effectiveness of these pro-women anti-abortion arguments can be found in South Dakota's recent attempt to ban virtually all abortions, and in what Ronald Dworkin has described as the 'grossly paternalistic' majority judgment in the recent Supreme Court case of *Gonzales v Carhart*.[27]

A. South Dakota

In 2006, South Dakota enacted a statute which would have outlawed all abortion procedures, except where an abortion was necessary to prevent the pregnant woman's death. The statute was ultimately struck down following a referendum, but what is important about South Dakota's direct challenge to *Roe v Wade*[28] was that it was grounded in the evidentially suspect claim that a ban on abortion would promote women's health and well-being. The South Dakotan statute resulted from a report produced by a Task Force set up to look at the question of abortion.[29] Most of the Task Force's Report is devoted to fleshing out the claim that women need to be protected from having abortions which they do not want, and which are bad for their health and well-being. Women, according to the

[25] AC Gilchrist, PC Hannaford, P Frank, and CR Kray, 'Termination of pregnancy and psychiatric morbidity' (1995) 167 *The British Journal of Psychiatry* 243.
[26] n 22 above.   [27] US 550 (2007).
[28] 410 US 113 (1973).
[29] 'Report of the Sourth Dakota Task Force to Study Abortion' (2005) at <http://www.voteyesforlife.com/docs/Task_Force_Report.pdf> (accessed 21 August 2007).

Task Force, are commonly misled or coerced into having abortions, often by the 'unjust and selfish demands of male sexual partners',[30] and they are damaged for years afterwards as a result.

The Task Force accuses abortion providers of misinforming women and mis-representing what abortion involves. It claims that 'in the overwhelming majority of cases, the decision to submit to an abortion is uninformed'.[31] But the solution advocated is not to insist that women should have access to clear and compre-hensive information. Rather the Task Force suggests that no amount of informa-tion could, in fact, enable a woman to give properly informed consent because a woman cannot make a truly informed decision about her relationship with her child until after the child is born.

Rejecting all of the data, referred to above, which suggests that abortion has no lasting health risks, the Task Force Report instead claims that abortion causes a long list of mental disorders, including bipolar affective disorder, psychosis, schizophrenia, depression, PTSD, and suicidal ideation. It maintains that women who have had abortions are more likely to have substance abuse problems; sexual and relationship difficulties; and that they are more likely to be abusive or failed mothers. All these ill effects occur because, according to the Task Force:

... it is simply unrealistic to expect that a pregnant mother [sic] is capable of being involved in the termination of the life of her own child without risk of suffering significant psycho-logical trauma and distress. To do so is beyond the normal, natural, and healthy capabil-ity of a woman whose natural instincts are to protect and nurture her child.

Rather than ground its claims in scientific evidence, the Task Force relies upon women's 'natural' maternal role in order to claim that it is axiomatic that abortion must hurt women, because it involves a woman (unnaturally) rejecting mother-hood. The 'relationship' a mother has with her child, 'at every moment of life', is celebrated in the Report for its inherently 'unselfish nature'.[32]

In order to remind women about the importance of this 'unselfish' relation-ship, the South Dakotan statute would have required abortion providers to advise the woman, two hours before any procedure, 'that abortion will termin-ate the life of a whole, separate and unique, living human being', with whom she has an existing relationship that enjoys protection under the law and the US Constitution. Despite being contrary to accepted medical knowledge, the stat-ute would also have demanded that doctors inform their patients about the risks to which the pregnant woman would be subject if she has an abortion including 'depression and related psychological distress, increased risk of suicide, and risks to the physical health of the woman including infection, hemorrhage [sic] and infertility'. In short, as Robert Post has succinctly explained, 'the objective of the Act is to use the concept of informed consent to eliminate abortions'.[33]

[30] ibid 31–2.   [31] ibid 37.   [32] ibid 67.
[33] R Post, 'Informed Consent to Abortion: A First Amendment Analysis of Compelled Physician Speech' (2007) *University of Illinois Law Review* 939, 941.

B. *Gonzales v Carhart*[34]

In the *Gonzales* case, by a 5 to 4 majority, the Supreme Court decided that a state law which banned a certain type of abortion procedure, used late in pregnancy, called intact D&X, did not impose an 'undue burden' on women's access to abortion, and hence was constitutional. The majority opinion, written by Justice Kennedy, claimed that women would be protected by a rule which prevents them from consenting to a particular sort of abortion. Women who have had abortions, Kennedy reasoned, come to regret them, and this regret is bound to be much more serious when they realize how the abortion was carried out. Intact D&X is, like many procedures used late in pregnancy, 'gruesome', and so Kennedy thought it likely that many doctors would not tell their patients precisely what it involves. This would compromise the woman's ability to give informed consent and, as a result, he maintained that the state was justified in banning the procedure.

With respect, surely a more logical response to any concern that doctors will withhold important facts from their patients is to insist that women *are* told what intact D&X entails, so that they can then make an informed choice. As Justice Ginsburg succinctly puts it in a footnote to her dissenting judgement: 'Eliminating or reducing women's reproductive choices is manifestly *not* a means of protecting them.'

The most significant aspect of the *Gonzales* decision is not, in practice, the prospect that doctors will no longer be able to conduct intact D&X procedures. This will have limited impact upon access to abortion because only about thirty American doctors use this method of abortion. Only about 2,200 of the 1.3 million abortions which take place in the United States each year involve intact D&X (less than 0.12 percent). Doctors who no longer have this option can, at the same late stage in pregnancy, choose to perform a D&E instead, and so the decision in *Gonzales* may not, in fact, prevent a single abortion from taking place.

Of course, it could be argued that the court should not be in the business of limiting doctors' clinical discretion. The evidence cited in Justice Ginsburg's vigorous dissent suggests that there are doctors who strongly believe that intact D&X poses less risk to women's health than the alternative, particularly for women with certain pre-exisiting conditions, such as uterine scarring, bleeding disorders, heart disease, or compromised immune systems. In these cases, the Supreme Court's decision in the *Gonzales* case will force doctors to act contrary to their clinical judgment, placing them, according to Justice Ginsburg, 'in an untenable position'.

This is, of course, serious, but the more important feature of the *Gonzales* judgment, in my view, is Justice Kennedy's argument that restrictions upon access to abortion are necessary in order to safeguard women's capacity to give informed

[34] No 05-380 (decided 18 April 2007).

consent. As Jack Balkin has argued, Kennedy's 'opinion opens the door for states to pass increasingly unreasonable versions of abortion restrictions designed to frighten, manipulate, and discomfit women under the guise of providing informed consent'.[35]

What is clear from the majority's judgment in *Gonzales* is that the unscientific claims of the anti-abortion lobby—the claim that abortion poses a risk to women's health—have exerted considerable influence over the highest court in America. Evidence, perhaps, that the strategic decision to focus on women's health rather than foetal life has worked. In a remarkable parallel with the South Dakota Task Force's Report, Kennedy assumes that, regardless of the evidence base, the ill-effects abortion has for women can simply be read across from women's natural maternal instincts: 'While we find *no reliable data* to measure the phenomenon, it seems unexceptionable to conclude some women come to regret their choice to abort the infant life they once created and sustained. Severe depression and loss of esteem can follow' (my emphasis).

VII. Neopaternalism?

There is an interesting parallel between the explicit paternalism evident in the South Dakota Task Force Report and the *Gonzales* judgment, and the arguments which were common currency in 1967 when abortion was partially decriminalized in the United Kingdom. As is well known, the passage of the Abortion Act 1967 did not emerge from concern about women's rights or women's reproductive autonomy, but rather from paternalistic concern about the risks abortion's illegality posed to women's health.[36] Abortion had to be legalized, not so that women could act autonomously, but so that doctors could act *paternalistically* in protecting the lives and interests of 'desperate' pregnant women, who would either be driven to distraction by having another mouth to feed, or would resort to unsafe and insanitary backstreet abortions.[37]

There is, however, at least superficially, a twist in these new pro-women arguments against abortion, which distinguishes them from the more straightforward paternalism of the past. This time the emphasis is not upon doctors taking decisions on behalf of their patients: it is not about 'doctor knows best'. Rather the emphasis is upon the female patient's *right* to make an informed choice. The rhetoric of the anti-abortion movement, here exemplified by David Reardon, is

---

[35] J Balkin, 'The Big News About Gonzales v. Carhart—It's the Informed Consent, Stupid', at <http://balkin.blogspot.com/2007/04/big-news-about-gonzales-v-carhart.html> (accessed 21 August 2007).
[36] See eg Sally Sheldon's seminal study on the background to the 1967 Act: Sheldon, *Beyond Control: Medical Power and Abortion Law* (London: Pluto Press, 1997).
[37] ibid.

attempting to enlist the language of autonomy, choice, and rights as reasons to *oppose* abortion. He argues that the anti-abortion movement needs to:

> ... take back the terms 'freedom of choice' and 'reproductive freedom' ... to emphasize the fact that we are the ones who are really defending the right of women to make an informed choice; we are the ones who are defending the freedom of women to reproduce without fear of being coerced into unwanted abortions.[38]

But are women really being addressed as choosing agents, capable of weighing up information and making decisions for themselves? The South Dakota Report, for example, suggested that women seeking abortions 'may be subject to pressures which can cause an emotional crisis, undue reliance on the advice of others, clouded judgment, and a willingness to violate conscience to avoid those pressures'. Rather than protecting women's choices and autonomy, *all* women's decision-making capacity is being questioned on the grounds, perhaps, either that the hormonal changes associated with pregnancy inevitably interfere with rational decision-making, or that the very fact that a woman is contemplating terminating her pregnancy reveals that she is mentally unstable. This is neopaternalism, in that the emphasis is upon women's freedom of choice and women's right to make informed decisions, but at the same time it is underpinned by some very old-fashioned assumptions about women's frailty, particularly in relation to reproduction.

VIII. Neopaternalism in Relation to Egg Donation?

That pro-life activists have mobilized some rather regressive and negative gender stereotypes in order to push forward their agenda of banning abortion is not necessarily surprising. What is more troubling, in my opinion, is that there is a remarkable parallel between feminist opposition to egg donation to stem cell research and the sort of neopaternalistic reasoning evident in the South Dakota Task Force's Report and Justice Kennedy's Supreme Court judgment. Rather than saying women need proper information and the option of making a decision for themselves, based upon full information, this new line of so-called feminist argument suggests that you protect women by taking choices away from them, on the grounds that they are overwhelmingly likely to make decisions which are bad for them.

Participants at a seminar, 'Feminist Issues in Contemporary UK Bioethics: Sourcing Eggs for Biomedical Research', organized by Cesagen ESRC genomics centre, published a 'Statement of concerns in response to the HFEA public consultation on donating eggs for research' in which they suggest that one reason to oppose egg donation for research is that it would be difficult for women to give

---

[38] Reardon (n 19 above) 96.

informed consent at a time of stress.[39] They claim that 'Social scientific research shows that people experiencing high level [sic] of stress find it difficult to process information and to make decisions'. As a result, they question what 'informed consent would mean in this context'.

If we were concerned that stress makes obtaining informed consent problematic, we should have to be suspicious about consent given to a wide range of medical procedures. Consent to the removal of a tumour comes at a time of extreme stress, yet there is no doubt that we assume stressed patients are still capable of weighing up the risks and benefits of treatment. Of course, it might be argued that the decision to consent to the removal of a tumour could be distinguished from the decision to consent to egg donation on the grounds that deciding to have a tumour removed is overwhelmingly in the patient's best interests. But it is important to remember that the patient's right to consent entails a right to refuse a treatment which might be beneficial, and even life-saving. Patients who are stressed therefore have the right to make decisions which might be likely to lead to their deaths, and yet the fact that such a decision is made at a time of stress does not mean that their decision-making autonomy is impugned.

It is hard to understand why feminists would want to argue that stressed women's decisions should not be binding upon them, or that women are not capable of weighing up the risks and benefits of taking part in research. The solution to the 'problem' of informed consent in the context of research on human subjects is normally to insist upon the provision of information, and upon other safeguards to ensure that potential participants are able to decide freely and without coming under undue pressure whether to participate. Why should egg donors be treated differently? Of course, one possible explanation is that egg donation is simply too risky, and the benefits from egg donation are too speculative to justify carrying out a research trial. Article 17 of the Helsinki Declaration, for example, states that 'Physicians should abstain from engaging in research projects involving human subjects unless they are confident that the risks involved have been adequately assessed and can be satisfactorily managed', and, under Article 18, 'research should only be conducted if the importance of the objective outweighs the inherent risks and burdens to the subject'.

It would be difficult to argue that egg donation is too risky, since the risk of OHSS is small, well-known, and can usually be properly managed by careful monitoring. It is a risk we permit women to bear repeatedly in their efforts to conceive a child. If egg retrieval is safe enough for a woman to choose to undergo it for one purpose, it is hard to see why a woman who wishes to undergo egg donation for another purpose should not be permitted to do so. In short, if the argument that egg donation is too risky is successful, it proves too much, because

---

[39] <http://www.cesagen.lancs.ac.uk/events/eventsdocs/HFEA_sourcing_eggs.pdf> (accessed 23 August 2007).

we should have to cast doubt on whether anyone should be permitted to consent to IVF, ICSI, or stimulated IUI.

What about the claim that the benefits of stem cell science are too speculative to justify egg donation? At present there is some dispute between prominent scientists in the United Kingdom over whether basic hESCR should be conducted using human or animal eggs. But none of them disagree that this basic research is vitally important, and that the potential benefits from hESCR are extraordinary. Certainly the potential benefits of hESCR far outstrip those in many clinical trials where volunteers have been known to expose themselves to considerable risks for marginal scientific benefits.

My point is simply that women who want to donate their eggs to research should be treated in the same way as other participants in research trials. Unlike the donors of spare or leftover eggs and embryos, altruistic egg donors are exposing themselves to small risks and a degree of discomfort and inconvenience in order to further scientific knowledge. This is a laudable enterprise, and we should not be in the business of patronizing women by assuming that they are incapable of weighing the risks and benefits of participation for themselves. We normally protect participants in research trials by insisting that they must be properly informed and that their consent must be given voluntarily and without duress. In addition research protocols must have the approval of an ethics committee, which has a duty to judge the information given to potential participants, and the consent process. For hESCR, there is an additional layer of protection, because the researchers must have a licence from the HFEA, and, again, the HFEA's Research Licence Committee scrutinizes information sheets and consent protocols especially carefully. Moreover, the HFEA's prohibition on payment for egg donation rules out, in the United Kingdom at least, the sorts of incentives commonly offered in clinical trials, such as the trial of TGN 1412 at Northwick Park Hospital, where it was evident that the participants only chose to expose themselves to risks much greater than those involved in the process of egg donation, in return for £2,000.[40]

If I feel very strongly about the importance of pursuing hESCR, and I decide that I would like to donate my eggs to such a project, I find it difficult to see what objection a feminist could have to me taking this decision for myself. Of course, if the objection to stem cell research is instead that it involves the destruction of embryos, then it is clear that there is no source of eggs which would render this sort of research acceptable. And this is the point at which the unholy alliance between feminists and pro-life activists may start to unravel. Using animal eggs might solve the problem for feminists whose concern is with risks to women's health, but it will not satisfy those whose real objection is, and will always be, the destruction of embryos.

---

[40] See MHRA, 'Investigation into Adverse Incidents during Clinical Trials of TGN1412' (2006).

17

Regulating the Reproductive Revolution: Ectogenesis—A Regulatory Minefield?

*Amel Alghrani**

I. Regulating Reproduction

12.7 It has been suggested that in the long term further development of current techniques could result in the maintenance of developing embryos in an artificial environment (ectogenesis) for progressively longer periods with the ultimate aim of creating a child entirely *in vitro*. This technique, it is argued would make it possible to study in detail normal and abnormal human development at the embryonic and foetal stages.

12.8 We appreciate why the possibility of such a technique arouses so much anxiety. There are however two points to make about this. First, such developments are well in to the future, certainly beyond the time horizon within which this inquiry feels that it can predict. Secondly, our recommendation is that the growing of a human embryo *in vitro* beyond fourteen days should be a criminal offence.[1]

The above statement was made by the Warnock Committee in its 1984 report, illustrating that when considering the legal and ethical issues raised by assisted reproductive technologies, the possibility of ectogenesis, an advance which could allow a foetus to be brought to term outside the womb, was not unheard of. The Warnock Committee, after briefly considering this possibility, was quick in dismissing it as a far off thing that might never happen. However, as scientists constantly strive to perfect this technology, and developments in neonatal care continue to reduce viability, the reality of ectogenesis may not be as far off as the Warnock Committee imagined. Some of those working within the field predict ectogenesis will be possible within the next twenty years.[2] Development of this technology is expected to be the next radical breakthrough in the arena of

* PhD Candidate and Research Associate at the University of Manchester.
[1] Warnock Report, *The Report of the Committee of Inquiry into Human Fertilisation and Embryology* (Cmnd 9314, 1984) 71–2.
[2] A Newson, 'From foetus to full term—without a mother's touch' *The Times*, 30 August 2005, at <http://www.timesonline.co.uk/article/0%2C%2C2-1755908%2C00.html>.

artificial reproductive technologies, and has aptly been labelled 'the third era of reproduction'.[3] If indeed ectogenesis is in the offing, ethicists, and lawyers need to begin thinking about how they may countenance the many difficult questions regulating this technology will pose.

In the United Kingdom, the principal means of regulating assisted reproductive technologies derives from the Human Fertilisation and Embryology Act 1990 (HFEA 1990). Despite the fact that the Act is only eighteen years old, recent advances have highlighted the inadequacies of that legislation to regulate both present and future reproductive advances. Legal challenges on numerous issues ranging from disputes over frozen embryos,[4] the creation of saviour siblings,[5] and the controversy surrounding reproductive cloning[6] have all exposed the weaknesses of the present legislation. As pointed out by Margaret Brazier: 'Warnock deliberated at a very early stage of the "reproductive revolution". Neither the science, nor the infrastructure which now underpins the 'reproductive business' was well developed.'[7]

Following a recent review of HFEA 1990,[8] the government belatedly accepted that it is time to redraft the legislation governing assisted reproduction, and the Human Fertilization and Embryology Bill is currently being considered.[9] In addition to this legislation being reviewed, the House of Commons Science and Technology Committee recently conducted an inquiry into scientific developments relating to the Abortion Act 1967, specifically addressing time limits.[10] As a new development in the realm of artificial reproduction, which will no doubt have a direct impact on the abortion debate, ectogenesis now merits serious consideration.

At the outset it is argued that the greatest challenge for regulating reproduction is the fact that the government legislates reactively as opposed to proactively. Warnock's response to ectogenesis, quickly dismissing it as a far off notion 'well in to the horizon', epitomizes the reactive approach often undertaken by the British government when it comes to regulating reproduction. It is only when

---

[3] S Wellin, 'Reproductive Ectogenesis: The third era of human reproduction and some moral consequences' (2004) 10 *Science and Engineering Ethics* 615.

[4] *Natalie Evans v Amicus Healthcare Ltd and Ors; Lorraine Hadley v Midland Fertility Services Ltd and Ors* [2003] EWHC 2161, [2004] 1 FLR 67 (Fam); *Natalie Evans v Amicus Healthcare Ltd and Ors* [2004] EWCA (Civ) 72, [2004] 2 FLR 766, CA; *Case of Evans v The United Kingdom* (Application No 6339/2005), [2006] 1 FCR 585 (ECtHR); *Evans v United Kingdom* (Application No 6339/05); [2007] 22 BHRC 190, 54 (ECtHR).

[5] *R (on the application of Quintavalle) v HFEA* [2003] 3 All ER 257, [2005] 2 All ER 555.

[6] *R v Secretary of State for Health, ex p Quintavalle* [2003] 2 WLR 692, reproductive cloning was deemed unlawful in the UK by the House of Lords interpretation of HFEA 1990.

[7] M Brazier, 'Regulating the Reproduction Business' (1999) *Medical Law Review* 166, 173.

[8] White Paper: *Review of the Human Fertilisation and Embryology Act—Proposals for revised legislation (including establishment of the Regulatory Authority for Tissue and Embryos)* (Cm 6989, 2006).

[9] See proposed Human Fertilisation and Embryology Bill.

[10] House of Commons Science and Technology Committee, *Scientific Developments Relating to the Abortion Act 1967,* volume 1 (Twelfth Report of Session 2006–07), 1045–1.

new technology is upon us that the government is jolted into legislative action. Consider the issue of reproductive cloning. The government was aware that scientists were researching the technology needed for this advance, but it was only when Dolly the sheep attracted mass media attention,[11] and the subsequent legal challenge was brought as to the legality of reproductive cloning[12] that the government reacted by swiftly rushing the Human Reproductive Cloning Act 2001[13] through Parliament. Regulating on an ad hoc basis is, arguably, not the most effective form of regulation. The only way to 'reconnect the Act with modern science' in accordance with the recommendations of the Science and Technology Committee,[14] is if the government is prepared for those future technologies looming on the foreseeable horizon.

In seeking to address how the government can be more proactive in its regulation of reproduction, I plan to consider the development of ectogenesis and how the British government can prepare itself for such a radical breakthrough. Legislators will have to address how ectogenesis could be regulated and how it will address many of the potential disputes that may arise. In developing a regulatory framework which accommodates this new technological advance it may well be the case that the government will have the barbed task of re-examining the status of the human embryo. Many of the cases that have generated legal rules and principles on the status of the unborn have developed in the context of the abortion debate[15], and cases of maternal–foetal conflict, where a foetus is being gestated in its mother's womb.[16] This is significantly different from the situation of foetuses that would have an independent physical existence, and that would be gestated in an ectogenic device.

In considering the complex myriad of legal and ethical questions that ectogenesis raises, my strategy for this chapter is as follows: I will begin by briefly describing how, contrary to Warnock's prediction, ectogenesis may arrive much sooner than anticipated and discuss how we already have a form of ectogenesis in the neonatal ward. The discussion will then be split into two parts; the first

---

[11] For a few of the articles featured in the media see L Rogers and J Harlow 'Science close to human clone' *Sunday Times*, 31 August 1997; S Dodd 'Human Cloning: "This stuff is straight out of the Nazis tinkering with Hitler clones in the jungle": Scientists predict human cloning in two years' *The Mirror*, 7 March, 1997; E Wilson 'Are clones such as Dolly programmed for an early death?' *Daily Mail* (London) 27 May 1999; C Arthur 'Laboratories are told they may produce embryo human clones' *The Independent* (London) 30 January 1998.

[12] See *R (Quintavalle) v Secretary of State for Health* [2001] EWHC 918 (Admin), [2001] 4 All ER 1013. For more on the cloning debacle, see J Herring, 'Cloning In The House Of Lords' (2003) 33 *Family Law* 663.

[13] The Act prohibits the act of placing in a woman a human embryo which has been created otherwise than by fertilization.

[14] House of Commons Science and Technology Committee, *Human Reproductive Technologies and the Law Volume 1* (Fifth Report of Session 2004–05) HC 7-I (24 March 2005) at 2.

[15] *Paton v BPAS* [1979] QB 276; *C v S* [1987] 1 All ER 1230.

[16] *Re MB* (1997) 38 BMLR 175, *St George's Health Care Trust v S* [1998] 1 All ER 673, *Rochdale Healthcare (NHS) Trust v C* [1997] 1 FCR 274, *Norfolk and Norwich Health Care (NHS) Trust v W* [1996] 2 FLR 613; *Bolton Hospitals NHS Trust v O* [2003] I FLR 824.

part examines partial ectogenesis, whereby conception and gestation initially take place within the woman's body but at some point during the pregnancy the foetus is transferred to an ectogenic device for the remaining gestation period. In this section I will briefly examine the law on abortion, considering how ectogenesis will impact on the controversial area. I will ask if, as Christopher Kaczor claims, ectogenesis and foetal transfer could be used in lieu of abortion and 'end the abortion debate'.[17] Having addressed this, I will then consider the parallel situation of how ectogenesis has the potential to increase the reproductive choices of women who may want to end their pregnancy but not the life of the foetus. I will argue that women should be permitted to do this as an alternative to either pregnancy or abortion.

The second part of this chapter will focus on complete ectogenesis, whereby a foetus is created outside a woman's body (via IVF) and then immediately transferred into an artificial womb where it is gestated for the entire forty-week period. The mother's body is never used in the gestation process. This section focuses on questions legislators will have to address in posing a regulatory framework. Here I examine (1) whether current legislation could be extended to such ectogenic foetuses; (2) what status and legal protection should be conferred on the independent foetus gestating outside the maternal womb; (3) disputes over the custody of an ectogenic baby; and (4) whether ectogenesis will signal a green light for foetal rescue.

II. Partial Ectogenesis

A. Ectogenesis—Far Off on the Horizon?

The Warnock Committee found false reassurance in the view that ectogenesis was 'well in to the future, certainly beyond the time horizon within which this inquiry feels that it can predict' and that in any event the problem would be abated by the recommendation 'that the growing of a human embryo *in vitro* beyond fourteen days should be a criminal offence'.[18]

As expounded by Peter Singer, ectogenesis is likely to come about by the gradual discovery of new methods of keeping the human embryo or foetus alive at the beginning or end of its gestational period in the womb: 'The period in which it is necessary for the human foetus to be in the womb is shrinking from both sides.'[19] The live human embryo can safely be kept in a petri dish for the first fourteen days. Beyond fourteen days, any research into complete ectogenesis which involves placing a fertilized embryo in an ectogenic device, designed to

---

[17] C Kaczor, 'Could Artificial Wombs End the Abortion Debate' (2005) 5(2) *National Catholic Bioethics Quarterly* 283.

[18] Warnock Report (n 1 above).

[19] P Singer and D Wells, *The Reproduction Revolution* (Oxford: Oxford University Press, 1984) 132.

carry the resulting foetus to term would be a criminal activity.[20] However partial ectogenesis, where the foetus is conceived in the maternal womb but spends some of the typical forty-week gestation period in an artificial womb or ectogenic device, already occurs around the world in the treatment of extremely premature babies. Advances in neonatal technology have reduced the amount of time that the foetus needs to spend in the mother's womb from the normal forty weeks, down to twenty-four weeks.[21] It has even been possible to salvage the lives of premature babies born earlier; consider the case of Amillia Taylor reported to be one of the world's most premature babies.[22] Amillia Taylor was conceived by natural reproduction, but at twenty-two weeks' gestation complications in the pregnancy arose. A caesarean section was performed, and the baby was delivered weighing a mere 280 grams and measuring 9.5 inches (around 24 cm). She was immediately transferred to a technologically advanced incubator in the neonatal intensive care unit for a further sixteen weeks. Against all odds, Amillia Taylor left the hospital 'healthy and thriving'.[23]

The technology deployed in the neonatal intensive care unit can be deemed to be ectogenic—it is technology which can mimic the functions of the maternal womb in the latter stages of pregnancy. When it comes to the treatment of premature babies, arguably very few dispute the use of such technology to rescue the lives of babies born on the thresholds of viability. It should be noted that at present such technology is not perfect, and while sophisticated technology may help to sustain the lives of extremely premature babies, those born at borderline viability are often afflicted with complications, disabilities, and a 50 per cent or less chance of survival.[24] But the fact remains that advances in neonatal technology continue to drive down the amount of time a foetus needs to spend in the maternal womb. The Nuffield Council recently noted that the limits of viability have fallen by approximately one week every decade over the past forty years which 'may be attributed at least in part to advances in technology and

---

[20] HFEA 1990, s 3(3) prohibits the use of embryos beyond the primitive streak. s 3(4): 'For the purposes of subsection (3)(a) above, the primitive streak is to be taken to have appeared in an embryo not later than the end of the period of 14 days beginning with the day when the gametes are mixed, not counting any time during which the embryo is stored.' The legislation also makes it mandatory to obtain a licence before any research in carried out on a human embryo. HFEA 1990, Sch 2 sets out what may be authorized by a licence.

[21] The Nuffield Council on Bioethics, 'Critical Care Decisions in Foetal and Neonatal Medicine: Ethical Issues', (November 2006) at <http://www.nuffieldbioethics.org/fileLibrary/pdf/CCD_web_version_8_November.pdf> (herein after 'Critical Care Decisions') states that viability is said to be at 24 weeks. Prior to viability, for instance at 23 weeks, normal practice would be to not resuscitate (para 9.18). Any attempts to resuscitate babies born below 22 weeks of gestation are to be regarded as experimental (para 9.19).

[22] J Moorhead 'Against All Odds', The Guardian, 21 Feburary 2007, at <http://www.guardian.co.uk/society/2007/fab/21/health.lifeandhealth> (accessed 1 June 2008).

[23] 'Most-premature baby allowed home', 21 February 2007, at <http://news.bbc.co.uk/1/hi/world/americas/6384621.stm> (accessed 25 August 2007).

[24] Nuffield Council on Bioethics, 'Critical Care Decisions' (n 21 above) para 5.4.

care'.[25] The incubators which help to treat premature babies are in essence ectogenic incubators mimicking the function of the maternal womb. It is anticipated
that as neonatal care continues to improve, viability will continue to be pushed
back to earlier stages of gestation, further reducing the amount of time the foetus needs to spend in the maternal womb. Through sustained improvement in
neonatal care, inadvertently we are discovering what ingredients are needed for
an ectogenic incubator which can gestate from fertilization to term. As noted
by Stephen Coleman: 'If premature newborns are saved from earlier and earlier
stages of gestation, then eventually the technique of ectogenesis may be discovered almost by default, without the necessity of any possibly unethical research
on the unborn'.[26]

This raises two important questions for regulators: first if the law is interested
in protecting foetal life, particularly after viability, and the current stance adopted
by the government is that both human embryo and foetus have a 'special status'
and thus should be afforded some protection in law,[27] could ectogenesis signal
an end to abortion? Could the state mandate that all unwanted foetuses must be
carried until it is safe for the foetus to be transferred in to an ectogenic incubator,
thereby prohibiting abortions which terminate the life of the foetus? Secondly,
and perhaps the reverse of this scenario, can women who wish to end their pregnancy but not the life of the foetus they are carrying, opt for ectogenesis?

B. Abortion Legislation—the Foetus is Protected

At this juncture it is necessary to set out the law on abortion in order to illustrate how, in England and Wales, the state has long had an interest in protecting
foetal life, and to consider how partial and complete ectogenesis may impact on
abortion.

It is clear that while English law bestows no rights on the foetus[28], the unborn
have long had the protection of the criminal law in England and Wales.[29] As far
back as 1803, procuring the miscarriage of a woman who was 'quick with child'
was a statutory offence subject to capital punishment.[30] The law remained the
same until 1861, when sections 58 and 59 of the Offences Against The Persons

---

[25] ibid para 5.1.

[26] S Coleman, *The Ethics of Artificial Uteruses: Implications for Reproduction and Abortion*
(Aldershot: Ashgate Publishing, 2004) 45.

[27] The Warnock Committee took the view that the embryo has a 'special status' and should thus
be accorded protection, The Warnock Report (n 1 above) 71–2. Similarly, *Review of the Guidance on
the Research Use of Fetuses and Fetal Material* (Cmnd 762, 1989) *(Polkinghorne Committee Review)*,
the Polkinghorne Report, stated that the foetus merits 'profound respect based upon its potential for
development into a fully-formed human being' (para 2.4); and consequently it is recommended that
the foetus be accorded a status 'broadly comparable to that of a living person' (para 3.1).

[28] Any rights are contingent upon being born alive; *Paton v BPAS* [1979] QB 276.

[29] For a discussion of the law, see J Keown, *Abortion, Doctors and the Law* (Cambridge: Cambridge
University Press, 1988); and J Fortin, 'Legal Protection of the Unborn Child' (1988) 51 *MLR* 54.

[30] Lord Ellenborough's Act 1803.

Act 1861 made it a criminal offence punishable by a maximum of life imprisonment for any person to do an unlawful act with intent to procure a miscarriage either in oneself or another. *In vivo* the foetus was protected throughout a pregnancy with no distinction with regard to gestational age. It was not until 1929 that a specific exclusion for therapeutic abortion was enacted with the Infant Life Preservation Act 1929. This Act made it an offence to destroy the life of a child 'capable of being born alive' unless done in good faith and in order to save the life of the mother.[31] Parliament was clearly concerned with protecting the foetus from the point at which it was viable, and thus capable of surviving outside the womb of its mother. The Act held that there was a presumption that a foetus was 'capable of being born alive' at twenty-eight weeks.[32]

Defences were later enshrined in the Abortion Act 1967. The 1967 Act permitted a pregnancy to be terminated by a registered medical practitioner if two registered medical practitioners were of the opinion, formed in good faith, that the grounds specified in the Act are met. The grounds under section one are as follows; (a) that the continuance of the pregnancy would involve risk to the physical or mental health of the pregnant woman or any existing children of her family,[33] (b) termination is necessary in order to prevent 'grave permanent injury to the pregnant woman',[34] (c) the continuance of the pregnancy would involve risk to the life of the pregnant woman; and (d) that there is a substantial risk that if the child were born it would suffer from some physical or mental abnormalities as to be seriously handicapped.[35]

As initially enacted, the Abortion Act 1967 set no time limit as to when an abortion could be lawfully performed, which effectively meant that a medical practitioner could still be liable for the destruction of a viable foetus which was 'capable of being born alive' under the 1929 legislation. This was remedied by section 37(4) of HFEA 1990 which inserted a fixed time limit of twenty-four weeks for abortions carried out in order to prevent risk to the health of the pregnant women or her children.[36] This removed the possibility, which existed between 1967 and 1990, of an offence being committed under the 1929 Act despite compliance with the 1967 Act.

Thus, under present legislation, a foetus is accorded a degree of protection and its destruction is permitted only under clearly invoked exceptions. There remains

---

[31] Section 1(1) of the 1929 Act reads: 'Any person who, with intent to destroy the life of a child capable of being born alive, by any wilful act causes a child to die before it has an existence independent of its mother, will be guilty of felony, to whit of child destruction, and shall be liable on conviction thereof on indictment to penal servitude for life. Provided that no person shall be found guilty of an offence under this section unless it is proved that the act which caused the death of the child was not done in good faith for the purpose only of saving the life of the mother.'

[32] Section 1(2) of the 1929 Act states: 'For the purposes of this act, evidence that a woman had at any material time been pregnant for a period of 28 weeks or more shall be prima facie proof that she was at the time pregnant of a child capable of being born alive...'

[33] Abortion Act 1967, s 1(1)(a).   [34] ibid s 1(1)(b).

[35] M Brazier, *Patients and The Law*, (London: Penguin Books, 3rd edn, 2003) 318.

[36] Abortion Act 1967, s 1(1)(a) as amended by HFEA 1990.

no right as such to an abortion, and a woman must be certified by two medical practitioners that she comes within one of the grounds under the Abortion Act.[37] The question which now merits attention is how ectogenesis will impact on the abortion legislation.

C. Ectogenesis and Meaning of 'Capable of Being Born Alive'

Once complete ectogenesis becomes a safe method of gestation, it will affect abortion legislation. As noted above, under section1(1)(a) of the Abortion Act 1967, abortion can be carried out in order to prevent risk to the health of the pregnant women or her children provided the pregnancy has not exceeded its twenty-fourth week. Section 1(1)(a), often referred to as the 'social ground' for the frequency with which it is invoked[38] is the only ground which imposes a twenty-four week time limit. This time limit was imposed as it was thought that this represented viability, the point at which a foetus was 'capable of being born alive'. After twenty-four weeks, as stated above, abortion is only permissible if continuance of the pregnancy would be a risk to the life of the pregnant woman,[39] or cause grave permanent injury to her physical or mental health,[40] or if there is a substantial risk that if the child were born it would suffer from some physical or mental abnormalities as to be seriously handicapped.[41] However, will section 1(1) (a) now have to be amended in the light of ectogenesis? Once complete ectogenesis becomes possible, a foetus could be seen as being viable from conception and, thus, being capable of being 'born alive'.

In England and Wales the state has chosen, through the criminal law, to protect the unborn once it 'is capable of being born alive'. The meaning of this phrase has come before the courts on two occasions. In the first case, *C v S*[42] a putative father sought to restrain his ex partner from undergoing a termination in accordance with the Abortion Act 1967 (prior to the 1990 amendment). He claimed the foetus, aged between eighteen and twenty-one weeks, was 'capable of being born alive'. In both the High Court and the Court of Appeal it was held that the foetus was not capable of being born alive, a term the judiciary declined to define, but held the interpretation of those words was a matter for the courts. The phrase was also considered in the case of *Rance v Mid-Downs Health Authority*[43] in which Brooke J held a child is 'born alive'

---

[37] Sally Sheldon criticizes the decision-making power granted to the medical profession by the Abortion Act 1967 in S Sheldon, *Beyond Control; Medical Power and Abortion Law* (London: Pluto Press, 1997).

[38] Abortion Statistics 2004 (2005) at <http.//www.dh.gov.uk/assetRoot/04/11/66/35/04116635.pdf>.

[39] Abortion Act 1967, s 1(1)(c).   [40] ibid s 1(1)(b).

[41] ibid s 1(1)(d).   [42] *C v S* [1987] 1 ALL ER 1230.

[43] [1991] 1 QB 587. Mr and Mrs Rance brought an action in negligence after Mrs Rance gave birth to a boy with spina bifida. They argued that Mrs Rance should have been given the opportunity to terminate the pregnancy. Brooke J held that since the diagnosis was only possible at 26 weeks,

'if, after birth, it exists as a live child, that is to say, breathing and living by reason of its breathing through its own lungs alone, without deriving any of its living or power of living by or through any connection with its mother'[44] Brooke J regarded the phrase as being interchangeable with viability, and stated: 'The primary dictionary meaning of the word "viable", which is derived from the French word "vie", is "capable of living"... In my judgment the word "viable" was simply being used [by Parliament] as a convenient shorthand for the words "capable of being born alive".'[45] He also noted the variety of interpretations accorded to the critical words 'a child capable of being born alive' citing paragraph 18(1) of the Report of the Select Committee on the Infant Life (Preservation) Bill (HL Paper (1987–88) No 50), which was chaired by Lord Brightman: 'The Committee think that, as a matter of legal interpretation, this expression probably means capable of being brought into the world alive independently of the mother, for a period however short, even a matter of minutes.'[46]

According to the above statements, the phrase 'capable of being born alive' is used interchangeably with viability. Using viability as a point from which to extend protection to the foetus is problematic for numerous reasons. The most pertinent reason being that viability is an ever-changing concept often dependant on the technology available and where in the world one lives. As Jonathan Herring notes, a 26-week-old foetus may be viable in Britain, but would not be viable in a developing country with limited medical facilities.[47] Using viability to confer moral status/protection on the foetus would lead to the illogical position that when a foetus becomes a person depends on where in the world it is being gestated.[48] As J K Mason points out:

... both medically and morally speaking, viability is an imprecise determinant of 'human' life in that it depends not only on maturity of the fetus but also on the technology that is available to support its extrauterine life and on the motivation with which that technology is put to use.[49]

Thus claims that protection and moral status can be grounded in viability are tenuous to say the least. Notwithstanding this, the fact remains that viability influences the legislation pertaining to abortion. As noted above, after viability, an abortion is possible only under the extreme circumstances that the life of the

---

at which point the foetus would be capable of being born alive—an abortion would have been unlawful under the 1929 Act.

[44] [1991] 1 QB 587, 622.   [45] ibid 621.

[46] ibid 607.

[47] J Herring, *Medical Law and Ethics* (Oxford: Oxford University Press, 2006) 253.

[48] ibid at 253.

[49] J K Mason, *Medico-Legal Aspects of Reproduction and Parenthood* (Aldershot: Dartmouth Publishing Co, 1990) 108.

pregnant woman is at risk[50] or the pregnancy may cause grave permanent injury to her physical or mental health,[51] or if there is a substantial risk that the child will be seriously handicapped.[52] Thus, should the law extend its protection to the foetus, with state abortions carried out in order to prevent risk to the health of the pregnant women or her children[53] being no longer permissible and instead a woman wishing to end her pregnancy on this ground being able to do so only by foetal extraction and transferral in to an ectogenic incubator, which will end the pregnancy but not foetal life?

D. The End of Abortion on 'Social Grounds'?

Some have questioned whether ectogenesis can 'end the abortion debate'.[54] The abortion debate has been polarized between differing views centred on the moral status of the foetus, and the protection it should be accorded. Sheila McLean summarizes the two main camps in the debate as follows:

For the anti-abortion lobby, all human life is sacred from the moment of conception (perhaps even from fertilization, as is evident from their concern about fertilized but not implanted ova) and therefore is worthy of protection. From this position it is logical to argue that no abortion should ever be conceded, with the possible exception of situations where there is a direct conflict between the mother's right to life and the rights which they would attribute to the embryo or fetus. Equally consistent is the view of the pro-choice lobby, which would argue that women have the right to make decisions about their own bodies, and that women's right to self determination is critically and irrevocably damaged by state intrusion into their right to choose to terminate a pregnancy.[55]

It has been asserted that these different schools of thought can now find a middle ground. Ectogenesis will provide both sides with 'what they desire',[56] for the foetus can be expelled from the maternal womb and transferred to an artificial womb where it can continue to gestate safely. Peter Singer and Deane Wells write:

Freedom to choose what is to happen to one's body is one thing; freedom to insist on the death of another human being that is capable of living outside one's body is another. At present these two are inextricably linked, and so the woman's freedom to choose conflicts

---

[50] Abortion Act 1967, s 1(1)(c).   [51] ibid 1967 s 1(1)(b).
[52] ibid 1967 s 1(1)(d).
[53] Abortion Act 1967, s 1(1)(a) was amended by HFEA 1990, s 37(4). This removed the possibility, which existed between 1967 and 1990, of an offence being committed under the 1929 Act for the destruction of a viable foetus which was 'capable of being born alive' despite compliance with the 1967 Act.
[54] P Singer and D Wells, 'Ectogenesis' in S Gelfand and J Shock (eds), *Ectogenesis* (Amsterdam/New York: Rodopi, 2006) ch 2 C Kaczor, 'Could Artificial Wombs End the Abortion Debate?' in C Kaczor, *The Edge of Life: Human Dignity and Contemporary Bioethics, Philosophy and Medicine, Vol 85*, Dordrecht: 105–121.
[55] S McLean, 'Abortion Law: is Consensual Reform Possible?' (1990) 17 *Journal of Law and Society* 106, 108.
[56] Kaczor (n 54 above).

head-on with the alleged right to life of the fetus. When ectogenesis becomes possible, these two issues will break apart, and women will choose to terminate their pregnancies without thereby choosing the inevitable death of the fetus they are carrying. Pro-choice feminists and pro-fetus right-to-lifers can then embrace in happy harmony.[57]

Similarly, Chrispoher Kaczor somewhat optimistically claims that 'if the right to abortion simply means the right not to be pregnant then partial ectogenesis would solve the problem'.[58] His contention is supported by the claim that among the most prominent philosophers defending abortion, most understand abortion as a right of evacuation, and not a right of termination. For instance, despite the apparently 'liberal' view espoused by Judith Jarvis Thomson that abortion is justified because of the violation on a woman's bodily autonomy, she makes it clear she supports abortion not because of any inherent right a woman has to end the life of a foetus; that is an incidental and unavoidable consequence. She states: 'A woman may be utterly devastated by the thought of a child, a bit of herself, put out for adoption and never seen or heard of again. She may therefore want not merely that the child be detached from her, but more, that it die... [But] the desire for the child's death is not one which anyone may gratify, should it turn out to be possible to detach the child alive.'[59] Similarly Mary Ann Warren comments '... if abortion could be performed without killing the fetus, she [the mother] would never possess the right to have the fetus destroyed, for the same reasons that she has no right to have an infant destroyed.'[60] Thus it is clear that Thomson and Warren advocate abortion merely as a right of evacuation. Thus, Christoper Kaczor, writing from a Roman Catholic perspective, claims that if defenders of abortion, such as Thomson and Warren, are consistent with what they have written, it would seem that the majority of these people could accept the use of artificial wombs in lieu of abortion.[61]

However, there are two weaknesses with this view that ectogenesis can be used in lieu of abortion, or end the debate.

Abortion is About the Right Not to Reproduce

It is presumed that once it becomes possible to expel the foetus without killing it, a woman's desire for foetal termination will automatically disappear. Singer and Wells argue: 'We do not allow a mother to kill her newborn baby because she does not wish to keep it or to hand it over for adoption. Unless we were

---

[57] Singer and Wells (n 54 above) 12.

[58] Kaczor (n 54 above)

[59] J Thomson, 'A Defense of Abortion' in R Wasserstrom (ed), *Today's Moral Problems*, (New York: Macmillan, 2nd edn, 1979) 106; C Overall, 'New Reproductive Technology: Some Implications for the Abortion Issue' in Patrick Hopkins (ed), *Sex Machine: Readings in Culture, Gender and Technology* (Bloomington Ind: Indiana University Press, 1998) 203.

[60] M Warren, 'On the Moral and Legal Status of Abortion' in R Wasserstrom (ed), *Today's Moral Problems* (New York: Macmillan, 1975) 136; Overall (n 59 above) 204.

[61] C. Kaczor, 'Could Artificial Wombs End the Abortion Debate' (2005) 5(2) *National Catholic Bioethics Quarterly* 283, 301.

to change our mind about this, it is difficult to see why we should give this right to a woman in respect in respect of a fetus she is carrying if her desire to be rid of the fetus can be satisfied without threatening the life of the fetus.'[62] But there is a crucial distinction between killing a newborn and killing a foetus. The former which has a separate existence to its mother can be protected independently, and is granted full legal status. The foetus however, is granted no legal rights while in the maternal womb, and instead it is the mother's autonomy which is the decisive influence. This has recently been confirmed by the courts in the context of caesarean section cases, where the courts have held that a competent woman's refusal to consent cannot be overridden in the interests of the foetus. This is so even after viability, when a foetus can be safely maintained safely outside the maternal womb.[63] In *Re MB* the court was clear on this point:

> The foetus up to the moment of birth does not have any separate interests capable of being taken into account when a court has to consider an application for a declaration in respect of a Caesarean section operation. The court does not have the jurisdiction to declare that such a medical intervention is lawful to protect the interests of the unborn child even at the point of birth.[64]

For many women seeking an abortion, it may be the case that a woman wants to end, not just her pregnancy, but also foetal life. As Stephen Ross contends, some women 'cannot be satisfied unless the fetus is killed: nothing else will do'.[65] This stems from the fact that the mother as a genetic progenitor has a 'deeply felt personal preference' that 'she and not anyone else ought to raise whatever child she brings into the world'; and that this failure to raise one's child can only be avoided by killing the foetus.[66] Thus, for these women there is a clear desire not to perpetuate their genetic material and become a biological mother. Foetal transferral and subsequent adoption would mean they still have a genetically related child out there in the world being raised by different parents. Even if no rearing duties or even contact result, the unwilling parent will still face the potentially significant psychosocial impact of the existence of biological offspring that may be from a failed relationship.[67]

Abortion is not merely about ending pregnancy, but about individuals having the right to determine whether or not they will reproduce. This notion of saying no to genetic parenthood was recently heard before the courts in England

---

[62] Singer and Wells (n 54 above) 12.

[63] *S v McC*; *W v W* [1972] AC 24; *Re T (Adult: Refusal of Medical Treatment)* [1992] 4 All ER 649, CA; *Re MB (An Adult: Medical Treatment)* [1997] 2 FCR 541, *St George's Healthcare NHS Trust v S* [1999] Fam 26, CA.

[64] [1997] 2 FCR 541, 558–61.

[65] S Ross, as cited by Overall (n 59 above) 208–9.   [66] ibid.

[67] J Robertson 'In The Beginning: The Legal Status of Early Embryos' (1990) 76 *Virginia Law Review* 437, 479; L Hemphill, 'American Abortion Law Applied to New Reproductive Technology' in (1992) 32 *Jurimetrics Journal* 361, 374.

and Wales in the case of *Evans v Amicus*.[68] The courts upheld Howard Johnson's decision to refuse his ex-partner, Natalie Evans, the use of the embryos they had created together through IVF, even though cancer had rendered this her last chance at genetic motherhood. Howard Johnson successfully argued that he did not want a child of his out there in the world that he was not actively raising with the child's mother,[69] that fatherhood was a life long commitment, and given that he and Ms Evans had separated, the child would be raised with an absent father, a position he did not wish to have foisted upon him.[70] His position was upheld by the European Court of Human Rights.[71] Thus, as cogently noted by Lisa Hemphill, 'abortion is not only about eliminating an unwanted pregnancy; it is also about an individual's right to reproductive control, as opposed to the exercise of that right by the state'.[72]

The Woman's Bodily Autonomy is Involved

The second difficulty with the argument posed, is that if the pregnancy has occurred naturally (through sexual intercourse) the foetus is located within the womb of a woman and her bodily autonomy is engaged. As noted by Dworkin, a pregnant woman is uniquely positioned in relation to her foetus: 'Her fetus is not merely "in her" as an inanimate object might be, or something alive but alien that has been transplanted in to her body. It is "of her and hers more than any-one's" because it is, more than anyone else's, her creation and her responsibility; it is alive because she has made it come alive.'[73] It is located in her body, thus she would have to consent to any procedure performed with the design to extract the foetus intact so that it may be transferred in to an ectogenic incubator. At present, the surgical procedure that would have to be performed to transfer the foetus intact would probably be akin to a caesarean section after twenty-four weeks' gestation—since this is the point from which we have technology that can gestate a foetus externally and mimic the functions of the maternal womb. As explained by David James:

A foetal transplant would be an elaborate surgical procedure aimed at the delicate removal of the fetus from the mother's placenta and its transfer and attachment to the external artificial womb . . . foetal transplantation would thus require general anesthesia as well as surgical incision through the abdominal wall and uterus, with all the risks and complications which accompany these more invasive procedures.[74]

---

[68]   *Evans v Amicus Healthcare Ltd and Ors* [2004] EWCA Civ 727, [2004] 2 FLR 766.

[69]   ibid at paras 32 and 89.

[70]   C Lind, 'Evans v United Kingdom—Judgments of Solomon: Power, Gender and Procreation' (2006) 18(4) *CFLQ* 576.

[71]   *Evans v The United Kingdom* (Application No 6339/05), 2006 1 FCR 585.

[72]   Hemphill (n 67 above) 385.

[73]   R Dworkin, *Life's Dominion: An Argument About Abortion, Euthanasia, and Individual Freedom* (New York: Knopf, 1993) 55; E Jackson, *Regulating Reproduction: Law, Technology and Autonomy* (Oxford: Hart, 2001) 114.

[74]   D James, 'Ectogenesis: A Reply to Singer and Wells' (1987) 1(1) *Bioethics* 87.

This differs drastically to an abortion in the early stages of pregnancy. Up until fourteen weeks after conception abortion is a relatively minor procedure,[75] which does not require surgery. Mandating fetal transfer would be to force women to endure the pain, inconvenience and risks of carrying a pregnancy for twenty-four weeks (or for the necessary period until ectogenic technology can safely mimic the functions of the maternal womb), then to have to undergo invasive surgery to transfer the foetus, de facto almost outlawing abortion. At the moment, a pregnant woman cannot be forced to consent to a caesarean section, even if it is necessary in order to save the life of the foetus. In *Re MB*[76] Butler Sloss P said: 'The law is... clear that a competent woman who has the capacity to decide may for religious reasons, other reasons, for rational or irrational reasons or for no reason at all, choose not to have medical intervention even though... the consequence may be the death or serious handicap of the child she bears, or her own death.'[77]

English law is clear on the point; a competent pregnant woman 'has an absolute right to choose whether to consent to medical treatment or refuse it or to choose one rather than another of the treatments offered'.[78] In *St George's Healthcare NHS Trust v S* the Court of Appeal also adopted the view that even if the foetus had interests, their protection could not justify an unwanted medical intervention in a competent woman.[79] Lord Justice Judge unequivocally stated:

...an unborn child is not a separate person from its mother. Its need for medical assistance does not prevail over her rights. She is entitled not to be forced to submit to an invasion of her body against her will, whether her own life or that of her unborn child depends on it. Her right is not reduced or diminished merely because her decision to exercise it may appear morally repugnant.[80]

---

[75] In the first 9 weeks of pregnancy an abortion can be obtained through the mere taking of a pill. The abortion pill actually involves taking two drugs 48 hours apart. The first drug (mifepristone, also known as RU486) blocks the action of the hormone that makes the lining of the womb suitable for the fertilized egg. The second drug (prostaglandin) is given 48 hours later and causes the womb to cramp and contract. The lining of the womb breaks down and is lost along with the embryo through bleeding from the vagina. This part of the process can be painful although pain-killing medication can be given. From 9 to 12 weeks of pregnancy, a process called vacuum aspiration (which means gentle suction) is used to remove the foetus from the womb. During this procedure, a narrow plastic suction tube is inserted into the womb through the neck of the womb (the cervix). A pump is then connected to the tube and this sucks out the foetus along with other tissue associated with the pregnancy. There may be a little bleeding for up to 14 days afterwards. Vacuum aspiration abortions can be carried out under a local or general anesthetic. It is not normally necessary to stay in the hospital or clinic overnight after a vacuum aspiration abortion. For more information see NHS Direct Online Health Encyclopedia: 'Abortion—How is it performed' at <http://www.nhsdirect.nhs.uk/articles/article.aspx?articleId=1&sectionId=14415>.

[76] *Re MB (An Adult: Medical Treatment)* [1997] 2 FCR 541; 38 BMLR 175. But note how the Court found the patient in this particular case was not competent to refuse consent. See I Kennedy, Commentary to *Re MB (Medical Treatment)* in (1997) 5 *Medical Law Review* 317.

[77] [1997] 2 FCR 541, 561.

[78] *St Georges Hospital NHS Trust v S* [1998] 3 All ER 673.

[79] [1998] 3 All ER 673, 692 *per* Judge LJ.

[80] [1998] 3 All ER 673, 691.

Applying these legal principles to ectogenesis, a woman should be able to choose to end her pregnancy through a termination in the early stages of pregnancy even though this may end foetal life. To coerce women to continue their pregnancies until foetal transfer into an ectogenic chamber is possible, is nothing short of a gross violation of one's bodily autonomy. The justifications Thomson offered in her hypothetical violinist scenario[81] still apply. The innocent reader was asked to consider that one morning they awaken to find they have been kidnapped by the Society of Music Lovers, who after canvassing all the available medical records discovered that you alone have the right blood type to cure a famous unconscious violinist. The violinist has a fatal kidney ailment, and so his circulatory system has been plugged in to yours so that your kidneys can be used to extract poisons from his blood as well as your own. It is only for nine months. To unplug him would be to kill him. Thomson assumes that the moral conclusion that most would draw is that you are entitled to unplug yourself. That no one should be morally required to make the sacrifice of freedom and bodily integrity that keeping the violinist alive would require. This argument applies to partial ectogenesis. No one should be forced to sacrifice her body for twenty-four weeks, or any period of time, and then undergo invasive surgery in order to save the life of a foetus.

For the very reason one cannot coerce a women to elect or refuse an abortion, the state should not mandate that a woman should transfer her unwanted foetus into an ectogenic chamber. As the foetus is located within the woman's body, it falls within the scope of a woman's right to privacy and autonomy that she alone should be able to decide whether it will be carried to term or aborted. Under English law the unborn have no legal rights, and as the European Court of Human Rights recently confirmed, even if the unborn do have a 'right to life', it is implicitly limited by the mother's rights and interests.[82]

Finally, even if the government were not convinced by the points above, any attempts to restrict abortion in the light of ectogenesis would incur grave difficulties when it came to enforcement. The Abortion Act was welcomed by some for remedying the situation occurring where women were resorting to self abortion, and aborting in unhygienic circumstances. In *R v Scrimaglia*[83], a case in which a backstreet abortion took place after legalization, the then Lord Chief Justice commented that 'one of the objects, as everyone knows, of the new Act was to try to get rid of back-street unsanitary operations'.[84] Thus regulators should be extremely cautious in trying to create any restrictive regulation of partial ectogenesis which would forbid terminations designed to end foetal life. Consideration ought to be given to 'whether the other evils that would flow from a restrictive regime would

[81] J Thomson, A Defense of Abortion (1971) 1(1) Philosophy and Public Affairs 47–66 at 48–49.
[82] *Vo v France* ECtHR (Application No 53924/00) [2004] 2 FCR 577, para 80.
[83] (1971) 55 Cr App R 280.
[84] See E Jackson, *Medical Law Text and Materials* (Oxford: Oxford University Press, 2006) 599.

outweigh any arguable benefits'.[85] As pointed out by Margaret Brazier: 'Women from countries which restrict abortion come to England now. Several still die, or irretrievably prejudice their health. English women with money, if we restrict abortion will go abroad. Others will resort to the backstreets. The embryo's "right to life" will not be significantly enhanced. Women's lives may be forfeit.'[86]

E. Can Women Elect for Partial Ectogenesis?

Can women who wish to end their pregnancy but not foetal life request partial ectogenesis? While at present we already have partial ectogenesis in the form of incubators in the neo-natal intensive care unit, transfer of the foetus from the maternal womb to a mechanical womb is reserved for cases of medical necessity, where a wanted pregnancy incurs complications which make early birth necessary in order to preserve the health of the mother. But what of the situation where the pregnancy is not incurring any complications and the mother merely requests that her foetus be transferred? The motivations for such a request may vary. It could stem from the fact a woman is having a horrible but not life-threatening pregnancy, to a change of circumstances, a break-up in her relationship, the death of a partner, a change of mind, and so on. The woman may wish to end the pregnancy but not the life of the foetus. Partial ectogenesis will mean she could achieve this. Is this something the law should sanction?

The Polkinghorne Committee, reporting in 1989, acknowledged that abortion is a decision of 'moral ambiguity and perplexity to many, reached only through a conflict of considerations'.[87] However, women wishing to end their pregnancy who may be interested in having their foetus transferred into an ectogenic incubator where it can continue to gestate and later be placed for adoption will be barred from doing so due to the operation of the 'separation principle' espoused in the Polkinghorne Report: 'Great care should be taken to separate decisions relating to abortion and to the subsequent use of fetal material. The prior decision to carry out an abortion should be reached without consideration of the benefits of subsequent use.'[88] Thus women who are seeking an abortion can not mandate what is to happen to their foetus after the procedure. A woman can abort using current methods which will end the life of the foetus. After the procedure the foetus will be disposed of. The mother can consent to research upon it, but the current Polkinghorne Code of Practice governing foetal research recommends that the woman, after she has given informed consent, should not be privy to further details regarding that research. Even if it is a late termination, guidelines recommend that foeticide (causing the death of the foetus) be carried out before

---

[85] M Brazier ' "Embryos" "Rights": Abortion and Research' in M Freeman (ed), *Medicine, Ethics and The Law* (London: Stevens & Sons, 1988) 9, 14.

[86] ibid 14.   [87] The Polkinghorne Report (n 27 above) para 2.8.

[88] ibid para 4.1

the initiation of labour in terminations after twenty-one weeks, six days of gestation to ensure that the foetus is not born alive.[89] But if, as both the Warnock
Committee and Polkinghorne Committee espouse, the human embryo/foetus
should be accorded respect, it is not clear why a woman can elect for an abortion
which would terminate the foetus but not a foetal transfer which will merely
end the pregnancy and not the life of the foetus. This is something the government needs to consider in the light of developments moving towards partial
ectogenesis.

In the early stages of ectogenesis, whilst the technology is still developing
there will also be ethical and legal problems in using ectogenesis to aid the survival of fetuses too premature to survive out of the womb. At present viability is
stated to be around twenty-four weeks, and the Nuffield Council is clear that any
attempt to resuscitate a baby born below twenty-two weeks is experimental.[90] A
foetal transfer may also pose grave risks for the woman. Caesarean sections at
pre-viability or at the borderline are more hazardous than near term caesarean
sections. As the Nuffield Council point out, at an early stage of pregnancy 'a classical caesarean section would be required, which involves opening the abdomen
at the upper part of the uterus, unlike the operation which is usually performed
at or near term in which only the lower part of the uterus is opened (lower segment caesarean section). The uterus is more likely to rupture in a future labour
if there is a scar from a previous classical caesarean section than from a lower
segment caesarean section'.[91] Thus while ectogenesis may expand reproductive
choice and the range of options available to pregnant women, at present the law
would not permit a woman to transfer her pre-viable fetus into an ectogenic
chamber.

Should ectogenesis and foetal transfer become safe, the government should
consider whether women who wish to end their pregnancies should be allowed
this option.

III. Complete Ectogenesis—From Embryo to Baby

A. Regulating Complete Ectogenesis

As noted earlier, should treatment of premature babies continue to advance and
reduce the amount of time that a foetus needs to spend in a maternal womb, it is
thought that ectogenesis is likely to be discovered by default through the treatment of premature babies. Notwithstanding the current prohibition on the use

---

[89] Royal College of Obstetricians and Gynaecologists, 'Termination of Pregnancy for Fetal
Abnormality in England, Wales and Scotland' (1996); Nuffield Council on Bioethics, 'Critical
Care Decisions in Foetal and Neonatal Medicine: Ethical Issues' (November 2006) 4.14.
[90] Nuffield Council on Bioethics, para 9.19.
[91] ibid para 5.5.

of an embryo after fourteen days, assuming that the law recognizes the potential benefits of ectogenesis it may decide it wishes to create an exception, and license research on complete ectogenesis.

Complete ectogenesis may be desired by women who, due to a genetic disorder, were born without a womb, or women for whom pregnancy poses grave health risks. The couple could opt for IVF and have their embryo placed in an ectogenic incubator for the forty-week gestation period. But as with all new technological advancements, the question then raised is how such technology would be regulated. Could present abortion laws be extended to cover this situation? Let us apply the current legislation to the following hypothetical scenario:

Henry and Ann have recently undergone IVF treatment. Ann was born with a congenital condition called Rokitansky's Syndrome[92] whereby she was born without a uterus. The couple thus decided to place one of their embryos in to an ectogenic incubator for gestation. Five months into the gestation the couple split. They both agree that they no longer wish to have a child together and write to the hospital requesting that the machine be switched off.

Can the Couple Simply Request that the Machine be Switched off?

Whether they would be allowed to ask for the machine to be switched off would depend firstly on whether switching the machine off would amount to 'procuring a miscarriage.' The courts have considered the phrase 'procuring a miscarriage' only in the context of a natural pregnancy. In the recent case of *R (On the Application of Smeaton) v Secretary of State for Health*[93] the courts held that the prescription, supply, administration, or use of the morning-after pill did not, and could not, involve the commission of any offence for it was not unlawfully 'procuring a miscarriage'. The court held that a miscarriage was the termination of post-implantation pregnancy. There could be no miscarriage if a fertilized egg was lost prior to implantation. If the placing of the embryo in to an ectogenic incubator is construed as being analogous to implantation in the maternal womb, then switching off the artificial womb could indeed be construed as procuring a miscarriage contrary to section 58 or section 59 of the Offences Against the Person Act 1861.

As mentioned earlier, any acts which cause a miscarriage or abortion are lawful only if two medical professionals certify that the conditions set out in the 1967 Act are satisfied. If the Abortion Act 1967[94] was extended to ectogenesis, this would mean that couples could request that the ectogenic chamber be switched off if the time the foetus has been in the ectogenic chamber has not exceeded its twenty-fourth week, and continuance of the ectogenic gestation would involve

---

[92] Patients with the Mayer-Rokitansky-Küster-Hauser syndrome, or Müllerian agenesis, have congenital absence of the uterus and vagina. Their ovaries, however, are present, with normal function and ovulation.

[93] [2002] EWHC 610 (Admin), [2002] 2 FLR 146, [2002] 2 FCR 193, 66 BMLR 59.

[94] As amended by Human Fertilisation and Embryology Act 1990.

risk of injury to the mental health of the progenitors (arguably this should be amended to extend to the father as much as the mother) or any existing child of their family, greater than if the ectogenic gestation were terminated.[95] Or at any point of the gestational period if there is a substantial risk that the child in the ectogenic incubator may suffer from some physical or mental abnormalities as to be seriously handicapped,[96] the couple could be allowed to request the machine be switched off. It is difficult to see how section 1(1)(b) and (c) of the Abortion Act which permit abortion post twenty-four weeks if there is a substantial risk to the life or health of the mother could extend to ectogenesis, since the woman will not be gestating the child.

But if the current abortion legislation is maintained and extended to cover ectogenic babies, the question then arises why retain twenty-four weeks as the cut-off point? As outlined earlier, at present that is used in abortion legislation, and for many is perceived as the point of viability.[97] But with complete ectogenesis, viability is from conception. Thus will the law protect all ectogenic babies, and state that as they are viable and can be gestated without violating the pregnant woman's bodily integrity, the life of the *in vitro* foetus cannot be ended prematurely?

It is likely that clear legislation will have to be drafted to regulate complete ectogenesis. When the Abortion Act was drafted, it was done so with the 'pregnant woman' and protection of the born child *in vivo* in mind. As noted by Jane Fortin: 'Since it was inconceivable until recently that a fetus could ever exist outside its mother's womb, hitherto the criminal law has only been concerned with the protection of the unborn child *in vivo* rather than *in vitro*.'[98]

Regarding the *in vivo* baby, English law is clear that a foetus is not a person until it is born.[99] The President of the Family Division stated: 'There can be no doubt, in my view, that in England and Wales the foetus has no right of action, no right at all, until birth.'[100] But the law is far from clear on the matter for while a foetus may not enjoy legal status, this does not mean a foetus is a 'nothing'.[101] As noted by Shaun Pattinson: 'While the fetus is not treated as having *full* status, neither is it treated as having *no status*.'[102] In *St George's*

---

[95] Abortion Act 1967, s 1(1)(a).

[96] ibid s 1(1)(d).

[97] Under English law, The Infant Life Preservation Act 1929 made it an offence to destroy the life of a child 'capable of being born alive'. Initially, a foetus was deemed to be 'capable of being born alive' at 28 weeks. Whilst the Abortion Act 1967 created statutory defences to the offences of procuring a miscarriage and the destruction of a viable foetus, it retained the clause in the 1929 Act, which stated that killing a foetus after 'viability' would constitute the offence of child destruction. Not surprisingly, few obstetricians would perform abortion after 22–24 weeks. HFEA 1990, s 37 reduced the time limit from 28 weeks to 24 weeks partly because of the increased viability of premature babies.

[98] Fortin (n 29 above) 61.

[99] *Paton v BPAS* [1979] Q B 276; *Re F (In Utero)* [1988] Fam 122.

[100] *Paton v BPAS* [1979] QB 276.   [101] Herring (n 47 above) 244.

[102] Pattinson, *Medical Law and Ethics* (London: Sweet & Maxwell, 2006) 227.

Healthcare NHS Trust v S[103] Judge LJ stated that a 36-week-old foetus is 'not nothing; it is not lifeless and it is certainly human'.[104] In *AG Reference (No 3 of 1994)*[105] the House of Lords rejected an argument by the Court of Appeal that a foetus should be regarded as a part of the mother, but instead regarded it as a unique organism. Lord Mustill declared the foetus was: 'An organism *sui generis* lacking at this stage the entire range of characteristics both of the mother to which it is physically linked and the complete human being to which it will later become.'[106]

When the courts have considered the status of the foetus, it has often been in the context of the unborn *in vivo*, the focus being predominantly focused on balancing protection of the foetus against the rights that must be accorded to the mother in whose womb the baby is located. This is drastically different from an *in vitro* foetus gestating in an artificial womb, extending protection to which would not be a direct violation of its mother's bodily autonomy. Thus what legal or moral status should be conferred on the *in vitro* foetus gestating in an ectogenic incubator?

B. The Status of the In Vitro/Ectogenic Baby

Whilst the unborn *in vivo* have no rights until they are 'born alive' and possess an independent existence, should the law grant the unborn *in vitro* full legal status?

None of the case law appears to envisage that it could one day be possible for a foetus to be gestated externally. In *Paton v BPAS*[107] Sir George Baker stated that a foetus does not have 'a right of its own at least until it is born and has a separate existence from its mother'.[108] But once ectogenesis becomes possible a foetus will have a separate existence, and arguably does have a 'right of its own'. Similarly in *Vo v France*[109] in declining to treat a foetus as a person under Article 2 of the Convention, the Court reasoned that the life of the foetus 'was intimately connected with that of the mother and could be protected through her'.[110] But if a foetus is conceived via IVF and directly placed in an ectogenic incubator for its gestation, this statement no longer applies.

The nearest we have on how the courts may treat an *in vivo* baby is to look at the protection accorded to embryos created via IVF. When it comes to the legal and

---

[103] [1998] 3 All ER 673.   [104] [1998] 3 All ER 673, 688.
[105] [1998] AC 245.
[106] [1998] AC 245, 255–56 *(per* Lord Mustil).
[107] [1979] QB 276.   [108] [1979] QB 276, 299.
[109] (Application No 53924/00) [2004] 2 FCR 577. This case concerned a female applicant who wanted to carry her pregnancy to term, but as a result of medical negligence was forced to have a therapeutic abortion. Relying on Article 2 of the Convention, the applicant complained of the authorities' refusal to classify the unintentional killing of her unborn child as involuntary homicide. She maintained that France had an obligation to pass legislation making such acts a criminal offence.
[110] [2004] 2 FCR 577, at para 86.

moral status of the *in vitro* embryo, it appears the government was unsure what status to confer upon it. The Warnock Committee avoided providing a definitive answer on the status of such embryos:

Although the questions of when life or personhood begin appear to be questions of fact susceptible of straightforward answers, we hold that answers to such questions in fact are complex amalgams of factual and moral judgments. Instead of trying to answer these questions directly we have therefore gone straight to the question of how it is right to treat the human embryo. We have considered what status ought to be accorded to the human embryo, and the answer we give must necessarily be in terms of ethical or moral principles.[111]

Parliament accepted the recommendations of the Warnock Committee that the embryo has a 'special status' and should be protected by the law after development of the primitive streak, said to occur at fourteen days.[112] Notwithstanding this special status, and limited protection, the courts have recently confirmed that an *in vitro* embryo does not have a 'right to life' under Article 2. In *Evans v Amicus Healthcare Ltd*[113] Natalie Evans unsuccessfully argued that an embryo had a qualified right to life, in a bid to preclude her partner from requesting embryos the couple had created together be destroyed as he was no longer consenting to their use. Wall LJ responded: 'In my judgment, an embryo has no qualified right to life. This court rejected the argument that a foetus had a right to life protected by art 2 in Re F (in utero) [1988] 2 All ER 193, [1988] Fam 122. So far as an embryo created by IVF is concerned, the claim to a right to life must be weaker.'[114]

But the certitude of Wall LJ's reliance on these authorities to aver that the *in vitro* embryo's claim to a right to life is weaker than that of the *in vivo* foetus is troublesome. Most of the jurisprudence on the status of the unborn has been in the context of the foetus *in vivo* where the interests of the mother are in conflict with those of the foetus. Rather than applying old legal principles to a new dilemma, perhaps regulators should have the temerity to consider this question anew, for an embryo/foetus which has an independent existence and which can be gestated entirely *in vitro* is substantially different for the *in vivo* unborn, as it no longer has to be subjugated to the rights of the pregnant woman.

Some may claim that the law should be consistent on the status conferred on the unborn, irrespective of where it is located. It could be argued that the mere fact that a mother's womb is a secret hidden place, unlike the ectogenic incubator in which you can see the baby growing over the nine months, does not provide sufficient justification for the law according different protection to the

---

[111] The Warnock Report (n 1 above) para 11.9.
[112] HFEA 1990, s 3 (3) states. 'A licence cannot authorise—(a) keeping or using an embryo after the appearance of the primitive streak'. The appearance of the primitive streak, stated to occur after fourteen days, was deemed significant as this is when the development of a nervous system begins.
[113] [2004] EWCA (Civ) 727.   [114] ibid para 107.

unborn. That the status conferred should not be based on what Rannon Gillion has labelled 'biological geography':

UK law, like that of many other jurisdictions, is explicit that a fetus is not legally speaking a person...whereas a born child is a person and does have a right to life. While in practical terms the simple criterion of birth is generally easy to apply and corresponds to a stage when what was previously hidden and private inside another human being is now a revealed, public, and clearly separate social entity, as a criterion for moral differentiation of a human being's intrinsic status it seems highly implausible. Essentially it is a criterion of what might be dubbed biological geography, asserting that a human being does not have a right to life if it lies north of the vaginal introitus but has a right to life once it has passed south and has (entirely) emerged from the vagina. What morally relevant changes can there have been in the fetus in its intrinsic passage from inside to outside its mother's body to underpin such a momentous change in its intrinsic moral status?[115]

Whilst consistency in the law is always desirable, perhaps the law cannot avoid according differential treatment to an unborn child based on where it is located. When housed in the maternal womb, the law is rightfully limited in the protection it can extend to the unborn, for it is situated within the body of an autonomous being, on whom it is dependent for survival. However, when gestating externally in the neutral territory of an ectogenic device *in vitro*, an embryo/foetus can be protected independently without violating a woman's bodily autonomy. On this basis, arguably a strong case can be made out for extending legal protection to the live *in vitro* foetus. Thus, ectogenesis will necessitate a re-examination of the moral and legal status of the unborn gestating in an ectogenic device. In this context the convoluted issue of moral and legal status can no longer be resolved by resorting to the fact it is located in a woman, whose bodily autonomy must prevail.

C. Disputes Over Custody of the Ectogenic Baby

In the course of relationships some couples do separate or disagree as to whether to go ahead with a pregnancy. However, as the woman's bodily autonomy is engaged, she normally has the ultimate say over the fate of her embryo. This is fundamentally altered with the use of an ectogenic incubator to gestate the child. In this context, assuming both have donated their gametes, both are arguably equally situated in relation to the embryo which can now be gestated in a neutral environment. In the unfortunate circumstance that a couple have their embryo implanted into an ectogenic incubator only to later separate, whose views should prevail regarding the fate of the foetus gestating in the ectogenic chamber?

Regulators may look to how such disputes are resolved when it comes to disputes concerning the disposition of frozen embryos. In America, the courts have

---

[115] R Gillon, 'Is There "A New Ethics of Abortion"?' (2001) *Journal of Medical Ethics* 115, 118; Jackson (n 84 above) 589–99.

looked to any prior agreements made between the parties. In *Davis v Davis*[116] the Tennessee Supreme Court set out a three-part test to be applied when a couple disagree over the disposition of their embryos: (1) the preferences of the progenitors; (2) if gamete donors disagree over the disposition courts are directed to enforce any prior agreements between the parties; and (3) in the absence of prior agreement, courts are advised to balance the relative interests of the parties. When those interests are in equipoise, courts are advised to favour the party wishing to avoid procreation, as long as the other party has a reasonable possibility of achieving parenthood by other means than the use of the embryo in question. Similarly in *Kass v Kass*[117], the New York Court of Appeal held that embryo agreements governing embryo disposition should be presumed valid and enforced.

In England, when couples have created embryos *in vitro* through IVF only to separate later, the courts have made it clear that prior agreements made between the parties will not be enforced and are not binding since the legislation which governs assisted reproduction, HFEA 1990, provides both gamete progenitors with the statutory right to withdraw or vary consent to the use of an embryo created through IVF until the moment of implantation into a woman.[118] Thus in *Evans v Amicus*[119] when such a dispute arose, the courts upheld the wishes of the partner wishing to avoid genetic parenthood and have the embryos destroyed, even though the embryos represented his former partner's last chance at genetic motherhood.[120]

Following on from this, should the placing of the embryo into an ectogenic incubator be construed as similar to implantation, a point from which consent cannot be revoked? This would have the advantage of being in line with IVF and the point of implantation into the biological womb. However, this leads to the disparity that a couple embarking on ectogenesis together can request that the machine is turned off up until twenty-four weeks, in accordance with abortion laws. But for a couple who separate during the time it is in the incubator, neither party can request it be turned off; for the point of no going back is the point at which it was placed in the ectogenic incubator. Arguably legislators should be consistent and stipulate that as in IVF consent is irrevocable upon implantation (the placing of the embryo in the ectogenic incubator). Should the couple change their minds, it will continue to be gestated and put up for adoption.

IV. A Green Light for Foetal Rescue?

Ectogenesis may also signal a green light for foetal rescue and allow governments to intervene to protect the foetus when necessary. It has been asserted that

[116] 842 S W 2d 588 (Tenn 1992).   [117] 673 NYS 2d 350 (NY 1988).
[118] The Human Fertilisation and Embryology Act 1990, Sch 3.
[119] *Evans v Amicus Healthcare* [2003] EWHC 2161 (Fam).
[120] ibid. See also A Alghrani, 'Deciding The Fate of Frozen Embryos: Natalie Evans v. Amicus Healthcare Ltd and Others' (2005) 13 *Medical Law Review* 244.

ectogenesis may be safer than a mother's womb. Edward Grossman contended: 'An efficient artificial womb, far from increasing the incidence of birth defects, would reduce them by keeping the foetus in an absolutely safe and regular environment; safe, for example from infection by German measles or drugs taken by the mother.'[121] Whilst Grossman has been criticized for his 'lack of confidence in the female body' and his failure to appreciate that 'women have successfully birthed the human species for millenia'[122] the fact remains that there is a small percentage of women who do endanger the health of their unborn child during the nine months of gestation. Pregnant women who continue to smoke and drink despite the warnings that harmful effects may cause irreversible harm to their unborn foetus. Drinking during pregnancy can cause Foetal Alcohol Syndrome (FAS), which is 'the combination of growth retardation, neurological impairment and abnormal facies shown by some infants born to alcoholic women'.[123] FAS is the biggest cause of non-genetic mental handicap in the Western world and the only one that is 100 per cent preventable.[124] Once ectogenesis is a viable method of gestation, the question may arise of whether pregnant women who are drug or alcohol addicted and whose foetuses are being severely impaired as a result should be made to have their foetuses transferred into ectogenic chamber to enable them to gestate in a safe and drug-free environment.

Unless the advent of ectogenesis alters the legal and moral status of the foetus, removal into an ectogenic incubator should only be done if it would benefit the mother, since currently the unborn have no legal status and thus healthcare professionals have no authority to seek to protect the unborn child.[125] Since a foetus is not a legal person[126] there is no basis for punishing a mother for any wrongdoing during the pregnancy. Mandating women whose foetuses appear to be distressed to have those foetuses transferred to an ectogenic device may deter pregnant women from seeking antenatal care and have a more detrimental effect.

Ectogenesis should not signal a green light to those hoping to set out on acts of foetal rescue, unless the law regarding the legal status of the unborn alters. Whilst it is located in a female womb, any attempts to force the pregnant woman to have the foetus transferred to an ectogenic device would violate her bodily autonomy and be unlawful.

---

[121] E Grossman, 'The Obsolescent Mother: A Scenario' (1971) 5 *The Atlantic* 48; S Eaton, 'The Medical Model of Reproduction' (2005) 1 *New Antigone* 28, 32.

[122] Eaton (n 121 above) 32.

[123] EME Poskitt, 'Foetal Alcohol Syndrome' (1984) 19(2) *Alcohol and Alcoholism* 159.

[124] FAS Aware UK, 'A Preventable Tragedy', at <http://www.fasaware.co.uk/> (accessed 28 August 2007).

[125] In English Law any legal rights of a foetus are contingent upon birth, *Paton v Trustees of the BPAS* [1979] QB 276; and *Paton v United Kingdom* [1980] 3 EHRR 408. *C v S* [1987] I All ER 123; *Vo v France* (Application No 53924/00).

[126] *Paton v Trustees of the BPAS* [1979] QB 260.

V. Conclusion

While the government may be reluctant to consider technology which would allow a foetus to be brought to term outside its mother's body, and which would re-open the intensely politicized debate surrounding abortion law, it would be irresponsible to dismiss ectogenesis as a far off advance confined to the realms of science fiction. We already have partial ectogenesis which can help to sustain the lives of extremely premature babies born as young as twenty-four weeks, and scientists continue to research how this may be reduced further. Should ectogenesis become a safe method of gestation it will have many ramifications, not least of all on the current abortion law. Ectogenesis will necessitate revising the legislation, in particular section 1(1)(a) of the Abortion Act 1967. Parliament should consider whether it does want to retain twenty-four weeks, deemed to be the point of viability, or when a foetus is 'capable of being born alive' as a cut-off point in the legislation for when a woman can abort in order to prevent risk to her health or that of her children.[127] On the flip side, consideration also needs to be given to whether partial ectogenesis should be allowed for women wishing to end their pregnancy but not the life of the foetus.

Complete ectogenesis raises a host of legal and ethical questions, the principal issue being the status that should be granted to the *in vitro* foetus. In view of this, regulators will have to re-examine the legal status of the human foetus. Many of the cases that have generated legal rules on the status of unborn children have originated in the context of the abortion debate,[128] caesarean cases,[129] and other instances concerning unborn children gestated in their mothers' wombs.[130] This is significantly different from the situation of the *in vitro* embryo/foetus that has a independent physical existence and can be gestated in an ectogenic incubator.

If the law in the United Kingdom is to be 'reconnected with modern science', it needs to be more proactive and consider not just present technologies, but those looming on the horizon. Given that we arguably already have partial ectogenesis, complete ectogenesis may not be as far off as the Warnock Committee imagined. Even if it is still far off, that does not justify ignoring the countless

---

[127] The Abortion Act 1967, s 1(1)(a) was amended by HFEA 1990, s 37(4). This removed the possibility, which existed between 1967 and 1990, of an offence being committed under the 1929 Act for the destruction of a viable foetus which was 'capable of being born alive' despite compliance with the 1967 Act.

[128] *Paton v BPAS* [1979] 1 QB 276; *C v S* [1988] 1 QB 135.

[129] *S v McC; W v W* [1972] AC 24; *Re T (Adult: Refusal of Medical Treatment)* [1992] 4 All ER 649, CA; *Re MB (An Adult: Medical Treatment)* [1997] 2 FCR 541; *St George's Healthcare NHS Trust v S* [1999] Fam 26, CA.

[130] *Attorney-General's Reference (No. 3 of 1994)* [1997] 3 WLR 421; *Re F (In Utero)* [1988] 2 All ER 193; *D v Berkshire County Council* [1987] 1 All ER 20.

legal and ethical questions this technology will give rise to. As one commentator prudently notes:

It may turn out that scientists just won't ever be able to perfect the technology to allow children to be born mechanically. It may turn out that society is unwilling to accept the mechanic bearing of children. However, it is irresponsible to wait until the first child is born of ectogenesis before discussing how the law will, or should, treat that new form of assisted, and collaborative, reproduction.[131]

If the United Kingdom wishes to capitalize on the benefits ectogenesis can offer, lawyers and ethicists need to start thinking about this technology now, and whether it is possible to create a comprehensive regulatory framework which will effectively monitor the advance in practice. It is conceded that at present the science is yet to be perfected, and it may even be the case that scientists will not discover how to achieve complete ectogenesis in our lifetime. However, given the advances that have already been made in this area, it is imprudent to wait until a child is born via ectogenesis before considering the plethora of legal and ethical questions this technology will give rise to.

---

[131] M Hibbert, 'Artificial Womb Technology and the Constitutional Guarantees of Reproductive Freedom,' at <http://www.law.asu.edu/Programs/Sci-Tech/Commentaries/ArtificialWomb Hibbert. aspx+law+and+ectogenesis&hl=en&gl=uk&ct=clnk&cd=1> (accessed 12 August 2007).

18

Surrogacy: Is there Room for a New Liberty Between the French Prohibitive Position and the English Ambivalence?[1]

Myriam Hunter-Henin

I. Introduction

Does a mother who gives a child over for adoption fail in a moral duty towards her child?[2]

A similar question is implicitly asked about surrogates who give 'their' babies away for adoption to a commissioning couple.[3] Unlike adoption, babies born under surrogacy arrangements are *ab initio* conceived for the very purpose of adoption. 'Even worse', would say most French lawyers who would interpret this deliberate abandonment from conception as a fraud against adoption rules.[4] The moral issues become even more complex when one considers that, unlike mothers who give away their child for adoption, surrogates do not necessarily carry 'their' babies in every sense of the term. Generally, the commissioning father and more and more often the commissioning mother as well will be the child's genetic parents. One may therefore argue that it is the surrogate who does *not* give the child over to the commissioning couple who fails in a moral duty towards the genetic parents and possibly towards the child who will not be raised by his genetic parents. Surrogacy therefore raises complex moral issues. It also raises questions about the meaning of taken for granted concepts such as 'mother'

[1] I would like to thank Alison Diduck for her useful comments on an earlier draft on the article which forms this chapter.
[2] J Eekelaar, 'Are Parents Morally Obliged to Care for their Children?' (1991) 11 *OJLS* 340, 350.
[3] Surrogacy was defined by the Warnock Committee as 'the practice whereby one woman carries a child for another with the intention that the child should be handed over after the birth', *Report of the Committee of Inquiry into Human Fertilisation and Embryology* (Cmnd 9314, 1984) para 8.1 (hereinafter 'Warnock Report'); see also M Warnock, *A Question of Life. The Warnock Report on Human Fertilization and Embryology* (Oxford and New York: Basil Blackwell, 1985) 42.
[4] See text accompanying note 63 below.

and 'natural'.[5] It fragments motherhood and challenges our traditional view that 'giving birth' is the basis for motherhood. Often seen as unnatural,[6] surrogacy is sometimes labelled as dangerous as fears of exploitation of surrogates and commodification of children arise. All the concerns and challenges raised by surrogacy have already led to many interesting studies.[7]

The purpose of this chapter is more specific. First and foremost, my aim will be to compare the French and English perspectives on surrogacy.[8] If similar fears and concerns have been voiced in both countries, the legal reaction in each country differs greatly. Most interestingly, in these diverging reactions seems to lie, to an unusual degree, a reflection of each country's legal traditions and core legal values. From a comparative point of view, surrogacy has therefore great value which I would like to explore.

Secondly, this chapter will seek a solution to surrogacy which could be acceptable to both legal systems and which in my view would be more respectful of individual liberties than the current pragmatic English approach or the present repressive French position. I will try and demonstrate that surrogacy should be treated as part of the fundamental liberty of women to recognize the child they have just given birth to (which would imply that the surrogate is allowed to renege) or not (thus confirming in the context of surrogacy the pregnant woman's initial intention to give the child away to the commissioning couple). Surrogacy and its unenforceability would thus be intrinsically linked and justified on the basis of principles rather than moral imperatives or the assumptions of 'nature'.

As the idea of this chapter stems from a conference on Bioethics, a preliminary issue needs to be addressed. Is surrogacy covered by Bioethics? Does surrogacy in other words have a place in a conference on Bioethics?

II. Surrogacy and Bioethics

If bioethics covers issues raised by the use of new technologies, surrogacy may seem an inappropriate topic. Indeed, surrogacy can involve little or no medical

---

[5] cf E Jackson, 'What is a Parent?' in A Diduck and KO'Donovan (eds), *Feminist Perspectives on Family Law* (Cavendish, 2006) 59,67.

[6] Despite having been practised for centuries. See eg in the Old Testament Book of Genesis, the story of Sara who suggested that her maid Hegar should bear a child conceived by her husband Abraham. Sara and Abraham's son, Ishmail, was born to Hegar as a result.

[7] See references quoted throughout this chapter.

[8] On the value of a comparison between Britain and France in the area of reproduction regulation, see M Latham, *Regulating Reproduction. A Century of Conflict in Britain and France* (Manchester University Press, 2002) 1–10. Several factors make the comparison between the two countries interesting:
  • the very different cultural and social heritage;
  • the different political and legal processes;
  • different legal systems with different views on the role of the state, seen as the guarantor of equality in France, as the guarantor of a sphere immune from public intervention in Britain;
  • different policy styles, pragmatic and reactive in Britain, in the form of 'heroic leadership in France' (p 6).

assistance. When the surrogate is artificially or *a fortiori* 'naturally' inseminated by the husband or partner of a sterile woman, no elaborate medical techniques are required. It is only when the surrogacy in question falls into the category of full or gestational surrogacies—ie when the surrogate does not, by contrast to the above-mentionned type of surrogacy known as partial surrogacies, provide her eggs but merely carries an embryo conceived with the gametes of the commissioning couple or of other donors that medical assistance becomes inevitable. This dichotomy between 'do-it-yourself' surrogacies and surrogacies which are heavily reliant on science is reflected in the *present English regime*. Only the latter surrogacies are covered by the Human Fertilisation and Embryology Act 1990 (HFEA 1990)[9] and in particular by section 13(5)[10] under which access to reproductive techniques is dependent on an assessment by the medical team of the child's welfare, including—for now[11]—the child's need for a father. By contrast, the former are not regulated at all and are thus open to anyone. It is only at a later stage, when the commissioning couple seeks to legalize its link with the child thus conceived, that consideration of the means of conception and in particular the issue of possible payment made to the surrogate will come into consideration. Under section 30 of HFEA 1990,[12] a parental order granting parental status and parental responsibility to the commissioning couple and severing all links between the baby and the surrogate can only be made where payments do not exceed reimbursement of expenses.

The issue of payment and the distaste for commercial arrangements appear also in the Surrogacy Arrangement Act 1985[13] prohibiting the intervention of profit-making agencies and advertisement, irrespective this time of the

---

[9] On the Act, cf D Morgan and RG Lee Blackstone, *Guide to the Human Fertilisation and Embryology Act 1990* (Blackstone Press, 1991); M Brazier, 'Regulating the Reproduction Business?' (1999) 7 *Medical Law Review* 166.

[10] HFEA 1990, s 13(5) stipulates that 'a woman shall not be provided with treatment unless account has been taken of the welfare of any child who may be born as a result of the treatment (including the need of that child for a father) and of any other child who may be affected by the birth'. For a strong argument for repeal of s 13(5), cf E Jackson, 'Conception and the Irrelevance of Welfare of the Child' (2002) 65 *MLR* 176. According to Emily Jackson, 'unlike factors that go to the heart of whether infertility treatment is, for example, clinically advisable or publicly affordable, the pre-conception welfare principle represents an invidious and opportunistic invasion of infertile people's privacy' (ibid 182).

For an assessment of section 13(5) in practice and a call on the HFEA to provide further guidance to clinics on what to take account of when considering the prospecting child's welfare: G Douglas, 'Assisted Reproduction and the Welfare of the Child' (1993) 46 *Current Legal Problems* 53.

[11] The *Review of the Human Fertilisation and Embryology Act* conducted by the Department of Health contains a proposal to remove the reference to the need for a father, Cm 6989, December 2006, para. 2.26.

[12] Section 30 allows for application by the commissioning parents to obtain a parental order in respect of the child. The section came into effect on 1 November 1994 (Regulations 1994, SI 1994/2767).

[13] On the Act, see MD Freeman, 'The Surrogacy Arrangements Act 1985' in *Current Law Statutes Annotated* (Sweet & Maxwell, 1986).

type of surrogacy concerned. But the prohibition is only aimed at intermediaries; the main protagonists, commissioning couple or surrogate, are explicitly immune from any criminal liability.[14] For the main protagonists, the only sanction lies in the refusal—subject to the court's willingness to allow payments retrospectively[15]—of a parenting order.[16]

The type of surrogacy (full or partial) will thus have an impact on the degree of medical assistance required and determine whether treatment needs to be given in a licensed clinic, but all surrogacy arrangements, whether carried out within or outside licensed clinics, will be accepted provided they are non-commercial agreements. However, in the event of a dispute, even altruistic surrogacies will be unenforceable in court[17] and only a married[18] commissioning couple genetically related to the child, either through one or both of the spouse's gametes, can apply for a parental order and avoid the more lengthy and uncertain adoption procedure.

This picture differs from other reproductive technologies where recourse to licensed clinics is the norm and where assessment of prospective parents is 'limited'[19] to a section 13(5) test, carried out by the medical profession, under HFEA 1990, and where no adoption procedure or parental order is required to secure parental status following medical intervention. In other words, scientific technologies are only (at the most) one aspect of surrogacy. If bioethics is to be reserved to challenges posed by science, then surrogacy had better be avoided in this context.

But does not the exclusion of surrogacy from other reproductive technologies reflect a preconceived idea about maternity rather than a reflection of surrogacy's true nature? For an infertile couple anxious to have a child genetically related to one of them, surrogacy is only the answer to certain forms of female sterility, just as artificial insemination with a donor's sperm is the answer to male sterility. However, depending on the cause of her sterility, a woman may or may not be able to fulfil her wish of maternity. Should she lack the capacity to bear the child, should she in other words require a surrogate mother, her medical condition

---

[14] Surrogacy Arrangements Act 1985, s 2(2).

[15] For a recommendation in favour of more stringent restrictions on payments, see the Department of Health's Brazier Report, *Surrogacy: Review for Health Ministers of Current Arrangements for Payment and Regulation* (Cmn 4068, 1998) para 7.22.

[16] eg *Re Q (Parental order)* 1996, 1 FLR 389, HC (Johnson J), under HFEA 1990, s 30(7).

[17] Surrogacy Arrangements Act 1985, s 1A.

[18] However, the government announced that it would consider the need to reflect the wider range of people who seek and receive assisted reproduction treatment, Select Committee on Science and Technology (2004) para 21.

[19] Assessment of those seeking treatment under section 13(5) has sometimes led to relatively extensive inquiries about the prospective patients' circumstances. See *Review of the Human Fertilisation and Embryology Act* (n 11 above) para 2.21 However, following a consultation exercise undertaken in 2005—HFEA 'Tomorrow's Children. A Consulation on guidance to licensed clinics on taking into account the welfare of children to be born of assisted conception treatment' (January 2005)—the HFEA has revised its guidance to clinics 'to focus on the likelihood of serious harm, with a general presumption in favour of providing treatment for patients who seek it'.

will not in itself justify her claim to motherhood. Only an adoption procedure (possibly simplified if she is entitled to apply for a parental order) may secure her maternal rights in law, even though she may be the child's genetic mother. Surrogacy is treated differently because it challenges our very understanding of motherhood. Fatherhood may rely on presumptions[20] but motherhood was supposed to rely on an established fact: the delivery.[21] Surrogacy threatens the idea that the natural mother is the pregnant woman who carries and gives birth to the child. The artificiality of surrogacy is not in the complexity of the medical act but in the ambiguity it sheds on traditional concepts. 'Surrogacy is problematic for so many societies because it renders the familiar ambiguous and forces us to think anew about our values.'[22] This is precisely why surrogacy deserves a place in the debate on bioethics.

A. The Current Position

In both the United Kingdom and France current laws seem inappropriate. UK legislation has reacted to the ambiguity of surrogacy by adopting an ambivalent attitude. The practice is lawful but prohibition of payments, the unenforceability of the contract, and the lack of proper regulatory mechanisms are designed to discourage parties from going down that route. Indeed, prohibition of payment will restrict the number of willing surrogates whereas the risk of the surrogate changing her mind and deciding to keep the baby will be a repellent for prospective commissioning couples. The Surrogacy Arrangements Act 1985 and the HFEA 1990 in the United Kingdom do not, as we have seen, provide any regulatory scheme but only interfere incidentally in the practice or its consequences. Surrogacy was addressed as such in two reports, Warnock[23] and Brazier,[24] but neither were ever acted upon by the government. Only recently has surrogacy been at last identified as an area warranting attention.[25] The government stated,

---

[20] See *Re F (A Minor: Paternity Test)* [1993] 1 FLR 598. However, the presumption that the mother's husband is the father is more and more easily opened to challenge. See Ward LJ in *Re H (Paternity: Blood Test)* [1996] 2 FLR 65 with a resulting fragmentation of social and biological fatherhood.

[21] In the context of a surrogacy arrangement, the legal mother will be the surrogate, whether the surrogacy is total or partial. HFEA 1990, s 27(1) states that 'the woman who is carrying or has carried the child as a result of the placing in her of an embryo or of sperm and eggs and no other woman is to be treated as the mother of the child'.

[22] R Cook, S Day Sclater, and F Kaganas (eds), *Surrogate Motherhood. International Perspectives* (Hart, 2003) Introduction 1, 4.

[23] The majority of the Warnock Report (n 3 above) was against the practice of surrogacy altogether. cf MDA Freeman, 'After Warnock—Wither the Law?' (1986) 39 *Current Legal Problems* 33.

[24] See n 15 above. See M Freeman, 'Does Surrogacy have a Future after Brazier?' (1999) 7 *Medical Law Review* 1.

[25] The Report from the House of Commons Science and Technology Committee, 'Human Reproductive Technologies and the Law,' (24 March 2005), recommended that a new assessment of surrogacy arrangements, based as a starting point on the Brazier Report, should be made

in December 2006, its intention 'through revision to legislation, to clarify the extent to which not-for-profit organisations may undertake activities for the facilitation of surrogacy arrangements including advertising their services'.[26]

In France, surrogacy is expressly mentionned in the law on bioethics[27] but only to be entirely prohibited.[28] No distinction is made as in the United Kingdom between commercial and altruistic agreements or between full or partial surrogacies or even, as suggested by the criteria set for applicants for a parental order, between married couples (at least partially) genetically related to the child and other commissioning couples. All types of surrogacy are illegal in France. Couples who brave the prohibition and nevertheless obtain a child from a surrogate abroad from more permissive countries or even in France in direct violation of the law will face criminal liability[29] and be precluded from adopting the child. A relatively recent 2002 case offers a good illustration of the French position.[30] Two French partners, Emmanuel and Isabelle, who could not have any children, fulfilled their wish of procreation in California thanks to a surrogate. Two twin girls were born and then registered in California as daughters of Emmanuel and Isabelle. Back in France, both parents officially recognized the girls as their children. But the French Consulate in San Francisco, at which the couple had made enquiries, grew suspicious and alerted the French authorities in France. Proceedings were consequently initiated in France and led to the nullity of Isabelle's declaration that she was the mother. Moreover, Isabelle was denied all possibility of ever establishing a link of motherhood with the twins. However, the illegality of the practice may easily remain hidden. Indeed, so long as the surrogate has respected her part of the bargain and has given birth anonymously[31]

(Recommendation 79). The Government's response 'Government Response's to the Report from the House of Commons Science and Technology Committee' swiftly excused its inaction: 'the Government has had to prioritise other matters above the review of surrogacy' (para 107) and was non-committal as to a specific legislation on surrogacy or even further review: 'However, we will consider the need to review surrogacy arrangements in the context of the review of the HFE Act' (ibid).

[26] *Review of the Human Fertilisation and Embryology Act* (n 11 above) 2.64.

[27] Loi Bioéthique of 29 July 1994 (L n°94–653) relative au respect du corps humain; Loi Bioéthique of 29 July 1994 (L n°94–654) relative au don et à l'utilisation des éléments et produits du corps humain, à l'assistance médicale à la procréation et au diagnostic prénatal; Law of 6 August 2004 (L n°2004–800) relative à la bioéthique, *JO* 7 août 2004, 14040.

[28] French Civil Code, art 16–7.

[29] Previous French criminal code, art 345. cf A Vitu, 'Le Crime de suppression d'enfant. Remarques pour servir à une refonte de l'article 345 du Code pénal' in *Mélanges en l'honneur du doyen Pierre Buzat* (Paris: Pedone, 1980) 383. Art 345 corresponds to art 227–13 of the new French Criminal Code which provides for up to 3 years' imprisonment and around a €50,000 fine for deception or secrecy relating to a child's civil status. Art 441–4 of the French Criminal Code (ex art 147) increases the sanctions to 10 years' imprisonment and around a €150,000 fine in case of forgery of a public official document.

[30] CA Rennes 4 juillet 2002, *D.*2002, 2902–2904, note F Granet.

[31] As is expressly allowed under French Law: Law of 22 January 2002 (L n°2002–93)— confirming and reforming the previous Law of 8 January 1993 (L n°93–22)—relative à l'accès aux origines des personnes adoptées et des pupilles de l'Etat, *JO* 23 janvier 2002, 1519. On this

and handed the child over, the commissioning father, whether he be genetically related to the child or not, may recognize the child as his own[32] and as sole legal parent be granted automatic parental responsibility for the child,[33] thus enabling the child to be raised, in practice, by the commissioning couple. Problems may arise though if the couple splits up or the father dies. Would the commissioning mother be entitled to invoke her continuing and undisputed role as a mother towards the child in order to obtain through *'possession d'état'*[34] what adoption could not give her, ie parental status or would the commissioning couple's fraud bar her claim as in the case of adoption? Current case law takes the view that motherhood by doing, ie through *'possession d'état'*, would be impossible because the caring mother never gave birth. Lack of delivery would irremediably taint the *'possession d'état'* with illegality.[35]

From this picture of Britain's and France's reactions to surrogacy, suffice it to say, for now, that to varying degrees, both countries manifest reluctance towards surrogacy. Reasons, justifications for, and criticisms of this prevailing negative attitude towards surrogacy have already given rise to several interesting studies,

---

possibility, see B Mallet-Bricourt, 'Réforme de l'accouchement sous X. Quel équilibre entre les droits de l'enfant et les droits de la mère biologique?' *JCP* 2002.I.119; J Rubellin-Devichi, 'La Recherche des origines personnelles et le droit à l'accouchement sous X dans la loi du 22 janvier 2002. A la mémoire de Brigitte Trillat' (mai 2002) *Droit de la famille* 7; M-C Le Boursicot, 'Consécration du droit à la connaissance de ses origines' (2002–3) RJPF 6; F Bellivier, 'D'Œdipe à Odièvre: les procédures administratives au secours de la tragédie des origines' (2002) RTD civ 368; *L'Accès aux origines personnelles* (2003) n° spécial A.J. fam. 86 ; N Lefaucheur, 'Tradition of Anonymous Birth: The Lines of Argument' (2004) 18 *International Journal of Law Policy and the Family* 319.

[32] Two authors have expressed the view that recourse to a surrogate should render future recognition of the child by his commissioning father void, even when the commissioning father is also the genetic father. See B Edelmann and C Labrusse-Riou, JCP 1991.II.21653. The practice is, however, that French authorities who suspect a surrogacy arrangement prior to recognition may challenge it before the courts. But the recognition will stand if it complies with the child's genetic heritage. The reasoning only applies to fatherhood. For the mother, genetic contribution is not enough to outweigh the bond created by pregnancy and recognition by the commissioning mother may be challenged whether it complies with the child's genetic heritage or not.

In Britain, the commissioning father will be the legal father if the surrogacy arrangement was conducted through a licensed clinic, the commissioning father was the sperm donor, and the surrogate is not married or her husband did not consent to the procedure: Section HFEA 1990, s 28(2). If the surrogacy arrangement was carried out outside a licensed clinic, the commissioning father, unless he applies to the courts, may only establish his paternity by inclusion of his name on the birth certificate with the agreement of the surrogate (Births and Deaths Registration Act 1953, para 10(1)(a)).

[33] French Civil Code, art 374 al.1.

[34] *Possession d'état* allows parenthood by doing (article 310–1 of the French Civil Code, at 310–1). If certain signs make a child appear to be the son/daughter of X, then he/she will become in law the son/daughter of X, provided no other claims to parenthood relating to the child are made. The required signs are, among others, the *'nomen'*, ie that the child is known under the name of X, the *'tractatus'*, ie the fact that the child is treated by X like X's son/daughter, the *'fama'*, ie the fact that the outside world (X's relatives, third parties, and public authorities) regard the child as X's son/daughter (see French Civil Code; art 311–1).

[35] cf CA Rennes 4 juillet 2002 (n 30 above) see also Ministerial instructions of 30 June 2006 on the 4 July 2005 Act and TGI Lille 22 March 2007, *Revue Dalloz*, 1251.

which I do not intend to repeat here. My aim is rather to compare how each country has manifested its reluctance differently. The difference I will suggest is not just one of degree (hostile tolerance in the United Kingdom, outright repulsion in France) but one of method based on underlying profoundly diverging ideologies. The prohibitive position adopted by France needs first to be explained further.

B. Analysis of the French Position

Prohibition of surrogacy was first[36] formulated by the Cour de Cassation in full assembly in 1991[37] before receiving Parliament's assent when the first Act on Bioethics was at last passed in 1994.[38] It has since been confirmed both by the legislator in 2004[39] and the courts.[40]

The basis for the 1991 decision was laid down by the Report made before the Court by Monsieur le Conseiller Yves Chartier and a brief reminder of its content is therefore necessary in order to understand the Court's decision to prohibit surrogacy altogether. But let us first look at the facts. The facts of the case were relatively straightforward and most exceptionally had never given rise to a dispute between the parties. In 1988, baby Marie-Louise was born through a surrogacy arrangement and handed over to the commissioning couple. The parties had met through a non-profit making association called 'Alma Mater' later declared to be illegal and hence dissolved by the courts.[41] The surrogate had carried a child conceived by artificial insemination with the commissioning father's sperm and had subsequently given birth without revealing her identity. The child was consequently registered as born of an unknown mother. The commissioning father recognized the child as his own and as sole legal parent was automatically granted parental responsibility for her.

The case came to the attention of the courts when the commissioning mother made a request to adopt her husband's child. The first instance court—the tribunal de grande instance of Paris[42]—rejected the adoption order. Despite admitting that the order would probably be in the child's present best interests, the court refused to allow the adoption because the surrogate had unlawfully surrendered her parental rights, in violation of the old article 311–9 of the French

---

[36] The first civil chamber had also expressed its disapproval: Première Chambre de la Cour de Cassation (Civ 1ère) 13 December 1989 *Association Alma Mater v Procureur Général d'Aix-en-Provence Bulletin Civil* I, n°387, p 260; JCP 1990.II.21526, note A Sériaux; *Revue Dalloz* 1990, 273, rapport J Massip; *Defrénois* 1990, 743, note J-L Aubert, RT Dciv 1990, 254, observations J Rubellin-Devichi. See also at appellate level, CA Aix en Provence 27 Avril 1988 JCP 1989. III.21191, note Ph Pedrot, 161 63 No 10.

[37] AP 31 May 1991, *Revue Dalloz* 1991, 417 ; JCP 1991.II.21752 ; RTD civ 1991, 517; RTD civ 1992, 489.

[38] See n 27 above.   [39] ibid.

[40] Civ 1ère 9 December 2003 (février 2004) *Droit de la famille*, 21–2.

[41] See n 36 above.

[42] TGI Paris, 28 June 1989.

Civil Code[43] and because granting the adoption request would endorse an illegal practice. The court was however willing to grant *'une adoption simple'*[44] in which the child's biological motherhood would be preserved. But the commissioning couple refused and appealed against the decision. The irrevocable nature of the type of adoption requested—*adoption plénière*—preventing the surrogate from ever playing a part in the child's life, seemed to have been a decisive factor in the first instance court's decision.

Before the Court of Appeal, the commissioning couple obtained the requested pleniary adoption order.[45] The Court of Appeal like the first instance court asserted that the issue of adoption could not be considered separately from that of the legality of the surrogacy arrangement itself since adoption was the very aim of the surrogacy arrangement but unlike the first instance court, it held that surrogacy arrangements were legal and consequently granted the adoption order. The Court of Appeal's reasoning was based on the legality of the procedure followed by the parties in order to secure a parental link with the child: the commissioning father was legally entitled to recognize the child, the surrogate was granted by law like any pregnant woman the possibility of giving birth anonymously, the commissioning father as sole legal parent was perfectly allowed and indeed obliged to take care of the child and exercise parental responsibility for her. As for the first steps, ie the conditions relating to conception itself, the Court of Appeal justified the practice in quite emphatic terms in the name of individual liberty and reproductive rights of sterile couples and added that to discriminate against children according to the circumstances of their conception would infringe Article 12 of the Universal Declaration on Human Rights and Article 8 of the European Convention on Human Rights. The hurdle of the *'principle of indisponibilité'*[46] was swept away with the following two comments: the inalienability of the human body which puts the human body outside the ambit of contract already suffers many exceptions such as organ donations, and surrogacy should be added to the list of derogations; the inalienability of individual status which prevents people from waiving their parental rights by contract is sufficiently guaranteed by the unenforceable and altruistic nature of the agreement. Provided that the surrogacy arrangement is made under non-commercial terms and remains unenforceable, it is therefore, under the Court of Appeal's view, legal and adoption should follow, so long as usual as it is in the child's best interests.

---

[43] According to the old art 311–9 (now French Civil Code, art 323) a person cannot surrender or transfer parental rights or duties to another.

[44] *'Adoption simple'* does not sever the links between the child and his biological parents.

[45] CA Paris, 15 June 1990, JCP 1991.II.21653, note B Edelmann and C Labrusse-Riou.

[46] According to this principle, the human body and individual status cannot be the object of agreements. On this principle, see A Jack, 'Les Conventions relatives à la personne physique' (1933) *Revue de critique législative et jurisprudentielle* 3; D Huet-Weiller, 'Réflexions sur l'indisponibilité des actions relatives à la filiation', *D.*1978, chronique 233; M Gobert, 'Réflexions sur les sources du droit et les principes d'indisponibilité du corps humain et de l'état des personnes. A propos des maternités de substitution' (1992) RTD civ 489.

The revolutionary approach adopted by the Court of Appeal was utterly condemned by the Cour de Cassation in a concise but powerful statement:

The agreement whereby a woman, albeit under non-commercial terms, consents to conceive and bear a child in the view of abandoning it at birth, violates both the principle
of inalienability of the human body and the principle of inalienability of individual
status.

By ordering a pleniary adoption by a woman where the adoption request was only the
ultimate phase of a global process designed to allow a couple to raise a child who had been
conceived in performance of a contract whereby the child's mother committed herself to
abandoning the child at birth, the Court of appeal violated articles 6 and 1128 of the civil
code together with article 353 of the same code and approved a process which distorted
the aim of the institution of adoption.[47]

The Court of Appeal's reasoning contained a few flaws: the assertion of a new
natural right to reproduction was a contradiction in terms; natural rights are
supposed to belong inherently to human nature and by definition are inalter-
able and unchangable. There cannot be any 'new' natural rights and in the tradition of Rousseau, only life and liberty count as natural rights.[48] But the Cour de
Cassation could have easily rectified the inappropriate drafting and still approved
the Court of Appeal's conclusion by merging reproductive rights into the concept
of liberty as an expression of bodily autonomy. This would however have violated
the fundamental principle of the inalienability of the human body and here lies
the other flaw in the Court of Appeal's approach; the Court of Appeal added
surrogacy too easily to the list of the derogations already made to the principle.
If organ donations are indeed a valid exception to the principle of human body
inalienability, the exception was the result of legislative intervention. Judges are
not entitled to put aside fundamental principles. But more deeply, the Cour de
Cassation and the Court of Appeal of Paris took strongly different views on the
problem of surrogacy.

The Court of Appeal of Paris and the Cour de Cassation could not have held
more extreme opposite views. Where the Court of Appeal looked at the facts
with a sympathetic eye, aware of and sensitive to sterile couples' needs to raise
a child genetically related to one of them, the Cour de Cassation implicitly

---

[47] The French goes as follows: 'La convention par laquelle une femme s'engage, fût-ce à titre
gratuit, à concevoir et à porter un enfant pour l'abandonner à sa naissance contrevient tant au
principe d'ordre public de l'indisponibilité du corps humain qu'à celui de l'indisponibilité de l'état
des personnes.
    A violé les articles 6 et 1128 du Code civil, ensemble article 353 du même code, la cour d'appel
qui a prononcé l'adoption plénière d'un enfant par une femme, alors que toute cette adoption
n'était que l'ultime phase d'un processus d'ensemble destiné à permettre à un couple l'accueil à
son foyer d'un enfant, conçu en exécution d'un contrat tendant à l'abandon à sa naissance par sa
mère, et que, portant atteinte aux principes susvisés, ce processus constituait un détournement de
l'institution de l'adoption.'
[48] See JJ Rousseau, *Discours sur l'origine et les fondements de l'inégalité,* Vol III (Pléiade, 1990)
184. (First published in 1755).

followed its Counsellor's view that there is no natural right to reproduction as such.[49] Access to reproductive technologies is dependent on a welfare test: the requested treatment must be proven to be in the patient's interest. However, who qualifies as a patient in a surrogacy arrangement? Logically, the sterile woman does and it is difficult to argue that the treatment would go against her interests. The Reporter before the Cour de Cassation did not attempt such a line of argument but underlined instead the risks run by the child-to-be and the surrogate mother. The child is said to be likely to suffer in his/her uterine life: either as a result of the surrogate's indifference towards him/her throughout the pregnancy or/and as a result of the trauma of separation when he/she is handed over to another woman, a total stranger.[50] The surrogate is also described as being at risk: besides the medical and physical risks related to pregnancy and giving birth, the surrogate is likely to suffer psychological problems later in her life as a result of having had to part with her baby. The little data available as to surrogates' motivation (desire to deal with their own abandonment as a child, way of 'paying back' past abortions or abandonments) only increases the likelihood of future psychological difficulties.[51]

Where the Court of Appeal swiftly disposed of the '*principle of indisponibilité*' of the human body and of individual status, the Cour de Cassation added a new vigour to the principle. A contractual model is for the Court of Cassation radically unsuited to rules of parenthood. If people's wishes are taken into account in the rules of parenthood, parenthood is above all grounded in law and biology, not in individual wishes. For the Cour de Cassation, there is a fundamental dichotomy between the sphere of contracts and the sphere of parenthood and the above-mentionned principle is there to preserve it.

Where the Court of Appeal invoked Article 8 of the European Convention on Human Rights and Article 12 of the Universal Declaration on Human Rights, the Cour de Cassation implicitly judged these international treaties to be irrelevant. Both protect the right to family life but, according to the Reporter before the Cour de Cassation, the best way to enhance that right would be to make sure that the child is brought up by his mother (ie the surrogate), not to sanction a practice which will artificially make a child a half orphan.[52] Obviously, what the Court of Appeal had in mind was the sterile couple's right to family life, construed in an extensive way as the right to create a family. By contrast, for the Cour de Cassation, only already existing family units deserve protection and after the child's birth, the only existing family unit is said to be that of the surrogate and the child, not that of the child and the commissioning couple. For the Cour de Cassation, the identification of the family unit is not only, as we have seen, independent from individual wishes—in compliance with the principle of inalienability of individual status—but also from the reality of the facts. Indeed,

---

[49] Rapport de M Yves Chartier, Conseiller à la Cour de cassation, *Revue Dalloz*, 1991, 417, 419.
[50] ibid.   [51] ibid.   [52] ibid 421.

in that case, the child was being raised by the commissioning couple and granting the adoption order would just have confirmed the status quo.

But this point was not central before the Cour de Cassation. Indeed, the Cour
de Cassation holds only on points of law and tends to a certain extent to undermine the importance of facts, or rather leave their appreciation to the discretion of lower courts. But undoubtedly, Cour de Cassation judges are still aware
of the potential factual consequences of their decisions and facts, in that sense,
usually have a bearing on solutions. However, in that case, the appeal lodged with
the Cour de Cassation was made following a specific procedure called *'pourvoi
dans l'intérêt de la loi'*[53] designed to resolve a contradiction in case law—in this
instance, the Court of Appeal of Paris' decision to recognize the legality of surrogacy and a previous decision by the first civil chamber of the Cour de Cassation
holding that surrogacy arrangements were contrary to public policy.[54] The specificity of this type of appeal is that it has no impact on the parties. In other
words, the adoption order already granted by the Court of Appeal could not be
affected by the Cour de Cassation's decision. This peculiar situation most probably prompted the Cour de Cassation to condemn the practice fully, knowing
that the present child would not be harmed by its extreme severity.

Moreover, the two issues of the legality of the surrogacy and the legitimacy of
adoption had already been seen as one single problem by the Court of Appeal.
Just as the Court of Appeal thought that the legality of surrogacy almost implied
the legitimacy of adoption, the Cour de Cassation was by symmetry tempted to
condemn both surrogacy and adoption in one strike. However, the issues could,
and in my view should, have been distinguished. Adoption is based on the welfare
of the child[55] and it is deeply disturbing to have the first court judgment acknowledge that adoption by the commissioning mother would be in the child's present
best interests and still refuse the order. Obviously, granting the adoption would
finalize the process and conclude to all parties' satisfaction a plan that the Cour
de Cassation specifically wants to condemn. There is a strong risk that granting
the adoption would send to commissioning couples the signal that surrogacy,
despite the Cour de Cassation's disapproval, is a worthwhile route. Nevertheless,
in adoption law, a child's interests should be paramount and have precedence

---

[53] Under of the Law of 3 July 1967, art 17 the Procureur Général près la Cour de Cassation
is entitled to appeal to the Cour de Cassation against a decision that has already been enforced
or against which none of the parties have decided to appeal. Decisions rendered by the Cour de
Cassation following this procedure have no effect on the parties' vested rights and obligations. The
Procureur Général may use this procedure where a Court of Appeal decision seems to be in violation of existing rules, here a previous decision of the first civil chamber of the Cour de Cassation of
13 December 1989 (*Bulletin civil* I, n°387, p 260).

[54] Civ 1ère 13 December 1989 (n 36 above). The 1989 decision was rendered in a different context. The legality of surrogacy came to be considered in a litigation against intermediaries who
helped surrogates and commissioning couples to meet. The illegality pronounced in 1989 thus left
open the question of whether to order the adoption by a commissioning mother of a child 'illegally'
conceived.

[55] French Civil Code, art 353.

over the need for the consistency and efficiency of the legal system. It is true that the Cour de Cassation's severity had no impact on the child in the present case but children in later case law were not so fortunate.

Mr and Mrs Lequesne thus, for example, later suffered from French law's harshness. The couple had obtained a child abroad through a Brazilian surrogate; they then secretly brought the baby back to France and declared it as their own. The baby was then raised for several years by Mrs Lequesne and her new partner Aaron Baron until the fraud was discovered and the parties prosecuted. The child was removed from his parents and put into care.[56] When the parties do not substitute a child for another or as in the 2000 case, hold a child out as the offspring of a woman who is not its mother by faking a delivery, the only (but already heavy) sanction will be a bar on adoption by the commissioning mother. This was confirmed by a 2003 decision of the Cour de Cassation.[57] In that case, Sarah was born in 1987 to an unknown mother and a married father who recognized the baby as his own. The baby was raised by her father and his wife. When the girl was 12 years old, the wife made a request to adopt her husband's child. The couple argued that the baby was born at a time when surrogacy arrangements had not yet been made illegal and that the best interests of the child should prevail. But the Cour de Cassation rejected the adoption request, stating, as in 1991, that surrogacy constituted a fraud to adoption rules. No concern as to the welfare of the child was allowed to soften the prohibition of surrogacy.

By contrast, in Britain, in the famous *Baby Cotton* case[58] which prompted the passing of the Surrogacy Arrangements Act 1985,[59] Latey J clearly distinguished the issue of the legitimacy of the arrangement and the issue of subsequent adoption of the child: 'Plainly, the methods used to produce a child as this baby has been and the commercial aspects of it, raise difficult and delicate problems of ethics, morality and social desirability. Are they relevant in arriving at a decision on what now and in the future is best for the child? In my judgment, they are not relevant. The baby is here. All that matters is what is best for her now that she is here and not how she arrived.' In the United Kingdom, if the future of the child is disputed, it will be governed by consideration of his/her welfare.[60] In practice, the surrogate is likely to keep the child if she changed her mind and refused to hand the baby over at birth.[61] But if the mother does not want the child and

---

[56] Crim 16 January 2000, *Bulletin criminel*, n°21; *Droit pénal* 2000, Commentaire 84, observations Véron.

[57] Civ 1ère 9 December 2003 (fevrier 2004) *Droit de la famille* 21–2.

[58] The *Baby Cotton Affair, Re C (A Minor)* [1985] FLR 846.

[59] See M Freeman, 'Legal and Philosophical Frameworks for Medical Decision Making' in M Freeman (ed), *Current Legal Problems. Medicine, Ethics and the Law* (London: Stevens & Sons, 1988) 1, describing the 1985 Act as a largely irrelevant panic measure. See also, C Dyer, 'Baby Cotton and the Birth of a Moral Panic' *The Guardian*, 15 January 1985.

[60] The Children Act 1989, s 1(1).

[61] See *A v C* [1985] 1 FLR 445; *Re P (Minors) (Wardship: Surrogacy)* [1987] 2 FLR 421.

the commissioning parents are able to offer a suitable home, the courts are more likely to allow the commissioning couple to keep and adopt the child.[62]

No similar distinction is drawn by French judges. The situation of the child is not even examined. A radical abstract and prohibitive approach is instead taken. As in its previous 1991 case, the Cour de Cassation in 2003 thus condemned the surrogacy and adoption order in one go, not only because allowing adoption by a commissioning mother would undermine the prohibition of surrogacy but also because the parties were said to have committed a fraud against adoption rules. Without openly violating the rules on adoption, the commissioning couple deliberately abused the law. 'The abuse of the law arises out of the arrangement between the parties to create a homeless child in order to take advantage of the legal provisions intended for genuine homeless babies.'[63] Adoption will only be possible in France if the existence of a prior surrogacy arrangement is ignored by the lower courts which, under article 353 of the French Civil Code, may grant an adoption request without having to state any particular reason or justification for their decision. If recourse to surrogacy is thus not alluded to in the lower courts' decision, censorship by the Cour de Cassation should be avoided.[64]

In neither France nor England is surrogacy thus completely assimilated to adoption. In the United Kingdom, the genetic tie seems to make surrogacy more susceptible than adoption to lead to a favourable outcome for the applicants, the commissioning couple. On the contrary, in France the deliberate and contractual nature of the child's conception through a surrogacy arrangement alienates it from the 'spirit' of the institution of adoption that is designed to provide families for orphans and not babies for childless families. Thus where the genetic link often present between the commissioning father and the child, if not both between the commissioning father and commissioning mother and the child, justifies in English Law a simplification of adoption procedures *via* access, under added conditions of entitlement, to the easier and quicker procedure of a parental order,[65] the distinction made between surrogacy and adoption is a further argument in France in favour of the prohibition of surrogacy and an irretrievable obstacle to adoption by a commissioning mother of a child born to a surrogate.

Reluctance with regard to surrogacy is therefore far deeper in France than it is in England. Whereas surrogacy is more and more seen in England as another

[62] *Re C (A Minor)* [1985] FLR 846, known as the '*Baby Cotton*' case.

[63] E Steiner, 'Surrogacy Arrangements in French Law' (1992) 41 *ICLQ* 866, 873. On this idea of a distortion of the institution of adoption, see F Boulanger, 'Fraude, simulation ou détournement d'institutions en droit de la famille', *JCP* 1993.I.3665.

[64] See J Rubellin-Devichi, 'Procréations assistées et stratégies en matière de filiation', JCP 1991.I.3505, p 185.

[65] HFEA 1990, s 30. The parental order is only open to married couples if one at least is the child's genetic parent and if the child is living with the applicants and the legal parents have consented to the order. Moreover, applications must be made within six months of the birth.

option for infertile couples,[66] surrogacy is seen as separate from other infertility treatments in France.[67] The extreme position adopted by France is not really linked to more acute concerns of the legal community towards surrogacy. In both countries, similar worries and fears have been raised. It is not the concerns surrounding surrogacy themselves but the way they have been translated into the legal debate that has brought these contrasting views. Let us now therefore turn to these concerns and more importantly to the way in which they were dealt with in both countries.

III. Fears of Exploitation

In both countries, fears of exploitation have been voiced. The surrogate is often described as a vulnerable person whose weakness is exploited to serve the commissioning couple's desire for a child. Concerns have also been raised regarding the commissioning woman, who may be under social pressure to provide her husband or partner with a child, using all possible means, including surrogacy: 'whether it is intended or not, the impression is given that a woman's primary function is to bear a child and failing in that function, she is a failure, becoming a net burden on family and society. Throughout history, women have all too often laboured under a duty to reproduce... We must be very careful that under the banner of women's rights, patriarchy does not triumph again.'[68] However, in the United Kingdom, there seems to be some scope for legitimate surrogacy arrangements where it can be proven that the surrogate genuinely consented to the contract. Rather than putting on the parties the burden of an impossible negative proof of the absence of all pressures on the surrogate's mind, English law draws a line between commercial agreements—presumed to be exploitative[69]— and altruistic arrangements—presumed to be risk free.[70] In France, on the other hand, fears of exploitation go to the heart of surrogacy itself as they are linked to the high involvement of the human body in a contract. In a surrogacy arrangement, the surrogate lends her bearing capacities for nine months at least, thus making her body the object of a contract. Whether her own dignity is affected or

---

[66] See *Review of the Human Fertilisation and Embryology Act* (n 11 above) para 2.64: 'Surrogacy, when all those involved are willing and well informed, can be an option for couples who cannot have children by other means. The government does not wish to restrict it unduly as a procedure for the alleviation of infertility, on a non-commercial basis.'

[67] At least in the eyes of the law. But a recent survey of French people's opinions revealed that 53% were in favour of surrogacy and considered it to be just another form of reproductive technique, quoted by X Labbée, comments on TGI Lille 22 March 2007, *Revue Dalloz*, 2007, 1251, 1255.

[68] M Brazier, 'Reproductive Rights: Feminism or Patriarchy?' in J Harris and S Holm (eds), *The Future of Human Reproduction* (Oxford University Press, 1998) 66, 76.

[69] See the Brazier Report (n 15 above) paras 4.25, 4.26.

[70] ibid para 4.36; see also, P Foot, *Virtues and Vices* (University of California Press, 1978); PM Slote, *From Morality to Virtue* (Oxford University Press, 1992).

not, the message it sends (were Parliament or the courts to sanction the validity of the arrangement) is that the human body is in general terms negotiable, thus opening the gates to a new market where body parts and reproductive abilities would be purely valued in financial terms.

In the United Kingdom, the discussion relating to fears of exploitation centres on *the issue of payment*. Altruistic arrangements seem to be devoid of any exploitative potential. The virtue of the 'gift' dispels all concerns. Only commercial arrangements appear suspicious as money, it is said, potentially distorts the surrogate's free will. Payments are seen as an inducement to engage in surrogacy arrangements without full understanding and realization of the physical and psychological risks involved.[71] Drawing a line between commercial and altruistic arrangements may, however, prove to be difficult. An altruistic arrangement may include payment of high expenses. Moreover, non-commercial agreements are not necessarily purely altruistic. Surrogates who enter into surrogacy arrangements with strangers for free will often seek to boost their self-confidence and hope to become, through this ultimate 'gift', someone special.[72] Besides, non-commercial agreements are no guarantee of free will. Are not subtle family pressures possibly more powerful to force a woman into a surrogacy arrangement?[73] There may be more ways of earning money than there are of contenting a sterile and frustrated sister for example. The concern for genuine free will and informed consent does not therefore justify the distinction drawn in Britain between altruistic and commercial surrogacies.

Some have consequently argued against the prohibition of commercial surrogacies. Why should surrogates deserve special treatment? Others who are economically as vulnerable are not deterred from entering into potentially exploitative or dangerous occupations.[74] Is prohibition of money in any case really more respectful of surrogates? Should they not be remunerated for the efforts they put in? How can banning payments protect women from exploitation when history shows that the lower status of women in society is inevitably linked to the fact that they undertake unpaid activities (like raising children, performing household chores, etc) or work in underpaid employment (like nursing or teaching)? Paying a woman to bear a child would force us to recognize the process as socially valuable.[75] On the contrary, prohibiting payments may reinforce the traditional gender inequity whereby women's work is kept out of the public sphere.[76]

---

[71] The Brazier Report (n 15 above) para 4.25.

[72] See A Stumcke, 'For Love or for Money: the Legal Regulation of Surrogate Motherhood' (1996) 3 *E Law-Murdoch University Electronic Journal of Law*, <http://www.murdoch.edu.au/elawl>.

[73] See J Oakley, 'Altruistic Surrogacy and Informed Consent' (1992) 6 *Bioethics* 269.

[74] cf M Freeman, 'Does Surrogacy have a Future after Brazier?' (n 24 above) 5.

[75] See L Purdy, *Reproducing Persons* (Cornell University Press, 1997) 47.

[76] MM Schultz, 'Reproductive Technology and Intent-Based Parenthood: An Opportunity for Gender Neutrality' (1990) *Wisconsin Law Review* 297, 301, n 11.

In France, fears of exploitation are not related to the possible lack of free consent of surrogates but to the mere use of the human body when '*the principle of indisponibilité*' tells us, the human body should remain outside the ambit of contracts. The human body should not be made an object of a deal. The issue is not whether there was free consent from all parties but that there was negotiation. Human dignity is at stake, not precisely from the perspective of a given surrogate but from the perspective of humanity as such, embodied in the behaviour of each of us. As Montaigne said '*je porte en moi l'entière condition humaine*'. Whether a surrogate truly freely consents to entering into a surrogacy arrangement or not, the arrangement cannot be made lawful because it shines unfavourably on all human beings.

Each line of arguments carries possible flaws. Focus on the surrogate's free will and autonomy in Britain undermines a more radical concern for the commodification of children. In the United Kingdom, if payments were allowed, we would run the risk of creating a market for babies. When faced with a particular surrogacy arrangement, risks for the particular child's well-being or for the particular surrogate's mental and physical health may not appear obvious. Fears of exploitation and commodification arise through the generalization of commercial surrogacy. If widespread, commercial surrogacy may change our perception of the value of life and human beings. Babies and surrogates would come to be valued in dollar terms with surrogates supposed to be able to offer the best genes and therefore the best babies being priced higher than those lower class women who supposedly (in the light of common prejudices) would not offer similar guarantees of gene quality and therefore be relegated to full surrogacy arrangements and face potentially more exploitative conditions.[77] The case-by-case approach favoured in Britain may therefore conceal the wider picture where the real risks of commodification lie. In France, on the other hand, prohibition of surrogacy relies on a broader conception of human dignity. But defending an idealistic view of humanity may disguise the oppression of minorities (in particular here, women who cannot bear a child) since the objective value of human dignity will be decided by Parliament on a majority basis. It is true to say that judges will be there to redress inequitable results in individual cases. But how reliable are they when the Cour de Cassation acts as a legislator and, as illustrated in the above-mentioned 1991 case,[78] rules in general terms, paying no attention to particular circumstances?

Various solutions have been suggested to resist the risk of exploitation. In the United Kingdom, the Brazier Report, still focusing on the issue of the surrogate's free will and the distinction between commercial and non-commercial arrangements, suggested that payments should be more strictly restricted to

---

[77] On the subject, see the important article by MJ Radin, 'Market Inalienability' (1987) 100 *Harvard Law Review* 1849. And for a contrary view, see EM Landes and RA Posner, 'The Economics of Baby Shortage' (1978) 7 *Journal of Legal Studies* 323.

[78] See n 37 above.

reimbursement of actual expenses.[79] As well as making sure that money would not be an incentive to surrogacy for a particular surrogate, the idea was to avoid the creation of professional surrogacies.[80] None of the proposals made by the report is yet in place and at the moment, despite the prohibition of commercial arrangements, judges, faced with a '*fait accompli*', at the time of a request for a parental order, are often willing retrospectively to allow payments made above expenses.[81] When the best interest of the child is to be raised by the commissioning couple, it is difficult to do otherwise, even though the couple may have acted in violation of the rules. Moreover, making rules too stringent may not avoid the creation of a market but only drive it underground.[82] A subtle and balanced solution needs therefore to be found. That is why the blanket prohibition in place in France is not satisfactory. It sacrifices individual freedom and drives protagonists underground where risks of exploitation are far greater than in a regulated lawful system.

The same extreme prohibitive attitude on the one hand and ambivalent pragmatism on the other explain the respective positions in France and in the UK on the issue of the enforceability of surrogacy arrangements.

IV. The Issue of Enforceability

In the United Kingdom, the debate on enforceability again revolves around questions of free will and the dangers of exploitation. Unenforceability is said to be more protective of the surrogate's interests. If surrogacy is presumed to be per se dangerous, unenforceability, like the prohibition of payments above expenses, acts as a further disincentive for parties to conclude surrogacy arrangements. Commissioning couples will think twice before entrusting a surrogate with the carrying of their genetic baby when they run the risk of her deciding in the end to keep the baby and ruin their hope of a child.[83] Moreover, unenforceability appears protective of the surrogate's free will. If the surrogate did not really freely consent to the arrangement, she thus still has the possibility of changing her mind. Unenforceability works as an extra safeguard for the surrogate's free decision: 'All non-enforcement does is to protect the woman who herself decides that she does not want to go through with the arrangement after all. Since the choices remain with the woman, it is hard to see how this recommendation may be called anti-feminist.'[84] But it may turn itself against the surrogate's interests

---

[79] The Brazier Report (n 15 above) paras 5.24–5.26.

[80] para 5.17.

[81] cf *Re Q (Parental Order)* [1996] 1 FLR 389, HC (*per* Johnson J), under HFEA 1990; s 30(7).

[82] See M Freeman, 'Does Surrogacy have a Future after Brazier?' (n 24 above) 7.

[83] This idea runs through the Brazier Report (n 15 above). For the recommendation that surrogacy arrangements should remain unenforceable, see ibid para 7.3.

[84] MA Field, 'Surrogate Motherhood' in J Eekekaar and P Sarcevic (eds), *Parenthood in Modern Society. Legal and Social Issues for the Twenty-first Century* (Martinus Nijhoff, 1993) 223, 227.

if the reneging party is the commissioning couple, for example because the baby they have ordered does not correspond to their expectations or because they have split up. In law, the surrogate is the mother of the child[85] and she will be the one entrusted with the responsibility of raising it or giving it up for adoption against her true wishes. Moreover, some have argued that unenforceability makes pregnant women appear capricious. If surrogates need to be allowed to change their minds, does it not reinforce stereotypes against women, particularly pregnant women, as unstable and unable to commit themselves?[86] Some authors have therefore opted for a defence of the contractual model with enforceable surrogacy arrangements.[87]

In France, the rule of unenforceability derives from the illegality of surrogacy. One can obviously not claim specific performance or damages for breach of an illegal contract, void *ab initio.*

Which view is to be favoured? How should surrogacy be treated in law? Can a common proposal be made for France and Britain or do the above outlined differences between the two countries require distinct approaches?

V. My Suggestion: Surrogacy, a Liberty

I suggest that surrogacy be treated as a liberty, both in Britain and France. Rather than tying the surrogate down to a contractual model giving rise to enforceable duties and rights on all parties, rather than presenting the parties with the hurdle of a prohibitive position, I would argue that the surrogate should be allowed to enter into a surrogacy arrangement lawfully but should also be allowed to change her mind, not for fears of possible pressures on her free will nor in the hope that the practice will wither as a result as in the United Kingdom but more positively, for the sake of a fundamental liberty: the liberty to recognize (or not) one's children as one's own. Let's now see how this proposal would stand in each country.

In my view, the French 'principle of *indisponibilité*', placing the human body outside the reach of contracts could allow expression of unilateral will. Surrogates could be free to use their bodies as they wish as an expression of a fundamental liberty: physical autonomy. Surrogacy would thus be justified as well as the rule of unenforceability. Using an analogy, individuals are free to become engaged to get married but their commitment to marry has no binding force. The liberty to wed is too fundamental to be waived by contract. Circumstances or feelings may change. It would be contrary to the fundamental liberty to wed to tie people

---

[85] HFEA 1990, s 27.

[86] See MM Schultz, 'Reproductive Technology and Intent-Based Parenthood: An Opportunity for Gender Equality' (1990) *Wisconsin Law Review* 297, 384.

[87] See MM Schultz (n 86 above) 349; JL Hill, 'The Case for Enforcement of the Surrogate Contract' (1990) *Politics Life Sciences* 147.

to their word. A similar reasoning may be in my view adopted for surrogacy.[88] Liberty to marry or to recognize one's child as one's own is so fundamental that it could not be restricted by contract: 'There are certain subject matters that are so important and so deeply personal that we as a society do not want the state to intervene to bind people—men *or* women—by their previous promises.'[89] This liberty could not even be restricted by a so-called right to procreation of the commissioning couple. There is a liberty to procreate which cannot or should not be interfered with by the state, for instance through forced sterilization,[90] but there is no right to demand from a third party (doctor, surrogate, sperm donor, state) the means enabling us to fulfil our reproductive desires. There is no right to a child as such, at least not from the French perspective. The United Kingdom, encouraged both by US case law on privacy[91] and more recently, by EU law, in the *Blood*[92] and *Grogan*[93] cases, which are imbued with a liberal stance, may take a different view. But the European Court of Human Rights in the *Evans*[94] case sent a more complex and balanced message which could support my proposal.

Under the right to privacy, individuals should be allowed, within a private sphere[95] which includes reproductive matters,[96] to do everything they like

---

[88] See, supporting this analogy, M Gobert, 'Réflexions sur les sources du droit et les "principes" d'indisponibilité du corps humain et de l'état des personnes. A propos de la maternité de substitution ' (1991) RTD civ 489, 519; F Terré, L'Enfant de l'esclave (Flammarion, 1987) 188 and JCP 1991.II.21752, p 383; J Rubellin-Devichi, 'Congélation d'embryons, fécondation *in vitro*, mères de substitution. Point de vue d'un juriste' in *Génétique, procréation et droit, Actes du Colloque* (Actes Sud, 1985) 314.

[89] Field (n 84 above) 225.

[90] The right to reproduce was recognized in the context of an application for sterilization of a 17-year-old ward of court with a mental age of 6 years: *Re B (A Minor) (Wardship: Sterilisation)* [1988] (*per* Lord Hailsham 203, *per* Lord Oliver 211). But sterilization was approved in this case in the woman's best interests. In France, the possibility of forced sterilization on adults deprived of their full mental capacities was recognized under the Law of 4 July 2001 (L n°2001–588), *JO* 7 July 2001; JCP 2001, *Actualités* n°30, 1477, Commentaire T Fossier and T Verheyde. But this is seen as an exception to the principle of reproductive autonomy and is subject to conditions, notably 'medical necessity'.

[91] *Skinner v Oklahoma* 316 US 535 (1942) in which it was held that the right to privacy covered the right to procreate. The decision confers legitimacy on surrogacy arrangements, at least in a non-commercial context. See R Rao, 'Surrogacy in the US: The Outcome of Ambivalence' in R Cook, S Day Sclater, and F Kaganas (eds), *Surrogate Motherhood. International Perspective* (Hart, 2003) 23, 25.

[92] Court of Appeal, *R v HFEA, ex p Diane Blood* [1997] 2 All ER 687 (CA).

[93] ECJ, 4 October 1991 *Society for the Protection of Unborn Children in Ireland Ltd (SPUC) v Stephen Grogan and Ors* Case C-159/90, Recueil 1991, I-04685.

[94] ECtHR, 7 March 2006 *Evans v UK* (2006) *RTD civ* 255–60, note J-P Marguénaud; S Sheldon, '*Evans v Amicus Healthcare*; *Hadley v Midland Fertility Services*—Revealing Cracks in the "Twin Pillars"?' (2004) 16 *CFLQ* 437. On the Court of Appeal's ruling, *Evans v Amicus Healthcare Ltd* [2004] EWCA Civ 727; [2005] Fam 1 (CA (Civ Div)), see S Sheldon, 'Gender Equality and Reproductive Decision-Making' (2004) 12(3) *Feminist Legal Studies* 303.

[95] On the difficulties of drawing a clear-cut public/private divide, see N Rose, 'Beyond the Public/Private Division: Law, Power and the Family' in P Fitzpatrick and A Hunts (eds), *Critical Legal Studies* (Blackwell, 1987) 61, 68.

[96] For a justification and a presentation of the concept of reproductive autonomy, see R Dworkin, *Life's Dominion* (London: Harper Collins, 1993) 148, 166–7.

provided it does not interfere with others' liberties. If individuals choose to bind themselves by contract, so be it. There is no right of privacy as such in English law, save via Article 8 of the European Convention on Human Rights, but this idea is contained in the concept of reproductive autonomy.[97] Applied to surrogacy, this philosophy favours contractual regulation over objective norms. It also favours *in fine* reproductive rights of the commissioning couple (less likely to change their minds) over the surrogate's (possibly changing) wishes. Statistics are often quoted to prove that surrogates rarely change their minds in practice. Indeed, it is estimated that in only 5 per cent of arrangements, the birth mother refuses to hand over the child.[98] But in a context where unenforceability is albeit authorized seen as a failure, where associations emphasize the importance to respect one's promise,[99] reneging surrogates are *'tuées dans l'oeuf'*, 'killed in the womb'. Moreover, how many of these successful arrangements hide regrets and despair? The mere description of the instances where the surrogates refuse to hand over the child as failed surrogacy arrangements reflect an unquestioned preference for the commissioning couple. If the surrogate were seen as exercising a fundamental liberty, if her claim to the child were therefore seen, irrespective of any deals, as paramount, one would not describe these instances as failures. The commissioning couple would no doubt be devastated but the child would still be brought up by a willing parent and individual liberties in my view would be better respected.

This conclusion can only be reached if the commissioning couple has no enforceable right to the child. Neither French nor British law grants the commissioning couple an enforceable right but one may argue that the present position violates the couple's right to procreation. Reproductive autonomy should in that view prompt a review of existing legislation in the direction of liberalization. Such a reasoning seems to have found an unexpected ally in EU law. In the *Blood* case,[100] Diane Blood challenged the Human Fertilisation and Embryology Authority's decision to deny her the right to export her dead husband's sperm to another EU country. Diane Blood's husband had died from a sudden meningitis. As he lay dying on his hospital bed, Mrs Blood persuaded the hospital staff to take some of his sperm in order to carry out a posthumous sperm insemination in the future. English law does not prohibit posthumous insemination but

---

[97] Reproductive autonomy does not, however, confer an absolute right to be provided with a child, see *Mellor v Secretary of State for the Home Department* [2000] QB 13, *per* Hale HL; the Brazier Report (n 15 above) para 4.32.

[98] ibid para 3.5.

[99] See COTS' emphasis on the surrogate's moral duty to keep her word: 'Finally and most importantly, it would be the final blow for your parents-to-be if you kept the child. *You would have robbed them of all hope they have placed in you.* You have your children to go home to, they are *empty handed.* It is a tremendous trust that your couple have placed on your shoulders, DO NOT BETRAY THAT TRUST' (original emphasis), COTS' Booklet, 'Information for Surrogates' (1987), quoted in the Brazier Report, (n 15 above) para 3.32, n 19.

[100] See n 92 above.

makes it conditional on the father's express consent.[101] Mrs Blood claimed that her husband would have consented[102] but it was clear that the requirement of an express consent had not been met. The taking of the sperm itself was described by the judge as an assault.[103] Unable to have a child from her dead husband under English law, Mrs Blood then sought to export the sperm to Belgium where artificial insemination would be permitted. The HFEA first refused but, after being urged by the Court of Appeal to review its decision in consideration of EU law, it finally granted Mrs Blood's request. The Court of Appeal indeed took the view that the HFEA's (initial) decision to refuse to make specific directions allowing access to the sperm for export was an interference with Mrs Blood's right to receive services and concomitant right to freedom of movement, under Articles 60 and 59 of the Treaty of Rome.[104] The reasoning partly relies on a previous European Court Of Justice (ECJ) case in which abortion was characterized as a service under EU law.[105] The solution could easily be transposed to surrogacy cases in order to allow a commissioning couple to enter into a surrogacy arrangement in another more permissive EU law country. Will French sterile women thus become familiar with the Eurostar? In my view, recourse to EU law in such instances is highly questionable. By characterizing any reproductive technology offered by professionals for remuneration as a 'service' to which access within the European Union should not therefore be restricted, unless a plea of derogation can be made by the Member State concerned, the ECJ is extending the construction of a free market beyond its legitimate boundaries. One may argue that all citizens of the European Union should freely have access to medical treatment and techniques throughout the Union but when these techniques affect rules of parenthood and the conception we have of babies, human beings, and reproduction, such an argument must rely on more than the goal of a harmonious and balanced development of economic activities. In the *Grogan* case, 'despite

---

[101] HEFA 1990, Sch 3, para 1.

[102] Mrs Blood and her husband had apparently discussed their intention to have a child and had specifically addressed the possibility of posthumous artificial insemination, see (1997) 35 BNLR 1, 8 *per* Sir Stephen Brown.

[103] [1997] 2 All ER 687, 690 *per* Lord Woolf.

[104] For comments on the case, see D Morgan and RG Lee, 'In the Name of the Father? *Ex Parte Blood*: Dealing with Novelty and Anomaly' (1997) 60 *MLR* 840; TK Hervey, 'Buy Baby: The European Union and Regulation of Human Reproduction' (1998) 18 *OJLS* 207; R Sefton-Green, 'La Procréation médicalement assistée entre droit national et droit communautaire. La controverse devant les cours anglaises' (2000) n° spécial *Revue générale de droit médical*, C Labrusse-Riou, B Mathieu and N-J Mazen (eds), *La Recherche sur l'embryon. Qualifications et enjeux*; J-S Bergé, 'Le Droit communautaire dévoyé. Le cas *Blood*' (1999) *Revue Europe* 4.

[105] The *Grogan* case (n 93 above). For comments on the case, see L Idot, 'A Propos de l'interruption de grossesse: premier bilan de la jurisprudence de la Cour relative à la libre prestation de services en 1991' (1991) Europe 4; H Gaudemet-Tallon, note (1992), RTD eu 167; DR Phelan, 'Right to Life of the Unborn v Promotion of Trade in Services: The European Court of Justice and the Shaping of the European Union' (1992) 55 *MLR* 670; S O'Leary, 'The Court of Justice as a Reluctant Constitutional Adjudicator: An Examination of the Abortion Information Case' (1992) 17 *European Law Review* 138; D Curtin, (1992) 29 *Common Market Law Review* 585.

the basis of SPUC's argument in national criminal legislation and unenumerated constitutional rights, and despite the Court's own engagement in moral issues by assuming a human rights jurisdiction, the Court characterised the argument that abortion was not a service under EC law as simply "moral" and therefore irrelevant'.[106] But moral arguments in such a context cannot simply be ignored. Pretending not to take a moral view in order to characterize abortion as a service, is in itself a moral statement: a refutation that some aspects of society can be immune from the logics and forces of the market. For countries such as France where in theory at least a strong divide still exits between the world of contracts and alienability and the world of '*indisponibilité*' in which certain elements and objects are placed beyond the scope of agreements, the statement is a direct threat to one of the most fundamental features of the legal system as well as to human dignity, which market inalienability is supposed to preserve. Besides, the ECJ's reasoning shows a curious disregard for fundamental rights. In the *Grogan* case, the right said to conflict with Treaty objectives was no less than the right to life and that right was entrenched in the Constitution, ie the highest norm of the Member State concerned (Ireland).[107] Relegating fundamental constitutional rights to precarious derogations amounts, in effect, to a re-shaping of human rights law as rights of the *homo economicus* to travel and pay for the services he/she longs for and a consecration of autonomy (provided individuals can afford it) as the supreme value across the European Union.

A pragmatic solution would be to have unified solutions across all Member States. Indeed EU law can only be invoked in order to benefit from a different (and presumably less stringent) legislation in another Member State. Should the gap between national legislations be reduced, the incentive to claim rights under the Treaty of Rome would also be diminished. In the area of reproductive technologies, oppositions between Member States are too acute to make the aim of a consensus realistic in the near future. But this consideration is an argument in favour of my proposal. If surrogacy could be accepted as a liberty in both Britain and France, a procreative tourism under the umbrella of EU law would not arise between Britain and France. A further justification may be found in European human rights law. In the *Evans* case,[108] the European Court of Human Rights recognized the right of respect of one's decision to have a child or not. Sadly for Ms Evans in that case, the right was used to justify her ex-partner's refusal to let her use the embryos they had created together prior to Ms Evans' treatment for cancer and loss of her reproductive capacities. Her ex-partner's right

---

[106]   Phelan (n 105 above); O'Leary (n 105 above) 693.

[107]   Constitution of Ireland art 40(3). For a recent presentation of the issue of abortion in Ireland, see S Mullally, *Gender, Culture and Human Rights, Reclaiming Universalism* (Oxford and Portland, Oregon: Hart, 2006) 141. Abortion can be allowed for Irish mothers in extreme cases, for instance most recently, in the case of Miss D, an Irish 17-year-old, was allowed by the High Court to travel to Britain for an abortion, *The Guardian*, 2 May 2007.

[108]   See n 94 above.

to decide not to have children (with her) prevailed over Ms Evans' desire for and last chance of a child. In the context of surrogacy, the assertion of a right to have one's decision to have a child or not respected may legitimate the argument whereby surrogates should have the liberty to recognize or not as their own the baby they have given birth to.

However, the *Evans* case may be distinguished from surrogacy cases. In the former, Ms Evans' ex-partner was the embryo's genetic father. In surrogacy cases, the surrogate may or may not be the genetic mother. Undoubtedly, my proposal therefore places gestational motherhood before genetic motherhood and the surrogate's wishes and continuing consent above those of the commissioning couple. Such a hierarchy needs to be justified. In the early stage of the surrogacy agreement, continuing consent from the surrogate would for many be seen as justified. Thus, a surrogate who changes her mind after a first failed attempt at IVF could not be compelled to try again. Prescriptive requirements as to specific conduct during pregnancy may also be seen as contrary to her privacy rights. Even such a view could be disputed. For those who defend full recognition of surrogacy and better regulation of the practice with possible screening of candidates, such conditions may appear to be reasonable restrictions on carefully selected and fully informed surrogates. In France, such intrusion into the surrogate's use of her own body would be difficult to justify. French judges are relatively willing to go against individual wishes to protect people against themselves[109] but they would be very reluctant to do so to foster others' wishes, even the baby-to-be's interests.

But assuming that non-interference with the surrogate's liberty is accepted throughout the pregnancy, why—it may be asked—should it extend after the birth of the child when all connection with her body has been by definition severed? Should surrogacy prompt us to review our understanding of motherhood and define it on a basis other than birth?

VI. Challenges to Our Understanding of Motherhood

In both the United Kingdom and France, motherhood is based on the fact of giving birth. France, despite its stronger repulsion for surrogacy, used to be more lenient with this 'birth rule'. Indeed, until very recently,[110] the rule only applied to married women. Unmarried women needed to recognize their child officially

---

[109]   See eg in Jehovah's Witness cases, CE 16 August 2002, (2002) RTD civ 781, note J Hauser, restricting the injunction to respect the patient's wishes not to have any blood transfusion to instances where his life was not at stake. More generally, see D Roman, ' "À Corps défendant". La protection de l'individu contre lui-même', *Revue Dalloz* 2007, 1284.

[110]   Since the Ordinance of 4 July 2005 (n°2005–759) which inserted a new art 311–25 into the French Civil Code. On the reform, see F Granet and J Hauser, 'Le Nouveau droit de la filiation', *Revue Dalloz* 2006, 17.

in a separate document called '*reconnaissance*'[111] in order to have their mother-hood established in law. *Possession d'état* or 'motherhood by doing' was intro-duced in 1982 to 'save' unmarried mothers who by ignorance or negligence had failed to perform this '*reconnaissance*' but who had always treated the child as their own.[112] The discrepancy between married and unmarried women was his-torically linked to the preferred status of marriage. Being an unwed mother and a child born out of wedlock was not an enviable situation and it was in conformity with nineteenth century mores not to deem than an unmarried woman would want to have a legal link established with the child she gave birth to even though she did not give the child away for adoption.[113] However, the difference survived long after procreation outside marriage became widely accepted[114] and after chil-dren born within and outside marriage were conferred the same rights.[115] The modern justification was that consent to wed carried with it consent to recognize all children to be born out of that marriage. In the absence of any expression of consent, of any formal celebration, unmarried couples therefore needed to mani-fest their acceptance of parenthood in a separate official document. For many it seemed outdated to suggest that children born out of wedlock were somehow less likely to be welcomed by their parents and needed an acknowledgement which children born within marriage did not need. But the idea that parenthood should be founded on an express and formal acknowledgement by parents could have introduced some flexibility in French family law by accomodating to a larger extent individual wishes.[116] Instead, the greater and greater emphasis put on 'sci-entific truth' and 'blood line'[117] combined with the new sacrosanct principle of equality have turned motherhood into a purely biological fact. The evolution started with the 1972 Act and was reinforced by European case law. The recent reform establishing motherhood by birth for all women, whether married or unmarried, is often linked[118] to the ECHR case of *Marckx*.[119] If women are still able to give birth in secret and deny their motherhood under the 1993 Act, it is because the biological truth is saved by a fiction—the woman is said never to have given birth—and by a cautious European decision in the *Odièvre* case.[120]

[111] Of the French Civil Code, 334–8 al 1 (now art 310–1).
[112] ibid 334–8 al 2 (now art 310–1).
[113] M Iacub, *L'Empire du ventre. Pour une autre histoire de la maternité* (Fayard, 2004) 103.
[114] In France, in 1999, it was estimated that 40% of births occurred outside marriage. The figure reached 50% for births of a first child. See percentages quoted in F Dekeuwer-Défossez, *Rénover le droit de la famille. Propositions pour un droit adapté aux aspirations et réalités de notre temps*, Rapport du groupe de travail (La Documentation française, 1999). In England, births outside marriage stood in 2002 at around 40% of the total live births, (2002) 108 *Population Trends*, Table 3.2.
[115] Law of 3 January 1972 (L n°72–3).
[116] Iacub (n 113 above) 351.
[117] cf F Bellivier, L Brunet, and C Labrusse-Riou, 'La Filiation, la génétique et le juge: où est passée la loi? En hommage à Marie-Thérèse Meulders-Klein' (1999) RTD civ 529.
[118] cf TGI Brive 30 June 2000, *Revue Dalloz* 2001, 27, note Ardeef.
[119] ECHR 13 June 1979 *Marckx v Belgium* Series A, n°31 (1979) 2 EHRR 330.
[120] ECHR 13 February 2003 *Odièvre v France* ECHR 2003-IV; (2003) RTD civ 276, note J Hauser; JCP 2003.II.10049, note A Gouttenoire and F Sudre; E Steiner, 'Desperately Seeking

In the context of surrogacy, motherhood based on intention would seem at first sight to designate the commissioning woman as the legal mother. This was the criterion applied by the Californian court in the famous case of *Johnson v Calvert*,[121] but the commissioning mother in that case also happened to have contributed genetically to the child and was already caring for it with her husband. The combination of intention, care, and genetics may thus have tipped the balance in favour of the commissioning couple. If intention is to be the only criterion, judges will still be helpless in the most problematic cases where one of the parties changes his/her mind. If the surrogate intends to give away the child but decides just after the birth to keep the baby, which of her intentions should be taken into account: the one expressed at the outset or the one expressed just after the birth? If the surrogate, despite the original agreement, and the commissioning woman both formally express their intention to be mothers, should we choose between the two on the basis of genes or prenatal bonding through pregnancy? Unless we adopt the contractual model which we have rejected for reasons explained above,[122] intention alone is therefore not enough in the context of surrogacy. The choice is inevitable between genes and pregnancy and my preference would go with the latter. It is in no way diminishing for women to state that pregnancy creates special links for many women. Even if some women will pass their pregnancy unaffected and will not form any special attachment to the foetus, the pregnant woman is the closest person to the foetus[123] and she should not consequently be bound by any decision made before the child is born. If after the birth, the surrogate is willing to raise the baby, she should in my view become his/her mother.[124] However, if the surrogate clearly and formally confirms her wish not to become mother to the child and if the commissioning mother expressly and formally acknowledges her desire to fulfil that role, a judge or a mere civil servant should declare the commissioning woman mother

Mother—Anonymous Births in the European Court of Human Rights' (2003) 15 *CFLQ* 425; A Pedain, 'Condemned to Life Long Ignorance' (2003) 62 *CLJ* 269.

[121] *Johnson v Calvert* 851 P 2d 776 (1993).

[122] Because when fundamental liberties are involved, people cannot waive their rights by contracts but should be allowed to change their minds, the only limit being the welfare of the child which requires stability. See text accompanying n 89 above.

[123] Some have suggested that the shared gestation is a much more intimate biological connection that shared genetics and more uniquely characteristic of motherhood as genes are shared between many different kinds of relations, see C Thompson, 'Relative Naturalizing; Kinship in an Infertility Clinic' in S Franklin and S McKinnon (eds), *Relative Values: Reconfiguring Kinship* (Durham, NC: Duke University Press, 2001) 175, 178, quoted in A Shaw, 'The Contingency of the "Genetic Link". Construction of Kinship and Inheritance—An Anthropological Perspective' in JR Spencer and A du Bois-Pedain (eds), *Freedom and Responsibility in Reproductive Choice* (Hart, 2006) 73, 75.

[124] cf arguing for the recognition of both the surrogate and commissioning mother as legal mothers but to a different degree, E Jackson, 'What is a Parent?'(n 5 above) 71. See also RF Kandel, 'Which Came First: the Mother or the Egg? A Kinship Solution to Gestational Surrogacy' (1994) 47 *Routledge Law Review* 165.

in law without the process of an adoption or even a parental order.[125] Is there not a fundamental discrimination in allowing sterile men to become fathers by sperm donation but to ask sterile mothers who cannot bear a baby to go through an adoption procedure (or at least request a parental order) before securing their maternal status in law? The difference may be explained in view of the poorer regulation in place for surrogacy compared to other reproductive treatments but it is also a reflection of the predominance of giving birth in our conception of motherhood. In my opinion, a more subtle position combining better regulation of surrogacy agreements on the one hand and a recognition of the special bond created by pregnancy as well as of the liberty to sever it on the other would be a better solution.

VII. Conclusion

In France, both forms of the principle of *'indisponibilité,'* that of the human body and that of individual status, combine to justify prohibition of all types of surrogacy. Under that principle, the human body and parental rights are beyond the reach of contracts. At present, in France, the surrogate is not allowed to relinquish any of her maternal rights at all. Such an approach stands at odds, though, with other provisions of French family law. Apart from adoption, any woman who gives birth may, under article 341–1 of the French Civil Code, request to do so anonymously. The child will be said to have been born 'under X' and all future proceedings to establish the maternal link between the woman and the child will be barred.[126] The difference with surrogacy is that the woman who gives birth anonymously is fictitiously said never to have given birth, whereas in the case of surrogates the fact of the delivery may be established. As Marcela Iacub pointed out,[127] both provisions (the possibility of anonymous births and the prohibition of surrogacy) far from being in contradiction actually both reinforce the importance of giving birth. Giving birth is so important that to allow anonymous births, the delivery itself had to be fictitiously denied. However, in practice, if a surrogate chooses to give birth anonymously and the commissioning father then recognizes the child as his own, no illegal act as such has been committed. The surrogate merely exercised her liberty to relinquish her maternal rights and the commissioning father his liberty to assert them. I find it therefore disproportionate to prosecute the parties for fraud for the reason that this liberty was not exercised spontaneously but was carefully planned between the protagonists. As long as the surrogacy is not made enforceable, I think that

---

[125] This would also solve the practical problem of informal transfers whithout any judicial proceedings, leading to children living with 'parents' who do not have any legal obligations towards them, cf Jackson (n 5 above) 64.

[126] Art. 341 of the French Civil Code, art 341.

[127] Iacub (n 113 above) 303–7.

surrogacy may thus respect both the principles of inalienability of the human body and of individual status.

From an English perspective, basing unenforceability on a liberty rather than on fears of exploitation will make it more acceptable. It is always difficult in the United Kingdom to justify protective measures against individual wishes, especially where these measures are inspired by fears of exploitation which are based on broad concerns relating to the practice of surrogacy in general rather than on the individual case concerned. The emphasis on individual liberty is seen to suffer too much from paternalistic attitutes imposed on adults.[128] On the contrary, if unenforceability is designed to promote a fundamental liberty, the rule will not be seen as a dubious paternalistic intrusion of the state but possibly as the priority given to some private interests over others. The difficulty is that historically in England there is no liberty to choose whether to recognize one's children or not. As Katherine O'Donovan and Jill Marshall have pointed out, 'even in feminist literature, motherhood is not often presented as a choice to be exercised after giving birth'.[129] But I suggest that such a restriction of choice is based on assumptions and ideal views of the perfect mother rather than on a logical and consistent reasoning.

But why should the surrogate's private interests prevail? Or in French terms, why not give up the principle of '*indisponibilité*' altogether? My suggestion, it may be argued, gives undue preference to the surrogate. If during pregnancy this superior status may be explained by the fact that giving precedence to the commissioning couple's wishes will intrude on the surrogate's bodily autonomy, no such objection may be raised after the birth. Why should the surrogate's freedom to relinquish her maternal rights be given priority over the commissioning mother's right to assert hers? Preference for the surrogate has the law on its side as in both countries the woman who gives birth is the legal mother. The obvious answer would therefore be that the commissioning mother has no maternal rights to assert until they are first recognized by adoption and that this implies that the surrogate has first relinquished her motherhood. But this leaves open the question as to whether the law ought to be changed or not. In my opinion, it should not. The surrogate should not be expected to commit herself in advance to the sacrifice of rights as essential as maternal rights. However, provided she

---

[128] In the name of autonomy, see J Harris, 'Rights and Reproductive Choice' in J Harris and S Holm (eds), *The Future of Human Reproduction* (Oxford University Press, 1998) 5; E Jackson, *Regulating Reproduction* (Oxford: Hart, 2001); For a more cautious view, M Fox, 'A Woman's Right to Choose? A Feminist Critique' in Harris and Holm (above) 77. Tensions between a libertarian approach and a more precautionary position appear in the two versions of the Report of the House of Commons Committee on Science and Technology. No consensus was found and the liberal approach triumphed, thanks to a 'guillotine' mechanism which curtailed the debate. Disapproval was expressed in the *Eighth Special Report of Session 2004–05* by Committee members.

[129] K O'Donovan and J Marshall, 'After Birth: Decisions About Becoming a Mother' in Diduck and O'Donovan (n 5 above) 101, 109.

truly consents to relinquishing her rights, the commissioning couple should be entitled to become the legal parents. To avoid harmful conflicts for the child, rather than screening the couple's fitness for parenthood and testing the surrogate's free will *after* the birth, through some form of adoption procedure, better regulation at the time of conception with a screening of surrogates and full information provided to all parties involved should in my view be encouraged. But this presupposes that surrogacy is put on the agenda for reform in both countries![130]

[130] A small step was taken in this direction in the UK, see *Review of the Human Fertilisation and Embryology Act* (n 11 above) 2.64 and the debate on surrogacy was recently re-opened in France, see B Debié and S Agacinski, 'Faut-il légaliser les mères porteuses en France?' *Le Figaro-Magazine*, 10 November 2007; M Bandrac, G Delaisi de Parseval, and V Depadt-Sebag, 'Repenser la prohibition de la gestation pour autrui?' *Revue Dalloz*, 2008, 434.

19

Children with Severe Disabilities and Their Families: Re-examining Private Responsibilities and Public Obligations from a Caring Perspective

Jo Bridgeman[*]

I. A Critique of the Narrow View

The number of children living with severe disabilities and complex needs has increased as a consequence of improvements in medical treatment and care which have enhanced the ability to sustain the lives of children born prematurely, with disabilities following a serious accident or illness, or with a life-limiting condition. In 2004, the Department of Health estimated that there were approximately 700,000 disabled children in Great Britain,[1] the majority of whom lived at home, cared for by their parents and families. Questions of *who decides* about future life-sustaining medical treatment of children with severe disabilities and *how* that decision is to be reached have been established through a small body of case law,[2] recently clarified by Hedley J and Wall LJ in the litigation concerning the treatment of Charlotte Wyatt.[3] As is well-known, treatment decisions are made by the child's parents (more accurately, the person(s) with parental responsibility) or, in the event that the treating doctors disagree with the child's parents, by a judge.

---

[*] Sussex Law School; University of Sussex.

[1] Department of Health, *National Service Framework for Children, Young People and Maternity Services*, Standard Eight (October 2004) para 2.1, referencing Department for Work and Pensions, 'Family Resources Survey 2002–3' (2004). Although this figure includes all disabled children. The NSF uses the term disabled to include children with learning disabilities, autistic spectrum disorders, sensory impairments, physical impairments, and emotional/behavioural disorders (para 1.5).

[2] *Re B (A Minor) (Wardship: Medical Treatment)* [1981] 1 WLR 1421; *Re J (A Minor) (Wardship: Medical Treatment)* [1991] 2 WLR 140; *Glass v United Kingdom* [2004] 1 FLR 1019.

[3] Principally *Portsmouth NHS Trust v Wyatt and Ors* [2004] EWHC 2247 and *Re Wyatt (a child) (medical treatment: continuation of order)* [2005] EWCA Civ 1181. See n 7 below, for a full list of the cases determining issues surrounding Charlotte Wyatt's care.

Either way, treatment decisions must be made in the best interests of the child, broadly conceived, informed by a view as to whether, from the perspective of the child, the child's life with continued treatment will be of a tolerable quality.[4] Judgments about best interests are wider than medical best interests, assessed through the mechanism of drawing up a balance sheet of known benefits and disadvantages and possible benefits and disadvantages.

In most cases referred to court for resolution, doctors seek a declaration as to the legality of withholding, or withdrawal of, medical treatment. Once granted, treatment is withdrawn or active treatment withheld and palliative care provided. Inevitably, private responsibilities and public obligations for the care of severely disabled children are not fully examined in the case law which, like the bioethical/legal literature, focuses upon questions of quality of life. For example, Ian Kennedy's discussion of the medical treatment of very low birth weight babies is centred upon questions of quality of life. He identifies beneficence, non-maleficence, respect for life, respect for dignity, and respect for autonomy as the moral principles to guide decision-making about medical treatment yet suggests that, 'the precise nature of the moral obligation—or, if you like, the operational meaning—of respect for life, or doing good and avoiding harm, turns on the baby's future "quality of life" '.[5] His essay concludes by acknowledging, without fully examining, two ethical dimensions with respect to the child's parents: the provision of information to enable them to make medical decisions in the best interests of their child and the obligation imposed upon all to support the parents.[6] It is these issues which I explore in this chapter: private responsibilities and public obligations for the care of children with severe disabilities and their families.

As noted above, Charlotte Wyatt's case offers the most recent authoritative explanation of the relevant legal principles applicable to the provision of life-sustaining treatment to children with severe disabilities. As her future took a different direction to that of the children in the earlier cases, Charlotte also offers the point of entry into the issues explored in this chapter. Born prematurely at twenty-six weeks' gestation, weighing 458 grammes and experiencing many of the physical (respiratory and kidney problems), and mental (poor neurological function), disabilities which may result from such a premature birth, Charlotte survived against the expectations of the doctors treating her at Portsmouth Hospital. The extent to which her impairments were reversible, her ability to

---

[4] *Portsmouth NHS Trust v Wyatt and Ors* [2004] EWHC 2247, para 24, 'intolerable to the child' is 'a valuable guide in the search for best interests in this kind of case'; Nuffield Council on Bioethics, 'Critical care decisions in fetal and neonatal medicine: ethical issues' (2006) Appendix 9; Royal College of Paediatrics and Child Health, *Withholding or Withdrawing Life Sustaining Treatment in Children: A Framework for Practice*, (2nd edn, 2004).

[5] I Kennedy, 'Ethics in Clinical Decision Making: The Care of the Very-low-birth-weight Baby' in *Treat Me Right: Essays in Medical Law and Ethics* (Oxford: Oxford University Press, 1988, reprinted 2001) 140, 144.

[6] ibid 152–3.

develop her capacities and to interact with those caring for her, and the extent to which she experienced pain or pleasure were uncertain matters upon which her doctors and her parents disagreed. The primary issue which the court was asked to resolve was whether she should be provided with aggressive artificial ventilation in the event, which her doctors considered inevitable, that she suffer a respiratory arrest. Her parents had more fundamental concerns about the treatment made available to their daughter. Charlotte's unexpected survival and the enduring inability of her parents and the hospital to agree upon aspects of her treatment resulted in numerous references to court during the first three years of her life.[7] Her discharge from hospital into foster care, rather than to the care of her parents who had fought so hard on her behalf, in December 2006 invites us to consider the ethical issues arising from the longer-term care of children with severe disabilities.

Before doing so, I wish to outline a recent and extremely controversial case from the United States which demands careful ethical examination. This is the series of procedures performed upon Ashley X born with brain damage, unable to walk or talk although alert and aware of people and her surroundings, fed by tube and entirely dependent upon those who care for her. Her cognitive, mental, and physical condition is not expected to improve nor is her condition progressive, giving her a normal life expectation. Ashley X is cared for at home by her mother and father with help from her grandmothers, attending daily a school for children with special needs. A hospital ethics committee at Seattle Children's Hospital, entrusting her parents to 'do the right thing' for Ashley, approved a 'treatment' plan for her. This involved a hysterectomy, removal of breast buds, appendectomy, and high-dose oestrogen therapy to restrict her height and weight. Her father explained that the guiding principle, upon which the plan was based, was the best interests of the child decided by the child's parents in consultation with their doctors: 'Clearly, a decision on the applicability of the Ashley Treatment needs to be made upon careful evaluation of their child's unique condition, with help

---

[7] Hedley J five times on the issue of whether it would be lawful to withhold artificial ventilation if her condition deteriorated to require mechanical ventilation to prolong her life: *Portsmouth NHS Trust v Wyatt and Wyatt, Southampton NHS Trust Intervening* [2004] EWHC 2247 (7 October 2004); *Portsmouth Hospitals NHS Trust v Wyatt and Ors* [2005] EWHC 117 (Fam) (28 January 2005); *Wyatt v Portsmouth NHS Trust and Wyatt (By her Guardian) (No 3)* [2005] EWHC 693 (Fam) (21 April 2005); *Re Wyatt* [2005] EWHC 2293 (Fam) (21 October 2005); unreported 23 February 2006. Court of Appeal twice—unreported [2005] EWCA Civ 185 (9 February 2005); *Re Wyatt (A Child) (Medical Treatment: Continuation of Order)* [2005] EWCA Civ 1181 (12 October 2005). In November 2004, Hedley J made an order permitting the administration of diamorphine to relieve the pain of a fractured leg (due to brittle bones), her parents having refused fearing that it would depress her breathing and in December 2004 made declarations giving directions in relation to palliative care, as well as orders granting anonymity to expert witnesses (13 September 2004) and forbidding identification of expert witnesses in the media (16 September 2004), later extended to all experts who gave evidence with regard to her care. Details of the unreported cases are set out in the Court of Appeal judgment *Re Wyatt (A Child) (Medical Treatment: Continuation of Order)* [2005] EWCA Civ 1181, paras 17–25. There have since been family proceedings regarding the care of Charlotte.

from their doctors, and careful evaluation of the benefits that might be obtained. We believe the parents are in the best position to make this evaluation and ultimately make this decision.'[8]

The procedures were viewed by Ashley's parents and treating physician as in the interests of her health on the grounds that they would enable maximum movement and, consequently, blood circulation thereby minimizing infections; and her well-being, because it would mean that she could continue to be lifted, and consequently be with her family, taken on trips, and held. Her father stressed that the procedures were not performed so that her parents could continue to care for her at home as they would do that anyway or for their convenience as her carers, but for her quality of life: to prevent discomfort which was the cause of much distress for Ashley and alleviate boredom by enabling her to participate as fully as possible in ordinary family life. Ashley's father suggested that criticism of them was 'gut reactions without depth or rational consideration of the situation, the treatment or the motivation behind it'.[9] Whether such a case within our shores would be reviewed by a court would depend upon the confidence of the treating doctors that the procedures were therapeutic and in the best interests of the child. Determination of best interests would be narrowly addressed without an examination of the child's rights, responsibilities to her, or the obligations of the state and society to children with severe disabilities.

II. Rights Of, or Obligations To, Children?

The cases of both Charlotte Wyatt and Ashley X could have been analysed from the perspective which Jane Fortin adopts in her commentary on *Re C*.[10] The court, she argues, in its judgment whether the withdrawal of artificial ventilation was in the best interests of 16-month-old C, who had been born with spinal muscular atrophy, should have examined the rights of the child to life or to a dignified death and the balance between the competing rights of the child, her parents, and doctors.[11] Jane Fortin argues that difficult decisions concerning the future treatment and care of acutely ill or dying children or those with life-limiting conditions are paradigm examples of decisions which should be informed by consideration of children's rights.[12] Fifteen years ago and soon after the *Gillick* case, the Children Act 1989, and the United Nations Convention on the Rights of the Child (UNCRC), Michael Freeman urged us to 'Tak[e] Children's Rights More Seriously'[13] in the interests of improving the conditions

---

[8] <http://ashleytreatment.spaces.live.com/blog/>.
[9] ibid.   [10] *Re C (Medical Treatment)* [1998] 1 FLR 384.
[11] J Fortin, '*Re C (Medical Treatment)* A baby's right to die' (1998) 10 *CFLQ* 411.
[12] ibid 411.
[13] M Freeman, 'Taking Children's Rights More Seriously' (1992) 6 *International Journal of Law and the Family* 52.

of children's lives. The incorporation of the European Convention of Human Rights and Fundamental Freedoms (ECHR) into English Law by the Human Rights Act 1998 may have indicated a change to the legal landscape through the adoption of rights-based perspectives to resolve conflicts. That children are moral and legal rights-holders is a view now more widely accepted and there is no doubt that the ECHR applies to children as much as to adults. But recognition of children as rights-holders has not had a discernable impact upon the legal regulation of the provision of medical treatment to children. For example, whilst Hedley J acknowledged Charlotte Wyatt's moral right 'to respect for her dignity',[14] the legal rights referred to in his judgment were those arising from parental responsibility: the right of Charlotte's parents to consent, or refuse to consent, to medical treatment.[15]

Shortly before incorporation of the ECHR into English law, Cazalet J expressed the view that a declaration that it would be lawful to withhold mechanical ventilation from baby D did not infringe his Article 2 'right to life' as this course of action was in his best interests. Furthermore, that withholding treatment positively respected the child's right to die with dignity protected under Article 3.[16] Following which, Hedley J noted in Charlotte's case that the ECHR had been referred to in argument and although 'key rights are undoubtedly engaged' and 'English domestic law has undoubtedly been significantly affected by the concept of Convention rights' submissions were not necessary given that it was accepted that English law was compliant.[17] Consequently, Convention rights have not been mentioned in any of the cases since: *Re L*,[18] *An NHS Trust v MB*,[19] or *K (A Minor)*.[20] As a result, there has been no examination of the implications of the landmark European Court of Human Rights (EctHR) judgment in *Glass v United Kingdom*[21] for the treatment of vulnerable and dependent children.[22] In that case, the ECtHR held that the administration of diamorphine to a child, without the consent of his mother or authorization of the court, amounted to an

---

[14] *Portsmouth NHS Trust v Wyatt and Ors* [2004] EWHC 2247, paras 22 and 27 *per* Hedley J.
[15] ibid para 16.
[16] *A National Health Service Trust v D* [2000] 2 FLR 677. Andrew Grubb has suggested that the case cited *D v UK* (1997) 24 EHRR 423 did not establish that Art 3 gave a right to die with dignity, Commentary, (2000) 8 *Medical Law Review* 339.
[17] n 14 above para 25.
[18] *Re L (Medical Treatment: Benefit)* [2004] EWHC 2713.
[19] *An NHS Trust v MB* [2006] EWHC 507 (Fam).
[20] *K (A Minor)* [2006] EWHC 1007.
[21] *Glass v United Kingdom* [2004] 1 FLR 1019. Discussed in Jo Bridgeman, 'Caring for Children with Severe Disabilities: Boundaried and Relational Rights' (2005) 13 *The International Journal of Children's Rights* 99.
[22] The Court of Appeal did consider *Glass* but in the context of the timing of reference to court for resolution in the face of different views held by doctors and parents rather than upon the more fundamental questions of the rights of the child and the respective roles of parents and professionals, *Re Wyatt (A Child) (Medical Treatment: Continuation of Order)* [2005] EWCA Civ 1181.

interference with his right to respect for private life[23] which was not necessary in a democratic society:[24] the hospital was aware that Carol Glass was opposed to the administration of diamorphine to her son, David, and could have sought an order of the court.[25] As noted above, Hedley J suggested that Charlotte Wyatt had a moral right to respect for her dignity which, in his Lordship's view, supported the claim that she had a right to a dignified death without medical intervention in the event that she suffer a life-threatening event. Inevitably, comparisons have been drawn between the invasive procedures performed upon Ashley X and the sterilization, without their consent, of women with learning difficulties: a procedure which has rightly been thoroughly subjected to academic criticism as contrary to the right to reproduce or to choose to reproduce. Arguments based upon Ashley X's dignity, relating to her size and intellectual development are as uncomfortable and fallacious as those which were made based upon the mental age of women with learning difficulties. Uncomfortably, because Ashley's right to dignity is denied in order to present an argument in support of the procedures, her parents quote with approval one commentator in the following terms:

If the concern has something to do with the girl's dignity being violated, then I have to protest by arguing that the girl lacks the cognitive capacity to experience any sense of indignity. Nor do I believe this is somehow demeaning or undignified to humanity in general; the treatments will endow her with a body that more closely matches her cognitive state—both in terms of her physical size and bodily functioning. The estrogen treatment is not what is grotesque here. Rather, it is the prospect of having a full-grown and fertile woman endowed with the mind of a baby.[26]

This is a similar argument to the one that women with learning difficulties did not enjoy rights because they lacked the capacity to enforce them and equally must be refuted. Both arguments are premised upon a limited view of moral personhood. Adopting this stance, Peter Singer has repeated, in this context, the argument he has made before that the terms of the debate are misunderstood if the question is asked whether the treatment violated Ashley's right to dignity or preserved it:

As a parent and grandparent, I find 3-month-old babies adorable, but not dignified. Nor do I believe that getting bigger and older, while remaining at the same mental level, would do anything to change that…We are always ready to find dignity in human beings, including those whose mental age will never exceed that of an infant, but we don't attribute dignity to dogs or cats, though they clearly operate at a more advanced mental level than human infants. Just making that comparison provokes outrage in some quarters. But why should dignity always go together with species membership, no matter what the characteristics of the individual may be?…. Lofty talk about human dignity should not

---

[23] ECHR, Art 8 and specifically his right to physical integrity, *Glass v United Kingdom* [2004] 1 FLR 1019, para 70.

[24] ibid paras 78–83.   [25] ibid para 81.

[26] <http://ashleytreatment.spaces.live.com/blog/>, quoting George Dvorsky.

stand in the way of children like her getting the treatment that is best both for them and their families.[27]

This view, that a right to dignity is enjoyed only by those who have the capacities traditionally associated with moral personhood, has been more generally expressed in the context of the medical treatment of children with severe disabilities[28] but is one which I would, for reasons given elsewhere, wholeheartedly reject.[29]

Given that the courts failed to embrace Charlotte Wyatt's moral and legal rights and that Ashley's right to dignity was invoked in criticism, and dismissed in defence, of the procedures, we should explore whether Onora O'Neill's infamous call for an obligations-based approach to protection of the interests of children is helpful to ethical analysis of these cases. Onora O'Neill, it will be remembered, argues that children's rights offer merely an 'indirect, partial and blurred picture'.[30] The protection of children's legal rights, she suggests, would be better framed in terms of obligations to children rather than claimed as fundamental rights of children. To have an obligation, she explains, means to be 'required to do or omit some type of action' and that this might be owed to all in the case of universal perfect obligations, to identified individuals, or to certain but not all others.[31]

When considering the care of children with severe disabilities we are first concerned with what Onora O'Neill identifies as specific perfect obligations which are owed by certain individuals to particular children. What the obligation-holder is required to do or omit to do depends upon their role within the particular set of social, cultural, and political circumstances. In the present context, therefore, parents of a child will have specific, perfect, obligations to their child, as will the doctors and nurses involved in providing care; although what parents and healthcare professionals are required to do will be different according to the social and cultural expectations of their role. For example, doctors are obliged to diagnose and order treatment, nurses to administer medical care, and parents to make decisions, advocate on their child's behalf, and provide for the child's basic needs, as far as his or her condition permits.

Where Onora O'Neill identifies the reach of obligations beyond that of rights is in relation to imperfect obligations which are not owed by identified individuals; rather, they 'may' be owed by all but cannot be claimed by specific children. This is the reason, because the recipient of the obligation is not identified and

---

[27] P Singer, 'A Convenient Truth' *New York Times*, 26 January 2007.

[28] P Singer and H Kuhse, *Should the Baby Live?* (Oxford: Oxford University Press, 1975), J Harris, *The Value of Life* (Routledge, 1985).

[29] J Bridgeman, *Parental Responsibility, Young Children and Healthcare Law* (Cambridge: Cambridge University Press, 2007), ch 1.

[30] O O'Neill, 'Children's Rights and Children's Lives' in P Alston, S Parker, and J Seymour (eds), *Children, Rights and the Law* (Oxford: Clarendon Press, 1992) 24.

[31] ibid 25–6.

consequently the benefit cannot be claimed, why imperfect obligations are of wider scope than rights. Imperfect obligations take the form of general obligations, which can't be owed to all children because that would be too onerous, and what is required cannot be specified because that depends upon the particular context. Imperfect obligations give rise to perfect obligations in the context of legal regulation, duties, or institutions. Onora O'Neill gives the examples of parents and teachers explaining that both will have perfect obligations to children but that if all they do is discharge their perfect obligations they will not be doing enough. In other words, in her view imperfect obligations are what are owed to children beyond their fundamental rights.[32] She claims that whilst rights may be sufficient to protect children they are not enough if children are owed a quality of life. She argues that whilst perfect obligations balance rights, the difference being one of perspective: 'When we speak of (perfect) obligations we adopt the perspective of the *agent* and consider what must be done if there is to be no moral failure; when we speak of rights we adopt the perspective of the *recipient* (of perfect obligations) and consider what must be received or accorded if there is to be no moral failure.'[33] As explained above, Onora O'Neill asserts that imperfect obligations are of wider scope. However, as David Archard has commented, the general duty which arises from imperfect obligation becomes specific only as a consequence of roles, legal duties, or policy at which point it is no longer imperfect. Moral principles alone 'do not always indicate who owes which obligations to whom, when, and to what extent';[34] rather, the content of imperfect obligations depends upon law or social practice. Secondly, David Archard has observed that the obligation of those with responsibilities to children to do more than the bare minimum is not confined to imperfect obligations.[35]

Onora O'Neill claims that she does not wish to deny the importance of fundamental or legal rights and indeed it is important to respect the rights of all children, including those who are particularly vulnerable and dependent as a consequence of their disabilities. As Michael Freeman expresses it in an article which details 'Why It Remains Important to Take Children's Rights Seriously': 'Rights are important because they recognise the respect their bearers are entitled to. To accord rights is to respect dignity: to deny rights is to cast doubt on humanity and on integrity.'[36] Respect for the rights of disabled children would recognize their equal entitlement not to have their life deliberately terminated, to dignity, to medical treatment, to a family life, or as Michael Freeman has argued to 'nurture, care and protection'.[37] To ask what it is that we are obliged to

---

[32] ibid 26–9.   [33] ibid 29 (emphasis in original).
[34] M Maclean and J Eekelaar, *The Parental Obligation: A Study of Parenthood Across Households* (Hart, 1997) 1.
[35] D Archard, *Children: rights and childhood* (Ashgate, 2nd edn, 2004) 123–4.
[36] M Freeman, 'Why It Remains Important to Take Children's Rights Seriously' (2007) 15 *International Journal of Children's Rights* 5, 7.
[37] M Freeman, 'Taking Children's Rights More Seriously' (n 13 above) 66.

do may provide another perspective helpfully broken down in Onora O'Neill's account into what is owed to children generally and to any particular child. But is it merely a difference of perspective? As Michael Freeman has argued, children should be understood to have rights to all those things which Onora O'Neill suggests we owe them.[38]

A different account of obligations to the Kantian approach employed by Onora O'Neill is one which adopts a contractual view of obligations freely entered into which contrasts with duties, which are that which is required of us.[39] Nancy Hirschmann has suggested that a contractual view of obligation is only possible because 'nonconsensual bonds—love, care, nurturance' are confined to the private realm.[40] Rather than choices, Nancy Hirschmann suggests that relationships should be viewed as central to obligations:

> ... if we take seriously the feminist notion of a moral reasoning that begins from premises of connection, responsibility, and response, an alternative formulation opens up. If relationship is the epistemological foundation, then connection is given, and obligation a presumption of fact. That is, perhaps obligation must be considered from the standpoint of a 'given' just as freedom is given in consent theory. From this perspective, 'recognition' of an obligation is not the same as 'consent' to it. Recognition involves the admission of an obligation that *already* exists. Consent theory, in contrast, bases its claims to legitimacy on the notion that choice creates obligation. It is precisely this notion of creation that women's historical experience of relationships challenges.[41]

It is surely unarguable that children with severe disabilities and their families have rights, or entitlements, which provide guarantees of the minimum protections and which can equally be understood in terms of obligations to them. Important as it is to recognize individual rights and to address what it is that others owe as a consequence of one person's rights, such a perspective only takes us so far. It is individualistic and isolationist when the vulnerability and dependency of children with severe disabilities invite us to adopt a relational perspective. Furthermore, it aims to identify what we must do, morally or legally, rather than what people do as a consequence of their responsibilities to another. I suggest that an alternative perspective should be adopted which respects individual rights but enriches the analysis through consideration of responsibilities arising out of relationships.

III. Relational Responsibilities

In *Parental Responsibility, Young Children and Healthcare Law*,[42] I argue that we need to develop a discourse of parental responsibility and a conceptual

---

[38] ibid.

[39] NJ Hirschmann, 'Rethinking Obligation for Feminism' in NJ Hirschmann and C Di Stefano (eds), *Revisioning the Political: Feminist Reconstructions of Traditional Concepts in Western Political Theory* (Boulder, Colorado: Westview Press, 1996) 157.

[40] ibid 169.   [41] ibid 169.

[42] Bridgeman (n 29 above).

framework of relational responsibility with respect to the care of children. As Hilde Lindemann Nelson has suggested, whilst some parental obligations arise from promises freely made, not all do. She offers the care provided by parents to a brain-damaged child as an example of obligations which are not based upon prior agreement. The functionally diffuse work[43] of parenting takes not the expected form of changing responsibilities as the needs of the child alter with their developing capacity, competency, and maturity, rather parents undertake a long-term commitment of caring responsibility for a dependent child: 'The ethics of care is ... hospitable to the relatedness of persons. It sees many of our responsibilities as not freely entered into but presented to us by the accidents of our embeddedness in familial and social and historical contexts. It often calls on us to *take* responsibility, while liberal individualist morality focuses on how we should leave each other alone.'[44]

Virginia Held has identified four features of the feminist ethic of care upon which Hilde Lindemann Nelson, above, is drawing.[45] First, the feminist ethic of care adopts an approach which understands the individual to be primarily connected or situated in relationships with others rather than first and foremost separate from others and thereby bringing to the fore questions of dependency, needs, and care. Secondly, the connected self takes responsibility for meeting the needs of others who are dependent upon them. Thirdly, an ethic of care approach highlights the importance of emotion and context in working out what we ought to do, rather than the abstract implementation of universal rules. Finally, it challenges accepted views of the public and private, examined further below. Ethics of care theorists seek to highlight the interdependency of all and the ways in which all individuals continue to be dependent upon others throughout their lives, albeit in different ways and to different extents at different times. However, the increased and enduring dependency and manifest needs of children with severe disabilities serve to highlight often hidden issues of caring responsibility and obligation.

So the responsibilities of parent to child should, it is suggested, be understood to arise out of their relationship and not promises or contract, such that Joan Tronto has proposed 'we are better served by focusing on a flexible notion of responsibility than we are by continuing to use obligation as the basis for understanding what people should do for each other'.[46] The responsibilities of parents to their children arise from the particular nature of the relationship, in this context the dependency of young and vulnerable children upon parents to meet their needs; and the particular circumstances of the child, such as having

---

[43] EF Kittay, *Love's Labor: Essays on Women, Equality and Dependency* (New York: Routledge, 1999) 39.

[44] V Held, *The Ethics of Care: Personal, Political, and Global* (New York: Oxford University Press, 2006) 14–15 (emphasis in original).

[45] ibid 10–15.

[46] J Tronto, *Moral Boundaries: the political argument for an ethic of care* (New York: Routledge, 1993) 133.

severe disabilities. As Katharine Bartlett has argued, to take responsibility is not merely to do that which is expected, rather it is to consider the particular needs of the person to whom there is responsibility and to be concerned with 'outcomes' whilst acting according to individual values and self-imposed limits.[47] How parents understand their responsibilities to their children is a matter of individual interpretation within a given social and cultural context and legal requirements of parents, fathers and mothers. Which means that it is necessary to develop a discourse of responsibility informed by practices of responsibility and consideration of differences between maternal and paternal responsibility.

The primary relationship and responsibility for young and dependent children is with their parents but others have relationships with children and responsibilities to them arising from their relationship, usually formed in a professional context. This is obviously so when a child is born with severe disabilities and may never have left hospital to be cared for at home by their parents, when the child will also be situated in relationships with professionals involved in their care. Recognition of responsibilities arising from professional relationships alongside the responsibilities of parents provides scope for recognition of the distinct roles, contributions, and perspectives of all those with relationships with the child. Doctors focus upon the medical needs of the child, arising at times of crisis or upon assessment of the data provided by those who continually care. As Eva Feder Kittay has identified, doctors offer intermittent and detached care, employing their medical expertise to respond to a particular problem of one child amongst all those to whom they have responsibility: focused upon the medical condition not the child and upon addressing consequences of the impairment.[48] Nurses caring for the child will have a deeper understanding of the child's interests and quality of life gained over a longer period of more personal care. As we witnessed with the parents of Charlotte Wyatt, theirs is a partial judgment, formed by personal experience and focused upon the needs of their child.

Preferring to adopt the concept of responsibility rather than obligation, I would agree with Nancy Hirschmann:

Thus the notion of given obligation should be treated as a methodological and epistemological proposition, urging us to focus on the questions we ask. If we take obligation as given, the issue becomes not *whether* an obligation exists—we do not try to determine whether a relationship has been created through consent—but *how* it is to be fulfilled. The question of 'how' *presupposes* relationship, because it automatically requires conversation and negotiation between individuals in relationship. Taking connection as given it tries to determine the relative spacing and placing of individuals within its constellation, and it does this through the participation of individuals who express desires and

---

[47] K Bartlett, 'Re-Expressing Parenthood' (1988) 98 *Yale Law Journal* 293, 295–6, 299–301.

[48] J McLaughlin, 'Conceptualising Intensive Caring Activities: the Changing Lives of Families with Young Disabled Children' Sociological Research Online, Volume 11, Issue 1, <http://www.socresonline.org.uk/11/1/mclaughlin.html>, paras 5.2–5.3.

preferences but understand that those exist within a context of necessary relationships that require their participation.[49]

The responsibility of parents of a child with severe disabilities is to make treatment decisions and care for their child as a separate individual, informed by their experience of their child and the knowledge of others involved in their care and drawing upon the support available to them. Informed by a feminist ethic of care, a conceptual framework of relational responsibilities would approach questions surrounding the treatment and care of the child by acknowledging the child as an individual with moral and legal rights, understanding the dependency of the child upon his or her parents and appreciating their expertise of the child gained through the caring relationship whilst understanding that the child is also related to others involved in their care whose expertise must be recognized. But also, that their ability to fulfil their caring responsibility is affected by external factors and the fulfilment of public obligations. The decision of the parents and doctors of Ashley X has, I suggest, to be examined in terms of the extent to which their decision was reached after careful consideration of the child's needs as an individual, in the light of the experience they had gained in caring for her and that of others involved in her care and the support available to them as they cared. The ethical and legal framework should support parents and professionals to work in partnership in the interests of the child respectful of the distinct roles and responsibilities of the other.[50]

IV. Public Obligations to Support Private Responsibilities

Feminists advancing the ethic of care have argued that it is not merely an approach to inform behaviour and decisions in the private sphere or in personal relationships, rather it offers an approach to evaluate the political and the public. As outlined above, a conceptual framework of relational responsibilities not only involves recognition of the child as an individual with rights and requires acknowledgement of responsibilities to the child arising from relationships with them but further, involves appreciation that there are external factors which limit the abilities of parents to meet their caring responsibilities. Analysis of legal and ethical issues surrounding the care of children with severe disabilities has to involve consideration of public obligations. It is not my intention, nor is it appropriate, to enter into discussion of social policy research studies which reveal the inadequacies in public services supporting parents caring for children with severe

---

[49] Hirschmann (n 39 above) 171 (emphasis in original).
[50] Nuffield Council on Bioethics, 'Critical care decisions in fetal and neonatal medicine: ethical issues' (2006) para 2.45 argues for a 'partnership of care' in which all involved present their view of the baby's best interests ('procedural justice') and the responsibilities which people have and responsibility for the decision are recognized ('personal and professional responsibility').

disabilities;[51] it is my purpose to consider the allocation of caring responsibilities between the private and public spheres. I adopt the analysis offered by Janice McLaughlin, whose study reveals that 'the minimalist approach that parents find within formal care provision keeps care in the private sphere and articulates public responsibilities towards care as a burden on the state and society, which mothers should take responsibility for'.[52] First, I briefly revisit the public/private divide before exploring the example of allocation of medical resources and caring from a public perspective.

A. Revisiting the Public/Private Divide

At its ideological extreme, the private is the place beyond the sphere of public life and, consequently, beyond the limits of state intervention or legal regulation. In this view, the private realm offers a retreat for the citizen from where rational, independent, equal selves participate in politics, government, and economic life.[53] The public/private dichotomy has been exposed in the work of liberal feminists who have offered a critique of the extent to which this polarization has operated to preclude recognition of work which occurs in the home (including caring responsibilities), had the consequence of presenting women as unfit for participation in political and public life, and kept behind closed doors inequalities of power and abuses which may occur in the home.[54] Furthermore, as the example of caring for children reveals very clearly, it is more a case of selective intervention rather than non-intervention. As has been noted, the primary responsibility for the care of children rests with their parents and parents enjoy a large degree of freedom in deciding how they wish to raise their children. The law imposes duties upon parents to achieve minimum standards of care, maintenance, and control of their children—to feed, clothe, provide a home, and secure medical treatment,[55] a duty to protect[56] and the common law duty to rescue. Parents must ensure that

[51] B Dobson, S Middleton, and A Beardsworth, *The impact of childhood disability on family life* (York: Joseph Rowntree Foundation, 2001); Mencap, *No ordinary life* (London, 2001); B Lamb and S Layzell, *Disabled in Britain: Behind closed doors, The carers' experience* (London: Scope, 1995); B Beresford, *Expert opinions: A national survey of parents caring for a severely disabled child* (Bristol: Policy Press, 1995); B Beresford, *Positively Parents: Caring for a Severely Disabled Child* (Social Policy Research Unit, HMSO, 1994).

[52] McLaughlin (n 48 above) para 5.1.

[53] MA Ackelsberg and ML Shanley, 'Privacy, Publicity, and Power: A Feminist Rethinking of the Public-Private Distinction' in Hirschmann and Di Stefano (n 39 above) 213, 214–15.

[54] ibid 213.

[55] Children and Young Persons Act 1933, s 1(2), failure by the child's parent, legal guardian, or other person 'legally liable to maintain a child' to provide, or to seek assistance with the provision of, medical treatment amounts to the offence of child neglect in s. 1(1). This section also makes it an offence for a person over the age of 16 with responsibility for the child to wilfully assault, ill-treat, neglect, abandon, or expose the child to unnecessary suffering or injury.

[56] The Domestic Violence, Crime and Victims Act 2004, s 5 makes it an offence for the child's parents or members of the household who are over the age of 16 and who have frequent contact with a child or vulnerable adult to cause their death by an unlawful act or to fail to take reasonable

their children are appropriately educated[57] and named;[58] and absent parents are required to provide financially for their children.[59] Legislation justifies the use of physical punishment[60] and increasingly seeks to hold parents to account for their children's behaviour, for example through Parenting Orders.[61] However, a child must be at risk of significant harm before the state takes over their care.[62] Children need to be cared for and children with severe disabilities have extreme dependence and magnified needs which, once the child is discharged from hospital, are considered to be the private responsibility of the child's parents with the assistance of professionals and services: the Children Act 1989 imposes a duty upon local authorities to provide services to support parents of children in need.[63] There may be greater intervention by medical and social services into the lives of families where there is a disabled child, but this is experienced by parents more as judgmental surveillance than practical support.[64] Caring for children with severe disabilities is not seen as a matter of public responsibility but a burden which is privatized within the family by 'refusals to care and rejections from both formal actors and agencies',[65] principally to be fulfilled by the child's mother.[66] I now consider the example of medical resource allocation before turning to examine public obligations to support caring responsibilities.

B. The Limits of Public Obligations?

Andje Pedain has argued that cases such as *Wyatt* should not be understood solely as examples of the application of the welfare principle, rather they should be understood as judicial review of the 'ethical defensibility' of the decisions of doctors to allocate scarce resources between patients.[67] Her argument is that doctors have a sense of the worthwhileness of treatment; an assessment of costs and benefits. Intervention by the court amounts to a review of that calculation:

Awareness of the finite nature of the National Health Service's resources is part of the framework in which doctors make their choices, internalised to a degree that certain

---

steps to protect them when they were aware, or ought to have been aware, that they were at significant risk of serious physical harm.

[57] Education Act 1996, ss 7, 8.
[58] Births and Deaths Registration Act 1953.
[59] Child Support Act 1991, s 1, currently being reformed with proposals in the Child Maintenance and Other Payments Bill.
[60] Children and Young Persons Act 1933, s 1(7); Children Act 2004, s 58.
[61] Anti-social Behaviour Act, ss 20, 26–27.
[62] Children Act 1989, s 31.
[63] Children Act 1989, s 17, specifically children with disabilities, s 17(10).
[64] Mc Laughlin (n 48 above) para 3.3.   [65] ibid para 5.1.
[66] J Read and L Clements, *Disabled Children and the Law* (London: Jessica Kingsley, 2002) 29.
[67] A Pedain, 'Doctors, parents, and the courts: legitimising restrictions on the continued provision of lifespan maximising treatments for severely handicapped, non-dying babies' (2005) 17 *CFLQ* 535.

treatments will seem "useless" to a doctor precisely because they secure a minimal extension of a miserable life at great cost and use of finite resources. The rationing dimension is implicit in the doctor's clinical judgment that this degree of effort is not worth it in terms of the limited benefits that can be secured.[68]

On a few occasions, the courts have been asked to review decisions about the allocation of scarce resources which have delayed or denied the provision of medical treatment to children. Both *Collier*[69] and *Walker*[70] were challenges by parents to decisions to delay children's heart surgery due to a shortage of paediatric intensive care beds and nurses. In both, doctors and parents were agreed that the operation was in the best interests of the child. *Re J (1992)*[71] and *Ex parte B*[72] raised both the issue of whether treatment was in the best interests of the child and that of the allocation of scarce resources; although whether ventilation in the event of a life-threatening episode was in his best interests was the primary issue in the former and the refusal of the health authority to fund experimental treatment for leukaemia in the latter. Supporting Andje Pedain's argument is the view expressed by Lord Donaldson MR that for the court to make an order requiring doctors to treat contrary to their professional judgment would fail to: 'adequately take account of the sad fact of life that health authorities may on occasion find that they have too few resources, either human or material or both, to treat all the patients whom they would like to treat in the way in which they would like to treat them. It is then their duty to make choices.'[73]

Noel Whitty, giving the example of Sir Bingham MR in *Ex parte B*, analyses the judicial adoption of the thinking and discourse of economics and the market, expressing their judgments in terms such as procurement, purchase, expenditure, and financial affairs.[74] What remains unarticulated, and perhaps unconsidered, Whitty points out, is any examination of care.[75]

Ethic of care feminists, Selma Sevenhuijsen and Eva Feder Kittay, offer critical perspectives on justice in resource allocation. Selma Sevenhuijsen has argued that, as the norm is that of the economically productive and self-sufficient citizen, healthcare resources are allocated for development to, or recovery of, that state. As with Whitty, what she identifies as being left out of the analysis is the

---

[68] ibid 544.

[69] *R v Central Birmingham Health Authority ex p Collier* (6 January 1988, CA) <http://web.lexis-nexis.com/professional/>.

[70] *R v Central Birmingham Health Authority, ex p Walker; R v Secretary of State for Social Services and Anor, ex p Walker*, QBD, 3 BMLR 32, 24 November 1987 <http://web.lexis-nexis.com/professional/>.

[71] *Re J (A Minor) (Child in Care: Medical Treatment)* [1992] 3 WLR 507.

[72] *R v Cambridge District Health Authority, ex p B* [1995] 1 WLR 898.

[73] n 71 above 517.

[74] Whilst at first instance in that case, Laws J adopted a human rights perspective to the 'chance of life' (n 72 above).

[75] N Whitty, '"In a Perfect World": Feminism and Health Care Resource Allocation' in S Sheldon and M Thomson (eds) *Feminist Perspectives on Health Care Law* (London: Cavendish Publishing Ltd, 1998) 135, 146–7.

need for care, when suddenly, unexpectedly and acutely ill, due to a chronic condition, or the daily care of dependents. All is rendered private, out of the public domain.[76] With a focus upon those with mental disabilities, Eva Feder Kittay observes that: 'The mentally retarded have at times been objects of pity, compassion, or abuse by their caretakers and society at large. But they have rarely been seen as subjects, as citizens, as persons with equal entitlement to fulfilment.'[77] People with mental disabilities, she argues, are considered dependent and unable to 'make [their] own way in the world',[78] that is, to become productive citizens. Justice, Kittay argues, will only be possible when there is recognition of caring dependency, dependency work, and the derivative dependency of carers. Furthermore, where the nature and extent of dependency, the responsibilities taken by those who care and the responsibilities of others for those in need of care remains unexamined neither is consideration given to the obligations of others to support those who care, to fulfil their caring responsibilities. Selma Sevenhuijsen argues that there needs to be a *comprehensive* political debate about the daily activity of unpaid care.[79] Recognition of caring responsibility and the concern of parents caring for children with severe disabilities to do their best for their child, like any other, requires questions to be asked, as Martha Fineman has suggested in a more general analysis of caring responsibility, about public, social, and collective obligations.[80] Eva Kittay's dependency work and Martha Fineman's derivative dependency expose the ways in which those caring for dependants themselves have to depend upon others where the work that they do is neither remunerated nor valued. There is another sense in which those providing care are dependent and that is their dependency upon others for support, advice, and services which they cannot provide themselves but which are necessary for quality care.

C. Caring Responsibilities

Whilst the parents of children with severe disabilities may become experts in their child's condition and develop a range of skills necessary for maximizing their child's health and well-being, parents cannot meet their child's needs alone. Whilst the primary responsibility for caring for children with severe disabilities

---

[76] Selma Sevenhuijsen, *Citizenship and the Ethics of Care: Feminist Considerations on Justice, Morality and Politics* (London: Routledge, 1998) 129–32.

[77] EF Kittay, 'When Caring is Just and Justice is Caring: Justice and Mental Retardation' (2001) 13 *Public Culture* 557, 558.

[78] ibid 560.

[79] Sevenhuijsen (n 76 above); Selma Sevenhuijsen, 'Caring in the Third Way: the Relation between Obligation, Responsibility and Care in the *Third Way* Discourse' (2000) 20 *Critical Social Policy* 5; J Herring, 'Where are the Carers in Healthcare Law and Ethics?' (2007) 27 *Legal Studies* 51.

[80] MA Fineman, *The Autonomy Myth: A Theory of Dependency* (New York: The New Press, 2004).

rests with their parents, the state has an obligation to provide services[81] and society also has an obligation to assist and support parents.[82] Bryony Beresford's study of twenty parents caring for a severely disabled child makes the powerful and simple point that the reason parents continue to care for their child is because they love them. Consequently, she argues, the focus of support provided to children with severe disabilities and their families should be upon sustaining the quality of the parent-child relationship through child-focused, parent-focused, financial, practical, and emotional support and opportunities for both parent and child.[83]

From her study of thirty-three families with a young disabled child, Janice McLaughlin identifies difficulties presented by:

... the wider social contexts that produce disability as tragedy and other; ... the material constraints that envelop their lives; ... the marginalisation and privatisation of care as a mothers' responsibility, which denies the role of wider society in the provision of care; ... the bureaucratic structures of state care that work within pathological models of disability. Where care provision is presented as individualistic, as focused only on the 'condition' rather than the child, as a form of charity and private responsibility rather than a public right and entitlement, families remain locked in marginalised positions that construct them as 'troubling' to society and enforce the caring role on the mother.[84]

Caring, she argues, is made more difficult where the diagnosis is delivered as if it amounts to a personal tragedy yet the parents are immediately expected to meet their children's needs, negotiate with professionals, and deal with negative attitudes of those around them. Further, parents are confronted with the expectation that they will explain their child's behaviour, needs, or condition. And many families experience being abandoned by family or friends. All factors which contribute to the 'channelling of caring responsibility' to the mother,[85] and 'into a marginalised and secluded private sphere'.[86] The experiences of parents with disabled children, Janice McLaughlin suggests, 'provide testimony to the lack of public responsibility to care'.[87] We have to take seriously the context such as that identified by the parents of Ashley X that her parents had been unable to find unrelated caregivers they considered were 'qualified, trustworthy, and affordable'. Furthermore, that the alternative of institutionalization was not one they could responsibly entertain. There needs to be recognition of caring responsibilities in order for the obligation of society to support parents to meet their responsibilities to be fulfilled and the rights of children with severe disabilities to be respected.

---

[81] Nuffield Council on Bioethics (n 4 above) para 2.42.
[82] Kennedy (n 5 above) 153.
[83] Beresford, (1994) (n 51 above) 113.
[84] McLaughlin (n 48 above) para 9.1.
[85] ibid para 5.7.   [86] ibid para 1.3.
[87] ibid para 1.3.

V. Conclusion

As questions about the care of children with severe disabilities enter the legal forum in the context of whether the provision of life-sustaining treatment is in their best interests, the wider questions surrounding the care of children with severe disabilities are rarely explored in the legal and bioethical literature. This limited sphere of analysis fits with an approach to disability as a personal tragedy to be coped with in private. We need to develop a discourse of parental responsibility and framework of relational responsibilities which respects the rights of others, recognizes responsibility-taking and public obligations to support parents and professionals to fulfil their responsibilities to children. Charlotte Wyatt's case was a private dispute played out very publicly through a legal framework which served to polarize the positions of the hospital and her parents rather than encourage them to work together in the shared endeavour of securing the best for Charlotte. The procedures performed upon Ashley X could be understood in terms of the privatization of caring responsibility to the family and the abrogation of public obligations to children with severe disabilities and their families.

20

Nanomedicine—Small Particles, Big Issues: A New Regulatory Dawn for Health Care Law and Bioethics?

Jean V McHale

I. Introduction

As with stem cell technology nanotechnology and nanomedicine have from the outset caused controversy. In his 2002 book *Prey*, Michael Crichton depicted a world where swarms of nanorobots which were equipped with memory, solar power generators, and powerful software began preying on living creatures.[1] In writing his 2002 book, Crichton, relied on a radical approach to nanotechnology which originated in a lecture by a theoretical physicist and nobel laureate, Richard Feynman.[2] He had written that 'ultimately in the great future we can arrange the atoms the way we want, the very atoms all the way down'.[3] This work was subsequently developed by Eric Drexler who had written of the 'grey goo' scenario, which refers to the destruction of mankind by 'omnivorous machines' that 'spread like blowing pollen replicate swiftly and reduce the biosphere to dust in a matter of days'.

Drexler had proposed a nanomachine 1,000 times thinner than a human hair which could copy itself in 1,000 seconds and then, in the next 1,000 seconds, two machines could build two more.[4] This replication could result in less than a day in machines which weighed a ton.

Concerns regarding nanoscience and nanotechnology were originally voiced by HRH Prince Charles in 2003.[5] Press reports suggested that he had raised the 'grey goo scenario'. Prince Charles, however, subsequently sought to distance himself from some of the more extreme claims made in relation to nanotechnology

---

[1] M Crichton, *Prey* (London: Harper Collins, 2006).
[2] RP Feynman, 'There's Plenty of Room at the Bottom' (1960) 23 *Engineering and Science.* 22.
[3] ibid.   [4] E Drexler *Engines of Creation* (New York: Anchor, 1986).
[5] T Radford, 'Brave new world or minature menace?' Why Charles fears grey goo nightmare' *The Guardian,* 29 April 2003.

in 2004. He stated that he had never used the expression 'grey goo' and commented: 'I do not believe that self-replicating robots smaller than viruses will one day multiply uncontrollably and devour our planet. Such beliefs should be left where they belong in the realms of science fiction.'[6] However, he went on to warn of some of the risks of nanotechnology and quoting one retired academic stated that it would not be surprising if nanotechnology did not 'offer similar upsets to thalidomide'.

Concerns regarding radical developments in scientific developments/technology, of course, are not new. From the early days of IVF and the concerns over cloning, through xenotransplantation to stem cell research, nanotechnology is another technology along the continuum which has raised the issue of 'moral panic'. But should we be 'panicking' and does nanomedicine really raise new legal/bioethical issues? Is it really different from other technological developments such as advancements in genetics?[7] A number of commentators have expressed concern that the speed at which the technology is advancing seems to be outpacing considerations of the social and ethical impact of this technology.[8] Does nanomedicine then represent the next 'big' challenge for health care law and bioethics?

II. What is Nanomedicine?

Before we can consider the potential benefits, problems, and regulatory challenges posed by the use of nanotechnology and nanoscience in medicine we need to explore what the terminology means. Nanoscience is a convergence of physics, chemistry, materials science, and biology, which deals with the manipulation and characterization of matter on length scales between the molecular and the micron size.

Nanotechnology is a technology which has a huge potential in the development of health technologies and medical treatment.[9] It concerns the use of particles at atomic or molecular or macro-molecular scale. It is an emerging engineering discipline that applies methods from nanoscience to create products. 'Nano' itself refers to 'one billionth'.[10] In the medical context, the use of this technology was facilitated by the scanning tunnelling microscope which enabled scientists not only to see atoms but also painstakingly move them around. *Nanomedicine* has

---

[6] BBC News, 'Prince warns of science risks', 11 July 2004.

[7] See FN Moore, 'Implications of Nanotechnology Applications: Using Genetics as a Lesson' (2002) 10(3) *Health Law Review* 9.

[8] A Mnyuiswalla, AS Daar, PA Singer, 'Mind the Gap: Science and Ethics in Nanotechnology' (2003) 14 *Nanotechnology*. 9.

[9] See eg the Royal Society and Royal Academy of Engineering, 'Nanoscience and Nanotechnologies, Opportunities and Certainties' (2004).

[10] It originates from the Greek, meaning 'dwarf'.

been defined as the application of nanotechnology in terms of making a medical diagnosis or treating or preventing diseases. It exploits improved and often novel physical, chemical, and biological properties of materials at nanometre scale.

It has been suggested that the potential of nanomedicine is huge. In their 2006 report, 'Nanotechnology for Health' the European Technology Platform commented that:

It is an extremely large field ranging from in vivo and in vitro diagnostics to therapy including targeted delivery and regenerative medicine

It has to interface nanomaterials (surfaces, particles or analytical instruments) with 'living' human material (cells, tissues and body fluids)

It creates new tools and methods that impact significantly existing conservative practices.[11]

The development of nanomedicine may result in more efficient interventions in relation to illness.[12] Nanotechniques can involve the use of technologies which are more cost-effective and more accurate, such as the ability to enhance resolution to a single-molecule analysis of a sample. Nanotechnology enables the development of minature devices which may be used in treatment itself. This can reduce the invasiveness of procedures and lead to the development of new forms of treatment. Use of nanowire arrays enables testing of a single-pinprick of blood.[13] This reduces the prospect of invasive procedures but still enables efficient testing results and can enable such tests to be undertaken at home easily and with little pain.[14] The use of nanotechnology in imaging, such as ultrasound may result in a much more precise diagnosis. In addition, the use of miniaturized imaging systems makes it possible for image-based diagnosis to be undertaken not simply in research centres but much more widely. This has the advantage that it may enable the earlier detection of disease with consequently less invasive and costly treatments being ultimately required.[15] Nanoimaging can be used in the context of the digestive system, for example, to identify ulcers.[16]

There is also considerable potential for the use of nanotechnology in the context of pharmaceuticals. Nanopharmaceuticals may deliver particular molecules through biological barriers such as blood-brain barriers.[17] Carriers on the shell of these molecules can be targeted at molecules which are typical for cancer. There is also the prospect of continuous medication through implants with controlled

---

[11] *'Nanomedicine: Nanotechnology for Health'*, European Technology Platform, (Brussels,2006) para 3.6.

[12] European Group on Ethics in Science and New Technologies to the European Commission, 'Opinion on the ethical aspects of nanomedicine', Opinion No 21, 17 January 2007.

[13] See discussion in 'Opinion on the ethical aspects of nanomedicine' (n 12 above) para 2.2.1.

[14] 'Nanomedicine: Nanotechnology for Health' (n 11 above) para 1.2.1.

[15] ibid para 1.2.2.

[16] See L Sheremeta, 'Nanotechnology and the Ethical Conduct of Research Concerning Subjects' G Hunt and M Mehta (eds), *Nanotechnology, Risk, Ethics and Law* (London: Earthscan, 2006) 252.

[17] See 'Opinion on the ethical aspects of nanomedicine' (n 12 above) para 2.2.4.

administration of drugs over a period of time. Pills are also being developed which have minature recording devices.

Nanotechnology may also facilitate regenerative medicine.[18] It may enable the improvement of the activation of genes which stimulate regeneration, through stem cell therapy with nanotechnology based upon magnetic cell sorting identifying/activating and guiding stem cells to the particular part of the body which needs regenerating. In addition, access to nanotechnology may also facilitate tissue engineering.[19] Tissue regeneration scaffolds which have been made from nanomaterials have been developed to grow complex human organs. A further use of nanotechniques is through the improvement of implantable devices, such as retinal implants which can restore vision through electronic stimulation of functional neurons in the retina.

III. Regulating Nanomedicine—Legal and Ethical Issues—Same or Different?

Nanomedicine may have great potential but the prospect of the use of such technology has led to controversy and debate. So does this new technology give rise to new ethical and legal issues and does this mean that we need to move sooner rather than later towards specific regulation of nanomedicine itself?

Is nanotechnology special/different? Ethicists Geoffrey Hunt and Michael Mehta seem to think that it may be regarded as such:

Nanotechnology is disruptive in that it puts pressure on other products/processes to realign themselves around its introduction. More importantly nanotechnology is transformative in the sense that it has the potential, at least in theory, to transform social relations, labour, international economies and to affect a range of institutions....Consequently the very existence of nanotechnology plays a role in shaping how we understand nature and ultimately affects how we redesign our regulatory, legal, social and ethical frameworks.[20]

However, the conclusions of a major study which was commissioned by the UK government in 2003 and was undertaken jointly by the Royal Society and Royal Academy of Engineering are a little more cautious.[21] The Royal Society/ Royal Academy report suggests that many of the social and ethical issues raised by nanomedicine are unlikely to be entirely new: 'For example many concerns about the overall impact of a rapidly changing science on society and the governance and regulation of the technology are likely to echo some of those raised previously about other developments in science and technology that

---

[18] ibid para 2.2.5.   [19] ibid para 2.3.2.
[20] G Hunt and M Mehta, 'What makes nanotechnologies special?' in G Hunt and M Mehta (eds), *Nanotechnology, Risk, Ethics and Law* (London: Earthscan, 2006) 275.
[21] 'Nanoscience and Nanotechnologies Opportunities and Certainties' (n 9 above).

have proved controversial such as nuclear energy, reproductive technologies or biotechnology...'[22] Nonetheless they go onto say: 'That does not make these concerns any the less significant or worthy of the attention of policy makers: indeed past experience with controversial technologies should predispose policy makers to pay timely and applied attention to these concerns rather than dismissing them as nothing new.'[23]

In terms of whether the technology is likely to give rise to new legal and ethical and indeed regulatory challenges the Royal Academy/Royal Society report suggests that: 'Precisely which social and ethical issues become a focus of concern will hinge upon the actual trajectories of change in particular nanotechnologies.'[24]

One obvious reason why we may be concerned to regulate nanomedicine, as with any new technology, are concerns regarding its safety. A UNESCO report on the ethics and politics of nanotechnology commented that nanotechnology and nanomedicine raised 'two concerns: the hazardousness of nanoparticles and the exposure risk. The first concerns the biological and chemical effects of nanoparticles on human bodies or natural ecosystems; the second concerns the issue of leakage, spillage, circulation, and concentration of nanoparticles that would cause a hazard to bodies or ecosystems.'[25] The Royal Society/Royal Academy report saw the need for recognition of the precautionary principle.[26] Nonetheless, to date, despite some expressed concerns regarding the safety of this technology, reports in this area have not recommended a moratorium on this issue.[27]

While some regulatory questions relate to safety, in addition there has also been much discussion as to whether nanomedicine raises new ethical issues. Are these matters which are essentially special or different from ethical concerns which may exist in relation to any new scientific development, and are they of such a degree as to require a specific distinct regulatory response? First, it has been suggested that the use of nanomedicine can have the effect of the medicalization of normal human conditions and thus blur the distinction between health and disease. It has also been suggested that the use of nanotechnology can further marginalize those in society who are seen to be disabled. The more extreme uses of nanomedicine such as the prospect that we may cross the human cyborg divide, have raised further concerns. One suggestion of an extreme use which would clearly give rise to regulatory controversy is that of the separation of human consciousness from the body and its relocation in a computer.

In addition, it has been suggested that nanotechnology has the potential to be used inappropriately to further human improvement. This argument has been

---

[22] ibid page 52.   [23] ibid.

[24] ibid para 6.1.

[25] <http://unesdoc.unesco.org/images/0014/001459/145951e.pdf>. See also, for discussion of the safety issues around nanotechnology, J Balbus, R Denison, K Florini, and S Walsh, 'Getting Nanotechnology Right the First Time' in G Hunt and M Mehta (eds), *Nanotechnology, Risk, Ethics and Law* (London: Earthscan, 2006).

[26] 'Nanoscience and Nanotechnologies Opportunities and Certainties' (n 9 above).

[27] Medicines and Healthcare Products Regulatory Agency (2006).

used by some disability rights groups in relation to the prospect of the use of nanomedicine in developing enhancement technology.[28] It can be argued, however, that these are risks which can arise in relation to many new medical technologies. The Royal Society/Royal Academy report noted that:

> All successful medical treatment of illness, including treatment of illness with a genetic basis, enhances the functioning and capacities of those who are treated. Even where an intervention—a drug, a prosthesis, a medical device, surgery—is not effective for all sufferers it can hardly be withheld from those who could benefit on the grounds that others cannot. There is no general case for resisting technologies or interventions that enhance human capacities.[29]

Nonetheless, they recognized the view of some disability groups that a 'technical fix' view of disability is not unproblematic. They noted that some disabled people may, for example, prefer money to be allocated to such things as anti-discrimination or human rights measures as opposed to developing technology in general.

Certain civil liberties concerns have been raised regarding the use of this technology.[30] One concern relates to the prospect of the invasion of personal privacy. The use of nanotechnology in medicine may lead to development of devices which enable information to be collected about the patient without consent. This could lead to surreptitious genetic profiling taking place.

A further concern regarding ethical issues raised in a review by the European Group on Ethics in Science and New Technologies on this issue was that of the implications of the overlap between medical and non-medical uses.[31] It noted that there was a possibility that 'the distinction between therapeutic goals and enhancement goals may become less clear, if for example, predisposition tests are available more easily and cheaply. Especially in the reproductive context of pre-implantation genetic diagnosis the line between "negative" and "positive" selection may be blurred.'

The Group noted the prospect that it may be the case that neurological stimulation of brain activity goes beyond therapeutic and diagnostic use. The Group suggested that appropriate monitoring and guidelines as to the use of nanotechnology in this particular area should be introduced. It was also of the view that priority should not be given to 'enhancement technologies', rather that health care concerns should be addressed first.

IV. Governmental Responses to the Challenge of Regulating Nanomedicine

As has already been noted, developments in nanomedicine have been the subject of consideration in a number of reports by national and international bodies.

---

[28] 'Nanoscience and Nanotechnologies, Opportunities and Certainties', (n 9 above) 54.
[29] 'Nanoscience and Nanotechnologies, Opportunities and Certainties', (n 9 above) para 6.5.
[30] ibid 53–4.
[31] See 'Opinion on the ethical aspects of nanomedicine' (n 12 above) para 5.13.

Following the Royal Society and Royal Academy of Engineering Report, the UK government made a series of commitments in relation to nanotechnology.[32] The Royal Society/Royal Academy report had identified the need for knowledge as to how nanoparticles operate. The government has committed itself to research in the area. It has created a Nanotechnology Issues Dialogue Group. This body is chaired by the Office of Science and Technology and contains members drawn from departments where nanotechnologies are an issue. It has the task of assisting in coordinating activities arising from nanotechnology. In addition, the Department of the Environment Food and Rural Affairs (DEFRA) chairs a Nanotechnology Research Coordination Group to work with bodies such as funding councils. However, this body does not have specific powers to commission funding. The government has also committed itself to a public dialogue on science and technology.

The Royal Society and Royal Academy report rejected the introduction of a moratorium at the present time, seeing it as inappropriate. But this was on the basis that the UK government should undertake an appropriate regulatory regime as rapidly as possible to deal with the prospect that nanoparticles may have considerably greater toxicity than they are thought to have at present. The government indicated that it would work with bodies such as the Health and Safety Commission and the Medicines and Healthcare Products Regulatory Agency (MHRA) to review current regulatory frameworks to ensure that the safeguards to public health are adequate and assess regulation of mechanisms concerning the release of nanoparticles into the environment. The government also supported the recommendation of the Royal Society/Royal Academy that existing bodies regulating aspects of this area, such as the Health and Safety Executive (HSE) should undertake reviews to see if there were any 'regulatory gaps'. The Royal Society/Royal Academy had also recommended that the funding councils should undertake a research programme investigating the social/ethical issues. In their response, the government indicated that it hoped that the research would be geared to practical guidance and advice as to how this could be used in policy-making.

Recently the Council for Science and Technology (CST) has been monitoring developments.[33] The Council undertook a two-year review of the commitments which the UK government had made in response to the Royal Society and Royal Academy of Engineering Report.[34] The review praised the UK government for driving forward issues internationally and it noted that the dialogue with industry had had the effect of limiting the presence of nanomaterials in waste streams.

---

[32] HM Government in Consultation with the Devolved Administration, 'Response to the Royal Society and Royal Academy of Engineering Report Nanoscience and Nanotechnologies: opportunities and uncertainties' (February 2005).

[33] <http://www2.cst.gov.uk>.

[34] CST, 'Nanosciences and Nanotechnologies: A Review of Government Progress on its policy commitments' (March 2007).

However, it was critical of the government's commitment in relation to research. It recommended greater strategic cross-government action.[35] It also stated that a department/body or agency should be given the responsibility to drive forward matters set out in the UK government's response to the Royal Society and Royal Academy of Engineering report. It also identified the need for nanotechnologies to be championed at ministerial level. It proposed a more proactive approach in relation to research spending. It recommended that the government should consider the possibility of involving the Nanotechnology Research Co-ordination Group more directly in awarding research funding. The CST also stated that the government should continue the momentum in its contact with the European Union and other international organizations.[36] It also proposed that it should streamline its relationship with industry.

The UK government has established a departmental group to maximize the benefits of nanotechnology while minimizing the risks. £90 million has been earmarked for nanotechnological research.[37] However, the CST review was critical on this point, commenting that there had been 'little tangible advance in knowledge since February 2005'.[38] They were also critical of the amount of funding and the absence of a substantial research programme in this area.[39] They examined the question of whether the response by the government could be seen as a precautionary approach and indeed whether only a moratorium could amount to a precautionary approach as suggested in some responses by Greenpeace and the Soil Association to the CST's review call for evidence.[40] The review defined the precautionary principle as one which should be invoked when

(i) there is good reason based on empirical evidence or plausible causal hypothesis, to believe that harmful effects might occur, even if the likelihood of harm is remote; and
(ii) a scientific evaluation of the consequences and likelihoods reveals such uncertainty that it is impossible to assess the risk with sufficient confidence to inform decision-making.'[41]

The CST review suggested that while there was sufficient concern to legitimize the application of the precautionary principle, nonetheless it was not of such a degree currently to justify the case for a moratorium.[42] While it accepted the conclusions of a review of the Medicines and Healthcare Products Regulatory Agency that existing trial procedures were sufficiently rigorous to include medicines and medical devices that incorporate nanotechnologies, it did have some concerns.[43] In particular it noted that it was unhappy that the Medicine and Healthcare Products Regulatory Agency was ending participation in a

---

[35] ibid para 36.   [36] ibid paras 72–75, 80, 135.
[37] See further M Wicks 'Unlocking the social and economic benefits of nanotechnologies safely' in *Media Planet: Nanotechnology* (Supplement) *The Times* 26 June 2007.
[38] CST Review (n 34 above) para 38.
[39] ibid para 39.   [40] ibid para 52.
[41] ibid para 53.   [42] ibid para 54.
[43] ibid para 127.

BSI NTI/1 Nanotechnologies Standardisation Committee and called for the authority to re-engage in the issue of nanotechnology standards.[44] The government has funded some research on the social-ethical issues of nanotechnology in general.[45] The CST review commented that as many of the current public engagement processes were coming to an end the government did need to engage further on these issues in the future given that public perceptions could change.[46] Furthermore the CST review suggested that the government should explore the possibilities of the involvement of industry with public engagement exercises.[47]

The UK government has also stated that it is aware that 'it is important to have good understanding of public attitudes to and supports the aim for public dialogue...to elicit and understand people's aspirations and concerns around the development of these technologies'.[48] The government has funded a Nanotechnology Engagement Group which is concerned to analyse public engagement with nanotechnology.[49] While the CST noted that public engagement outputs have been useful, nonetheless it commented that there was a discrepancy in public perception as to what steps the government is taking in relation to funding research into the risks of nanotechnology and what happens in practice.[50] In addition, it recommended that the Nanotechnologies Issues Dialogue Group should improve links between those who operate public engagement programmes and policy makers in government departments.[51] The operation of public dialogue here is itself not uncontroversial. Macnaughten, Kearnes, and Wynne suggest that increased public dialogue may lead to conflict with concerns such as 'global competitiveness and economic potential of scientific systems'.[52]

V. EU Responses to Nanomedicine

Domestic regulatory responses to nanomedicine in the future will inevitably be affected by developments at EU level. The European Union has engaged with nanotechnology in general and in relation to health in particular. In the Commission Communication 'Towards a European Strategy for nanotechnology'

---

[44] ibid para 128.
[45] University of Sheffield, 'The Social and Ethical Challenges of Nanotechnology' at <http://www.shef.ac.uk/physics/people/rjones/PDFs/SECNanotechnology.pdf>: 'Nanotechnology Risk and Sustainability: Moving Engagement Upstream', at <http://www.sustainabletechnologies.ac.uk/Projects/nanotechnology.htm>.
[46] See CST Review (n 34 above) para 145.
[47] ibid paras 90–93.
[48] HM Government Response to the Royal Society and Royal Academy Report, 'Nanoscience and Nanotechnologies: opportunities and uncertainties' (2005).
[49] See further <http://www.involve.org.uk/aboutneg>.
[50] See CST Review (n 34 above) para 142.
[51] ibid paras 143.
[52] P Macnaghten, M Kearnes, and B Wynne, 'Nanotechnology, Governance and Public Deliberation. What Role for the Social Sciences?' (2005) 27(2) *Science Communication* 1.

in 2004, while highlighting the potential of nanotechnology the Commission also recognized its risks.[53] It pinpointed the need for the early identification and resolution of safety concerns along with effective R&D support. It recommended the effective coordination of national measures through mechanisms such as the 'Open Method of Co-ordination'. This document also highlighted the need for recognition of ethical principles in accordance with the EU Charter of Fundamental Rights and Freedoms and other European and international documents.[54] It also identified the need for effective communication of such information within the scientific community.

Following the Communication from the Commission to the Council, the European Parliament and the Economic and Social Committee, 'Nanosciences and nanotechnologies: an action plan for Europe 2005–2009' the European Group on Ethics in Science and New Technologies was asked to undertake an ethical review of nanomedicine which would enable the future appropriate ethical review of proposed projects concerning nanoscience and nanotechnology.[55] As noted earlier, the report considered many of the issues already discussed in this chapter. The Group highlighted one uncertainty in this area namely that there was no clear legal definition of nanomedicine.[56] It also identified a major practical problem in attempting to take a holistic approach to the regulation of nanotechnology, namely that there is a diverse range of forms of legal regulation of such technologies. So, for example, at EU level regulation of nanotechnology may arise in the context of the regulation of pharmaceuticals,[57] and medical devices,[58] and other health care law principles are applicable, such as consent, confidentiality, and data protection.[59] Nonetheless whilst the Group recognized the range of regulatory issues, it rejected the introduction of a new broad regulatory structure for nanomedicine.[60] Instead it was thought that changes should be made within the existing structures.[61]

Nonetheless the Group was concerned to ensure that the differences within the range of regulations which existed were addressed by the regulatory bodies. It was noted that while many of the problems associated with new materials are addressed through product liability legislation at the same time there are difficulties in ascertaining the risks and related liability from negligence. It was suggested that given that given such problems with risk assessment, then ascertaining liability in negligence could be a serious problem and one which needed

[53] Commission of the European Communities, Communication from the Commission 'Towards a European Strategy for nanotechnology' COM (2004) 338 final, Brussels, 12 May 2004.

[54] ibid para 3.5.1.

[55] COM (2005) 243 final. Section 5.1.(b).

[56] See 'Opinion on the ethical aspects of nanomedicine' (n 12 above) para 3.5.

[57] Directive (EC) 2004/726.

[58] See Directive (EEC) 93/42; Directive (EEC) 90/385.

[59] Directive (EC) 95/46.

[60] See 'Opinion on the ethical aspects of nanomedicine' (n 12 above) para 5.51.

[61] ibid para 5.5.1.

to be addressed. The Group also suggested a review of the patent system, as it was concerned that the use of unduly broad patents in this area could hinder therapeutic availability.

The Group expressed concern at the prospect of internet tests using nanotechnology becoming available. It suggested that in the interest of consumer protection, policies should be developed to monitor the introduction of tests directly marketed to customers.[62] As with any new technology, there are challenges in terms of the provision of information as part of an 'informed consent' process and the Group suggested that these needed to be addressed by Member States.[63]

The Group emphasized the need for transparency and public trust.[64] Recognizing the on-going nature of the challenges faced by nanotechnology, the Group suggested that there was a need for inter-disciplinary research on the ethical, legal and social implications of this technology.[65] It proposed that there should be a dedicated European network on nanotechnology ethics established and financed by the Commission under FP7. The Group also suggested that initiatives should be developed to enhance information exchange between research ethics committees in different Member States. Interestingly it also proposed that measures should be taken at a European level to establish databases not only for the scientific aspects of nanomedicine but also on the ethical, legal, and social implications of nanomedicine.

VI. How Should We Regulate Nanomedicine?

If nanomedicine does raise at least some potentially problematic legal/ethical and regulatory issues, is this then a case for us to develop specific regulation of nanotechnology in general or nanomedicine in particular? And if we do, just how should we regulate at a domestic level in particular? As Black notes, interest in regulatory techniques has grown against a backdrop of increasing scepticism regarding the role of the state,[66] particularly in the context of a globalized society. Regulation may be seen as a means of safeguarding individual interests, concerns, and rights and also the public interest.[67] One reason for regulation in the context of a new technology such as in the area of nanomedicine is that of the 'public interest'. There may be a perceptible public interest in safeguarding individual rights and values such as dignity. Without at least some degree of regulation, individual autonomy may be undermined and human rights principles ignored. In addition, safeguarding the public interest here can also be seen through the use of mechanisms designed to protect health and safety interests.

---

[62] ibid para 5.6.   [63] ibid para 5.7.
[64] ibid para 5.9.   [65] ibid para 5.10.
[66] See J Black 'Proceduralising Regulation: Part 1' (2000) 20(4) *OJLS* 597, 600.
[67] ibid.

How then should we regulate? One option is to create a single regulatory body—a 'Nanomedicine Regulatory Authority'. The Human Fertilisation and Embryology Authority (HFEA), which currently regulates modern reproductive technology services, provides one possible model. There are certain perceptible advantages in the creation of such a body. First, such a regulator may be seen as having independence. This means that they can be seen to have the ability to stand outside the pressures of the scientific community and to be divorced from the commercial imperative to develop such technology. Secondly, and linked to the first aim, a regulator may be able to foster public trust and confer legitimacy. However, the simple establishment of a regulatory body will not necessarily achieve this role. Much will depend upon the construction of the body and how it operates in practice. Thirdly, the regulator may be able to ensure accountability— though this again would depend upon how the regulatory body was constructed. The HFEA, for example, operates a statutory licensing procedure in relation to those reproductive technology procedures within its remit and also in relation to embryo research. A similar licensing approach is now operated by the Human Tissue Authority in relation to tissue banks consequent upon the Human Tissue Act 2004. However, in practice the diversity of the issues under consideration would suggest that to operate a similar licencing system in the case of nanomedicine at the present time would not be feasible in practical terms.

Fourthly, the establishment of a regulator might have the effect of facilitating public participation in decision-making through the prospect of a broader dialogue on these issues. It might also facilitate regular consultation exercises. There has been recent concern to ensure that such technology goes forward with public acceptance. Some recent social science discourse suggests that participation with social/ethical issues may not simply facilitate acceptance but may assist in formulating and developing the technology itself.

But is a regulatory body at present premature? Do we really need such a body if we can be convinced that what we have here is really something new, rather than, as has been suggested in some reports, simply an extension—albeit an important extension of—existing technology? After all, just how likely is Drexler's scenario? Drexler has suggested that 'nanorobots are envisaged that could destroy viruses and cancer cells and repair damaged structures', of course not all the scientific community accept Drexler's prognosis. Richard G Smalley, Chemist and Nobel Prize winner, writing in an article, 'Of Chemistry, Love and Nanorobots' in the journal *Scientific American* in 2001, argued that nanorobots/assemblies 'are simply not possible in our world because of constraints caused by limitations of scale'.[68] Even at the nanolevel there is simply not room for such developments— what he calls the 'fat fingers' problem. It remains to be seen how the science develops, nonetheless two decades from Drexler's thesis we are still some considerable way from nanorobots.

---

[68]   RG Smalley, 'Of Chemistry, Love and Nanorobots' (2001) *Scientific American* 68.

Secondly, a further practical issue here is that of the diverse nature of regulatory issues which arise. The range of issues here is considerably broader even than that facing a regulatory body such as the HEFA. This raises the practical issue of whether a single regulator would be feasible. If not a regulator, then how should we regulate? There is currently some regulation of nanomedicine, however, it is not at present the subject of a single regulatory structure. One of the practical difficulties in regulating this technology relates to the diversity of issues which are under consideration. These include the regulation of pharmaceuticals, medical devices, the law as it relates to informed consent, data protection, and patient confidentiality.

Nonetheless, there are clearly some pertinent safety and ethical and legal challenges raised by the prospect of nanomedicine. A better approach may be to establish a specific standing advisory body specifically concerned with nanomedicine, as opposed to the current reviews provided by the CST and various other nanotechnology bodies which have been created by the government. Here one possible model is the Human Genetics Commission. The terms of reference of the Human Genetics Commission include the requirement

To analyse current and potential developments in human genetics and advise Ministers on
   — their likely impact on human health and healthcare
   — their social, ethical, legal and economic implications.[69]

The Commission advises on strategic priorities in the delivery of genetic services by the NHS and on strategic priorities for research. It is also charged with the development and implementation of strategy to involve and consult and encourage debate among the public and other stakeholders regarding the development and use of genetic technologies, and also to advise on methods of increasing public knowledge and understanding. The Commission is also charged with co-ordinating and exchanging information with relevant bodies in order to identify/advise regarding the effectiveness of existing guidance in relation to European/international approaches.

Members are usually appointed for terms of three years. They are drawn from a range of relevant disciplines—currently genetics, ethics, law and consumer affairs. These terms are renewable. The Commission has undertaken work on a wide range of issues related to genetics. This currently includes identity testing, genetic discrimination, intellectual property and genetics, databases and genetic services. The Commission has no licensing and enforcement powers and its role is—although influential—advisory. In 2005, the Joint Select Committee on Science and Technology suggested that the role of the Human Genetics Commission be combined with the ethical and policy role of the HFEA and placed on a statutory basis however, this recommendation was not followed by the government.[70]

[69] <http://www.hgc.gov.uk/Client/Content_Wide.asp?ContentId=79>.
[70] House of Commons Select Committee on Science and Technology, 5th Report (2005), recommendation 102.

Although the Human Genetics Commission is simply advisory, the creation of a specific analogous body in relation to nanomedicine would have the advantage of providing a central point for the review and coordination of these diverse issues and could provide a basis for leading to more structured review and regulation in the future should this prove necessary. It also could provide a higher profile for consideration of this type of issue than has been the case in relation to current bodies, such as the Nanotechnologies Issues Dialogue Group.

VII. Conclusions

Will the development of nanomedicine present a new regulatory dawn for medical research and medical technologies? As we have noted above, there are differing views as to whether nanotechnology can be truly regarded as 'special' or 'different'. It is really too early to resolve the question of whether this is truly a brave new regulatory dawn for health care law and bioethics. There is certainly a range of pertinent issues which need to be addressed as pinpointed at both national and EU level in the many reviews as to the validity of such technologies, their safety, and the broader implications in relation to issues as diverse as patenting, informed consent, and confidentiality. The United Kingdom's own approach here is likely to be considerably affected by developments at EU level here in the future. Much will of course, in practice, depend on precisely how this new technology develops. If Drexler's views are correct then perhaps we are in a brave new world of regulation. However, the manner in which the technology has developed to date may suggest that there is the prospect of a much less dramatic solution. This does not, however, mean that there are not regulatory challenges which we do need to address. If nanomedicine does develop but in a more gradual and piecemeal fashion, then we need to ensure that those areas where it is currently regulated are sufficiently robust and effectively structured to deal with the task of regulation. The UK government has attempted to engage with the broad scope of the area of nanotechnology, however, it is suggested that it may now be time for the government seriously to consider establishing a specific advisory body in the area of nanomedicine. This could ultimately operate as a transitional body to a more formal regulator in the future, should this be appropriate given future scientific developments in nanomedicine. What is certain is that a measured proactive regulatory approach is preferable to the risk of the rise of moral panics which can be fuelled by an unchecked regulatory response.

21

The Place of Carers

Jonathan Herring

I. Introduction

Current medical law and ethics is plagued with individualism. Medical law students are usually introduced to medical law and ethics with the principles of autonomy: *my* right to make decisions about *my* medical treatment; and of beneficence: that *I* should receive the treatment that is appropriate for *me*.[1] But this is highly individualistic. As Martha Minow points out, the question 'who is the patient?' goes unasked.[2] The obvious answer is: 'Why, it is the person in front of the doctor'. But we cannot separate the interests of someone from those they are in interdependent relationships with. We cannot pretend there are such things as 'our' choices. What we decide about medical decisions will often impact on those we are in relationship with. We cannot decide how much benefit a treatment provides simply by looking at the individual, but we must take into account those around them, and particularly those who care for them. In medical ethics, as in many other areas of academic and public life, the work of carers has been invisible.[3]

But that is just starting to change. Although it has taken a long time, at last the work that carers perform is receiving some recognition.[4] Sadly, it is the economic value of carers that often captures the headlines: £87 billion per year in one recent estimate.[5] Of course, the real value of care lies not in monetary terms, but the impact is has on people's lives. Whatever the reason, the government now openly acknowledges the importance of the role carers perform. It has declared: 'What carers do should be properly recognised, and properly

---

[1] See eg the hugely influential T Beauchamp and J Childress, *The Principles of Biomedical Ethics* (Oxford: Oxford University Press, 5th edn, 2001).

[2] M Minow, 'Who's the Patient?' (1994) 53 *Maryland Law Review* 1173.

[3] M Henwood, *Ignored and Invisible* (London: Carers' National Association, 1998).

[4] The Princess Royal Trust for Carers, 'Eight Hours a Day and Taken for Granted' (London: PRTC, 1998); P Smith, 'Elder Care, Gender, and Work: The Work-Family Issue of the 21st Century' (2004) 25 *Berkeley Journal of Employment and Labour Law*, 351.

[5] L Buckner and S Yeandle, *Valuing Carers—Calculating the Value of Unpaid Care* (London: Carers UK, 2007).

supported—and the Government should play its part. Carers should be able to take pride in what they do. And in turn, we should take pride in carers. I am determined to see that they do—and that we all do.'[6] This has led to a 'National Strategy for Carers' and a range of benefits being made available to them.[7] The effectiveness of these measures is open to question, but carers are now clearly on the political agenda.

Despite the increased public attention that carers are being given there are still a host of unsatisfactory aspects to their legal treatment. The law tends to regard people as single entities with individual rights and responsibilities. In the context of caring relationships (ie much of life) this is inappropriate. This chapter will first develop the claim that an individualized approach to caring relationships is inappropriate. It will then consider in more detail two specific issues which demonstrate this issue. The first is the relevance of carers when issues of rationing health care resources. The second is the relevance of the interests of carers when decisions are made concerning people who lack capacity.

II. The Law and Carers

Legal and ethical writings often express issues as involving an isolated patient and the medical professionals who interact with him.[8] Much has been written on the 'regulation of the doctor-patient relationship'. Nowadays many medical lawyers are proud that the patient is armed with his rights (well, a few) against the might of the medical profession. Here, as often in legal writing, the law presumes an autonomous competent man who can enforce his rights. The reality is that we are ignorant, vulnerable, interdependent individuals, whose strength and reality is not in our autonomy, but our relationships with others.[9]

The law's approach should, then, be based on a norm of interlocking mutually dependent relationships, rather an individualized vision of rights. Many of those sympathetic to such a claim have turned to ethics of care as an alternative to traditional rights-based approaches.[10] It promotes a vision of people

---

[6] Department of Health, 'Caring About Carers' (1999) 1.

[7] F Carmichael, G Connell, C Hulme, and S Sheppard, *Meeting the Needs of Carers; Government Policy and Social Support* (Salford: University of Salford, 2005).

[8] I use the male pronoun deliberately because the image of the isolated rational-driven male patient is the image that dominates in much of the writing.

[9] C Meyer, 'Cruel Choices: Autonomy and Critical Care Decision-making' (2004) 18 *Bioethics* 104; J Tronto, *Moral Boundaries* (London: Routledge, 1993) 167–70.

[10] eg C Gilligan, 'Moral Orientation and Moral Development' in E Kittay and D Meyers (eds), *Women and Moral Theory* (Lanham, Md: Rowman and Littlefield, 1987); M Friedman, *Liberating Care* (Ithaca: Cornell University Press, 1993); S Sevenhuijsen, *Citizenship and the Ethics of Care* (London: Routledge, 1998); R Groenhout, *Connected Lives: Human Nature and an Ethics of Care* (Lanham, Md: Rowman and Littlefield, 2004); V Held, *The Ethics of Care* (Oxford: Oxford University Press, 2006); D Engster, *The Heart of Justice. Care Ethics and Political Theory* (Oxford: Oxford University Press, 2007).

with interdependent relationships as the norm around which legal and ethical responses should be built. The values that are promoted within an ethic of care are not isolated autonomy or the pursuance of individualized rights, but rather the promotion of caring, mutuality, and interdependence. This is not the place to fully flesh out how an ethic of care might work, nor indeed the dangers with it. But I want to highlight five aspects relating to an ethic of care which will be relevant in the discussion which follows:

(1) Dependency and care are an inevitable part of being human.[11] Caring relationships are the stuff of life.[12] Although the extent of caring may vary there is probably no point in our lives at which we are neither cared for nor are caring for another. As Jo Bridgeman has recently emphasized, it is wrong to assume that the only kinds of dependencies are those between parents and children; or in respect of those with disabilities. There are wide ranging forms of dependencies that we all have with each other, even between friends.[13] In failing to acknowledge care work properly the law is missing an important and inevitable aspect of life.

(2) Not only is care an inevitable part of life; it is a good part of life. Care should be treasured and valued. As Robin West puts it:

Caregiving labor (and its fruits) is the central adventure of a lifetime; it is what gives life its point, provides it with meaning, and returns to those who give it some measure of security and emotional sustenance. For even more of us, whether or not we like it and regardless of how we regard it, caregiving labor, for children and the aged, is the work we will do that creates the relationships, families, and communities within which our lives are made pleasurable and connected to something larger than ourselves.[14]

The value of care is not, of course, simply for the individuals themselves. Without caring relationships the burden that would fall onto society would be impossible to bear.[15] As Martha Fineman[16] has argued, for too long society has benefited from caring without giving the activity is due value and support. She calls for a reworking of legal and social attitudes so that caring becomes an activity of central significance. Others have argued that the time has come to recognize that there is a right to care.[17]

---

[11] M Fineman, *The Autonomy Myth* (New York: New Press, 2004) xvii; T Levy, 'The Relational Self and the Right to Give Care' (2007) 28 *New Political Science* 547.
[12] F Williams, 'The Presence of Feminism in the Future of Welfare' (2002) 31 *Economy and Society* 502.
[13] J Bridgeman, 'Book Review' (2006) 14 *Feminist Legal Studies* 407. See also J Herring and P-L Chau, 'My Body, Your Body, Our Bodies' (2007) 15 *Medical Law Review* 34.
[14] R West, 'The Right to Care' in E Kittay and E Feder (eds), *The Subject of Care: Feminist Perspectives on Dependency* (Lanham, Md: Rowman and Littlefield, 2002), 89.
[15] L McClain, 'Care as a Public Value: Linking Responsibility, Resources, and Republicanism' (2001) 76 *Chicago-Kent Law Review* 1673; M Daly, 'Care as a Good for Social Policy' (2002) 31 *Journal of Social Policy* 251.
[16] M Fineman (n 11 above).
[17] Levy (n 11 above); West (n 14 above) 90.

(3) Much of medical law emphasizes the importance of rationality and intellect. The concepts of mental capacity; informed consent; compliance with standards expected by a responsible body of opinion; all privilege in legal discourse logical thought and sound judgment. There is nothing wrong in that, but the emotional side of health is lost. The love which goes on caring and caring; the grief, disappointment, frustration, anger and despair, find no place. Occasionally it peeps through (see the refusal of the medical team who had done so much work to care for the patient in *Re B (Adult: Refusal of Medical Treatment)*[18] that they felt unable to switch off her life support machine as the court ultimately ordered) and when it does it seems somehow inappropriate. The exclusion of emotion means the voice of carers talking about how their cared for one should be looked after finds no ready legal mouthpiece. An ethic of care seeks to acknowledge the role that emotion and rationality plays in relationships. We do not live by rational thoughts alone.

(4) In relationships of caring and dependency interests become intermingled.[19] We do not break down into 'me' and 'you'. To harm a carer is to harm the person cared for; to harm the person cared for is to harm the carer. There should be no talk of balancing the interests of the carer and the person cared for, the question rather should be emphasizing the responsibilities they owe to each other in the context of a mutually supporting relationship.[20]

Indeed it is simplistic to imagine we can identify in a caring relationship who is the carer and who the cared for. Their relationship is marked by interdependency. The 'cared for' provides the 'carer' with gratitude, love, acknowledgement, and emotional support which will be of great emotional value to them. Indeed often a 'carer' will be 'cared for' in another relationship. As Diane Gibson has argued, our society is increasingly made up of overlapping networks of dependency.[21] Further, Clare Ungerson has convincingly argued that it is wrong to see the relationship between 'carer' and 'cared for' as one where the 'carer' has power over the 'cared for'.[22] The 'cared for' might have a range of powers they can exercise. The emotional well-being of the carer can depend on the attitude and response of the 'cared for' person to the carer. The 'cared for' has the power to make the life of the carer unbearable.

(5) Ethics of care emphasizes the importance of responsibilities within caring relationships. Supporters of the ethic of care argue that rather than the focus of the enquiry being whether it is my right to do X, the question is what is my

---

[18] [2002] All ER 449.
[19] T Shakespeare, *Help* (Birmingham: Venture, 2000) and T Shakespeare, 'The social relations of care' in G Lewis, S Gewirtz, and J Clarke (eds), *Rethinking Social Policy* (London: Sage, 2001).
[20] G Clement, *Care, Autonomy and Justice: Feminism and the Ethic of Care* (New York: Westview, 1996) 1. Held (n 10 above) 1.
[21] D Gibson, *Aged Care: Old Policies, New Solutions* (Melbourne: Cambridge University Press, 2005).
[22] C Ungerson, 'Social Politics and the Commodification of Care' (1997) 4 *Social Policy* 362.

proper obligation within the context of this relationship.[23] Virginia Held makes the point by contrasting ethics of care and an ethic of justice:

An ethic of justice focuses on questions of fairness, equality, individual rights, abstract principles, and the consistent application of them. An ethic of care focuses on attentiveness, trust, responsiveness to need, narrative nuance, and cultivating caring relations. Whereas an ethic of justice seeks a fair solution between competing individual interests and rights, an ethic of care sees the interest of carers and cared-for as importantly intertwined rather than as simply competing.[24]

It should be added that Held makes it clear that an ethic of care includes justice: 'There can be care without justice. There has historically been little justice in the family, but care and life have gone on without it. There can be no justice without care, however, for without care no child would survive and there would be no persons to respect.'[25]

It is easy in a discussion of an ethic of care to glamorize care. No one should overlook the sheer exhaustion and exasperation that caring brings.[26] Caring can be mucky, nasty, and frustrating.[27] Care is hard work; extremely hard work.[28] Carers can often feel trapped: their life goals come to an end and they must adopt the role of carer while the rest of their life is put on hold.[29] Caring can become abusive for both the carer and cared for. As Robin West puts it: 'Relationships of care, untempered by the demands of justice, resulting in the creation of injured, harmed, exhausted, compromised, and self-loathing "giving selves," rather than in genuinely compassionate and giving individuals, are ubiquitous in this society.'[30] But this is why it is so important that those sympathetic to an ethic of care emphasize the importance of upholding justice within relationships. An ethic of care which promotes mutual obligation and support within a relationship should never be used to permit abuse to foster. Indeed a relationship-based approach can be more alert than any other to the dangers of misuse of a relationship.[31]

This chapter will now focus on two issues where the law and bioethics' individualist approach which fails to take account of our relational identity is manifest.

---

[23] Held (n 10 above) 15.

[24] ibid 15.   [25] ibid 17.

[26] M Goldsteen, T Abma, and B Oeseburg, 'What is it to be a Daughter? Identities under Pressure in Dementia Care' (2007) 21 *Bioethics* 1.

[27] K Abrams, 'The Second Coming of Care' (2001) 76 *Chicago-Kent Law Review* 1605; J Oliver and A Briggs, *Caring Experiences of Looking after Disabled Relatives* (London: Routledge, 1985).

[28] A Hubbard, 'The Myth of Independence and the Major Life Activity of Caring' (2004) 8 *Journal of Gender, Race and Justice* 327; Ungerson 'Social Politics and the Commodification of Care'.

[29] Department of Health, 'Caring about Carers' (1999) para 69.

[30] R West, *Caring for Justice* (New York: New York University Press, 1997) 81.

[31] See M Chen-Wishart, 'Undue Influence: Vindicating Relationships of Influence' in J Holder and C O'Cinneide (eds), *Current Legal Problems 2006* (Oxford: Oxford University Press, 2007).

III. Quality Adjusted Life Years

The rationing of medical treatment is a controversial and complex topic.[32] Not surprisingly attempts have been made to produce a formula that will ensure that decisions are made which take on board in an appropriate way the benefits and costs of different treatments and enable a comparison to be made between alternatives. Such formulas provide also, perhaps, the smallest of fig leaves to hide behind in the face of a patient being denied treatment:[33] 'Computer says no'.

In the debates surrounding the correct formula much attention has understandably focused on Quality Adjusted Life Years (QALY). This is probably the most popular way of analysing the cost-effectiveness of treatments and is widely used in decision-making in rationing healthcare. It is used by the National Institute for Health and Clinical Excellence (NICE),[34] although not as the only factor to be taken into account.[35]

QALY, as used in rationing decisions, requires an assessment of three factors:

- How many extra years of life will the treatment provide this patient?
- What will the quality of those extra years be?
- How expensive is the treatment?

A treatment that provides a year of perfect health scores as one; however, a year of less than perfect health will score less than one. Death is equivalent to 0. Under QALY, therefore, a treatment which provides a patient with an extra year of perfect health would be preferred to a treatment which provides a patient with an extra year, but a year of pain and low quality of life. A treatment which offered a large number of QALYs for a small amount of money would be highly cost-effective, while one that produced a low number of QALYs for a large amount of money would not be. Someone required to ration health services can therefore examine a range of different services and consider how many QALYs for how much money is possible.[36] NICE indicates that if a treatment gives £20,000 per QALY it is likely to be approved, whereas if it is more than £30,000 there will need to be a strong justification before approval.[37] There are many ways in which one could argue that QALYs are problematic. For the current purposes my

---

[32] J King, 'The Justiciability of Resource Allocation' (2007) 70 *Modern Law Review* 197; K Syrett, 'Nice Work? Rationing, Review and the "Legitimacy Problem" in the New NHS' (2002) 10 *Medical Law Review* 1.

[33] For discussion of needs in this context, see A Hasman, T Hope, and L Østerdal, 'Health Care Need: Three Interpretations' (2006) 33 *Journal of Applied Philosophy*.

[34] National Institute for Health and Clinical Excellence, *The Guidance Manual* (London: NICE, 2006) para 8.2.1; J Fox-Rushby, *Disability Adjusted Life Years (DALYs) for Decision-Making?* (London: Office of Health Economics, 2002).

[35] National Institute for Health and Clinical Excellence, *Social Value Judgements* (2005) para 4.1.

[36] NICE, *The Guidance Manual* (n 34 above) para 8.1.3.

[37] NICE, *Social Value Judgements* (n 35 above) para 4.3.

complaint will be that they are too often used in a way which ignores the significance of carers.

QALY is normally used in a highly individualistic fashion, focusing just on the impact of the treatment on a particular patient. The improvement in the patient's quality of life alone is considered and the impact on their carers counts for nothing. Imagine, for example, a drug which prevents incontinence. It may be that with a highly incapacitated patient receiving excellent care, the benefit of the drug will be very limited. It might therefore score very low indeed on a QALY scale. The fact that the drug might have a dramatic impact on the quality of life for their carer would not be relevant under a traditional analysis of QALY, unless it can be shown that the impact on the carer is such as to affect the quality of care and thereby harm the patient.

The issue of the importance of carers in the assessment of the benefits of a drug for carers has come to a head in disputes over NICE's response to drugs for the treatment of dementia.[38] In 2005, NICE proposed that certain drugs should not be authorized for NHS Alzheimer's patients because their cost was too high and 'outside the range of cost effectiveness that might be considered appropriate for the NHS'.[39] This provoked John Harris to comment: 'It is difficult to think of this as anything but wickedness or folly or more likely both.'[40] NICE's decision was based on a QALY assessment: the improvement in quality of life for Alzheimer's patients per year was insufficient to justify the expenditure. In January 2006 NICE, acknowledging the controversy that had arisen, revised its decision and issued further guidance. However, NICE still rejected the use of Ebixa for late stages of Alzheimer's disease and recommended that anti-cholinesterase treatments[41] not be available for people with a mild version of the disease. In October and November 2006, the appeal panel at NICE rejected an appeal launched against the guidelines.[42] In July 2007, a court challenge to the NICE ruling was made, which was largely unsuccessful.[43]

Much controversy surrounds the NICE recommendations. In this chapter the focus will be on the relevance of the interests of carers when making the decision. A number of different issues arose.

First, there is the point already made that QALYs assess the impact of the proposed treatment on the patient, but they normally place little weight on the impact for the carer. For carers of those suffering from Alzheimer's the distress of seeing an individual they love change their personality, memory and become, in

[38] J Harris, 'Its Not NICE to Discriminate' (2005) 31 *Journal of Medical Ethics* 373.
[39] National Institute for Health and Clinical Excellence, *Appraisal Consultation Document: Donepezil, Rivastigmine, Galantamine and Memantine for the Treatment of Alzheimer's Disease* (London: NICE, 2005) para 4.3.5.
[40] Harris (n 38 above).
[41] Donepezil, rivastigmine, and gelantamine.
[42] National Institute for Health and Clinical Excellence, *Donepezil, Galantamine, Rivastigmine (Review) and Memantine for the Treatment of Alzheimer's Disease* (London: NICE, 2006).
[43] *Eisai v NICE* [2007] EWHC 1941 (Admin).

a sense, a different person is hard to bear. This is particularly so where the disease manifests itself in aggression. Medication which may inhibit the progress of this condition is of huge benefit, not just to the individual patient, but for those caring for him or her. However, traditional use of QALY takes no account of such matters. In the January 2006 guidance, the NICE Committee did consider the benefit of the treatment to carers. It stated:

The Committee considered that although at any point in time a carer may have a higher utility if they were caring for a person responding to drug treatment than if the person were not on the drug or not responding to the drug, the effect of the drug would be to delay progression of the condition, in which case the carer would still be faced at some time in the future with the same difficulties caused by disease progression. Exceptions could be if the person did not progress to later and more difficult stages of the disease within 5 years or because of death.[44]

This argument is, with respect, unconvincing. The claim appears to be that if someone is going to have the burdens of caring of a relative suffering from Alzheimer's at some point in one's life then it matters not whether that is now or at some future point in time. So medication which simply delays the inevitable onset of Alzheimer's does not benefit the carer. However, delaying the onset of the condition provides the benefit of the carer having a longer time with their loved one before the condition takes its toll. Maybe in purely financial terms the loss of the carer is no different, but in terms of quality of life there is certainly a loss.

A second, and linked, point is that the NICE report went on to say that the QALY assessment should be conducted from the perspective of the NHS: 'The Committee therefore concluded that it would not be appropriate to include carer costs in the augmented base case or sensitivity analyses on the augmented base case.'[45] So costs to the NHS count, costs to carers do not. Yet the costs to the individual carer are costs to real people whose lives bear the blight of caring. By contrast, any cost to the NHS and society is spread across everyone. To count for nothing the sacrifices of carers and to consider only the monetary loss to the NHS in allocating health care resources is unjustifiable. Politically, of course, the approach is understandable. Costs to the NHS are in the public eye and impact on the sensitive issue of levels of taxation. Costs to carers go unnoticed in the public arena, although they are real enough to those who suffer them, and real enough in their effect on society as a whole.

Thirdly, the initial decision by NICE did not include in its calculation of QALYs an assessment of behavioural symptoms, although this was later requested by the Appraisal Committee.[46] The original thinking was that if the treatment did not alter the health of the individual, even though it might alter their behaviour, this was not a benefit for the purposes of a QALY calculation. The significance of this

---

[44] National Institute for Health and Clinical Excellence, *Donepezil, Galantamine, Rivastigmine (Review) and Memantine for the Treatment of Alzheimer's Disease (Appraisal Consultation)* (London: NICE, 2006) para 4.3.10.2.
[45] ibid para 4.3.10.3.   [46] ibid para 4.2.6.

is that behavioural symptoms can have a huge impact on the quality of life of a carer. Their initial omission from the standard use of QALYs reflects the individualistic approach that can be used with QALY. If the behaviour does not affect the patient it counts for nothing.

Fourth, the appeal Committee did finally agree that in this unusual case the interests of carers should be considered. 'The Panel heard that costs for informal carers are not normally included in assessing a technology's cost-effectiveness, but it was in recognition of the particular and important role that carers play in the care of people with dementia that a carer utility was included in the analysis for this technology.'[47]

It is not explained why some carers are included in NICE's assessments and not others. What is it about care of dementia that makes this care special? Why are other carer's burdens not relevant for NICE?

However, while accepting that the costs to carers should be taken into account the Committee went on to say: 'The Committee agreed that when the effect on carers is to be considered in an economic evaluation, it should only be incorporated as either carer benefits, in the form of improvements in quality of life (utilities), or carer costs in the form of some (monetary) valuation of the opportunity costs of caring, but not both because of the potential for double counting.'[48]

The double counting argument referred to is dubious. There appear to be two quite distinct issues from a carer's point of view. The first is the financial cost they suffer from caring, most obviously the loss of an income. The second is the quality of life while they are caring. Imagine two drugs, both have such a good effect that during the day the carer is no longer required to be with the patient and is able to return to work. However, one drug means that night-times are disturbed and burdensome for the carer; while with the other night-times are peaceful and unproblematic. Surely treating them as equally effective for the carer because they produce the same financial benefit is inappropriate. Improvements to quality of life and improvements to financial position are two very separate issues.

Fifth, even accepting there should be some assessment of the gain of the treatments to carers NICE found it very difficult to produce a figure to represent it. It relied on an admittedly limited study. As one pressure group noted:

Based on this NICE chose to assign the very small utility gain of 0.01 to carers when calculating a cost per QALY. We believe NICE should not have accepted this finding unquestioningly, particularly given the strength of evidence from carers contradicting this. NICE must address how to properly incorporate benefits to carers if they are to produce equitable evaluations of interventions. Certainly, in the case of treatments for Alzheimer's disease NICE's evaluation methods have failed carers.[49]

Despite all of this the appraisal document makes welcome comments on the significance of the contribution of carers. Indeed in November 2006 guidance

---

[47] ibid para 3.2.4.   [48] ibid para 3.2.5.
[49] Evidence to Select Committee on Health from Alzheimer's Association, March 2007.

was issued on the help and support that should be made available to carers of those suffering dementia. In particular counselling services should be made available.[50]

A legal challenge was issued against the NICE ruling, *Eisai v NICE*.[51] The claimants failed, except in respect of an argument that the NICE guidelines failed to take sufficient account of the difficulties facing those for whom English was not a first language and those with learning difficulties. In relation to arguments that inadequate account had been taken of the interests of carers, Justice Dobbs had this to say:

> There was an exercise of judgement by the expert Appraisal Committee in view of the paucity of scientific evidence, which the Appeal Panel acknowledged. It is a decision with which the Appeal Panel and the court should be slow to interfere in the absence of compelling evidence to the contrary. The fact that thousands of carers gave testament as to the beneficial effect to them does not of itself provide a scientific basis for allocating a calculation. The calculation must bear some relationship to the benefit to the sufferer, and also must show health-related utility gains, as opposed to assessing quality of life more generally.[52]

It is interesting that one of the major difficulties facing NICE was the lack of scientific evidence of the impact of caring. As the judge noted this made it very difficult for the panel to assess the benefits of the drugs to carers. The very fact that caring has been ignored by researchers meant that their interests could not properly be taken into account. This is not to criticize NICE, it could only deal with the evidence before it. A second factor emphasized by Justice Dobbs was the fact that the focus of NICE's approach was the health-related gains rather than quality of life more generally. The difficulty is that for carers, the impact of caring on their health is variable and can be hard to ascertain. The impact of caring can be similar to that of serious illness. It can restrict movement; inhibit social interaction; and produce exhaustion.

It must not be thought, however, that including the costs to carers when making rationing decisions is without difficulty. There are dangers that it will mean that those cared for by a large number of carers or a more vulnerable carer will be regarded as having a greater call on health care resources than a person who is alone, with no family or carers.[53] In the *Rogers*[54] case the use of social and personal characteristics for determining which patients should be given

---

[50] National Institute for Health and Clinical Excellence, *Supporting People with Dementia and their Carers in Health and Social Care* (London: NICE, 2006). For a discussion of the health impact of care, see I Cormac and P Tihanyi, 'Meeting the Mental and Physical Healthcare Needs of Carers' (2006) 12 *Advances in Psychiatric Treatment* 162.

[51] [2007] EWHC 1941 (Admin).

[52] ibid para 131.

[53] Although see D Shickle, 'Public Preference for Health Care' (1997) *Bioethics* 277 for some evidence that surveys of the general public suggest that the number of dependants should be a factor in rationing health care. Contrast P Anand and A Wailoo, 'Utility versus rights to Publicly Provided Rights: Augments and Evidence from Health Care Rationing' (2000) 67 *Economica* 543.

[54] *R (Rogers) v Swindon Primary Care Trust* [2006] EWCA Civ 392.

Herceptin was seen by the court as problematic. It is interesting that the Court of Appeal noted that if the Primary Care Trust had accepted that financial considerations were relevant then this could produce 'a decision by a trust which was subject to financial constraints and which decided that it could not fund all the patients who applied for funding for Herceptin treatment, to make the difficult choice to fund treatment for a woman with, say, a disabled child and not for a woman in different personal circumstances'.[55]

Jo Bridgeman has rejected such an approach.[56] She has argued: 'The needs of a child with disabilities are no different whether they are met by her mother or another. The needs of a woman with breast cancer are no different, whether she is the carer of a child with disabilities or not.' In some ways this is a surprising comment in the light of her comments in the same article which reflect many of the views expressed in this chapter, that we should not view patients in isolation, but in the context of a network of dependencies. The problem with saying 'The needs of a woman with breast cancer are no different, whether she is the carer of a child with disabilities or not' is that it imagines we can assess the needs of a patient without looking at their network of relationships in which they find themselves.

However, this may be to misinterpret Bridgeman's point. Her argument is that we all exist in a network of dependencies. So all women with breast cancer have people who are dependent on them and we should not be in the job of giving greater preference to some dependent relationships over others. Indeed, as she says, there is a danger that the woman's own identity becomes subsumed within a highly visible 'caring role'. Bridgeman notes that it is interesting that the Primary Care Trust in *Rogers* regarded as an exceptional case for treatment for breast cancer, 'caring for a disabled child'; rather than, say, outstanding success in a career, or other criterion.

There is as Bridgeman argues something unpleasant about seeking to compare 'the worth of the lives of women centred around their caring responsibilities'. However, if there is to be rationing of health care resources there must be some way of ranking the needs of patients. The choice is between either ignoring the network of those in caring relations with the patient; or comparing them. Whilst sharing Bridgeman's distaste I would rather do the comparison without ignoring the relationship patients are in.[57]

So, we have seen in this discussion that the primary method of allocating health care resources, the QALY approach, fails appropriately to take into account the interests of carers. In the allocation of health resources, it has been argued, the benefits to those caring for and being cared for by the patient should be taken

---

[55] At para. 77.

[56] J Bridgeman, ' "Exceptional" women, healthcare consumers and the inevitability of caring' (2007) 15 *Feminist Legal Studies* 235.

[57] This discussion opens the debate over whether an alternative to the consequentialist QALY approach is preferable. See eg J Harris, 'Justice and Equal Opportunities in Health Care' (1999) 13 *Bioethics* 392.

into account, as well as the benefits to the patient themselves. Indeed it has been argued that there is no way of separating the benefits to the patient and those they are in caring relationships with. It has, however, been acknowledged this is not straightforward. There is a lack of research into the benefits for carers of particular medication and in particular a lack of a theoretical model of giving appropriate weight to those benefits when rationing decisions are made. Further, there are the difficulties inherent in seeking to compare different sets of caring relationships. Despite these difficulties, it is argued that rationing decisions should not be restricted to considering the benefit to an individual patient, without recognition being given to the network of relationships within which they live.

IV. Mental Capacity Act 2005

The second area I wish to examine concerns the treatment of people who lack mental capacity. This is governed by the Mental Capacity Act 2005. An overriding principle of the Act is that when making decisions about a person who lacks capacity these decisions should be made on the basis of what is in the incompetent person's best interests. Can the interests of a carer be taken into account? The answer, at first sight, is a clear 'no'. Only the interests of the patient in question can be considered.

Section 4 provides some requirements for a person, or court, seeking to ascertain what is in a person's best interests. Of particular note, for present purposes, is section 4(7):

He must take into account, if it is practical and appropriate to consult them, the views of —

...

(b) anyone engaged in caring for the person or interested in his welfare

...

as to what would be in the person's best interests...

While it is good to see a statutory acceptance of the relevance of the views of carers as to what should happen to those they care for, it is important to realize the limited nature of this. Most significantly, the carer can only speak as to what would be in the incapacitated person's best interests. Their views as to what would assist them as carers is not a relevant consideration, unless it can be 'dressed' up as being about the benefit of the individual. So, if the carer can say 'if my views on this issue are not listened to I will cease to care for the individual and hence it is in their interests that my views are accorded weight', then her views can be taken into account.[58]

---

[58] See *Re Y (Mental Patient: Bone Marrow Donation)* [1997] 2 WLR 556 (FD) for an example of a case where the courts used some rather convoluted reasoning to find a benefit to the person lacking capacity in donating bone marrow to a relative. I have discussed this case further

Let us consider a case of a severely demented 80-year-old woman. Her primary carer is her daughter, but this is supplemented at night by paid professional carers. The daughter lives 50 miles away from the mother. The daughter proposes that her mother move to live with her. There is some evidence that this change of home will cause a little confusion and disturbance to her mother. Of course for the daughter the task of caring will be greatly eased. If the daughter were to say that the long journey is exhausting her and the quality of care she is able to offer her mother is greatly improved by moving her it would be possible to make an argument that the move would promote the mother's best interests. Let us say, however, that the daughter goes to the utmost length to ensure she offers her mother the best of care despite the long journey. In all honesty she cannot say that the care will be any better in her own home, it will just greatly ease her task of caring. At first sight we must conclude that although in the carer's best interests the move is not in the patient's best interests and so should not be permitted.

I will argue, first, that such a conclusion does not necessarily follow from a reading of the Mental Capacity Act. Second, that the law ought indeed to permit such a move, by taking into account the interests of carers when considering the best interests of a person lacking capacity.

A. Interpreting the Mental Capacity Act

A straightforward reading of the Act suggests that a carer's interests cannot be taken into account. The sole criterion is the interests of the individual patient. Earlier reference was made to the Mental Capacity Act 2005 and the fact that although carers' views about what would be in the best interests of the patient can be taken into account, the decision can only be made based on what is in the best interests of the patient. This narrow understanding of best interests has found its way into the Act's *Code of Practice*. This is most powerfully shown by its discussion of the case of Pedro:

Pedro, a young man with a severe learning disability, lives in a care home. He has dental problems which cause him a lot of pain, but refuses to open his mouth for his teeth to be cleaned. The staff suggest that it would be a good idea to give Pedro an occasional general anaesthetic so that a dentist can clean his teeth and fill any cavities. His mother is worried about the effects of an anaesthetic, but she hates to see him distressed and suggests instead that he should be given strong painkillers when needed. While the views of Pedro's mother and carers are important in working out what course of action would be in his best interests, the decision must *not* be based on what would be less stressful for them. Instead, it must focus on Pedro's best interests.[59]

---

in J Herring, 'The Welfare Principle and Parent's Rights' in A Bainham, S Day Sclater, and M Richards (eds), *What is a Parent?* (Oxford: Hart, 1999).

[59] Department of Constitutional Affairs, *Mental Capacity Act 2005. Code of Practice* (London: TSO, 2007) para 5.7.

Despite this apparently clear statement in the Guidance, I will argue that the Act should be interpreted in a way which includes the interests of carers.

First, section 4(6) requires the decision-maker, when deciding what is in the best interests of the individual to consider:

(a) the person's past and present wishes and feelings (and, in particular, any relevant written statement made by him when he had capacity)

(b) the beliefs and values that would be likely to influence his decisions if he had capacity, and

(c) the other factors that he would be likely to consider if where able to do so.

There are very few people indeed, I suggest, who would want decisions about them when incapacitated to be made entirely based on their own best interests and with no consideration being given to the person caring for them, especially where that is a loved one. At the very least surely there are few people who want a decision to be made which caused enormous harm to the carer because it procured for them the most marginal of gains. And surely not where a choice is made to prefer an option which benefits them, and hugely helps the carer; over an alternative which would benefit them slightly more, but hugely harm the carer. Section 4(6) enables the decision-maker to take into account the relationship between the patient and carer when making decisions. The values of altruism, however limited, will mark most intimate relationships. The Act does not tell us what weight is to be attached to the values an individual exhibited in their life but in earlier case law we are told that the view of a patient could be major factor.[60] Indeed the Code of Practice accepts this: 'Section 4(6)(c) of the Act requires decision-makers to consider any other factors the person who lacks capacity would consider if they were able to do so. This might include the effect of the decision on other people, obligations to dependants or the duties of a responsible citizen.'[61]

The fact that the individual will not be competent and so unable to receive the benefit of the relationships should not negate this argument. In *Ahsan v University Hospitals Leicester NHS Trust*[62] it was confirmed that an incompetent person should be treated in accordance with their religious beliefs, even if they now lacked awareness of what was happening to them. The argument that because they did not know what was happening to them it was of no benefit to be treated in accordance with their beliefs was rightly rejected.

Second, it should be recalled that 'best interests' is not defined in the Act. It is not, however, an entirely materialistic concept. In *Re MB*[63] it was made clear that best interests are not restricted to medical best interests. Butler Sloss P in *JS v An NHS Trust* stated the court should define best interests 'in the widest possible

---

[60] *Re MB* [1997] 2 FLR 426, 439 (CA).
[61] *Mental Capacity Act 2005. Code of Practice*, (n 59 above) 5.47.
[62] *Ahsan v University Hospitals Leicester NHS Trust* [2006] EWHC 2624 (QB).
[63] [1997] 2 FLR 426 (CA).

way'.[64] In *Re A*[65] it was held that 'best interests encompasses medical, emotional, and all other welfare issues'. Munby J has explained that best interests require a consideration of 'ethical, social, moral emotional and welfare considerations'.[66]

The *Code of Practice* states:

The Act allows actions that benefit other people, as long as they are in the best interests of the person who lacks capacity to make the decision. For example, having considered all the circumstances of the particular case, a decision might be made to take a blood sample from a person who lacks capacity to consent, to check for a genetic link to cancer within the family, because this might benefit someone else in the family. But it might still be in the best interests of the person who lacks capacity. 'Best interests' goes beyond the person's medical interests.[67]

It seems, then, that a consideration of best interests can take into account the obligations towards others that a person properly has. Would you say it would be in your best interests to be waited on hand and foot by an army of slaves, meeting your every need? Would we want our friends to be undertaking enormous sacrifices to achieve relatively minor gains for us? Would anyone find such a way of life rewarding or beneficial?[68] We should not impose that on those who are incompetent. Indeed the Mental Capacity Act itself recognizes that people lacking capacity can be treated in a way which does not directly benefit them, when in Chapter 11 of the Act it permits an incompetent person to be involved in research.

Third, an approach which fails to take account of the interests of carers is liable to infringe the European Convention rights of the incapacitated individual and carer. Those in a caring relationship must have their relationship respected as part of their private or family life under Article 8.[69] Under the Human Rights Act 1998 the concept of best interests must be interpreted and given effect to in a way which respects their rights as far as is possible. It is true that any right that a carer may claim under Article 8 can be interfered with under Article 8(2) in the interests of the patient. However, it needs to be shown that the interference is necessary in the interests of the incompetent patient. If a decision will hugely interfere in the private life of the carer, but provide a tiny benefit to the person lacking capacity, I suggest it is unlikely this will be sufficient to justify the interference.[70]

---

[64]   [2002] EWHC 2734 (Fam), para 60.

[65]   *Re A (Male Sterilisation)* [2000] 1 FLR 549 (CA).

[66]   *E v Channel Four* [2005] EWHC 1144 (Fam), para 57 and *Sheffield CC v S* [2002] EWHC 2278 (Fam), para 7.

[67]   *Mental Capacity Act 2005. Code of Practice* (n 59 above) para 5.48.

[68]   J Piliavin and H-W Charng, 'Altruism: A Review of Recent Literature and Research' (1990) 16 *Annual Review of Sociology* 27 discusses recent evidence that true altruism does exist in human nature.

[69]   *Sheffield CC v S* [2002] EWHC 2278 (Fam).

[70]   *B Borough Council v Mrs S, Mr S* [2006] EWHC 2584 (Fam) [2007] 1 FCR 574; *A Local Authority v Mr BS* [2003] EWHC 1909 (Fam). In *Sheffield CC v S* [2002] EWHC 2278, para 48, (Fam) Munby J said that although the best interests applied, common sense dictates that mentally

So, although at first glance the Mental Capacity Act appears to make it clear that only the interests of the person lacking capacity are to be taken into account and the interests of the carers are to count for nothing, the situation is not so straight forward. The view of the patient when they had capacity must be taken into account; the term best interests must be understood very broadly; and the human rights of the carer and person cared for need all to be considered. This means that in many, if not all, the interests of carers can be considered. The Mental Capacity Act should not, for example, be interpreted to mean that a decision is made which hugely harms a carer, while providing only a minimal benefit to the patient.

B. Theoretical Issues

My argument now moves onto the more theoretical level which is assessing whether we should seek to promote the best interests of the incompetent person without taking into account the interests of their carers. It is not possible to consider the incompetent person without considering the well-being of the incompetent person's carer. The interests of the two are intertwined. No carer could possibly undertake the task of caring if every decision which has to be made was solely on the basis of what is in the interests of the cared for person. As the President's Council on Bioethics puts it:

As a simple rule of thumb, caregivers should do the best they can do; they are never compelled to do what they cannot do, but they are obligated to see how much they can do without deforming or destroying their entire lives. But in practice, this rule of thumb rarely leads to any fixed rules, because every person faces different demands and has different capacities. And inevitably, we cannot do our best simultaneously in every area of our life: that is to say, we cannot do our best for everyone all the time; we cannot be there for everyone all the time; we cannot devote resources to everyone equally all the time. To be a caregiver is to confront not only the limitations of the person with dementia who relies upon us entirely, but our own limitations as human beings who are more than just caregivers or who are caregivers in multiple ways for multiple people.[71]

No one would want to be cared for in a relationship in which the carer's interests counted for nothing. The relationship of caring does, and should, involve give and take. It would not be in the interests of a cared for person to be in a relationship which was utterly oppressive of their carer. What *is* in their interests is to be in a relationship with their carer which promotes the interests and well-being of both of them.[72] It is, therefore, argued that when considering

incapacitated adults were normally better cared for within their family. Although there was no formal legal presumption to that effect.

[71] President's Council on Bioethics, *Taking Care* (Washington, DC: President's Council on Bioethics, 2005), 198.

[72] For a development of this approach in relation to parents and children see J. Herring, 'The Human Rights Act and the Welfare Principle in Family Law—Conflicting or Complementary?' [1999] *CFLQ* 223.

the best interests of an incompetent person such an assessment must consider their well-being in the context of their relationships. This might involve making decisions which in a narrow way do not explicitly promote the incompetent person's welfare or even slightly harm it, if that is fair aspect of a caring relationship which is a necessary part of the incompetent person's well-being. An important aspect of the ethic of care, but one that is often overlooked by care ethicists, is that part of valuing and promoting caring relationships is the protection of people who are rendered vulnerable in caring relationships. We need to promote 'just care'.[73]

In Ronald Dworkin's influential discussion of making decisions for incompetent people he draws a much discussed distinction between experiential interests and critical interests.[74] Critical interests are those things which make a person an individual. The things that make a person's life worthwhile. Experiential interests may produced pleasure and fun (for example skiing) but are not part of a person's life goal. If this is used I would argue that for many people lacking capacity their relationship with their carer, especially where that has been someone with whom they have been in a close relationship, will be part of their critical interest. Their partnership; marriage; sibling relationship; or friendship will have been a defining part of their lives. Their interest in promoting that as a relationship of give and take will be a part of their critical interest which should continue after losing capacity.

So can we be more precise about how the interests of carers should be taken into account? I argue that the key is to examine the decision at issue in the context of the relationship between two people. How does this decision fit in with the giving and taking involved in this relationship. This will mean that carers will not be treated 'as objects to be manipulated as part of patient care'.[75] The relationship between carer and dependant must not be one-sided. Of course, it is extremely difficult, if not impossible to imagine that a decision that severely harms either the carer or the dependent could be seen as justified in the context of a relationship.

It may help to add what I am not saying.[76] I am not claiming that treating a person lacking capacity in a way which is not in their best interests but promotes altruism creates a moral good. Altruism which is forced is probably not properly described as altruism. At least it does not exhibit the characteristics which

---

[73] C Koggel, 'Care and Justice; Re-Examined and Revised' (1999) *Paideia* 24. For an excellent discussion on the importance of responsibilities in medical law and ethics, see M Brazier, 'Do no harm—Do patients have responsibilities too?' [2006] *CLJ*, 397.

[74] R Dworkin, *Life's Dominion* (London: Harper Collins, 1993) 224.

[75] Minow (n 2 above).

[76] P Lewis, 'Procedures that are against the Medical Interests of Incompetent Adults' (2002) 22 *OJLS* 575.

we admire in altruism.[77] Nor am I saying that the procedure is justified because making decisions which benefit the carer can be shown to create benefits for the dependent person in the long run.[78]

Rather my claim is that the incompetent person cannot be viewed in isolation. They must be viewed in the context of the relationship which they are in. This will be a fair and just relationship which promotes the rights and interests of both parties. As with all healthy relationships this will involve give and take. Under the orthodox analysis there will be some decisions which are in the interests of the person lacking capacity and some which are in the interests of the carer. This is how it is in real life in a well working caring relationship and this is how it should be.

A common objection to the argument that it is permissible when making a decision on behalf of an incompetent person to take into account the interests of others is that in so doing the incompetent person may simply be used to benefit others. The incompetent person ends up being used as a means to an end and not an individual in their own right.[79] I would suggest two arguments in reply to such a claim. First, that to view a person outside the context of their relationships; to view them as an isolated vessel of gain or loss is even more dehumanizing. When decisions are made about an individual in the context of their relationship, this is regarding them as truly human. Second, it is, of course, common to impose obligations, some of them quite heavy, on people in order to benefit others. Taxation and jury service are two common examples.[80] These are not normally regarded as infringing a fundamental principle of ethics, but rather part of the responsibilities of a good citizen.

A slightly different argument is to challenge whether it is appropriate to require sacrifices of an incompetent person without their consent due to their relationship with their carers, while at the same time not making the same requirement of a competent person. In short, is this not discriminatory against incompetent people? One response to this is to suggest (as I have elsewhere)[81] that we should not enable a competent person to make a decision in the context of medical treatment which imposes intolerable burdens on carers. More moderately I simply question whether or not there is a 'sacrifice' here. As already indicated a good argument can be made for saying that an incompetent person benefits from being in just and mutually supportive relationships.

---

[77] J Seglow, 'Altruism and Freedom' (2002) 5 *Critical Review of International Social and Political Philosophy*, 145.

[78] M Goodwin, 'My Sister's Keeper?: Law, Children, And Compelled Donation' (2007) 29 *Western New England Law Review* 357.

[79] L Harmon, 'Falling Off The Vine: Legal Fictions and the Doctrine of Substituted Judgment' (1990) 100 *Yale Law Journal*, 1.

[80] J Harris, 'In Praise of Unprincipled Ethics' (2003) 29 *Journal of Medical Ethics* 303.

[81] J Herring, 'Where are the Carers in Health Care Law and Ethics?' (2007) 27 *Legal Studies* 51.

V. Conclusion

To conclude, this chapter refutes the notion that we can consider the interests of the patient in isolation from those who are in caring relations with them. However proudly the law may seek to trumpet our autonomy, our self-sufficiency, and our rights, that is a false pictures of our lives. We are not self-sufficient, we are dependent on others and others are dependent on us. We are not all-knowing autonomous people in control of our lives, but subject to the obligations, ties, and joys of our relations with others. We must therefore in the law recognize that 'patients' come in a web of relationships. Their interests cannot be disentangled from those around them.

Unfortunately this all makes medical law and ethics harder, not easier! What restrictions are justifiably imposed on an individual's decision to take medical decisions? To what extent can we make decisions which are not in an incompetent person's best interests bearing in mind those who are in dependent relationships with them? These are hard questions, because relationships are hard. They involve the struggles of daily life. Problematic; but that's life.

22

Gender Inequities in Health Research: An Australian Perspective

Belinda Bennett, Isabel Karpin,
Angela Ballantyne, and Wendy Rogers[1]

I. Introduction

Health research plays an important role in informing the treatment choices made by patients and their health care providers, and in the decisions made by those who fund health care. Research provides the evidence that enables us to distinguish effective treatments from those that do not work or are harmful. For women and men to benefit equally from health research, it is necessary that research populations accurately reflect the gender mix of those populations likely to need the relevant treatments and that analysis of data by sex or gender[2] is integrated into the programme of health research. Since 'sex and gender are complex concepts—influenced by cultural, social and political contexts—which cannot be equated simply with biology and culture'[3] it is not adequate to regulate simply for the inclusion of men and women in equal numbers. Rather, considered attention needs to be given to the kinds of regulations that could be put in place to ensure that gender and sex are also utilized as analytical tools, thereby ensuring that both men and women benefit equally from health research.

[1] Research for the paper which forms this chapter was supported by a Legal Scholarship Support Fund Grant, Faculty of Law, University of Sydney to Belinda Bennett in 2003 and by the Australian Research Council Discovery Grant (DP0666279) (Chief Investigators: B Bennett, W Rogers, I Karpin; Research Fellow: A Ballantyne). The authors would like to thank Leisa Burrell, Natasha McCarthy, Myra Cheng, Claire Deakin, Marta Iljadica, Aliza Podwol, and Jo Sutton for their research assistance.
[2] Although sex and gender are separate concepts, they are used interchangeably in the research literature which, in general, does not distinguish between biological and social features.
[3] Institute of Gender and Health, 'What's Sex and Gender Got To Do With It? Integrating Sex and Gender into Health Research' (2004) <http://www.cihr-irsc.gc.ca/e/25131.html> (accessed 10 December 2007) 'Executive Summary', and see further 'What's Sex and Gender Got to Do With It?'.

II. What is Sex and Gender?

When deciding whether to regulate for equitable participation of women and men in clinical research we need to understand what is meant by the terms male and female and sex and gender more generally. However, the meaning of these terms depends on the context in which they are being used. Legal definitions of male and female and sex and gender differ markedly from definitions provided by health research institutions. The Office of Research on Women's Health in the United States, for instance, defines sex as 'being male or female according to reproductive organs and functions assigned by chromosomal complement' whereas gender 'refers to socially defined and derived expectations and roles rooted in biology and shaped by environment and experience.'[4] Similarly, Health Canada defines sex as 'biological characteristics such as anatomy and physiology that distinguish males and females' whereas 'gender refers to the array of socially constructed roles and relationships, personality traits, attitudes, behaviours, values, relative power and influence that society ascribes to the two sexes on a differential basis. Gender is relational.'[5] The legal definition of sex, however, tends to merge these two concepts of sex and gender and adds a further dimension: 'psychological sex'.[6]

In Australia, formal legal definitions of sex are rarely provided despite the importance of sexual distinctions in a number of legal categories such as passports and other documents. For instance, the Commonwealth Sex Discrimination Act 1984 (SDA), merely states that a man is a member of the male sex and a woman is a member of the female sex.[7] Most often sex and gender are not distinguished in legal cases and statutes. In the United States, however, the idea of gender non-conformity was raised as a potential ground for discrimination. In *Price Waterhouse v Hopkins*, for example, a woman was held to have suffered sex discrimination when she was treated badly because she did not conform to sex stereotypes in the workplace.[8] The Opinion of Brennan J said:

---

[4] VW Pinn, 'Expanding the Frontiers of Women's Health Research—US Style' (2003) 178 *Medical Journal of Australia* 598.

[5] Health Canada, 'Gender Based Analysis Policy' (Ottawa: Minister of Public Works and Government Services, 2000) 14.

[6] eg, in *R v Harris and McGuiness* (1988) 17 NSWLR 158 the Supreme Court of NSW held that a person's sex 'is to be determined by a combination of psychological sex identification and physical attributes', and that 'psychological sex identification alone was not sufficient'.

[7] See Sex Discrimination Act 1984 (Cth), s 4.

[8] At first instance, Judge Gesell in the Federal District Court for the District of Columbia, held that the female employee (a senior manager) suffered sex discrimination: see *Hopkins v Price Waterhouse* 618 F Supp 1109 (1985). This finding of liability was affirmed upon appeal by the Court of Appeals for the District of Columbia Circuit: see 263 US App DC 321, 825 F 2d 458 (1987). The Supreme Court subsequently heard an appeal on the question as to the burden of proof owed by the employer, remitting the matter to the District Court: *Price Waterhouse v Hopkins* 490 US 228 (1989). Upon remand and applying the revised legal test, the District Court again found

As for the legal relevance of sex stereotyping, we are beyond the day when an employer could evaluate employees by assuming or insisting that they matched the stereotype associated with their group, for '[i]n forbidding employers to discriminate against individuals because of their sex, Congress intended to strike at the entire spectrum of disparate treatment of men and women resulting from sex stereotypes.' (at 251)[9]

In the United Kingdom, the United States, and New Zealand a number of different approaches to determining sex identity have been considered and endorsed by the courts. On the one hand, courts have found that sex is determined physiologically at birth and cannot be changed. In the United Kingdom, before the passing of the Gender Recognition Act 2004 (UK), the courts had been unwilling to consider social and psychological factors as relevant to determining sex: *Corbett v Corbett* [1970] 2 WLR 1306.[10] In Texas, too, social and psychological factors have been held to be irrelevant: *Littleton v Prange* 9 SW3d 223 (1999). On the other hand, there has been case law in other jurisdictions where the courts have held that sex can be changed naturally or surgically, and that social and psychological factors are relevant: *W v W* [2001] Fam 111 (England and Wales), *MT v JT* 355 A 2d 204 (1976) (New Jersey, US), and *AG v Otahuhu Family Court* [1995] NZLR 603 (NZ). Some jurisdictions have also introduced legislation that aims to facilitate the recognition of sex change in some limited circumstances.[11] New Zealand legislation governing the alteration of the recorded sex on birth certificates recognizes psychological factors and non-surgical medical treatments.[12] The Gender Recognition Act 2004 (UK) has removed the requirement for surgical alteration or hormonal treatment. A person who has been living in an acquired gender for at least two years and intends to continue to do so until death can apply for a gender recognition certificate (ss 1(1) and 2(1)). The application must be supported by either two reports by registered medical practitioners practising in the field

that Ms Hopkins had failed to receive partnership because of sex discrimination: see *Hopkins v Price Waterhouse* 737 F. Supp 1202 (1990).

    [9] The Supreme Court quoted from *Los Angeles Dept. of Water and Power v Manhart*, 435 US 702, 707, n 13 (1978), which quoted *Sprogis v United Air Lines, Inc* 444 F2d 1194, 1198 (CA7 1971).

    [10] In Corbett, the biological sexual constitution of an individual was considered to be fixed at birth and sex was determined by considering chromosomal, gonadal, and genital factors: *Corbett v Corbett* [1970] 2 WLR 1306, at 1323, 1325. The UK Gender Recognition Act 2004, ss 1(1) and 2(1). For a very interesting discussion of the impact of the Gender Recognition Act on the sex/gender distinction in law, see A Sharpe 'Endless Sex: The Gender Recognition Act 2004 and the Persistence of a Legal Category' (2007) 15 *Feminist Legal Studies* 57.

    [11] Sexual Reassignment Act 1988 (SA); Gender Reassignment Act 2000 (WA); Gender Recognition Act 2004 (UK). See the more detailed discussion of the South Australia and Western Australia legislation below.

    [12] The New Zealand Family Court can issue a declaration of the sex to be shown on the birth certificates of adults and children if it is satisfied the applicant has assumed and intends to maintain the gender identity of a person of the nominated sex and 'has undergone such medical treatment as is usually regarded by medical experts as desirable [to enable the acquisition of a physical conformation that accords with the gender identity of] a physical conformation that accords with the gender indentity of a person of the nominated sex' or, in the case of a child, that the child's guardian 'intends to bring up the child as a person of the nominated sex' and that the child has undergone, or will undergo, such treatment (NZ, Births, Deaths, and Marriages Registration Act 1995, ss 28 and 29).

of gender dysphoria, or by a report by a chartered psychologist practicing in that field and a report by a registered medical practitioner (s 3(1)).

In Australia, recent case law has exhibited a willingness to depart from a biological understanding of sex.[13] Australian courts have on occasion emphasized the 'importance of psyche in determining sex and gender',[14] and have stated that undue emphasis on the chromosomal make-up of the person 'makes no contribution to the physiological or psychological self'.[15] Importantly, the Full Court in *Attorney-General (Cth) v 'Kevin and Jennifer'* also gave weight to the evidence of societal acceptance of the transsexual in question as a man.[16] In the matter of *Re Alex,*[17] Nicholson CJ of the Family Court was prepared to authorize hormonal treatment (the first step in the sex change process) despite 'no ambiguity in sexual characteristics [in the young adult in question]; [the presence of] normal female chromosomes... [and] female reproductive organs.[18] Notwithstanding these biological factors, Nicholson CJ gave greater weight to evidence demonstrating the young adult's 'long-standing, unwavering and present identification as a male'.[19]

Remarks within more recent case law suggest growing criticism of a requirement of surgical operation before recognition of one's desired sex/gender. In *Attorney-General (Cth) v 'Kevin and Jennifer'*, the Full Court was sympathetic to the difficulties faced by transgender people forced to undergo surgery, referring to the oral submissions of the Human Rights and Equal Opportunity Commission (HREOC) (which outlined the especial difficulty in female to male surgical intervention) and querying 'If one accepts... the evidence given in this case, Kevin has always perceived himself to be a man. One then asks the rhetorical question as to why he must subject himself to radical and painful surgery to establish this fact.'[20] In *Re Alex* Nicholson CJ considered the 'requirement of surgery... to be a cruel and unnecessary restriction upon a person's right to be legally recognized in a sex which reflects the chosen gender identity and would appear to have little justification on grounds of principle'.[21] Instead, Nicholson CJ considered the requirement of surgical intervention as inconsistent with human rights and capable of amounting to a form of indirect discrimination in certain circumstances.[22] The latter possibility was premised on the greater difficulties

---

[13] See *Attorney-General (Cth) v 'Kevin and Jennifer'* (2003) 172 FLR 300, *Kevin and Another v Attorney-General (Commonwealth)* (2001) 165 FLR 404 (the first instance judgment).

[14] *Attorney-General (Cth) v 'Kevin and Jennifer'* (2003) 172 FLR 300, 348.

[15] The Full Court stated its agreement with this view expressed by Thorpe LJ (dissenting) in *Bellinger v Bellinger* [2001] 2 FLR 1048: see *Attorney-General (Cth) v 'Kevin and Jennifer'* (2003) 172 FLR 300 348.

[16] ibid 364–5.   [17] *Re Alex* (2004) 180 FLR 89.

[18] ibid 103.

[19] ibid 103, and further at 104–7.

[20] Obiter remarks made by the Court in *Attorney-General (Cth) v 'Kevin and Jennifer'* (2003) 172 FLR 300, 365–6.

[21] *Re Alex* (2004) 180 FLR 89, 131.

[22] ibid 131.

associated with successful female-to-male surgery. While 'surgical intervention for a male to female transsexual person in relation to the construction of a vagina may be common place, surgical intervention which requires the construction of a penis is much more problematic'.[23] Therefore the legal requirement for surgical alteration to achieve the desired sex in female-to-male transgender people might be characterized as indirect discrimination. Females wishing to become male will find it harder to comply with the condition than males wishing to become female and therefore will suffer a disproportionate burden.

While in Australia there is an increasing trend to take into account psychological factors, self-identification, and social context when determining legal sex, in addition to considering human rights and indirect discrimination, it nevertheless appears that at this point in time surgery is required to recognize the desired sex of preoperative transexuals.[24] For example, the law in New South Wales exemplifies the dominant approach taken by Australian States and Territories with its requirement for gender reassignment surgery before alteration of the recorded sex on a person's birth certificate. In South Australia and Western Australia, a person who has undergone a reassignment procedure can apply for a recognition certificate.[25] In considering the application, the magistrate (in South Australia) or Gender Reassignment Board (in Western Australia) must be satisfied the person believes that his or her true sex is the sex to which the person has been reassigned; has adopted the lifestyle and has the sexual characteristics of a person of the sex to which the person has been reassigned; and has received proper counselling in relation to his or her sexual identity.[26] These matters are not considered by the Registrar of Births, Deaths and Marriages in the other States and Territories. These differing approaches to the recognition of psychological elements of sex across State and Territory jurisdictions in Australia present a challenge to assumptions that sex can be defined definitively.

[23] Nicholson CJ in *Re Alex* referring to submissions made by the Human Rights and Equal Opportunity Commission (which outlined these surgical difficulties) in the earlier case of *Attorney-General (Cth) v 'Kevin and Jennifer': Re Alex* (2004) 180 FLR 89, 131.

[24] Gender reassignment surgery is a prerequisite for an application to alter the record on a birth certificate of a person's sex under legislation in the following jurisdictions: *Births, Deaths and Marriages Registration Act* 1997 (ACT), ss 24(1)(c), 24(2)(b), and 25(a); Births, Deaths and Marriages Registration Act 1995 (NSW), ss 32B(1)(b), 32B(2)(b), and 32C(a); Births, Deaths and Marriages Registration Act 1996 (NT) ss 28B(1)(b), 28B(2)(b), and 28C(a); Births, Deaths and Marriages Registration Act 2003 (Qld), s 23(4)(b)(i); Births, Deaths and Marriages Registration Act 1999 (Tas), ss 28A(1)(b) and 28B(a); Births, Deaths and Marriages Act 1996 (Vic), ss 30A(1)(b) and 30B.

[25] Sexual Reassignment Act 1988 (SA), s 7; Gender Reassignment Act 2000 (WA), s 14. The recognition certificate identifies the applicant as being the sex to which the person has been reassigned and is conclusive evidence that the person has undergone the reassignment procedure and is the sex stated in the certificate: Sexual Reassignment Act 1988 (SA), ss 4, 8; Gender Reassignment Act 2000 (WA), ss 3, 16.

[26] Sexual Reassignment Act 1988 (SA), s 7(8)(b) and Gender Reassignment Act 2000 (WA), s 15(1)(b).

Within the context of this project, which examines the inclusion of women in health research in Australia, a further question arises as to how we account for other vulnerable populations, specifically people with diverse gender identity.[27] For instance, while we can count the numbers of male and female participants in a particular medical research study there is rarely an accounting of the number of intersex or transex persons. This is despite the fact that estimates of the numbers of intersex people ranges from 0.18 to 1.7 per cent of the population.[28] Figures can be higher depending on how one defines genital ambiguity.[29] In this context, assumptions made in clinical trials about which physical characteristics and psychological elements constitute sex are untenable. An intersex person is generally broadly defined as someone who is chromosomally one sex and gonadally and genitally another sex, or both sexes. Where a person is intersex their psychological sex may accord with either their chromosomes, or their genital sex. A transexual person is someone who has external genitalia and secondary sexual characteristics of one gender, but whose personal identification and psychosocial configuration are those of the opposite gender. Such a person may or may not undergo surgery to align their physical and psychosocial sex. If the consent forms in research protocols require self-identification between two options: male and females, the participant rates of other gendered and sexed identities will not be ascertainable.

Importantly, the same trend towards taking into account psychological factors, self-identification, and social context when determining sex in law is now occurring in clinical medicine. Medical experts are increasingly unsupportive of the binary sex paradigm in the field of intersexuality.[30] Nevertheless there are few indications that the understandings of sex and gender reflect this complexity.[31]

---

[27] For instance, the Australian Medical Association noted in its submission to the Australian Human Rights and Equal Opportunity Commission's *Same-Sex Entitlements Inquiry* that 'anecdotal research indicates that experiences or expectations of discriminatory treatment [for intersex people] may lead to decreased accessing of healthcare facilities. This has flow on effects for untreated mental and physical health problems.' See Human Rights and Equal Opportunity Commission, 'Stories of discrimination experienced by the gay, lesbian, bisexual, transgender and intersex community' (October 2007) at <http://www.humanrights.gov.au/pdf/human_rights/gay_lesbian/stories.pdf> (accessed 19 December 2007).

[28] The Australian Bureau of Statistics allowed intersex and androgynous people to make a notation on the 2006 census to that effect; however, they did not count the numbers of those who did.

[29] D Salt, 'Intersex: The Space Between the Genders' *Cosmos: The Science of Everything*, 15 June 2007. Salt notes that 'Peter Koopman, a celebrated geneticist at the University of Queensland in Brisbane, suggests intersexuals may be surprisingly common. "About four per cent of live births are affected by these disorders, which can result in infertility, genital abnormalities, gender misassignment and long-term psychological trauma."'

[30] See eg M Holmes, 'Rethinking the Meaning and Management of Intersexuality' (2002) *Sexualities*, 159.

[31] An example of this kind of failure within the medical/legal context, though not in the research context, was discussed in the submission of the Western Australian (WA) Gender Project to the recent inquiry by the Australian Human Rights and Equal Opportunity Commission into *Same-Sex Entitlements*. The WA Gender Project noted that 'the Health Insurance Commission will not recognise the affirmed sex of a transgender individual unless surgery has been performed. In many

As indicated previously, the terms 'sex' and 'gender' are largely used interchangeably in the medical research literature, without reference to those who may not be covered by this binary distinction. There is also ambiguity about equity and inequality in relation to research participation. In this chapter, we use the term 'gender inequity' to refer to exclusions of research participation or failures in analysis that are unfair on the grounds that they do not generate results that will apply equally to all members of the affected population. Exclusions of participation mean that the research population does not reflect that of the affected population, while failures of analysis by sex mean that any important differences in the ways that males and females respond to the intervention will remain undetected.

Gender inequity intersects with and can compound other research inequities. For instance, the exclusion of elderly people from clinical trials[32] leads to a lack of evidence about effective interventions for the elderly. This has a disproportionate effect on women as they form a greater proportion of the elderly population. The end result is a lack of evidence about effective interventions for elderly women, with subsequent health impacts.[33] Any measures aimed at reducing gender inequity in health research must therefore take account of the whole range of ways in which sex and gender intersect with other socio-political contexts.

III. Recognizing the Relevance of Sex and Gender

In recent years there has been growing recognition of the relevance of sex and gender to the construction of health and health care. There is a combination of biological and social factors that have important sex and gender dimensions.[34] Reviews of gender bias in, for example, international cardiovascular and

---

circumstances this denies transgender people appropriate medical treatment. For example, a preoperative transsexual woman may be denied Medicare rebates for mammograms. This is alarming, given that transsexual women, like all women, are at risk of breast cancer.' Human Rights and Equal Opportunity Commission, 'Stories of discrimination experienced by the gay, lesbian, bisexual, transgender and intersex community' (October 2007) <http://www.humanrights.gov.au/pdf/human_rights/gay_lesbian/stories.pdf> (accessed 19 December 2007).

[32] K Hall and R Luepker, 'Is Hypercholesterolemia a Risk Factor and Should it be Treated in the Elderly?' (2000) 14(6) *American Journal of Health Promotion* 347; L Hutchins, J Unger, J Crowley, C Coltman, and K Albian, 'Underrepresentation of Patients 65 Years of Age or Older in Cancer-Treatment Trials' (1999) 341(27) *New England Journal of Medicine* 2061.

[33] J Gurwitz, N Col and J Avorn, 'The Exclusion of the Elderly and Women from Clinical Trials in Acute Myocardial Infarction' (1992) 268(11) *JAMA* 1417.

[34] M Inhorn and K Whittle, 'Feminism Meets the "New" Epidemiologies: Towards an Appraisal of Antifeminist Biases in Epidemiological Research on Women's Health' (2001) 53(5) *Social Science and Medicine* 553; J Kaiser, 'Gender in the Pharmacy: Does It Matter?' (2005) 308 *Science* 1572; VW Pinn, 'Research on Women's Health: Progress and Opportunities' (2005) 294(11) *JAMA* 1407; TM Wizeman and ML Pardue, *Exploring the Biological Contributions to Human Health: Does Sex Matter?* (Washington, DC: National Academy Press, 2001).

HIV/AIDS research, have consistently found underrepresentation of women.[35] Despite the growing recognition of the relevance of sex and gender to health, health research has been slow to ensure that women and men are represented in equal numbers, or to analyse results in ways that ensure that significant differences between men and women are identified.

A. Sex Differences

There are recognized sex differences in the causes, incidence, response to treatment, and prognosis of diseases,[36] such as HIV/AIDS,[37] coronary heart disease,[38] depression,[39] tropical infectious diseases,[40] and tuberculosis.[41]

These differences assume particular importance in the development of new pharmaceutical treatments as men and women respond differently to drugs in a number of ways. First, there are pharmacokinetic differences in the way that drugs are processed. Women are on average smaller than men, women's kidneys filter excreted drugs more slowly, and women tend to have a higher proportion of body fat which may mean that fat soluble drugs stay in their

---

[35] S Ebrahim and G Davey Smith, 'Systematic Review of Randomised Controlled Trials of Multiple Risk Factor Interventions for Preventing Coronary Heart Disease' (1997) 314 *BMJ* 1666; E Mills, S Nixon, S Singh, S Dolma, A Nayyar, and S Kapoor, 'Enrolling Women into HIV Preventive Vaccine Trials: An Ethical Imperative But a Logistical Challenge' (2006) 3 *PLoS Medicine* e94; R Raine, T Crayford, K Chan and J Chambers, 'Gender Differences in the Treatment of Patients with Acute Myocardial Ischemia and Infarction in England' (1999) 15 *International Journal of Technology Assessment in Health Care* 136; P Rochon, J Clark, M Binns, V Patel, and J Gurwitz, 'Reporting of Gender-Related Information in Clinical Trials of Drug Therapy for Myocardial Infarction' (1998) 159 *Canadian Medical Association Journal* 321; N Wenger, 'Coronary Heart Disease in Women: Highlights of the Past 2 Years—Stepping Stones, Milestones and Obstructing Boulders' (2006) 3(4) *Nature Clinical Practice. Cardiovascular Medicine* 194.

[36] L Doyal, *What Makes Women Sick: Gender and the Political Economy of Health* (Basingstoke, Hampshire: MacMillan Press Ltd, 1992).

[37] A Moore, A Mocroft, S Madge, H Devereux, D Wilson, AN Phillips, and M Johnson, 'Gender Differences in Virologic Response to Treatment in an HIV-Positive Population: A Cohort Study' (2001) 26(2) *Journal of Acquired Immune Deficiency Syndromes* 159.

[38] J Hung, 'Aspirin for Primary Prevention of Cardiovascular Disease in Women: Does Sex Matter?' (2006) 184 *Medical Journal of Australia* 260; S Kjeldsen, R Kolloch, G Leonetti, JM Mallion, A Zanchetti, D Elmfedt, I Warnold, and L Hansson, 'Influence of Gender and Age on Preventing Cardiovascular Disease by Antihypertensive Treatment and Acetylsalicylic Acid: The HOT Study-Hypertension Optimal Treatment' (2000) 18(5) *Journal of Hypertension* 629; D Lawlor, S Ebrahim and G Davey Smith, 'Sex Matters: Secular and Geographical Trends in Sex Differences in Coronary Heart Disease Mortality' (2001) 323 *British Medical Journal* 541; L Mosca, C McGillen and M Rubenfire, 'Gender Differences in Barriers to Lifestyle Change for Cardiovascular Disease Prevention' (1998) 7(6) *Journal of Womens Health* 711.

[39] J Ussher, 'Women and Mental Illness' in L Sherr and J St Lawrence (eds), *Women, Health and the Mind* (Chichester: John Wiley and Sons, Ltd, 2000) 77.

[40] C Vlasshoff and E Bonilla, 'Gender-Related Differences in the Impact of Tropical Diseases on Women: What Do We Know?' (1994) 26(1) *Journal of Biosocial Science* 37.

[41] MW Uplekar, S Rangan, MG Weiss, J Ogden, MW Borgdorff *et al*, 'Attention to Gender Issues in Tuberculosis Control' (2001) 5(3) *International Journal of Tuberculosis and Lung Disease* 220.

bodies for a longer period.[42] Second, there are pharmacodynamic differences concerning the manner in which men and women's bodies react to a drug once it is in the bloodstream. Recent research indicates that this is likely to be the most significant source of clinical difference in drug response between men and women. For example, drugs that affect the heart's rhythm, including some antihistamines, antibiotics, antiarrythmics, and antipsychotics exert greater effects in women than in men. More than two-thirds of reported arrhythmias from these drugs occur in women.[43] Research conducted only with male populations therefore cannot reliably identify appropriate and safe doses for women.

B. Gender Differences

Gender differences may be more difficult to identify than physiological differences, but can be just as important in terms of health outcomes. Women and men access health care in different ways, and are treated differently by health care systems. Research consistently demonstrates differences between men and women in levels of self-reported medical symptoms, medical care utilization, morbidity and mortality. Women visit healthcare professionals more frequently than men for reasons including increased sensitivity to symptoms, greater interest in health, and being subject to a greater number of morbidities than men.[44] Once at the doctor's, female patients are typically subjected to greater scepticism from their medical practitioners than male patients. For example, there is a significant body of literature demonstrating that women's self reports of pain are discounted and as a result female patients are systematically under treated for pain.[45] In areas such as preventive health care, screening, and compliance with treatment, men and women behave differently, with implications for health outcomes. These kinds of gender differences have significant implications for health, and require investigation using research methods that are capable of identifying just how men and women behave and are treated in relation to health care.

---

[42] M Anthony and MJ Berg, 'Biologic and Molecular Mechanisms for Sex Differences in Pharmacokinetics, Pharmacodynamics and Pharmacogenetics: Part I' (2002) 11 *Journal of Women's Health and Gender-Based Medicine* 601.

[43] Kaiser (n 34 above).

[44] CA Green and CR Pope, 'Gender, Psychosocial Factors and the Use of Medical Services: A Longitudinal Analysis' (1999) 48(10) *Social Science and Medicine* 1363; A Redondo-Sendino, P Guallar-Castillón, JR Banegas, and F Rodríguez-Artalejo, 'Gender Differences in the Utilization of Health-Care Services among the Older Adult Population of Spain' (2006) 6 *BMC Public Health* 155.

[45] C Bouchardy, E Rapiti, S Blagojevic, AT Vlastos, and G Vlastos, 'Older Female Cancer Patients: Importance, Causes, and Consequences of Undertreatment' (2007) 25 *Journal of Clinical Oncology* 1858; DE Hoffmann, and AJ Tarzian, 'The Girl Who Cried Pain: A Bias Against Women in the Treatment of Pain' (2001) 29 *Journal of Law, Medicine and Ethics* 13.

IV. Exclusion of Women from Research

Gender bias in participation in research, especially in clinical trials, has been documented consistently over many years.[46] There is clear evidence of the historical exclusion of women from landmark research studies such as the Multiple Risk Factor Intervention Trials (known as Mr. Fit) and The Physician's Health Study.[47] It is worrying to note that recent research reviews have continued to demonstrate the under-representation of women over the age of 65 in research and the over-representation of men in studies of heart disease and colorectal and lung cancer trials.[48]

Three connected factors have lead to the exclusion of women from research: explicit policies of exclusion; practical considerations of research efficiency and cost; and false assumptions about the relevance of sex and gender differences. From 1977 to 1993 the Food and Federal Drug Administration (FDA) in the United States prohibited researchers from including women of childbearing potential in early (phase 1) drug trials to avoid potential harm to reproductive capacity or their foetus if they became unintentionally pregnant.[49] This policy was extremely influential, leading to a de facto exclusion of women from almost all pharmaceutical research irrespective of their reproductive potential.[50]

Practical considerations for excluding women include the alleged need for homogenous populations, the cost of including women, and the purported difficulty of recruiting women.[51] These justifications reflect what we call the 'distortion paradigm', which defines the male body as normal and considers female biological processes as distortions of this norm. This attitude underlies the exclusion of women from research on the grounds that female hormonal rhythms will 'distort' the otherwise normal findings generated from research with male participants. The distortion paradigm results in research with male

[46] R Dresser, 'Wanted: Single, White Male for Medical Research' (1992) 22(1) *Hastings Center Report* 24; E Kinney, J Trautmann, J Gold, E Vesell, and R Zelis, 'Underrepresentation of Women in New Drug Trials: Ramification and Remedies' (1981) 95(4) *Annals of Internal Medicine* 495; VH Murthy, HM Krumholz, and CP Gross, 'Participation in Cancer Clinical Trials: Race-, Sex-, and Age-based Disparities' (2004) 291 *JAMA* 2720; L Sherr and J St Lawrence, *Women, Health and the Mind* (Chichester: John Wiley and Sons, Ltd, 2000).

[47] General Accounting Office (US), Testimony: National Institutes of Health: Problems in Implementing Policy on Women in Study Populations (Washington DC: General Accounting Office, 1990) (GAO/T-HRD-90-38).

[48] Murthy (n 46 above). Hutchins *et al* (n 32 above).

[49] RB Merkatz, R Temple, S Sobel, K Feiden, and DA Kessler, The Working Group on Women in Clinical Trials, 'Women in Clinical Trials of New Drugs—A Change in Food and Drug Administration Policy' (1993) 329(4) *New England Journal of Medicine* 292.

[50] A Lippman, *The Inclusion of Women in Clinical Trials: Are We Asking the Right Questions?* (Health Canada, Women and Health Protection, 2006).

[51] Dresser (n 46 above); PR Fergusson, 'Selecting Participants When Testing New Drugs: The Implications of Age and Gender Discrimination' (2002) 70(3) *Medico-Legal Journal* 130.

populations, but when it comes to applying the results of research, there are problems with gender blindness. Gender blindness refers to the tendency of some researchers to ignore gender despite the potential for sex and/or gender-related differences in aetiology, treatment, responses, and experiences in many conditions that affect both men and women.[52] Paradoxically, female hormones and other biological processes are thought to interfere with research to a sufficient degree to justify the exclusion of women, and yet men and women are thought to be sufficiently homogeneous to apply research results from male studies to the treatment of women.

V.   Unasked Questions and Misleading Assumptions

Current research agendas tend to reflect an uneasy combination of biological essentialism and gender blindness. Biological essentialism refers to the focus on women as reproducers, resulting in a large proportion of women's health research concentrating primarily on reproductive capacity and function.[53] Health issues related to fertility and reproduction are important causes of mortality and morbidity for women, but defining women's health solely in relation to reproductive biology ignores the ways in which the social as well as the biological effects of gender impact upon women's health across a wide range of disorders.

Biological essentialism marginalizes women's health issues that are not related to biological aspects of reproduction despite the morbidity and mortality associated with non-reproductive illnesses. Coronary heart disease (CHD) continues to be the leading cause of death among women in the United States.[54] There have been significant reductions in mortality due to CHD in men, but mortality from CHD has not declined in women in the last twenty years.[55] Women with diabetes are a subgroup at particular risk of CHD. A 2005 study demonstrated that women with diabetes received less treatment for modifiable coronary risk factors (for example elevated lipids and hypertension) than men, and as a result were less likely to achieve lipids and blood pressure targets.[56] This inequity points to the need for specific prevention interventions for women. Despite increasing recognition of sex and gender differences in CHD in the scientific and medical literature, most contemporary guidelines for prevention, diagnostic testing, and

---

[52]   Inhorn and Whittle, (n 34 above).

[53]   ibid.

[54]   NK Wenger, 'Preventing Cardiovascular Disease in Women: An Update' (2007) 31(3) *Clinical Cardiology* 109.

[55]   American Heart Association, Heart Disease and Stroke Statistics—2006 Update (Dallas, TX: American Heart Association, 2006).

[56]   DJ Wexler, RW Grant, JB Meigs, DM Nathan, and E Cagliero, 'Sex Disparities in Treatment of Cardiac Risk Factors in Patients with Type 2 Diabetes' (2005) 28 *Diabetes Care* 514.

medical and surgical treatments for cardiovascular disease are still based on studies conducted predominately on middle-aged men.[57] Research is required to demonstrate which prevention and treatment strategies are effective for women and medical guidelines must reflect these findings.

VI. Current Participation Rates—What Do We Know?

Over the last fifteen years increasing efforts have been made to include women in clinical research. A number of countries have introduced policies and guidelines, and in the United States legislation, to encourage the inclusion of women in all phases of clinical research (see section below on International Regulatory Developments). These policies aim to achieve fair and appropriate inclusion of women in health research.

Teasing out the current participation rate of women in research is a complex process. Gender inequity is multifaceted and does not simply occur when women are not included in clinical trials in equal numbers. A comprehensive examination of the issue requires information about (a) the overall proportion of male to female research participants; (b) the proportion of male to female research participants in non-sex specific clinical research; (c) the proportion of male and female research participants in sex-specific versus non-sex specific research; and (d) the nature of research that is conducted with male or female only research participants.

The United States is the only country that systematically tracks the inclusion of men and women in clinical research. The National Institutes of Health (NIH) has a comprehensive monitoring system for tracking the inclusion of men and women in NIH funded research (see the section on International Regulatory Developments). A 2000 review conducted by the US General Accounting Office reported that in 1997 women represented 62 per cent of subjects in NIH extramural trials and 52 per cent of subjects in non sex-specific research.[58]

Outside of the United States the lack of data about the inclusion of men and women in clinical research inhibits the ability of researchers and research funders to assess systematically whether national research agendas are adequately addressing questions of men's and women's health. Most analysis therefore relies on one-off reviews conducted by individual research teams. The situation is further complicated by the lack of a standard method of data collection in these individual studies, which impedes inter-study comparison.

---

[57] N Wenger (n 35 above).
[58] General Accounting Office (US), *Women's Health: NIH Has Increased its Efforts to Include Women in Research* (Washington, DC: General Accounting Office, 2000) (GAO/HEHS-00-96).

Meinert and Gilpin published a historical analysis of male-only and female-only clinical trials registered with MEDLINE in 2001.[59] They found that overall there were more female research participants than male research participants. However, the exception to this general rule was cardiovascular research. Their review also suggested that large-scale trials were more frequently female-only. Such large-scale studies are more likely to be epidemiological or health system surveys rather than randomized controlled drug trials with the capacity to identify differences between men and women.[60] Recent research in Australia also indicates that there are more female than male participants in clinical research. However, assumptions of biological essentialism persist, with research involving women only continuing to focus predominantly on their reproductive capacity and function, while research with men continues to investigate non-sex specific conditions.[61]

VII. Analysis of Gender and Sex Differences in Research Results

Gender equity in research is not simply a matter of including equal numbers of women as research participants; research data must be systematically analysed for evidence of sex or gender differences in response to the interventions. Sex analysis of results ranges from analysis of sex as a variable (including covariate adjustment and subgroup analysis by sex) to sex-specific reporting of results.[62] Sex-specific reporting requires the reporting of primary outcomes for males and females in a format that allows for the data to be directly abstracted, such as for use in a systematic review or meta-analysis.[63]

A study by Geller *et al* of forty-six randomized control trials published in influential medical journals in 2004 found that 87 per cent of studies did not report any outcomes by sex or include sex as a covariate in modeling.[64] A recent study by Blauwet *et al* found that only 24 per cent of published cardiovascular trials reported sex-specific results;[65] this low figure is of concern given the recognized

[59] CL Meinert and AK Gilpin, 'Estimation of Gender Bias in Clinical Trials' (2001) 20 *Statistics in Medicine* 1153.

[60] ibid.

[61] W Rogers and A Ballantyne, 'When is Sex-Specific Research Appropriate?' (2008) 1(2) *International Journal of Feminist Approaches to Bioethics* 36.

[62] SF Assman, SJ Pocock, LE Enos, and LE Kasten, 'Subgroup Analysis and Other (Mis)uses of Baseline Data in Clinical Trials' (2000) 355 *Lancet* 1064; LA Blauwet, SN Hayes, D McManus, RF Redberg, and MN Walsh, 'Low Rate of Sex-Specific Result Reporting in Cardiovascular Trials' (2007) 82(2) *Mayo Clinic Proceedings* 166.

[63] Blauwet *et al* (n 62 above).

[64] SE Geller, MC Adams, and M Carnes, 'Adherence to Federal Guidelines for Reporting of Sex and Race/Ethnicity in Clinical Trials' (2006) 15(10) *Journal of Women's Health* 1123.

[65] Blauwet *et al* (n 62 above).

sex differences in cardiovascular disease. Marrocco and Stewart examined clinical research ethics applications submitted to a tertiary care Canadian university teaching hospital between 1995 and 2000 to assess investigator intention to perform analysis of results by sex.[66] Only 20.2 per cent intended to conduct this analysis and this proportion decreased from 29.9 per cent in 1995–1996 to 16.9 per cent in 1999–2000. Only 17 per cent of non-sex specific drug studies planned to perform analysis by sex and this is a particular cause for concern given the well-recognized difference in drug absorption and metabolism between males and females.

One limitation of these approaches is that they only capture analysis of results by sex in published research. It is possible that in some cases analysis of results by sex was conducted but not reported, perhaps because sex was not found to be a significant variable. Marrocco and Stewart's study is restricted to researchers' intentions to analyse by sex and does not record actual rates of sex analysis performed. Short of contacting research teams directly it is impossible for those interested in sex and gender differences to know whether this analysis has been conducted but not reported. To address this, we support the call for journals to require all authors to submit analysis of results by sex, even if such analysis is not published.[67] This issue is complicated by the recognized problem of poor understanding and reporting of appropriate statistical methods.[68]

VIII. Harms Resulting from the Exclusion from Research

The lack of evidence about the effectiveness of interventions in women can lead to both withholding treatment and inappropriate or harmful treatment. If there are no clinical trials to demonstrate that particular interventions are effective in women, this may contribute to the under-treatment of women with that intervention.[69] Alternatively, there may be harmful consequences for patients if practitioners use an intervention in populations that were not included in the trials (for example, all women, fertile women, or pregnant women) for whom the safety has not been demonstrated.[70] As Rebecca Dresser has argued, 'the choice is whether

[66] A Marroco and DE Stewart, 'We've Come a Long Way, Maybe: Recruitment of Women and Analysis of Results by Sex in Clinical Research' (2001) 10(2) *Journal of Women's Health and Gender-Based Medicine* 175.

[67] Assman *et al* (n 62 above); Meinert and Gilpin (n 59 above).

[68] SJ Pocock, SE Assmann, LE Enos, and LE Kasten, 'Subgroup Analysis, Covariate Adjustment and Baseline Comparisons in Clinical Trial Reporting: Current Practice and Problems' (2002) 21 *Statistics in Medicine* 2917; DI Cook, VJ Gebski, and AC Keech, 'Subgroup Analysis in Clinical Trials' (2004) 180(6) *Medical Journal of Australia* 289–91.

[69] W Rogers, 'Evidence-Based Medicine: Do the Principles and Practice of EBM further Women's Health?' (2004) 18(1) *Bioethics* 50.

[70] Kaiser (n 34 above); D Krummel, D Koffman, Y Bronner, J Davis, and K Grennlund *et al*, 'Cardiovascular Health Interventions in Women: What Works?' (2001) 10(2) *Journal of Women's Health and Gender-Based Medicine* 117.

to expose some consenting members of these groups [women and people of colour] to risk in the closely monitored research setting, or to expose many more of them to risk in the clinical setting without these safeguards'.[71]

The issue of gender bias in health research has reached a new urgency with the increasing use of evidence-based medicine (EBM) to guide both clinical practice and health policy decisions.[72] EBM is a method of synthesizing research results from multiple trials to give a result that can be considered the definitive best available information about an intervention.[73] Internationally this approach has been widely adopted, leading to an influential role in informing health policy, commissioning resources, and directing clinical practice through mechanisms such as evidence-based guidelines. However, EBM relies upon the results of existing research, so that any inequities in that research will be repeated and reinforced through the processes of research synthesis and guideline generation.[74] If women are excluded from the original trials, then the resulting guidelines will similarly omit information about any relevant differences between the sexes.

IX. International Regulatory Developments

There are a number of possible ways of trying to regulate male and female participation in research. The United States has taken a legal approach, regulating the inclusion of women and minorities through a combination of legislation and guidelines. Other countries rely upon research ethics guidelines, with varying statutory force.

In Australia, the research community is guided primarily by the National Health and Medical Research Council's (NHMRC) *National Statement on Ethical Conduct in Research Involving Humans* ('*National Statement*'). There is no express requirement for the equal inclusion of men and women and there is no express requirement of analysis of the research results by sex. The *National Statement 2007* states in section 1.4:

In research that is just:
(a) taking into account the scope and objectives of the proposed research, the selection, exclusion and inclusion of categories of research participants is fair, and is accurately described in the results of the research;

---

[71] Dresser (n 46 above) 27.

[72] Rogers (n 69 above); DL Sackett, M William, C Rosenberg, JA Muir Gray, RB Haynes, and WS Richardson, 'Evidence Based Medicine: What it is and What it isn't' (1996) 312 *British Medical Journal* 71.

[73] Sackett *et al* (n 72 above).

[74] Rogers (n 69 above); P Shekelle, S Woolf, M Eccles, and J Grimshaw, 'Clinical Guidelines: Developing Guidelines' (1999) 318 *British Medical Journal* 593; E Annandale and K Hunt, 'Gender Inequities in Health: Research at the Crossroads' in E Annandale and K Hunt (eds), *Gender Inequities in Health* (Buckingham: Open University Press, 2000) 1.

(b) the process of recruiting participants is fair;

(c) there is no unfair burden of participation in research on particular groups;

(d) there is fair distribution of the benefits of participation in research;

(e) there is no exploitation of participants in the conduct of research; and

(f) there is fair access to the benefits of research.

The *National Statement* operates as a guideline only and lacks the force of specific legal regulation,[75] although there is the capacity to penalize non-compliant institutions by suspension of any research moneys received from the NHMRC. While the NHMRC does gather information in funding applications on the anticipated breakdown of research participants by sex, there has, to date, been no public reporting summarizing that data or reflecting on its import. The *National Statement* is supported by the 2002 *Human Research Ethics Handbook* ('the *Handbook*')[76] which provides commentary and additional information and resources. The *Handbook* has two sections on women in research providing guidance on inclusion, recruitment and retention of women in research, and collection of gender-specific data. This guidance provides cogent arguments for gender equity in research, but there is no statutory requirement to adhere to the advice, and no overt mechanism for checking on compliance. The *Handbook* also has a section on the potential for breach of discrimination law if subjects are unreasonably excluded from a clinical trial on the grounds of sex, however, the *Handbook* does not include amendments made to the SDA in 2003 after the handbook was completed.

In Canada, gender equity is guaranteed under the provisions of the Canadian Charter of Rights and Freedoms. In 1995, the Canadian government's *Federal Plan for Gender Equality* stated the federal government's commitment 'to ensure that all future legislation and policies include, where appropriate, an analysis of the potential for different impacts on women and men'.[77] In 1999, Health Canada's *Women's Health Strategy* articulated a strategy for responding to the health needs of Canadian women, and in 2000, Health Canada adopted a policy of gender-based analysis as a tool for determining the links between gender and health.[78] In 1993, the Women's Health Bureau was established with responsibility for implementing the *Women's Health Strategy* and the *Gender Based Analysis Policy* within Health Canada and in 1996 the Centres for Excellence in Women's Health were established.[79]

The 1996–97 Health Canada guideline on the 'Inclusion of Women in Clinical Trials' aimed to encourage the inclusion of women in clinical trials and

---

[75] Although clinical trials are required to have approval from a Human Research Ethics Committee: Therapeutic Goods Act 1989 (Cth), s 18, 19; Therapeutic Goods Regulations 1990 (Cth), reg 12AD, Sch 5A.

[76] National Health and Medical Research Council, *Human Research Ethics Handbook* (2002).

[77] Women's Health Bureau, Health Canada, *Exploring Concepts of Gender and Health* (Health Canada, 2003), 56.

[78] ibid 57.   [79] ibid 6.

to identify sex-differences.[80] In a recent paper Abby Lippman noted 'it is possible to conclude that despite the good intentions of the 1997 Canadian guidelines, there is no systematic monitoring of conformity to them. Nor is there strong evidence from reported research that the appropriate inclusion of women in drug trials is happening.'[81]

Currently, Canada has a similar non-statutory regulatory structure for ethics review to that in Australia. The Tri-Council Policy Statement, *Ethical Conduct for Research Involving Humans* describes the joint policy of the Canadian Institutes of Health Research (CIHR), the Natural Sciences and Engineering Research Council of Canada, and the Social Sciences and Humanities Research Council of Canada. This states at Article 5.2, 'Women shall not automatically be excluded from research solely on the basis of sex or reproductive capacity' and thus imposes obligations of equitable treatment of potential subjects.

In the United States, a series of regulatory measures were introduced during the 1980s and 1990s to ensure that women and minority groups were not excluded from medical research and to ensure that clinical trials were carried out in such a way that it was possible to analyse any differences in the effects of interventions for women and minority groups.[82] These regulatory initiatives marked a move away from earlier policies which had limited the inclusion of women in clinical trials.[83]

The Office of Research on Women's Health (ORWH) at the National Institutes of Health, created in 1990, has had a significant role in these initiatives. The NIH Revitalization Act 1993, Public Law 103–43 made the inclusion of women and minorities in clinical trials a legal obligation for research undertaken or funded by the NIH. This requirement does not apply if the inclusion would be inappropriate for the health of the research subjects, inappropriate for the purpose of the research, or inappropriate for other reasons designated by the Director of the NIH.[84] The legislation also requires that clinical trials are carried out in a way that makes it possible to provide a valid analysis of any differences for women and members of minority groups in the variables being studied. The Director of the NIH must issue guidelines on the circumstances in which the inclusion of women and minorities as research subjects in clinical research would be inappropriate, and the manner for conducting clinical

---

[80] Health Canada, Therapeutic Products Directorate, *Therapeutic Products Programme Guidelines: Inclusion of Women in Clinical Trials* (1997) discussed in J Caron, *Report on Governmental Health Research Policies Promoting Gender or Sex Differences Sensitivity* (Canadian Institutes of Health Research, 2003), 52–3.

[81] Lippman (n 50 above) 11.

[82] General Accounting Office (2000) (n 58 above); General Accounting Office (US) (2001). *Women's health: Women sufficiently represented in new drug testing, but FDA oversight needs improvement* (GAO-01-754).

[83] See nn 49 and 50 above.   [84] NIH Revitalization Act 1993, s 131.

research in order to allow valid analysis of differences in the results.[85] The US legislative requirement for federally funded research to include appropriate numbers of men and women is associated with a comprehensive monitoring system for tracking the inclusion of men and women in research.

In Europe, the European Union's Seventh Research Framework Programme (FP7) for research provides recognition of the relevance and importance of gender for health. The objectives of FP7 are divided into four broad groupings: Cooperation, Ideas, People, and Capacities.[86] Within the Cooperation Programme:

Support will also be provided to initiatives aimed at engaging the broadest possible public beyond the research community in the debate on scientific issues and research results, and to initiatives in the field of scientific communication and education, including the involvement, where appropriate, of civil society organisations or networks of such organisations. The integration of the gender dimension and gender equality will be addressed in all areas of research.[87]

The theme of Health is one of ten themes contained with the Cooperation Programme. Within the Health theme: 'Gender aspects in research will be considered and integrated in the projects[88] whenever appropriate. Special attention will be given to communicating research outcomes and engaging in dialogue with civil society, in particular with patient groups, at the earliest possible stage, of new developments arising from bio-medical and genetics research. A wide dissemination and use of the results will also be assured.'

The Council of Europe's Additional Protocol to the Convention on Human Rights and Biomedicine, Concerning Biomedical Research, (2005), states in Article 18 that 'Research on a pregnant woman which does not have the potential to produce results of direct benefit to her health, or to that of her embryo, foetus or child after birth,' may only be undertaken under certain limited conditions. Article 18 also requires that 'Where research is undertaken on a breastfeeding woman, particular care shall be taken to avoid adverse impact on the health of the child.'

Despite the commitment in EU policy to promotion of gender equity in EU-funded research,[89] challenges still remain. Moerman *et al* studied research

---

[85] ibid.

[86] Decision (EC) 1982/2006 of the European Parliament and of the Council of 18 December 2006 concerning the Seventh Framework Programme of the European Community for Research, Technological Development and Demonstration Activities (2007–2013) [2006] OJ L 412, 2, para 13.

[87] ibid LU412/8.

[88] 'Risk factors, biological mechanisms, causes, clinical manifestation, consequences and treatment of disease and disorders often differ between women and men. Therefore, all activities funded within this theme must reflect the possibility of such differences in their research protocols, methodologies and analysis of results.' Council Decision (EC) 2006/971 of 19 December 2006, concerning the Specific Programme 'Cooperation' Implementing the Seventh Framework Programme of the European Community for Research, Technological Development and Demonstration Activities (2007–2013) [2007] OJ LU54/30, 40.

[89] CJ Moerman, JA Haafkens, M Söderström *et al*, 'Gender Equality in the Work of Local Research Ethics Committees in Europe: A Study of Practice in Five Countries' (2007) 33 *Journal of Medical Ethics* 107.

ethics committees in five European countries (Austria, Germany, Ireland, the Netherlands, and Sweden) in 2003 to see how they dealt with issues relating to gender equity. In relation to assessment of research protocols, Moerman *et al* note that: '[T]he main reason given [by research ethics committees] for paying specific attention to female study participants in protocol evaluation is the ethical principle that pregnant women or women of childbearing age should be excluded from studies to protect unborn children from potential harm.'[90] Moerman *et al* recommended that the EU Directive on clinical research should include provisions to promote gender equity in health research, in part by requiring that evaluation of research protocols is sensitive to the health needs of women and to the potential for differences that are sex or gender specific.[91]

Finally, at the international level, the *International Ethical Guidelines for Biomedical Research Involving Human Subjects* published by the Council for International Organizations of Medical Sciences (CIOMS) expressly provide for the inclusion of women in biomedical research. Guideline 16 of the 2002 CIOMS Guidelines provides, in part, that: 'Investigators, sponsors or ethical review committees should not exclude women of reproductive age from biomedical research. The potential for becoming pregnant during a study should not, in itself, be used as a reason for precluding or limiting participation.'

As is clear from the above, formal regulatory mechanisms such as legislation or guidelines play an important role in shaping the framework for health research and the inclusion of women and sex and gender specific analysis within that research. The crafting of regulatory frameworks necessarily involves making decisions about the objectives, scope, and content of regulation. As the analysis in this chapter has shown, even key concepts such as 'sex' can present definitional challenges in the context of contemporary understandings of the body.

It is also important to realize that regulatory outcomes can be achieved without formal legal regulation. The decision by the International Committee of Medical Journal Editors to require registration of clinical trials in a publicly accessible trial registry as a condition of publication in some of the world's leading medical journals[92] has had a dramatic impact on the number of trials registered.[93] A requirement by medical journal editors for sex-specific reporting of results from clinical trials[94] could also be expected to have a significant impact. As Blauwet *et al* point out: 'Implementation of universal sex-specific reporting of trial results may reveal unexpected sex differences worthy of further study and, at the least, provide data for subsequent meta-analyses.'[95]

[90] Moerman *et al* (n 89 above) 110.
[91] Moerman *et al* (n 89 above) 111.
[92] C de Angelis, JM Drazen, FA Frizelle *et al*, 'Clinical Trial Registration: A Statement from the International Committee of Medical Journal Editors' (2004) 354 *Lancet* 911.
[93] C Laing, R Horton, C de Angelis *et al*, 'Clinical Trial Registration: Looking Back and Moving Ahead' (2007) 298(1) *JAMA* 93.
[94] Blauwet *et al* (n 62 above).
[95] Blauwet *et al* (n 62 above) 169.

X. Anti-Discrimination Laws

Apart from specific laws, another legal avenue for addressing gender inequity in research lies with anti-discrimination laws. Using Australian federal sex-discrimination law as a case study we can see that these laws might give rise to a legal right not to be excluded from a trial where such exclusion can be described as less favourable treatment on the grounds of sex, pregnancy, potential pregnancy, breastfeeding, or marital status in the provision of goods and services. For example the SDA was specifically relied upon in a 1995 case involving the exclusion of a woman from a clinical trial. The complainant, who was HIV positive, had been denied admission to a clinical drug trial because she was still capable of menstruating and there was a consequent risk of pregnancy. The complainant claimed that there was no risk of her becoming pregnant because she had not engaged in sexual activity with men for many years, and that in any case she was prepared to have a tubal ligation. The complainant died before the matter was properly heard and the President of the HREOC determined that the proceedings had abated on her death: *Alyschia Dibble (Estate of the Late) v St Vincents Hospital Sydney Ltd* (1995) EOC 92–702. The decision that the matter abated on death was overturned on appeal to the Federal Court and referred back to the HREOC for consideration of the question of discrimination: *Stephenson v HREOC and Another* (1996) 68 FCR 290. The complaint was not, however, taken any further.

At the Federal level in Australia, the SDA proscribes direct discrimination, including on grounds of sex,[96] pregnancy,[97] and marital status.[98] Direct discrimination occurs where the complainant (with a particular trait) is afforded less favourable treatment than a member of the non-trait group in similar circumstances. In other words, such discrimination occurs where the discriminator treats the complainant less favourably than a person of the opposite sex, a non-pregnant (or non-potentially pregnant) person, or person of a different marital status. Furthermore, this less favourable treatment must have been meted out 'by reason of' the complainant's trait (sex, (potential) pregnancy or marital status).[99] Unlike in circumstances of indirect discrimination (discussed

---

[96] As to what constitutes direct discrimination on grounds of sex, see Sex Discrimination Act 1984 (Cth), s 5(1). It should be noted that breastfeeding is included in this category as a characteristic that appertains generally to women (s 5(1A)).

[97] As to what constitutes direct discrimination on grounds of pregnancy or potential pregnancy, see Sex Discrimination Act 1984 (Cth), s 7(1).

[98] As to what constitutes direct discrimination on grounds of marital status, see Sex Discrimination Act 1984 (Cth), s 6(1).

[99] The discriminator must have meted out the less favourable treatment 'by reason of' the complainant's trait, and this includes having treated the complainant less favourably based on a characteristic generally appertaining to members of that group (eg, women) or a characteristic generally

below), no defence of reasonableness is available to the perpetrator of direct discrimination.

However, if the discrimination is indirect as set out in sections 5(2), 6(2), and 7(2) an argument that the discriminatory condition is reasonable in the circumstances can be made. Indirect discrimination occurs where a condition, requirement, or practice is imposed that has, or is likely to have, the effect of disadvantaging persons of the same sex, who are also pregnant or potentially pregnant or of the same marital status as the aggrieved person.

An example of indirect discrimination may be an exclusionary condition for a trial that no one who was taking an oral contraceptive could be enrolled in the trial. Given that this condition is more likely to have the effect of disadvantaging women since only women take oral contraceptives, this is a clear instance where reasonableness in the context would need to be shown. A researcher might argue that the oral contraceptive would have an impact on the validity of any results. However, a counter argument may be that it is important to obtain research data about the efficacy of remedies in conjunction with oral contraceptive use since the numbers of women likely to be using oral contraceptives while undergoing treatment are high. According to some US research there has been inadequate attention to the question of risks of contraceptives and 'interference with drug metabolism by hormonal contraception'.[100]

Given that drugs may have harmful effects on male gametes, and that it is equally possible that a man may give rise to a pregnancy while undergoing a clinical trial, it is difficult to argue that the exclusion of women on the ground that she is not using a contraceptive is necessary or reasonable.

Arguably, excluding women of childbearing capacity who are not using a form of contraceptive from research trials, would not be necessary or reasonable where the woman has indicated that she is not sexually active, or that she has no intention of becoming pregnant. Holdcraft notes for instance, that in a survey done by an Institutional Board in the United Kingdom, of those protocols requiring the use of contraceptives: '[A]lmost 10% of protocols allowed no exclusions for contraceptive use (eg celibacy or sexual orientation).'[101] In the Australian context, Leanna Darvall has argued that if adequately informed a woman should be permitted to decide for herself whether to participate.[102]

Although anti-discrimination law might found a legal right not to be excluded from research, the practical utility of these laws is likely to be limited.

imputed to persons of that group (again, eg, women): see, Sex Discrimination Act 1984, ss 5(1), 6(1), and 7(1) (Cth).

[100] Anita Holdcroft citing Anthony and Berg (n 42 above), in A Holdcroft, 'Gender Bias in Research: How Does it Affect Evidence Based Medicine?' (2007) 100(1) *Journal of the Royal Society of Medicine* 2, 3.

[101] Holdcroft (n 100 above).

[102] L Darvall, 'Autonomy and Protectionism: Striking a Balance in Human Subject Research Policy and Regulation' (1993) 11(2) *Law in Context (Special Issue: Law and Medicine)* 82.

Anti-discrimination law is complaint-based and unlikely to be taken up by women who are not aware of their exclusion from research. It would also do little to address the broader issues around research agendas.

XI. Conclusion: Moving Forward

We have presented the current challenges facing legislators, regulators, researchers, and ethics committees in determining how and when to include women appropriately in research and ensure that sex analysis of research results is routinely performed. In conclusion, we offer five issues that require attention in order to address these challenges.

(1) As this chapter has argued, definitional clarity over the meaning of 'sex', 'gender' and 'gender equity' is elusive. National regulatory statements, whether policy, guidelines, or legislation, could provide guidance to researchers by providing a definition of these terms in research, and by presenting more detailed normative instruction regarding what sorts of inclusions and exclusions of men and women are appropriate.

(2) Ideally sex and gender analysis should be built into research protocols for health research. Research funders could require researchers to consider the sex and gender aspects of their studies during protocol development. For example, researchers could be required to present targets for male and female recruitment, justify why this is appropriate given the nature of the study, and report regularly on whether these targets are being met.

(3) The lack of internationally comparable data regarding the rates of inclusion of men and women presents a major hurdle for analysing the efficacy of different regulatory strategies. There is mounting international pressure for Clinical Trials Registries to present key trial results. If CTRs develop in this way, the inclusion of publicly accessible data regarding the number of male and female participants will facilitate international comparisons of regulatory strategies.

(4) The accessibility of data would also be facilitated by a requirement by medical journal editors for publication of the results of health research to include descriptions of sex analysis performed on research data, including descriptions of any covariate adjustment and/or subgroup analysis by sex.

(5) The available research[103] suggests that institutional review boards, research ethics committees, and researchers themselves require better education about the scientific and ethical importance of including of women in clinical research.

---

[103] AJ Ballantyne and WA Rogers, 'Fair inclusion of men and women in Australian clinical research: views from ethics committee Chairs' (in press 2008) *Medical Journal of Australia*.

(6) Further comparative analysis should be undertaken examining the efficacy of different regulatory models including direct legislation, health regulations, discrimination laws, and guidelines aimed at gender equity.

Research is the gateway for access to effective health care treatments. Without equitable participation in research, women are disadvantaged in terms of accessing the benefits, and potentially denied equal access to positive health outcomes. However, equitable participation in research alone is not sufficient. There must also be sub-sample analysis by gender and that analysis must take account of intersecting factors such as race/ethnicity, socio-economic status, sexuality, sex identification, and age. Without this we will still lack important information on any differential impact of drugs and diseases.[104]

There is a challenge in devising a regulatory framework that will achieve equity for women in research together with appropriate subgroup analyses. To date, with the exception of the United States, guidelines and minimalist regulatory approaches have tended to stand in for statutory or legislative solutions in Australia, Canada, and other jurisdictions. Such responses are unlikely to achieve gender equity in research, especially where there is no mandated requirement to report data on gender participation rates and analyses in research. We need new regulatory responses and new legal paradigms that are tailored to the specifics of this intersection between health and law.

[104] Marroco and Stewart (n 66 above); Pinn (n 4 above); Pinn (n 34 above).

23

Pandemic Planning and Distributive Justice in Health Care*

Leslie P Francis, Margaret P Battin, Jay A Jacobson, and Charles B Smith

Pandemic planning poses stark and potentially tragic issues of distributive just-ice. Who should receive scarce supplies of vaccines or antivirals? Who among the seriously ill should be triaged to home care, admitted to hospitals, or given ventilator support? Some of the pandemic planning process has emphasized efforts to avoid or blunt the impact of scarcity: the development of new, much quicker molecular techniques of vaccine manufacture, stockpiling of antivirals, and increases in hospital 'surge capacity' are the primary examples. All plans, however, recognize that under a worse case scenario, and perhaps also under fairly bad case scenarios, choice may be inevitable. Some—perhaps many—people will die who might otherwise have lived, had prevention or treatment been available for them.

The triage choices in pandemic planning for the distribution of vaccines and antivirals are open, coordinated, and institutionally adopted. Perhaps this is one reason why they have drawn so much attention. Yet in today's world, vast numbers of deaths occur annually from diseases that could be treated quite easily, were resources only available. For example, the WHO estimates that about 1,000 children die every hour of diseases that are largely preventable or treatable with low-cost interventions.[1] Pneumonia and diarrheal diseases are primary culprits, but so is malaria: one African child dies of malaria every thirty seconds. These deaths are not subsequent to institutionally-adopted, written-out prioritiza-tions of the sort found in pandemic planning, decisions that a scarce resource should be given to some who meet carefully-chosen criteria but not to others, but they are the result of multiple decisions and non-decisions that have critical

---

* This chapter draws on Chapters 17, 18, and 19 of MP Battin, LP Francis, JA Jacobson, and CB Smith, *The Patient as Victim and Vector: Ethics in Infectious Diseases* (New York: Oxford University Press, 2009).

[1] WHO, 'What are the Key Health Dangers for Children?' (October 2007), available at <http://www.who.int/features/qa/13/en/index.html> (accessed 26 January 2008).

distributive justice consequences nonetheless. Because they have so many points of entry—from the legal regime of intellectual property rights over vaccines and pharmaceuticals, to displacement from strife and conditions in crowded refugee camps—identifying these decisions as a matter of distributive justice is a far more protean problem than discussion of pandemic triage. Thus the justice *of* pandemic planning—of the decisions to devote resources to counter a prospective harm in a context of many actual harms—has drawn less ethical attention than the questions of justice *within* pandemic plans.

No doubt there are other explanations, too, for the apparent assumption that devoting resources to pandemic planning is just. There is the frightful thought of a widespread disease with a 60 per cent mortality rate, and there are the descriptions of the 1918 pandemic that make the avian influenza threat seem personally real to people in the developed world in a way that neglected tropical diseases do not. People in the developed world can see themselves dying of pandemic influenza—as members of their grandparents' or great-grandparents' generations died. The proclivity in the United States to devote resources to saving identified victims but concomitant difficulties in developing policies to deal effectively with the protection of statistical victims is well known among political theorists.[2]

Nonetheless, there are serious questions of justice to be asked about the allocation of extensive resources to pandemic threats. Every state in the United States has a coordinated pandemic plan to address a potential emergency—albeit incomplete—but only a handful of states, Massachusetts and Hawaii among them, have made similar coordinated efforts to address the health needs of their share of the estimated 46.5 million residents of the United States without health insurance.[3] In the United States, the initial federal appropriation for influenza planning was US$3.8 billion, including $1.8 billion for vaccine development,[4] and the second year's appropriation was $2.3 billion.[5] At the same time, states have reportedly been cutting back on the funding available for the purchase of vaccines for uninsured or underinsured children in the United States; one estimate is that 1.2 million children in the United States are unable to receive funded meningococcal conjugate vaccine from public or private sources and that there are similar problems with pneumococcal conjugate vaccine and hepatitis A vaccine.[6] By comparison,

[2] See G Calabresi and P Bobbitt, *Tragic Choices* (New York: Norton, 1978); and N Daniels, *Just Health Care* (New York: Cambridge University Press, 1985).

[3] Kaiser Family Foundation, 'The Uninsured: A Primer' (October 2007), available at <http://www.kff.org/uninsured/upload/7451-03.pdf> (accessed 26 January 2008).

[4] Department of Health and Human Services, 'Pandemic Planning Update' (13 March 2006), available at <http://www.pandemicflu.gov/plan/pdf/panflu20060313.pdf> (accessed 6 February 2008).

[5] Department of Health and Human Services, 'Pandemic Planning Update III' (November 2006), available at <http://www.pandemicflu.gov/plan/pdf/panflureport3.pdf> (accessed 6 February 2008).

[6] GM Lee *et al*, 'Gaps in Vaccine Financing for Underinsured Children in the United States' (2007) 298(6) *JAMA* 638.

the funding for the entire expansion of the state children's health insurance plan (S-CHIP) vetoed by President Bush in the fall of 2007 was US$35 billion— and this was a proposal that would have extended health insurance availability to approximately 10 million children in the United States.[7] Although ignoring a genuine pandemic risk would surely be unwise, there are questions to be raised about the justice of how resources have been allocated to pandemic planning.

I. Justice *Within* Pandemic Planning

A predominant focus of attention within pandemic planning in the developed world has been the allocation of vaccines and antivirals. A second focus has been triage, especially as a function of what is called 'surge capacity'—the ability to handle a far larger influx of patients than normal, whether due to a pandemic, a natural disaster, or a terrorist attack. On the view we defend here, the most important missing element in some of these discussions has been attention to the situation of the 'deprioritized': victims or potential victims of pandemic disease who are low on lists for vaccines, antivirals, or stepped-up treatment. A note-worthy and admirable exception is the recent European emphasis putting plans into place for delivery of supplies and needed services, a predominant initiative of pandemic planning in the European Community for 2008–10.[8] We should preface this discussion, however, with the caveat that pandemic planning rec-ommendations change virtually daily. Nonetheless, reflection on some features of current plans, we think, is instructive for understanding global health justice more generally.

A. Allocating Vaccines and Antivirals

Vaccines provide immunity to infection from a pathogen; immunity may be partial or complete. To provide protection, vaccines must be administered suf-ficiently in advance of exposure for immunity to take hold: approximately two weeks in the case of influenza vaccines. Antivirals such as Tamiflu interfere with viral replication and thus reduce the likelihood that exposure will result in infec-tion, as well as mitigating the severity of infection and contagiousness of the host. For maximum effectiveness, antivirals need to be administered either before infection or early in the course of an infection—the earlier the better—before viral replication has taken extensive hold. These different modes of operation suggest different bases for prioritization of these two preventive methods.

---

[7] eg, S Issenberg, 'House fails to override veto of SCHIP—Democrats vow to continue pushing a bill' *Boston Globe,* 19 October 2007, A2.

[8] European Centre for Disease Prevention and Control, '*Technical Report: Pandemic Influenza Preparedness in the EU/EEA*' (December 2007), available at <http://ecdc.europa.eu/Health_topics/ Pandemic_Influenza/pdf/Pandemic%20prepare%20web%20l.pdf> (accessed 4 February 2008) 17.

Vaccine Prioritization

In the United States, the initial federal framework for the prioritization of vaccines gave first priority to vaccine and antiviral manufacturers, health care workers, and essential service personnel. Following these groups for priority were people who were thought most likely to suffer adverse outcomes from influenza infection: the elderly, those with co-morbidities, and the very young.[9] This prioritization also recognized that groups at greatest mortality risk might vary with the type of pandemic—after all, in 1918 it was healthy young adults who had the highest death rate from infection—and concomitant need to reassess these priorizations as more became known about any particular pandemic. The policies reflected in these prioritizations were maintaining public health and medical care infrastructures, together with protecting the most vulnerable victims. The prioritizations were criticized, however, for being somewhat self-serving—the definition of 'essential services' was at best unclear—and for paying inadequate attention to the role of vaccination in preventing potential disease transmission by targeting those who were most likely to be vectors, such as school-age children.[10]

In the fall of 2007, the United States issued revised draft guidance for allocating vaccines for public comment.[11] The draft guidance attempts both to introduce more precision into the definition of categories and to strike a balance among the competing interests of people in different category types. Thus the structure of the guidance is to identify general categories, 'levels' of equal priority within categories, and 'tiers' of priority within levels for vaccine administration depending on the severity of a pandemic. There are four categories: homeland and national security, health care and community support services, critical infrastructure, and the general population. Within each category, some groups have 'level A' priority for vaccination—ie highest priority for vaccination. In the level of homeland and national security, the level A group is 'deployed and mission critical personnel'; in the category of health care and community support services, it is public health personnel, in-patient health care providers, out-patient and home health providers, and health care providers in long-term care facilities; in the category of critical infrastructure, it is emergency medical service personnel, law enforcement personnel, fire services personnel, manufacturers of pandemic vaccine and antivirals, and key government leaders; and in the category of the general population it is pregnant women and infants between six and thirty-five

---

[9] US Department of Health and Human Services, 'HHS Pandemic Influenza Plan', Appendix D (November 2005), available at <http://www.hhs.gov/pandemicflu/plan/pdf/AppD.pdf> (accessed 6 February 2008) D-13.

[10] By Tom May (paper in draft) and by Mark Rothstein (paper in draft).

[11] US Federal Government, 'Draft Guidance on Allocating and Targeting Pandemic Influenza Vaccine', available at <http://www.pandemicflu.gov/vaccine/prioritization.html> (accessed 6 February 2008). The comment period closed on 31 December 2007.

months. Within level A, there are tiered sub-rankings for administration depending on pandemic severity; for example pregnant women and infants between six and eleven months are in the sixth tier, and other infants are in the final, seventh tier within level A.[12]

In reaching these priorities, the guidance attempts to strike a balance among several values: reciprocity and vaccinating those placed at risk in their jobs; maintaining essential services such as law enforcement and fire protection and vaccinating those who provide them; and protection of the vulnerable and vaccinating those who are likely to become sickest from infection. In the judgment of the draft guidance, this balance reflects values of reciprocity, fairness in the sense of treating everyone as an equal, and flexibility.[13] The fairest observation to make about these priorities is that they attempt to strike a balance among these and other competing values. But it is not at all clear that this is the right balance. To be sure, the emphasis on keeping public health, health care, and other essential services functioning would appear to be well placed, assuming these functions are carefully defined: without these services, efforts to prevent disease spread are more likely to collapse and victims are also more likely to go unsupported. There are important questions to ask about this newest prioritization, however.

One central problem is whether the most recent priorities have paid sufficient attention to targeted use of vaccination to prevent spread. An easy concern to raise is that, like the earlier recommended prioritization, this guidance will allocate vaccines to states on the basis of population—surely a strategy that is not the best way to think about prevention even though it may be politically necessary in a federalist system. A more complex question is whether the priorities pay sufficient attention to how pandemic disease might spread—and to the need to reassess this in the face of actual pandemic circumstances. To take one example: if people are still mobile during the onset of a pandemic, use of public transport is a likely means of disease spread, yet transport workers are not listed in top priority of 'critical infrastructure' groups—they are only in level C of three levels within the critical infrastructure category.[14] To take another: depending on the speed and distribution of pandemic spread (vaccines take two weeks to become effective), a plan to deploy vaccination quickly to areas of initial disease identification—and to couple it with a two-week course of antivirals—may be a more successful strategy than a plan to vaccinate people by occupational or disease-risk groups. And to take a final example: from the perspective of prevention, it is not at all clear that the way to protect the most vulnerable—say, infants—is through vaccination of them or whether it is through vaccination of those with whom they might come into contact—say, their parents who go out into the world.

Another central question to ask is whether it really is defensible from the perspective of justice to concentrate on those who fall into groups now thought to

---

[12] US Federal Government, *Draft Guidance*, 5.
[13] ibid 11.   [14] ibid 5.

be most vulnerable to serious illness from an anticipated influenza pandemic. Suppose we assume a hypothetical Rawlsian veil of ignorance, as Norman Daniels did in asking about whether age should be taken into account in the distribution of health care resources. From the perspective of someone who does not know her actual circumstances of vulnerability, it is not at all clear that allocation to the most vulnerable would be the most justified policy. Obviously, one important goal would be to try to protect everyone: for example by increasing vaccine manufacture capability. But if a pandemic is sufficiently severe and swift, this strategy is unlikely to be available. But there are other strategies to reduce the overall possibility of victimhood. One strategy is transparency: to make sure that people are fully aware of what the scarcities are and what the implications of those scarcities are for them—so that they may take precautions to the extent that they are available, for example by self-shielding until vaccine supplies increase. Another is to try to allocate scarce supplies of vaccine to minimize disease spread. Still another is to employ preventive strategies such as social distancing: for example, nursing home residents can be protected by requiring everyone who enters to have been vaccinated or to be on a regimen of prophylactic antivirals, rather than by vaccination. Mostly home-bound, frail elderly can be protected by adequate social systems for the delivery of meals, medications, and other necessities—so that their need to go out into places of exposure is reduced until pandemic risk has passed.

Antivirals

Antivirals that are designed to interrupt the replication process of viruses may be given either as prophylaxis starting before infection occurs or as treatment that interrupts the course of the disease. As prophylaxis before infection, they must be given on an ongoing basis; thus prophylactic use may consume larger dose numbers and be less efficient overall when supplies are scarce, unless prophylaxis is carefully limited to those at known risk. On the other hand, prophylaxis is effective in preventing infection, and such prophylaxis before infection may be the most efficient way to protect people at ongoing risk of exposure, such as health care workers—at least, until vaccines can be administered and become effective. Because antivirals interrupt replication, once infection occurs they are more effective the earlier they are initiated. 'Effective' here is a statistical term, meaning on average 'more effective' than no intervention. One estimate of the magnitude of impact for antivirals administered within the first twenty-four hours of onset of symptoms is the reduction of a degree of temperature and a day of illness—in healthy people with seasonal influenza; there is insufficient evidence to predict what the efficacy of antivirals might be in otherwise healthy people who become ill with pandemic flu.[15]

[15] UK Department of Health, 'Pandemic Flu', 75; N. Kawai *et al*, 'A comparison of the effectiveness of oseltamivir for the treatment of influenza A and influenza B: a Japanese multicenter study of the 2003–2004 and 2004–2005 influenza seasons,' (2006) 43(4) *Clinical Infectious Diseases*.

An initial point to make about antivirals in pandemic planning, therefore, is that it may not be most sensible to consider the distribution of vaccines and antivirals as separate strategies. From the perspective of prevention, it may be most effective to deploy antivirals in tandem with vaccine, giving antivirals to people such as those care-providers who are at known exposure risk until vaccine becomes available and takes effect. It is also noteworthy that antivirals are quite expensive. For example, one 'discount' price advertised over the internet in early 2008 for Roche's Tamiflu was US$90 for a ten-tablet (75mg) package;[16] dosage is two tablets a day, so the effective cost per person of Tamiflu prophylaxis purchased in this way would be $18 a day. An ongoing concern about antivirals as well is the possibility of resistance; there are recent, alarming reports about strains of seasonal influenza that are resistant to Tamiflu.[17] Strategies of stockpiling antivirals for treatment purposes thus consume scarce economic resources that might otherwise be devoted to developing faster techniques for vaccine manufacture, for a gain that is at least somewhat uncertain.

Recommendations for the allocation of antivirals, however, see treatment as the primary goal. The British plan, for example, comments that prophylactic use of antivirals is in general inefficient because it will consume large amounts of scarce dosage. Britain thus plans to use antivirals in initial containment efforts but primarily for treatment of symptomatic patients.[18] With treatment as one central goal in the allocation of antivirals, the US federal plan recommendations allocate to priority groups in the following order: hospitalized patients, health care workers and emergency service workers with direct patient contact, high risk out-patients (for example people who are immune-compromised), pandemic health responders and government officials, increased risk out-patients, residents of nursing homes, and residents in homes where there has been an outbreak, and so on.[19] The justifications for this priority list begin with protecting people at greatest risk of mortality and morbidity—hence the allocation to hospital in-patients for treatment even when they are outside the window in which administration of antivirals is most likely to be effective and at a point

---

[16] Mail-RX.com, <http://www.mail-rx.com/shop/home.php?cat=255> (accessed 9 February 2008).

[17] European Centre for Disease Prevention and Control, 'Emergence of seasonal influenza viruses type A/H1N1 with oseltamivir resistance in some European Countries at the start of the 2007–8 influenza season' (27 January 2008), available at <http://ecdc.europa.eu/pdf/080127_os.pdf> (accessed 3 February, 2008); Lawrence K Altman, 'Mutant Flu Virus is Found that Resists Popular Drugs,' *New York Times*, 31 January 2008, A-10, col.0. For mathematical modelling of the effects of population structure on the development of resistance with the use of treatment and prophylaxis during a pandemic, see F Debarre, S Bonhoeffer, and RR Regoes, 'The effect of population structure on the emergence of drug resistance during influenza pandemics' (2007) 4 *Journal of the Royal Society Interface* 893, doi10.1098/rsif.2007.1126. (argues that in fragmented populations, development of resistance is less).

[18] UK Department of Health, 'Pandemic Flu', 75–8.

[19] US Department of Health and Human Services, *HHS Pandemic Influenza Plan*, Appendix D, 21.

at which efficacy is unknown.[20] Protecting those who are most likely to suffer mortality and morbidity is also the rationale for prioritizing high and increased risk groups.[21] Maintaining health care services, encouraging health care workers to come to work, and reciprocal obligations to those who incur risks are all given as justifications for providing scarce antivirals to health care workers—as is the observation that this allocation might be publicly acceptable because of the recognition that health care workers incur risks by virtue of their jobs.[22]

As with vaccines, there are important questions about these allocations. Targeting prophylactics quickly to cases of known exposure will have the greatest impact in reducing viral replication and thus diminishing risks of transmission—but this is not an emphasis in US prioritization. Giving highest priority to hospital patients—those whose disease has already become severe— also appears problematic. This allocation runs the very real risk of benefiting no one at all—or at least providing very limited benefit. This result surely is not what would be justified from the perspective of someone who does not know his or her actual circumstances of vulnerability. From this perspective, the most justified policy is that which makes best use of antivirals in interrupting disease processes—and this is trying to target their use to cases of known exposure as well as early symptoms, when there is a very real chance of changing the course of the disease. The prioritization of health care workers reflects this concern to the extent that it is aimed at those who might have suffered exposures; it also responds to obligations of reciprocity to those who take risks in protecting others from disease.

Priority level 6 in the US recommendations, targeting antivirals as a response to outbreaks in care facilities and in residences, represents a clear effort to intervene where it might be most effective in interrupting the course of disease. However, it is noteworthy that this category groups together widely different cases: residents of long-term care facilities are in the same category as home caregivers for people who are ill, and people who are subject to home quarantine because of known exposures. Long-term care residents may be highly likely to die from disease—but there are also questions about whether the administration of antivirals after symptoms have appeared is likely to be effective in altering their disease course and thus to be beneficial to them. Moreover, arguably there are far better ways to protect these residents, for example, by ensuring that during a time of pandemic they are cared for only by people who have been vaccinated or who are taking antiviral prophylaxis and who have followed proper hygienic practices such as handwashing.

By contrast, home caregivers are being relied on by patients; indeed, in a pandemic of any degree of severity, it is likely that such care will be an integral part of efforts to attend to the circumstances of victims. Arguably, home caregivers are

[20] ibid Appendix D, 22.   [21] ibid Appendix D, 24.
[22] ibid Appendix D, 23.

taking on some of the responsibilities of health care providers, to the extent that they are filling in for health care capacities that are insufficient to meet need, and therefore any obligations of reciprocity that extend to health care workers may extend to home carers as well.

Because of their mechanism of action, antivirals must be deployed rapidly to people who have become symptomatic, if they are to be effective at all. Many US plans, at least in published versions to date, appear uninformative about how rapid distribution is to take place. Mechanisms for identifying exposure or illness in early stages, for example by using information from hotlines, are provided in some plans.[23] Methods of delivery need to be clear as well. In the United States, Alaska's plan is somewhat of an exception—it actually lists the planned locations and distribution amounts for Tamiflu.[24] But it, too, does not set out pick up and delivery mechanisms for getting Tamiflu actually into the hands of people who need it. By comparison, Europe has recently made it an 'acid test' for EEA countries in pandemic planning whether social services can deliver antivirals to all who need them within forty-eight hours of the onset of symptoms.[25] This comparison does not imply complete success in Europe, however, either: apparently an attempt to create a European stockpile of antivirals was unsuccessful, and different EEA nations have varying levels of supplies available.[26]

B. Surge Capacity and Palliative Care: Victims Without Care

A second, ethically critical issue in pandemic planning is allocation of treatment for the seriously ill. Pandemic planning models recognize that even in medium-bad case scenarios, some—perhaps even many—people will not receive optimal treatment, or even very good treatment, or even any treatment at all. One plan, Idaho's, has chosen a remarkably honest epigram for its pandemic plan: the newspaper description of how Idaho hospitals were overwhelmed in the 1918 pandemic and had to turn to schools and churches as alternative facilities.[27] Many

[23] State of Massachusetts, 'Massachusetts Influenza Pandemic Preparedness Plan' (October 2006), available at <http://www.mass.gov/dph/cdc/epii/flu/pandemic_plan_8.pdf> (accessed 9 February 2008) 113; New Jersey Department of Health and Senior Services, 'Influenza Pandemic Plan' (draft, 1 February 2006), available at <http://www.state.nj.us/health/flu/documents/pandemic_draft_022006.pdf> (accessed 9 February 2008) 55.

[24] State of Alaska, Division of Public Health, 'Pandemic Influenza Response Plan' (July 2007), available at <http://www.epi.hss.state.ak.us/id/influenza/fluinfo/pandemicfluplan.pdf> (accessed 1 February 2008) 35.

[25] European Centre for Disease Prevention and Control, 'Technical Report: Pandemic Influenza Preparedness in the EU/EEA' (December 2007) 15.

[26] European Centre for Disease Prevention and Control, 'Report for Policymakers: Pandemic Preparedness in the European Union, Autumn 2007,' available at <http://ecdc.europa.eu/pdf/2007_12_05_Pandemic%20preparedness%20for%20policymakers.pdf> (accessed 4 February 2008) 3.

[27] 'Idaho Pandemic Influenza Response', available at <http://www.healthandwelfare.idaho.gov/DesktopModules/Documents/DocumentsView.aspx?tabID=0&ItemID=4523&MId=11634&wversion=Staging> (accessed 27 January 2008) vi.

plans make quite clear that care facilities may be utterly inadequate should a pandemic become serious. The US Department of Health and Human Services (HHS) in grim fashion advises health care facilities that they should make provisions for security to deal with long lines and patients who 'because [of] triage or treatment decisions' do 'not receiv[e] the care they think they require'.[28] Others contain milder messages about the need to communicate with the public about where to seek alternative care facilities. Yet many plans—at least published ones available on the Internet—are not fully transparent about the scenarios that may develop. Plans do not spell out where people should go, or where they will not be able to go, as rates of illness increase. Few plans are transparent about the prioritization of hospital admission or intensive care services, either, yet this information is critically important to people as potential victims—both so that they know what they might or might not be able to receive and so that they are aware of the nature of the choices being made.

Expanding 'Surge Capacity'

Beyond transparency, how should pandemic planning approach issues of scarcity in treatment? One possibility, of course, is to attempt to expand capacities for treatment. The US HHS high-end estimate is that, nationwide, 1.5 million people will need intensive care unit treatment in a predictable avian flu epidemic.[29] This will require extensive 'surge capacity', ie the ability of facilities in a community to respond to a sudden patient load. California planning assumes that by the fifth week of a worst-case pandemic, demand for critical care beds will exceed surge capacity by 1212 per cent and for ventilators by 1350 per cent![30] Other than relying on the Joint Commission on Accreditation of Healthcare Organizations(JCAHO) recommendation for 'sufficient' care in emergencies, however, California had not yet laid out further recommendations for the allocation of scarce treatment.[31] Massachusetts and Minnesota have perhaps the most developed plans, seeing hospitals as critical care facilities operating in tandem

---

[28] 'HHS Pandemic Influenza Plan Supplement 3 Healthcare Planning', available at <http://www.hhs.gov/pandemicflu/plan/sup3.html#secur> (accessed 9 February 2008).

[29] 'HHS Pandemic Influenza Plan' (2005), available at <http://www.hhs.gov/pandemicflu/plan/pdf/HHSPandemicInfluenzaPlan.pdf> (accessed May 2007).

[30] California Department of Health Services, 'Pandemic Influenza Preparedness and Response Plan', available at <http://www.healthyarkansas.com/pandemic_influenza/pandemic_influenza_plan.pdf> (accessed 12 February 2008) 54.

[31] California Department of Health Services, 'Pandemic Influenza Preparedness and Response Plan', 58. The JCAHO reference is JCAHO, 'Surge Hospitals: Providing Safe Care During Emergencies' (2006), available at <http://www.jointcommission.org/NR/rdonlyres/802E9DA4-AE80-4584-A205-48989C5BD684/0/surge_hospital.pdf> (accessed 12 February 2008). Other illustrative plans clearly recognizing the problem of surge capacity but stopping short of making recommendations include the District of Columbia plan, available at <http://dchealth.dc.gov/doh/frames.asp?doc=/doh/lib/doh/information/influenza/pdf/dc_pandemic_influenza_plan.pdf> (accessed 12 February 2008) 63.

with intermediate care satellite facilities providing surge capacity.[32] New Jersey has innovative plans for mental health services, including counselling by telephone, as well as plans for out-patient rehydration stations to reduce the need for hospitalization in some cases.[33] At the time of writing, none of these states has allocated funding for these or other resources, however.

In the United States, as health care costs have risen, hospitals and health care systems have cut back on the numbers of available beds and occupancy rates of 100 per cent or higher are now common.[34] Emergency room capacity has fallen as well. Despite some attention to coordinated disaster planning, estimates now are that the United States falls far short of reasonable levels of disaster preparedness. 'Surge capacity' requires not only facilities, but also supplies and adequate staffing. Especially given current pressures on health care financing in the United States, expanding surge capacity is a very difficult task. One problem is the acute shortage of personnel, especially nurses. Another problem is the lack of adequate primary care networks as well as support for primary care that result in increased burdens on existing emergency departments. In other words, in the judgment of a recent analysis by Kaji, Koenig, and Lewis, the problem of surge capacity is deeply intertwined with other problems in the delivery of health care in the United States. Development of more adequate surge capacity may rest on attending to some of these more systemic problems, and not on a simpler solution such as purchasing additional ventilators or identifying alternatives to hospitals, such as closed schools, where very ill patients can be housed. In the United States, the Veterans' Administration medical system is attempting to implement a coordinated system-wide response, which includes improved primary care infrastructure (such as ensuring high rates of vaccination), attention to staffing needs, and the identification of alternative care facilities.[35] This need to embed surge capacity planning into issues of access to health care more generally is but one suggestion of how issues of justice within pandemic planning may raise larger questions of distributive justice in health care, a point to which we return below.

Seeing the issue of surge capacity in the context of health infrastructure more generally is not just a practical matter of developing an effective strategy, however. It is morally required as well. To view distributive justice in this context from the immediate perspective of the person who is ill is myopic. We are all in some

[32] 'Massachusetts Influenza Preparedness Plan', available at <http://www.mass.gov/dph/cdc/epii/flu/pandemic_plan_4.pdf> (accessed 12 February 2008) 50; Minnesota Department of Health, 'Pandemic Influenza Plan', available at <http://www.health.state.mn.us/divs/idepc/diseases/flu/pandemic/plan/mdhpanfluplan.pdf> (accessed 12 February 2008) 133–62.

[33] New Jersey Department of Health and Senior Services, Pandemic 'Preparedness Plan', available at <http://www.state.nj.us/health/flu/documents/pandemic_draft_022006.pdf> (accessed 12 February 2008) 59, 72.

[34] The discussion in this paragraph is based on AH Kaji, KL Koenig, and RJ Lewis, 'Current Hospital Disaster Preparedness,' (2007) 298(18) *JAMA* 2188.

[35] Department of Veterans Affairs, 'VA Pandemic Influenza Plan', available at <https://idea.iupui.edu/dspace/bitstream/1805/750/1/Veterans%20Administration%20pandemic%20influenza%20plan.pdf> (accessed 8 February 2008) 12.

respects potential victims or vectors, behind a kind of naturalized Rawlsian veil of ignorance from which we do not know when or how disease will strike; from that perspective, practices are most justifiable that reduce overall burdens of disease, as well as addressing the range of possible situations of people who become ill. Efforts to develop primary care structures that identify disease early and that increase the likelihood that patients will be treated while disease is incipient and more easily addressed would be most important from this justificatory perspective. Thus attention to the infrastructure that can support surge capacity is both a useful strategy and a moral imperative.

Allocating Care

Unfortunately, it remains all-too-likely that the United States—or the world more generally—will not have addressed issues of health infrastructure effectively before the advent of a pandemic. Moreover, even with improved infrastructure, it remains possible that natural—or bioterrorism-caused—pandemic conditions may obtain. In such circumstances, on what bases should available care be allocated? These situations are what John Rawls called 'partial compliance' contexts—situations in which ideal justice does not prevail. In his discussion of partial compliance theory, Rawls considered two importantly different kinds of partial compliance contexts, without discussion of the difference between the two:[36] those that are infused by social injustice, in this case the injustice of failures to address issues of health infrastructure; and those that are in the main the result of disasters, either natural or man-made. An important final question to address, therefore, is the relevance of background injustice—whether social or natural—to pandemic allocation decisions.

Drawing from the Toronto Centre's *Stand on Guard for Thee*, several pandemic plans have begun to address quite directly prioritization of higher-level care on a principled ethical basis. In the United States, the Tennessee plan is an early example. Tennessee proposes to base allocation decisions on the values of 'stewardship' and 'reciprocity'. Stewardship in the sense of careful use of scarce resources recommends giving lesser priority to people who are not expected to benefit from hospitalization, people with less than five years of expected survival, and people who are expected to need scarce resources for longer periods of time. The value of reciprocity leads Tennessee to give priority to health care workers and others who have risked infection in pandemic control.[37]

A more recent example is a Canadian proposal,[38] also developed on the basis of *Stand on Guard for Thee* and later incorporated in a plan for

[36] John Rawls, *A Theory of Justice* (Cambridge, Mass.: Harvard University Press, 1971) 244–5.

[37] Tennessee Department of Health, 'Pandemic Influenza Response Plan', available at <http://health.state.tn.us/CEDS/PDFs/2006_PanFlu_Plan.pdf> (accessed 1 February 2008) 129–30.

[38] The proposal is Christian M.D., 2006 *et al*, 'Development of a triage protocol for critical care during an influenza pandemic', *Canadian Medical Association Journal* 175, no. 11 (21 November): 1337–81. Although this protocol claims to be based on *Stand on Guard for Thee*, commentators

Utah.[39] This proposal utilizes the values of equality of access and fairness of treatment. Equity of access is understood to mean that all have an equal claim to treatment evaluated in terms of inclusion and exclusion criteria. These criteria are developed through an assessment tool for survival and need for care. People will have low priority on the one hand if they have limited chances of survival even with treatment, and on the other hand if they have very high chances of survival without treatment. Reassessment is on an ongoing basis; a patient who might have qualified for intensive care on one day may no longer qualify on the next.

The decision of both Tennessee and the Canadian proposal to understand equal treatment in terms of stewardship of resources is a reasonable one. Such prioritization husbands resources to give people overall the best chance that effective treatment will be available for them. However, several aspects of these decisions are noteworthy. First, it is especially important for the 'deprioritization' that is contemplated not to mean 'being ignored'. The Canadian document, followed by Utah's proposal, mentions the importance of palliative care for those who are not prioritized. Yet while there is extensive attention in the proposals to assessment methods for triage, there is no further discussion of what palliative care might be required or how it might be provided. 'Discharge to home' is the contemplated strategy when even ordinary hospital floors are full or patients do not meet triage criteria for hospital admission—but surely an adequate account of what this might involve includes pain management, methods to deal with distress from air hunger, and psychosocial support for both victims and their care-givers.

A second issue that is not attended to at all in pandemic advance care triage is raised by the possibility of partial compliance contexts that result from injustice in health care. When care is triaged according to the proposed medical criteria of survivability and need, certain distributive patterns may emerge.[40] One pattern is that groups already disadvantaged in access to health care may be further disadvantaged in pandemic prioritization. For example, African-Americans for a variety of reasons may be over-represented among patients who are so severely ill when they come to medical attention that their probabilities of survival are lower than the survival probabilities of patients in other groups. African-Americans are

have questioned whether the values in the latter are fully represented in the former. Melnychuk, Ryan H., and Nuala P. Kenny, 'Pandemic triage: The ethical challenge,' (2006) 175(11) *Canadian Medical Association Journal* 175, no. 11 (21 November): 1393.

[39] Utah Hospitals and Health Systems Association, 'Utah Pandemic Influenza Hospital and ICU Triage Guidelines' (draft 12/07/07), available at <http://www.pandemicflu.utah.gov/plan/med_triage120707.pdf> (accessed 9 February 2008).

[40] This point is also made in J Tabery, CW Mackett III, and the University of Pittsburgh, Pandemic Influenza Task Force's Triage Review Board, 2008. 'The Ethics of Triage in the Event of an Influenza Pandemic' *Disaster Medicine and Public Health Preparedness* 2(2) (June). These authors defend a hybrid ethical model of triage, emphasizing utility (who can most benefit), narrow social utility (who is most needed to maintain health care and social infrastructure during a pandemic), and egalitarianism (who is most needy; egalitarian considerations also temper utility when unintended patterns of racism or other forms of discrimination become apparent).

less likely to have a source of primary care and so less likely to receive vaccines or to be seen early in the course of disease; they are more likely to live in crowded urban areas and to be dependent on modes of public transport where exposure might be more expected (especially if, as we have noted, prophylaxis is not prioritized to transport workers); and they are more likely to be in poor health and thus experience greater severity of disease. Depending on the type of pandemic, African-Americans thus might be over-represented among the sickest—and under-represented among those triaged to care. To be sure, the likelihood of any pattern such as this will depend on the nature and distribution of a pandemic. We are not arguing here for addition of a kind of 'affirmative action' criterion to pandemic triage that disrupts attention to the effort to triage care where it will be most effective. What we do claim is that the possibility of a result such as this has gone virtually unnoticed in pandemic triage planning and that this is a matter of concern. At a minimum, we think, reducing the likelihood that pandemic triage will compound existing patterns of injustice is another argument for attention to basic health care infrastructure: to the kind of primary care networks and trust in the health care system that decrease existing injustice and thus the probability that pandemic planning could compound it.

Palliative Care

Pandemic plans in the United States take quite different positions about responsibilities for home care. Some have attempted to identify agencies such as the Red Cross that may be available to help out. Others, however, view stockpiling essential supplies and home remedies as fundamentally an individual responsibility. By contrast, Britain's plan devotes far more attention to the development of the infrastructure that may be needed to deliver essential supplies to people in home isolation or quarantine. Whether home care is a social or an individual responsibility looms with great urgency when people are triaged not to receive advanced care and sent home because there is insufficient surge capacity to include everyone who might otherwise receive treatment in hospitals or intensive care units.

These 'deprioritized'—people who are sent home because treatment is not available for them—will include the sickest victims. Consideration of palliative care modalities that might be available for them in an out of hospital setting is thus an especially pressing matter. For example: might it be possible to develop methods of dealing with respiratory distress that do not require the sophistication of hospital personnel and equipment? What kinds of pain medication might be appropriate to ease distress, and how can it be administered at home? Depending on the type of pandemic illness, what other forms of care might be needed to relieve distress: for example, is there likely to be vomiting or diarrhea, with the need for medication to relieve nausea or other forms of abdominal distress? Is there likely to be bleeding, with all the needs for care that might involve? These are questions that, as far as we know, have not been addressed extensively in pandemic planning to date.

II. The Justice of Pandemic Planning and Global Health Security

There are a number of respects in which pandemic planning decisions require further attention to health infrastructure in order to be justified. Global surveillance—critically important to the early identification of possible pandemic infection—depends both practically and ethically on structures that can offer treatment. Adequate health infrastructures are important in vaccine development, too: countries have been unwilling to share the viral samples needed for vaccine research and development without assurance that they also will benefit.[41] Without access to primary care, people are less likely to identify disease, receive vaccine or prophylaxis when needed, or identify symptoms early enough to permit antiviral treatment to be effective. Pandemic planners in Europe, for example, have judged that attention to the health infrastructure needed to provide ordinary care for people in the case of seasonal influenza is a critical strategy for preparation for pandemic influenza.[42] Arizona's effort in its pandemic plan to understand ways of communicating with special populations—the elderly, people with disabilities, and people who do not speak English—is an excellent example of how infrastructures might be developed to help build the trust that is essential for health care delivery to be effective in crisis situations.[43] The development of surge capacity to improve health care delivery in pandemics or in other emergencies likewise requires attention to health infrastructure. Allocation of scarce intensive care to patients who are most likely to benefit may compound patterns of disadvantage, if attention is not paid to these patterns in the first place.

Questions of justice within pandemic planning thus cannot be considered without attention to the justice *of* pandemic planning as well. By this claim, we do not mean that pandemic planning should be ignored. Rather, we mean that questions of justice within pandemic planning cannot be addressed in an ethically satisfactory manner without attention to health care justice more generally, ie that 'pandemic myopia' is misguided.

From the perspective of their immediate circumstances, people who have relatively secure access to health care may seem to have little interest in what happens to others and thus little interest in more robust systems of health security. As

---

[41] USINFO.STATE.GOV, 'Indonesia Agrees to Resume Sharing Avian Flu Samples' (27 March 2007), available at <http://www.america.gov/st/washfile-english/2007/March/200703271518131 cnirellep0.7828638.html> (accessed 9 February 2008).

[42] European Centre for Disease Prevention and Control, 'Technical Report: Pandemic Influenza', 18.

[43] Arizona Department of Health Services, 'Demographics and Effective Risk Communication' (April 2005), available at <http://www.azdhs.gov/phs/edc/edrp/es/pdf/adhsspecialpopstudy.pdf> (accessed 26 January 2008).

long as individuals are immunized, or otherwise unlikely to catch communicable diseases from others because of where they live or the health and living choices they make, it might seem that it does not matter to them how those others fare. But such insulated health security is unstable at best. The possibility of pandemic influenza is perhaps the most powerful illustration of this for people in the developed world today, but so are possibilities of measles, whooping cough, and other transmissible infectious diseases for which immunization rates fall below levels that confer herd immunity.

What this uncertainty suggests is the importance of a robust public health infrastructure, where people get treated for diseases that they or others might catch, even in areas of the developed world where health security for some is relatively good. Critical here is funding for vaccination and vaccine development, as well as for inexpensive and widely-available modes of treatment for infectious disease. Critical also is the presence of the kind of primary care system that encourages people to be vaccinated, as well as to seek treatment early for conditions that might prove contagious.

By contrast, would the intensive investment in the United States in treatment for diseases that are not communicable—heart disease, cancer, even diabetes—command a lesser priority, despite the use of the rhetoric of 'epidemic' in referring to conditions such as diabetes? To conclude that the answer to this question is 'yes' might be too hasty; there are important arguments for the expansion of health security that this analysis so far overlooks. The more that public facilities or public funding are available for the treatment of common ailments such as diabetes for people who could not afford treatment, for example, the higher the likelihood that people will receive primary care more generally. Robust health infrastructures such as this increase the likelihood of access to more general primary care and thus to routine immunization. Access to primary care also makes it more likely that people will have a source and the trust to seek care if they become ill with diseases that are communicable. Influenza surveillance is an example of the importance of such access to primary care. To take but one example, the current strategy for monitoring influenza infections in the United States involves identified sentinel providers submitting samples to state health department laboratories that in turn report infection sub-types to the CDC.[44] Unless patients access providers—whether for diabetes or for the flu—this system will not function to identify novel viral strains.

For many in the developed world, it might also seem that much of the untreated burden of diseases in the developing world is of little consequence. The diarrheal diseases that kill so many infants in areas of the world with unsanitary water, for example, seem unlikely to spread to the United States,

---

[44] The White House, 'National Strategy for Pandemic Influenza Implementation Plan One Year Summary' (July 2007), available at <http://www.whitehouse.gov/homeland/pandemic-influenza-oneyear.html> (accessed 26 January 2008).

even as air travel increases. Yet some of this sense of safety may be illusory. West Nile fever, unheard of in the United States twenty years ago, has now been reported in mosquito and avian populations in all states but Alaska, Hawaii, and Maine; in 2007, human cases were reported in every state but these three, New Hampshire, Vermont, Washington, and West Virginia.[45] Dengue fever, hardly a disease familiar to most Americans, is now regarded as a potential threat to public health in the United States; the mosquito vectors of the disease have been multiplying and spreading at remarkable rates, perhaps owing to global climate change, and are now found in thirty-six states.[46] Gostin has recently argued that both narrow and enlightened self-interest support a moral interest of the developed world in the health status of people in the developing world.[47] The argument from narrow self-interest is the point we have just made about dengue fever: no one, anywhere in the world today, is safe from infectious diseases, both familiar and emerging ones. Gostin's argument from enlightened self-interest is that improving health status in impoverished countries benefits travel, world trade, and national security.

Gostin's argument from self-interest, even from enlightened self-interest, however, is based on how individuals from their real-life circumstances perceive themselves as victims or vectors, threats or the objects of threats. This perspective is inherently unstable, for it depends on current perceptions of apparent safety or apparent danger. These perceptions may be accurate—or they may be dangerously wrong. From the perspective on an infectious disease veil of ignorance that we have suggested here—that of people who cannot really know at any given time that they are secure from the web of transmissible disease that affects us all—failure to attend to health security against the burden of infectious disease is unjustifiable. To be sure, this conclusion is but a starting place for enormous questions about how such attention should ethically be achieved. Even establishing that this is a worldwide, human responsibility, however, is an important beginning, one that suggests several issues that should come to the fore.

First, as vaccination is the best preventive—after all, someone who is vaccinated is unlikely to get sick and pass disease on to others, thus interrupting the chain of disease transmission—far more attention to vaccine development and vaccination is critical. Yet even in wealthy countries such as the United States, funding for vaccination and development of new vaccines is lagging to say the least.[48] And elsewhere in the world, vaccination rates remain low for diseases

[45] CDC, '2007 West Nile Virus Activity in the United States' (reported as of 8 January 2008), available at <http://www.cdc.gov/ncidod/dvbid/westnile/Mapsactivity/surv&control07Maps. htm> (accessed 27 January 2008).

[46] D Morens and AS Fauci, 'Dengue and Hemorrhagic Fever: A Potential Threat to Public Health in the United States', (2008) 299(2) *JAMA* 214.

[47] LO Gostin, 'Why Rich Countries Should Care About the World's Least Healthy People', (2007) 298(1) JAMA 89.

[48] See eg GM Lee *et al*, 'Gaps in Vaccine Financing for Underinsured Children in the United States' (2007) 298(6) *JAMA* 638.

such as measles,[49] or even polio[50] in some remaining areas. The strategic plan of the Initiative for Vaccine Research of the WHO emphasizes the need for the development of vaccines against diseases that are major killers of people in poverty: HIV/AIDS, malaria, and tuberculosis especially.[51]

Second, investment in other forms of disease prevention remains problematic as well. Beyond poverty itself, poor sanitation and unclean water are major sources of infection, from infant diarrhea to cholera.[52] Bednets—the cheap and highly effective means for interrupting mosquito-borne malaria transmission, especially for infants[53]—are still far from universally available.

Third, inexpensive forms of treatment are all too scarce in the developing world, but also in areas of the developed world. Treatment for HIV infection, as well as other essential medications, remains unaffordable in many areas of the developing world.[54] Over 45 million residents of the United States lack health insurance, many of them children. The problem of anti-microbial resistance continues to grow as well, and with insufficient attention to the development of replacement drugs. In many areas of the world, simple primary care infrastructures—storefront clinics, mobile units, public clinics, and the like—are utterly unavailable; yet these are, as we have suggested, critical to encouraging people to seek care and thus to the early identification of emerging disease.

Admittedly, identification of these priorities does not provide an argument from justice for advanced treatment of advanced cancer or of non-communicable or degenerative conditions such as Alzheimer's disease. Admittedly, on the argument we have been developing, these priorities—so much the concern of health care in the United States—should take something of a back seat. But we should note that this back seat is not a vacant seat. For one thing, many of the infrastructural reforms that we are suggesting—cleaner water, for example—may reduce other disease risks. Better access to primary care may result in earlier diagnosis of non-infectious diseases as well. Arguably, access to at least a decent minimum of care overall—however this is to be defined in the wide variety of societies across

[49] The WHO vaccine campaign against measles resulted in a 68% drop in the death rate from measles worldwide between 2000 and 2007; however, 600 children still die every day from this disease that is preventable with a vaccine that costs less than US$1. Measles Initiative, available at <http://www.measlesinitiative.org/index3.asp> (accessed 11 February 2008).

[50] Although progress continues to be made, in 2006 the WHO estimated immunization rates of below 50% in some areas of sub-Saharan Africa and rates hovering between 50 and 75% in areas of Africa and south-east Asia. WHO, 'Immunization coverage with 3rd dose of polio vaccines in infants, 2006', available at <http://www.who.int/immunization_monitoring/diseases/Polio_coverage_map.jpg> (accessed 11 February 2008).

[51] WHO Initiative for Vaccine Research, 'Strategic Plan 2006–2009' available at <http://www.who.int/vaccine_research/documents/Final_version.pdf> (accessed 11 February 2008) 6.

[52] WHO, 'Cholera Prevention and Control', available at <http://www.who.int/topics/cholera/control/en/index.html> (accessed 11 February 2008).

[53] See eg CDC, 'Malaria: Vector Control' available at <http://www.cdc.gov/malaria/control_prevention/vector_control.htm> (accessed 11 February 2008).

[54] R Steinbrook, 'Closing the Affordability Gap for Drugs in Low-Income Countries', (2007) 357(20) *New England Journal of Medicine* 1996.

the globe—is critical to the trust needed for the health care infrastructure that, we have argued, is ultimately critical to improving global health security against infectious disease.

Nearly fifty years ago, in the context of racial discrimination, the Reverend Martin Luther King, Jr, wrote this about social interconnectedness: 'We are caught in an inescapable network of mutuality, tied in a single garment of destiny. Whatever affects one directly affects all indirectly.'[55] Although King was writing about social interconnectedness, his language captures perfectly our biological interconnectedness in the face of infectious disease. This interconnectedness, we have argued, is the basis for attending not just to justice within pandemic planning, but to the justice of pandemic planning in the light of pressing issues of global health security in the world today.

[55] Rev Martin Luther King, Jr, 'Letter from Birmingham City Jail', available at <http://www.crisispapers.org/liberty/king-letter.htm> (accessed 19 February 2008).

24

Humanitarian Intervention and Medical Epidemics

Bruce M Landesman

I. Medical Epidemics and Unresponsive Governments

There is a type of humanitarian military intervention that has not been much considered, but is very likely to be an important topic in the near future. Suppose there is a deadly epidemic in a country, and many are dying or will die if nothing is done. The epidemic can be stopped and people saved by appropriate medicines, which are available to the government. The government, however, refuses to do anything, perhaps even refuses to admit there is a problem. One might imagine such an epidemic spreading through North Korea or Myanmar with an enormous loss of life, but a stubborn government refuses to provide or accept any aid.[1]

Or suppose that the government is willing to treat the disease but only for the 'favoured' part of its population. It fails to provide treatment to the citizens of a minority ethnic group it would like to be rid of. Consider, for example, a Serbian government saving Serb lives from an epidemic in pre-intervention Kosovo, but not Albanian lives. This would be 'genocide' or 'ethnic cleansing' by epidemic. Is humanitarian intervention permissible or obligatory in cases like these?

To answer these questions, I will first discuss humanitarian intervention in general and examine what can be said for and against it. Humanitarian intervention has been much discussed and its pros and cons canvassed. My main question will be whether medical epidemics pose any new issues for the validity of such intervention. I will argue that intervention is sometimes permissible or mandatory in the face of medical epidemics. I will conclude, however, that humanitarian intervention is a tool that can be effectively used only on rare occasions. As a result, we need a better way of dealing with the recurrent problems of the world's poor, medical and otherwise.

---

[1] This chapter was written before the cyclone that devastated Myanmar, but the government's reaction to that disaster is an analogous case.

II. Humanitarian Intervention

Humanitarian intervention occurs when one state or a group of states intervenes militarily in another state, without invitation, to prevent a large-scale human tragedy. The NATO intervention to stop ethnic cleansing in Kosovo, and the US intervention to feed starving people in Somalia are examples. Preventing the massacre of Tutsis in Rwanda is a humanitarian intervention that did *not* happen.

Politicians and scholars debate the legitimacy of this kind of intervention. It appears to transgress international law, since it violates the United Nations charter which allows only defensive wars.[2] Humanitarian intervention also violates a nation's sovereignty. We still exist in a world of sovereign states, each of which has the right to independence and territorial integrity. Each is accorded the freedom to manage its own affairs, free from external interference. Humanitarian intervention is thus an infringement of both international law and state sovereignty.

Despite this, such interventions have occurred in the recent past, and there has been much debate about changing international law and limiting sovereignty to allow it. When a state violates the human rights of its citizens, or stands idly by while this happens, or is unwilling or unable to prevent large-scale loss of life, it is difficult to do nothing and let this happen. In such cases many find intervention at least permissible, and some find it mandatory.

With regard to humanitarian intervention to stop a medical epidemic, we can imagine two different cases in which a government refuses to fight a disease. In one case, the disease is confined to the borders of that country and poses no threat to other countries. If it spreads, it is treatable and other countries will be able to avoid disaster. Since the problem is almost solely internal in such a case, intervention would be purely humanitarian.

In a second type of case, the disease is very likely to spread to countries which will have difficulty controlling it. Intervention here would have humanitarian aims, but it would not be a pure case of humanitarian intervention. It would also be a matter of self-defence, a type of preventive war. Cases of this type would be an epidemic of Avian flu or Severe Acute Respiratory Syndrome (SARS) which, if uncontained in the country where it begins, will almost certainly spread to other countries.

My aim is to discuss intervention with respect to the sort of medical epidemic that poses little threat to other countries. This will be pure humanitarian intervention. The topic of intervention with respect to contagious diseases raises issues about preventive war which I leave for another occasion.

---

[2] Charter of the United Nations, Arts 2(4) and 51, Enacted 1945. See <http://www.un.org/aboutun/charter/>, Chs II and VII.

II. Humanitarian Intervention: Basic Grounds

Many people are moved to support humanitarian intervention when terrible things are happening to people in other nations. I want to suggest three reasons for this motivation: a *sentiment*, an abstract *value*, and a certain minimalist understanding of *the human good*.

The *sentiment* is the desire to help those in need and the aversion to standing by when other people are in trouble and can be helped without undue cost to oneself. In an illuminating discussion, David Luban points out that we are shamed when we fail to live up to our principles. He calls this 'bystander shame'.[3] Luban suggests that failing to help stop certain human rights violations 'calls into question our very commitment to civilization over barbarism'.[4]

The *value* I have in mind is human equality, the notion that people are equal by nature. No one is born better than anyone else—there are no higher castes or statuses that make some fit to be rulers or masters and others fit only to be ruled or enslaved. Most abstractly, it is the idea that people are equal in their intrinsic value, independent of the ways they become unequal as they live their lives. We express this when we say of another that 'he may be richer, smarter, more handsome, more accomplished than me but he is no better than me as a human being'. We have equal value.

This value of course is abstract and difficult to define.[5] It is best explained, I think, as having the following implications: that all people should be treated as equals; that people should be treated with equal concern and respect; that when policies are enacted everyone's interests count and count equally; that discrimination and prejudice are wrong; that a just state follows the rule of law and treats all as the law requires, with no exceptions for the rich and powerful. The idea of human equality is essential to the modern liberal tradition and underlies many of its practices[6]. A distant stranger in great need is, though distant, my equal and has a claim on my help.

The notion of *the human good* I have in mind is that without certain fundamental goods, life cannot be lived decently. The first of these is life itself. The others include food, shelter, and a degree of autonomy. By the latter I do not mean full-scale civil liberty protected in liberal democracies. I mean sufficient freedom to pursue one's aims in life without being subject to arbitrary arrest or persecution, coercion, discrimination, etc. I mean the minimal freedom to

---

[3] David Luban, 'Intervention and Civilization: Some Unhappy Lessons of the Kosovo War' in P De Grieff and C Cronin (eds), *Global Justice & Transnational Politics* (Cambridge, Mass.: MIT Press, 2002) 98.

[4] ibid 101.

[5] An early statement of this idea can be found in G Vlastos, 'Justice and Equality' in R Brandt (ed), *Social Justice*, (Englewood Cliffs, NJ: Prentice Hall, 1962).

[6] I would also argue, as many have, that it is essential to morality.

live one's life in accord with one's values. These are basic and necessary human goods.

The three things I have mentioned—the *sentiment* to help those in need, the *value* of equality, and the conception of *necessary human goods*—set the background for humanitarian intervention. None of them, separately or jointly, entail that humanitarian intervention is either permissible or mandatory. One might claim that the sentiment to help is a mere psychological fact that has no moral import. And one might accept human equality and necessary human goods without believing we have duties to help those unconnected to us. We also have duties to take care of ourselves, and to friends and relations, and it may be argued that these exhaust the moral claims on us.

These items nevertheless provide reasons for thinking that humanitarian intervention is either permissible or obligatory. These reasons are strengthened if we take the second and third items as a basis for claims about human rights. If all people are of equal value and all need security, subsistence, and limited autonomy to lead a decent human life, it is reasonable to argue that persons have a right to these things. These rights are basic rights in a sense that Henry Shue has clarified: without protection of these rights no other rights can be enjoyed.[7] I will not argue here that people should be considered to have these rights. I note only that doing so explains the tendency to see humanitarian intervention as appropriate. If there are any human rights, surely they are violated by such things as ethnic cleansing, genocide, and mass murder.

The reasons given above are moral reasons for humanitarian intervention. I want to note that there are two different ways one can support such intervention. One can argue that it is permissible, at least sometimes, but it is never obligatory. In the right circumstances a nation may intervene to prevent a tragedy, but it does no wrong if it chooses not to do so. Alternately, one can argue that it is sometimes not merely permissible but obligatory, that there are cases in which one cannot stand by in the face of such things as genocide and mass killing. For the moment I will not distinguish between these two claims. I will come back to them later.

III. Humanitarian Intervention: Basic Reasons Against

The most basic reason to oppose humanitarian intervention is that it is illegal, that it violates international law, as expressed in the UN Charter. Some have argued that the Charter is ambiguous enough to allow humanitarian intervention.[8] I want, however, to avoid this issue. I assume that as currently understood such intervention, unless authorized by the UN, violates international law.

---

[7] H Shue, *Basic Rights: Subsistence, Affluence and U.S. Foreign Policy* (Princeton, NJ: Princeton University Press, 2nd edn, 1996).

[8] For a discussion of the arguments, see JL Holzgrefe, 'The Humanitarian Intervention Debate', in JL Holzgrefe and RO Keohane, *Humanitarian Intervention: Ethical, Legal and Political Dilemmas* (Cambridge: Cambridge University Press, 2003) 37–43.

This, of course, does not settle the moral issue. There can be good moral reasons to violate a law if it is a bad law or if following it has very bad consequences in particular instances. The UN Charter, it is arguable, reflects the time of its composition, after a terrible war among nations. Its main aim was to outlaw war among states. Consequently, it permits military conflict only as a matter of defence. Times have changed, both because of the growing worldwide recognition of basic human rights and the existence of failed or autocratic states inclined towards massive rights violations. Humanitarian intervention may now be important in a way it was not earlier.

The second main reason against intervention is the fact that it violates sovereignty. When a state is *voluntarily* invited to enter another state by its legitimate government to stop or prevent a tragedy, it is not humanitarian intervention. It is fully consistent with the notion of sovereignty. Humanitarian intervention is unilateral intervention, against the will of the intervened state.[9] In such a case, there is a clear infringement of a state's independence and territorial integrity. Sovereignty no longer has the normative force it once had, if it ever had it.[10] We now recognize many limitations on sovereignty as the result of the development of international law, the growth of global and regional organizations, including judicial courts, and extensive global trade agreements.

Morally, it is arguable that sovereignty is justified for specific purposes. When a state's government no longer fulfils that purpose, its sovereignty is suspect. There are two prime purposes. One is to protect and promote the welfare of its citizens. When it fails to do that, the moral importance of its sovereignty is diminished.[11] Some would say it is forfeited.

The other main purpose is peace. When sovereignty exists, states recognize a duty not to use military means to promote their interests against other states. Aggressive war is seen as a violation of international norms and the result is that war and its horrors are diminished. Against this, it can be argued that humanitarian intervention is not the sort of aggressive war that the system of sovereignty is meant to constrain. It is in fact a response to the failure of sovereignty to satisfy its primary purpose.

Illegality and sovereignty are thus not enough to make humanitarian intervention morally impermissible. A strong case against it will have to be based on different grounds.

IV. Other Objections to Humanitarian Intervention

One important objection to humanitarian intervention is the difficulty of deciding just when a situation calls for it. There are no saintly governments.

---

[9] Complications arise when the state is invited in by one party to a conflict.

[10] For scepticism about sovereignty, see S Krasner, *Sovereignty: Organized Hypocrisy* (Princeton, NJ: Princeton University Press, 1999).

[11] David Luban has given two effective critiques of sovereignty in 'Just War and Human Rights' (1980) 9(2) *Philosophy and Public Affairs*, and 'The Romance of the Nation-State'(1980) 9(5) *Philosophy and Public Affairs*. See also Charles Beitz, *Political Theory and International Relations* (Princeton, NJ: Princeton University Press, 1979, 1999 expanded version) Part Two, sections 1–30.

Governments not only make mistakes but perpetrate injustices and rights violations. In almost any state at any time, there are morally problematic practices perpetrated or allowed by the government and often vigorously opposed by critics.

If any state misbehaviour justified intervention, no state would be immune.
The world would be full of violence. The standard response is to limit humanitarian intervention to gross violations of human rights. One problem with this is the
difficulty of determining what rights we have. Richard Norman has argued that
human rights are 'epistemologically indeterminate'.

> ...how do we establish whether human rights are correctly listed as 'life, liberty and
> the pursuit of happiness' (according to the United States Declaration of Independence),
> or as 'liberty, property, security and resistance to oppression' (according to the French
> Declaration of the Rights of Man and Citizen), or as the 13 rights recognised in the
> European Convention on Human Rights, or as the more than thirty rights recognised in
> the United Nations Declaration of Human Rights?[12]

If we have a fulsome account of human rights, this may allow too much humanitarian intervention; a weak account would allow too little. It is tempting to say
about occasions for humanitarian intervention what Supreme Court Justice
Potter Stuart said about obscenity: 'I shall not... attempt... to define the kinds of
material I understand to be [obscene]... [b]ut I know it when I see it...'[13] There is
the further difficulty that people disagree about what basic rights people possess.
Some include rights to subsistence; others limit basic rights to non-interference.[14]
There are further disagreements within each camp.

I will not go further into this question. David Luban has suggested that injustice warrants humanitarian intervention when it amounts to uncivilized and
barbaric behaviour. Luban asks which rights are worth going to war over. 'The
answer is: those human rights the violation of which is uncivilized, so that standing idly by while they are violated calls into question our very commitment to
civilization over barbarism.'[15] Critics will find this criterion too vague and will
note that ideas of what is civilized and barbaric differ from society to society. I
think, however, that there is general consensus to limit humanitarian intervention to the worst cases, the most egregious violations of human rights, the greatest human tragedies. There will be much agreement on specific cases, for example
Rwanda, and we can argue about others on a case-by-case basis.

In my view, the strongest argument against permitting humanitarian intervention *in principle* is that permitting it will motivate a great deal of unjustified military conflict in its name. Nations always have multiple motives and are liable to
abuse any reason for war if it is in their interest. The restriction of war to self-defence
makes war more difficult. A humanitarian principle provides a loop-hole that will

---

[12] Richard Norman, 'War, Humanitarian Intervention and Human Rights' in R Sorabji and
D Rodin (eds), *The Ethics of War* (Aldershot: Ashgate, 2006) 193.
[13] 1 *Jacobellis v Ohio* 378 US 184, 197 (1964).
[14] Shue (n 7 above).   [15] Luban (n 3 above) 100.

be exploited. If we permit humanitarian intervention, there will be too much of it, most of it unjustified, and the world will be a more violent place.

There is cogency to this criticism, but it is not decisive. It we do not permit humanitarian intervention, there will also be serious violence through genocide, ethnic cleansing, and mass violations of basic rights. The principle has its dangers, but not permitting humanitarian intervention also has dangers. It allows tragedies to occur and permits those bent on genocide to believe that they can get away, literally, with murder. A blanket condemnation of humanitarian intervention is not warranted.

The hard issues arise, I believe, when we consider particular instances of intervention. Military intervention always has unexpected consequences. Those who intervene may not understand the internal dynamics of the country and the intervention can unleash conflict that was under control. There is always a chance that a humanitarian intervention will do more harm than good.

This objection needs to be taken seriously when intervention is contemplated. The American intervention in Somalia appears to have been intended solely to feed starving people. But once one intervenes, one takes on a commitment to improve the conditions that warranted the intervention. In Somalia, that led to 'mission creep' and hasty withdrawal, as the American military found themselves in the middle of disputes among rival clans. This intervention may have been a bad idea, or at least badly managed.

In Rwanda, on the other hand, there was no intervention. A terrible genocide occurred. The resulting refugee flights to Congo led to military conflict in that country that is still going on and has led to millions of deaths. It is difficult to imagine that an intervention could have had worse consequences.

Critics are correct that any given instance of humanitarian intervention will raise difficult issues. That does not make it always wrong. It makes it difficult.

A further problem with humanitarian military intervention is the issue of asking the citizens of one state to risk their lives for the welfare of foreigners. Can this be legitimate? As Allen Buchanan has noted, it seems to go against the 'dominant understanding of the nature of the state' as a 'discretionary association' which exists for the mutual advantage of its members.[16] Of course a state may perceive an instance of humanitarian intervention as being partially in its own interest, as a way of providing stability in a region where instability can become a threat to it. Further, its own people may support the intervention. But it is not enough that the intervention be supported by a democratic procedure, as it is arguable that risking military lives for the sake of non-citizens is inappropriate, even if approved by a democratic legislature.

In response to this, Buchanan suggests that there is a natural duty incumbent on all humans to promote or preserve justice and this leads to an alternate view of

---

[16] A Buchanan, 'The Internal Legitimacy of Humanitarian Intervention' (1999) 7(1) *Journal of Political Philosophy* 73, 75.

the state as an 'instrument of justice'. This understanding permits the state to risk its citizens' lives through humanitarian intervention.[17]

These are difficult issues which I cannot address fully here. On the one hand the state has a fiduciary responsibility for its citizens and it is difficult to see how it can risk their lives solely for the sake of non-citizens. On the other hand, the state represents its people who have duties to aid those in distress. Limited humanitarian intervention will sometimes be the most efficient way for citizens to satisfy this obligation.

I have now canvassed what I take to be the main arguments against the permissibility of humanitarian intervention. They all have some cogency but I do not think they amount to decisive reasons against it. What we have seen, however, is that any particular case of intervention will be morally problematic. It should never be done lightly. We must consider that it can go wrong, do more harm than good, and it risks the lives of soldiers whose primary responsibility is to protect their own citizens.

V. Obligatory or Only Permissible

I have argued then that humanitarian intervention is sometimes permissible. But is it ever obligatory? As I noted earlier, one might hold that a state may engage in such intervention but it is never *obligated* to do so. Humanitarian intervention is never a duty. I am inclined to argue that once an action is understood to be permissible, it is difficult to argue that it is never a duty. If it is permissible, then there are good reasons for doing it. To claim that it is never a duty would be to claim that the reasons against it are always stronger. No one can say this in advance. I conclude that intervention can sometimes be obligatory.

If humanitarian intervention is obligatory, it seems reasonable at first sight to classify it as what Kant called an imperfect duty.[18] This is a duty towards other people but no particular persons can claim a right to be the beneficiary of that duty. If I make a promise to A, I have a duty to A to keep that promise. This is a perfect duty because A can claim my performance of what I promised as a right. I do not, however, owe that duty to anyone else.

I also believe that I have a duty to help people in need. There are, however, many people in need and I cannot help them all. I should help some and I have a choice as to whom to help. Thus I violate the duty if I help no one, but if I help some, those I do not help cannot claim that I have violated a duty to them. That is why it is an imperfect duty.

[17] ibid 82–7.
[18] I Kant, *The Metaphysics of Morals*, ed M Gregor (ed), (Cambridge: Cambridge University Press, 1996) Part II, The Metaphysical Principles of Virtue, Introduction, section VII, 153.

Since there are many cases that seem to call for humanitarian intervention, it seems reasonable to think of it as an imperfect duty. It is something a nation may do but is not obligated to do. This may be true for many cases but I doubt it is true for a nation with ample resources with regard to the greatest crimes. The failure of the UN and other developed countries to intervene in Rwanda cannot be thought of as merely passing up an acceptable option. If the evil is bad enough, the duty is actual and perfect.

I have argued that the reasons for humanitarian intervention can outweigh those against it so that it is, on occasion, obligatory. But how should it be conducted?

VI. Humanitarian Intervention and the Rules of War

The theory of just war is a framework for thinking about the morality of war. I will accept this framework and point out some important ways it applies to humanitarian intervention.

The first part of just war theory is the *Jus ad Bellum* which addresses the question of when it is justifiable to engage in military conflict. Among other things, it requires that a war have a just cause. I have argued that humanitarian intervention is a just cause. The *Jus in Bello*, the second part of Just War Theory, is a set of rules about how a war must be fought. The idea is that both sides must adhere to the rules, whether their resort to war is just or unjust.

I want to emphasize some special ways in which the requirements of just war theory apply to humanitarian intervention. I start with the rules of war. The most important provision of the *Jus in Bello* is sometimes called the *Principle of Discrimination*, sometimes the principle of *Non-Combatant Immunity*. The idea is that civilians—non-combatants—may not be the direct target of military attack. Intentionally killing or injuring civilians is prohibited, even if it would produce military advantages, such as the demoralization of the population.

Civilian deaths, however, are allowed, but only as a foreseen but unintended side-effect of a legitimate attack. In addition, the death of civilians must conform to a principle of proportionality. The benefits of the military attack must be great enough to significantly outweigh civilian death and injury. This rules out, for example, an attack which kills many civilians but brings only minor military gains. Even if the gains are great, the attack will be unjustified if there are a great many civilian deaths.

Humanitarian Intervention is meant to help those oppressed by their own country. A military intervention which ends up killing many of the people it is supposed to help makes no sense. The requirement of non-combatant immunity is especially important in humanitarian intervention.

One problem with allowing unintended civilian deaths is the difficulty of distinguishing intended versus unintended deaths. To deal with this, Michael

Walzer has argued that the requirement of proportionality needs to be under-stood as involving duties of care and restraint. He argues that

> ...simply not to intend the death of civilians is too easy; most often, under battle condi-tions, the intentions of soldiers are focused narrowly on the enemy. What we look for in such cases is some sign of a positive commitment to save civilian lives... if saving civilian lives means risking soldiers' lives, that risk must be accepted... I think it best to say that civilians have a right that 'due care' be taken.[19]

The most important part of this is that nations must be willing to risk the lives of their own soldiers to minimize civilian casualties. This requirement applies with special force to humanitarian intervention. The civilian population is to be rescued. Any civilian deaths are a set-back to its aims.

This brings to light one of the paradoxes of humanitarian intervention. As we have seen, it is difficult to justify because it puts at risk soldiers who are not defending their own citizens. Yet they must take even greater risks to satisfy proportionality. Thus the United States chose to intervene to save the Albanians in Kosovo with high altitude military bombings in Serbia, which caused many civilian deaths. This is difficult to justify, but putting US fighters at greater risk would have endangered support at home. Still, I believe that a justified humani-tarian intervention must increase military risk in order to minimize civilian casualties.

The *Jus ad Bellum* requires that a justified war be fought with a 'right intention'. It should not be an excuse for waging a war really motivated by other aims. Right intention also means that the ultimate aim of the war should be a just and lasting peace. Humanitarian intervention often occurs in failed societies filled with hos-tile groups. Stopping the killing and leaving quickly may lead to its immediate resumption if the underlying social issues are not addressed. This can be difficult and can mean that the intervening nation must stay for some time and engage in nation-building. This, however, can become, or come to be perceived as, an occu-pation, especially if harsh means are taken to prevent new hostilities. A humani-tarian intervention, when justified, must involve a realistic plan for producing peace and stability in the society invaded.

It is difficult to do humanitarian intervention properly. The American inter-vention in Somalia looked like an easy thing, a matter of delivering food to starving people. But it meant getting involved in a deeply troubled society and it ended badly. Somalia's troubles continue to this day. The likelihood of stepping into a quagmire may account for some of the reluctance of powerful nations to get involved when tragedies occur. Much can go wrong. But sometimes the risk needs to be taken.

[19] M Walzer, *Just and Unjust Wars* (New York: Basic Books, 1977, 2006 expanded version) 155–6.

VII. Humanitarian Intervention and Medical Epidemics

I now turn to the question I raised at the beginning. Is humanitarian military intervention acceptable when people are dying because of a medical epidemic? As I suggested, let's imagine a case in which an epidemic involving a fatal disease is raging, there are available medicines to treat it and save people, but the government refuses to distribute them or allow others to do so. The local government by its inaction allows large numbers of its citizens to die.

This may seem far-fetched but we know that North Korea let large numbers die of famine rather than seek aid, and a scarlet fever pandemic is now said to be raging in that xenophobic country. South Africa has until recently failed to treat its AIDS epidemic because of unscientific beliefs about AIDS medication on the part of its President and leading health ministers. And malaria and other epidemics rage through Africa.

This phenomenon would be particularly poignant in a country full of ethnic strife. Suppose there is a ruling group and a disfavoured group. A serious disease breaks out and the government provides aid to members of the favoured group, but prevents aid from getting to the disfavoured group. This is a case of 'genocide by epidemic'.

In most cases in which a nation needs aid to battle a disease, the local government is willing to help. The problems are that the medications are unavailable or too expensive, doctors and nurses are in short supply, and health centres are far from the people who need aid. The infrastructure to provide help is lacking. The government is not recalcitrant but overwhelmed, resource-poor, or incompetent. But it is willing to accept aid, and international NGOs can operate freely. In such a case, help is needed but not military intervention.

Let us return, then, to the recalcitrant government that refuses aid. We do not naturally think of such cases as candidates for humanitarian intervention. I want to suggest several reasons why these cases seem different from the cases that warrant military intervention.

First, in ordinary cases of humanitarian intervention, military conflict already exists. The government has sent soldiers to attack a disfavoured group or supports a paramilitary organization like the Janjaweed in Sudan. There may be rebels on the other side. Humanitarian intervention in such cases means getting involved in a military conflict already under way, trying to stop the conflict and protect those most victimized. In the epidemic case, there is no such conflict under way. Thus military intervention does not come quickly to mind. It would be initiating a conflict, rather than trying to stop one.

A second difference is that the recalcitrant state is not actively killing or injuring the victims of disease. It is not engaged in acts of massacre and oppression. It is letting something bad happen. This difference will not appeal much to those who find little significance in the distinction between doing and allowing. But it may affect our tendency not to think of this as a case for intervention.

A third difference can be brought out best by example. Consider the current situation in Zimbabwe. This is a country run into the ground by a ruthless auto-crat. According to the Lowy Institute, an international policy think-tank in Sydney, Australia, the following is currently true of Zimbabwe:

Inflation rate of +2,200%, will rise to 5,000%.
Only 20% of people formally employed.
60–70% of the workforce in the Diaspora.
Lowest life expectancy on earth: 34 years for women and 37 for men.
One of highest HIV rates: over 20%.
GDP has shrunk by over 40% in six years.
Urban poverty has quadrupled in five years.
Health, education and food production collapsed.
The health development index has sunk below the levels of sub-Saharan Africa.[20]

There have been rigged elections and beatings and imprisonments of opposition candidates. The situation is dire, yet there is no talk of intervention. Why? Here is a humanitarian disaster of the first proportion. It is unlike the standard cases in which humanitarian intervention is contemplated. There is no large-scale massacre of civilians, no oppressed ethnic group, no ethnic cleansing. There is, instead, an autocratic elite determined to maintain its power, privileges, and wealth at the expense of the population.

I suggest that our main reason for not considering intervention here is a deep-seated commitment to the concept of sovereignty. The world is carved into independent nations and we expect each to manage its own problems.[21] Every state, even rich ones, has problems it must deal with, such as managing its econ-omy, providing security and a judicial system, educating the young, etc. The notion of sovereignty means that each state wrestles internally with the prob-lems of its common human life. When a state fails to manage well, intervention is inappropriate. If a state, for example, makes poor economic decisions that lead to serious economic set-backs for its citizens, we do not automatically consider intervention.

We have deeply internalized the norms of the Westphalian system of sover-eignty and that helps to explain why we do not consider intervention in cases like Zimbabwe and in cases of medical pandemics. I do not want to underestimate other relevant factors. Intervention in a state like Zimbabwe or North Korea will be met with armed resistance and the consequences can be very bad. Even if

[20] Lowy Institute for International Policy, Sydney, Australia. This is from a PowerPoint Presentationat<http://72.14.253.104/search?q=cache:35VqBuBlOgUJ:lowyinstitute.richmedia-server.com/sound/The_current_situation_in_Zimbabwe.ppt+Zimbabwe+current+situation&hl=en&ct=clnk&cd=5&gl=us>.
[21] This is a fundamental theme of John Rawls's book on global justice, *The Law of Peoples* (Cambridge, Mass.: Harvard University Press, 1999).

intervention is thought prima facie acceptable, the consequences must be considered and they may not promise an acceptable outcome.[22]

We are moved to consider intervention when citizens are massacred, but we lack such motivation when harm occurs through tyranny or mismanagement. Does this distinction make sense? In each case, large numbers of people die or have their lives entirely destroyed. The outcome for individuals in the same. Should we be more inclined to consider humanitarian intervention in these cases?

I do not have a good answer. I am inclined to think that we should be more willing to consider intervention in the face of neglect, mismanagement, and recalcitrance than we have been. But even then intervention will be limited. It works best when one invades a country with a weak military, the aims are clear and achievable, casualties in both countries can be kept low, and extensive 'nation-building' is not required. It may be justifiable or obligatory in some cases of this sort. But these cases may be the exception.

Humanitarian intervention is a poor substitute for the existence of international institutions which have the power to protect the human rights of each and every citizen. We are far from developing the institutions (including international law) that can achieve this end. The problem is part of the more general problem of dealing with worldwide poverty and injustice. We need norms and institutions that move us to some degree out of the worldwide state of nature.[23] Is this a utopian and impractical hope? I do not know, but it is our best alternative for dealing with problems we now face as a worldwide human community.

---

[22] I do not consider the American-initiated war in Iraq a humanitarian intervention, even though it toppled a ruthless dictator. Its awful consequences are an object lesson of the dangers of unleashing military force even for the best of reasons.

[23] Hobbes discusses the international situation as a 'state of nature' in *Leviathan*, (1651): R Tuck (ed), *Leviathan* (Cambridge University Press, 1991) ch 13.

25

The Age of Deference—A Historical Anomaly

*Margaret Brazier**

I. Introduction

Medical Law is still a comparatively young subject.[1]

Few have argued with this opening sentence from the third edition of *Kennedy and Grubb's Medical Law*, published in 2000. The authors go on to note the emergence of medical law in the last two decades of the twentieth century as a distinct subject '... both as an area of importance in legal practice and as an academic discipline'.[2] The publication of Ian Kennedy's Reith Lectures *The Unmasking of Medicine*,[3] in 1981 is often seen as a key moment in the birth of 'modern' medical law.

In the earlier part of the twentieth century, few cases relating to medical practice reached the courts. University courses on medical law were virtually unknown. Although a short textbook on *Medical Negligence* had been published in 1957,[4] and practitioner tomes on the liability of hospitals were available,[5] medical law had a low profile. Neither the courts nor legal scholars paid much critical attention to the law's relationship with medicine. When English judges did engage with challenges to medical practice, they tended to be very wary of expressing any criticism of 'medical men'.[6]

* Of the Centre for Social Ethics and Policy, University of Manchester.
[1] A Grubb (ed), *Kennedy and Grubb's Medical Law* (Butterworths, 3rd edn, 2000) 3.
[2] ibid.   [3] I Kennedy, *The Unmasking of Medicine* (Allen & Unwin, 1981).
[4] PC Nathan and AR Barrowclough, *Medical Negligence* (Butterworths, 1957).
[5] See eg SR Speller, *Law relating to hospitals and kindred institutions* (Lewis, 1956); J Finch (ed), *Speller's law relating to hospitals* (Chapman and Hall Medical, 7th edn,1994). AS Taylor and FJ Swaine, *The Principles and Practice of Medical Jurisprudence* (J & A Churchill, 5th edn, 1905) dealt principally with issues of forensic medicine.
[6] See *Hatcher v Black, The Times*, 2 July 1954; and see JL Montrose, 'Is Negligence an Ethical or a Sociological Concern?' (1958) 21 *MLR* 259; J Montgomery, 'Medicine, Accountability and Professionalism' (1989) 16 *Journal of Law and Society* 319.

The consequences of the lack of attention to law's historical engagement with medicine are two-fold. First, it seemed to be assumed that law and medicine lacked much of a history of engagement—that in truth medical law was 'comparatively young'. Second, it is often suggested that when the two did meet, a tradition of judicial deference had from 'time immemorial' dominated those encounters. So scholars and judges in the final decade of the twentieth century perceived themselves as battling against a tradition of deference to medicine entrenched over centuries.[7] I seek to show that such an era was short-lived. Deference to doctors was principally a product of two developments in the Victorian age. The Medical Act 1858 established the dominance of one model of 'healing'. The birth of modern biomedical science created an aura of power enjoyed solely by its practitioners. Thus as Harrington says '... medicine attained a position of unprecedented prestige and influence'.[8]

The history of medical law has been little explored, at least by legal scholars. The distinguished medical historian, Roy Porter, said of the history of medicine generally:[9] 'The historical record is like the night sky: we see a few stars and group them together in mythic constellations. But what is chiefly visible is the darkness.' The history of law and medicine is darker still. Very few stars glimmer in the night sky, and no constellations have yet been glimpsed.

Medical historians have not ignored medico-legal history altogether. However, they have tended to focus primarily on what we might describe today as public health law, mental health law, forensic medicine,[10] or the history of a particular issue within medical law, for example abortion.[11] In an excellent collection of essays, *Legal Medicine in History*,[12] eight of the thirteen essays address forensic medicine. Little space is devoted to, for example, the legal obligations inherent in the doctor-patient relationship. Historians of medicine seek to address medicine in a broader context than the insular tradition of the common law in England and Wales, thus references to English medico-legal history are often necessarily brief. Paradoxically, papers discussing the history of medical ethics come closer to offering some light on the history of medical law.[13]

---

[7] J Miola, 'The Need for Informed Consent: Lessons from the Ancient Greeks' (2006) 15 *Cambridge Quarterly of Healthcare Ethics* 152.

[8] JA Harrington '"Red in Tooth and Claw": The Idea of Progress in Medicine and the Common Law' (2002) *Social and Legal Studies* 211, 213.

[9] R Porter, *The Greatest Benefit to Mankind: A Medical History of Humanity from Antiquity to the present* (Fontana Press, 1997) 13.

[10] See eg the questions addressed in C Crawford, 'Medicine and the Law' in WF Bynum and R Porter (eds), *Companion Encyclopaedia of the History of Medicine* (Routledge, 1993) 1619.

[11] See B Brookes, *Abortion in England 1900–1967* (Croom Helm, 1988); B Brookes and P Roth '*R v Bourne* and the medicalisation of abortion' in M Clarke and C Crawford (eds) *Legal Medicine in History* (Cambridge University Press, 1994); J Keown, *Abortion, Doctors and the Law* (Cambridge University Press, 1988) (a rare historical work by an English legal scholar).

[12] M Clarke and C Crawford (eds), *Legal Medicine in History* (Cambridge University Press, 1994). Of the remaining five essays, three address mental health law.

[13] See E Shorter, 'The History of the Doctor-Patient Relationship' in Bynum and Porter (n 10 above) 783.

Why should neglect of its history matter to the study of medical law today? Medicine in the twenty-first century is so vastly different to the physic practised two or three hundred years ago. Seventeenth-century doctors suggested that the whole of a little human (*homunculus*) was present in its father's sperm,[14] simply seeking a seedbed in the mother's womb. Bleeding was a popular remedy for nearly any complaint. What can a study of such times teach us about the wonders of scientific medicine? The 'medicine' may be very different. Nevertheless, even a brief excursion into past centuries demonstrates that many of the fundamental questions of medical law and ethics today have an ancient lineage. By treating too many developments as wholly 'new', we fail to learn from the past. Human kind has not changed that much. Our bodies remain fallible and we seek 'cure'. Kennedy and Grubb claim medical law to be 'young' in 2000, but travel back in time over 3000 years and consider the Code of Hammurabi in ancient Mesopotamia[15] 'If a physician has performed a major operation on a lord with a bronze lancet and has saved the lord's life... he shall receive ten shekels of silver... if he causes the death of the lord his hand shall be chopped off'. Charges of medical malpractice are as old as medicine itself. And the conditions that to some extent insulated medicine from legal 'assaults' for much of the twentieth century are in 2008 rapidly disappearing. Medicine, healing, is again becoming a diverse marketplace.[16]

II. Responsible 'Medical Men': Who Were They?

The context in which medical law in England became a distinct subject of study in the final quarter of the twentieth century assumed the existence of a single and powerful medical profession. It was the dominance of that profession especially in defining what constituted ethical and lawful practice that was challenged. Critics argued that medical practitioners could not be the sole judges of what constituted good medicine for the individual patient and the public good. Lord Scarman (writing extra-judicially) noted that:...'the law's standard is, in effect, set by the medical profession. If a doctor can show that his advice or treatment, reaches a standard of each which has been accepted by a reasonable and responsible body of medical opinion as adequate, he cannot be made liable in damages if anything goes wrong. It is a totally medical proposition erected into a working rule of law'.[17] To put it crudely, the notion that 'doctor knows best' came under attack. Such assumptions that 'doctor knew best' depended on a prior knowledge

---

[14] See Porter (n 9 above) 226.   [15] ibid 45.

[16] See M Brazier and N Glover, 'Does Medical Law Have a Future?' in D Hayton (ed), *Law(s) Future(s)* (Hart Publishing, 2000) 371; J Montgomery, 'Law and the demoralisation of medicine' (2006) 26 *Legal Studies* 185–210.

[17] L Scarman, 'Law and Medical Practice' in P Byrne (ed), *Medicine in Contemporary Society* (King Edward's Hospital Fund for London, 1987) 131, 134.

of who was 'doctor'. Such assumptions equally (if unconsciously) presumed that judges (and patients) had always perceived doctors as pillars of society, repositories of knowledge that should not be challenged.

So the first decade or so of 'modern medical law' was dominated by criticisms of the pervasive *Bolam* test. MacNair J's ruling[18] that a doctor was not to be found negligent if he acted 'in accordance with a practice accepted as proper by a responsible body of medical men skilled in that particular area' was attacked for handing over to the doctors control of what amounted to good practice. The *Bolam* test came under even more intensive fire when it broke the bounds of its original context in negligence. *Bolam* became, for a while, the touchstone for the propriety of virtually all medical practice.[19] Decisions about the lawful treatment of mentally incapacitated patients,[20] whether or not to withdraw life support from patients in a persistent vegetative state,[21] and how much information about proposed treatment doctors must volunteer to patients,[22] all were *Bolamized*. The roots of *Bolam*, whether it was orthodoxy or heresy, need to be explored.

A hundred and sixty years prior to the *Bolam* case, judicial deference to expert medical opinion may be seen in its infancy.[23] Until 1858, however, and the creation of the General Medical Council,[24] any uncritical *Bolam* approach would have encountered difficulty. How would one identify the responsible 'medical man'?[25]

Prior to 1858, the medical profession in England was far from unified. Three principal 'professions' competed in the market for patients. The physicians enjoyed the highest social status. The London College of Physicians[26] obtained its Charter from Henry VIII in 1518, and revels in its claim as the oldest of the Royal Colleges.[27] The Charter, confirmed by an Act of Parliament in 1522 'The Privileges and Authority of Physicians in London', granted the College powers to license those permitted to practise 'physic' in London, or within a seven-mile circuit around London. There were two distinct classes of licensed physicians, Fellows who controlled the College, and mere licentiates allowed to practise and controlled by the College. The College enjoyed the power to determine who was

---

[18] *Bolam v Friern Hospital Management Committee* [1957] 2 All ER 118.

[19] See J Miola, *Medical Ethics and Medical Law: A Symbiotic Relationship* (Hart Publishing, 2007); M Brazier and J Miola, 'Bye-Bye Bolam: A Medical Litigation Revolution' (2000) 8 *Medical Law Review* 85. And see M Davies, 'The "New Bolam" Another False Dawn for Medical Negligence' (1996). 12 *Professional Negligence* 10.

[20] *F v West Berkshire Health Authority* [1990] 2 AC 1 HL.

[21] *Airedale NHS Trust v Bland* [1993] 1 All ER 821, HL.

[22] *Sidaway v Royal Bethlem Hospital* [1985] 1 All ER 643, HL.

[23] See eg *Slater v Baker and Stapleton* (1797) 95 ER 860.

[24] See M Davies, *Medical Self-Regulation* (Ashgate, 2007) 15–17.

[25] There is evidence that a number of women did practise medicine before and well into the sixteenth century. Parliament and the male professional colleges and guilds devoted great effort to excluding women from the public practice of medicine; see Porter (n 9 above) 128–30.

[26] It became the Royal College in the reign of Charles II.

[27] See T Gelfand, 'The History of the Medical Profession' in Bynum and Porter (n 10 above) 1119–50.

qualified to practice 'physic',[28] and via its censors, claimed draconian powers to seek out and punish unlicensed practice or *mala praxis*[29] (malpractice). Unlawful practice attracted a fine of £5 for each month of unlicensed practice. An earlier statute of 1511 had entrusted licensing powers outside London to the bishops in each diocese.[30] Those licensed by the College could lawfully practise both in London and throughout the realm. The physicians sought to dominate medical practice but were limited in their personal practice by their self-imposed prohibition on drawing blood,[31] and thus administering one of the favoured remedies of blood-letting. The physician would diagnose (perhaps by sniffing the patient's urine or consulting his astrological charts), he might then 'prescribe'.

Should blood-letting be prescribed, the actual procedure would be carried out by a surgeon. Surgeons in medieval and Tudor England 'played second fiddle to physic'.[32] They were perceived as more akin to the craftsman than the gentleman. Yet the first guild of master surgeons (or Fellowship of Surgeons) was founded in 1368.[33] And evidence exists that the guild developed (for its time) a sophisticated code of ethics emphasizing the imperative to do no harm. The forced marriage of the surgeons to the barbers to form the Barber-Surgeons Company in 1540 did the social status and academic credentials of the surgeons little good.[34]

Apothecaries[35] were the lowest in the official pecking order. In 1607, they obtained separate status within the Grocers' Company and established the Apothecaries Society in 1617. Sometimes seen as the forebears of the modern pharmacists, apothecaries were much more than just mixers and purveyors of potions. Their role in most towns and villages in England resembles more closely that of the modern general practitioner. Their fees, while not cheap, were in the reach of more people than those charged by physicians or surgeons. In addition to the physicians, surgeons, and apothecaries, other 'healers' crowded the marketplace. Herbalists peddled their wares, some deliberately choosing to evade the restrictions imposed in gaining the status of the apothecary.[36] Midwives did more than simply deliver babies. Forbidden as women to practise medicine formally, the local midwife (like the apothecary) often took on the role of general practitioner. Most importantly, any self-respecting wife and mother was expected to have a basic knowledge of medicine and be able to treat her family and, if she

[28] Graduates of Oxford and Cambridge automatically qualified to become Fellows of the College.

[29] See *Dr Groenvelt's Case* (1697) 9 Will 3 BR.

[30] An Act designed to exclude 'a great multitude of persons', including women and witches, from practising medicine.

[31] Derived from a ruling of the Lateran Council 1215.

[32] See Porter (n 9 above) 186.

[33] ibid.

[34] See B Wooley, *The Herbalist* (Harper Perennial, 2005) 36–9. And see also his discussion of the 'Quacks' Charter and the machinations of the College of Physicians at 38.

[35] See Porter (n 9 above) 198.

[36] See Wooley (n 34 above).

were lucky enough to have them, her servants.[37] Medical advice circulated as freely in the sixteenth century as in the media of today. The lady of the manor might be seen as the medieval forebear of NHS Direct.

III. Physicians Seek Dominence

Our ancestors worried as much about their health as we do (and with more cause). Thus medicine was a lucrative market. Within the market 'official' healers competed with each other and sought to fight off the 'unlicensed' competition. The spectacle did not inspire patient confidence or deference. John Gay jested in *The Beggar's Opera*:[38] 'Man may escape from rope and gun. Nay, some have outlived the doctor's pill.' More serious authors addressed the 'unhappy condition of the practice of physic in London'[39] and begged patients 'to take heede of... "unskilful chryrurgians"'.[40] The College of Physicians had many advantages in seeking to dominate that market. Their proximity to the Royal Court and generous Charter should have assisted them. The College acquired exclusive licensing rights in London. But it allowed the pursuit of social status to undermine its advantage. Porter comments 'The Royal College of Physicians of London subsided into a gentleman's club, reserved for the fashionable.'[41] Entry to the College for any aspirant lacking a degree from Oxford or Cambridge was laborious.[42] From 1687, surgeons, drug compounders or 'any other artificer' were barred from candidacy to the College. Their exercise of 'any illiberal art' was seen as prejudicial to the dignity of the College and the honour of the great universities. Any licentiate of the College who engaged in the 'trade of a drug seller' forfeited his licence. The College tended to eschew the developments in Continental Europe flourishing within the 'anatomical Renaissance'.[43] Its members remained resolutely old-fashioned. A vast effort focused on control of its own members and what physicians regarded as the lower orders of the profession 'defending only the perks and privileges of the metropolitan elite'.[44] The playwright Webster noted: 'Physicians are like kings, they brook no contradiction.'[45]

---

[37] See Silvia De Renzi, 'The sick and their healers' in P Elmer (ed), *The Healing Arts* (Manchester University Press, 2004).

[38] *The Beggar's Opera* SC Viii air Xxvi. And see Miola (n 19 above) 28–30.

[39] Jonathan Goddard, *A discourse setting forth the unhappy condition of the practice of physic* (Wing 15914, 1670).

[40] Johann Oberndorf, *The anatomyes of the true physition* (STL, 2nd edn 1875) (first published, 1602).

[41] See Porter (n 9 above) 288.

[42] See Gelfand (n 27 above) 1125–7.

[43] See J Sawday, *The Body Emblazoned* (Routledge, 1995).

[44] See Porter (n 27 above) 354.

[45] *The Duchess of Malfi* Act Vii 72.

The College enjoyed draconian powers. The Censors could present doctors charged with *mala praxis* to the courts and thus subject the errant doctor to hefty fines and imprisonment. The Censors of the College sought out, and punished unlicensed healers. The fines were forfeit to the College. They purported to control the apothecaries so that no apothecary could provide medicine or treatment in London except under the supervision of a physician. By 1700, the College, despite their obsession with social pretentions, looked set to become the overarching regulatory authority for medicine, at least in the capital. An enterprising apothecary put an end to their hopes. William Rose challenged the College and won.[46]

Mr Rose had attended John Seale, a butcher. He had made up and administered proper medicines for him. Mr Seale disputed the bills submitted by Apothecary Rose. He complained to the College which prosecuted Mr Rose as it had many other apothecaries. The College argued that an apothecary could only lawfully provide medicines under the direction of a physician licensed by the College. An apothecary acting independently of a physician's direction acted unlawfully and stood to be fined £5 for every month of unlawful practice. Mr Rose was convicted by a jury and his conviction was upheld by the Court of Queen's Bench. The statute provided no appeal process. Supported by his colleagues in the Society of Apothecaries, Rose moved for a writ of error before Parliament. As with so many landmark judgments in the common law in the sixteenth and seventeenth centuries, the case formally turned on something of a technicality. The jury, finding Mr Rose guilty of unlawfully practising physic, found as to the facts that, while Rose provided medicines for Mr Seale without the direction of a physician, and charged Mr Seale for the medicine, he claimed no fee for advice. Therefore, Rose argued that his conviction was in error in that simply selling medicines could not constitute practising physic.

Every Fellow of the Royal College of Physicians was summoned to attend the hearing before the House of Lords. Counsel for both sides declined to limit their eloquence to the precise interpretation of the College Charter and statutes. Rose's counsel mounted an attack on the College's claim to a monopoly of lawful medical practice. They argued that 'constant usage and practice' sanctioned the sale of medicine and the provision of gratuitous advice by apothecaries. The physicians sought to strain the interpretation of their Charter and of statute, seeking to 'monopolise all manner of physic to themselves'. Were they to succeed, the social consequences would be ruinous. No medicine would be accessible without payment to a physician. Sick people would have to call the physician and pay his fee for his advice, and then summon the apothecary to sell them the medicine. This would be 'a great oppression upon poor families who, not being able to bear the charge of a fee, would be deprived of all kinds of assistance in their necessities'.

---

[46] See Sir G Clark, *A History of the Royal College of Physicians of London* (Clarendon Press, 1964–66) 476–9 for a full account of the history of the case.

It would be dangerous to health, for those taken suddenly ill most commonly summoned the apothecary who, if Rose's conviction were upheld, 'should not dare to apply the least remedy without running the hazard of being ruined'.

The College fought back. First, their Counsel stressed that the College imposed on its members an obligation to treat the poor for free. Every physician had a duty to visit the 'sick poor' in his neighbourhood in their own lodgings. So the apothecaries' argument that the 'poorer sort of people would be lost for want of proper remedies had not the least foundation'. In emergency, the College conceded that any person might lawfully do his best to treat a sick neighbour. But this concession should not be allowed to permit apothecaries to 'undertake at leisure all dangerous diseases', especially as in London a skilful physician would be accessible to all. Apothecaries were not '*bred* to have suitable skill'. Moreover, declared Counsel for the College, it was the apothecaries who sought to exploit their patients by over prescribing whereas a 'distemper—by the discreet advice of a physician might, by one proper medicine, have been eradicated at the beginning'.

Counsel presented two contrasting pictures of medicine in 1703. In the one, the practical, kindly apothecary provided accessible low cost medicine to all patients in need, whereas the physician lined his pockets in the service of the rich. In the other, greedy business men of a lower class aimed solely to maximize sales, while the gentlemen physicians devoted themselves to the vocation of healing. The House of Lords reversed the judgment of Queen's Bench, finding for the apothecaries.[47] As was the custom of those times, no reasons are given.

Rose's case is of immense significance to the history of the relationship of law and medicine. Had the College of Physicians succeeded in their prosecution of Rose, the development of a unified professional hierarchy would have begun over a century and a half prior to the Medical Act 1858. Gelfand comments: 'The Rose case virtually ended the physicians' efforts to regulate other healers.'[48] The success of the apothecaries also indicates that, despite the physicians' social credentials, the judges had little regard for the College. The evidence suggests that the House of Lords accepted the apothecaries' substantive arguments as well as their technical legal case.

Internecine warfare in the courts between the warring 'medical professions' continued through the eighteenth and nineteenth centuries.[49] In 1861, the apothecaries and physicians met in court yet again. In its by-laws prior to 1858, the College barred its Fellows and licentiates from making up prescriptions or selling medicines. That function was seen to belong to the apothecary. The Apothecaries' Act 1815 had provided for the licensing of apothecaries and granted what the apothecaries saw as a monopoly on pharmacy practice to them. The 1858 Medical

---

[47] *William Rose (Plaintiff in Error) v The College of Physicians (London)* (1703) English Reports 857.
[48] Gelfand (n 27 above) 1126.
[49] ibid 1134–5; and see Porter (n 9 above) 354–6.

Act was less than radical in its unification of the medical professions. Each profession, the Royal College of Physicians, the College of Surgeons, and the Society of Apothecaries, retained independent licensing powers. Licensing by any of the three granted the 'doctor' registration by the newly created General Medical Council as a duly qualified medical practitioner. But each 'doctor' remained part of his own separate 'species'.

The physicians then, in 1860, sought to change their own rules removing the absolute prohibition on doctors licensed by the College to make up medicines, thus enlarging their share of the market. Fellows of the College were still barred from such activity. The College, however, proposed to create a new class of licentiate not bound by that prohibition. This, the Society of Apothecaries argued, was creating a new class of licences—'purporting to allow them to act as apothecaries'. The College was poaching in the apothecaries' territory. The revised by-laws of the College would allow admission of a new category of licentiates with a much shorter period of training who would not be restricted 'by any bye-law from supplying medicines to their patients'. The Society of Apothecaries brought an action akin to a modern application for judicial review invoking the Attorney-General to challenge the Royal College's new rules: The apothecaries lost this round of the war.[50] In a complex judgment, the judge in 1861 (*inter alia*) took the view that ancient laws gave the College the 'whole medical domain'. They may have chosen to limit their jurisdiction ceding certain sorts of medicine to the apothecaries and the surgeons. The College remained entitled to claim back their territory. The judge also saw the 1858 Act as moving towards a common scheme of regulation with which judges and other 'outsiders' should not interfere. Inexorably, the model of medicine we knew in the twentieth century emerged.

IV. Responsible Medical 'Men' Gain Control

The emergence of one dominant and unified medical profession was paralleled by a number of other developments that set the scene for *Bolamization*. From 1858, medicine became much more respectable. Writing in 2001, Lord Woolf spoke of judicial reluctance 'to make findings of negligence against any honourable profession'.[51] Pillorying doctors in literature receded as the twentieth century dawned. The Manchester physician, Thomas Percival, eloquently advanced the case to allow ethics to be defined by the benevolent paternalism of the gentleman physician.[52]

[50] *Attorney-General v Royal College of Physicians* (1861) 70 English Reports 868.

[51] The Right Honourable The Lord Woolf, 'Are the Courts Excessively Deferential to the Medical Profession?' (2001) 9 *Medical Law Review* 1, 2.

[52] In his seminal book *Medical Ethics*, first published in 1803 ; see now CD Leake (ed), *Percival's Medical Ethics* (Williams & Wilkins, 1927); Porter (n 9 above 286), points out that Percival's

Percival promoted the model of medicine as an *art* emphasizing the doctor's vocation and obligation to do good. We (the patients) should trust the good intentions of doctors and resist questioning what was good for us. Cynicism about doctors did not immediately decline. Belloc (who lived from 1870–1953) still quipped: 'Physicians of the utmost fame were called at once but when they came, They answered, as they took their fees, There is no cure for this disease.'[53]

By Belloc's death, doctors had acquired a better reputation. Two other developments prepared the ground for the era of deference to medicine. First as Harrington[54] has eloquently explained, scientific progress in the nineteenth and twentieth centuries elevated the status of medicine. Judges bought into the notion of medical mystique. Medical science was too complex to be challenged by lay people (even judges). Medicine as an art, or medicine as a science,[55] was hotly debated, but in the courtroom and popular opinion doctors seemed to reap the benefit of both. Judgments about the rights and wrongs of treatment decisions could not be challenged because judges did not know enough about the science of medicine.[56] Judgment about what was in the best interests of a patient should not be challenged, because the benevolent doctor exercising his art knew best.[57] Second, and most importantly, with the establishment of the National Health Service in 1948, medicine largely moved out of the marketplace for nearly half a century. Physicians (for the most part) no longer, to quote Belloc again, 'took their fees', save from those private patients who actively chose to pay. The historic notion of the money-grubbing 'quack' evaporated. Literature and the media began to put doctors on a pedestal. The judges, as Lord Woolf put it, operated a 'presumption of beneficence' towards doctors.[58]

The conditions of the society in which *Bolamization* and deference took hold included the following. Registered medical practitioners dominated 'healing'. Self-regulation largely governed medical practice. The laity had limited access to medical knowledge, save via their doctor. Money and markets became peripheral to medicine.

Many of those conditions are now in a state of flux. 'Healing' in 2008 is once again a competitive field of business. More and more tasks which were once a medical monopoly are now devolved to nurses[59] and paramedics.[60] A growing

---

famous work, *Medical Ethics,* developed from his earlier less known work, *Medical Jurisprudence,* published in 1794.

[53] *Jim.*   [54] See n 8 above.

[55] ibid at 213.

[56] See eg *Maynard v West Midlands Health Authority* [1984] 1 WLR 634, HL.

[57] See eg *F v West Berkshire Health Authority* [1989] 2 All ER 545, HL.

[58] See Woolf (n 51 above) 2.

[59] An increasing number of nurses take on advanced and extended roles taking over jobs earlier reserved for medicine; see 'Maxi nurses. Advanced and specialist nursing roles. Results from a survey of RCN members in advanced and specialist nursing roles'; accessible at<http://www.rcn.org.uk>.

[60] Paramedics now fall within the regulatory jurisdiction of the Health Professions Council and have wide powers to carry out medical procedures in emergencies. See <http://www.britishpara-medics.org>.

cadre of medical assistants, 'quasi-doctors', take on procedures once the domain of the doctor.[61] Other models of medicine have received the blessing of the state, notably osteopathy[62] and chiropractic.[63] In January 2008, the Department of Health offered support to the creation of a voluntary Complementary and Natural Healthcare Council (CNHC). The Council (established by the Prince's Foundation for Integrated Health and thus strongly backed by the Prince of Wales) will regulate a bewildering range of alternative therapies including Alexander technique, massage technique, homeopathy, and yoga therapy.[64] The model of regulation chosen mirrors that of medicine. It is suggested that 'mainstream alternative therapies' such as acupuncture will remain outside the CNHC and be subject to statutory regulation, as are osteopathy, and chiropractic. The picture of regulation creates a possible future in which registered medical practitioners (or nurses) could simply become one of a selection of 'healers' with little greater status than the osteopath or the reflexologist.

Self-regulation is set to be diluted both by proposed radical reforms of the General Medical Council itself[65] and the growing clout of the super-regulator, the Council for Healthcare Regulatory Excellence (CHRE).[66]

Nor are doctors any longer seen as sole repositories of medical knowledge. Not only have the internet and self-help manuals persuaded many people to consider themselves to be equally knowledgeable, but government, and sometimes doctors themselves, actively encourage self-care. The Department of Health promotes the concept of the expert patient.[67] When doctors refuse to provide the treatments chosen by the patient, they may face anger and demands to accede to the patient's rights.[68] Doctors may be expected to defer to their patients, rather as their eighteenth-century forbears were expected to pander to the whims of their wealthy clientele.[69]

---

[61] eg Operating Department Practitioners (ODPs) now undertake procedures formerly reserved for anaesthetists and theatre nurses. Interestingly, their professional association acknowledges their 'ancestors' as being the 'surgerymen' of the 16th and 15th centuries. See <http://www. aode.org>.

[62] Osteopaths Act 1993; and see <http:// www.osteopaths.org.uk>.

[63] Chiropractors Act 1994; see <http://www.scc-uk.org>. Both osteopaths and chiropractors now practise within the NHS as well as in the private sector.

[64] See *The Times,* 5 January 2008.

[65] See the White Paper, *Trust, Assurance and Safety—The Regulation of Health Professions* (Cm 7013). And see M Brazier and E Cave, *Medicine, Patients and the Law* (Lexis Nexis/Penguin, 4th edn, 2007) ch 1.

[66] See <http://www.chre.org.uk> and see Brazier and Cave (n 65 above) para 1.12.

[67] See <http://www.expertpatients.nhs.uk>.

[68] Nonetheless the Court of Appeal has made it clear that patients have no legal right to treatment on demand—patients cannot insist their doctors provide treatment that the doctor judges adverse to the patient's clinical needs; *R (on the Application of Burke) v GMC* [2005] EWCA Civ 1005, at para 15.

[69] See the extract from Tobias Smollett, *Humphrey Clinker* (1771) in P Elmer and Ole Grell, *Health, Disease and the Society in Europe 1500–1800* (Manchester University Press, 2004) discussed by LR Brockliss in 'Organisation, Training and the Medical Marketplace in the Eighteenth Century' in P Elmer (ed) (n 37 above) 344, 375–6; and see Miola (n 19 above) 29.

Finally, money is once again an overt factor in medicine. NHS doctors still do not yet charge NHS patients fees, but no patient can be unaware that cost plays a role in what treatment will be offered to them. Discussion of NHS 'markets' is commonplace.

The picture of medicine in 2050 seems paradoxically to be more likely to resemble the 'medical marketplace' of 1700, than medicine in 1960. Doctors may be seen as simply another service industry no more entitled to deference or revered for special wisdom than plumbers or beauticians. Whether this turn of the wheel of history will benefit either doctors or their patients remains to be seen. Before it is too late, medico-legal scholars should perhaps take a greater interest in medico-legal history.

Index